T0344799

Corruption and Fraud in Financial Markets

Corruption and Fraud in Financial Markets

Malpractice, Misconduct and Manipulation

Carol Alexander

Douglas Cumming

WILEY

Library of Congress Cataloging-in-Publication Data is Available:

ISBN 978-1-119-42177-1 (hardback)

Cover Design: Wiley
Cover Image: © Comstock/Stockbyte/Getty Images

Set in 10/12pt, OptimaLTStd by SPi Global, Chennai, India

Printed in Great Britain by TJ International Ltd, Padstow, Cornwall, UK

10 9 8 7 6 5 4 3 2 1

Contents

About the Editors

Carol Alexander

Carol Alexander is Professor of Finance at the University of Sussex and Co-Editor of the *Journal of Banking and Finance*. Carol has been back at Sussex (her alma mater) since 2012. She was appointed the John von Neumann Chair at TU Munich for the year 2018 and in January 2019 she became visiting professor at the Oxford campus of Peking University Business School.

Prior academic appointments were as Chair of Financial Risk Management at the ICMA Centre in the Henley Business School at Reading (1999–2012) and lecturer in Mathematics and Economics at the University of Sussex (1985–1998). She holds degrees from the University of Sussex (BSc First Class, Mathematics with Experimental Psychology; PhD Algebraic Number Theory) and the London School of Economics (MSc Econometrics and Mathematical Economics). She also has an Honorary Professorship at the Academy of Economic Studies in Bucharest, Romania.

Carol has also held several positions in financial institutions: Fixed Income Trader at UBS/Phillips and Drew (UK); Academic Director of Algorithmics (Canada); Director of Nikko Global Holdings and Head of Market Risk Modelling (UK); Risk Research Advisor, SAS (USA). She also acts as an expert witness and consultant in financial modelling. From 2010–2012 Carol was Chair of the Board of PRMIA (Professional Risk Manager's International Association).

She publishes widely on a broad range of topics, including volatility theory, option pricing and hedging, trading volatility, hedging with futures, alternative investments, random orthogonal matrix simulation, game theory and real options. She has written and edited numerous books in mathematics and finance and published extensively in top-ranked international journals. Her four-volume textbook on Market Risk Analysis (Wiley, 2008) is the definitive guide to the subject.

Douglas Cumming

Douglas Cumming, J.D., Ph.D., CFA, is the DeSantis Distinguished Professor of Finance and Entrepreneurship at the College of Business, Florida Atlantic University in Boca Raton, Florida. Douglas is also a Visiting Professor of Finance at Birmingham Business School, University of Birmingham, UK, and the Royal Melbourne Institute of Technology, Australia. Previously, Douglas was a Professor and the Ontario Research Chair at the Schulich School of Business, York University, in Toronto, Canada from 2007–2018. He has held prior visiting appointments at Essex Business School, Kobe University, University of Bergamo, and EMLyon, among others.

Douglas has published over 180 articles in leading refereed academic journals in finance, management, and law and economics, such as the *Academy of Management Journal, Journal of Financial Economics, Review of Financial Studies, Journal of Financial and Quantitative Analysis*, and *Journal of International Business Studies*, and has been cited over 15,000 times according to Google Scholar. He is the Editor-in-Chief of the *British Journal of Management* (2020–2022) and the *Journal of Corporate Finance* (2018–2020). He is the Founding Editor-in-Chief of *Review of Corporate Finance*, and a former Co-Editor of *Finance Research Letters and Entrepreneurship Theory and Practice*.

Douglas has published 18 academic books. His most recent book is *Crowdfunding: Fundamental Cases, Facts, and Insights* (Elsevier Academic Press, 2019) complete with companion materials. He is the coauthor of *Venture Capital and Private Equity Contracting* (Elsevier Academic Press, 2nd Edition, 2013), and Hedge Fund Structure, Regulation and Performance around the World (Oxford University Press, 2013). He is the Editor of the *Oxford Handbook of Entrepreneurial Finance* (2013), the *Oxford Handbook of Private Equity* (2013), the *Oxford Handbook of Venture Capital* (2013), the *Oxford Handbook of Sovereign Wealth Funds* (2018), the *Oxford Handbook of IPOs* (2019), the *Research Handbook of Finance and Sustainability* (2018), and the *Research Handbook of Investing in the Triple Bottom Line* (2019).

Douglas has consulted for various private and governmental organizations in Australia, Canada, China, Europe, and the U.S. on projects ranging from stock market regulation, mutual fund fees, valuation, damages, and venture capital, among others. Douglas is a regular speaker at academic and industry conferences around the world. He has given recent keynote speeches at the British Academy of Management Corporate Governance Conference, Entrepreneurial Finance Association, Financial Research Network Corporate Finance Conference, French Finance Association, Infiniti Conference on International Finance, Vietnam Symposium in Banking and Finance, the Budapest Liquidity and Financial Markets Conference, and the Humbolt University of Berlin Fintech Conference, among numerous others.

Douglas' work has been reviewed in numerous media outlets, including the *Chicago Tribune, The Economist, The New York Times*, the *Wall Street Journal*, the *Globe and Mail, Canadian Business*, the *National Post*, and *The New Yorker*.

List of Contributors

Mike Aitken	Rozetta Institute
Anita Anand	University of Toronto
Sam Baker	SJB Capital Limited
Christina Bannier	Justus Liebig University Giessen
Jonathan A. Batten	RMIT University, Melbourne, Australia
Gennaro Bernile	University of Miami
Mary Condon	Osgoode Hall Law School
Ryan J. Davies	Babson College
Ai Deng	NERA Economic Consulting and John Hopkins University
F. Alexander de Roode	Robeco
Stephen G. Dimmock	Nanyang Technological University
Arman Eshraghi	Cardiff University
Corinna Ewelt-Knauer	Justus Liebig University Giessen
Joseph D. Farizo	University of Richmond
Michael Firth	Lingnan University
Priyank Gandhi	Rutgers Business School
William C. Gerken	University of Kentucky
Jens Hagendorff	University of Edinburgh
Shan Ji	Capital Markets Consulting
Jonathan M. Karpoff	University of Washington
Ann Leduc	Capital Markets Consulting
Johannes Lips	Justus Liebig University Giessen
Chelsea Liu	University of Adelaide
Igor Lončarski	University of Ljubljana
Andrew Mann	University College London and Coinstrats

Joseph A. McCahery	Tilburg University
Duc Duy Nguyen	King's College London
Stefano Paleari	University of Bergamo
Tālis J. Putniņš	University of Technology Sydney and Stockholm School of Economics in Riga
Oliver M. Rui	China Europe International Business School
Alexis Stenfors	University of Portsmouth
Johan Sulaeman	National University of Singapore
Andrea Signori	Catholic University of Milan
Peter G. Szilagyi	Central European University
David Twomey	Coinstrats
Silvio Vismara	University of Bergamo and Ghent University
Peter Winker	Justus Liebig University Giessen
Wenfeng Wu	Shanghai Jiao Tong University
Alfred Yawson	University of Adelaide

Foreword

This book is intended for finance practitioners, regulators, lawyers, academics, and students in advanced undergraduate and graduate business school programs. Financial market manipulation and fraud covers all aspects of finance. The book includes chapters written by academics in finance, management, and law, as well as by practitioners with experience in trading, surveillance, and regulation. All the chapters are digestible by a wide audience and not written specifically for one type of reader. The timely nature of the material in this book is perhaps exhibited by the fact that one of the chapters had to be removed a few months before going to print due to a gag order associated with on-going litigation; as such, we made sure to cover the pertinent material in other ways to ensure as timely and comprehensive examination of fraud and manipulation as possible.

At a broad level, the book has two main parts: (1) market manipulation and (2) other types of fraud. Market manipulation refers to a wide array of trading practices on stocks, bonds, derivatives, commodities and currencies (including cryptocurrencies). These practices include price manipulation, volume manipulation and insider trading. Other types of fraud are money laundering, credit card fraud, financial statement fraud, options backdating, breach of contract, self-dealing, financial and intellectual property theft, procurement fraud, regulatory or compliance Breach, Ponzi schemes, and computer-intrusion fraud and hacking.

The coverage is very comprehensive: identifies and defines the full array of manipulative activities; discusses the different markets in which manipulation most commonly occurs; analyses misconduct amongst different types of players such as banks and advisors; deals with detection methods including quantitative techniques and surveillance; and describes regulation and enforcement.

Everyone with an interest in financial markets should be concerned with fraud and market manipulation. Navigating financial markets necessarily involves the assessment of risks, of which fraud and manipulation are the most serious and pronounced. An understanding of the causes and consequences of fraud and manipulation is a necessary step to investing in financial markets, studying the behaviour of players in these markets and designing appropriate surveillance systems and regulatory structures.

The concern with fraud and manipulation is particularly timely as this book goes to print in March 2020 with the COVID-19 pandemic spreading over the world. Panic and hysteria are the fuel of financial market volatility and Wall Street's fear gauge, the VIX, has just hit an all-time high as we write, exceeding the peak of the so-called 'great financial crisis' of 2008-9. The financial bomb of US toxic debt (or, more specifically, its derivatives) that was launched by the collapse of Lehman brothers seems nothing compared with consequences of the market activity at this time.

Since 2008 most central banks have employed quantitative easing, raising cash by issuing government securities and selling them to domestic and foreign investors. The US has about $19 trillion debt of which about $7 trillion is held by foreigners and of that over $2 trillion is held by China and Japan. However, since the US trade wars began in 2019 the demand for US government securities has fallen. China, for instance, built up their gold bullion reserves by 6% during 2019. So, in September 2019 the Federal Reserve re-introduced repurchase (repo) operations for the first time since the 'great financial crisis'. That is, they buy their own securities from banks, hedge-funds and this way, they inject liquidity to financial markets for a limited period. At the time of writing, in March 2020, the Federal Reserve have cut benchmark rates and announced an unprecedented level and duration of repo operations that are worth trillions of US dollars. But still, as we write this forward and the book goes to press, the seventh circuit-breaker this month has been applied to attempt to limit the losses on the New York Stock Exchange.

As funds flow out of equities one would expect demand for safe havens like gold and bitcoin to increase. But gold and bitcoin have fallen at the same time. Manipulating the price of gold downwards by dumping huge naked shorts on COMEX gold futures has been documented for years yet, despite the Market Abuse Directive (which is described in Chapter 10) it still continues. With high-frequency trading algorithms now the norm, manipulation techniques are becoming even more advanced. For instance, on Friday 13 March 2020 a distributed denial of service attack, very similar to the Kraken attack documented in Chapter 8 during 2017, occurred on the BitMEX cryptocurrency derivatives exchange. Indeed bitcoin, originally termed 'digital gold' because of its safe-haven properties, has fallen well over 50% on the openly manipulative spoofing trades that are explained in many chapters in this book. The layering, spoof and pinging techniques described Chapter 7, on foreign exchange markets, could also be associated with the astonishing rise in the US dollar. This seems counter-intuitive because the US economy is struggling to cope with the impact of COVID-19 just as China appears to have recovered from the virus.

We encourage you to explore in detail each one of the chapters in this book. We hope this book will help improve the state of knowledge amongst investors, lawyers, regulators, students and academics alike. In turn, we hope that improved an understanding facilitates better due diligence amongst investors and better surveillance to mitigate the frequency and severity fraud and market manipulation. And we hope the material will inspire more in-depth analyses of fraud and market manipulation in the future.

Acknowledgements

We are foremost indebted to the authors of each of the chapters of this book. The authors are, alphabetically, Michael Aitken, Anita Anand, Sam Baker, Christina Bannier, Jonathan Batten, Gennaro Bernile, Mary Condon, Ryan Davies, Ai Deng, Alexander de Roode, Steve Dimmock, Arman Eshraghi, Corinna Ewelt-Knauer, Joseph Farrizo, Michael Firth, Priyank Gandhi, Will Gerken, Jens Hagendorff, Shan Ji, Jonathan Karpoff, Ann Leduc, Johannes Lips, Chelsea Liu, Igor Lončarski, Andrew Mann, Joe McCahery, Duc Duy Nguyen, Stefano Paleari, Tālis Putniņš, Oliver Rui, Alexis Stenfors, Johan Sulaeman, Andrea Signori, Peter Szilagyi, David Twomey, Silvio Vismara, Peter Winker, Wenfeng Wu, and Alfred Yawson. These authors are all world-leading experts on the subject matter covered in their chapters. It was a privilege working with them and having the opportunity to integrate their timely analyses into this book.

Carol Alexander would like to thank the University of Sussex Business School, and her colleagues in the Department of Accounting in Finance in particular, for such a friendly and supportive workplace. Douglas Cumming wishes to thank Sofia Johan for helpful comments on some of the work prepared here. Douglas Cumming is grateful to the Florida Atlantic University College of Business, and Dean Dan Gropper in particular, for offering a professional work environment consistent with the best practices in university administration.

Carol Alexander and Douglas Cumming, March 2020.

Chapter 1

Introduction

Carol Alexander
University of Sussex

Douglas Cumming
Florida Atlantic University

This book covers two general areas of financial market misconduct:

1. Market manipulation in the course of financial trading on stock exchanges (hereafter referred to as "market manipulation" in this chapter), and
2. Financial fraud, or non-trading related fraud (hereafter referred to as "financial fraud" in this chapter).

The CFA Institute (2014) survey of its members shows that most practitioners believe that market manipulation and financial fraud are among the most important issues facing financial markets around the world. Indeed, market manipulation and both types of financial fraud are commonplace. For instance, Cumming, Dannhauser and Johan (2015) report that roughly 1.9%, 4.5%, and 5.1% of NYSE, NASDAQ, and pink sheet companies, respectively, face enforcement actions from the Securities and Exchange Commission (SEC) each year. Similarly, detected fraud cases affect approximately 3.8% of listed companies in China each year. But detected fraud is just the tip of the iceberg, so to speak, and Dyck, Morse and Zingales (2010, 2014) estimated that up to 14% of all US firms have engaged in fraud.

Enforcement varies significantly across countries. In fact, there are enormous differences in enforcement rates in Europe, despite countries having similar market misconduct rules (Cumming, Groh, and Johan, 2018). And there is scant enforcement in some emerging markets such as Brazil, which had its first ever reported insider trading case in 2011. Even in Germany, the (now defunct) Neur Markt, a small-company growth market, reported only four cases of fraud (Cumming et al., 2015).

The consequences of fraud are extremely severe to managers and shareholders alike. Karpoff et al. (2008a) shows that fraud costs firms 20–38% of a firm's long-term stock market value. Karpoff et al. (2008b) show significant negative career consequences to managers that engage in market manipulation and financial fraud: 93% lose their jobs, and 28% face criminal prosecution, serving an average of 4.3 years of jail time.

This book offers a unifying look at the different types of market manipulation and financial fraud. The chapters in this book:

- Explain the various types of market manipulation and financial fraud;
- Describe the factors that mitigate or exacerbate their occurrence;
- Discuss their consequences in terms of penalties and/or financial market impact;
- Provide evidence for the presence of fraud in specific markets, such as cryptocurrencies, LIBOR and foreign exchange;
- Summarize the lessons to be learned about detection and enforcement of market manipulation and financial fraud.

The book is organized into five sections. Part I provides a general overview, where different types of market misconduct and financial fraud are defined, and the market and reputational penalties are explained. Part I comprises 5 chapters (Chapters 2–6) from leading authors around the world. The scope of the chapters is explained in Table 1.1, Panels A (for market manipulation) and B (for financial fraud). Chapter 2 by Tālis J. Putniņš provides a comprehensive overview of the different types of market manipulation. Chapter 3 by Ai Deng and Priyank Ghandi includes additional information on market manipulation and extends the discussion to financial fraud. Chapter 4 by Chelsea Liu and Alfred Yawson offers a comprehensive review of the market and reputational penalties associated with market manipulation and financial fraud. Chapter 5 by Jonathan Batten, Igor Lončarski and Peter Szilagyi provides detailed explanations of various issues in price manipulation and insider trading and describes detected cases of such misconduct. Chapter 6 by Jonathan Karpoff offers critical insights into the consequences of financial fraud based on findings from precisely compiled large-sample evidence.

Part II provides analyses of specific contexts and markets. Chapter 7 by Alexis Stenfors provides insights into the foreign exchange market based on his first-hand practical experience as well as his research on topic. Chapter 8 by David Twomey and Andrew Mann examines the cryptocurrency market. Chapter 9 by Ryan Davies offers a detailed look at the context of closing prices, which are frequently the subject of manipulation, since closing prices are used in determining various other things in financial market, such as executive compensation, whether options trade in or out of the money, and M&A prices and terms. Chapter 10 by Sam Baker provides insights into market manipulation and financial fraud cases from the experience and perspective of a financial market trader who has dealing with regulations on a daily basis for many years.

Part III considers different financial market players that engage in market manipulation and financial fraud. Chapter 11 by Duc Duy Nguyen, Jens Hagendorff and Arman Eshraghi analyses fraud among banks. Chapter 12 by Steven Dimmock, Joseph Farizo, and William Gerken examines fraud by investment advisors. Chapter 13 by Johan Sulaeman and Gennaro Bernile discusses how options backdating is a form of fraud. Stefano Paleari, Andrea Signori and Silvio Vismara provide an empirical analysis of misconduct in the context of pricing Initial Public Offerings, in Chapter 14. And in Chapter 15, Joseph McCahery and Alexander Roode examine the role of financial fraud through financial outsourcing to third parties and provide comprehensive survey evidence of the extent of the problems.

Part IV covers detection of market manipulation and financial misconduct. Chapter 16 by Mike Aitken, Anne Leduc and Sian Ji describes computer surveillance and technologies for detecting manipulation, and the computer software that is used by exchanges and their regulators. Chapter 17 by Ai Deng and Priyank Ghandi explains econometric and statistical tools to detect financial fraud. Chapter 18 by Professors Bannier, Ewelt-Knauer, Lips, and Winker provides an empirical review of Benford's Law and its application to detecting financial misconduct, with an illustration using data pertaining to the LIBOR scandal.

Part V provides an overview of financial market regulation relating to manipulation and fraud. Chapter 19 by Anita Indira Anand explains that empirical evidence around the world is consistent with the view that financial market regulation improves market efficiency and integrity and provides an in-depth analysis of regulation and enforcement issues in Canada and the UK. Chapter 20 by Mary Condon reviews issues surrounding registrant misconduct. Finally, Chapter 21 by Michael Firth, Oliver Rui and Wenfeng Wu provides empirical evidence supporting differential rates of enforcement depending on potential institutional biases, such as a "home court" advantage.

The coverage of each area of market manipulation and financial fraud in this book is summarized in Table 1.1. The range of topics is not completely exhaustive in this book. In some cases topics were excluded because authors faced confidentiality restrictions that precluded their publication. Nevertheless, we hope the broad range of materials in this book better informs and guides financial market participants, regulators, students, and academics alike. Individual cases of misconduct and outright fraud are reported frequently, whereas price and volume manipulation are so common that their occurrence is not usually conveyed to the general public. However, it is important to inform everyone about these practices, not only those directly participating in financial markets, because prices of final assets have a direct effect on the well-being of the global economy. We are, therefore, extremely indebted to the world leading authors that have contributed herein. We expect their analyses will continue to guide practice and policy for years to come.

Table 1.1 Summary of Coverage in Chapters

This table summarizes the topics in each chapter, and the scope of the chapters in terms of definitions, analyses of causes and/or consequences of fraud and misconduct, and case analyses or data. Panel A summarizes topics in financial market misconduct, Panel B summarizes topics in fraud. The different types of misconduct and fraud in the table are explained in detail in the chapters enumerated here.

Panel A. Topics in Financial Market Misconduct

Chapter	Authors	Topics	Price Manipulation, Reference Price Manipulation, and Benchmark Rigging	Circular Trading (e.g., wash, pool, matched or compensation trades; painting the tape; or warehousing), or Spoofing	Insider Trading, Collusion and Information Sharing	Improper Order Handling and Frontrunning	Misleading Customers	Abuse of Market Power, Corners, or Squeezes	Momentum Ignition, Pump and Dump, or Slur and Dump	Marking the Open (or Close or Set), Pegging or Capping	Layering, Advancing the Bid, Quote Stuffing, "Abusive liquidity detection", "pinging", or "phishing"
Section I. General											
2	Putnins	Defining Fraud, Causes, Consequences	X	X	X	X		X	X	X	X
3	Deng and Ghandi	Defining Fraud, Causes, Consequences	X	X	X	X	X				
5	Batten, Lončarski and Szilagyi	Definitions, Case Studies, and Regulations	X								

Section II. Markets

#	Author	Title								
7	Stenfors	Foreign Exchange Markets	x	x	x	x	x		x	
8	Twomey and Mann	Cryptocurrency Markets	x	x	x	x	x	x	x	x
9	Davies	Closing Prices	x		x	x				
10	Baker	Regulator's Perspective and Case Studies	x	x	x	x	x	x	x	x

Part III. Players

#	Author	Title								
12	Dimmock, Farizo and Gerken	Investment Advisors. Data: SEC filings, Form ADV filing	x							
13	Sulaeman and Bernile	Causes and Consequences of Options Backdating	x							
14	Paleari, Signori and Vismara	IPO Valuation Bias: Data: Euronext, Germany, and Italy, from the EurIPO Database	x							
15	McCahery and Roode	Third Party Financial Outsourcing; Authors' Survey Data	x				x			

(continued)

Table 1.1 (Continued)

Chapter	Authors	Topics	Price Manipulation, Reference Price Manipulation, and Benchmark Rigging	Circular Trading (e.g., wash, pool, matched or compensation trades; painting the tape; or warehousing), or Spoofing	Insider Trading, Collusion and Information Sharing	Improper Order Handling and Frontrunning	Misleading Customers	Abuse of Market Power, Corners, or Squeezes	Momentum Ignition, Pump and Dump, or Slur and Dump	Marking the Open (or Close or Set), Pegging or Capping	Layering, Advancing the Bid, Quote Stuffing, "Abusive liquidity detection", "pinging", or "phishing"
Part IV. Detection											
16	Aitken, Leduc and Ji	Surveillance in Connection to Regulation	x	x	x	x	x	x	x	x	x
17	Deng and Ghandi	Quantitative Techniques for Detection			x						
Part V. Regulation											
19	Anand	Enforcement in Canada and the UK	x		x						
20	Condon	Registrant Misconduct	x		x						

Panel B. Topics in Financial Fraud

Chapter	Authors	Topics	Money Laundering, Credit Card Fraud	Financial Statement Fraud	Options Backdating	Breach of Contract or Loan Covenant	Self Dealing, Financial Theft, or Intellectual Property Theft	Vendor, Supplier, or Procurement Fraud	Regulatory or Compliance Breach	Ponzi Scheme	Computer Intrusion Fraud and Hacking
Section I. General											
3	Deng and Ghandi	Defining Fraud, Causes, Consequences	x	x							x
4	Liu and Yawson	Market/Reputational and Regulatory Penalties		x							
5	Batten, Lončarski and Szilagyi	Definitions, Case Studies, and Regulations		x			x				
6	Karpoff	Reputational Penalties		x			x				
Section II. Markets											
8	Twomey and Mann	Cryptocurrency Markets	x	x							x

(continued)

Table 1.1 (Continued)

Chapter	Authors	Topics	Money Laundering, Credit Card Fraud	Financial Statement Fraud	Options Backdating	Breach of Contract or Loan Covenant	Self Dealing, Financial Theft, or Intellectual Property Theft	Vendor, Supplier, or Procurement Fraud	Regulatory or Compliance Breach	Ponzi Scheme	Computer Intrusion Fraud and Hacking
Part III. Players											
11	Nguyen, Hagendorff and Eshraghi	Misconduct in Banking (Data on regulatory enforcement actions issued by the FDIC, FRB and OCC)					X				
12	Dimmock, Farizo and Gerken	Investment Advisors. Data: SEC filings, Form ADV filing		X			X			X	
13	Sulaeman and Bernile	Causes and Consequences of Options Backdating			X						
14	Paleari, Signori and Vismara	IPO Valuation Bias: Data: Euronext, Germany, and Italy, from the EurIPO Database							X		

15	McCahery and Roode	Third Party Financial Outsourcing; Authors' survey data	x		x	x	x
Part IV. Detection							
16	Aitken, Leduc and Ji	Surveillance in Connection to Regulation	x				x
17	Deng and Ghandi	Quantitative Techniques for Detection	x				
18	Bannier, Ewelt-Knauer, Lips, and Winker	Benford's Law; Libor Case Study	x				
Part V. Regulation							
19	Anand	Enforcement in Canada and the UK	x		x		
20	Condon	Registrant Misconduct	x		x		x
21	Firth, Rui and Wu	Home Court Bias; 5,436 Cases from China	x	x	x		

References

CFA Institute (2014). Global Market Sentiment Survey 2015: Detailed Survey Results. CFA Institute. http://www.cfainstitute.org/Survey/gmss_2015_detailed_results.pdf.

Cumming, D.J., Dannhauser, B. and Johan, S. (2015). Financial market misconduct and agency conflicts: A synthesis and future directions. *Journal of Corporate Finance* 34: 150–168.

Cumming, D.J, Groh, A. and Johan, S. (2018). Same rules, different enforcement: Market abuse in Europe. *Journal of International Financial Markets, Institutions, & Money* 54: 130–151.

Dyck, A., Morse, A. and Zingales, L. (2010). Who blows the whistle on corporate fraud? *Journal of Finance* 65: 2063–2253.

Dyck, A., Morse, A. and Zingales, L. (2014). How pervasive is corporate fraud? Working Paper, University of Chicago.

Karpoff, J., Lee, D.S. and Martin, G.S. (2008a). The consequences to managers for cooking the books. *Journal of Financial Economics* 88: 193–215.

Karpoff, J.M., Lee, D.S. and Martin, G.S. (2008b). The consequences to managers for financial misrepresentation. *Journal of Financial Economics* 85: 66–101.

## Part I

What Are Manipulation and Fraud and Why Do They Matter?

Chapter 2

An Overview of Market Manipulation

Tālis J. Putniņš
University of Technology Sydney
Stockholm School of Economics in Riga

2.1   Introduction

Market manipulation is as old as markets. Joseph de la Vega's description of the Amsterdam Stock Exchange in 1688 provides a vivid illustration:

> Among the plays which men perform in taking different parts in this magnificent world theatre, the greatest comedy is played at the Exchange. There, . . . the speculators excel in tricks, they do business and find excuses wherein hiding places, concealment of facts, quarrels, provocations, mockery, idle talk, violent desires, collusion, artful deception, betrayals, cheatings, and even tragic end are to be found. – Joseph de la Vega (1688).

Many of the practices described by de la Vega would in today's markets be classed as market manipulation and in most jurisdictions would be illegal. Numerous other examples of market manipulation exist in history, such as when the influential Rothschilds sold large amounts of stock to create the false impression that Napoleon had defeated Wellington. Their actions caused prices to crash and allowed them to repurchase the stock at depressed prices (Griffin, 1980).

Today, market manipulation can be found in markets all around the world, in almost all asset classes, and in a wide variety of forms. The magnitude of manipulation's effects can be extraordinary; for example, the price of nearly bankrupt NEI Webworld Inc. shot up by 11,400% within a day in response to manipulators spreading rumours on the internet.[1] Manipulation is not confined to small and illiquid companies; for example, multibillion dollar Lucent Technologies was successfully manipulated (Leinweber and Madhavan, 2001). The amount of funds used in manipulation and scale of profits can be immense; for example, in 2004 Citigroup netted €18.2 million profit from manipulation that involved placing €12.9 billion worth of sell orders in 200 different government bonds within 18 seconds and later repurchasing them.[2] Manipulation is also not confined to sophisticated market participants; for example, Jonathan Lebed, a teenager from New Jersey successfully manipulated stocks 11 times by posting messages on Yahoo Finance message boards and made profits of $800,000 (Lewis, 2001). Similarly, Navinder Sarao made profits in excess of $10 million from manipulating S&P500 futures contracts, trading from his parents' home in London.[3] Nor is manipulation confined to individual securities; for example, in 1996, Nomura Int. Plc. manipulated an entire market index (Australian All Ordinaries) by selling a $600 million basket of stocks (more than the average daily market turnover) within minutes of the close of trading.[4]

Recent examples of manipulation illustrate just how enormous the impact of market manipulation can be. Regulators and law enforcement agencies have uncovered manipulation of major financial benchmarks including LIBOR, other "IBOR" benchmarks such as EURIBOR and TIBOR, and foreign exchange rate benchmarks such as

---

[1] See "Stock pump-n-dump fraudsters settle suit, earn jail time", by Brian Krebs, Newsbytes, 24 January 2001.
[2] See "The day Dr Evil wounded a financial giant", by Avinash Persaud and John Plender, Financial Times, 23 August 2006.
[3] See US CFTC v. Navinder Singh Sarao (Case No. 15-cv-3398), Consent Order.
[4] See "The financial monster that tried to eat Australia", by Ben Hill, *Sydney Morning Herald*, 11 December 1998.

the key WM/Reuters forex benchmark rates. These benchmarks underpin the pricing of hundreds of trillions of dollars' worth of financial contracts and securities such as floating rate loans/bonds, swaps, forward rate agreements, futures, and options (e.g., Duffie and Stein, 2015). To put this into context, the notional value of the affected securities and contracts exceeds the total value of US GDP. It also exceeds the total market capitalization of all companies listed on US stock markets. In fact, it exceeds the value of global GDP and the value of all listed companies globally. The outcomes of decade-long investigations and legal proceedings include billions of dollars of fines, criminal sanctions including jail sentences, and reforms including new legislation and benchmark setting mechanisms. The direct losses to affected parties are in the billions of dollars. Yet the indirect costs of such manipulation cases, including loss of confidence and participation in markets, impacts on market liquidity, and regulatory/compliance costs, could be even larger.

Market manipulation takes many forms. Markets can be manipulated by trading or by placing orders in markets. But they can also be manipulated by releasing false information or performing misleading actions. Some forms of market manipulation involve inflating prices, some involve depressing prices, and some involve both, but at different times. Some manipulation schemes are contained within a single market, yet others involve multiple related markets (e.g. an underlying and derivative market, or a transparent and dark market) with manipulators making losses in one market in order to profit in another. Financial securities within markets can be manipulated, but so too can indices and financial benchmarks. Market manipulation occurs at many frequencies with some manipulations taking years to execute, while others are completed within seconds. Manipulation can be conducted manually, programmed and automatically executed by a computer algorithm, or involve human–computer collaboration. Some market manipulation schemes are carried out by a single individual, yet others involve complex collaborations by teams of market manipulators. Section 2.3 of this chapter develops a taxonomy of the different types of market manipulation and explains the main ways in which market manipulation is conducted.

Market manipulation is difficult to precisely define. In part, this is because it encompasses a very broad collection of highly varied trading strategies as noted above. But another reason, in particular for the vagueness in legal definitions, is to minimize the risk that manipulators circumvent the law by devising schemes that fall outside of a precise and narrow legal definition. The unifying feature of market manipulation techniques is that they involve trading, placing orders, or releasing information for the purpose of creating a false or misleading appearance of the supply of, demand for, or price of a financial security or benchmark. It follows that an important distinguishing feature of market manipulation is the *intent* to mislead others or influence market prices or volumes. Section 2.2 of this chapter discusses the issue of defining market manipulation, provides examples of how manipulation is dealt with in legislation, and provides perspectives from the law and economics literature.

Finally, research on market manipulation has made considerable advances in terms of understanding how manipulation is conducted and what its effects are, but there are still many areas in which our understanding of market manipulation is limited. These include issues such as how widespread is market manipulation, how it responds to various forms of regulation, and how it affects corporate investment decisions and the real economy. Research on market manipulation is made difficult by the fact that manipulators often go to great length to conceal their actions and therefore there is often a lack of information about instances of market manipulation other than those prosecuted by regulators. Prosecution samples usually reflect a small non-random subset of all manipulation, which further complicates empirical research. Section 2.4 of this chapter provides an overview of the theoretical and empirical research on market manipulation and suggests future research directions.

2.2   Definitions of Market Manipulation

There is no generally accepted definition of market manipulation. This may seem surprising given the long history of manipulation in world financial markets[5] and the fact that more than three quarters of a century has passed since the inception of the US federal securities regulation against market manipulation.[6] Legal definitions are often intentionally not explicit, and much of the finance and economics literature uses the term "market manipulation" in an imprecise manner. This situation has led to a long-standing debate over the definition of market manipulation.

2.2.1   Legal Interpretation and Provisions against Market Manipulation

Legal definitions vary across jurisdictions and in many cases are not explicit about what constitutes market manipulation. One reason for the vagueness in legal definitions is to minimize the risk that manipulators can circumvent the law by devising schemes that fall outside of a precise and narrow legal definition. The task of defining manipulation is largely left to the courts on a case-by-case basis.

For example, in the US, statutory law states that it is unlawful "to use or employ, in connection with the purchase or sale of any security . . . any manipulative or deceptive device or contrivance".[7] In Australia, statutory law prohibits "transactions that have or are likely to have . . . the effect of . . . creating an artificial price".[8] EU statutory law stipulates, "market manipulation shall mean transactions or orders to trade which give, or are likely to give, false or misleading signals as to the supply of,

---

[5] For example, one of the most famous of the early manipulation prosecutions during the Napoleonic wars involved a group of manipulators spreading false rumours about the death of Napoleon and that the allies had entered Paris. The Court of King's Bench in England ruled that it was an offence to conspire to raise the price of Government securities by false rumours with the intent of injuring purchasers (Rex v De Berenger in Maule and Selwyn's reports 67 (1814), see Baxt et al. (1996)).

[6] A common view is that regulation against market manipulation in the US began in the 1930s with the Securities Act of 1933, the Securities Exchange Act of 1934, and the creation of the Securities and Exchange Commission (SEC) in 1934, largely in response to the massive losses suffered by the public in the Great Depression. However, Berle (1938) points out that while the reforms of the 1930s contributed significantly to bringing legal action against market manipulators, the forms of manipulation banned by the Acts of 1933–1934 were already effectively outlawed by the courts through common law.

[7] Section 10(b), Securities Exchange Act 1934. For a detailed discussion see Thel (1990) and Goldwasser (1999).

[8] Section 1041A, Corporations Act 2001.

demand for or price of financial instruments, or which secure . . . the price of one or several financial instruments at an abnormal or artificial level".[9]

Given that statutory law does not provide a precise definition of manipulation, one must turn to case law to understand what is viewed as manipulation by courts. For example, in the US, where perhaps the largest number of market manipulation cases have been brought to courts, case law has established a four part test for manipulation involving ability, intent to deceive, causation, and artificiality (Johnson, 1981).

Across a number of jurisdictions, arguably the two most important elements of market manipulation in case law, and often the most difficult to prove, are intent and artificiality. Intent distinguishes manipulative from non-manipulative trading. Legitimate, non-manipulative market participation can cause an increase in market activity or alteration of the market price. Therefore, both manipulative and legitimate trading can have the same effects on the market, but are distinguished by the fact that manipulation involves an impermissible purpose (Goldwasser, 1999). The purpose of trading in the case of market manipulation is to mislead or deceive others, or to influence (sometimes referred to as "set" or "maintain") a price or volume. Because intent can rarely be determined with certainty, this element causes significant difficulties in identifying and prosecuting market manipulation. Prosecution cases often rely on communications between market participants to infer their intention or purpose of trading.

The second element, artificiality, can be with respect to trading activity (e.g. creating the appearance of more trading than what would naturally take place), or price (e.g. altering the price by raising or depressing it). Generally speaking, an "artificial price" is created when two things occur. First, a market participant with an impermissible intention or purpose for trading engages in one or more trades or submits one or more orders to a market. And second, the orders or trades of that market participant have an effect on the market price. Consequently, the resulting market price does not reflect only genuine demand and supply, but also the "artificial" supply or demand injected by the market manipulator. It is widely accepted in the financial economics literature that buying or selling, or even signalling one's desire to buy or sell, is likely to have an effect on the market price, particularly when buying or selling in sufficiently large quantities relative to the market's liquidity. Therefore, evidence about the effects of a given market participant's trading or order submissions can involve quantifying whether the participant traded in sufficient quantities or placed order in such a way so as to impact prices. Artificial prices can also be created when false information disseminated for an impermissible purpose such as to deceive others or to influence the price received by market participants, who alter their orders or trades and thereby cause the price to be influenced by the false information.

Two recent developments in the scope of market manipulation provisions and definitions in the law are noteworthy. The first is the provisions introduced with the Dodd–Frank Act prohibiting a form of market manipulation known as "spoofing" and

---

[9] Section 1(2)(a) Market Abuse Directive 2003. Similar wording is found in the more recent European Market Abuse Regulation 2014 (Article 12).

adding further prohibitions on reckless or disorderly trading at the close.[10] Spoofing involves placing orders with the intention to cancel those orders before they execute and is often implemented with a computer algorithm (more details in the next section of this chapter). While spoofing existed well before the Dodd–Frank Act and may have been illegal under existing legislation, the addition of anti-spoofing provisions increased clarity about the legal stance in relation to this form of market manipulation. Furthermore, the rapid increase in algorithmic trading made it important that the legal framework be up to date with respect to manipulation techniques that are used by algorithmic traders, such as spoofing.

The second recent legislative development is the enactment of the Market Abuse Regulation (MAR) in Europe, which came into effect in July 2016.[11] The MAR updates the regulatory framework for market abuse in Europe, establishing new offences, and facilitating easier enforcement. Importantly, with respect to market manipulation provisions, it expands the prohibited activities to include benchmark manipulation and attempted manipulation. These provisions address the difficulties faced by prosecutors taking action against the recent benchmark manipulations (LIBOR, EURIBOR, the WM/Reuters foreign exchange benchmark rate, and so on). In some jurisdictions, financial benchmarks, although highly important to the financial system and susceptible to manipulation, fall outside of market manipulation provisions that focus on traded financial instruments. The new provisions in MAR address this shortcoming. The inclusion of provisions against attempted market manipulation increases the power of prosecutors by facilitating prosecution of cases in which the intent to manipulate can be established but the actual outcomes are difficult to measure or the manipulator is unsuccessful in influencing the price. Similar to the anti-spoofing provisions introduced in the US, the MAR also explicitly prohibits a range of market manipulation techniques that could be undertaken by algorithmic or high-frequency traders using order submissions and cancellations as the core part of the strategy.

In summary, the law in most developed markets generally considers market manipulation as actions or trades undertaken for the purpose of influencing a price or creating a misleading appearance of the supply of or demand for a financial security.

2.2.2   Economics and Legal Studies Perspective

The law and financial economics literature contains considerable debate about how to define manipulation. In a departure from mainstream legal thought, Fischel and Ross (1991) argue that market manipulation is too vague a concept to form the basis for criminal charges. They point out that there is no objective definition of manipulation and suggest that manipulation could only be defined as dishonest intent to move stock prices. In a sense, this definition is consistent with the essence of many laws in force today against market manipulation, in which intent to influence prices is one of the most important elements. Fischel and Ross argue that irrespective of intent, trades

---

[10] Dodd–Frank Wall Street Reform and Consumer Protection Act (the "Dodd–Frank Act"), resulted in a new section 4c(a)(5) of the Commodity Exchange Act, prohibiting certain disruptive trading practices.
[11] See Regulation (EU) No. 596/2014 in the Official Journal of the European Union. Although most provisions came into effect in 2016, the MiFID II-dependent provisions come into effect on January 2018.

should not be prohibited as manipulative; but fictitious trades (e.g. trades in which the buyer and seller is the same person) and spreading false information should be classified as fraud. Their reasoning is that (i) purely trade based manipulation is unlikely to be successful; and (ii) rules that prohibit manipulation deter some legitimate trading. Dozens of subsequent prosecution cases that show purely trade-based market manipulation is not just a theoretical possibility, but can be highly profitable, casts doubt over their reasoning.

Thel (1994) delivers a strong rebuttal. Based on evidence in the economics literature Thel argues that manipulation is easier to accomplish than Fischel and Ross claim and provides some striking examples. Thel points out that manipulators can sometimes control prices with trades and in doing so profit either from pre-existing contracts that are contingent on prices, or by inducing other market participants to trade at manipulated prices.

Thel uses the term "manipulation" to mean trading undertaken with the intent of increasing or decreasing the reported price of a security. Cherian and Jarrow (1995) define manipulation as trading by an individual (or group of individuals) in a manner such that the share price is influenced to his advantage. Many subsequent papers implicitly use the term "market manipulation" to refer to trading strategies or actions taken to influence the price to one's advantage.

In forming their view about what forms of trading should or should not be prohibited, Kyle and Viswanathan (2008) consider the welfare effects of trading. They propose that trading strategies should only be illegal if they undermine economic efficiency both by decreasing price accuracy and reducing liquidity. Unless both of these conditions are satisfied, the trading strategy is not unambiguously socially harmful and therefore, according to Kyle and Viswanathan, should not be prohibited.

2.3   A Taxonomy of the Types of Market Manipulation

The term "market manipulation" encompasses a wide variety of different strategies. To map out the relations between the various forms of market manipulation, Figure 2.1 provides a taxonomy of the most common types of market manipulation. The taxonomy is an expanded version of the framework set out in Putniņš (2012), accounting for recent forms of market manipulation. This section first describes the two broad levels on which manipulation can be grouped into categories and then defines the individual techniques.

2.3.1   Categories of Market Manipulation

At the broadest level, manipulation can be divided into four categories: runs, contract-based or benchmark manipulations, spoofing, and market power techniques. Within these groups, manipulation can be further broken down according to the main mechanism used to facilitate the manipulation: trade-based, information-based, action-based, submission-based, and order-based forms. And within these mechanisms are a number of individual manipulation techniques. These categories and mechanisms are not mutually exclusive and there are also hybrid manipulation strategies that combine several of the individual techniques or elements of the techniques.

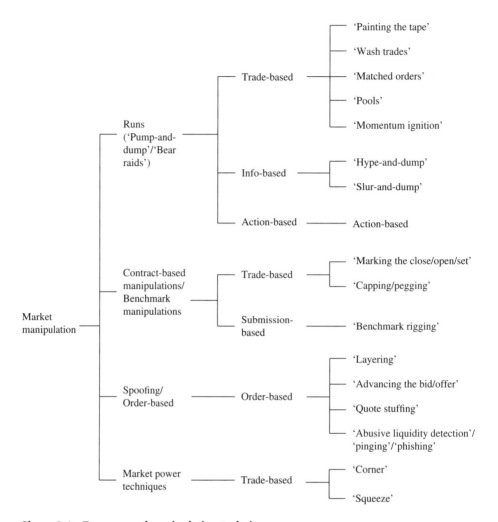

Figure 2.1   Taxonomy of manipulation techniques.

In the first category of market manipulation, "runs", the manipulator takes either a long or a short position in a stock, inflates or deflates the stock's price while attracting other traders, and finally reverses his position at the inflated or deflated price. While runs are commonly observed in the stock market, in principle they could be conducted in any financial security. Runs that involve the manipulator taking a long position and then inflating a stock's price are often referred to as "pump-and-dump" manipulation, whereas the reverse strategy of first taking a short position and then manipulating the price downwards is known as a "bear raid". The stock "pumping" or "raiding" can take anywhere from a matter of seconds to several years and involve techniques such as spreading rumours, executing wash trades, and coordinated pooling by several manipulators.

A feature of runs is that the manipulator profits directly from the manipulated market by exploiting other investors that buy at inflated prices or sell at depressed prices. The main challenge in conducting this form of manipulation is having to induce other market participants to buy or sell the manipulated security.

The second category of market manipulation, "contract-based manipulation" or "benchmark manipulation" or "reference rate manipulation" contrasts with a run in that it involves the manipulator profiting from a contract or market that is *external* to the manipulated market. For example, a manipulator might take a position in a derivatives contract and then manipulate the underlying stock price to profit from the derivatives position. Or a manipulator might have positions in securities whose cash flows or prices are determined by a financial benchmark (e.g. floating rate loans, swaps, futures) and then manipulate the benchmark to profit from the external positions.

An important difference between runs and contract-based or reference rate manipulation is that the latter does not require the manipulator to induce others to trade at manipulated prices. This category of manipulation therefore tends to be more mechanical.

The third category of manipulation is "spoofing" and other order-based techniques. Generally speaking, spoofing involves submitting orders to a market with the intention to cancel the orders before they execute. The defining feature of this category is that orders play a central role in the manipulation, although they are often accompanied by trades as part of the strategy. Although spoofing can be performed manually, this type of market manipulation naturally lends itself to being implemented by a computer algorithm that manages the entry, amendment, and cancellation of the manipulative orders. Automating the strategy allows it to be scaled and repeated many times. While each instance of spoofing might make only a small profit, repetition can be used to accumulate a sizable profit. This category of manipulation is often implemented at relatively high frequencies, with positions typically opened and closed intraday.

Due to the growth in algorithmic and high-frequency trading, spoofing and order-based market manipulation techniques have gained increasing attention in recent years. Regulators have brought a number of prosecution cases against such manipulation, lawmakers have made legislative amendments to account for this form of manipulation, and market/surveillance system operators have developed algorithms to detect such strategies.

The fourth broad category of manipulation techniques involves the manipulator exploiting market power by, for example, taking a controlling position in the supply of a security. Like contract-based manipulation, market power techniques are more mechanical in nature than runs. However, they are similar to runs in that the manipulator profits by exploiting participants of the manipulated market.

Within the four broad categories, manipulation techniques can be further grouped according to the five main mechanisms used in their implementation. Allen and Gale (1992) define three of the five techniques: trade-based, information-based, and action-based techniques, which I augment by adding order-based and submission-based techniques. Trade-based manipulation involves influencing the price of a financial instrument through trading. In information-based manipulation, a manipulator releases false information or rumours about a company in order to inflate or depress its share price. Action-based manipulation involves taking actions to affect the value or perceived value of a firm. For example, a company director may shut down a factory to depress the share price. Order-based manipulation involves using order submissions, amendments, and cancellations as a core part of the strategy, with orders that are not intended to execute. Submission-based manipulation involves making false or misleading submissions to a financial benchmark calculation.

2.3.2   Market Manipulation Techniques

Each of the broad categories of market manipulation encompasses a range of individual techniques, particularly trade- and order-based manipulation.[12] Runs, such as pump-and-dump or bear raids, can be implemented using one or several of the following trade-based manipulation techniques.

(i)   Painting the tape
Involves engaging in a series of transactions that are reported on a public display facility (the "tape") to give a false impression of the degree of trading activity or interest in the stock or its price. Painting the tape often involves "wash sales" and "matched orders", which are defined below.

(ii)   Wash trades
Are improper transactions in which the buyer and seller is the same person such that there is no genuine change in ownership. Such trades are usually intended to inflate the appearance of trading activity or to print misleading prices to the tape that records or displays trade prices. Sometimes, to circumvent broker-level controls or to reduce the probability of detection, a manipulator will execute wash trades using several different accounts or multiple brokers.

(iii)   Matched orders
Are related to the practice of wash sales and involve pairs of buy and sell orders placed by different but colluding parties at the around same time for the same price and similar volume. Manipulators using matched orders usually seek to have the same effect as when using wash trades, but merely separate the buying and selling entities to avoid conducting prohibited wash trades.

(iv)   Pools
Are when a group of manipulators trade shares back and forth among themselves to influence prices and create the appearance of trading volume.

(v)   Momentum ignition
Involves executing a series of buys or sells in quick succession, often at progressively increasing/decreasing prices. The objective is to induce others to trade, in particular

---

[12] For a list of the techniques targeted by market surveillance authorities, see Cumming and Johan (2008). For a (non-exhaustive) list of techniques considered by European securities market regulators, see the European Securities and Markets Authority Final Report ESMA/2015/224.

short-term trend followers (momentum traders). The manipulator then reverses their position by selling to or buying from the trend followers. While momentum ignition can be implemented manually, it can also be implemented algorithmically and can be designed to prey on other trading algorithms that are programmed to respond to price movements. Momentum ignition can also sometimes exploit stop loss orders to mechanically induce others to trade in a given direction. For example, margin traders with a long position might have a stop loss to sell their position if the price falls below some threshold, whereas short sellers might have a stop loss to repurchase the position if the price rises above some threshold. Either of these stop loss orders could be targeted by a manipulator to try and ignite momentum. The process of searching for stop-loss thresholds is sometimes referred to as "stop hunting".

Runs can also be facilitated with information-based or action-based manipulation techniques that can be used instead of, or in conjunction with, any of the above trade-based techniques.

(vi) Hype-and-dump
Involves dissemination of positive, false information or positive rumours via the media, internet, phone calls/emails, or other means to inflate a security's price.

(vii) Slur-and-dump
Is like hype-and-dump but instead involves spreading negative, false information to cause a decrease in the security's price.

(viii) Action-based
Manipulation, although rarely seen in practice, involves taking real actions (e.g. operational changes within a company) to affect its price, rather than merely disseminating false information or trading.

The second category, contract-based or reference-price manipulation can be implemented with a few different trade-based manipulation techniques including the following.

(ix) Marking the close
Also known as "closing price manipulation", "high closing", "banging the close", and "punching the close", involves buying or selling securities at or shortly before the close of trading to alter the closing price. The price distortions are particularly harmful because of the widespread use of closing prices – they are widely followed by investors and used in a large number of contracts and derivatives as a reference price or benchmark.[13] Their widespread use is also what creates the incentive for closing price manipulation. Marking the close is more mechanical than runs because the manipulator only needs to sustain a price distortion for a short time period at the close and does not necessarily need to induce others to trade. However, marking the close can also be used in conjunction with other techniques to facilitate runs.

---

[13] For example, stock closing prices are used to determine payoffs from derivative securities such as options, evaluate broker execution quality, calculate mutual fund net asset values and therefore determine fund manager performance and remuneration, pricing seasoned equity offerings, determining merger/takeover prices, deciding index inclusion, evaluating stock exchange minimum price requirements, margin calls, and so on (see Comerton-Forde and Putniņš, 2011a,b, 2014).

(x)   Marking the open
Is similar to marking the close, but involves influencing the opening price rather than closing price.

(xi)   Marking the set or *banging the set*
Is also similar to closing price manipulation but involves trading to influence a particular reference rate set, which might not be at the close or open. For example, in a 24-hour market, such as the global foreign exchange market, key reference rates are set at predetermined times, which are not necessarily the open or close of trading.

(xii)   Pegging and *capping*
Refer to placing orders that effectively prevent a price from moving up or down beyond a particular threshold, thereby setting a floor or ceiling price. This is often done to ensure a derivatives contract expires in or out of the money, or that a reference rate or benchmark does not move in an unfavourable direction. For example, a manipulator that wants to prevent a stock price from moving below $5.00 might place large buy orders at a price of $5.00 to prevent any trades from occurring below this price. Pegging and/or capping can be implemented dynamically with a threshold that is adjusted by the market manipulator in response to changing conditions. For example, if the manipulator in the above example encounters very heavy selling against his $5.00 order, he might retreat (amend his buy order) to a price of, say, $4.95 and seek to prevent further declines. Such a retreating defence can be used to reduce the extent of adverse price movements.

Benchmarks that are based on submissions of a select group of benchmark panellists (e.g. the mechanism used for setting LIBOR at the time of the recent LIBOR manipulations) rather than an actual underlying market can be manipulated through submission-based manipulation techniques:

(xiii)   Benchmark rigging
Achieved through submission-based manipulation involves making false or misleading submissions as inputs to a financial benchmark calculation. When there are many parties whose submissions are used in calculating the benchmark, and/or when the benchmark calculation involves a trimmed mean whereby the highest and lowest submissions is excluded from the average, submitters might collude to influence the benchmark as the impact of one individual submission can be small.[14]

Spoofing and other order-based manipulation strategies, which are often but not always implemented via a computer algorithm, include the following techniques.

(xiv)   Layering
Is a form of spoofing that involves placing one or several orders on one side of a visible limit order book (the bid or the offer side) at one or several price steps to create a false or misleading impression with respect to the real demand or supply in a given security. Being a form of spoofing, the manipulator's intention is for the orders not to execute and therefore most spoofing orders result in cancellations. The term

---

[14] For example, at the time of the recent manipulations, USD LIBOR was based on submissions from around 20 banks, taking an average that excludes the highest one-quarter and lowest one-quarter of the submissions.

"layering" stems from the fact that often the manipulator's orders are placed in layers across several price steps or on top of one another at a given price step. Layering could also be done with a single large order. Collectively, the layering orders often represent a substantial proportion of the orders on one side of the limit order book. They are often placed close to the best quotes at the time, and sometimes dynamically amended (or cancelled) as the market moves closer to the layering orders to avoid execution. Layering can be used to help obtain a more favourable execution price for a trade that the market participant wants to execute for an unrelated reason. For example, a trader wanting to sell out of a long position could use layering buy orders to temporarily inflate the market price by misleading other market participants and then sell the actual position at an inflated price. However, layering can be, and often is, used repeatedly in a cycle together with other orders that profit from distorted prices. A typical layering cycle is as follows: (i) place a small sell order at or near the best ask price, (ii) layer the bid side of the order book until the market moves up and the small sell order executes, (iii) cancel the layering bid orders and repeat the above steps in the opposite direction.

(xv)   Advancing the bid/offer

Involves placing a buy or sell order within the prevailing best quotes for the purpose of setting a new best bid or best offer price. These orders are often not intended to execute and are therefore much like an aggressive layering strategy. Advancing the bid or offer can be used to give other market participants a false signal about the security's demand or supply and therefore can be used in conjunction with other techniques to cause a run. Alternatively, advancing the bid or offer can be used in manipulating a benchmark or reference price. The bid and ask quotes, or their half-way point (the "midquote") are often used as reference prices for pegged dark/hidden orders, dark pools, crossing systems, and some alternative trading venues. Therefore, advancing the bid or offer on a transparent reference market can be done as part of a strategy that exploits orders or trading venues that reference the manipulated market's quotes. For example, a manipulator that detects the presence of a dark sell order pegged to the midquote can place an order that lowers the offer and thus midquote on the transparent reference market, then buy in the dark at the artificially low midquote, and finally cancel the order that lowered the offer.

(xvi)   Quote stuffing

Involves jamming a financial market's infrastructure, such as the matching engine that processes incoming order messages or the systems that disseminate market data to participants, by submitting an enormous number of order submission, amendment, and cancellation messages in a short period of time (typically, second or sub-second horizons). By overwhelming the financial market's processing capacity, quote stuffing can increase latency for anyone trying to submit legitimate orders to the market, or deny other participants timely information on the actual state of the orders in a market. It appears possible to slow down an entire market (such as the NYSE) by quote stuffing only one or a subset of the stocks traded on that market. Thus, quote stuffing allows a manipulator to control the latency of markets to their advantage. While intense bursts of order submissions and cancellations that appear consistent with quote stuffing are frequently observed in today's markets (e.g. Egginton et al., 2016), it is less clear exactly how this manipulation technique is used in conjunction with other strategies to make a profit. Quote stuffing has nevertheless been acknowledged as a form of market manipulation in several jurisdictions, in particular if the orders are submitted with the intention of being cancelled before execution.[15]

(xvii)   Abusive liquidity detection, pinging, or *phishing*
Involves submitting small probing orders for the purpose of detecting hidden or latent liquidity. While such orders can result in trade executions, that is not their dominant purpose. Rather, their dominant purpose is to gather information about other market participants' trading intentions, which is then exploited to make a profit (often at the expense of those traders whose intentions were inferred). For example, to gauge whether there are buyers, sellers, or neither buyers nor sellers waiting to trade in a dark pool or trade with dark orders pegged to the midquote, a trader might submit a small probing order (for as little as one share if allowed by the trading protocol) to buy at the midquote. If the order executes, the trader knows that others are trying to sell at the midquote. If the order does not execute, the trader might cancel the order and place a small probing order to *sell* at the midquote. If that order executes, the trader knows there are buyers wanting to buy at the midquote. And if that order does not execute, the trader knows that there are no resting dark orders waiting to trade at the midquote. The trader then uses the information about others' trading intentions to earn a profit. This often involves trading in the direction of others' intentions, but before them, exploiting the impact that their future orders will have on market prices. Such techniques have gained popularity with the growth in algorithmic and high-frequency trading and regulatory responses are still emerging. So far, Canadian and European regulators have expressed views that such trading is considered market manipulation.[16]

The final category of market manipulation exploiting market power involves two trade-based manipulation techniques, which have been used in markets for decades if not centuries.

(xviii)   Corners and *squeezes*
Are techniques in which the manipulator secures a controlling position in the supply of an asset and/or a derivative contract. The manipulator then uses this position to manipulate the price by exploiting investors that need the underlying asset to close out short positions or deliver on a derivative contract.

2.4   Research on Market Manipulation

This section provides an overview of the academic research on market manipulation. If focuses on identifying what we know about market manipulation from the literature, as well as highlighting deficiencies and future research directions. The section

---

[15] For example, the Investment Industry Regulatory Organization of Canada (IIROC) Rules Notice Guidance Note 13-0053 confirms IIROC's position that quote stuffing is "considered a manipulative and deceptive trading practice". Similarly, the US Commodity Futures Trading Commission (CFTC) Interpretative Guidance and Policy Statement (RIN 3088-AD96) concerning the anti-spoofing provisions introduced into US legislation with the Dodd–Frank Act provides quote stuffing as one of the examples of trading that is considered spoofing and therefore prohibited.

[16] See IIROC Rules Notice Guidance Note 13-0053 and ESMA Final Report 2015/224.

starts with an overview of the theoretical literature, followed by the empirical litera-ture. It then summarizes what we know and don't know about market manipulation based on the literature and points out some future research directions.

2.4.1   Theoretical Literature

The theoretical market manipulation literature provides insights about the conditions under which manipulation is possible and profitable. The literature, which spans the past 30 years, is fairly extensive, particularly regarding trade-based manipulation, and to a lesser extent information-based techniques. Although action-based manipu-lation is not explicitly studied in the literature, it can often be viewed as a type of information-based strategy because the manipulator's actions create a false signal similar to false information. Consequently, many of the findings about information-based manipulation are relevant for action-based manipulation. There is a deficiency when it comes to theoretical models of order-based manipulation techniques such as spoofing and layering. This deficiency is in part because these techniques have only in recent years gained significant regulatory attention, but also because of the difficulties in forming tractable and realistic limit order book models.

(i)   Trade-based manipulation

Early theoretical trade-based manipulation literature establishes very general condi-tions under which pure trade-based manipulation in a single market (e.g. a series of buys followed by a series of sells) is and is not profitable. Fischel and Ross (1991), among others, argue that trade-based manipulation is not possible in an efficient mar-ket. Jarrow (1992), Cherian and Kuriyan (1995) and Cherian and Jarrow (1995) build on the model of Hart (1977) and derive conditions under which trade-based manipu-lation is not possible. In Cherian and Kuriyan's model, manipulation is not possible with rational agents when price responses to trades are symmetric. Jarrow demon-strates that a sufficient condition to exclude market manipulation strategies is that the price response function depends only on a trader's aggregate stock holdings and not on his past sequence of trades, in other words, when prices do not exhibit momen-tum. Huberman and Stanzl (2004) demonstrate that uninformed trading strategies that generate infinite expected profits (in effect, trade-based market manipulation strate-gies) are ruled out when the price impacts of trades are time independent and linear.

Empirically, price impacts are not linear, nor are they time-invariant, nor are they always symmetrical. Thus, the conditions shown by theory to be necessary to rule out profitable trade-based market manipulation are not satisfied in practice, suggesting that some trade-based manipulation strategies should be profitable in real markets. Actual trade-based strategies can exploit non-linearity, time variation, or asymmetry in price impacts.

Many theoretical studies seek to prove that trade-based manipulation is possible in variations of the seminal models of Kyle (1985) and Glosten and Milgrom (1985). For example, Allen and Gorton (1992) argue that the natural asymmetry between liquidity purchases and liquidity sales gives rise to profitable trade-based manipula-tion. If liquidity-motivated sales are more likely than liquidity-motivated purchases, buy orders are more informed on average and therefore have a larger effect on prices. In a Glosten and Milgrom (1985) model, this asymmetry allows an uninformed manipulator to generate a profit by executing a series of buys to bid up the price and then sell the stock, causing a relatively smaller decrease in price. Allen and Gale (1992) similarly use a Glosten and Milgrom (1985) framework, but in their model an uninformed manipulator mimics an informed trader with positive information about the stock. The uninformed trader's manipulation is profitable under certain restrictions on the strategy of the informed trader. Of critical importance to the success of such a strategy is information asymmetry. Investors are uncertain whether a large trader who buys the stock does so because he knows it is undervalued or because he intends to manipulate the price. Aggarwal and Wu (2006) extend this model and provide the insight that although information seekers (or arbitrageurs) generally make markets more efficient, when manipulation is possible more information seekers imply greater competition for shares, making it easier for an uninformed manipulator to enter the market and harm market efficiency.

An important insight from the literature above is that the information asymmetry that is present in almost all financial markets to varying degrees is one of the enablers of profitable trade-based market manipulation. Market manipulators can exploit the fact that other market participants will not be able to tell for sure whether their trades are informed or uninformed.

Unlike the previous studies that examine *uninformed* manipulators, Chakraborty and Yilmaz (2004a, 2004b) demonstrate that in Glosten and Milgrom (1985) and Kyle (1985) models, *informed* traders can also benefit from manipulating the market by bluffing. When the existence of an informed trader is uncertain and there is a large number of trading periods before all private information is revealed, long-lived informed traders will manipulate the market in every equilibrium by initially trading in the opposite direction to their information. This bluffing strategy results in short-term losses for the informed traders; however, the increased noise in the trading process allows them to retain their informational advantage for longer and extract more profit from their information. Intuitively, the value of confusing the market exceeds the costs of trading against one's own private information. When there are many competitive rational traders who hold coarser information than the insider but finer information than the market maker, the manipulator has added incentive to manipulate because the competitive rational traders follow the insider's trades in equilibrium (Chakraborty and Yilmaz, 2008).

A number of studies model how specific securities (e.g. derivatives), events (e.g. seasoned equity offerings), or market design features (e.g. trade reporting requirements) give rise to profitable trade-based manipulation. Jarrow (1994) provides evidence of manipulation strategies that arise from derivative securities. In Gerard and Nanda (1993), strategic informed traders short sell a stock just prior to a seasoned equity offering to place downward pressure on the price. The manipulators then more than cover their position by purchasing stocks in the offering at a discount price, and finally liquidate their positions at a profit when the stock price is eventually restored to its fair value. In Fishman and Hagerty (1995), a manipulator takes advantage of the Securities Exchange Act (1934) mandatory disclosure rule for large trades. The manipulator declares large buys, thereby forcing prices up, and then sells the position anonymously in a series of small trades. John and Narayanan (1997) and Huddart et al. (2001) also examine the effect of mandatory disclosure laws on the insider's incentive to manipulate. Kyle (1984), Vila (1987), and Allen et al. (2006)

model corners and squeezes in which manipulators control prices by obtaining a large fraction of the supply. Pirrong (1993) shows that squeezes hinder price discovery and create deadweight losses. In Vila (1989) and Bagnoli and Lipman (1996), a manipulator trades to give the impression of a takeover bid, misleading the market and allowing the manipulator to profit by selling at an inflated price.

Theory suggests that another mechanism manipulators can exploit to their advantage is feedback from financial markets to the real value of a firm. One form of such feedback occurs when directors use their company's stock price as a signal in making decisions about the company's investment. In Goldstein and Guembel's (2008) model, manipulators aggressively short sell shares to depress share prices, thereby negatively influencing companies' investment decisions, harming fundamentals and allowing the short sellers to cover their positions at depressed prices. Khanna and Sonti (2004) demonstrate that feedback from stock prices to fundamental values can also be exploited in the other direction. In their model, long-term shareholders manipulate prices upwards to encourage value creating investment. These studies illustrate that manipulation can reduce economic efficiency by distorting resource allocation.

In contrast to much of the theoretical literature, Hanson and Oprea (2009) do not seek to demonstrate the possibility or profitability of manipulation, but rather they examine the effects manipulators have on price accuracy. They find that in a Kyle (1985) model adapted to an illiquid prediction market setting, an agent with an exogenous preference for manipulation has the somewhat counter-intuitive ex-ante effect of *increasing* price accuracy. This effect arises because informed trading is more profitable in the presence of a manipulator and so more traders are willing to incur the costs of becoming informed.

A few studies specifically analyse closing price manipulation. Kumar and Seppi (1992) use a Kyle (1985) framework to model a manipulator that takes a substantial long position in the futures market and then aggressively bids up the spot price before the close to profit from a more favourable futures settlement price. In Hillion and Suominen (2004), brokers manipulate closing prices to alter customers' perceptions of their execution quality. Their model demonstrates that closing call auctions reduce manipulation and enhance price efficiency. In a model of a mutual fund manager's investment decision, Bernhardt and Davies (2009) show that fund managers have incentives to use short-term price impacts to manipulate closing prices at the ends of reporting periods.

(ii)   Information-based and action-based manipulation
Vila (1989) uses game theory to model a simple scenario in which a manipulator short sells a stock, releases false and damaging information about the stock, and then covers his position at the depressed price. Bagnoli and Lipman (1996) analyse a model in which a manipulator announces a false takeover bid to drive up the price of a stock. The profitability of both strategies hinges on the credibility of the information released by the manipulator. In repetitions of such games, if market participants are able to deduce that false information originated from a manipulator, the manipulator will quickly be discredited and the manipulation strategy will cease to be profitable.

To overcome the problem of credibility in repeated games, Benabou and Laroque (1992) and Van Bommel (2003) model the use of imprecise information to influence stock prices. In Benabou and Laroque (1992), noise in private information restricts the ability of traders to verify the truthfulness of a piece of information. Consequently traders, such as company insiders, journalists or stock analysts, can manipulate stock prices over a long period of time without losing credibility by mixing truth and lies in the information they release. Van Bommel (2003) uses a Kyle (1985) framework to model informed investors that manipulate prices by spreading imprecise rumours. In equilibrium, rumours are informative and therefore rational profit maximizing agents trade on them. Because the rumours are imprecise, prices occasionally overshoot. This allows the informed rumourmonger to profit not only from trading on their information, but also from trading against overshot prices. Eren and Ozsoylev (2006) use a similar model to Van Bommel (2003) and find that hype-and-dump manipulation increases market depth and trading volume, but decreases market efficiency.

2.4.2   Empirical Literature

The theoretical literature is valuable, particularly in: (i) providing insights about the conditions under which manipulation is possible; and (ii) identifying circumstances in which profitable manipulation opportunities may exist even if no such cases have yet been reported. However, many manipulation strategies are too complicated to be modelled theoretically and the assumptions and simplifications made in order for theoretical models to be tractable lead to questions about the validity of their results in real markets. For these reasons empirical research plays an important role in understanding market manipulation. Compared to the theoretical literature, empirical studies are fewer and more recent. This is largely due to the difficulties in obtaining data. This section provides an overview of studies that report circumstantial or indirect evidence on manipulation, followed by studies of known manipulation cases, and finally, the small number of experimental studies.

(i)   Indirect empirical evidence
Early empirical asset pricing and market microstructure studies identify various abnormalities in closing prices, but do not link the abnormalities to market manipulation.[17] More recently, however, several studies attribute seasonal patterns and anomalies in day-end trading to closing price manipulation. Felixson and Pelli (1999) examine whether closing prices are manipulated in the Finnish stock market using regression analysis. Although their results are consistent with the hypothesis that closing prices are manipulated, they concede that further research is required to be conclusive. Hillion and Suominen (2004) find on the Paris Bourse that significant rises in volatility, volume, and bid-ask spreads occur mainly in the last minute of trading and they attribute this effect to manipulation. Carhart et al. (2002) find more conclusively that in US equities markets, price inflation is localized in the last half hour before the close

---

[17] See Keim (1983) and Ariel (1987) on seasonal patterns and Wood et al. (1985) and Harris (1989) on intraday anomalies.

and that it is more intense on quarter-end days. They report that 80% of funds beat the S&P 500 Index on the last trading day of the year, but only 37% do so on the first trading day of a new year. They attribute this phenomenon to manipulation by fund managers. Similarly, Ben-David et al. (2013) conclude that hedge funds also manipulate closing stock prices. This conclusion is based mainly on the fact that stocks held in large quantities by hedge funds exhibit abnormal returns in the last minutes of trading on quarter-end days, followed by return reversals.

Empirical studies that analyse stock prices around options expiration generally find that effects of manipulation can be found in the last hour before options expire and that the price effect is reversed in the first half hour of trading after expiration (Stoll and Whaley, 1987; Chamberlain et al., 1989; Stoll and Whaley, 1991). Ni et al. (2005) find evidence that on option expiration dates the closing prices of stocks with listed options cluster at option strike prices. They attribute this finding to closing price manipulation. McDonald and Michayluk (2003) examine whether manipulators exploit the trading halt mechanism on the Paris Bourse, where trading is halted in a stock when an order is submitted outside the daily price limits. They document suspicious trading characteristics around some trading halts, consistent with manipulators submitting trade-ending orders to secure the most recent trade price as the closing price. Zdorovtsov, Tang, and Onayev (2017)) find patterns of abnormal returns around the reconstitution of the Russell 3000 index. They suggest the patterns of returns are caused by closing price manipulation that is intended to influence the index reconstitution.

The literature also provides some indirect evidence about relatively high-frequency (intraday) spoofing manipulation. For example, Lee et al. (2013) analyse account-level limit order book data from the Korean stock exchange. They find patterns of order submissions and cancellations consistent with spoofing, and more specifically, layering. Their results suggest that manipulators exploited a particular feature of the Korean stock exchange as part of their spoofing strategies; namely, until 2002, the Korean stock exchange displayed the total quantity of orders on each side of the order book without displaying prices, which meant that displayed volume could be easily manipulated by placing orders very far from the best quotes with little chance of the orders executing.

Griffin and Shams (2018) provide a collection of circumstantial evidence that suggests the VIX Volatility index is manipulated around the time that VIX futures and options settle. VIX is calculated from the prices of S&P 500 index options, including highly illiquid deep out-of-the-money options. The evidence suggests traders manipulate the VIX index by aggressively trading the illiquid deep out-of-the-money S&P 500 index options, presumably to profit from the settlement of VIX derivatives.

Some studies find evidence of manipulation by examining the trading records of likely manipulators, rather than market prices. Khwaja and Mian (2005) find evidence of pump-and-dump market manipulation by brokers in Pakistan's main stock exchange. Brokers earn at least 8% higher returns on their own trades and neither market timing nor liquidity provision offer sufficient explanations for this result. They conclude that traders in developing markets resist stronger regulation to maintain high rents, suggesting poor regulatory systems hinder market development. Gallagher et al. (2009) support the earlier findings of Carhart et al. (2002) that some fund managers manipulate closing prices to influence their fund's reported performance. Gallagher et al. (2009) find that on the last day of the quarter, fund managers tend to purchase illiquid stocks in which they already hold overweight positions. Unlike in Carhart et al. (2002), however, Gallagher et al. (2009) find that poor performing managers are more likely to manipulate prices.

A limitation of studies that are based on indirect or circumstantial evidence of manipulation is that usually there are alternative explanations for their results and it is virtually impossible to eliminate all alternative explanations. Despite this limitation, they are useful in providing an indication of the magnitude of price distortions caused by manipulation (e.g. in the order of 0.5% to 2.0% in Carhart et al. (2002)) and the scale of profits earned by a manipulator (e.g. in an emerging market, 50% to 90% higher annual returns than the average investor (Khwaja and Mian, 2005)). These studies also provide evidence of manipulation in a wide range of settings; some studies support theoretical models (e.g. models of stock price manipulation related to derivatives), while others identify motivations for manipulation that are not considered in the theoretical literature (e.g. manipulation around index reconstitutions). They also suggest factors that can mitigate the propensity for manipulation, for example, high-frequency trading can attenuate closing price dislocations that are indicative of manipulation (Aitken et al., 2015).

(ii)   Empirical studies of known manipulation cases
Studies of known manipulation cases are relatively few and in several instances resemble case studies due to the lack of larger and more representative datasets. A significant study in this area for pioneering the approach of hand collecting a relatively large sample of manipulation prosecution cases is Aggarwal and Wu (2006). Aggarwal and Wu analyse pump-and-dump manipulation cases obtained from the US Securities and Exchange Commission (SEC) litigation releases. They identify 142 cases of manipulation, of which they are able to obtain data on 51 manipulated stocks during the period 1990–2001. The minimum length of a manipulation period is two days, the median is 202 days and the maximum is 1,373 days, highlighting the variation in the nature of pump-and-dump manipulation. They find that in their sample of prosecution cases stocks generally experience a price increase during the manipulation period, a subsequent decrease during the post-manipulation period, and increased volatility. Their sample of cases is more concentrated in illiquid stocks and most of the manipulation is conducted by informed insiders such as company managers, substantial shareholders, market-makers, and brokers.

Aggarwal and Wu (2006), like most empirical studies of prosecution cases, do not address the sample selection bias arising from incomplete and non-random detection and prosecution. Results from such studies should be interpreted as characteristics of *prosecuted* manipulation, not manipulation in general.

Comerton-Forde and Putniņš (2011a) study a sample of 184 instances of closing price manipulation that were prosecuted by the SEC between 1997 and 2009. The manipulation in their sample is conducted mainly by fund managers, top managers of companies, brokers, and substantial shareholders. They find that the instances of closing price manipulation are associated with large increases in day-end returns, subsequent return reversals, increased trading volume, and wider bid–ask spreads.

Based on these findings, they construct an index of the probability of closing price manipulation, which can be used to analyse manipulation in the large number of markets and time periods in which prosecution data are not available.

Unlike the forgoing studies of market manipulation prosecution cases, Comerton-Forde and Putniņš (2014) explicitly account for the non-randomness of manipulation detection and prosecution. They analyse a hand-collected sample of prosecuted closing price manipulations using Detection Controlled Estimation (DCE) methods pioneered by Feinstein (1989, 1990). DCE involves jointly estimating a model of violation, in this case the probability of market manipulation, and a model of detection, in this case the probability that an instance of market manipulation is detected and prosecuted by regulators. By estimating the two processes jointly and using instrumental variables, the model provides unbiased estimates of the drivers and characteristics of *all* closing price manipulation, not just the prosecuted subset. Using this approach, they show that manipulation is more likely to occur in stocks with a high level of information asymmetry, consistent with theory; on quarter- and month-end days, consistent with manipulation by fund managers; and in stocks with a medium to low level of liquidity.

Furthermore, the DCE model used in Comerton-Forde and Putniņš (2014) also estimates the characteristics of detection and the prevalence of market manipulation. The estimates of the prevalence of manipulation explicitly account for the fact that not all manipulation is detected. In fact, as the study shows, only a tiny fraction (around one in three hundred cases) of market manipulation is detected by regulators and brought to prosecution. The important insight from this is that prosecuted market manipulation is just the tip of the iceberg. Their estimates reveal that approximately 1% of all closing stock prices in the US and Canada are manipulated, but the vast majority of these manipulations are not prosecuted. These are the first and perhaps only estimates to date of the prevalence of a particular type of market manipulation. While anecdotal accounts of market manipulation are plentiful, there is very little hard evidence on how widespread various forms of manipulation are, largely due to the difficulties in detecting/observing manipulation.

A small number of studies examine corners, squeezes, and the stock pools of the 1920s. Although the widespread manipulation through stock pools before the crash of 1929 is vividly documented in Galbraith (1972) and one of the main reasons for the introduction of the US federal securities legislation in the 1930s, Mahoney (1999) and Jiang et al. (2005) find little evidence of manipulation in the alleged stock pools of the 1920s. They conclude that these pools did not harm investors. Their sample consists of 55 stock pools identified from a US Senate report. Allen et al. (2006) examine several well-known stock and commodity market corners which occurred between 1863 and 1980. They find that manipulation by large investors and corporate insiders using market power increases market volatility and has an adverse price impact on other assets. They also find that the presence of large investors makes it risky for would-be short sellers to trade against the mispricings, which in some cases are severe. Merrick et al. (2005) examine a case of manipulation involving a delivery squeeze on a bond futures contract traded in London, while Jegadeesh (1993) and Jordan and Jordan (1996) examine the Salomon brothers' market corner of a Treasury note auction in 1991.

Some market designs are more susceptible to manipulation than others. It is widely recognized that closing prices and other key reference/benchmark prices are particularly susceptible because of the strong manipulation incentives that arise from external contracts/securities and the fact that the price only needs to be distorted in a short interval of time around the setting of the reference price, for example, at the close. Market design mechanisms can be used to mitigate the manipulation of closing prices. For example, closing call auctions can reduce the ability for the closing price to be manipulated by consolidating liquidity at the close. Despite this, Comerton-Forde and Rydge (2006) identify a sample of 25 prosecuted closing auction manipulations from six developed markets. Auction manipulators tend to submit large, unrepresentative orders in the final seconds of the auction. The design of the closing auction algorithm influences how easily the closing price can be manipulated. Some algorithm designs are more effective than others in reducing the impact of manipulation (Cordi et al., 2017).

Having a small number of market participants that interact manually can also make a market more susceptible to manipulation. Atanasov et al. (2015) show that in such circumstances, traders might engage in tacit collusion to benefit from the manipulator's desire to trade at distorted prices, rather than competing to exploit the manipulator's price distortions and thereby attenuate the manipulator's actions. Their evidence is based on analysis of an alleged case of closing price manipulation by a hedge fund manager in platinum and palladium futures.

In addition to designing markets so they are less susceptible to manipulation, it is also possible to design contracts to reduce the incentives for closing price manipulation. For example, by using the volume weighted average price (VWAP) in place of the closing price or using "manipulation-proof" measures of performance such as those suggested by Goetzmann et al. (2007) for evaluating fund managers.

Besides the somewhat obvious limitation of small sample sizes, a less obvious limitation of most of the studies of prosecution cases discussed in this section is non-randomness of their samples that arises as a result of incomplete detection and prosecution. Despite this limitation, studies of known manipulation cases provide rich insights about manipulation that cannot be gained using other approaches.

(iii) Experimental studies

In an unusual field experiment, Camerer (1998) attempts to manipulate horse racing odds by making bets and then cancelling them shortly before the race. In essence, this is a form of spoofing. Although making and then cancelling bets is costless, this is not widely known by bettors at the time. Camerer finds that the bets placed by the experimenter do not distort prices.

Hanson et al. (2006) conduct the first laboratory work on price manipulation. In their study, 12 participants trade stock and cash in an electronic limit order book market. In their manipulation treatment, half of the participants are given monetary incentives to manipulate the stock price *during trading*. Their main result is that manipulators are unable to distort price accuracy because other traders counteract the manipulator's actions.

In a follow-up experimental market study, Comerton-Forde and Putniņš (2011b) demonstrate that when traders are given incentives to manipulate the *closing price* as opposed to the price throughout an entire trading session, they harm both the accuracy of prices and the liquidity of the market. Thus, these two experimental studies taken together suggest that some prices are more susceptible to manipulation than others. In particular, key reference prices that are measured at a specific point in time, such as closing prices, are more susceptible to manipulation than other prices such as those during a full window of trading.

Another interesting question that lends itself to analysis in a laboratory is how manipulation strategies respond to the introduction of possible detection and penalties. By introducing a "regulator" into the experimental market and penalties if a manipulator is correctly detected by other market participants, Comerton-Forde and Putniņš (2011b) show that manipulators respond by trading less aggressively and earlier before the close in an effort to better conceal their actions and price impact. An implication of this finding for empirical studies of how changes in rules, penalties or surveillance affect market manipulation is as follows. Any changes in the frequency or severity of indirect measures of market manipulation (e.g. abnormal day-end returns) could be a result of manipulators changing their trading patterns to increase concealment, rather than a change in the frequency of manipulation.

An important but difficult to answer research question is how does market manipulation affect market efficiency and liquidity? While several studies such as those analysing prosecuted cases have been able to document the *ex-post* effects of market manipulation, including distorted prices and wider spreads, understanding the *ex-ante* effects, that is, the effects of the mere possibility that someone will manipulate the market, is more difficult. Does the possibility of manipulation discourage participation in markets and thereby make them less liquid and less efficient as some have argued? Or does it make markets more efficient ex-ante by incentivizing participants to become better informed? The difficulty arises from not having a counterfactual manipulation-free market in practice as a benchmark.

Laboratory settings, however, can overcome this challenge and create a manipulation-free benchmark market by controlling trader incentives and thereby establish the counterfactual. Taking this approach, Comerton-Forde and Putniņš (2011b) show that the mere possibility of manipulation has the ex-ante effect of harming liquidity. Consistent with this notion, Cumming et al. (2011) show that more detailed rules prohibiting practices such as market manipulation tend to increase market liquidity by increasing confidence in markets.

Experimental studies are able to overcome many of the limitations of other empirical methods because the experimenter is able to observe and control information, incentives, and fundamental asset values, as well as being able to overcome the problems caused by incomplete detection of manipulation. The main limitation in this type of research is in the ability to construct the experimental setting in a sufficiently realistic manner so that results have external validity and offer meaningful insights for real markets. Despite this limitation, experimental studies are a promising and underutilized method for enhancing our understanding of market manipulation.

2.4.3   Conclusions from the Research on Market Manipulation

(i)   What do we know about manipulation?
Broadly speaking, from the research we know that manipulation is possible in a wide variety of markets and circumstances. Information-based manipulation can be profitable if the manipulator has credibility, which the manipulator can maintain indefinitely by mixing truth and lies. Pure trade-based manipulation, e.g. a series of buys followed

by sells, can be profitable (i) if price responses to buys and sells are asymmetric, non-linear, or time dependent; (ii) under particular asymmetric information sets; and (iii) in the presence of feedback from financial markets to firm value. Specific securities (e.g. derivatives), events (e.g. seasoned equity offerings), market design features (e.g. trade reporting requirements), and contracts (e.g. mutual fund management, broker-age) also give rise to profitable trade-based manipulation strategies.

Patterns of price and volume irregularities around market closing times and trad-ing records of brokers provide indirect or circumstantial empirical evidence of clos-ing price manipulation and pump-and-dump manipulation, respectively. Prosecuted cases of pump-and-dump and closing price manipulation are more frequent in illiq-uid stocks and often involve management, substantial shareholders, market-makers, or brokers. The cases are associated with abnormal returns, subsequent return rever-sals, increased volume, and volatility. Market corners tend to involve large investors and corporate insiders, and they tend to increase volatility.

We also know that prosecuted cases of market manipulation are just the tip of the iceberg – many more cases exist but are not detected or prosecuted by authorities (e.g. for closing price manipulation only about one in three hundred cases is prose-cuted in the US and Canada). Accounting for the detection bias, manipulation is more likely in stocks with high information asymmetry, low to mid liquidity, and on month/quarter-end days. The mere possibility of manipulation can decrease market liquidity.

Some markets and mechanisms are more susceptible to manipulation than oth-ers. For example, a lack of liquidity makes it easier to manipulate a market. Markets with few participants are likely to be more susceptible to manipulation. Simple clos-ing mechanisms such as the last trade price are generally easier to manipulate than more robust mechanisms, such as well-designed closing auctions. Benchmark mech-anisms that rely on submissions can be more readily manipulated than those that rely on prices in a liquid market, and those that rely on prices at a single point in time are generally more susceptible than those based on a longer period of time. Markets/prices that underpin external contracts or the pricing of other securities/markets are particularly susceptible to manipulation.

(ii)   What don't we know about manipulation?

We know relatively little about (i) the prevalence of manipulation, (ii) its ex-ante and real effects, (iii) how it responds to regulation, and (iv) some of the more recent algo-rithmic manipulation techniques. I briefly discuss each of these below.

It is difficult to infer how much manipulation occurs from indirect manipula-tion proxies such as abnormal price and volume patterns because the estimates of frequency are highly dependent on how the proxies are defined and the thresholds used to classify observations as manipulation. Prosecuted manipulation cases also do not provide much evidence on the prevalence of manipulation unless the incomplete detection and prosecution processes are also modelled and the number of prosecu-tions is scaled up accordingly. While this approach has been used to estimate the prevalence of a particular type of manipulation in specific markets (Comerton-Forde and Putniņš, 2014), we do not have estimates of the prevalence of other types of manipulation or manipulation's prevalence in other markets.

The distinction between *ex-ante* and *ex-post* effects of manipulation is an important one. It is generally accepted that manipulation, ex-post, distorts prices, but far less is known about the ex-ante effects of manipulation, i.e. how the possibility of manipulation affects markets. There are theoretical arguments that the possibility of manipulation has a positive effect on liquidity and informational efficiency because it increases the incentives for market participants to become informed and trade to exploit the distorted prices from manipulation. But there is also some evidence from experimental markets and from the effects of securities market rules against manipulation that the possibility of manipulation can decrease market liquidity, consistent with the notion that manipulation discourages investor participation in markets. The effects, both ex-ante and ex-post, are important because price accuracy affects economic efficiency via resource allocation and liquidity affects the usefulness of markets thus the welfare gains that they facilitate. Furthermore, there is very limited evidence on the "real" effects of market manipulation, for example, the effects on company cost of capital, corporate investment decisions, and so on.

Other than general predictions from the economics of crime literature, such as the prediction that higher detection probabilities or increased penalties should deter manipulation, we know little about how regulation affects manipulators' behaviour. An exception is some evidence from laboratory markets. Difficulties in estimating the frequency of manipulation and the inability to observe manipulators' actions limit the ability to analyse the effects of regulation.

Finally, manipulation techniques evolve through time, particularly in response to changes in markets. Fragmentation of trading across multiple competing trading venues and the emergence of algorithmic and high-frequency trading has given rise to new types of market manipulation and changes in how some of the earlier manipulation techniques are implemented. Relatively little is known about some of these more recent techniques, including quote stuffing, cross-market manipulation involving multiple trading venues, order reference price manipulation such the prices referenced by dark pools and pegged orders, layering strategies implemented algorithmically, pinging/abusive liquidity detection, and manipulation techniques that exploit predictable responses of other market participants' trading algorithms.

(iii)   Future Research

Further evidence on the issues identified above would be valuable. Three methodological approaches to overcoming some of the limitations of existing empirical studies are (i) collecting more comprehensive datasets of manipulation cases, (ii) using detection controlled estimation methods to address the incomplete detection problem, and (iii) conducting controlled laboratory and field experiments.

Tackling the issue of the prevalence of different forms of market manipulation can be most directly achieved using comprehensive data sets of prosecution cases coupled with econometric techniques that take into account the incomplete and non-random detection of manipulation. Feinstein's (1989, 1990) detection controlled estimation is an example of a suitable method. This approach is also effective in characterizing manipulation's ex-post effects on markets, avoiding the biases present in most existing studies of prosecution cases.

Analysis of manipulation's ex-ante effects, real effects, and how it responds to regulation requires exogenous variation in the probability of manipulation. While such variation could be obtained by analysing regulatory changes, it is difficult to disentangle manipulation's effects from unrelated contemporaneous changes. Laboratory experiments overcome the endogeneity and contemporaneous effect problems and have been underutilized in studying manipulation. The main downside of laboratory experiments is the questionable ability to generalize their results to real markets. A related alternative is to conduct controlled field experiments. Prediction markets and crypto-asset markets have grown rapidly in number, diversity of instruments, and liquidity. Because they are often subject to less restrictive regulations, they could provide opportunities for field experiments to better understand market manipulation (e.g. see Rhode and Strumpf, 2009).

The spate of recent high-profile benchmark manipulation cases including LIBOR, EURIBOR, and foreign exchange benchmark rates, calls for research on optimal or robust benchmark design. Such research might seek to better understand what types of benchmark are more susceptible to manipulation and how to design better benchmark setting mechanisms.

Empirical analysis of recent algorithmic market manipulation techniques (quote stuffing, layering, abusive liquidity detection, and so on) could begin with circumstantial evidence highlighting possible cases and characterizing the settings in which circumstantial evidence exists. After all, empirical analysis of other manipulation techniques started with circumstantial evidence before more direct analysis became possible. An example of such an approach is the empirical characterization of quote stuffing by Egginton et al. (2016). Such studies could help guide regulatory efforts in detecting and prosecuting these more recent forms of market manipulation.

Our understanding of recent algorithmic market manipulation techniques would also benefit from theoretical modelling to illustrate when, why, and how such strategies can be used by market manipulators. Such analysis might also guide the regulation of these trading strategies by identifying their likely effects on other market participants and on overall market efficiency.

Finally, the increased use of machine learning (ML) and artificial intelligence (AI) in devising trading strategies raises a number of legal, ethical, and economic considerations regarding the possibility of manipulation by machines. As an example of one of the many questions, suppose a ML/AI system tasked with maximizing trading profits devises a trading strategy that involves aggressively buying a stock, followed by selling soon after, or placing many buy orders in the limit order book, but then cancelling them and immediately selling the stock. Such strategies might be profitable because other market participants might consider the buys or orders to buy as signalling higher future prices. The machine that developed the strategy might know that the strategies are profitable but not know *why* these trading strategies are profitable. Is the machine guilty of market manipulation? Is the human that tasked the machine and let it trade guilty? One might say the machine should be held to the same standards as humans and the human must take ultimate responsibility for the machine's actions. But recall, a key element that distinguishes market manipulation from other forms of legitimate trading is the *intent* to deceive others or to affect the price. Here, the intent of the human and the machine was to profit, not to deceive others, and the resulting prices are only artificial if the machine traded for an impermissible purpose. Complicated issues such as these arise when machines make trading decisions, and future work on market manipulation should explore these issues.

2.5   Summary and Conclusions

Market manipulation always has, and probability always will, be a feature of markets. It takes many forms and can be found in a wide range of different markets all around the world. Market manipulation evolves through time, with new forms of market manipulation emerging in response to changes in market structure. Recent, high-profile cases, such as the manipulation of LIBOR, foreign exchange benchmark rates, and S&P 500 futures indicate that no market or benchmark is immune to market manipulation – even the most widely used financial benchmarks and the world's most liquid markets are susceptible to market manipulation, with extremely widespread consequences.

This chapter provides a taxonomy of the various forms of market manipulation, highlighting how they are related. At the broadest level, manipulation can be divided into four main categories: (i) runs, such as pump-and-dump manipulation in which the manipulator takes a position and then inflates or deflates the price to benefit their position; (ii) contract-based or benchmark manipulations, in which the manipulator profits from an external contract or security whose payoff is determined by an underlying manipulated market or benchmark; (iii) spoofing and other order-based manipulation techniques; and (iv) market power techniques such as corners and squeezes. Within these groups, manipulation can be further broken down according to the mechanism used to facilitate the manipulation (trade-based, information-based, action-based, submission-based, order-based) and then into a number of individual manipulation techniques.

Although there is substantial variation across the different forms of market manipulation, they share a common foundation – they generally all involve the intent to mislead other market participants with respect to supply or demand, or the intent to influence the price of a financial instrument or benchmark. The intent to deceive or to influence prices is central to definitions of market manipulation in legislation and in the economics/law literature. Notable recent changes in the legislation concerning market manipulation in Europe and North America include new provisions against attempted manipulation, against benchmark manipulation, and against algorithmic and order-based manipulation techniques. These changes reflect the efforts of lawmakers in keeping up with the evolution in market manipulation techniques and addressing difficulties that regulators faced in prosecuting recent cases of market manipulation under existing legislation.

A large body of theoretical, empirical, and experimental research has made considerable advances in understanding market manipulation. The literature shows that manipulation occurs in a wide variety of markets and circumstances. It also shows that manipulators can exploit many different mechanisms, including asymmetric or non-linear price impacts, information asymmetry, feedback from financial markets to firm values, mixing truth and lies, and leveraged exposure to an underlying market or benchmark, which can arise from derivative securities or external contracts. Existing research provides evidence on the ex-post effects of market manipulation, including the price distortions and subsequent reversals that are typical of manipulation as well as the elevated volatility and volume. Studies show that prosecuted cases of market manipulation are just the tip of the iceberg and represent a very small fraction of all market manipulation. The literature has quantified the prevalence of manipulation, at least for a specific form of manipulation, showing that approximately 1% of closing prices in North American stock markets are manipulated. Research also identifies the characteristics that make some stocks more likely to be manipulated than others and the features that make some markets and mechanisms more susceptible to manipulation than others.

Despite these advances, there are still a number of areas in which our understanding of market manipulation is limited and there are several new issues that require further research. Besides evidence for one type of market manipulation, it is generally not known how widespread market manipulation is. Our understanding of how manipulation responds to regulation, surveillance, and penalties is limited to laboratory evidence and indirect measures. While we have a reasonable amount of evidence on the ex-post effects that manipulation has on markets, less is known about the ex-ante effects of market manipulation or its effects on company cost of capital, investment, and so on. Some of the market manipulation techniques that have recently emerged together with algorithmic and high-frequency trading are also not yet well understood. Finally, the use of machine learning and artificial intelligence in developing trading strategies, which can sometimes be a "black box" yet resemble manipulative strategies, raises a number of legal, ethical, and economic issues to be explored by future research.

References

Aggarwal, R., and Wu, G. (2006). Stock market manipulations. *Journal of Business* 79: 1915–1953.

Aitken, M., Cumming, D. and Zhan, F. (2015). High frequency trading and end-of-day price dislocation. *Journal of Banking and Finance* 59: 330–349.

Allen, F. and Gale, G. (1992). Stock price manipulation, *Review of Financial Studies* 5: 503–529.

Allen, F. and Gorton, G. (1992). Stock price manipulation, market microstructure and asymmetric information. *European Economic Review* 36: 624–630.

Allen, F., Litov, L. and Mei, J. (2006). Large investors, price manipulation, and limits to arbitrage: An anatomy of market corners. *Review of Finance* 10, 645–693.

Ariel, R. (1987). A monthly effect in stock returns, *Journal of Financial Economics* 18: 161–174.

Atanasov, V., Davies, R.J. and Merrick, J.J. Jr. (2015). Financial intermediaries in the midst of market manipulation: Did they protect the fool or help the knave? *Journal of Corporate Finance* 34: 210–234.

Bagnoli, M. and Lipman, B. (1996). Stock price manipulation through takeover bids, *RAND Journal of Economics* 27, 124–147.

Baxt, R., Ford, H.A.J. and Black, A. (1996). *Securities Industry Law*. 5th ed. Sydney: Butterworths.

Benabou, R. and Laroque, G. (1992). Using privileged information to manipulate markets: Insiders, gurus and credibility. *Quarterly Journal of Economics* 105: 921–958.

Ben-David, I., Franzoni, F., Landier, F.A. and Moussawi, R. (2013). Do hedge funds manipulate stock prices? *Journal of Finance* 68: 2383–2434.

Berle Jr., A.A. (1938). Stock market manipulation, *Columbia Law Review* 38: 393–407.

Bernhardt, D. and Davies, R.J. (2009) Smart fund managers? Stupid money? *Canadian Journal of Economics* 42: 719–748.

Camerer, C.F. (1998). Can asset markets be manipulated? A field experiment with racetrack betting. *Journal of Political Economy* 106: 457–481.

Carhart, M., Kaniel, R., Musto, D. and Reed, A. (2002). Leaning for the tape: Evidence of gaming behaviour in equity mutual funds. *Journal of Finance* 57: 661–693.

Chakraborty, A. and Yilmaz, B. (2004a). Informed manipulation. *Journal of Economic Theory* 114: 132–152.

Chakraborty, A. and Yilmaz, B. (2004b). Manipulation in market order models, *Journal of Financial Markets* 7: 187–206.

Chakraborty, A. and Yilmaz, B. (2008). Microstructure bluffing with nested information. *American Economic Review* 98: 280–284.

Chamberlain, T.W., Cheung, C.S. and Kwan, C.C.Y. (1989). Expiration-day effects of index futures and options: Some Canadian evidence. *Financial Analysts Journal* 45: 67–71.

Cherian, J.A. and Jarrow, R.A. (1995) Market manipulation. In *North-Holland handbooks of operations research and management science: Finance* (eds. R.A. Jarrow, V. Maksimovic, and W.T. Ziemba), 611–630. New York: Elsevier.

Cherian, J.A. and Kuriyan, V.J. (1995). Informationless manipulation in a market type economy. Unpublished manuscript.

Comerton-Forde, C. and Putniņš, T.J. (2011a). Measuring closing price manipulation. *Journal of Financial Intermediation* 20: 135–158.

Comerton-Forde, C. and Putniņš, T.J. (2011b). Pricing accuracy, liquidity and trader behavior with closing price manipulation. *Experimental Economics* 14: 110–131.

Comerton-Forde, C. and Putniņš, T.J. (2014). Stock price manipulation: Prevalence and determinants. *Review of Finance* 18: 23–66.

Comerton-Forde, C. and Rydge, J. (2006). Call auction algorithm design and market manipulation, *Journal of Multinational Financial Management* 16, 184–198.

Cordi, N., Foley, S., Putniņš, T.J. and Félez Viñas, E. (2017). Closing time: The effects of closing mechanism design on market quality. Working paper.

Cumming, D. and Johan, S. (2008). Global market surveillance. *American Law and Economics Review* 10: 454–506.

Cumming, D., Johan, S. and Li, D. (2011). Exchange trading rules and stock market liquidity. *Journal of Financial Economics* 99: 651–671.

De la Vega, J.P. (1688). *Confusión de confusiones* (trans. H. Kellenbenz), reprinted in M.S. Fridson (ed.), 1996, Extraordinary popular delusions and the madness of crowds & Confusión de confusions. New York: Wiley.

Duffie, D. and Stein, J.C. (2015). Reforming LIBOR and other financial market benchmarks. *Journal of Economic Perspectives* 29: 191–212.

Egginton, J.F., Van Ness, B.F. and Van Ness, R.A. (2016). Quote stuffing, *Financial Management* 45: 583–608.

Eren, N. and Ozsoylev, H.N. (2006). Hype and dump manipulation. Unpublished manuscript.

Feinstein, J.S. (1989). The safety regulation of US nuclear power plants: Violations, inspections, and abnormal occurrences. *Journal of Political Economy* 97: 115–154.

Feinstein, J.S. (1990). Detection controlled estimation. *Journal of Law and Economics* 33: 233–276.

Felixson, K. and Pelli, A. (1999) Day end returns – stock price manipulation. *Journal of Multinational Financial Management* 9: 95–127.

Fischel, D. and Ross, D. (1991). Should the law prohibit manipulation in financial markets? *Harvard Law Review* 105: 503–553.

Fishman, M.J. and Hagerty, K.M. (1995). The mandatory disclosure of trades and market liquidity. *Review of Financial Studies* 8, 637–676.

Galbraith, A.J. (1972). *The Great Crash, 1929.* Boston: Houghton Mifflin.

Gallagher, D.R., Gardener, P. and Swan, P.L. (2009). Portfolio pumping: An examination of investment manager quarter-end trading and impact on performance. *Pacific-Basin Finance Journal* 17: 1–27.

Gerard, B. and Nanda, V. (1993). Trading and manipulation around seasoned equity offerings. *Journal of Finance* 48: 213–245.

Glosten, L.R. and Milgrom, P.R. (1985). Bid, ask and transaction prices in a specialist market with heterogeneously informed traders. *Journal of Financial Economics* 14: 71–100.

Goetzmann W., Ingersoll, J., Spiegel, M. and Welch, I. (2007). Portfolio performance manipulation and manipulation-proof performance measures. *Review of Financial Studies* 20: 1503–1546.

Goldstein, I. and Guembel, A. (2008). Manipulation and the allocation role of prices. *Review of Economic Studies* 75: 133–164.

Goldwasser, V. (1999). *Stock market manipulation and short selling.* Sydney: CCH Australia/The Centre for Corporate Law and Securities Regulation.

Griffin, D. (1980). *Descent into slavery?* Colton: Emissary Publications.

Griffin, J.M. and Shams, A. (2018). Manipulation in the VIX?, *Review of Financial Studies* 31: 1377–1417.

Hanson, R. and Oprea, R. (2009). Manipulators increase information market accuracy. *Economica* 76: 304–314.

Hanson, R., Oprea, R. and Porter, D. (2006). Information aggregation in an experimental market. *Journal of Economic Behavior & Organization* 60: 449–459.

Harris, L. (1989). A day-end transaction price anomaly. *Journal of Financial and Quantitative Analysis* 24: 29–45.

Hart, O. (1977). On the profitability of speculation. *Quarterly Journal of Economics* 90: 579–596.

Hillion, P. and Suominen, M. (2004). The manipulation of closing prices. *Journal of Financial Markets* 7: 351–375.

Huberman, G. and Stanzl, W. (2004). Price manipulation and quasi-arbitrage. *Econometrica* 72: 1247–1275.

Huddart, S., Hughes, J.S. and Levine, C.B. (2001). Public disclosure and dissimulation of insider trades. *Econometrica* 69: 665–681.

Jarrow, R.A. (1992). Market manipulation, bubbles, corners, and short squeezes. *Journal of Financial and Quantitative Analysis* 27: 311–336.

Jarrow, R.A. (1994). Derivative security markets, market manipulation, and option pricing theory. *Journal of Financial and Quantitative Analysis* 29: 241–261.

Jegadeesh, N. (1993). Treasury auction bids and the Salomon squeeze. *Journal of Finance* 48: 1403–1419.

Jiang, G., Mahoney, P. and Mei, J. (2005). Market manipulation: A comprehensive study of stock pools. *Journal of Financial Economics* 77: 147–170.

John, K. and Narayanan, R. (1997). Market manipulation and the role of insider trading regulations. *Journal of Business* 70: 217–247.

Johnson, P.M. (1981). Commodity market manipulation. *Washington and Lee Law Review* 38: 725–732.

Jordan, B. and Jordan, S. (1996). Salomon Brothers and the May 1991 Treasury auction: Analysis of a market corner. *Journal of Banking and Finance* 20: 25–40.

Keim, D. (1983). Size-related anomalies and stock return seasonality: Further empirical evidence. *Journal of Financial Economics* 12: 13–32.

Khanna, N. and Sonti, R. (2004). Value creating stock manipulation: feedback effect of stock prices on firm value. *Journal of Financial Markets* 7: 237–270.

Khwaja, A. and Mian, A. (2005). Unchecked intermediaries: Price manipulation in an emerging stock market. *Journal of Financial Economics* 78: 203–241.

Kumar, P. and Seppi, D. (1992). Futures manipulation with cash settlement. *Journal of Finance* 47: 1485–1502.

Kyle, A.S. (1984). A theory of futures market manipulation. In *The industrial organization of futures markets* (ed. R.W. Anderson). Massachusetts: Lexington.

Kyle, A.S. (1985). Continuous auctions and insider trading. *Econometrica* 53: 1315–1335.

Kyle, A.S. and Viswanathan, S. (2008). How to define illegal price manipulation, *American Economic Review* 98, 274–279.

Lee, E.J., Eom, K.S. and Park, K.S. (2013). Microstructure-based manipulation: Strategic behavior and performance of spoofing traders. *Journal of Financial Markets* 16: 227–252.

Leinweber, D.J. and Madhavan, A.N. (2001). Three hundred years of stock market manipulations. *Journal of Investing* 10: 7–16.

Lewis, M. (2001). *Next: The future just happened.* New York: Norton.

Mahoney, P. (1999). The stock pools and the Securities Exchange Act. *Journal of Financial Economics* 51: 343–369.

McDonald, C.G. and Michayluk, D. (2003). Suspicious trading halts. *Journal of Multinational Financial Management* 13: 251–263.

Merrick Jr, J., Naik, N. and Yadav, P. (2005). Strategic trading behavior and price distortion in a manipulated market: Anatomy of a squeeze. *Journal of Financial Economics* 77: 171–218.

Ni, S., Pearson, N. and Poteshman, A. (2005). Stock price clustering on option expiration dates. *Journal of Financial Economics* 78: 49–87.

Pirrong, S.C. (1993). Manipulation of the commodity futures market delivery process. *Journal of Business* 66: 335–369.

Putniņš, T.J. (2012). Market manipulation: A survey. *Journal of Economic Surveys* 26: 952–967.

Rhode P.W. and Strumpf, K.S. (2009) Manipulating political stock markets: A field experiment and a century of observational data. Unpublished manuscript.

Stoll, H.R. and Whaley, R.E. (1987). Program trading and expiration-day effects. *Financial Analysts Journal* 43: 16–28.

Stoll, H.R. and Whaley, R.E. (1991). Expiration-day effects: What has changed? *Financial Analysts Journal* 47: 58–72.

Thel, S. (1990). The original conception of section 10(b) of the Securities Exchange Act. *Stanford Law Review* 42: 385–464.

Thel, S. (1994). $850,000 in six minutes – The mechanics of securities manipulation. *Cornell Law Review* 79: 219–298.

Van Bommel, J. (2003). Rumors. *Journal of Finance* 58: 1499–1520.

Vila, J.-L. (1987). The role of information in the manipulation of futures markets. Unpublished manuscript.

Vila, J.-L. (1989). Simple games of market manipulation, *Economics Letters* 29, 21–26.

Wood, R., McInish, T. and Ord, J. (1985). An investigation of transactions data for NYSE stocks. *Journal of Finance* 40: 723–739.

Zdorovtsov, V. M., Tang, X. and Onayev, Z. (2017). Predatory trading around Russell reconstitution. Unpublished manuscript.

Chapter 3

A Taxonomy of Financial Market Misconduct

Ai Deng
NERA Economic Consulting and John Hopkins University

Priyank Gandhi
Rutgers Business School

3.1   Introduction

What is financial market misconduct? Generally speaking, any practice that is 'unfair' to market participants can be considered financial market misconduct, but a precise definition of the term is difficult to specify.[1] As such the range of activities that potentially fall under the scope of financial market misconduct is quite broad. To paraphrase the words of a cotton trader from a testimony before a Senate Committee in the 1920s, the term 'financial market misconduct' is so broad that it can include any operation in financial markets that does not suit the person who is speaking at the moment.[2]

Concerns related to financial market misconduct have bedevilled market participants since the dawn of financial markets. The first recorded incident of financial market misconduct was sometime in the third century BCE, when a Greek merchant named Hegestratos took out a large loan, secured by the cargo on his boat. Hegestratos planned to sink his empty boat, keep the loan, and sell the cargo. In modern terms, this would be an instance of misrepresentation and loan fraud.

The earliest known cases of financial market misconduct in the United Kingdom was in 1814, when Charles Random de Berenger landed in Dover, and widely proclaimed the death of Napoleon. It was later discovered that De Berenger had bought UK government bonds and that his fraudulent announcement resulted in ill-gotten gains of GBP 0.5m (some GBP 70m today). In modern terms, this would be an instance of price manipulation, i.e. the deliberate attempt to interfere with the free and fair functioning of financial markets with misleading information or appearances.

Financial market misconduct started in the United States just a few years after it officially became a nation. During the late 1700s, prices of bonds issued by the US Federal government or (former) colonies were volatile, much like how emerging market debt is today. William Duer, the assistant secretary of the Treasury at the time, was privy to all the Treasury's actions, and used his insider information to trade on his own account, before selectively leaking such information to the public. In modern terms, this would be an instance of insider trading.

In more recent times, concerns related to financial market misconduct have significantly heightened or even skyrocketed, especially after the financial crisis of 2007–2009. A Google search for the term 'financial market misconduct' that we ran in December 2017 produced more than 14,300,000 hits. A related search for academic articles on the topic indicates that more than 80,400 academic papers have been published on financial market misconduct.[3]

For financial economists, the recent attention paid to financial market misconduct raises two important questions. What methodologies exist to detect financial market misconduct? How does one quantify the effects of financial market misconduct on market participants? In two related chapters, we survey the current empirical

---

[1] Kyle and Viswanathan (2008) note that even 'illegal price manipulation' – just one particular type of financial market misconduct – is difficult to define. Generally, all activities viewed by market participants as illegal or unethical are considered as instances of misconduct.

[2] Federal Trade Commission, 2 The Cotton Trade 20 (Senate Document 100, 68th congress, 1st Session, 1924).

[3] Both searches were run on Google on 31 December 2017.

and theoretical literature on financial market misconduct in an attempt to answer these questions.

There are several reasons why such a survey is of interest. First, financial market misconduct is systemic and pervasive in scale. For example, Dyck, Morse, and Zingales (2010) find that in the US, as many as one in seven publicly traded companies engage in financial market misconduct in any given year. They estimate the probability of a large firm in the US engaging in misconduct in any given year to be 14.50%.

Studies that estimate the incidence or frequency of financial market misconduct in other countries are more limited. One recent survey by the Association of Certified Fraud Examiners (ACFE) does estimate the incidence of financial fraud (which is just one particular type of financial market misconduct) in other countries. ACFE examined 2,410 confirmed instances of financial fraud in 114 different countries over 10 months from January to October 2015. The results of this survey are summarized in Table 3.1 and shows that financial fraud is widespread, affecting almost all the countries in the world.[4]

Figures 3.1 and 3.2 (also from the 2016 ACFE Global Fraud Study) depict the incidence of financial fraud by industry, firm size, and firm type. Figure 3.1 indicates that

Table 3.1   Frequency of fraud by country.

Notes: This table is based on the results of the 2016 Global Fraud study by the Association of Certified Fraud Examiners (ACFE). The report is available on ACFE's website at http:\www. acfe.com. The report confirmed 2,410 instances of financial fraud over the months of January 2015 to October 2015. This table depicts the frequency of fraud cases by geographic region. Column 1 indicates the geographic region. Columns 2 and 3 indicate the number and percentage of fraud cases in each region. Finally, Column 4 indicates the median loss (in US dollars) for fraud cases in each region.

Region	Number of cases	Percent of cases	Median loss (USD)
United States	1,038	48.80	120,000
Africa	285	13.40	143,000
Asia-Pacific	221	10.40	245,000
Latin America	112	5.30	174,000
Western Europe	110	5.20	263,000
Eastern Europe	98	4.60	200,000
Southeast Asia	98	4.60	100,000
Canada	86	4.00	154,000
Middle East	76	7.70	275,000

---

[4] Table 3.1 shows that nearly 50% of cases of financial fraud occurred in the US. At first sight, this seems surprising, as the US is one of the few countries with strict standards for financial market conduct and enforcement. The reason for the high frequency for the US may be that the report is based on a survey of ACFE members and reflects the geographical distribution of its members, of which the US has the most. Perhaps a variable that better reflects the geographical distribution of financial market misconduct is median loss. Table 3.1 indicates that the median loss due to financial fraud in any country is close to about $150,000 (USD), despite stark variations in the size of economies and financial markets.

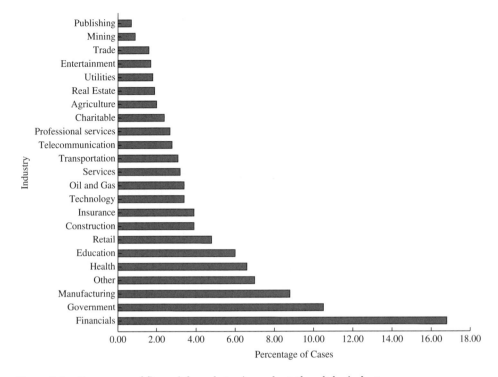

Figure 3.1   Frequency of financial market misconduct (fraud) by industry.
Notes: This chart is based on the results of the 2016 Global Fraud study carried out by the Association of Certified Fraud Examiners (ACFE). The report is available on ACFE's website at http:\\www.acfe.com. The report examined 2,410 instances of financial fraud over the months of January 2015 to October 2015. This figure depicts the percentages of cases by industry.

fraud affects firms in all industries, but that most cases occur in the financial services industry. In addition, Figure 3.2 indicates that while private sector firms experience higher incidence of fraud, firms in all sectors of the economy, regardless of their ownership status, suffer from such misconduct. Thus, financial market misconduct impacts all economic agents and entities in the economy. Finally, the ACFE Global Fraud Study also shows that fraud affects firms of all sizes and the percentage of cases hardly varies by firm size.

Second, the impact of financial market misconduct on market participants can be economically large. In 2002, the US Government Accountability Office (henceforth the GAO) analysed the stock market reaction of financial statement restatements.[5] They found that on the initial restatement announcement, stock prices of the restating companies fell almost 10% on average and the restating companies lost about $100 billion in market capitalization (See US Government Accountability Office 2002).

_____

[5] A financial statement restatement occurs when a company, either voluntarily or prompted by auditors or regulators, revises public financial information that was previously reported.

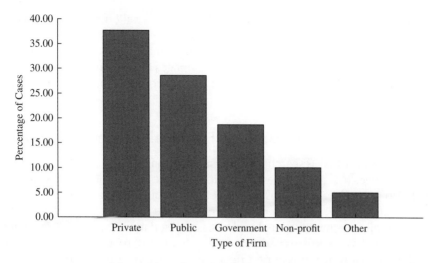

Figure 3.2 Frequency of financial market misconduct (fraud) by firm type.
Notes: This table is based on the results of the 2016 Global Fraud study carried out by the Association of Certified Fraud Examiners (ACFE). The report is available on ACFE's website at http:\\www.acfe.com. The report examined 2,410 instances of financial fraud over the months of January 2015 to October 2015. This figure depicts the median loss and percentage of cases by firm type.

More recently, Karpoff, Lee, and Martin (2008) show that firms that engage in financial market misconduct in the US on average lose 38% of their value (i.e. market capitalization) as a reputation penalty when such misconduct is revealed. In general, Dyck, Morse, and Zingales (2010) estimate that financial market misconduct destroys on average one-fifth of firm value, giving rise to an average cost of financial market misconduct in large corporations in the US estimated at $380 billion per year. In yet another study, Gee and Button (2015) estimate that a typical firm loses 5.6% of its annual revenue due to financial market misconduct. Applying this percentage to the corporate revenues for all the countries in the world yields a figure of nearly $3.7 trillion lost worldwide due to activities related to financial market misconduct.

Incredible as these numbers are, they only reflect direct losses suffered by firms when they engage in financial market misconduct. These estimates do not include indirect costs of financial market misconduct, such as losses due to erosion of trust among market participants, or their reluctance to participate in financial markets if misconduct becomes widespread. Guiso, Sapienza, and Zingales (2008) study one such indirect cost and argue that when investor trust in markets is low (i.e. when the likelihood of financial market misconduct is high) people do not participate in the stock market. The resulting lack of investor demand for equity in such countries makes it difficult for firms to float their stock and raise capital.

Finally, our survey can perhaps even help those who have engaged in financial market misconduct. As an example, consider the typical case of a firm that faces an allegation of financial market misconduct. Ex-post, that is after misconduct is discovered (or proven), the risk of potential litigation for the firm can be much like the 'Sword of Damocles', hanging over its future operating decisions. Under these circumstances, it may be helpful for existing (or new management) at this firm to quickly quantify the extent of its potential losses and damages (using some of techniques outlined in this chapter), thereby ascertaining the extent of litigation risk stemming from the alleged misconduct.[6]

3.2 Challenges in Research on Financial Market Misconduct

Our review reveals that researchers interested in financial market misconduct face several challenges that are perhaps unique to this topic. First, there is the issue of data. Regulators often collect enormous amount of data about financial markets.[7] However, this data is often not available to researchers. In some instances, regulators post data only periodically, often with a lag. In other cases, regulators aggregate data, so it cannot be attributed to a particular entity. In still other cases, regulators fear that sharing detailed information may reveal proprietary methods that criminals may then use to develop more sophisticated misconduct techniques or to avoid detection of misconduct. While these concerns are understandable, this limited information exchange constrains not only the detection of misconduct but also the development of new misconduct detection technologies.

Second, in any study of financial market misconduct, prevalent laws are important as they influence the conduct of financial market participants. In fact, it is difficult to make progress on many issues related to financial market misconduct without understanding the enormous variation in laws across markets and time. On the one hand, such variation in laws poses difficulties for studies on financial market misconduct as what may be deemed as misconduct during one period/jurisdiction, may be an accepted practice in another. On the other hand, variation in laws can also help as researchers can use variation to identify the causes of misconduct, and the effect of enforcement on misconduct. This rich variation in laws and regulations is only now beginning to be exploited by financial economists, and seems a likely fruitful area for further work.[8]

---

[6] Henry (2008) finds that the total cost of litigations for Fortune 500 companies in the US equals one-third of their profits in a given year. Typically, a firm under investigation for financial market misconduct identifies potential litigation costs and regulatory fines as a key future risk factor in its annual reports. For example, several large global banks identified litigation risk and regulatory fines as a key risk factor in their annual reports for 2008–2010, after they faced allegations of manipulating interest and foreign exchange rates.

[7] For example, in the US, the Securities Exchange Commission (SEC), the Commodities and Futures Trading Commission (CFTC), the Federal Reserve (FED), the Federal Deposit Insurance Corporation (FDIC), the Financial Industry Regulatory Authority (FINRA), the Office of the Comptroller of the Currency (OCC), and the Consumer Financial Protection Bureau (CFPB) collect accounting and price information from all market participants.

[8] While research that exploits the time-series variation in laws and regulations is limited, researchers have utilized the cross-sectional variation (across countries) in laws, regulations, and enforcement action and its effect on financial markets. One example is Jackson and Roe (2009), who study the effect of disclosure and private enforcement on financial market development. Similarly, Cumming, Groh, and Johan (2017) collect enforcement data from the European Securities Market Authority and show that the same rules are applied with different intensity in different markets.

Finally, a study of financial market misconduct is inherently cross-disciplinary in nature, perhaps much more so than other areas of finance. Many questions in the area of financial market misconduct cannot be addressed appropriately within the confines of individual disciplines and must draw from the body of knowledge in areas as diverse as finance, economics, law, mathematics, statistics, decision sciences, sociology, and so on. Cross-disciplinary work of course presents challenges and frustrations of its own. For one thing, researchers wishing to draw on the body of knowledge in diverse disciplines must learn the set of rules and assumptions that are particular to each of these disciplines. In addition, it is difficult enough to keep abreast with the ongoing developments in any one discipline. When one conducts cross-disciplinary research, however, one also needs to stay current in multiple areas.

3.3   Defining Financial Market Misconduct

As we attempt a comprehensive review of the current empirical and theoretical literature on detecting and quantifying financial market misconduct, a key challenge for us is the issue of scope.

In particular, how does one define financial market misconduct, and what activities and practices fall under its domain? The range of potential financial market misconduct is limitless and its scope so wide that regulators often resort to use of computer surveillance algorithms to search for such activities (Cumming and Johan 2008). The US Seventh Circuit Court of Appeals aptly summarized this issue in its decision in Cargill v. Hayden wherein it stated that: 'The methods and techniques of manipulation are limited only by the ingenuity of man'. Financial market misconduct comes in many different forms and includes several classes of activities, and at first sight, a comprehensive review does not even seem possible.

Consider, for example, the bevy of allegations of financial market misconduct levied against financial intermediaries in the aftermath of the financial crisis of 2007–2009. A non-comprehensive list of such misconduct includes rating agencies providing favourable ratings to lenders to help them sell risky mortgages (Acharya and Richardson 2009), banks selectively moving risky mortgages off their balance sheets (Keys et al. 2010), instances of lenders issuing mortgages while allegedly wilfully disregarding the borrower's ability to repay the mortgage (Agarwal et al. 2014), and banks rigging an important interest rate benchmark (Gandhi et al. 2018). Each of these practices were commonplace prior to the financial crisis of 2007–2009, and can be classified as financial market misconduct. Each of these activities is also quite unique, and requires the use of distinct empirical techniques to detect and quantify its extent.

However, it seems that new data combined with novel analytical and computational techniques can help resolve the issue of limitless scope of potential misconduct activities and indicate that the number of misconduct techniques is perhaps more limited. For example, recently, the Fixed Income, Currencies, and Commodities Markets Standards Board (FMSB) – established in 2015 as a private sector response to the conduct problems revealed in global wholesale fixed income currencies and commodities (FICC) markets after the financial crisis – carried out an analysis that

Figure 3.3   Classifying types of financial market misconduct.

Notes: In 2015, the Fixed Income, Currencies, and Commodities Markets Standards Board (FMSB) analysed 400 recorded cases of financial market misconduct from 19 countries over a 200-year period. FMSB classified these 400 recorded cases of financial market misconduct into 25 different patterns. This figure depicts the 25 distinct patterns of financial market misconduct. For more information visit their website at http:\\www.fmsb.com.

demonstrates that the same misconduct techniques are repeated, and it is rare that a genuinely new ploy is invented.

FMSB reached this conclusion based on its analysis of more than 400 recorded cases of financial market misconduct from 19 different countries over a 200-year period. This information, although publicly available, had not been used in studies of financial market misconduct. Only recently did FMSB analyse and disseminate this information on patterns of financial market misconduct. Most importantly, FMSB found that all financial market misconduct activities can be classified into just 25 patterns that repeat over time, across markets, asset classes and jurisdictions. These 25 patterns are summarized in Figure 3.3 taken from their report. FMSB refers to this analytical technique as Behavioural Cluster Analysis (or BCA).

Figure 3.3 shows that the 25 patterns identified by FMSB can be further grouped into seven broad categories of behaviour. For example, patterns of *spoofing, new issue support, ramping, squeeze,* or *bull* or *bear raids* all fall under the category of price manipulation. Similarly, the other 21 patterns can be classified either under *circular trading, collusion and information sharing, inside information, reference price influence, improper order handling,* or *misleading customers.* Next, we discuss each of these categories of financial market misconduct, and illustrate each category with a recent example from financial markets.[9]

3.3.1 Price Manipulation

The possibility of artificially influencing market prices has always been an important concern for market participants. Soon after the inception of the Amsterdam Stock Exchange, brokers discovered that they could profitably manipulate stock prices by engaging in concentrated bouts of selling. Such heavy selling would spook other investors who would then also sell, causing a further drop in prices. Eventually, the brokers would buy back stock at lower prices to cover their original positions. While this particular example highlights a bear raid, all other patterns classified as price manipulation, such as spoofing (creating false pessimism or optimism), new issue or mergers and acquisition support (supporting a new security's offering price), ramping (raising the market price), and squeezing or cornering (acquiring a large market share to influence prices) have one thing in common: they all involve trading strategies in which violators attempt to create a false impression regarding market prices, liquidity, or both.

Historical reviews by Bernheim & Schneider (eds.) (1935) and Sobel (1965), among others indicate that during the early years, price manipulation occurred in all kinds of markets and was widespread. By one account several fortunes were made and lost on Wall Street during the nineteenth century through stock price manipulation. One story is that of Jacob Little, who was nicknamed the 'Great Bear of Wall Street' and is said to be the greatest speculator in the history of markets. These historical reviews show that not all attempts at price manipulation are successful. There is always a possibility that a manipulator could be outwitted by another speculator or manipulator. Allen and Gale (1992) cite one famous instance. At the beginning of 1863, Commodore Cornelius Vanderbilt had bought Harlem Railway stock for around $9 a share. Under his management the stock price increased to $50 per share. In April 1863, the New York City Council passed an ordinance allowing Harlem Railway to build a streetcar system and on this news its stock price increased to $75. Members of the council then conspired to sell the stock short and repeal the ordinance, to subsequently cover their short positions. Vanderbilt got wind of the plot, managed to buy the entire stock in secret, and squeezed the members of the council when they tried to cover their short positions (after repealing the ordinance). It is rumoured that Vanderbilt forced the Council members to settle at $179 per share.[10]

---

[9] As we note above there is no precise definition of activities classified as financial market misconduct. In fact, the definition and categorization of such activities varies from one study to the next. A notable alternative definition and categorization of financial market misconduct is provided by Cumming, Johan, and Li (2011), who identify different categories or patterns of financial market misconduct. These include insider trading, price manipulation, volume manipulation, spoofing, and false disclosures, among others. Cumming, Johan, and Li (2011) also note that rules and regulations concerning activities that are (or are not) considered market manipulation vary widely from one country to the next.

[10] See Eiteman, Dice, and Eiteman (1966) for an account of this episode.

Over time, allegations of manipulation have spurred serious investigations, and the enactment of rules and laws to make almost all such activities illegal in many countries. In the US, in the aftermath of the Great Depression, the Senate Committee on Banking and Currency conducted extensive investigations and enacted extensive provisions in the Securities Exchange Act of 1934 to eliminate price manipulation. The Securities Exchange Act (and other similar Acts in other countries) have by and large been successful in reducing the frequency and incidence of manipulation, although such behaviour has not been eradicated from the financial market entirely.

As recently as 2008, well-known banks such as HSBC and J.P. Morgan faced allegations of manipulating silver prices. In particular, a London-based whistleblower alleges that both HSBC and J.P. Morgan made large, coordinated trades to artificially lower the price of silver at key times when the commodity should have been trading at a higher price. In an even more recent case, both Porsche's and Tesla's management are accused of making misleading statements in an attempt to manipulate the stock prices of their respective firms. In 2008, Porsche's management revealed that they owned 75% of Volkswagen (VW) stock (in stock and option positions combined). In Germany, this level of ownership usually implies an impending take over. The expectation of a turnover led to a surge of 336% in VW's share price, which hurt several hedge funds that were short the stock. Later, Porsche announced it had no intention of taking over VW. In August 2018, Tesla's CEO, Elon Musk tweeted that he had secured funding to take his firm private at a price of $420 per share at a time when its stock was trading close to $330 per share. Musk's tweet led to an 11% jump in the stock price and likely caused large losses for investors who had shorted the stock. As reported by many outlets, it soon became apparent that Musk had not secured any such funding, and his announcements are reportedly currently under investigation by the Securities and Exchange Commission (SEC) as a form of price manipulation.[11]

3.3.2   Circular Trading

Activities classified as circular trading (i.e. wash trades, matched trades, compensation trades, or warehousing) refer to trading strategies that aim to keep the beneficial ownership of a financial asset unchanged, but inflate its trading volume or liquidity in order to influence its price. For example, a typical wash trade involves simultaneous transactions for the sale and purchase of the exact same quantity of a financial asset at the exact same price between the same counterparties. Similarly, a matched trade is nothing but a wash trade that is intermediated by a third party, such as a broker acting on the behalf of the trading participants.

It has been observed that newly listed assets or innovative financial markets are particularly at risk of circular trading. This is because manipulators can multiply their illicit gains if they can create the appearance of intense trading activity and a buzz around these novel assets or markets. One recent example of a typical circular trade comes from the recently established market for Bitcoin derivatives. On 9

---

[11] See, Robert Ferris, SEC reportedly investigating whether Elon Musk tweeted about take-private deal to hurt short sellers, available at https://www.cnbc.com/2018/08/16/sec-reportedly-investigating-whether-elon-musk-tweeted-about-take-private-deal-to-hurt-short-sel.html.

October 2014, TeraExchange – one of the first federally regulated platforms for Bitcoin derivatives – announced that the first Bitcoin derivatives transaction had been completed on its exchange. This transaction was widely publicized. Several commentators noted that this transaction could lead to an active, liquid market for Bitcoin derivatives and would effectively allow investors to hedge the wild price fluctuations in Bitcoin. However, in 2015, the Commodities and Futures Trading Commission (CFTC) revealed that the reported transaction was nothing more than a wash trade. Specifically, TeraExchange had contacted two firms (who did not know each other and had not been accused of wrongdoing) and suggested that they execute a roundtrip trade as a way to test the system. At TeraExchange's request, one party entered a buy order with a notional amount of $500,000 which was accepted by the second party. Within minutes an offsetting sell order was executed and accepted between the same counterparties. Although CFTC's system immediately flagged this transaction, which led CFTC to questioning TeraExchange, the latter explained that the trade was only a test, which is allowed under the current CFTC regulations. However, the very next day, TeraExchange issued a press release celebrating the transaction was the first Bitcoin derivative transaction on its exchange. CFTC eventually settled with TeraExchange.[12]

3.3.3 Collusion and Information Sharing

If financial market misconduct is carried out by several market participants acting together in concert, while spreading false or misleading information, then it can be classified as collusion or (mis)information sharing. Pooling is one example of such behaviour. A pool involves several participants whose activities are coordinated by one or few key individuals, commonly referred to as the pool managers. In a typical pool, a particular kind of transaction (either purchase or sale) of a target asset is undertaken at progressively higher or lower prices, in smaller quantities, until a predetermined target price is reached. At the target price all pool positions are liquidated and the market is left to adjust on its own. By its very nature, pooling tends to be a longer-term strategy that takes place over several days, weeks, or months.

Pool members may also engage in spreading misinformation by publishing false research, media reports, or other marketing materials to generate interest in the target asset among investors who are not members of the pool. Pool members may also engage in other kinds of misconduct behaviour, such as circular trading to achieve their goal.

In a recent case, the Securities and Exchange Commission (SEC) Thailand charged seven conspirators with manipulating the share price of Union Petrochemical (UKEM). The SEC alleges that the perpetrators engaged in circular trading and were successful in ramping the stock price from 2.60 Baht per share (as of July 18, 2008) to 6.20 Baht (as of August 20, 2008). In yet another case, federal authorities arrested fourteen people involved in a pooling scheme that led to more than 20,000 investors losing over $30 million when artificially inflated stock prices collapsed. According to authorities, the perpetrators gained control of the majority of the stock of some publicly traded

---

[12] CFTC Settles with TeraExchange LLC, a Swap Execution Facility, for Failing to Enforce Prohibitions on Wash Trading and Prearranged Trading in Bitcoin Swap. https://www.cftc.gov/PressRoom/PressReleases/pr7240-15,September24,2015.

companies. They concealed their control by transferring shares to offshore accounts. Subsequently, the group spread misleading information and engaged in circular trading to fraudulently inflate the stock prices of the target firms. The actors then allegedly coordinated the sale of their positions at the peak of the manipulated markets.[13]

3.3.4   Inside Information

Insiders are a unique class of traders who, by definition, have favoured access to private information about certain firms. The group of misconduct activities by this group which relate to the improper use of information to generate illicit gains or profits are particularly difficult to detect and quantify. This is because by law, insiders are not barred from trading, and are legally permitted to buy and sell shares of the firms that employ them. To demonstrate misconduct, the SEC must prove that the insider 'traded while in possession of material non-public information in violation of a duty to withhold the information or refrain from trading' – which is not an easy standard to meet.

Because of their preferential access to information and the increased risk of financial market misconduct, insiders are subject to increased scrutiny, regulation, and restrictions regarding their trading activities. In particular, all transactions by insiders related to firm stock must be properly declared, and registered with the SEC.

The rash of high-profile insider trading cases in recent years, notably the government's investigation into the Galleon Group – the largest hedge fund insider trading case in US history – indicates that the SEC continues to expend substantial resources trying to address this difficult problem. In 1997, billionaire Sri Lankan–American businessman Raj Rajaratnam co-founded hedge fund management company Galleon Group. In October 2009, he was arrested and charged with leading a team of insider traders. US Attorney Preet Bharara estimated that the scam yielded more than $60 million. Authorities allege that between 2006 and 2009, Rajaratnam made his money by illegally using inside information to trade stocks of Google, eBay, Hilton Worldwide, and Goldman Sachs, among others. In May 2011, a jury found Rajaratman guilty of 14 counts of conspiracy and securities fraud. And in October the same year, he received a sentence of 11 years in prison, which at that time was the longest jail term every imposed for insider trading. Rajaratman was also ordered to pay a $10 million fine and relinquish $53.8 million in assets.

3.3.5   Reference Price Influence

When misconduct activities aim to manipulate reference prices, i.e. prices at which financial assets are valued, this is referred to as reference price influence. In other words, reference price influence is similar to price manipulation (discussed above), but particularly targets financial instruments that help determine cash flows for other assets or positions.

---

[13] The details of the case are available at https://archives.fbi.gov/archives/losangeles/press-releases/2013/fourteen-arrested-for-market-manipulation-schemes-that-caused-thousands-of-i

Reference price influence can notably affect markets for derivatives, interest rates, commodities, and foreign exchange. One technique of reference price influence is 'marking or banging the close'. This technique involves buying or selling securities or derivatives contracts at or near the close of the market in an attempt to alter the closing price of the security or derivatives contract. This technique is particularly effective if buying and selling orders are concentrated on dates when derivatives contracts are set to expire, or when financial assets are set to be valued using the reported reference prices.

In one recent example, Andrew Kerr is accused of manipulating the reference price for coffee derivatives on the London International Financial Futures and Options Exchange (LIFFE) at the behest of his client. Kerr's client held a large position in September 2017 option contracts with a strike price of $1,750. The client wanted the reference price of coffee to be greater than $1,750 for these contracts. The reference price for coffee contracts is determined between 12:29 and 12:30 on the third Wednesday of the preceding month, which was 15 August 2017 in this case.

At 12:29 on 15 August 2017 (i.e. the day when the reference price was to be determined) coffee contracts were trading at $1,745. The authorities allege that Kerr's client instructed him to buy 600 coffee contracts just seconds before 12:30 to push its price above $1,750. Kerr executed the order, the price of coffee momentarily rose to $1,757, and the reference price was set at $1,752, just what the client wanted.[14]

3.3.6   Improper Order Handling

In almost all countries and financial markets, regulations require market participants (such as brokers or advisors) who are authorized to execute orders on behalf of clients to ensure that clients' orders are executed in a prompt, fair, and expeditious manner. Specifically, once clients' orders are received they should be promptly and accurately recorded and allocated. Client orders should be executed sequentially. Clients should be informed right away about any difficulty in execution of their contracts. A broker or advisor should not misuse information relating to pending client orders. For example, the broker or advisor cannot use client order information to trade on its own account. Further, order execution should be in the best interests of the client. For instance, client orders must be executed individually and at lowest execution or transaction costs. Once executed, brokers and advisors must ensure that any instruments or funds are promptly and correctly delivered to the client's account.

When any or all of these conditions are not met, they are referred to as improper order handling. Examples or improper order handling include front running and cherry picking. Front running is a practice in which the broker who receives a large buy or sell order from a client holds the client's order until after personally executing an order for the same stock for his or her own account. Later when the client's request is executed, there is a rise or a fall in the share price (due to its large size) and this

---

[14] See Javier Blas, Broker fined for market abuse in FSA crackdown, available at https://www.ft.com/content/16e786d4-6e93-11df-ad16-00144feabdc0.

creates an instant profit (or prevents an instant loss) for the broker. Similarly, cherry picking is a practice in which an investment advisor executes a large number of trades (perhaps on multiple stocks) and then allocates those trades to accounts based on their relative profitability to the advisor.

A recent case illustrates the cherry-picking technique. In 2009, the SEC indicted Melhado, Flynn and Associates, an investment firm based in Massachusetts for engaging in cherry-picking over the period January 2001–April 2005. According to the SEC, the president and CEO of the firm, George M. Motz, would place trades every morning, and would wait several hours before telling the trading desk which accounts to allocate particular trades. Over the period January 2001–September 2003, profitable trades (i.e. those that appreciated during the course of the day), were placed in the firm's proprietary trading account. Loss-making trades (i.e. those that depreciated during the day) were allocated to client (or advisory) accounts. The SEC further alleges that, over the summer of 2003, profitable trades were allocated to favour one particular client – a hedge fund affiliated with Melhado, Flynn, and Associates. In the fall of 2003, Motz altered records in an attempt to cover up the trade allocations.[15]

3.3.7 Misleading Customers

A final category of misconduct activity refers to any behaviour via which market participants attempt to misrepresent the value of financial assets or liabilities to mislead customers. One example is window dressing, which refers to the strategy used by asset managers near the end of the reporting period to improve the appearance of the fund's performance to clients or shareholders. To window-dress performance, fund managers may sell stocks with large losses, or purchase stocks with large gains near the end of the quarter. These transactions create the appearance that the fund manager was prescient enough to avoid losses or pick winning investments.

Attempts to mislead customers are not limited to fund managers. Recently, Betterment, a popular robo-advisor platform, was fined $400,000 by Financial Industry Regulatory Authority (FINRA) for window-dressing its financial obligations, to make them appear lower. FINRA alleges that over several months between 2012 and 2015, Betterment structured its transactions on days when it was required to calculate customer reserve account obligations differently than on other days when it was not required to perform this computation. By doing so, Betterment was allegedly able to reduce the funding which was required to maintain its customer reserve account obligations under FINRA regulations, making its financial position appear better than it really was.[16]

---

[15] Full details of the indictment are available at https://www.sec.gov/litigation/admin/2007/34-55356-o.pdf.
[16] For further details of the case, see http://www.finra.org/sites/default/files/fda_documents/2015048047101%20MTG%20LLC%20dba%20Betterment%20Securities%20BD%2047788%20AWC%20jm.pdf.

3.4 Defining Financial Fraud

A quick search of academic databases (Google Scholar, ABI/INFORM, Academic Search Premier, Business Source Premier, Emerald, IEEE Transactions, Science Direct, Springer-Link Journals, and World Scientific Net) suggests that interest in techniques to detect and quantify financial market misconduct extends beyond financial economists, and includes important contributions by researchers in other disciplines such as law, computer science, statistics, decision sciences, and information management. However, the focus of researchers in these other disciplines is somewhat different – they are primarily interested in financial fraud, which is only one particular type of misconduct analysed by financial economists.

Kou et al. (2004) and Bolton and Hand (2002) provide a detailed description of fraudulent activities. This list includes credit card fraud, money laundering, financial statement manipulation, and computer intrusion fraud. A brief description of these activities from their papers follows.[17]

3.4.1 Credit Card Fraud

Credit card fraud includes outright theft (the offender attempts to spend the maximum amount before theft is discovered and the card is disabled), application fraud (the offender attempts to obtain new credit cards using false information), and creation and usage of counterfeit cards (the offender has access to credit card data but not the actual card itself). All credit card fraud can be classified into two broad categories: one in which the offender possesses the physical card, and one in which the offender only has the card details, but not the actual card. Hand and Blunt (2001) comprehensively review the definition of credit card fraud and how it is perpetrated.

According to Kou et al. (2004) and Bolton and Hand (2002), credit card fraud is difficult to quantify as card issuers do not publicly release figures related to such fraud. Card issuers fear that releasing such information publicly may needlessly frighten customers, and make them reluctant to apply and use credit cards. Occasionally, researchers have been able to quantify the extent of credit card fraud in some markets. Leonard (1993) suggests that in Canada credit card fraud amounted to Canadian $19 million, $29 million and $46 million from 1989 to 1991. Ghosh and Reilly (1994) and Aleskerov, Freisleben, and Rao (1997) estimate credit card fraud losses in the US to be of the order of $700–$800 million per year. The latter study also estimates worldwide credit card fraud losses to be close to $10 billion in 1996. In the UK, credit card fraud losses are publicly provided by the Association of Payment Clearing Services and are estimated to be GBP 400 million in 2001.[18]

---

[17] Researchers in other disciplines also focus on telecommunication fraud, insurance fraud, and e-commerce fraud. We omit these for space constraints, and also because techniques to detect telecommunication, insurance, or e-commerce fraud are similar to those described below to detect credit card, money laundering, or financial statement fraud.

[18] In an interesting study, Patient (2000) notes that Expedia Inc. set aside $6 million for credit card fraud in 1999. Thus, analysing the expenditure related to credit card fraud of publicly listed entities may be one way to quantify the extent of such activity in the future.

3.4.2   Money Laundering

Money laundering is the process of obscuring the source, ownership, or use of cash that is obtained from illicit activity. A typical money laundering scheme involves three steps. The first step is 'Placement', i.e. the introduction of the cash into a bank or a legitimate business. For example, cash obtained from illicit transactions may be converted into a cashier's cheque, or mixed with proceeds from a regular business. Yet another common technique is to over-invoice (i.e. pay inflated prices) for goods or raw materials. The second step is 'Layering', whereby multiple transactions are routed through multiple bank accounts, each at a different financial institution, with a different account holder, to obscure the source of funds. The last step is 'Integration', whereby illicit funds are merged with money that is obtained from other legitimate activities.

By its very nature, the extent of money laundering activities is hard to quantify. One good estimate is available from the US Office of Technology Assessment (OTA) in 1995. This report estimates that in 1995 nearly $300 billion was laundered worldwide. Of this, $40–$80 billion related to illicit activities in the US. To obtain this estimate, the OTA analysed incoming wire transfers, which are commonly used money launderers.[19]

3.4.3   Financial Statement Fraud

Beasley (1996) and Schilit (2010) provide an exhaustive list of financial statement fraud techniques. They base their list on the analysis of 204 cases of financial statement fraud documented in the SEC's Accounting Auditing Enforcement Releases (AAERs) from 1987 to 1997. According to Beasley (1996) and Schilit (2010) financial statement fraud includes overstatement of assets or revenues, understatement of expenses or liabilities, and misappropriation of assets, among others. Schilit (2010) categorizes financial statement fraud techniques into seven groups, namely (a) recording revenue too soon or of questionable quality, (b) recording bogus revenue, (c) boosting income with one-time gains, (d) shifting current expenses to a later or earlier period, (e) failing to record or improperly reducing liabilities, (f) shifting current revenue to a later period, and (g) shifting future expenses to the current period as a special charge.

The ACFE presents yet another list of financial statement fraud techniques and defines financial statement fraud either as the intentional misstatement (or omission) of material facts or as the presentation of misleading accounting data which would cause investors to alter their investment decisions. ACFE's definition includes manipulation of financial records; intentional omission of events, transactions, accounts, or other significant information; and misapplication of accounting principles used to measure, recognize, report, and disclose business transactions.

---

[19] In 1995, US financial institutions collectively received 500,000 wire transfers, amounting to nearly $2 trillion. OTA estimated that around 0.05–0.1% of these transactions related to money laundering.

3.4.4   Computer Intrusion Fraud

Computer intrusion fraud is defined as the deliberate unauthorized attempt to access, manipulate, or steal financial information or resources using computer systems. Computer intrusion fraud and its detection and quantification is an extensive and active area of research, with several papers devoted to this topic. A comprehensive review of this topic is beyond the scope of this chapter and interested readers may refer to Denning (1997), who lists eight different kinds of computer intrusion fraud techniques, and the methodologies to detect, quantify, and prevent them.

Computer intrusion fraud can be either financial or non-financial in nature, and to the extent we cover it in this section, we focus only on the former. A recent example of computer intrusion financial fraud is the 'Bangladesh Bank Heist' in February 2016.[20] In this case, offenders capitalized on the weaknesses of the computer security of Bangladesh's Central Bank and attempted to steal $951 million from the Bangladesh central bank's account with the Federal Reserve Bank of New York (FRBNY). The offenders gained access to the bank's credentials for payment transfers and used it to authorize the FRBNY to transfer funds from the Bangladesh bank's account to several accounts in Sri Lanka and the Philippines. Fortunately, the system of checks at the FRBNY blocked most of the fund transfers. Still, close to a $100 million was transferred without authorization from Bangladesh Central Bank's account with the FRBNY.

3.5   Conclusion

This chapter provided a detailed list and description of activities classified as financial market misconduct and analysed how pervasive such misconduct is in financial markets. Researchers have now started to apply novel analytical and computational techniques to classify financial market misconduct activities into broad categories. Such analysis reveals that the number of misconduct techniques is more limited, that misconduct techniques are often repeated, and it is rare that a genuinely new ploy is invested. In Chapter 17, we review the empirical literature and catalogue and categorize various econometric techniques utilized to detect, monitor, and quantify financial market misconduct related to price manipulation, information manipulation, or fraud[21].

References

Acharya, V.V. and Richardson, M. (2009). Causes of the financial crisis. *Critical Review* 21: 195– 210.

Agarwal, S., Amromin, G., Ben-David, I., Chomsisengphet, S. and Evanoff, D.D. (2014). Predatory lending and the subprime crisis. *Journal of Financial Economics* 113: 29–52.

---

[20] 21See, for example, Jim Finkle, Bangladesh Bank hackers compromised SWIFT software, warning issued, Reuters, Apr 25, 2016, available at https:// www.reuters.com/article/us-usa-nyfed-bangladesh-malware-exclusiv/bangladesh-bank-hackers-compromised-swift-software-warning-issued-idUSKCN0XM0DR.

[21] We also do not cover any studies of financial market misconduct in the commodity markets or in the foreign exchange markets, as separate chapters in this volume deal with misconduct in both of these special markets.

Aleskerov, E., Freisleben, B. and Rao, B. (1997). Cardwatch: A neural network based database mining system for credit card fraud detection. In *Computational Intelligence for Financial Engineering (CIFEr), 1997, Proceedings of the IEEE/IAFE 1997*, pp. 220–226. IEEE.

Allen, F. and Gale, D. (1992). Stock-price manipulation. *The Review of Financial Studies* 5: 503– 529.

Beasley, M.S. (1996). An empirical analysis of the relation between the board of director composition and financial statement fraud. *Accounting review* 71(4): 443–465.

Bernheim, A.L. and Schneider, M.G. (eds) (1935). *The Security Markets: Findings and Recommendations of a Special Staff of the Twentieth Century Fund*. Twentieth Century Fund.

Bolton, R.J. and Hand, D.J. (2002). Statistical fraud detection: A review. *Statistical science* 17(3): 235–249.

Cumming, D. and Johan, S. (2008). Global market surveillance. *American Law and Economics Review* 10: 454–506.

Cumming, D., Johan, S. and Li, D. (2011). Exchange trading rules and stock market liquidity. *Journal of Financial Economics* 99: 651–671.

Cumming, D.J., Groh, A.P. and Johan, S. (2017). Same rules, different enforcement: Market abuse in Europe. *Journal of International Financial Markets, Institutions, and Money* 54: 130–151.

Denning, D.E. (1997). Cyberspace attacks and countermeasures. In: *Internet Besieged* (eds. D.E. Denning and P. Denning), 29–55. New York: ACM Press/Addison-Wesley Publishing.

Dyck, A., Morse, A. and Zingales, L. (2010). Who blows the whistle on corporate fraud? *The Journal of Finance* 65: 2213–2253.

Eiteman, W.J., Dice, C.A. and Eiteman, D.K. (1966). *The Stock Market*. New York: McGraw-Hill.

Gandhi, P., Golez, B., Jackwerth, J.C. and Plazzi, A.J. (2018). Financial market misconduct and public enforcement: The case of Libor manipulation. *Management Science, forthcoming*.

Gee, J. and Button, M. (2015). The Financial Cost of Fraud 2015. Resreport, PKF Accountants and Business Advisers.

Ghosh, S. and Reilly, D.L. (1994). Credit card fraud detection with a neural-network. In *System Sciences, 1994. Proceedings of the Twenty-Seventh Hawaii International Conference on*, vol. 3, pp. 621–630. IEEE.

Guiso, L., Sapienza, P. and Zingales, L. (2008). Trusting the stock market. *The Journal of Finance* 63: 2557–2600.

Hand, D.J. and Blunt, G. (2001). Prospecting for gems in credit card data. *IMA Journal of management Mathematics* 12: 173–200.

Henry, J.B. (2008). Fortune 500: The total cost of litigation estimated at one-third of profits. *The Metropolitan Corporate Counsel* February.

Jackson, H.E. and Roe, M. (2009). Public and private enforcement of securities law: Resource-based evidence. *Journal of Financial Economics* 93: 207–238.

Karpoff, J.M., Lee, D.S. and Martin, G.S. (2008). The cost to firms of cooking the books. *The Journal of Financial and Quantitative Analysis* 43: 581–611.

Keys, B.J., Mukherjee, T., Seru, A. and Vig, V. (2010). Did securitization lead to lax screening? Evidence from subprime mortgages. *The Quarterly Journal of Economics* 125: 307–362.

Kou, Y., Lu, C.-T., Sirwongwattana, S. and Huang, Y.-P. (2004). Survey of fraud detection techniques. In *Networking, sensing and control, 2004 IEEE international conference on*, vol. 2, pp. 749–754. IEEE.

Kyle, A.S. and Viswanathan, S. (2008). Price manipulation in financial markets. *American Economic Review* 98: 274–279.

Leonard, K.J. (1993). Detecting credit card fraud using expert systems. *Computers & industrial engineering* 25: 103–106.

Patient, S. (2000). Reducing online credit card fraud. *Web Developer's Journal*.

Schilit, H. (2010). *Financial Shenanigans*. New York: Tata McGraw-Hill Education.

Sobel, R. (1965). *The Big Board*. Washington: Beard Books.

US Government Accountability Office (2002). Financial Statement Restatements, Trends, Market Impact, Regulatory Response, and Remaining Challenges. Resreport, Government Accountability Office.

Chapter 4

Financial Misconduct and Market-Based Penalties

Chelsea Liu and Alfred Yawson
University of Adelaide

4.1   Introduction

Financial fraud and misconduct can attract significant penalties imposed by both legal processes and market forces. Legal penalties only account for a small fraction of the overall consequences incurred for the firms, executive officers, and directors involved. In the United States (US), Karpoff et al. (2008a) document that the legal penalties imposed on firms for financial misrepresentation only average $23.5 million per firm, whereas the average reputational penalty, as captured in the loss of market valuation, amounts to $380.50 million per firm. Similarly, in the United Kingdom (UK), losses of market value triggered by financial misconduct are nearly nine times the size of regulatory fines and compensation paid (Armour et al. 2017). In light of the significance of the penalties imposed by markets, we provide a synthesis of the empirical literature on the market-based penalties for financial fraud and misconduct.

In this chapter, we review the empirical evidence on the existence of market-based penalties for financial fraud and misconduct, with a primary focus on misconduct relating to financial reporting and disclosure. While most empirical studies are conducted in the US setting, we also review evidence from other jurisdictions around the world, including Canada, UK, Australia, European Union (EU) nations, China, and other Asian countries. Specifically, we begin by reviewing recent notable cases of financial reporting fraud. Next, we discuss the legal penalties for financial reporting fraud, and highlight the importance of examining non-legal, market-imposed penalties. We then discuss the empirical evidence on market-based penalties for corporate financial fraud and misconduct. Firm-level penalties include losses of market value, increased costs of operations, reduced innovation, financial constraints, and heightened risk of hostile takeovers. At the individual level, fraud-tainted executive officers and directors face consequences such as increased turnover, impaired career prospects, decreased compensation, and damaged reputations. We next discuss related areas of empirical research, including evidence on the incentives driving and risk factors predicting corporate financial misconduct, the role of public and private enforcement, and how the penalties for financial misconduct differ from those following other types of corporate misconduct. Finally, we provide some concluding remarks.

We examine several forms of market-related financial fraud and misconduct. Securities fraud refers to intentional deceptions in the financial market, causing detriment to users who justifiably rely upon the false information (Hennes et al. 2008; Duarte et al. 2014; Karpoff et al. 2017). The legal definition of financial fraud varies across jurisdictions. In the US, Section 10(b) of the *Securities Exchange Act* of 1934 prohibits 'any manipulative or deceptive device or contrivance'. Specifically, Rule 10b-5 makes it unlawful 'to make any untrue statement of a material fact or to omit to state a material fact'. Similarly, in the UK, Sections 89–91 of the *Financial Services Act* 2012 render it illegal to 'make a false or misleading statement', 'dishonestly conceal material facts', or 'create a false or misleading impression as to [. . .] the price or value of any relevant investments' (Roberts 2013; Gullifer and Payne 2015). Similar statutory prohibitions exist in Canada and Australia. Section 12DA of the *Australian Securities and Investments Commission Act* 2001 outlaws 'misleading or deceptive' conduct in relation to financial services; likewise, in Canada the *Securities Act* 1990 of Ontario prohibits 'misrepresentation' affecting both primary and secondary markets for financial securities.

Financial fraud and misconduct can damage investor confidence (Giannetti and Wang 2016; Gurun et al. 2018), distort allocation of resources (Kedia and Philippon 2009), and undermine the efficiency of capital markets (Karpoff et al. 2017). Common types of financial market misconduct include misrepresentation in financial reporting, insider trading, market manipulation, and other dissemination of false information (Cumming and Li 2011; Cumming et al. 2015a). Cumming et al. (2015a) provide an overview of different types of financial misconduct. For example, front-running is a form of insider trading which involves brokers trading on client information in advance of the client's trade (Markham 1988; Cumming et al. 2015a; Scopino 2015; Manahov 2016). 'Pump-and-dump' refers to a type of price manipulation, whereby the manipulator introduces misleading information to the market (Putniņš 2012; Withanawasam et al. 2013). For example, in early 2018, the Securities and Exchange Commission (SEC) cracked down on numerous 'pump-and-dump' schemes involving initial coin offerings in the cryptocurrency market (Eaglesham and Vigna 2018; Rubin 2018).[1] Wash trading is another form of financial misconduct, which involves manipulating trading volume by having the same client as both buyer and seller in a transaction (Cumming et al. 2011). In 2012, US regulators accused the Royal Bank of Canada of engaging in a 'wash trading scheme of massive proportion' for tax benefits (Eaglesham et al. 2012).[2]

To prove a case of financial misrepresentation, under US law plaintiffs must establish several elements, including 'a misstatement or omission of a material fact made with intent that the plaintiff justifiably relied on causing injury in connection with the purchase or sale of a security' (Jacobs 1973; Skinner 1994, p. 41; Donelson et al. 2012). Although the legal definitions of securities fraud vary across jurisdictions, one typical requirement is the presence of *scienter*, or the state of mind which

---

[1] Rubin, G.T. 2018. 'Investors Warned of Cryptocurrency "Pump-and-Dump" Schemes.' The Wall Street Journal, February 15, 2018. https://www.wsj.com/articles/investors-warned-of-cryptocurrency-pump-and-dump-schemes-1518724576.
Eaglesham, J., Vigna, P. 2018. 'Cryptocurrency Firms Targeted in Sec Probe; Regulator Issues Subpoenas to Parties Engaged in Booming Market for Initial Coin Offerings.' *The Wall Street Journal*. February 28, 2018. https://www.wsj.com/articles/sec-launches-cryptocurrency-probe-1519856266.
[2] Eaglesham, J., Trindle, J., Van Hasselt, C. 2012. 'CFTC Deals out Royal Pain; Canadian Bank Is Accused of Massive "Wash" Scheme to Garner Tax Benefits.' *The Wall Street Journal*, April 3, 2012. https://www.wsj.com/articles/SB10001424052702303816504577319990588467360.

accompanies the act. To establish fraud, the misstatement or omission must be proven to be intentional (or reckless in some jurisdictions). Similarly, in the UK and Australia, an equivalent requirement is built into the statutory provisions, which prohibit 'intentional' ('knowing') or 'reckless' misstatements. An exception exists in Canada, where *scienter* is not required to establish fraud (Gelowitz et al. 2015). In most jurisdictions, the presence of a culpable state of mind is an important factor that distinguishes securities fraud from mere misconduct (if negligent) or innocent mistakes.[3]

Empirical researchers have adopted different proxies to represent securities fraud and misconduct, which capture various levels of severity and culpability (a comprehensive discussion is provided by Karpoff et al. 2017). At one end of the spectrum, Agrawal et al. (1999) examine corporate fraud by identifying 'fraud or crime-related' news articles reported in the *Wall Street Journal*. This is a narrow proxy, as it captures only extreme cases of fraud which attract media attention, while excluding other lower-profile incidences not reported in the press (potentially resulting in 'false negatives'). At the other end of the spectrum, accounting misstatements are frequently used as a broader proxy for financial misconduct (Desai et al. 2006; Agrawal and Cooper 2017). This is a wide proxy which captures all financial reporting errors, whether fraudulent or innocent, and may result in 'false positive' cases where unintentional mistakes are regarded as misconduct. In the middle of the continuum, securities litigation constitutes a commonly used proxy for financial misconduct. Specifically, researchers observe public or private enforcement through securities class actions or SEC enforcement lawsuits (e.g. Helland 2006; Dechow et al. 2011; Correia and Klausner 2012; Humphery-Jenner 2012; Karpoff et al. 2017).

However, these empirical proxies have common limitations. First, actual fraud committed by corporations is inherently unobservable (Wang 2013). Empirical researchers typically use detected fraud to proxy all fraud committed, which disregards undetected fraud (Wang 2013). Second, empirical researchers often use *accusations* of misconduct to proxy actual misconduct. This is also inaccurate because accused firms are presumed innocent until proven otherwise at trial, which rarely happens given that a vast majority of cases are settled out of court.[4] Consequently, there is no consensus in the literature as to what is the correct proxy for financial fraud, as no empirical proxy perfectly aligns with the legal definition of fraud. Karpoff et al. (2017) caution researchers to carefully select empirical proxies that best reflect the constructs of financial misconduct examined, as the choice of empirical proxies has a significant bearing on the research findings.

An extensive and growing body of literature examines the causes and consequences of corporate financial fraud and misconduct (e.g. Srinivasan 2005; Desai et al. 2006; Fich and Shivdasani 2007; Karpoff et al.,2008b; Cheng et al. 2010; Brochet and Srinivasan 2014; Amel-Zadeh and Zhang 2015; Arena and Julio 2015). Several recent surveys discuss the methodological issues in financial misconduct research and provide directions for future studies (Karpoff et al. 2017; Amiram et al. 2018; Cumming et al. 2018a). In particular, there is considerable academic attention devoted

---

[3] In many cases the distinction is a legal or evidentiary one.
[4] For example, Schrand and Zechman (2012) find that in three quarters of SEC enforcement actions for financial misreporting, the executives involved lack the requisite intent to defraud.

to investigating market-imposed consequences of financial fraud and misconduct, in addition to legal penalties such as fines and imprisonment. Understanding these market-imposed consequences is important to provide a holistic view of the overall penalties for fraud or misconduct (Alexander 1999). This enables regulators and policymakers to assess the adequacy of the legal penalties and to prescribe the optimal level of disincentives to deter future misconduct (Alexander 1999; Karpoff 2011).

4.2   Notable Cases of Financial Reporting Fraud

Notorious incidents of financial reporting fraud, such as the scandals involving Enron and WorldCom, have shocked stock markets worldwide in recent decades. These revelations of fraud not only resulted in significant losses of shareholder and debtholder wealth, but also undermined investor confidence in the markets generally (Giannetti and Wang 2016; Karpoff et al. 2017).

Enron's accounting fraud constitutes one of the most notorious corporate scandals this century (Brennan and McGrath 2007; Soltani 2014). Enron Corporation was an energy giant and the seventh largest US company by revenue in December 2000, with market capitalization of $75.2 billion (Soltani 2014). Enron announced restatements of its 1997–2000 earnings on 16 October 2001, revealing glaring accounting irregularities. These revelations triggered a freefall in Enron's share price from which it never recovered (Baker and Hayes 2005; Gillan and Martin 2007). The ensuing influx of securities lawsuits resulted in legal settlements of $7.2 billion in 2006, paid by Enron, its executive officers, auditor Arthur Andersen (including individual partners and employees), and former legal counsel, Vinson & Elkins. Enron's demise severely impaired market confidence. Subsequent forensic examination of its financial records revealed sophisticated and well-disguised accounting malpractices (Baker and Hayes 2005; Soltani 2014). For example, Enron failed to include three of its special purpose entities (SPEs) in its consolidated financial statements, in violation of the applicable accounting rules. This enabled Enron to use these SPEs as vehicles to overstate earnings, conceal losses, and remove liabilities from its balance sheet (Baker and Hayes 2005; Soltani 2014). Enron's scandal prompted regulatory changes in the US and worldwide during the ensuing decade (Rockness and Rockness 2005).

Another well-known case of financial reporting fraud involves WorldCom, a leading telecommunications company in the 1990s. During 2000 and 2001, facing a downturn in the telecommunications market and declines in long distance rates and revenue, WorldCom adopted fraudulent accounting practices to disguise expenses as capital expenditure and to overinflate its earnings (Soltani 2014). In July 2000, WorldCom's stock price began to fall after its attempted merger with Spring was blocked by the Department of Justice. Internal auditors at WorldCom discovered the fraudulent accounting practices in 2002. This discovery prompted an enforcement action by the SEC alleging $3.8 billion of overstatement of WorldCom's 2001–2002 earnings. The lawsuits against WorldCom and its chief executive officer (CEO), chief financial officer (CFO), controller, and accounting director, eventually settled for $6.2 billion in 2005.

Corporate fraud is by no means unique to US corporations. Numerous financial reporting scandals worldwide have gained notoriety over the past decades, including

Canadian manufacturer Nortel Networks, Japan's cosmetic producer Kanebo Ltd, UK-based retailer Tesco, Australian telecommunications group OneTel, and the Italian food producer Parmalat (Lehman and Okcabol 2005; Jones 2011; Farrell 2015). For example, Nortel Networks, a Canadian manufacturer of telecommunications equipment, settled a civil fraud lawsuit initiated by the SEC in 2007 for allegedly falsifying accounting entries to overstate sales revenue for 2000–2001 and 2003–2004. Nortel's stock price fell from C$124 to C$0.47 from September 2000 to August 2002, causing its market capitalization to plunge from C$398 billion to C$5 billion. In the Australian context, the collapse of retailer Harris Scarfe in 2001 left outstanding debt totalling AUD$265 million. Subsequently, the Australian Securities and Investments Commission (ASIC) prosecuted its CFO and executive chairman for overinflating consolidated earnings (ASIC 2005). Parmalat, an Italian food producer, committed 'one of largest and most brazen corporate financial frauds in history' (SEC 2003), the total value of which exceeded the combined size of Enron and WorldCom (Soltani 2014). In December 2003, the then eighth-largest industrial group in Italy admitted to overstating assets by €3.95 billion and was declared insolvent within the same month (Soltani 2014). These notable scandals illustrate the significant extent to which corporate financial reporting fraud can deplete market value, harm investor trust, and disrupt capital markets.

4.3   Financial Reporting Misconduct and Legal Redress

Misrepresentation in financial reporting constitutes a common type of corporate misconduct (Cumming et al. 2015a; Cumming et al. 2018a), which is prohibited under Rule 10b-5 of the *Securities Exchange Act* 1934 and Section 17(a) of the *Securities Act* 1933:

> Rule 10b-5: Employment of Manipulative and Deceptive Practices:
> It shall be unlawful for any person, directly or indirectly, by the use of any means or instrumentality of interstate commerce, or of the mails or of any facility of any national securities exchange,
>
> **a.** To employ any device, scheme, or artifice to defraud,
> **b.** To make any untrue statement of a material fact or to omit to state a material fact necessary in order to make the statements made, in the light of the circumstances under which they were made, not misleading, or
> **c.** To engage in any act, practice, or course of business which operates or would operate as a fraud or deceit upon any person, in connection with the purchase or sale of any security.

Violations of Rule 10b-5 can attract enforcement through public or private mechanisms. As public enforcement, the SEC or the Department of Justice (DOJ) can initiate regulatory actions against violators, commonly in the event of serious or high profile cases (Nourayi 1994; Dechow et al. 1996; Correia and Klausner 2012). Securities law violations can also be enforced through private mechanisms including securities class actions (McTier and Wald 2011; Humphery-Jenner 2012; Caskey 2014) and derivative lawsuits (Fischel and Bradley 1986; Loewenstein 1999; Ferris et al. 2007; Davis 2008).

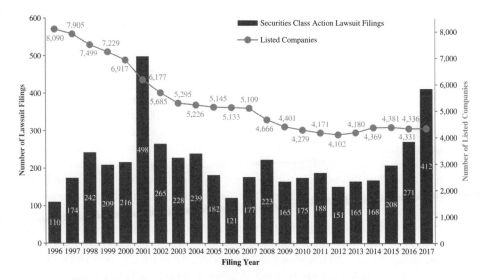

Figure 4.1   Lawsuit filings and number of companies listed in the United States.

Note: the number of federal securities class action lawsuit filings is sourced from Stanford Law School's Securities Class Actions Clearinghouse; the number of companies listed in the US is sourced from The Global Economy.

Securities class actions constitute an important avenue of private enforcement of securities law, particularly in relation to violations of Rule 10b-5 (Kennedy 1977; Banoff and DuVal 1984; Thompson and Sale 2003). Shareholders have the right to file private legal actions for alleged securities fraud. Federal courts have exclusive jurisdiction to hear 10b-5 related securities lawsuits under Section 27 of the *Securities Exchange Act* 1934 (Choi 2007, p. 1489). Securities class actions remain a relatively unique feature of the US legal environment (Warren 2012), even though some elements of this legal process have been adopted by European nations (Grace 2006).

Legal actions accusing firms of financial misrepresentation have increased over time (Boettrich and Starykh 2017; Karpoff et al. 2017). The annual number of federal securities class action lawsuits has more than tripled from 1996 to 2017, despite a decrease in the total number of listed companies by over 40% during that time, as illustrated in Figure 4.1. This indicates that firms on average are becoming more frequently accused of financial wrongdoing.

4.4   Evolution of US Financial Regulations

'An ounce of prevention is worth a pound of cure – in few other business contexts is that as true as with financial statement fraud' (Young 2000, p. 211). The prevention of financial fraud is crucial to maintaining the efficiency of capital markets. Since the passage of the *Securities Exchange Act* of 1934, which established the Securities and Exchange Commission (SEC) to regulate securities issuance and trading, the modern financial system has been gradually constructed through legislative developments, with significant overhauls occurring in the 1980s and 1990s and additional fine-tuning since 2000 (Komai and Richardson 2014). In this section, we briefly review several significant changes in financial market regulations enacted over recent decades.

4.4.1   Private Securities Litigation Reform Act (1995)

Prior to the Private Securities Litigation Reform Act (PSLRA) of 1995, plaintiffs were able to file securities lawsuits with limited evidence of wrongdoing and use the discovery process as a 'fishing' expedition to seek evidence to support the claim filed. Consequently, defendants were frequently forced to settle any filed lawsuits at a 'nuisance' value to avoid high litigation costs (Spier 2007). PSLRA was introduced with the aim of reducing the number of frivolous securities lawsuits (Choi and Thompson 2006; Choi et al. 2009) to 'address the problems plaguing securities class action litigation' (Choi 2007, p. 1489). The passage of this legislation raised pleadings standards and limited the ability of plaintiffs to file nuisance lawsuits.

Empirical studies have documented the effects of PSLRA on corporations, executives, and investors. As PSLRA restricted investors' ability to file securities lawsuits, in the short term stock markets reacted negatively to its enactment, particularly in litigation-prone industries including computers, electronics, pharmaceutical and biotech, and retailing (Ali and Kallapur 2001). In the long-run, PSLRA has reduced securities lawsuits, consistent with its intended purpose of limiting nuisance claims (Choi et al. 2009). However, Choi (2007) finds that PSLRA also reduces the filings of meritorious lawsuits, and that non-nuisance claims are more likely to be dismissed or receive low-value settlements in the post-PSLRA era. This evidence suggests that PSLRA may have the unintended consequence of hampering meritorious securities lawsuits.

4.4.2   Sarbanes–Oxley Act (2002)

The *Sarbanes–Oxley Act* of 2002 (SOX) was enacted in the wake of the high-profile corporate scandals including Enron and WorldCom. SOX introduced changes aimed at improving financial reporting transparency and increasing investor protection. These changes include heightened disclosure requirements and corporate governance mandates (Romano 2004). For example, SOX prescribes a minimum proportion of independent directors on the board and prohibits auditing firms from providing advisory services. Section 404 of the Act mandates various internal controls. Section 403 requires more timely disclosure of insider trades by reducing the filing period from the next calendar month to two business days.

Debates persist over whether SOX is effective in protecting investors and capital markets, and whether any benefits are sufficient to justify the costs of compliance incurred by firms (Romano 2004; Ge et al. 2017). To investigate the benefits of SOX, researchers have examined its impact on capital markets, management behaviour, and executive and director labour markets (e.g. Romano 2004; Zhang 2007; Cohen et al. 2008; Linck et al. 2009; Brochet 2010). In the capital markets, the enactment of SOX is followed by reduced accrual-based earnings management (Cohen et al. 2008), decreased firm information opaqueness (Arping and Sautner 2013), and increased accounting conservatism, especially in firms with internal control weaknesses (Mitra et al. 2013). Additionally, more timely disclosures of insider trades help facilitate security pricing in the market (Brochet 2010), and firms experience lower costs of equity given the reduced information risk post-SOX (Ashbaugh-Skaife et al. 2009). In the executive and director labour markets, SOX is expected to enhance corporate governance quality and increase penalties for financial fraud. Empirical evidence shows that director and officer (D&O) insurance premiums have doubled since the passage of SOX (Linck et al. 2009). Post-SOX boards are larger and more independent, and audit and nominating committees meet more frequently (Linck et al. 2009). However, there is mixed evidence on whether CEO and CFO turnover is more sensitive to accounting restatements (Hennes et al. 2008; Collins et al. 2009; Burks 2010). Nonetheless, CEOs are more likely to experience reductions in bonus compensation in response to accounting misstatements post-SOX (Burks 2010), and CFOs incur greater ex post settling up when seeking re-employment after losing their jobs amidst fraud allegations (Collins et al. 2009).

SOX imposes significant costs of compliance on firms (Ge et al. 2017). As a result, stock prices reacted negatively to the enactment of SOX, particularly for firms with weak shareholder rights (Zhang 2007). The costs of compliance are especially burdensome on smaller firms, potentially reducing their value (Zhang 2007; Iliev 2010) and discouraging unlisted firms from going public (Piotroski and Srinivasan 2013). Furthermore, SOX also impacts on the incentives for foreign firms to list on US stock exchanges. In particular, small foreign firms are less likely to list in the US (Piotroski and Srinivasan 2013). Duarte et al. (2014) argue that it is more costly for insider investors of foreign firms to extract value from minority shareholders, whose interests are better protected after the passage of SOX.

4.4.3 Dodd–Frank Act (2010)

In the wake of the Global Financial Crisis, the *Dodd–Frank Wall Street Reform and Consumer Protection Act* was enacted in 2010 to further strengthen investor protection. Notable changes include tougher consequences for executive officers who have committed fraud, and increased incentives for fraud reporting. For example, Section 954 of the Act establishes the 'clawback' provisions, which enable firms to recoup excessively paid compensation from their executive officers following accounting restatements. Furthermore, the Act amends the *Securities Exchange Act* of 1934 by adding Section 21F on 'Securities Whistleblower Incentives and Protection'. This 'bounty' programme provides whistleblowers with financial rewards ranging from between 10% and 30% of the value recovered.

A growing number of academic studies examine the impacts and effectiveness of the Dodd–Frank Act (DFA). For example, Balasubramanian and Cyree (2014) find that following the passage of the Act, the size discount on bank yield spreads (in particular the too-big-to-fail discount) has decreased amongst secondary market subordinate debt transactions. This indicates that the DFA has strengthened market disciplining of banks. However, Dimitrov et al. (2015) document that, in the wake of the DFA, credit rating agencies such as Standard & Poor's and Moody's tend to issue lower ratings, more false warnings, and less informative downgrades. Dimitrov et al. (2015) argue that the DFA creates incentives for credit rating agencies to be overprotective of their own reputations and impede the informativeness of credit ratings. Further, deHaan et al. (2013)

find that voluntary adoption of clawback provisions prior to the enactment of DFA was associated with better financial reporting quality. This evidence potentially sheds light on the likely impacts of the clawback provisions mandated under the DFA. Overall, securities regulations in the US and worldwide will continue to evolve over time in response to new challenges. Academic research provides important evidence to inform policymakers and regulators of the effectiveness of these laws.

4.5   Legal versus Market-Based Penalties for Financial Misconduct

Financial fraud and misconduct can attract an array of consequences. These include legal penalties arising from lawsuits or regulatory enforcement proceedings, and non-legal penalties imposed by the operation of market forces. In this section, we provide an overview of the legal penalties for the accused firms and their executive officers and directors. We then discuss the role and relevance of market-imposed penalties.

4.5.1   Common Forms of Legal Penalties

Violations of securities law can result in public or private enforcement actions. Legal penalties may be levied against the accused firms, or their individual executive officers and directors (Karpoff et al. 2008b). Monetary penalties constitute the main form of firm-level penalty (Karpoff et al. 2008b). Regulatory bodies such as the SEC can impose fines on the accused firms. If any wrongdoing is proven at trial, defendants would be ordered to pay damages for any losses sustained by the plaintiffs from relying on the fraudulent information. In addition to the compensatory damages for the actual losses incurred, punitive damages may be awarded for the purpose of penalizing the offenders (Karpoff and Lott 1999). However, a majority of securities class actions are settled out of court before damages are awarded at trial (Cox and Thomas 2005). The amount of the settlement represents the firm's economic value in terminating the lawsuit, factoring in the estimated damages, the likelihood of losing, and any additional reputational losses arising from continuing a court trial (Haslem 2005).

Serious or high-profile violations can attract SEC enforcement actions. Researchers show that the risk of being targeted by the SEC is lower if firms have political connections established through lobbying and campaign donations (Yu and Yu 2011; Correia 2014). Furthermore, politically connected firms tend to incur significantly lower monetary penalties in enforcement actions (Correia 2014). Cooperation with the SEC increases the likelihood of receiving sanctions, but cooperation and timely disclosure through prompt restatements are both associated with lower monetary penalties (Files 2012).

At the individual level, executive officers and directors may be personally named in lawsuits and regulatory enforcement proceedings (Karpoff et al. 2008b; Crutchley et al. 2015). The SEC or Department of Justice (DOJ) may initiate criminal prosecutions against officers and directors (Karpoff et al. 2008b). In civil proceedings, accused individuals may face monetary sanctions, such as fines and disgorgement, and debarment from professional activities (Karpoff et al. 2008b). For example, Karpoff et al. (2008b) examine regulatory enforcement actions during 1978 to 2006, and find that 34% of accused executive officers were barred from serving as officers or directors of public or SEC-registered companies. The average monetary sanctions amounted to $6.7 million per individual (Karpoff et al. 2008b). Criminal prosecutions against individual executive officers and directors are relatively rare and only occur in serious cases (Brennan and McGrath 2007). Karpoff et al. (2008b) find that 28% of responsible individuals face criminal charges. Convicted individuals receive imprisonment averaging 4.3 years with an average 3-year probation period (Karpoff et al. 2008b).

4.5.2 Role of Market-Based Penalties

Many believe legal penalties to be insufficient to deter corporate misconduct. According to *Time*, 'the threat of fines . . . has proved laughably inadequate in producing better behaviour.' (Karpoff 2011, p. 361). In particular, personal fines levied against executives and directors are typically covered by the companies' D&O insurance, and therefore serve as an ineffective penalty. Consequently, in the absence of debarment and imprisonment, executives and directors may incur negligible out-of-pocket expenses from fraud accusations.

Given the perceived inadequacy of legal penalties as a means of effectively penalizing executives and directors, researchers have looked to market-based penalties to determine whether other disincentives exist to deter firms from committing financial fraud. This body of research aims to inform policymakers as to the extent to which legislative changes are needed to provide sufficient deterrence to prevent corporate fraud (Alexander 1999).

Market-based penalties form an essential part of the sanctions incurred by corporations and their officers following alleged fraud and misconduct (Alexander 1999). Fama (1980) argues that such ex post settling-up in the labour market can discipline managers and consequently provide ex ante disincentives to deter managers from wrongdoing. In light of perceived insufficient legal penalties, it is imperative to examine market-based penalties to gain a full understanding of these ex post consequences and their potential deterrent effects (Cox 1997; Coffee 2006; Desai et al. 2006; Mitchell 2009).

4.6 Firm-Level Penalties for Corporate Financial Misconduct

In the next two sections, we discuss the empirical evidence on market-imposed penalties for financial fraud and misconduct. Market-based penalties can be divided into two broad categories: penalties incurred at the firm level, and penalties incurred personally by executive officers and directors. Most of the empirical studies examining these market-based penalties are conducted in the US setting. However, we also discuss studies examining securities misconduct in other institutional settings, including countries in Europe (Grace 2006; Brennan and McGrath 2007; Armour et al. 2017), Asia (Chen et al. 2006; Jia et al. 2009; Tanimura and Okamoto 2013; Chen et al. 2016; Hass et al. 2016; Stuart and Wang 2016; Wang et al. 2017), and Oceania (Chapple et al. 2014; Capezio and Mavisakalyan 2016).

In this section, we discuss the firm-level penalties imposed by the markets. We provide a summary of a number of prior empirical studies in this literature in Table 4.1.

Table 4.1 Overview of studies on firm-level penalties.

This table summarizes the papers that examine firm-level penalties for financial fraud incurred by the accused firms. The authors, data sources, countries, time periods, variables, and main findings are summarized. The main findings are largely paraphrased and/or copied from the abstracts of the papers to best and succinctly represent the authors' contributions, but are not meant to exhaustively represent all of the findings from the papers.

Author(s)	Data Source(s)	Country	Time Period	Dependent Variables	Main Explanatory Variables	Main Findings
Market Reactions and Reputational Loss						
Karpoff and Lott (1993)	Searches for 'fraud' or 'crime' listings in *The Wall Street Journal* Index.	US	1978–1987	Market reactions to fraud allegations	Fraud allegations; legal penalties	Reputational costs significantly exceed legal penalties for firms accused or convicted of fraud. Initial allegations of fraud trigger an average 1.34% decline in market value (or 5.05% for fraud against government agencies). Penalties and criminal fines account for only 1.4%, and court-imposed costs 6.5%, of the loss of market valuation.
Bhagat et al. (1998)	Lawsuit filings or settlements reported in *The Wall Street Journal*.	US	1981–1983	Market reactions to lawsuit filings and settlements	Corporate lawsuits (lawsuit issues and nature of plaintiffs)	Lawsuit announcements trigger significant negative market reactions. The two-day abnormal returns differ depending on the nature of lawsuits: environmental suits (−3.08%), product-liability suits (−1.46%), and violations of security laws (−2.71%) result in significantly greater wealth losses for defendant firms, compared to disputes involving antitrust (−0.81%) or breach of contract (−0.16%) issues.
Alexander (1999)	Federal court criminal cases, news from *Wall Street Journal*, Dow Jones News Retrieval Service, *LexisNexis*, Westlaw, and government publications.	US	1984–1990	Market reactions; customer relationships; CEO turnover	Corporate crimes	Corporate crimes give rise to reputational penalties reflected in the average 2.26% loss of firm value), but losses in market valuation associated with crimes against related parties (e.g. customers) are significantly larger than losses associated with third-party crime (e.g. environmental violations). Firms facing criminal allegations also experience terminated or suspended customer relationships, and management and employee turnover.

Study	Method	Country	Period	Variables	Event type	Findings
Karpoff and Lott (1999)	Searches for 'punitive' in *LexisNexis* Library.	US	1985–June 1996	Size of punitive damages awards; market reactions	Punitive damages lawsuits	Punitive damages lawsuits trigger larger market valuation losses for the defendant firms than compensatory damages lawsuits and actual punitive damages awarded. Initial lawsuit filings trigger an average loss of −1.02% market value during the two-day window. An announcement of a plaintiff verdict triggers a further valuation loss of 0.62%.
Palmrose and Scholz (2004)	Restatements from *LexisNexis* News Library, Lexis Disclosure of other corporate events, and Form 8-Ks on Lexis using keyword (e.g. 'restat', 'revis', 'adjust', 'error') for specific accounting issues.	US	1995–1999	Market reactions; bankruptcy and delisting; litigation likelihood	Accounting restatements of core earnings	Firms with core restatements have higher frequencies of intentional misstatements (fraud), material restatements, subsequent bankruptcy or delisting, more negative security price reactions to restatement announcements, more negative security price changes over the six months pre- and post-restatement, and greater likelihood of securities lawsuits.
Palmrose et al. (2004)	Restatements from *LexisNexis* News Library, Lexis Disclosure, and Form 8-Ks on Lexis by searching for keywords (e.g. 'restat', 'revis', 'adjust', 'error') and for specific accounting issues.	US	1995–1999	Market reactions	Accounting restatements	The market reactions to restatement announcements average approximately 9% over the two-day event window. Returns are more negative if the restatements involve fraud, affect more accounts, decrease reported income or are attributed to auditors or management.
Karpoff et al. (2008a)	Securities and Exchange Commission (SEC) and Department of Justice (DOJ) enforcement actions from *LexisNexis*, Academic Business News, General News, and Legal Cases libraries, and SEC and DOJ websites.	US	1978–2002	Market reactions to lawsuits	SEC/DOJ enforcement actions for financial misrepresentation	Penalties imposed on firms through the legal system average only $23.5 million per firm, compared with the average loss of $330.50 million in market valuation per firm. For each dollar that a firm misleadingly inflates its market value, on average, it loses this dollar when its misconduct is revealed, plus an additional $3.08. Of this additional loss, $0.36 is due to expected legal penalties and $2.71 is due to lost reputation.

(continued)

Table 4.1 (Continued)

Author(s)	Data Source(s)	Country	Time Period	Dependent Variables	Main Explanatory Variables	Main Findings
Gande and Lewis (2009)	Securities class actions from Stanford Securities Class Action Clearinghouse (SCAC).	US	1996–2003	Market reactions; market reactions of non-sued industry-peer firms	Securities class action law-suits	Firms sued for securities class actions experience significant negative price reactions, averaging −4.66% during the three-day window around filing dates, and −9.79% in the two-week period preceding filings, indicating that the market partially anticipates the lawsuits. High litigation-risk firms experience greater anticipation effects and correspondingly smaller filing-date effects. Non-sued firms operating in the same industry as the accused firms also experience declines in valuation upon lawsuit announcements, indicating an industry spillover effect.
Tanimura and Oka-moto (2013)	Factiva searches (*Jiji Press English News Service* and *Kyodo News*) for fraud*, false*, cheat*, conceal*, cover* up, manipulate* or misrepresent*.	Japan, US	2000–2008	Market reactions	Corporate scan-dals	Japanese firms involved in corporate scandal experience significant losses of market valuation upon revelations, despite negligible legal and regulatory penalties. The negative abnormal stock price reactions are larger in Japan than in the US, which is attributable to the trust-based culture underlying the business environment in Japan.
Armour et al. (2017)	Press statements relating to enforcement actions by the Financial Services Authority (FSA) and London Stock Exchange (LSE).	UK	Jan 2001–Jan 2011	Market reactions	Regulatory enforcement actions	Reputational losses, as captured by the losses of market valuation upon announcements of violation and penalties, are nearly nine times the size of fines. However reputational losses are confined to cases where the wrongdoing is against related parties (customers or investors) but not third parties.
Access to Financing and Cost of Capital						
Lowry and Shu (2002)	Securities class actions from *Securities Class Action Alert* Newsletters and Database; SEC filings from EDGAR or Nexis; Gilardi and Co. class action administration (http://www.gilardi.com/index. html); IPO data from Securi-	US	1988–1995	Initial IPO returns; subsequent litigation risk for securities class actions	Securities class action law-suits; initial IPO returns	Firms with higher litigation risk experience greater IPO underpricing. Higher underpricing lowers expected subsequent litigation risks, especially for lawsuits occurring closer to the IPO dates.

Study	Data source	Country	Dependent variable	Sample period	Topic	Findings
Hribar and Jenkins (2004)	Restatements from the U.S. General Accounting / Government Accountability Office (GAO) Database.	US	Cost of equity capital	1997–2002	Accounting restatements	Accounting restatements lead to decreased expected future earnings and increased cost of equity capital for the restating firms, averaging 7%–19% in the month immediately following a restatement. The increase dissipates as time passes and after controlling for analyst forecast biases, but continues to average between 6% and 15% in the most conservative setting. This increase in the cost of capital is larger if the restatement is initiated by the auditor, or if the firm has high leverage.
Graham et al. (2008)	Restatements from GAO. Bank loan data from Dealscan, a Loan Pricing Corporation (LPC) Database.	US	Cost of debt capital (loan spreads); loan terms (maturities, security, restrictive covenants)	1997–2002	Accounting restatements	Restating firms experience significant increases in loan spreads. Lenders also impose stricter loan terms on the restating firms, such as shorter maturities, greater likelihood of secured loans, and more stringent restrictive covenants. The increase in loan spread is significantly larger for fraudulent restating firms than other restating firms. After restatement, the number of lenders per loan declines and firms pay higher upfront and annual fees.
Kravet and Shevlin (2010)	Restatements from GAO.	US	Fama and French factor loadings on Information Risk (IR) (discretionary and innate)	1997–2002	Accounting restatements	Restating firms experience a significant increase in the factor loadings on the discretionary information risk factor after a restatement announcement, resulting in increased estimated cost of capital. Other non-restating industry-peers of the restating firms also experience a smaller increase in the pricing of discretionary information risk.
Bai et al. (2010)	Settled securities class actions from Public Access to Court Electronic Records (PACER), SEC Litigation Releases, *LexisNexis*, restatements from GAO.	US	Liquidity ratio, bankruptcy risk (Altman's Z), market-to-book	1996–2008	Securities class action settlements; financial restatements	Defendant companies in securities class action lawsuits experience reduced operating efficiency during the lawsuits. After lawsuit settlements, defendant firms experience greater liquidity constraints and increased bankruptcy risk (proxied by Altman's Z score).

(continued)

Table 4.1 (Continued)

Author(s)	Data Source(s)	Country	Time Period	Dependent Variables	Main Explanatory Variables	Main Findings
Autore et al. (2014)	Securities lawsuits from the University of Michigan's Inter-University Consortium for Political and Social Research (ICPSR) and Stanford SCAC.	US	1987–2009	Net equity issue; net debt issue; long-term net debt issue	Securities lawsuits	Firms with a history of securities lawsuits are less likely to seek external debt and equity financing, particularly following more severe litigation and for firms with high information asymmetry. Sued firms experience a decline in capital expenditure and research and development (R&D) expenses during the three-year period following a litigation filing.
Arena et al. (2015)	Securities class actions from Stanford SCAC; Non-securities lawsuits from Audit Analytics.	US	1996–2006	Cash holdings; cash holdings of industry peer-firms; capital expenditure; value of cash	Securities class actions; other lawsuits (product liability, copyright, patent, antitrust, and trade regulation)	Firms with higher securities litigation risk hold significantly more cash in anticipation of future lawsuits and settlements, and lower market value of cash holdings. Additionally, high litigation-risk firms reduce investments and have lower capital expenditures. Non-sued industry-peers of the sued firms also increase their cash holdings in response to securities class action lawsuit filings.
Yuan and Zhang (2015)	Lawsuits from Institutional Shareholder Services (ISS) Securities Class Action Database.	US	1996–2009	Loan spread; restrictive covenants	Securities class action lawsuits	Sued firms experience increased loan spreads (averaging 19%) and stricter covenants following securities class action lawsuits.
Chu (2017)	Bank loan data from DealScan.	US	1995–2003	Loan spreads	Ninth Circuit Court ruling in 1999 increasing the difficulty of securities class actions	Using a natural experiment based on a ruling by the Ninth Circuit Court of Appeals, increasing the difficulty of class action suits is found to decrease loan spreads. The effect is stronger for firms with higher institutional ownership.

Author	Data source	Country	Period	Variables	Topic	Findings
Arena (2018)	Corporate lawsuits from Audit Analytics; debt issue data from Thomson One-Banker (SDC Global Issues).	US	2000–2013	Credit ratings; yield spread	Corporate lawsuits	Litigation affects a firm's creditworthiness and debt costs in two stages. Before a lawsuit filing, firms at higher risk of litigation have lower credit ratings, are more likely to be rated speculative grade, pay higher yields on loans and bonds, and are less likely to rely on debt financing. After the lawsuits, firms facing larger settlement disbursements relative to their available cash experience a decline in credit ratings and an increase in yield spread.

Operating Performance, Innovation, and Costs of Operations

Author	Data source	Country	Period	Variables	Topic	Findings
Baker and Griffith (2007a)	Qualitative data from interviews with underwriters, actuaries, brokers, lawyers, and corporate risk managers.	US	2004–2006	D&O insurance premiums (qualitative)	Corporate governance risk (qualitative)	Insurers seek to price D&O policies according to the risk posed by each prospective insured and underwriters focus on corporate governance in assessing risk, with a focus on the idiosyncratic culture of firms beyond what is captured by traditional corporate governance indices.
Murphy et al. (2009)	Corporate misconduct from *WSJ Index* keyword searches (antitrust, breach of contract, bribery, business ethics, conflict of interest, copyright/patent infringement, fraud, kickbacks, price-fixing, securities fraud, and white-collar crime).	US	1982–1996	Profitability (reported earnings, analyst forecasts); risk (stock returns volatility; analyst forecast concordance)	Corporate misconduct (against related vs. unrelated party)	Corporate misconduct against related parties (e.g. customers, suppliers, investors) is followed by deteriorations in operating performance as measured by earnings and analyst earnings forecasts. Corporate misconduct is also associated with increased stock return volatility and reduced concordance amongst analyst forecasts, indicating an increase in risk.
Johnson et al. (2014)	Securities class actions from Stanford SCAC.	US	1996–2009	Customer relation termination; change in ROA; market reactions.	Securities class action lawsuits	Customers impose significant reputational sanctions on firms accused of securities fraud, resulting in a decline in operating performance through increased selling costs. The size of these decreases in earnings corresponds to the loss of market valuation upon initial lawsuit filings.

(continued)

Table 4.1 (Continued)

Author(s)	Data Source(s)	Country	Time Period	Dependent Variables	Main Explanatory Variables	Main Findings
Gillan and Panasian (2015)	D&O insurance, governance, ownership, and compensation data hand-collected from proxy statements. Lawsuit data from Stanford SCAC and LexisNexis legal sources.	Canada (largest 350 firms listed on the Toronto S.E.)	1995, 2000, 2005	Securities litigation likelihood	D&O insurance coverage and premium	Firms with D&O insurance coverage are more likely to be sued and the likelihood of litigation increases with increased coverage. Higher premiums are associated with the likelihood of litigation, indicating that insurers price this behaviour.
Cumming et al. (2019)	Patent data from the EPO's Worldwide Patent Statistical (PATSTAT) Database. Manipulation data from SMARTS Group Inc, Capital Markets Cooperative Research Centre (CMCRC) and SIRCA.	9 countries (Australia, Canada, China, India, Japan, New Zealand, Singapore, Sweden, and US)	2003–2010	Innovation (patents and citations)	End-of-day manipulation; Liquidity	Financial misconduct of market manipulation (through end-of-day dislocation) is associated with reduced innovation due to the firms' short-term orientation and impaired employee incentives to innovate. There is a positive relationship between liquidity and innovation which, however, is offset by the presence of end-of-day dislocation.

Mergers and Acquisitions

Author(s)	Data Source(s)	Country	Time Period	Dependent Variables	Main Explanatory Variables	Main Findings
Humphery-Jenner (2012)	Securities class actions from Stanford SCAC.	US	1996–2007	CEO/CFO turnover; change in compensation; disciplinary takeover	Securities class action lawsuits	Following securities class action suits for financial misrepresentation, CEOs and CFOs are more likely to experience turnover or a decrease in compensation, and the firm is more likely to sustain a disciplinary takeover.
Amel-Zadeh and Zhang (2015)	Accounting restatements from GAO. M&A data from Securities Data Corporation (SDC)	US	2001–2008	Mergers and acquisitions (M&A); deal duration	Accounting restatements	Firms that have issued accounting restatements are substantially less likely to receive takeover bids and, when they do, the bids are more likely to be withdrawn and the M&A process take longer to complete.

The penalties incurred by firms accused of securities misconduct range from loss of market value, to restricted access to financing resulting in reduced investments and innovation, to threats to their survival through disciplinary takeovers.

At firm level, revelations or allegations of financial fraud can lead to negative stock market reactions (Karpoff and Lott 1993; Palmrose and Scholz 2004; Gande and Lewis 2009), increased costs of operations (Hribar and Jenkins 2004; Autore et al. 2014; Caskey 2014; Chu 2017), reduced liquidity and access to financing (Bai et al. 2010; Kravet and Shevlin 2010; Cumming et al. 2011; Arena 2018), hampered innovation (Autore et al. 2014; Arena and Julio 2015; Cumming et al. 2019), and greater risks of hostile takeovers (Humphery-Jenner 2012).

4.6.1 Direct Economic Costs Captured in Loss of Market Value

Allegations of fraud cause declines in market valuation for the accused firms (Feroz et al. 1991; Karpoff and Lott 1993; Palmrose et al. 2004; Palmrose and Scholz 2004; Bhagat and Romano 2007; Gande and Lewis 2009). Bhagat et al. (1998) observe a 3% stock price decline for sued firms during the two-day period surrounding securities lawsuit filings. Feroz (1991) documents a 13% loss of market value over the two-day period in response to SEC enforcement actions. SEC enforcement proceedings signal the serious nature of the claims and therefore trigger greater declines in the sued firm's share price.

This decline in valuation is attributable to several factors, including the direct costs of litigation, reduced productivity from disruptions of operating activities, and a residual loss attributable to damage to firm reputation (Karpoff and Lott 1993; Karpoff et al. 2008a).

The loss of market value reflects the market's anticipation of future outflows of wealth directly associated with the lawsuits. These include legal fines, damages, or settlements paid to the plaintiff(s) (Cutler and Summers 1987; Fields 1990; Hertzel and Smith 1993). In addition, a defendant firm incurs substantial legal expenses, which rise exponentially as a lawsuit proceeds towards trial (Coffee 1986; Romano 1991; Haslem 2005). Further, successful litigation may also encourage other potential plaintiffs to sue and open the floodgates for further lawsuits (Grace 2006).

Finally, defending fraud allegations can disrupt a firm's productivity. Preparations for legal defence consume time and divert manager and employee attention from their ordinary duties. Executive officers, directors, and employees may be needed in the discovery and deposition process. Legal counsel commonly brief witnesses before depositions and trials. These activities prevent managers and employees from conducting their normal operating activities, thus hindering the firm's productivity (Johnson et al. 2000; Black et al. 2006; Dai et al. 2014).

4.6.2 Loss of Firm Reputation

The decline in shareholder wealth that cannot be explained by observable legal or regulatory penalties is attributed to a loss of reputation. Only a small portion of the losses of market value is attributable to the direct costs associated with legal penalties (Karpoff and

Lott 1993; Karpoff et al. 2008a). Karpoff et al. (2008a) find that, in SEC enforcement actions, the loss of market value exceeds the amount of legal penalties (which averaged $23.5 million) by more than 7.5 times. This suggests that the loss of reputation can be substantial.

Karpoff (2011) defines reputation as 'the value of the quasi-rent stream that accrues when counterparties offer favourable terms of contract because they believe the firm will not act opportunistically towards them'. The reputational penalty imposed by the capital market captures 'the expected loss in the present value of future cash flows due to lower sales and higher contracting and financing costs' (Karpoff et al. 2008a, p. 581). The reputational penalty serves to increase a firm's future costs of operation (Karpoff et al. 2008a; Murphy et al. 2009). Empirical evidence shows that in the wake of financial misconduct and accounting restatements, firms experience poorer operating performance (Murphy et al. 2009; Johnson et al. 2014), restricted access to financing (Autore et al. 2014; Arena 2018), greater liquidity constraints (Bai et al. 2010), and increased risks as captured by higher cost of capital (Hribar and Jenkins 2004; Murphy et al. 2009; Kravet and Shevlin 2010; Yuan and Zhang 2015) and higher insurance premiums (Baker and Griffith 2007a; Caskey 2014). These increases in operating and financing costs do not arise from a conscious choice by other businesses to penalize the fraudulent firms. Instead, they arise because providers of finance and other business resources take measures to protect their own self-interest when dealing with the fraudulent firms, in light of heightened information uncertainty (Karpoff 2011). Such collective actions result in market-imposed penalties embodied in the loss of reputation (Lin et al. 2013). Fraud-committing firms can repair their reputational damage by engaging in reputation-building activities targeting their most salient stakeholder groups (Chakravarthy et al. 2014).

4.6.3   Spillover of Reputational Effect

The loss of reputation can also affect non-sued firms through perceived connections or commonality with the accused firms. For example, non-accused firms operating in the same industry as the accused firms also experience declines in valuation upon fraud revelations (Gande and Lewis 2009). This contagion effect extends to interlocked firms that share directors with the accused firms (Srinivasan 2005; Fich and Shivdasani 2007), industry peers (Gande and Lewis 2009; Arena and Julio 2015; Yuan and Zhang 2015), and country peers (Huang et al. 2017). Srinivasan (2005) finds that, following accounting restatements, non-restating firms which share directors with the restating firms experience an average loss of 0.24% market value during the two-day period. Similarly, Fich and Shivdasani (2007) find that interlocked firms experience an average one-day abnormal return of −3.25% upon securities class action lawsuit filings. Further, when foreign firms are accused of securities violations in the US, other non-sued US firms that are cross-listed in the same foreign countries also lose market value, particularly if these countries have poor institutional governance (Huang et al. 2017). Such spillover effects reflect the markets' reassessment of the information risk of the non-sued firms, in light of newly revealed information about their interlocked directors' monitoring capabilities, or the industry- and country-level risks.

4.6.4 Governance Risk and Insurance Premiums

One source of the increase in operating costs experienced by accused firms originates from insurance providers. Director and officer (D&O) liability insurance covers a substantial portion of settlement costs in securities litigation (Klausner et al. 2013). D&O insurance premiums reflect a firm's corporate governance risks (Boyer and Stern 2012). Following securities fraud allegations, insurance providers calibrate to the increased litigation risks associated with a firm's corporate governance failures and accordingly increase insurance premiums (Baker and Griffith 2007b; Boyer and Stern, 2012; Gillan and Panasian 2015). Baker and Griffith (2007b, 2014) argue that D&O insurance providers can impose deterrence on firms through the underwriting process, in particular through their risk assessment of firms in deciding whether to provide coverage and the pricing of premiums. However, the increased price of insurance alone is insufficient to provide effective deterrence, in the absence of disclosure of the insurance details to the market (Baker and Griffith 2007b, 2014).

4.6.5 Reduced Liquidity

Securities fraud and misconduct may also impact on firm liquidity (e.g. Bai et al. 2010; Cumming et al. 2011; Arena and Julio 2015). At the macro-level, Cumming et al. (2011) document that more detailed stock exchange trading rules prohibiting false disclosure are associated with greater liquidity in the market. At the firm-level, Bai et al. (2010) find the firms sued in securities class actions are more likely to experience reduced liquidity and liquidity constraints following lawsuit settlements. The authors attribute this to the out-of-pocket settlement costs paid in cash or liquid assets, which are not fully covered by litigation insurance. Consistent with this view that lawsuit settlements reduce liquidity, Arena and Julio (2015) find that firms facing higher risks of securities litigation pre-emptively increase their cash holdings in anticipation of future settlements. Additionally, this effect of litigation risk on liquidity spills over to other non-sued peers that operate in the same industries as the sued firms (Arena and Julio 2015).

4.6.6 Access to Financing

Firms accused of fraud tend to experience restricted access to capital (Autore et al. 2014; Chu 2017) and increased cost of capital (Hribar and Jenkins 2004; Kravet and Shevlin 2010; Yuan and Zhang 2015). Firms sued for securities violations are less likely to obtain both debt and equity financing during the post-lawsuit period (Autore et al. 2014), and more likely to experience IPO underpricing (Lowry and Shu 2002). Specifically, following accounting restatements, firms experience increased cost of equity, which reflects investors' higher risk assessment of the restating firms (Hribar and Jenkins 2004).

Firms that are accused or suspected of financial fraud also incur higher cost of debt (Graham et al. 2008; Arena 2018). Following accounting restatements, lending institutions not only increase loan spreads, but also impose stricter loan terms on the restating firms, such as shorter maturities, greater likelihood of secured loans, and more stringent restrictive covenants (Graham et al. 2008). Yuan and Zhang (2015) find evidence of increased loan spreads and stricter covenants following securities class action lawsuits, and that these consequences also extend to industry peers of the sued firms. Finally, lawsuits alleging securities violations may lead to substantial settlements, causing the credit ratings of the sued firms to deteriorate, thus rendering it more difficult for sued firms to obtain future financing (Arena 2018).

4.6.7   Reduced Innovation

Securities fraud allegations can also hinder the accused firms' innovative activities and investments. Following securities class action lawsuits, sued firms experience a decline in capital expenditure and research and development (R&D) expenses during the subsequent three-year period (Autore et al. 2014; Arena and Julio 2015). These changes are attributable to limited external financing (Autore et al. 2014) and the firms' need to increase cash reserves in anticipation of future lawsuits and settlements (Arena and Julio 2015). Beyond the US context, Cumming et al. (2019) investigate the impacts of suspected market manipulation on firm innovation by examining patents and patent citations in nine countries, specifically Australia, Canada, China, India, Japan, New Zealand, Singapore, Sweden, and US, and find that financial misconduct is associated with reduced innovation due to the firms' short-term orientation and impaired employee incentives to innovate.

4.6.8   Mergers and Acquisitions

Hostile takeovers constitute an additional mechanism of corporate governance when board governance fails to prevent fraud (Shivdasani 1993). In a market where managers constantly compete for corporate control, disciplinary takeovers serve as a mechanism to remove unfit management (Jensen and Meckling 1976; Jensen and Ruback 1983; Shivdasani 1993). Securities fraud revelations may expose managerial actions that are detrimental to investors, and trigger disciplinary takeovers to replace the existing management. Consistently, Humphery-Jenner (2012) finds evidence that firms sued for securities violations face increased likelihood of hostile takeovers in the year following the lawsuits.

By contrast, other empirical evidence suggests that firms with prior financial misstatements are *less* likely to successfully complete mergers (Amel-Zadeh and Zhang 2015). Amel-Zadeh and Zhang (2015) find that firms that have issued accounting restatements are substantially less likely to receive takeover bids and, when they do, the bids are more likely to be withdrawn and the M&A process take longer to complete. The authors attribute these observations to the increased information risk surrounding the restating firms (e.g. Kravet and Shevlin 2010), which makes them less attractive as potential targets.

Overall, at the firm level, penalties include losses of market valuation, which encompass anticipated direct litigation costs and a loss of reputation, which captures increased future costs of operations for the accused firms.

4.7   Individual-Level Penalties for Corporate Financial Misconduct

In this section, we discuss the second type of penalties for corporate financial fraud and misconduct, which are incurred personally by executive officers and directors of the accused firms. As discussed in the previous section, the direct legal costs in the form of fines or financial settlements are unlikely to lead to significant out-of-pocket expenses for the executive officers and directors, who are covered by D&O insurance (Klausner et al. 2013; Baker and Griffith 2014). At the other end of the scale, imprisonment and debarment constitute extreme forms of legal penalty which are relatively rare. Nevertheless, the executive and director labour markets can impose a variety of consequences on officers and directors following allegations of financial fraud. At the individual level, executive officers and directors experience increased turnover, impaired career prospects and reputation, decreased or restructured compensation, and more stringent future board monitoring. Such ex post settling-up is important to deter executive officers and directors from engaging in future fraud or misconduct or allowing fraud to be committed in their corporations (Fama 1980; Alexander 1999). In Table 4.2, we provide a summary of select papers examining individual-level penalties for fraud and misconduct.

4.7.1   Executive and Director Turnover

Forced turnover is a severe form of ex post settling-up for executive officers of public firms (Fama 1980). When facing corporate fraud allegations, the board of directors of the accused firm has significant incentives to replace the top managers in order to restore market confidence and stakeholder goodwill (Agrawal et al. 1999). Given that a key function of the board is to monitor the CEO (Fama and Jensen 1983), fraud may also indicate a failure in board governance, which motivates the shareholders to replace existing board members. Therefore, fraud revelations can result in increased executive *and* director turnover.

Early empirical evidence showed increased CEO turnover following securities lawsuits (Romano 1991) and SEC enforcement actions (Feroz et al. 1991). Since then a large body of empirical studies have examined the relationship between allegations of financial fraud and executive and director turnover (Agrawal et al. 1999; Beneish 1999; Niehaus and Roth 1999; Persons 2006; Karpoff et al.,2008b; Correia and Klausner 2012).

A majority of studies focus on chief executive officers (CEO) (e.g. Agrawal et al. 1999; Beneish 1999; Niehaus and Roth 1999; Persons 2006; Karpoff et al. 2008b; Correia and Klausner 2012; Aharony et al. 2015). Some researchers document increased CEO turnover associated with fraud and lawsuit revelations (Romano 1991; Persons 2006; Karpoff et al. 2008b), whereas others find no empirical evidence of increased executive turnover in the wake of fraud charges (Agrawal et al. 1999), securities class actions (Niehaus and Roth 1999; Correia and Klausner 2012) and SEC enforcement actions (Beneish 1999).

One key determinant of the market-based consequences is whether the executive officers are personally named in the lawsuits (Karpoff et al. 2008b). Karpoff et al. (2008b)

Table 4.2 Overview of studies on individual-level penalties.

This table summarizes the papers that examine individual-level penalties for financial fraud incurred by executive officers and directors. The authors, data sources, countries, time periods, variables, and main findings are summarized. The main findings are largely paraphrased and/or copied from the abstracts of the papers to best and succinctly represent the authors' contributions, but are not meant to exhaustively represent all of the findings from the papers.

Author(s)	Data Source(s)	Country	Time Period	Dependent Variables	Main Explanatory Variables	Main Findings
Executive Turnover						
Romano (1991)	Shareholder lawsuits in SEC filings.	US	1966–1987	Executive turnover, board turnover	Shareholder lawsuits	Sued firms experience top management turnovers significantly more frequently both before *and* during the litigation than the matched controls, with 55% of lawsuit firms experiencing a change in CEO or chair in the years surrounding litigation. Board turnover is significantly higher for lawsuit firms whose suits settled compared to their matches, but not for those whose suits were dismissed.
Feroz et al. (1991)	SEC enforcement actions from Accounting and Auditing Enforcement Releases (AAER).	US	Apr 1982–Apr 1989	Executive turnover	SEC enforcement actions	42 out of 58 sample firms (72%) experienced subsequent firing or resignation of high-level executives.
Agrawal et al. (1999)	'Fraud' and 'Crime' listings in the 'General News' and 'Corporate News' sections of the *Wall Street Journal Index*.	US	1981–1992	Executive (CEO and Top 3) turnover; board turnover	Fraud allegations	Little systematic evidence that firms suspected or charged with fraud have unusually high turnover among senior managers or directors.
Beneish (1999)	SEC enforcement actions from AAER; *LexisNexis* searches for executive turnover.	US	1987–1993	Executive turnover; SEC-imposed monetary penalties	SEC enforcement actions	Managers' employment losses subsequent to discovery of financial misstatements are similar in firms that do and do not overstate earning.

Niehaus and Roth (1999)	US	Securities class actions (*Securities Class Action Alert Newsletters*); LexisNexis searches for CEO reemployment.	Apr 1989–Dec 1994	CEO turnover; Subsequent reemployment	Securities class action lawsuits	Sued firms experience significantly higher CEO turnover than matched control firms. No departing defendant CEO gained a new and comparable position as CEO, president, or chair at another exchange-listed firm within three years after leaving the defendant firm.
Hennes et al. (2008)	US	Accounting restatements from the U.S. General Accounting / Government Accountability Office (GAO) Database, divided into 'errors' and 'irregularities' based on the wording of the restatement (8-K filings), and/or the existence of any SEC, DOJ, or other investigations.	2002–2005	CEO/CFO turnover; market reactions to restatements	Classification of accounting restatements as 'errors' (unintentional) or 'irregularities' (deliberate)	Restating firms experience significantly higher executive turnover in the 13 months surrounding the restatements (six months before to six months after) if the restatements are 'irregularities' (49% and 64% for CEO and CFO, respectively) rather than 'errors' (8% and 12%, respectively). During the four-year period surrounding irregularities restatements (two years before and two years after), 67% of CEOs and 85% of CFOs experience turnover.
Karpoff et al. (2008b)	US	Securities and Exchange Commission (SEC) and Department of Justice (DOJ) enforcement actions from *LexisNexis*, Academic Business News, General News, and Legal Cases libraries, and SEC and DOJ websites.	Jan 1, 1978–Sept 30, 2006	Executive turnover; financial penalties, criminal penalties	SEC/DOJ enforcement actions for financial misrepresentation.	93% of individuals who are named in SEC and DOJ enforcement actions lose their jobs by the end of the enforcement periods. Most are explicitly fired. The likelihood of ouster increases with the cost of the misconduct to shareholders and the quality of the firm's governance. 28% face criminal charges and penalties, including jail sentences that average 4.3 years.
Collins et al. (2008)	US	Restatements from GAO.	Jan 1, 1997–June 30, 2002	CFO, CEO, COO turnover; bonus compensation	Accounting restatements; Securities class action lawsuits	Increased CFO, CEO, and COO turnover and lower CFO bonus compensation associated with income-decreasing earnings restatements, but only when the restatements give rise to securities class action lawsuits.

(continued)

Table 4.2 (Continued)

Author(s)	Data Source(s)	Country	Time Period	Dependent Variables	Main Explanatory Variables	Main Findings
Aharony et al. (2015)	Environmental, intellectual property, antitrust, and contractual lawsuits from Public Access to Court Electronic Records (PACER).	US	2000–2007	CEO and director turnover; CEO compensation	Corporate lawsuits	Contractual lawsuits are followed by increased turnover of CEOs and inside directors, whereas following environmental and IP lawsuits, only outside directors tend to depart.
Chen et al. (2016)	Regulatory enforcement actions against corporate fraud and firm data from China Centre for Economic Research (CCER/Sinofin) or China Stock Market and Accounting Research (CSMAR).	China	1999–2008	CEO turnover	Corporate fraud; state-owned enterprises; split share structure reform	Following corporate fraud enforcement actions, the likelihood of CEO turnover is lower amongst state-owned enterprises (SOE) than among non-SOE listed firms. After the Split Share Structure Reform, there is an increase in CEO turnover likelihood following fraud enforcements against SOE listed firms, indicating strengthened incentives of SOE controlling shareholders to replace fraudulent management.
Agrawal and Cooper (2017)	Earnings-decreasing restatements from GAO.	US	1997–2002	CEO turnover; CFO turnover; Auditor turnover	Accounting restatements	CEOs, top management, and CFOs of restating firms experience higher turnover compared to the control sample, but there is no evidence of significantly higher auditor turnover. CEOs and CFOs face, on average, a 14% and 10% greater probability of being replaced in restating firms over the three-year period surrounding the year of restatement announcement. The risk of turnover is larger for restatements that are more serious, have worse effects on stock prices, result in negative restated earnings. are initiated by outside parties, are accompanied by Accounting and Auditing Enforcement Releases (AAERs), or trigger securities class action lawsuits.

Career Progression

Study	Data source	Country	Period	Topic	Event	Findings
Desai et al. (2006)	Restatements from GAO.	US	1997–1998	Executive turnover; CEO career progression	Accounting restatements	Restating firms experience higher executive turnover (60%) within 24 months following the restatement compared with matched controls (35%). Displaced CEOs are less likely to be reemployed by another public firm as (1) the CEO, president, chairman of the board, (2) a senior executive officer, or (3) an independent director.
Collins et al. (2009)	Restatements from GAO.	US	1997–2003	CFO turnover; CFO career progression	Accounting restatements; Sarbanes–Oxley Act (SOX)	Firm's restating earnings have higher rates of involuntary CFO turnover. Displaced CFOs face impaired likelihood of finding comparable reemployment. The passage of SOX does not change the rate of CFO turnover, but the labour-market penalties are more severe post-SOX.
Correia and Klausner (2012)	Stanford Securities Class Action Clearinghouse (SCAC) – 'Classic' category 'alleged material misstatement or omission'. Accounting restatements from GAO, Glass Lewis and Audit Analytics Databases.	US	2000–2011	Executive turnover; career progression	Securities class action lawsuits for financial misrepresentation	CEOs, CFOs and other officers experience an increased likelihood of turnover, and conditional on leaving the firm, have a lower probability of finding a comparable position in a public company.
Liu et al. (2016)	Environmental, intellectual property, antitrust, and contractual lawsuits from Public Access to Court Electronic Records (PACER).	US	2000–2007	CEO career progression; CEO reputation (outside directorships)	Corporate lawsuits	CEOs of sued firms experience poorer reemployment prospects following contractual lawsuits. There is no decrease in the number of outside directorships following politically sensitive lawsuits such as environmental violations.

(continued)

Table 4.2 (Continued)

Author(s)	Data Source(s)	Country	Time Period	Dependent Variables	Main Explanatory Variables	Main Findings
Condie et al. (2017)	SEC enforcement actions from AAER.	US	2005–2014	CFO turnover; CFO career progression	SEC enforcement actions	CFOs of accused firms experience higher turnover than non-implicated CFOs within two years of the end of the fraud. CFOs face impaired job prospects when seeking reemployment, which persist through three subsequent changes of employment.
Director Turnover and Reputation						
(Srinivasan, 2005)	SEC enforcement actions from AAER.	US	1997–2001	Independent director turnover; outside directorships; CAR of interlocked firms	SEC enforcement actions; interlocking directors	Director turnover is higher, particularly audit committee members, for restating firms during the three years after the restatement (46% following earnings-reducing restatements). Directors serving on audit committees lose an average of 25% of existing board seats in three years following accounting restatements. Interlocked firms which share directors with the restating firms experience significant negative market reactions upon restatement announcements.
Arthaud-Day et al. (2006)	Restatements from GAO.	US	Jan 1, 1997–June 30, 2002	Executive turnover; director (audit committee) turnover	Accounting restatements; CAR	CEOs and CFOs of restating firms experience higher turnover than matched controls (twice as likely to depart). Directors and audit committee members are approximately 70% more likely to exit in restatement firms.
Helland (2006)	Lawsuits from Securities Class Action Alert Newsletters and SEC enforcement actions from AAER.	US	1994–2002	Director reputation (proxied by number of outside directorships)	Securities class action lawsuits; SEC enforcement actions	Directors generally experience an increase in the number of directorships held in other firms following securities class actions. Directors lose outside board seats only following serious lawsuits, i.e. those in the top quartile of settlements or prosecuted by the SEC.

Study	Data source	Country	Period	Dependent variables	Independent variables	Findings
Fich and Shivdasani (2007)	Securities class actions from Stanford SCAC.	US	1998–2002	Independent director turnover; outside directorships; CAR of interlocked firms	Securities class action lawsuits	Independent directors do not face abnormal turnover on the board of the sued firm but experience a significant decline in outside board seats held in other firms (a loss of 50% of outside directorships during the three-year period following securities class actions). Interlocked firms that share directors with the sued firm also exhibit valuation declines at the lawsuit filing.
Marcel and Cowen (2014)	Restatements from Pro-Quest Newspapers database; Director capital from Corporate Library Board Analyst Database.	US	2001–2004	Director turnover following restatements	Director capital	Low-capital directors are more likely to leave restating firms than high-capital directors, indicating that the post-fraud director turnover is driven by 'cleaning house' rather than 'jumping ship' motives.
Brochet and Srinivasan (2014)	Securities class actions from Stanford SCAC.	US	1996–2010	Directors' likelihood of being named in securities class actions; re-election votes; turnover	Audit committee membership; selling stock during class period; securities class lawsuits	Independent directors are more likely to be named in securities class actions if they serve on the audit committee or sell stock during the class period. Named directors receive more negative recommendations, receive worse voting outcomes from shareholders, and are more likely to leave the sued firms.

Executive Compensation

Study	Data source	Country	Period	Dependent variables	Independent variables	Findings
Persons (2006)	Fraud/lawsuit revelation in the *Wall Street Journal* (*WSJ*) Index.	US	1992–2000	CEO turnover; CEO compensation	Fraud/lawsuit revelations in the *WSJ*	No evidence of increased CEO turnover following fraud/lawsuit revelations. CEOs receive an increase in cash compensation after fraud/lawsuit revelations.
Humphery-Jenner (2012)	Securities class actions from Stanford SCAC.	US	1996–2007	CEO/CFO turnover; change in compensation; disciplinary takeover	Securities class action lawsuits	Following securities class action lawsuits for financial misrepresentation, CEOs and CFOs are more likely to experience turnover or a decrease in compensation, and the firm is more likely to sustain a disciplinary takeover.

(continued)

Table 4.2 (Continued)

Author(s)	Data Source(s)	Country	Time Period	Dependent Variables	Main Explanatory Variables	Main Findings
Crutchley et al. (2015)	Securities class actions from Stanford SCAC.	US	1997–2009	CEO/director incentive compensation; board restructuring	Securities class action lawsuits	Following class action lawsuits naming directors, boards of the sued firms increase CEO incentive pay, but decrease director incentive compensation. Additionally, naming directors results in a greater change in board composition, including reduced board size and director busyness.

Strengthened Monitoring

Author(s)	Data Source(s)	Country	Time Period	Dependent Variables	Main Explanatory Variables	Main Findings
Farber (2005)	SEC Accounting and Auditing Enforcement Releases (AAER), filtered for financial statement misrepresentation.	US	1982–2002	Board composition and monitoring; institutional holdings; analyst following; stock price performance	SEC enforcement actions (financial misrepresentation); board composition and monitoring	Firms accused of financial statement fraud experience improvements in corporate governance. Three years after the fraud events, accused firms have similar board independence as non-accused firms, but exceed the non-accused firms in the number of audit committee meetings. These corporate governance improvements are associated with superior stock price performance, but not increased analyst following or institutional holdings.
Ferris et al. (2007)	Derivative lawsuits filings from *The Wall Street Journal* and Lexis-Nexis.	US	1982–1994	Board restructuring; director turnover	Shareholder derivative lawsuits	Derivative lawsuits are followed by significant increases in the proportion of independent directors and reduced incidence of CEO–Chair duality within the sued firms. Directors are more likely to depart during the three years following the lawsuits.
Cheng et al. (2010)	Lawsuits from Securities Class Action Services (SCAS) of Institutional Shareholder Services (ISS).	US	1996–2005	Securities class action outcomes; post-lawsuit board restructuring	Institutional investors (as lead plaintiffs)	Securities class action lawsuits led by institutional investors are more likely to lead to improvements in board monitoring, through the appointment of new outside directors to increase board independence. Securities class actions with institutional lead plaintiffs are more likely to survive the motion to dismiss than class actions with individual lead plaintiffs.

find that as high as 93% of individuals who are named in SEC and DOJ enforcement actions lose their jobs by the end of the enforcement periods. This figure is higher than the 60% corresponding figure documented by Desai et al. (2006) and the 38% turnover rate amongst CEOs observed by Persons (2006). The difference could be explained by the degree of culpability attributed to the individual officers by the executive labour market.

Another subset of turnover studies examines CFOs, documenting higher CFO turnover in the wake of financial misreporting (Collins et al. 2008; Collins et al. 2009; Correia and Klausner 2012; Agrawal and Cooper 2017; Condie et al. 2017). Collins et al. (2008) find increased CFO turnover associated with income-decreasing earnings restatements, but only when the restatements give rise to securities class action lawsuits. Involuntary CFO turnover has not increased in the wake of the Sarbanes–Oxley Act, which introduced more stringent corporate governance requirements (Collins et al. 2009).

The final strand of turnover research focuses on directors (e.g. Arthaud-Day et al. 2006; Fahlenbrach et al. 2014; Baum et al. 2016). When firms encounter fraud scandals, executive directors and independent directors are motivated by different incentives to exit or remain in the firms. Executive directors have similar career incentives to the CEO. Their rate of turnover is documented to be comparable to CEO turnover (Romano 1991). In contrast, independent directors may be driven by concerns for their own reputation to pre-emptively depart from the fraudulent firms (Fahlenbrach et al. 2014; Baum et al. 2016). Consistent with this narrative, Fahlenbrach et al. (2014) document increased independent director turnover preceding earnings restatements and class action lawsuits. Further, Baum et al. (2016) find that independent directors are more likely to exit prior to settled lawsuits compared with dismissed lawsuits. This indicates that independent directors have private information regarding the seriousness of impending fraud allegations, and choose to exit the firms before the more serious claims are brought to light. As an alternative view, Marcel and Cowen (2014) argue that post-litigation fraud turnovers are primarily driven by firms' motives to 'clear house' and repair organizational legitimacy, rather than individual directors' motives to 'jump ship' and protect their own reputations.

4.7.2 Impaired Career Progression

For turnover to effectively discipline executive officers, the managerial labour market must impose ex post settling up which prevents displaced executives from acquiring comparable reemployment post-turnover (Fama 1980; Desai et al. 2006). If executive officers are debarred from serving in public companies, they would be automatically prevented from obtaining re-employment in similar positions. However, such legal penalties are relatively rarely imposed. Nonetheless, even in the absence of debarment, empirical evidence shows that executive officers exiting from firms accused of fraud face impaired subsequent career opportunities (e.g. Desai et al. 2006; Correia and Klausner 2012; Liu et al. 2016; Condie et al. 2017). For example, Desai et al. (2006) examine the career paths of CEOs following financial misreporting that violates accounting rules. They track the displaced CEOs' subsequent employment in other public firms, and document that CEOs are less likely to be re-employed for all three tiers of positions examined, including as (i) the CEO, president, chair of the board; (ii) a senior executive officer; or (iii) an independent director. Similarly, Condie et al. (2017) focus on CFOs who exit their previous firms amidst fraud scandals. They find that CFOs face impaired career opportunities when seeking re-employment, and such impaired job prospects persist through three subsequent changes of employment. Furthermore, executive officers who have not been personally accused of fraud can still experience impaired career prospects after their firm experiences an event of fraud (Condie et al. 2017). This reflects the market penalizing the executive officers for their failure to discover and prevent the corporate fraud or misconduct.

4.7.3   Loss of Reputation

In the executive labour market, executive officers and directors trade on their reputational capital. Fama (1980) argues that the executive labour market prices executive officers' human capital based on their performance. Consequently, well-performing managers of large firms are more likely to receive additional board appointments, reflecting a high demand for their services and expertise. Independent directors are also priced by the labour market and assessed based on their demonstrated abilities (Fama 1980). Studies use the number of outside directorships as a proxy for the reputational capital of both executive officers (Lee 2011; Liu et al. 2016) and directors (Srinivasan 2005; Helland 2006; Fich and Shivdasani 2007).

Financial fraud can impair the reputations of both directors and executive officers. For independent directors, this reflects the market's reassessment of their monitoring capabilities in light of the fraud revelations. However, executive officers and independent directors have different reputational incentives (Fahlenbrach et al. 2014; Baum et al. 2016). Independent directors can be motivated to use their insider knowledge to avoid damage to their personal reputation by pre-emptively departing from firms ahead of imminent revelations of fraud or misconduct (Fahlenbrach et al. 2014). This represents a breakdown in their monitoring function, but there is limited evidence on whether this 'jumping ship' strategy is effective in deflecting the reputational harm associated with corporate misconduct.

In the wake of financial fraud allegations, shareholders can also force implicated directors to depart by voting against their re-election during annual general meetings (Brochet and Srinivasan 2014). Independent directors experience significant declines in reputation following fraud and accounting restatements, as evidenced by both increased turnover from the fraudulent firms, and a loss of outside directorships in other firms (Srinivasan 2005; Brochet and Srinivasan 2014). The likelihood of losing board seats is particularly high for directors who serve on audit committees (Srinivasan 2005) and for those personally named in the securities lawsuits (Brochet and Srinivasan 2014).

However, studies have not reached any consensus in quantifying this loss of reputation. For example, Srinivasan (2005) finds that directors serving on audit committees lose an average of 25% of existing board seats in three years following accounting restatements. Fich and Shivdasani (2007) observe a loss of 50% of outside directorships held by directors during the three-year period after securities class actions. In contrast, Helland (2006) documents a slight increase in the number of directorships held by sued firms' directors, which the author attributes to the outside-director labour market rewarding 'yes-man' behaviour. In addition, Helland (2006) finds that directors lose outside board seats only following serious lawsuits, as proxied by high settlements in the top sample quarter of filed lawsuits. This suggests that the director labour market can distinguish between meritorious and frivolous fraud allegations. Overall, directors incur reputational penalties in the wake of allegations of financial fraud or misconduct, as proxied by losing outside directorships. This loss of reputation occurs because other firms in the market have incentives to dissociate themselves from the fraud-tainted individuals, by removing them from their boards (Srinivasan 2005; Fich and Shivdasani 2007).

4.7.4   Executive Compensation

Legal penalties in the forms of fines and awards of damages are insufficient to punish executive officers and directors for committing or failing to detect fraud, because a substantial portion of the litigation and settlement costs is covered by D&O insurance (Baker and Griffith 2007b, 2007a; Klausner et al. 2013; Baker and Griffith 2014). Nevertheless, executive officers may still incur monetary penalties in the form of reduced compensation beyond the fines, damages, or settlements imposed by the legal system (Collins et al. 2008; Jones and Yan 2010; Humphery-Jenner 2012).

Empirical studies document significant decreases in executive compensation following securities fraud allegations (Collins et al. 2008; Jones and Yan 2010; Humphery-Jenner 2012). Evidence shows that CEOs, CFOs, and chief operating officers (COO) experience reductions in bonus compensation, which are driven by the performance-linked component (Collins et al. 2008; Humphery-Jenner 2012). Apart from reducing the level of compensation, firms also change compensation structure in the wake of fraud allegations (Dai et al. 2014; Crutchley et al. 2015). Crutchley et al. (2015) find that, following fraud lawsuits, boards increase CEO incentive pay to strengthen the alignment of manager–shareholder interests, but decrease *director* incentive compensation to enhance the independent monitoring by the board (Crutchley et al. 2015). In different country settings such as China where institutional enforcement is relatively weak, executive equity incentives are linked to higher fraud likelihood (Hass et al. 2016). To discourage fraud driven by incentive compensation, the *Dodd–Frank Act* in the US introduces 'clawback' provisions which require executive officers to repay any compensation obtained under misrepresentation of financial information.[5]

4.7.5   Strengthened Monitoring

Accused firms may undergo internal restructuring to strengthen board governance. Following allegations of fraud, firms change their board composition to rebuild legitimacy

---

[5] Previously this remedy was available at common law rather than as a statutory remedy (see Collins et al. 2008).

and restore lost reputational capital (Fich and Shivdasani 2007; Crutchley et al.,2015). These restructurings typically involve increasing the proportion of independent directors, reducing board size, and reducing director busyness (by reducing the number of outside board positions held by directors) (Farber 2005; Ferris et al. 2007; Cheng et al. 2010; Crutchley et al. 2015). Extant corporate governance literature shows more effective monitoring by smaller boards (Yermack 1996; Eisenberg et al. 1998; Coles et al. 2008), more independent boards (Hermalin and Weisbach 1998; Farrell and Whidbee 2000; Boone et al. 2007; Duchin et al. 2010), and less busy directors (Ferris et al. 2003). Consistently, firms that have experienced securities lawsuits tend to increase their proportion of independent directors (Farber 2005; Ferris et al. 2007; Cheng et al. 2010), increase the frequency of audit committee meetings (Farber 2005), reduce board size (Ferris et al. 2007), and hire less busy directors (Crutchley et al. 2015), in order to improve the monitoring effectiveness of their boards.

The likelihood of such restructurings of board composition depends on the severity of the legal actions (Crutchley et al. 2015) and the strength of institutional monitoring, which constitutes a complementary governance mechanism (Cheng et al. 2010). Improvements in board independence are more likely to occur when the directors are named as defendants in securities fraud lawsuits (Crutchley et al. 2015) and when large institutional investors serve as lead plaintiffs in securities lawsuits (Cheng et al. 2010).

Strengthened board monitoring represents a potential penalty for future executive officers, who face reduced scope to engage in opportunistic conduct to the detriment of shareholders. These improvements in corporate governance are found to increase firm value in the wake of corporate financial misconduct (Farber 2005; Crutchley et al. 2015).

4.8   Causes, Risks, and Moderators of Financial Misconduct

In this section, we discuss the incentives and risk factors that determine the likelihood of financial misconduct, and the role of institutional enforcement in detecting and prosecuting securities violations. Firms' internal corporate governance mechanisms and external regulatory environments both play important roles in preventing financial fraud and misconduct. We first discuss incentives that motivate executive officers to engage in financial reporting fraud or misconduct. We then provide an overview of firm- and executive-level risk factors which exacerbate or mitigate fraud likelihood. Finally, we discuss public and private enforcement of securities law, including the impact of regulatory and judicial stringency on the effectiveness of financial regulations, and the role of surveillance in detecting fraud and misconduct in the markets. Table 4.3 provides a summary of prior studies investigating the causes and risk factors predicting the likelihood of financial fraud or misconduct. Table 4.4 summarizes the key papers in the literature pertaining to the enforcement, surveillance, and detection of financial fraud.

4.8.1   Fraud Incentives

Managers are motivated by various incentives to misrepresent firms' financial information. These incentives fall into two broad categories: obtaining personal gains and fundraising motives. First, managers can derive personal gains from manipulating the firms'

Table 4.3 Overview of studies on the causes, risks, and deterrents of fraud and misconduct.

This table summarizes the papers that examine the causes, risks, and deterrents of financial fraud and misconduct. The authors, data sources, countries, time periods, variables, and main findings are summarized. The main findings are largely paraphrased and/or copied from the abstracts of the papers to best and succinctly represent the authors' contributions, but are not meant to exhaustively represent all of the findings from the papers.

Author(s)	Data Source(s)	Country	Time Period	Dependent Variables	Main Explanatory Variables	Main Findings
Incentives: Personal Gains						
Denis et al. (2006)	Securities class actions from *Securities Class Action Alert* Newsletters and Stanford Securities Class Action Clearinghouse (SCAC). Compensation data from ExecuComp.	US	1993–2003	Securities class action lawsuits	Executive stock option incentives	Firms with higher executive incentive compensation in the form of stock options experience greater likelihood of securities class action lawsuits. This relationship is stronger in firms with higher outside blockholding and higher institutional ownership.
Burns and Kedia (2006)	Restatements from U.S. General Accounting / Government Accountability Office (GAO) and *LexisNexis*.	US	1997–2002	Accounting restatements	Sensitivity of CEO compensation to stock price	Firms' propensity to issue accounting restatements is positively associated with the sensitivity of CEO's option portfolio to stock price (but not the price-sensitivity of other components of CEO compensation, i.e. equity, restricted stock, long-term incentive payouts, and salary plus bonus).
O'Connor et al. (2006)	Accounting restatements from Pro-Quest Newspapers Database.	US	2000–2004	Earnings-decreasing accounting restatements	CEO stock options; CEO duality; director stock options	Large CEO stock option grants are associated with lower likelihood of financial misreporting when the CEO is also the chair of the board, or when the CEO does not chair the board and the directors do not hold options. In other circumstances, large CEO stock option grants are associated with increased likelihood of financial misreporting.

(continued)

Table 4.3 (Continued)

Author(s)	Data Source(s)	Country	Time Period	Dependent Variables	Main Explanatory Variables	Main Findings
Johnson et al. (2009)	SEC Accounting and Auditing Enforcement Releases (AAER) and *LexisNexis*.	US	1992–2005	SEC enforcement actions	Unrestricted stockholdings; restricted stock-holdings; stock options	Likelihood of corporate fraud is positively related to incentives from unrestricted stockholdings and is unrelated to incentives from restricted stock and unvested and vested options.
Armstrong et al. (2010)	Accounting restatements from Glass-Lewis & Co.; Securities class action lawsuits from Woodruff-Sawyer and Co; and SEC actions from AAER.	US	2001–2005	Accounting restatements; class action lawsuits; SEC enforcement actions.	CEO equity incentives	No evidence of a positive relationship between CEO equity incentives and the incidence of accounting-related restatements, shareholder lawsuits alleging accounting manipulation, and SEC enforcement actions. To the contrary, high CEO equity incentives are associated with reduced likelihood of accounting irregularities.
Crutchley and Minnick (2012)	Director-aimed derivative lawsuits (federal and state) from the 'Corporate Officer and Director Liability Litigation Reporter'.	US	1996–2001	Shareholder derivative lawsuits targeting individual officers and directors	Director incentive compensation; cash compensation	High director incentive compensation is linked to increased incidence of shareholder lawsuits targeting individual officers and directors. Greater director cash compensation is associated with reduced likelihood of lawsuits.
Agrawal and Cooper (2015)	Restatements from GAO; 10-Q, 10-K, and 8-K SEC filings, ProQuest Newspapers and LexisNexis Databases.	US	1997–2002	Executive insider trading (sales, purchases, and net sales)	Earnings-decreasing restatements	Executive officers of restating firms tend to sell more stocks during the misstated period preceding income-decreasing accounting restatements than during the pre-misstated period.

Study	Data	Country	Period	Dependent variable	Independent variables	Findings
Hass et al. (2016)	Regulatory actions from CSRC Enforcement Actions Research Database (excluding buybacks, embezzlement, price manipulation, fraudulent listings, illegal guarantees, and illegal speculation). Firm data from China Stock Market and Accounting Research (CSMAR) Database.	China	2000–2010	Regulatory enforcement actions	Executive equity incentives; board equity incentives	Firms with higher executive equity incentives are more likely to face regulatory enforcement actions for fraud. This effect is more pronounced for state-owned firms. There is no evidence that equity incentives of supervisory board members increase firms' propensity to commit fraud.

Incentives: Capital Raising

Study	Data	Country	Period	Dependent variable	Independent variables	Findings
Dechow et al. (1996)	SEC enforcement actions from AAER.	US	1982–1992	SEC enforcement actions	Free cashflow; financing; insider trading; bonus compensation; debt covenants	Firms' desire to raise external financing at low cost and to avoid debt covenant restrictions constitute important motivations for earnings manipulation. No evidence suggests that managers are manipulating earnings to obtain a larger earnings-based bonus, or to gain from selling their stockholdings at inflated prices.
Dechow et al. (2011)	SEC enforcement actions from AAER.	US	1982–2005	SEC enforcement actions	Financing activities; off-balance-sheet activities; accrual quality; performance	Firms which are investigated for financial misreporting are more likely to be engaging in financing activities and related off-balance-sheet activities during the misstatement periods, indicating that raising financing is a motivation for financial misreporting. Sued firms also have lower accrual quality and deteriorating performance compared to control firms.

(continued)

Table 4.3 (Continued)

Author(s)	Data Source(s)	Country	Time Period	Dependent Variables	Main Explanatory Variables	Main Findings
Teoh et al. (1998b)	IPO data from Securities Data Co. (SDC). Accounting data from Compustat.	US	1980–1992	Post-IPO stock returns; seasoned equity offerings	Accounting accruals	IPO firms with higher discretionary accruals in the IPO year experience poor stock return performance in the subsequent three years, and are less likely to issue seasoned equity offerings, indicating that firms are motivated by IPO fund-raising incentives to manipulate accounting accruals.
Teoh et al. (1998a)	Seasoned equity offering data from SDC. Accounting data from Compustat.	US	1976–1989	Stock returns post-seasoned equity offers	Accounting accruals	Higher accounting accruals in firms issuing seasoned equity are associated with poorer post-issue long-run stock performance and net income, indicating that firms manipulate accounting information to achieve better fund-raising outcomes.
DuCharme et al. (2004)	Securities class actions from *Securities Class Action Alert* Newsletters and *LexisNexis*. Seasoned equity offering data from SDC.	US	1988–2001	Stock returns post-equity offers; lawsuits	Accounting accruals	Managers increase accounting accruals before equity stock offers, and such accruals subsequently reverse to negatively affect post-offer returns. Abnormal accruals are positively associated with the likelihood of firms being sued in securities class actions.
Wang et al. (2010)	SEC enforcement actions from AAER; securities class actions from SCAC (excluding dismissed cases and settlements < $2 mil). IPO data from SDC.	US	1995–2005 (IPO); 1996–2007 (law-suits)	Securities lawsuits	Investor optimism pre-IPO	Firms are more likely to commit fraud before IPOs that result in securities lawsuits when investors are optimistic about the firms' industry prospects. However, when facing extreme investor optimism, firms have reduced likelihood of committing fraud, as they are able to raise capital without engaging in financial misrepresentation.

Study	Country	Years	Dependent variable	Risk factor	Data sources	Findings
McTier and Wald (2011)	US	1996–2005	Securities class action lawsuits likelihood; post-lawsuit investment and payout policies	Pre-lawsuit overinvestment; securities class actions	Securities class actions from Stanford SCAC. Restatements from GAO.	Firms which overinvest are more likely to be sued in securities class actions. Following the lawsuits, sued firms tend to decrease investments and payouts, increase leverage and cash holdings, and reduce diversification.

Executive-Level Risk Factors

Study	Country	Years	Dependent variable	Risk factor	Data sources	Findings
Biggerstaff (2015)	US	1992–2009	Financial misrepresentation	CEO options backdating	Options data from Thomson Financial Network Insider Filing Data Feed. SEC/DOJ enforcement actions from Federal Securities Regulation (FSR) Database.	Firms led by CEOs who backdate their option grants and/or exercises are more likely to engage in financial misrepresentation.
Cline et al. (2018)	US	1978–2012 (misconduct); 1996–2012 (lawsuits)	Securities class action lawsuits; DOJ/SEC enforcement actions; market reactions; operating performance	Executive personal misconduct	Cases of personal misconduct from searching Factiva, LexisNexis, and ProQuest news retrieval services. Securities class action lawsuits from SCAC.	Executive officers' private misconduct, such as substance abuse, sexual scandals, or violence, is associated with an increased likelihood of unrelated securities class action lawsuits, DOJ and SEC enforcement actions, and earnings management. CEO indiscretions trigger significant negative market reactions averaging 4.1% of firm value, and are followed by losses of customers and poorer performance. CEOs and boards face increased turnover, pay cuts, and lower shareholder votes at re-election.
Yu and Yu (2011)	US	1998–2004	Fraud detection; period before detection	Lobbying expenditure	Lobbying expenditure from Political Money Line (PML) of Congressional Quarterly Inc Database. Securities class actions from Stanford SCAC, filtered by settlement size (>$2.5M) and firm size (total assets >$750M).	Firms which engage in lobbying have a significantly lower hazard rate of being detected for fraud, their frauds remain undetected for an average period of 117 days longer, and are 38% less likely to be detected by regulators.

(continued)

Table 4.3 (Continued)

Author(s)	Data Source(s)	Country	Time Period	Dependent Variables	Main Explanatory Variables	Main Findings
Correia (2014)	PAC contribution data from Federal Election Commission's (FEC) website (www.fec.gov) and Charles Stewart III and Jonathan Woon's Congressional Committee Assignments, 1993–2007, and Garrison Nelson's Committees in the U.S. Congress, 1947–1992, databases (http://web.mit.edu/17.251/www/data_page.html). SEC enforcement actions from Karpoff et al. (2008)'s Federal Securities Regulation (FSR) Database.	US	1979–2006	SEC enforcement actions; penalties imposed by SEC	PAC contributions and lobbying expenditures	Firms with political connections (established through lobbying and campaign contributions) are less likely, on average, to encounter SEC enforcement actions. If pursued in regulatory actions, politically connected firms tend to receive lower penalties imposed by the SEC. Firms' lobbying expenditure spend on the SEC directly or through lobbyists who have prior employment links to the SEC are most significantly associated with reduced enforcement costs.
Sun et al. (2016)	Director political connections manually coded by GTA Information Technology (provider of the China Stock Market and Accounting Research (CSMAR) Database). Firm data from China Listed Firm's Corporate Governance Research and Shareholder Research Databases.	China	2008–2011	Blockholder appropriation (tunnelling proxied by blockholders-intercorporate loans recorded as 'other receivables')	Ratio of politically connected directors (independent directors)	In Chinese firms with politically connected boards, blockholders are more likely to engage in expropriation of minority shareholder interests through tunnelling in the form of intercorporate loans.
Wang et al. (2017)	Enforcement actions by the China Securities Regulatory Commission (CSRC) and/ or Shanghai and Shenzhen Stock Exchanges; China Securities Markets and Accounting Research (CSMAR).	China	2007–2012	Regulatory enforcement actions for financial fraud; penalties.	Manager ability; political connectedness	High managerial ability (efficiency to generate revenue) is associated with lower likelihood of the firm experiencing regulatory enforcement actions for financial misreporting. However, this relationship is weaker in politically connected firms. Firms led by more capable managers also receive less severe regulatory penalties in the

Study	Data	Country	Period	Dependent variables	Independent variables	Findings
Stuart and Wang (2016)	Chinese technology firms data from Ministry of Science and Technology (MOST) and State Administration of Industry and Commerce (SAIC). Firm political connections hand-collected from founder resumes. Grant data from Innofund website.	China	2005–2010	Financial misreporting (discrepancy between profits reported to MOST vs. SAIC); Innovation Fund Grant	Firm founder political connections; venture capital investment	Chinese technology firms with politically connected founders and those backed by venture capital are more likely to engage in financial misreporting. However, these firms are rewarded by experiencing increased likelihood of receiving government-sponsored innovation grants.
Khanna et al. (2015)	SEC/DOJ enforcement actions from Karpoff et al.'s (2008b) Federal Securities Regulation (FSR) Database, supplemented by SEC's Litigation Releases and Stanford SCAC; filtered by naming CEO as a respondent.	US	1996–2006	SEC/DOJ enforcement actions; CEO turnover	CEO appointment-based connections (fraction of top 4 executives and directors appointed by the CEO)	CEO connectedness within the firm, established through their appointments of other top executives and directors of the firm, is associated with increased likelihood of committing fraud and decreased likelihood of fraud detection. Following fraud discovery, well-connected CEOs are less likely to experience turnover. Connections based on network ties through past employment, education, or social organization memberships are not significantly associated with fraud likelihood.
Kuang and Lee (2017)	Directors social connections data from BoardEx. Securities lawsuits from SEC's AAER and Stanford SCAC.	US	1999–2013	Securities lawsuits; fraud detection; period before detection; number of individuals charged for fraud	Independent directors' social connectedness	Well-connected independent directors are not associated with increased likelihood of committing fraud, but are associated with significantly reduced likelihood of fraud detection, longer period before fraud detection, and fewer individuals charged for the fraud. Independent directors connected to fraudulent firms are associated with higher likelihood of committing fraud and fraud detection.

(continued)

Table 4.3 (Continued)

Author(s)	Data Source(s)	Country	Time Period	Dependent Variables	Main Explanatory Variables	Main Findings
Banerjee et al. (2018)	Securities class actions from Stanford SCAC.	US	1996–2012	Securities class action; subsequent CEO appointments	Executive overconfidence (holding deep in-the-money (>67%) options)	Overconfident CEOs and senior executives are more likely to misrepresent their firms' financial information giving rise to securities class actions. However, this relationship is weaker following the passage of the Sarbanes-Oxley Act which improved corporate governance. Following a class action, firms with overconfident CEOs reduce their litigation risk. Sued firms are also less likely to hire overconfident CEOs.
Schrand and Zechman (2012)	SEC enforcement actions from AAER.	US	1996–2003	SEC enforcement actions	CEO overconfidence (holding deep in-the-money (>67%) options)	Overconfident executives are more likely to misrepresent their firms' financial information due to an optimistic bias, which may lead to intentional misstatements in subsequent periods.

Firm-Level Risk Factors

Author(s)	Data Source(s)	Country	Time Period	Dependent Variables	Main Explanatory Variables	Main Findings
Beasley (1996)	SEC enforcement actions from AAER, supplemented WSJ Index 'Crime – White Collar Crime' listings.	US	1980–1991	SEC enforcement actions + fraud reported in WSJ	Board independence	Increased proportion of independent directors is associated with reduced likelihood for the firm to be accused of fraud. The presence of an auditing committee is not significantly associated with fraud likelihood.
Uzun et al. (2004)	WSJ Index 'Fraud' and 'Crime – White Collar Crime' listings.	US	1987–2001	Fraud reported in WSJ	Board independence; audit and compensation committee independence	Increased proportion of independent directors is associated with reduced likelihood of corporate fraud. The presence of outside directors who were not independent because they had business or personal ties to the company significantly increased the likelihood of fraud. The presence of a compensation committee is associated with increased fraud likelihood.

Study	Data source	Country	Period	Outcome	Variables	Findings
Agrawal and Chadha (2005)	News search using 'restat' or 'revis'. In LexisNexis, Newspaper Source, and Proquest Newspapers.	US	2000–2001	Accounting restatements	Director financial expertise; founding CEO; board and audit committee independence; non-audit services	The presence of independent directors with financial expertise is associated with a lower likelihood for the firm to issue accounting restatements. The likelihood to issue restatements is higher if the CEO belongs to the founding family, and is not significantly related to board independence, audit committee independence, or auditors providing non-audit services.
Zhao and Chen (2008)	SEC enforcement actions from AAER relating to 'fraudulent,' 'defraud,' and 'antifraud'; accrual data from Compustat.	US	1995–2001	Accounting accruals; SEC enforcement actions	Staggered board	Staggered boards are associated with lower likelihood of being accused of fraud in SEC enforcement actions and smaller magnitudes of abnormal accruals. Staggered boards are also associated with lower firm value. Consistent with the quiet-life perspective, managers insulated by staggered boards may be less motivated to increase firm value or manipulate earnings.
Perino (2012)	Class actions from Securities Class Action Services (SCAS) of Institutional Shareholder Services (ISS), Stanford SCAC and PACER.	US	1984–2005	Securities class action outcomes	Institutional investors (as lead plaintiffs)	Securities class actions with institutional investors as lead plaintiffs result in greater settlement amounts, and lower attorney fee requests and fees awarded. This indicates that institutional plaintiffs have greater ability to monitor class action attorneys.
Chapple et al. (2014)	Lawsuits from Factiva, NERA Report, law firm websites, Australian Securities and Investment Commission (ASIC), Signal G disclosure to Australian Stock Exchange (ASX), legal databases for reported cases (Austlii), Firm data from Morningstar, Connect4, and Worldscope.	Australia	1999–2010	Securities class action lawsuits	Compliance culture (ASX queries); corporate governance	Firms which receive more frequent queries from the Australian Stock Exchange (ASX) are more likely to experience securities class action lawsuits. The presence of a nomination committee and insider stock ownership are associated with increased lawsuit likelihood.

(continued)

Table 4.3 (Continued)

Author(s)	Data Source(s)	Country	Time Period	Dependent Variables	Main Explanatory Variables	Main Findings
Cumming et al. (2015c)	Detected fraud data from China Securities Regulatory Commission (CSRC); board data from China Securities Market and Accounting Research (CSMAR).	China	2001–2010	Securities violations (inc. regulatory enforcement actions); market reactions	Female board representation	Firms with high board gender diversity are less likely to commit financial fraud. The presence of female directors is associated with both reduced frequency and severity of fraud. The effect of women is more pronounced in male-dominated industries. Market reactions to fraud revelations are less pronounced when the firms have high board gender diversity.
Capezio and Mavi-sakalyan (2016)	Fraud data from KPMG fraud surveys in 2004, 2006, and 2008, supplemented by Australian Securities and Investment Commission (ASIC) annual reports.	Australia	2002–2007	Fraud	Female board representation	Higher board gender diversity is associated with decreased likelihood of fraud.
Pukthuan-thong et al. (2017)	Securities class actions from Stanford SCAC, Securities Class Action Alert (ISS), and PACER.	US	1996–2008	Securities class action lawsuit likelihood	Institutional investor horizon	Institutional investors with short-term horizons pursue litigation as an ex post monitoring mechanism, resulting in higher likelihood of securities class actions. In contrast, institutional investors with long-term horizons tend to engage in ex ante monitoring through board oversight and compensation structure, thus resulting in fewer securities class action lawsuits.

Table 4.4 Overview of studies on the enforcement, surveillance, and detection of financial fraud.

This table summarizes the papers that examine the enforcement, surveillance, and detection of financial fraud and misconduct. The authors, data sources, countries, time periods, variables, and main findings are summarized. The main findings are largely paraphrased and/or copied from the abstracts of the papers to best and succinctly represent the authors' contributions, but are not meant to exhaustively represent all of the findings from the papers.

Author(s)	Data Source(s)	Country	Time Period	Dependent Variables	Main Explanatory Variables	Main Findings
Cumming and Johan (2008)	Survey data from questionnaires sent to 75 jurisdictions worldwide with responses from 25 jurisdictions.	25 jurisdictions (in North, Central and South America, Western and Eastern Europe, Africa, and Asia)	2002–2005	Trading velocity, the number of listed firms, market capitalization	Single- and cross-market surveillance	Surveillance is positively associated with trading velocity, and cross-market surveillance is associated with the number of listed firms and market capitalization. The scope of cross-market surveillance shows a stronger positive association with trading velocity, the number of listed companies, and market capitalization than single-market surveillance. Compared with securities commissions, exchanges engage in a greater range of single-market surveillance, but both engage in cross-market surveillance activity of similar scope. Cross-market surveillance is more effective with information-sharing arrangements, and securities commissions are more likely to engage in information sharing than exchanges are.

(continued)

Table 4.4 (Continued)

Author(s)	Data Source(s)	Country	Time Period	Dependent Variables	Main Explanatory Variables	Main Findings
Dyck et al. (2010)	Class actions from Stanford SCAC, filtered by settlement size (>$3M) and firm size (total assets >$750M) and Factiva articles.	US	1996–2004	Identity of fraud detectors (e.g. investors, SEC, auditors, media, employees)	Securities class actions; SOX	Interral and external actors play important roles in fraud detection. Employee whistleblowing accounts for approximately 17% of fraud detection, other major detectors include analysts (14%), regulators (13%), short-sellers (15%), media (13%), auditors (10%), and SEC (7%). The passage of SOX (increased whistleblower protection) did not increase the employees' incentives to reveal fraud.
Cumming et al. (2011)	Trading rules from the webpage of each stock exchange (or regulatory body). Trading data from World Federation of Exchanges and Thomson Reuters Datastream.	42 stock exchanges worldwide	Feb 2006–Oct 2008	Market liquidity (velocity, volatility, and bid-ask spread)	Exchange trading rules indices (insider trading; market manipulation; broker-agency conflict)	Regulatory strength of stock exchange trading rules (as proxied by indices that capture the level of detail and explicitness of the rules prohibiting insider trading and market manipulation) are significantly associated with increased market liquidity on the stock exchange. There are close connections between the Volume Manipulation Rules Index and trading velocity, the Price Manipulation Rules Index and volatility, and the Insider Trading Rules Index and bid-ask spreads.
Humphery-Jenner (2013)	Intraday trade data from SIRCA/Reuters. Firm data from Compustat Global.	China (treatment: Shanghai and Shenzhen Stock Exchanges); Hong Kong, Korea, and Taiwan Stock Exchanges (control)	Nov 2002–Dec 2003	Probability of informed trading; absolute order imbalance; adverse selection component of bid-ask spread	Principled reforms to China's market manipulation law in 2003 by the Supreme People's Court (SPC) guideline judgment	Difference-in-difference results show that informed trading increases following the Court judgment, indicating that adopting stringent securities regulations without altering the regulatory environment may worsen the market's information environment.

Study	Data	Sample	Period			Findings
Cumming and Johan (2013)	Enforcement actions recorded by CSA (Canada), FSA (UK), and SEC (U.S.).	Canada, UK, US, (comparison sample: Brazil, China, Germany)	2005–2011	Fraud lawsuits characteristics	Junior vs. senior stock exchanges; different countries	Litigated fraud cases vary significantly by nature across different countries, and across different stock exchanges within the country. Outside the US there is relatively weak enforcement in other jurisdictions.
Aitken et al. (2014)	Market data from Capital Market Cooperative Research Centre (CMCRC).	24 stock exchanges in 19 countries	2003–2011	Average trade size; colocation services	High-frequency trading (HFT); colocation services	High-frequency trading (HFT) predates colocation by at least eight months on most exchanges, and has strong power in explaining the introduction of colocation services, indicating that colocation services are the result of HFT.
Aitken et al. (2015a)	Surveillance data from Cumming and Johan (2008). Exchange trading rules data from Cumming et al. (2011).	22 stock exchanges worldwide	2003–2011	Insider trading; number of cases, severity (profit) per case	Trading rules indices (insider trading; market manipulation; broker-agency conflict; surveillance index	Domestic and cross-market surveillance, and more detailed exchange trading rules, significantly reduce the number of suspected insider trading cases over time and across markets, but increase the profits per suspected case.
Cumming et al. (2015b)	Trading data from Compustat Global and CRSP. World Bank governance indicators, ICRG's composite risk ratings, S&P sovereign risk ratings, and Spamann's (2010) revised ADRI. Exchange trading rules data from Cumming et al. (2011).	26 countries	1999–2008	Location of trade for non-US firms cross-listed in the US.	Exchange trading rules indices; country-level sovereign governance; EU's implementation of Markets in Financial Instruments Directive (MiFID)	Stronger exchange trading rules outside the US increase the proportion of trading on non-US exchanges for stocks cross-listed in the US. Specifically, the EU's adoption of the Markets in Financial Instruments Directive, which strengthened trading rules, has increased the relative amount of trade in the EU for stocks cross-listed in the US.

(continued)

Table 4.4 (Continued)

Author(s)	Data Source(s)	Country	Time Period	Dependent Variables	Main Explanatory Variables	Main Findings
Christensen et al. (2016)	Entry-into-force dates of Market Abuse Directive and Transparency Directive from publications by the European Commission and by Linklaters LLP, an international law firm.	European Union (EU) countries	2001Q1–2011Q2	Market liquidity	New EU securities regulations; country-level regulatory quality; Directive-level enforcement strength	EU's adoption of new regulations, including the Market Abuse Directive and Transparency Directive, is associated with significant increases in market liquidity. The effects are stronger in countries with stricter implementation and more stringent securities regulations.
Neupane et al. (2017)	IPO and firm data from Bombay Stock Exchange (BSE) and the National Stock Exchange (NSE) websites.	India	2006–2011	Post-listing trading volume; number of bulk trades; post-listing returns	Suspected IPO manipulation: bulk trades on the first day of trading by syndicate traders involved in 7 prosecuted IPOs	IPCs which are suspected to be manipulated exhibit abnormally high volumes of large trades, a significant fraction of which originates from a syndicate of traders present in the prosecuted IPOs. Stock price in the manipulated IPOs rises initially before declining significantly, consistent with the pump-and-dump scheme.
Cumming et al. (2018b)	Enforcement data from the European Securities Market Authority (ESMA) report on the use of sanctioning powers under the Market Abuse Directive.	28 European Union countries	2008–2010	Number of detected offenses (or transmitted cases)	Number of supervisors; formalized cooperation; minimum imprisonment	Following the harmonization of market abuse regulations across the EU countries, country-level enforcement plays a significant role in predicting fraud. A greater number of supervisors in the regulatory institution is associated with a higher number of detected fraud cases, indicating that having more supervisors improves detection efforts. Formalized cooperation between the competent authorities and the judiciary is associated with fewer fraud cases through improving surveillance. Minimum duration of imprisonment for fraud offenses, which facilitates deterrence, is associated with a lower number of fraud cases.

financial information, including obtaining performance-linked compensation and profiting from insider trading (Agrawal and Cooper 2015). From an agency perspective, accounting information serves an important role to 'monitor and constrain the decision behaviour of agents and specify the performance criteria that determine rewards' (Fama and Jensen 1983, p. 310). However, given the information asymmetry underlying the manager-shareholder relationship, managers have incentives to manipulate accounting information to maximize performance-based compensation (Goldman and Slezak 2006; Crocker and Slemrod 2007; Peng and Roell 2014). Empirical evidence shows that executive incentive compensation (such as stock options) increases the likelihood of securities fraud (Burns and Kedia 2006; Denis et al. 2006; O'Connor et al. 2006; Hass et al. 2016). Furthermore, director incentive pay is also linked to increased fraud, as directors receiving incentive compensation experience greater interest alignment with managers, and therefore provide less effective independent monitoring (Crutchley and Minnick 2012). However, there is mixed empirical evidence on how different types of incentive pay affect fraud propensity. For example, Johnson et al. (2009) find that managerial incentives to commit fraud are driven by unrestricted stockholdings rather than restricted stocks or options. Armstrong et al. (2010) find no evidence of increased securities fraud associated with CEO equity compensation; to the contrary, they document fewer accounting irregularities associated with CEO equity incentives. Apart from incentive compensation, securities fraud is also precipitated by insider trading. Executive officers tend to sell more stocks preceding income-decreasing accounting restatements (Agrawal and Cooper 2015), consistent with the view that managers benefit from overinflated stock prices resulting from misstated financial information.

The second category of incentives for financial misconduct relate to fundraising activities. Managers have incentives to manipulate accounting information to obtain better capital raising outcomes through initial public offerings (IPO) (e.g. Teoh et al. 1998b; Wang et al. 2010) and stock offerings (e.g. Teoh et al. 1998a), as well as to avoid defaults on debt covenants (DeFond and Jiambalvo 1994; Dechow et al. 1996). For example, Dechow et al. (1996) find that fraud-committing firms tend to have higher leverage. DuCharme et al. (2004) observe that managers manipulate accounting accruals to boost earnings before equity stock offers, and such accruals subsequently reverse to negatively affect post-offer returns. Wang et al. (2010) find that firms have greater incentives to commit fraud before IPOs when investors are optimistic about the firms' industry prospects.

The existing literature shows that both corporate fund-raising incentives and private gains can motivate managers to misrepresent firms' financial information. Further, managers may engage in insider trading in conjunction with financial misreporting to derive personal gains. In the next section, we discuss executive- and firm-level idiosyncrasies, including corporate governance characteristics, which can affect the likelihood of financial fraud and misconduct.

4.8.2 Risk Factors

Personal characteristics of CEOs, such as overconfidence and social or political connectedness, play a significant role in determining a firm's likelihood of engaging in financial wrongdoing. At the firm level, corporate governance quality serves as an important safeguard to mitigate the risk of fraud and misconduct. In this section, we discuss the empirical evidence on these risk factors.

Idiosyncrasies of individual managers significantly predict the risk of securities fraud litigation against their firms. Overconfident managers are more likely to misrepresent their firms' financial information (Laux and Stocken 2012; Schrand and Zechman 2012; Banerjee et al. 2018). Additionally, firms are more likely to be sued for securities violations when their CEOs have poor personal ethics, as evidenced by option-backdating scandals (Biggerstaff et al. 2015) or other private misconduct such as substance abuse, sexual scandals, or violence (Cline et al. 2018). Further, well connected CEOs are more likely to commit fraud (Khanna et al. 2015). Political connectedness increases fraud likelihood, particularly in countries like China with weak institutional enforcement (Stuart and Wang 2016; Sun et al.,2016; Wang et al. 2017). However, social and political connectedness of CEOs and directors also reduces the risk of fraud detection and enforcement (Yu and Yu 2011; Correia 2014; Khanna et al. 2015; Kuang and Lee 2017). Finally, managers' cultural values can play a role in predicting firms' fraud likelihood. Liu (2016) examines corruption attitudes held by executive officers, based on the cultural values associated with their countries of ancestry. Liu (2016) finds that firms with high corruption culture are more likely to commit accounting fraud.

At the firm level, the nature of their operating activities and environments are relevant in determining fraud litigation risk. In particular, industry membership is an important predictor of the likelihood of securities class action lawsuits, along with firm size, growth, and stock volatility (Kim and Skinner 2012). Firms which engage in overinvestment are more likely to be accused of securities fraud (McTier and Wald 2011). This is consistent with the aforementioned evidence that firms in need of financing are motivated to manipulate earnings (DeFond and Jiambalvo 1994; DuCharme et al. 2004). By contrast, Lennox et al. (2013) find that tax aggressive firms are less likely to be accused of accounting fraud, however, the authors concede that this finding is sensitive to the choice of empirical proxies for tax aggressiveness.

Firm-level corporate governance quality can mitigate the risk of financial fraud and misconduct (e.g. Agrawal and Chadha 2005; Chapple et al. 2014). Board monitoring constitutes an important internal governance mechanism (Fama and Jensen 1983). Reduced risk of securities litigation is linked to greater independence of boards and audit committees (Beasley 1996; Uzun et al. 2004), the presence of directors with financial expertise (Agrawal and Chadha 2005), and board gender diversity (Cumming et al. 2015c; Capezio and Mavisakalyan 2016). Staggered boards are also associated with lower likelihood of financial fraud and misconduct (Zhao and Chen 2008). The authors argue that staggered boards reduce the performance pressure on managers, which lessens their incentives to manipulate earnings (Zhao and Chen 2008). By contrast, securities litigation risk is higher for firms in which the CEOs belong to the founding families (Agrawal and Chadha 2005).

Institutional holdings provide a complementary governance mechanism to board monitoring, which also ameliorates the risk of financial fraud and misconduct. The presence of institutional investors not only reduces the likelihood of fraud accusations, but also enhances the disciplining effect of securities lawsuits (Barabanov et al. 2008; Cheng et al. 2010; Perino 2012; Pukthuanthong et al. 2017). In particular, securities class actions with institutional investors as lead plaintiffs are more likely to succeed (Cheng et al. 2010; Perino 2012). This higher success rate is in part attributable to institutional plaintiffs' greater ability to monitor class action attorneys (Perino 2012). Furthermore, securities lawsuits led by institutional investors are more likely to lead to improvements in board monitoring, by appointing new outside directors to increase board independence (Cheng et al. 2010). Pukthuanthong et al. (2017) provide further insights into how institutional holding affects fraud litigation likelihood. Specifically, institutional investors with short-term horizons pursue litigation as an ex post monitoring mechanism, whereas institutional investors with long-term horizons tend to engage in ex ante monitoring through board oversight and compensation restructuring, thus resulting in fewer shareholder lawsuits. Overall, monitoring by institutional investors serves as a complementary governance mechanism that reduces the likelihood of financial misconduct and strengthens disciplining of managers, whether through ex post litigation or through ex ante fraud prevention.

4.8.3 Public Enforcement: Regulatory and Judicial Stringency

External institutional environments play an important role in deterring and preventing financial market fraud and misconduct. Strong institutional enforcement is essential to ensure the effectiveness of securities laws and regulations (Jenner-Humphery 2013; Cumming et al. 2015a; Cumming et al. 2018b). For example, Humphery-Jenner (2013) finds that adopting stringent securities regulations in a weak enforcement environment may even worsen market conditions. Moreover, Dyck et al. (2010) provide a holistic view of the roles of various actors (e.g. employees, auditors, regulators, and the media) in fraud detection, which suggests that the regulatory environment extends beyond laws and legal institutions, but rather 'takes a village'. In this section, we discuss both public and private enforcement mechanisms, and their impacts on the causes and consequences of financial misconduct.

Regulatory enforcement stringency varies widely across countries (Cumming et al. 2011; Cumming and Johan 2013; Christensen et al. 2016; Cumming et al. 2017; Cumming et al. 2018b), as a result of their different institutional environments (La Porta et al. 2006; Djankov et al. 2008; La Porta et al. 2008) and levels of resources devoted to securities law enforcement (Jackson and Roe 2009). The strength of enforcement has direct impacts on the risks and consequences of corporate financial fraud and misconduct (Tanimura and Okamoto 2013; Chapple et al. 2014; Stuart and Wang 2016).

In countries with strong legal enforcement such as the UK and Japan (La Porta et al. 1998; La Porta et al. 2008), firms that have committed fraud experience significant market-based penalties (Tanimura and Okamoto 2013; Armour et al. 2017). In contrast, in emerging economies such as China with unique institutional characteristics, state ownership plays a role in determining the executive-level penalties for corporate misconduct (Chen et al. 2016). The CEOs of state-owned enterprises are less likely to turnover following fraud revelations. However, following the Split Share Structure Reform, which converted non-tradable shares to tradable, controlling shareholders of state-owned enterprises experience stronger incentives to initiate CEO turnover following fraud revelations (Chen et al. 2016). Culture also plays an important role. For example, in Japan where honour and trust are highly valued and businesses operate in a reputation-based environment, firms accused of fraud experience greater reputational penalties and thus losses of firm value compared with their US counterparts (Tanimura and Okamoto 2013).

The strength of regulatory enforcement also moderates the role of political connectedness in predicting the likelihood and consequences of fraud. In countries such as China where legal enforcement is relatively weak (Allen et al. 2005; La Porta et al. 2008), firms with politically connected founders or managers are more likely to commit financial fraud (Stuart and Wang 2016; Sun et al. 2016; Wang et al. 2017). Further, some evidence suggests that firms are rewarded for committing financial misreporting, which improves their chances of receiving government-sponsored innovation grants (Stuart and Wang 2016). Even in the US where institutional enforcement is strong, political and social connections of CEOs and directors can significantly reduce the likelihood of fraud detection and the risk of regulatory enforcement actions (e.g. Yu and Yu 2011; Correia 2014; Kuang and Lee 2017).

In addition to country-level variations, the regulatory environment can also differ across different stock exchanges (Cumming and Johan 2013; Cumming et al. 2015b), court districts (Cheng et al. 2017), and geographical locations (Kedia and Rajgopal 2011). For example, Aitken et al. (2015a) examine 22 stock exchanges worldwide and find that more detailed trading rules significantly reduce the incidence of insider trading but increase the illegal profits obtained per trade. Even within the US, some Federal District Courts exhibit greater judicial stringency than others in interpreting securities fraud law (Cheng et al. 2017). Additionally, firms' proximity to the SEC headquarters and the locations of its past enforcement activities also significantly determine their likelihood of being targeted in enforcement actions (Kedia and Rajgopal 2011). However, empirical research produces inconsistent evidence on how the perceived risk of enforcement affects firm behaviour. Kedia and Rajgopal (2011) find that firms located closer to the SEC are less likely to restate earnings. In contrast, Cheng et al. (2017) find that firms headquartered in districts with greater court enforcement stringency are more likely to issue accounting restatements, in the attempt to promptly correct any misstatements to avoid litigation.

4.8.4   Public Enforcement: Detection and Surveillance

Financial market fraud and misconduct are not readily observable. Wang (2013) points out that empirical researchers use detected fraud to proxy all fraud committed, which is not accurate because many incidents of fraud remain undetected.

Fraud detection is an important issue in securities law enforcement. Across the common types of financial fraud and misconduct, misreporting of financial information is typically revealed through subsequent accounting restatements, which correct market misinformation and trigger legal actions. Karpoff and Lou (2010) document that, prior to fraud discovery, short-sellers in the markets anticipate the occurrence and severity of financial misconduct and serve to curb the overinflated stock price. In contrast, insider trading and market manipulation are difficult to detect and require regulatory surveillance (Neupane et al. 2017; Cumming et al. 2018b).

Computer surveillance forms a necessary component of the public enforcement of securities laws (Austin 2017; Cumming and Johan 2019). Technological developments have had significant impacts on trading activities and created greater potential for market manipulation (Aitken et al. 2014; Li et al. 2015). As a part of the enforcement process, stock exchanges and securities commissions commonly use computer algorithms to facilitate surveillance and to search for activities that indicate fraud or misconduct, such as insider trading and market manipulation (Cumming and Johan 2008; Comerton-Forde and Putniņš 2011; Aitken et al. 2015a, 2015b; Cumming et al. 2015a).

The importance of surveillance in preventing financial market fraud has been documented globally (Aitken and Siow 2003; Comerton-Forde and Rydge 2006; Cumming et al. 2011; Domowitz 2012; Aitken et al. 2015b, 2015a; Li et al. 2015). For example, Cumming and Johan (2008) examine market surveillance conducted by stock exchanges and commissions in 25 jurisdictions worldwide to detect manipulative trading, including in North, Central and South America, Western and Eastern Europe, Africa, and Asia. The authors find that surveillance is positively associated with trading velocity, and cross-market surveillance is strongly related to the number of listed firms and market capitalization. Aitken et al. (2015a) investigate insider trading activities on 22 stock exchanges around the globe, documenting that domestic and cross-market surveillance reduce the incidence of insider trading. Furthermore, there is significant interplay between regulatory stringency and surveillance efforts (e.g. Aitken et al. 2014, 2015a). For example, in environments of comparatively weak institutional enforcement, a large number of trade-based market manipulations may remain undetected and escape enforcement (Neupane et al. 2017). Overall, surveillance plays a crucial role in fraud detection and securities law enforcement.

4.8.5 Private Enforcement

Apart from public enforcement, a significant portion of fraud cases rely on private enforcement through shareholder litigation. Regulators have limited resources and only prosecute the most serious and high-profile violations, which account for a small percentage of all cases, leaving the remainder to be litigated by private plaintiffs.

Potential plaintiffs are motivated by their own incentives in deciding whether to litigate their claims. Plaintiffs' decisions to file lawsuits depend on their assessment of the private costs and benefits (Spier 2007). In an environment of uncertainty and asymmetric information, a plaintiff may choose to litigate a frivolous claim, which can appear more credible than it is, forcing the defendant to reach a settlement (Spier 2007). In the US, two institutional factors further remove barriers to sue and render it easier to file frivolous claims. First, attorneys are permitted to charge contingent legal fees. Contingent fees are calculated as a percentage of the damages awarded to the plaintiff(s), and conditional upon the success of the litigation (no fees are paid if the litigation is unsuccessful). This removes the initial financial outlay of legal fees incurred by potential plaintiffs. This risk-sharing between plaintiffs and their attorneys encourages more lawsuits to be filed. Secondly, fee awards (also known as cost recovery) are rare in the US compared with other jurisdictions, such as the UK and Australia. In those countries, the losing party in a lawsuit is usually required to pay the legal fees incurred by the winning party (Baker et al. 2015). Such fee awards discourage plaintiffs from filing lawsuits, because of the risk of paying the defendant's legal fees in the event of losing the lawsuit. The absence of such cost recovery practices further encourages more lawsuits to be filed.

Plaintiffs are more likely to file suits against 'deep pocket' corporations with large market capitalization and abundant funds, to maximize the plaintiffs' chances of receiving payouts (Choi 2004; Coffee 2006). Plaintiff attorneys also play an important role in the litigation process (Coffee, 1986). Since the passage of PSLRA, institutional investors play an important role as lead plaintiffs in securities class action lawsuits. Institutional investors are more effective in monitoring class action attorneys (Perino 2012), capable of developing repeat relationships with top-tier law firms, and can negotiate lower attorney fees (Choi et al. 2011).

Given the myriad incentives affecting a plaintiff's decision to sue, some legitimate claims of fraud against firms may never result in lawsuits. Conversely, not all securities fraud lawsuits filed are meritorious, as plaintiffs and their attorneys may use litigation as a means to force defendant firms into settling their claims for a nuisance value.

4.9   Other Non-Financial Misconduct

Financial misconduct constitutes only one subset of corporate misbehaviour. Corporate wrongdoings can take various forms, such as environmental violations (Karpoff et al. 2005), breaches of contract (Bhagat et al. 1998), infringements of intellectual property rights (Meurer 2003; Posner 2005), and antitrust transgressions (Griffith 2013; Krishnan et al. 2014). Unlike securities violations which are typically perpetrated against the firms' investors, other types of corporate misconduct impact on broader stakeholder groups. For example, environmental lawsuits can affect local communities; contractual disputes may disturb supplier or customer relations; and intellectual property and antitrust challenges often involve the firms' competitors and regulators.

Securities lawsuits are followed by significant market-imposed penalties at both firm- and executive-levels. In contrast, the consequences of other types of corporate misconduct are less obvious and seldom studied (e.g. Bhagat et al. 1998; Aharony et al. 2015; Liu et al. 2016). For example, following environmental transgressions, Karpoff et al. (2005) find that the loss of market value experienced by sued firms is limited to the amount of the legal penalties incurred, indicating that there is no additional reputational penalty for firms accused of environmental misconduct. Similarly, at the executive level, researchers have examined CEO turnover and reputational impairments following different types of litigation, but find no penalties incurred by individual officers in the wake of environmental lawsuits (Aharony et al. 2015; Liu et al. 2016).

Karpoff et al. (2005) propose an important distinction between corporate misconduct affecting parties who have existing contractual relationships with the accused firms versus misconduct affecting external parties with no such contractual relationships. Through the process of future repeated contracting, parties such as shareholders, suppliers, and customers are able to penalize the offending firms by increasing their costs of operations (e.g. Karpoff et al. 1999). In contrast, alleged victims in environmental lawsuits usually lack such contractual recourse to impose penalties on the accused firms. This argument is further supported by empirical evidence documented by Armour et al. (2017), who find that firms in the UK experience significant reputational damage following misconduct against customers and investors, but not following misconduct against third parties who do not trade with the firms. In this respect, financial fraud constitutes a special type of corporate misconduct that is most likely to attract market-imposed consequences, due to the direct relationship between the accused firms and defrauded investors.

4.10   Concluding Remarks

Financial misconduct disrupts capital markets and harms investor confidence. The past two decades have witnessed numerous cases of high-profile corporate scandals, which prompted legislative changes aimed at fraud prevention. To gauge the adequacy of legal penalties in deterring corporate fraud, it is crucial to understand the full extent of market-imposed penalties incurred by corporations and responsible individuals. Indeed, the evidence suggests that market-based penalties are of much greater magnitude than legal fines and compensation. This chapter has provided a comprehensive review of the empirical evidence on the economic, reputational, and personal consequences for accused firms and their executive officers and directors.

At the corporate level, firms accused of securities fraud experience a variety of negative consequences. Short-term consequences include losses of market value, which incorporate the market's assessment of the firms' future impaired reputational capital. Long-term consequences include restricted access to financing, higher cost of capital and insurance premiums, reduced innovation, and increased risk of hostile takeovers. At the individual level, executive officers of firms facing securities allegations are more likely to experience turnover and subsequent impairment in their career progression. Executive officers who retain their jobs nonetheless experience reduced compensation and strengthened board monitoring. Directors are also more likely to exit fraud-tainted firms, though debates persist as to whether this is driven by the firms' motives to restore organizational legitimacy or the directors' motives to protect their personal reputations.

The existing literature has also provided insights into incentives that motivate fraud and misconduct, including fund-raising objectives and executives' motives to obtain personal gains through insider trading or incentive compensation. Effective corporate governance, such as monitoring by boards and institutional investors, mitigates the risk of fraud. Regulatory enforcement environments also play a significant role in the detection, prevention, and punishment of financial market fraud. Compared with other forms of corporate wrongdoing such as environmental violations or intellectual property infringements, securities misconduct attracts more significant market-based penalties for the accused firms and their executives.

The body of literature on the consequences of corporate fraud and misconduct has significant implications for policymakers, investors, and practitioners. The empirical evidence on market-based penalties imposed on corporations, executive officers, and directors provides regulators and lawmakers a holistic view of the total penalties incurred by those who commit fraud, beyond those imposed in the legal and regulatory systems. Moreover, understanding the causes, motivators, and inhibitors of fraud also contributes valuable insights into the prevention of corporate fraud and misconduct.

Apart from the need to be aware of the methodological issues in financial fraud-related research, such as the choice of empirical proxies and the distinction between committed and detected fraud, there remain a number of unanswered questions to be explored in future research. First, it is important to distinguish between allegations of fraud and actual fraud committed. While prior researchers have sought to filter lawsuit filings to exclude frivolous claims (e.g. by the size of settlements), most prior studies employ litigation-based variables (e.g. securities class actions, regulatory enforcement actions) as proxies for fraud. In the absence of data on actual convictions, it may be a misnomer to characterize and interpret allegations of fraud as indicating actual fraud committed. Careful attention devoted to developing a more nuanced approach to explore the connection between allegations and convictions of fraud may yield fruitful avenues for future research.

Second, corporate fraud does not occur in a vacuum, but is the product of a myriad of social-political, cultural, and ideological factors that coexist at the individual, firm, and institutional levels. It is worthwhile investigating the interplay of these factors in influencing corporate behaviour, and providing motivators and inhibitors of fraud and misconduct.

Finally, more attention should be devoted to understanding what remedial measures are undertaken by firms following the revelations of fraud to rebuild their reputations and to safeguard the firms against fraud in the future. It is useful to investigate whether these measures are effective in preventing future fraud. Given the importance of understanding the causes and consequences of corporate financial misconduct, future research will continue to contribute to this tapestry of multifaceted evidence to assist policymakers to formulate optimal regulations to facilitate fraud prevention.

References

Agrawal, A. and Chadha, S. (2005). Corporate governance and accounting scandals. *Journal of Law and Economics* 48 (2): 371–406.

Agrawal, A. and Cooper, T. (2015). Insider trading before accounting scandals. *Journal of Corporate Finance* 34: 169–190.

——— (2017). Corporate governance consequences of accounting scandals: Evidence from top management, CFO and auditor turnover. *Quarterly Journal of Finance* 07 (01): 1650014.

Agrawal, A., Jaffe, J.F. and Karpoff, J.M. (1999). Management turnover and corporate governance changes following the revelation of fraud. *Journal of Law and Economics* 42 (1), 309–342.

Aharony, J., Liu, C., Yawson, A. (2015). Corporate litigation and executive turnover. *Journal of Corporate Finance* 34: 268–292.

Aitken, M., Cumming, D. and Zhan, F. (2014). Trade size, high-frequency trading, and colocation around the world. *The European Journal of Finance*, 1–21.

——— (2015a). Exchange trading rules, surveillance and suspected insider trading. *Journal of Corporate Finance* 34: 311–330.

————— (2015b). High frequency trading and end-of-day price dislocation. *Journal of Banking & Finance* 59: 330–349.

Aitken, M. and Siow, A. (2003). Ranking Equity Markets on the Basis of Market Efficiency and Integrity. In *Hewlett-Packard Handbook of World Stock, Derivative & Commodity Exchanges* (ed. H. Skeete), xliv–lv. Dubin: Mondo Visione.

Alexander, C.R. (1999). On the nature of the reputational penalty for corporate crime: Evidence. *Journal of Law and Economics* 42 (1): 489–526.

Ali, A. and Kallapur, S. (2001). Securities price consequences of the Private Securities Litigation Reform Act of 1995 and related events. *The Accounting Review* 76 (3): 431–460.

Allen, F., Qian, J. and Qian, M. (2005). Law, finance, and economic growth in China. *Journal of Financial Economics* 77 (1): 57–116.

Amel-Zadeh, A. and Zhang, Y. (2015). The Economic Consequences of financial restatements: evidence from the market for corporate control. *Accounting Review* 90 (1): 1–29.

Amiram, D., Bozanic, Z., Cox, J., Dupont, Q., Karpoff, J. and Sloan, R. (2018). Financial reporting fraud and other forms of misconduct: A multidisciplinary review of the literature. *Review of Accounting Studies* 23 (2): 732–783.

Arena, M. and Julio, B. (2015). The effects of securities class action litigation on corporate liquidity and investment policy. *Journal of Financial & Quantitative Analysis* 50 (2): 251–275.

Arena, M.P. (2018). Corporate litigation and debt. *Journal of Banking & Finance* 87: 202–215.

Armour, J., Mayer, C. and Polo, A. (2017). Regulatory sanctions and reputational damage in financial markets. *Journal of Financial and Quantitative Analysis* 52 (4): 1429–1448.

Armstrong, C.S., Jagolinzer, A.D. and Larcker, D.F. (2010). Chief executive officer equity incentives and accounting irregularities. *Journal of Accounting Research* 48 (2): 225–271.

Arping, S. and Sautner, Z. (2013). Did SOX Section 404 make firms less opaque? Evidence from cross-listed firms. *Contemporary Accounting Research* 30 (3): 1133–1165.

Arthaud-Day, M.L., Certo, S.T., Dalton, C.M. and Dalton, D.R. (2006). A changing of the guard: executive and director turnover following corporate financial restatements. *Academy of Management Journal* 49 (6): 1119–1136.

Ashbaugh-Skaife, H., Collins, D.W., Kinney Jr, W.R. and Lafond, R. (2009). The effect of SOX internal control deficiencies on firm risk and cost of equity. *Journal of Accounting Research* 47 (1): 1–43.

ASIC, Australian Securities and Investments Commission. (2005). Financial Statement Fraud – Corporate Crime of the 21st Century. Presentation by J. Cooper.

Austin, J. (2017). *Insider Trading and Market Manipulation: Investigating and Prosecuting across Borders*. Cheltenham: Edgar.

Autore, D.M., Hutton, I., Peterson, D.R. and Smith, A.H. (2014). The effect of securities litigation on external financing. *Journal of Corporate Finance* 27: 231–250.

Bai, L., Cox, J.D. and Thomas, R.S. (2010). Lying and getting caught: An empirical study of the effect of securities class action settlements on targeted firms. *University of Pennsylvania Law Review* 158 (7): 1877–1914.

Baker, C.R. and Hayes, R. (2005). The Enron fallout: Was Enron an accounting failure? *Managerial Finance* 31 (9): 5–28.

Baker, L.A., Perino, M.A. and Silver, C. (2015). Is the price right? An empirical study of fee-setting in securities class actions. *Columbia Law Review* 115 (6): 1371–1452.

Baker, T. and Griffith, S.J. (2007a). Predicting corporate governance risk: Evidence from the directors' & officers' liability insurance market. *The University of Chicago Law Review* 74 (2): 487–544.

———— (2007b). The missing monitor in corporate governance: The directors' & officers' liability insurer. *Georgetown Law Journal* 95: 1795–1842.

———— (2014). *Ensuring Corporate Misconduct: How Liability Insurance Undermines Shareholder Litigation*. Chicago: University of Chicago Press.

Balasubramanian, B. and Cyree, K.B. (2014). Has market discipline on banks improved after the Dodd–Frank Act? *Journal of Banking & Finance* 41: 155–166.

Banerjee, S., Humphery-Jenner, M., Nanda, V. and Tham, M. (2018). Executive overconfidence and securities class actions. *Journal of Financial and Quantitative Analysis* 53 (6): 2685–2719.

Banoff, B.A. and DuVal, B.S., Jr. (1984). The class action as a mechanism for enforcing the federal securities laws: An empirical study of the burdens imposed. *Wayne Law Review* 31 (1): 1–134.

Barabanov, S.S., Ozocak, O., Turtle, H.J. and Walker, T.J. (2008). Institutional investors and shareholder litigation. *Financial Management* 37 (2): 227–250.

Baum, C.F., Bohn, J.G. and Chakraborty, A. (2016). Securities fraud and corporate board turnover: New evidence from lawsuit outcomes. Working paper.

Beasley, M.S. (1996). An empirical analysis of the relation between the board of director composition and financial statement fraud. *The Accounting Review* 71 (4): 443–465.

Beneish, M.D. (1999). Incentives and penalties related to earnings overstatements that violate GAAP. *The Accounting Review* 74 (4): 425–457.

Bhagat, S., Bizjak, J.M. and Coles, J.L. (1998). The shareholder wealth implications of corporate lawsuits. *Financial Management* 27 (4): 5–27.

Bhagat, S. and Romano, R. (2007). Empirical Studies of Corporate Law. In *Handbook of Law and Economics* (eds. A.M. Polinsky and S. Shavell), 945–1012. Amsterdam: Elsevier.

Biggerstaff, L., Cicero, D.C. and Puckett, A. (2015). Suspect CEOs, unethical culture, and corporate misbehavior. *Journal of Financial Economics* 117 (1): 98–121.

Black, B., Cheffins, B.R. and Klausner, M. (2006). Outside director liability. *Stanford Law Review* 58: 1055–1160.

Boettrich, S. and Starykh, S. (2017). Recent Trends in Securities Class Action Litigation: 2016 Full-Year Review. NERA.

Boone, A.L., Casares Field, L., Karpoff, J.M. and Raheja, C.G. (2007). The determinants of corporate board size and composition: An empirical analysis. *Journal of Financial Economics* 85 (1): 66–101.

Boyer, M.M. and Stern, L.H. (2012). Is corporate governance risk valued? Evidence from directors' and officers' insurance. *Journal of Corporate Finance* 18 (2): 349–372.

Brennan, N.M. and McGrath, M. (2007). Financial statement fraud: Some lessons from US and European case studies. *Australian Accounting Review* 17 (42): 49–61.

Brochet, F., 2010. Information content of insider trades before and after the Sarbanes–Oxley Act. *The Accounting Review* 85 (2): 419–446.

Brochet, F. and Srinivasan, S. (2014). Accountability of independent directors: Evidence from firms subject to securities litigation. *Journal of Financial Economics* 111 (2): 430–449.

Burks, J.J. (2010). Disciplinary measures in response to restatements after Sarbanes–Oxley. *Journal of Accounting and Public Policy* 29 (3): 195–225.

Burns, N. and Kedia, S. (2006). The Impact of performance-based compensation on misreporting. *Journal of Financial Economics* 79 (1): 35–67.

Capezio, A. and Mavisakalyan, A. (2016). Women in the boardroom and fraud: Evidence from Australia. *Australian Journal of Management* 41 (4): 719–734.

Caskey, J. (2014). The pricing effects of securities class action lawsuits and litigation insurance. *Journal of Law, Economics, and Organization* 30 (3): 493–532.

Chakravarthy, J., de Haan, E. and Rajgopal, S. (2014). Reputation repair after a serious restatement. *The Accounting Review* 89 (4): 1329–1363.

Chapple, L., Clout, V.J. and Tan, D. (2014). Corporate governance and securities class actions. *Australian Journal of Management* 39 (4): 525–547.

Chen, G., Firth, M., Gao, D.N. and Rui, O.M. (2006). Ownership structure, corporate governance, and fraud: Evidence from China. *Journal of Corporate Finance* 12 (3): 424–448.

Chen, J., Cumming, D., Hou, W. and Lee, E. (2016). CEO accountability for corporate fraud: Evidence from the split share structure reform in China. *Journal of Business Ethics* 138 (4): 787–806.

Cheng, C.S.A., Huang, H.H., Lei, A.Z. and Lu, H. (2017). District Court stringency and firm restatement policy. Working Paper.

Cheng, C.S.A., Huang, H.H., Li, Y. and Lobo, G. (2010). Institutional monitoring through shareholder litigation. *Journal of Financial Economics* 95 (3): 356–383.

Choi, S.J. (2004). The Evidence on Securities Class Actions. *Vanderbilt Law Review* 57 (5), 1465–1526.

Choi, S.J. (2007). Do the merits matter less after the Private Securities Litigation Reform Act? *Journal of Law, Economics, & Organization* 23 (3): 598–626.

Choi, S.J., Johnson-Skinner, D.T. and Pritchard, A.C. (2011). The price of pay to play in securities class actions. *Journal of Empirical Legal Studies* 8 (4): 650–681.

Choi, S.J., Nelson, K.K. and Pritchard, A.C. (2009). The screening effect of the Private Securities Litigation Reform Act. *Journal of Empirical Legal Studies* 6 (1): 35–68.

Choi, S.J. and Thompson, R.B. (2006). Securities litigation and its lawyers: changes during the first decade after the PSLRA. *Columbia Law Review* 106 (7): 1489–1533.

Christensen, H.B., Hail, L. and Leuz, C. (2016). Capital-market effects of securities regulation: Prior conditions, implementation, and enforcement. *The Review of Financial Studies* 29 (11): 2885–2924.

Chu, Y. (2017). Shareholder litigation, shareholder–creditor conflict, and the cost of bank loans. *Journal of Corporate Finance* 45: 318–332.

Cline, B.N., Walkling, R.A. and Yore, A.S. (2018). The consequences of managerial indiscretions: Sex, lies, and firm value. *Journal of Financial Economics* 127 (2): 389–415.

Coffee, J.C., Jr. (1986) Understanding the plaintiff's attorney: The implications of economic theory for private enforcement of law through class and derivative actions. *Columbia Law Review* 86 (4): 669–727.

Coffee, J.C., Jr. (2006). Reforming the securities class action: An essay on deterrence and its implementation. *Columbia Law Review* 106 (7): 1534–1586.

Cohen, D.A., Dey, A. and Lys, T.Z. (2008). Real and accrual-based earnings management in the pre- and post-Sarbanes–Oxley periods. *The Accounting Review* 83 (3): 757–787.

Coles, J.L., Daniel, N.D. and Naveen, L. (2008). Boards: Does one size fit all? *Journal of Financial Economics* 87 (2): 329–356.

Collins, D., Masli, A.D.I., Reitenga, A.L. and Sanchez, J.M. (2009). Earnings restatements, the Sarbanes–Oxley Act, and the disciplining of chief financial officers. *Journal of Accounting, Auditing & Finance* 24 (1): 1–34.

Collins, D., Reitenga, A.L. and Sanchez, J.M. (2008). The impact of accounting restatements on CFO turnover and bonus compensation: Does securities litigation matter? *Advances in Accounting* 24 (2): 162–171.

Comerton-Forde, C. and Putniņš, T.J. (2011). Measuring closing price manipulation. *Journal of Financial Intermediation* 20 (2): 135–158.

Comerton-Forde, C. and Rydge, J. (2006). Market integrity and surveillance effort. *Journal of Financial Services Research* 29 (2): 149–172.

Condie, E.R., Convery, A.M. and Johnstone, K.M. (2017). Being in the wrong place at the wrong time? Labor market implications for non-implicated CFOs of fraud firms. Working Paper.

Correia, M. and Klausner, M. (2012). Are securities class actions 'supplemental' to SEC enforcement? An empirical analysis. Working Paper.

Correia, M.M. (2014). Political connections and SEC enforcement. *Journal of Accounting and Economics* 57 (2): 241–262.

Cox, J.D. (1997). Private litigation and the deterrence of corporate misconduct. *Law and Contemporary Problems* 60 (4): 1–38.

Cox, J.D. and Thomas, R.S. (2005). Letting billions slip through your fingers: Empirical evidence and legal implications of the failure of financial institutions to participate in securities class action settlements. *Stanford Law Review* 58 (2): 411–454.

Crocker, K.J. and Slemrod, J. (2007). The economics of earnings manipulation and managerial compensation. *RAND Journal of Economics (Wiley-Blackwell)* 38 (3): 698–713.

Crutchley, C.E. and Minnick, K. (2012). Cash versus incentive compensation: Lawsuits and director pay. *Journal of Business Research* 65 (7): 907–913.

Crutchley, C.E., Minnick, K. and Schorno, P.J. (2015). When governance fails: Naming directors in class action lawsuits. *Journal of Corporate Finance* 35: 81–96.

Cumming, D., Dannhauser, R. and Johan, S. (2015a). Financial market misconduct and agency conflicts: A synthesis and future directions. *Journal of Corporate Finance* 34: 150–168.

Cumming, D., Filatotchev, I., Knill, A., Reeb, D.M. and Senbet, L. (2017). Law, finance, and the international mobility of corporate governance. *Journal of International Business Studies* 48 (2): 123–147.

Cumming, D., Hou, W. and Wu, E. (2015b). Exchange trading rules, governance, and trading location of cross-listed stocks. *The European Journal of Finance*, 24:16, 1453–1484.

Cumming, D. and Johan, S. (2008). Global market surveillance. *American Law and Economics Review* 10 (2): 454–506.

——— (2013). Listing standards and fraud. *Managerial & Decision Economics* 34 (7/8): 451–470.

——— (2019). Capital-Market Effects of Securities Regulation: Prior Conditions, Implementation, and Enforcement Revisited. *Finance Research Letters* 31.

Cumming, D., Johan, S. and Li, D. (2011). Exchange trading rules and stock market liquidity. *Journal of Financial Economics* 99 (3): 651–671.

Cumming, D., Johan, S. and Peter, R. (2018a). Developments in financial institutions, governance, agency costs, and misconduct. *Journal of International Financial Markets, Institutions and Money* 54: 1–14.

Cumming, D., Leung, T.Y. and Rui, O. (2015c). Gender diversity and securities fraud. *Academy of Management Journal* 58 (5): 1572–1593.

Cumming, D. and Li, D. (2011). Run-up of acquirer's stock in public and private acquisitions. *Corporate Governance: An International Review* 19 (3), 210–239.

Cumming, D., Peter Groh, A. and Johan, S. (2018b). Same rules, different enforcement: Market abuse in Europe. *Journal of International Financial Markets, Institutions and Money.* 54: 130–151.

Cumming, D.J., Ji, S. and Peter, R. (2019). Market manipulation and innovation. Working Paper.

Cutler, D.M. and Summers, L.H. (1987). The costs of conflict resolution and financial distress: Evidence from the Texaco-Pennzoil litigation. *RAND Journal of Economics* 19 (2): 157–172.

Dai, Z., Jin, L. and Zhang, W. (2014). Executive pay-performance sensitivity and litigation. *Contemporary Accounting Research* 31 (1): 152–177.

Davis, K.B., Jr. (2008). The forgotten derivative suit. *Vanderbilt Law Review* 61 (2): 387–452.

Dechow, P.M., Ge, W., Larson, C.R. and Sloan, R.G. (2011). Predicting material accounting misstatements. *Contemporary Accounting Research* 28 (1): 17–82.

Dechow, P.M., Sloan, R.G. and Sweeney, A.P. (1996). Causes and consequences of earnings manipulation: An analysis of firms subject to enforcement actions by the SEC. *Contemporary Accounting Research* 13 (1): 1–36.

DeFond, M.L. and Jiambalvo, J. (1994). Debt covenant violation and manipulation of accruals. *Journal of Accounting and Economics* 17 (1-2)– 145–176.

deHaan, E., Hodge, F. and Shevlin, T. (2013). Does voluntary adoption of a clawback provision improve financial reporting quality? *Contemporary Accounting Research* 30 (3): 1027–1062.

Denis, D.J., Hanouna, P. and Sarin, A. (2006). Is there a dark side to incentive compensation? *Journal of Corporate Finance* 12 (3): 467–488.

Desai, H., Hogan, C.E. and Wilkins, M.S. (2006). The reputational penalty for aggressive accounting: Earnings restatements and management turnover. *The Accounting Review* 81 (1): 83–112.

Dimitrov, V., Palia, D. and Tang, L. (2015). Impact of the Dodd-Frank Act on credit ratings. *Journal of Financial Economics* 115 (3): 505–520.

Djankov, S., La Porta, R., Lopez-de-Silanes, F. and Shleifer, A. (2008). The law and economics of self-dealing. *Journal of Financial Economics* 88 (3): 430–465.

Domowitz, I. (2012). Market Abuse and Surveillance. Foresight, Government Office for Science.

Donelson, D.C., McInnis, J.M. and Mergenthaler, R.D. (2012). Rules-based accounting standards and litigation. *The Accounting Review* 87 (4): 1247–1279.

Duarte, J., Kong, K., Siegel, S. and Young, L. (2014). The impact of the Sarbanes–Oxley Act on shareholders and managers of foreign firms. *Review of Finance* 18 (1): 417–455.

DuCharme, L.L., Malatesta, P.H. and Sefcik, S.E. (2004). Earnings management, stock issues, and shareholder lawsuits. *Journal of Financial Economics* 71 (1): 27–49.

Duchin, R., Matsusaka, J.G. and Ozbas, O. (2010). When are outside directors effective? *Journal of Financial Economics* 96 (2): 195–214.

Dyck, A., Morse, A. and Zingales, L. (2010). Who blows the whistle on corporate fraud? *The Journal of Finance* 65 (6): 2213–2253.

Eaglesham, J., Trindle, J. and Van Hasselt, C. (2012). CFTC deals out royal pain; Canadian bank is accused of massive 'wash' scheme to garner tax benefits. *The Wall Street Journal* (April 3, 2012).

Eaglesham, J. and Vigna, P. (2018). Cryptocurrency firms targeted in SEC probe; Regulator issues subpoenas to parties engaged in booming market for initial coin offerings. *The Wall Street Journal* (February 28, 2018).

Eisenberg, T., Sundgren, S. and Wells, M.T. (1998). Larger board size and decreasing firm value in small firms. *Journal of Financial Economics* 48 (1): 35–54.

Fahlenbrach, R., Low, A. and Stulz, R.M. (2014). The dark side of outside directors: Do they quit ahead of trouble? Working Paper.

Fama, E.F. (1980). Agency problems and the theory of the firm. *Journal of Political Economy* 88 (2): 288–307.

Fama, E.F. and Jensen, M.C. (1983). Separation of ownership and control. *Journal of Law and Economics* 26 (2): 301–325.

Farber, D.B. (2005). Restoring trust after fraud: Does corporate governance matter? *The Accounting Review* 80 (2): 539–561.

Farrell, Kathleen A., Whidbee and David A. (2000). The consequences of forced CEO succession for outside directors. *The Journal of Business* 73 (4): 597–627.

Farrell, S. (2015). The world's biggest accounting scandals. *The Guardian* (22 July 2015).

Feroz, E.H., Park, K. and Pastena, V.S. (1991). The financial and market effects of the SEC's accounting and auditing enforcement releases. *Journal of Accounting Research* 29 (3): 107–142.

Ferris, S.P., Jagannathan, M. and Pritchard, A.C. (2003). Too busy to mind the business? Monitoring by directors with multiple board appointments. *The Journal of Finance* 58 (3): 1087–1111.

Ferris, S.P., Jandik, T., Lawless, R.M. and Makhija, A. (2007). Derivative lawsuits as a corporate governance mechanism: Empirical evidence on board changes surrounding filings. *Journal of Financial and Quantitative Analysis* 42 (2): 143–166.

Fich, E.M. and Shivdasani, A. (2007). Financial fraud, director reputation, and shareholder wealth. *Journal of Financial Economics* 86 (2): 306–336.

Fields, M.A. (1990). The wealth effects of corporate lawsuits: Pennzoil v. *Texaco. Journal of Business Research* 21 (2): 143–158.

Files, R. (2012). SEC enforcement: Does forthright disclosure and cooperation really matter? *Journal of Accounting and Economics* 53 (1): 353–374.

Fischel, D.R. and Bradley, M. (1986). The role of liability rules and the derivative suit in corporate law: A theoretical and empirical analysis. *Cornell Law Review* 71 (2): 261–297.

Gande, A. and Lewis, C.M. (2009). Shareholder-initiated class action lawsuits: Shareholder wealth effects and industry spillovers. *Journal of Financial and Quantitative Analysis* 44 (4): 823–850.

Ge, W., Koester, A. and McVay, S. (2017). Benefits and costs of Sarbanes-Oxley Section 404(B) exemption: Evidence from small firms' internal control disclosures. *Journal of Accounting and Economics* 63 (2): 358–384.

Gelowitz, M.A., Coleman, A.D. and Carson, R. (2015). Securities litigation in Canada. In: *The Securities Litigation Review* (ed. W. Savitt), 50–63. London: Law Business Research.

Giannetti, M. and Wang, T.Y. (2016). Corporate scandals and household stock market participation. *The Journal of Finance* 71 (6): 2591–2636.

Gillan, S.L. and Martin, J.D. (2007). Corporate governance post-Enron: Effective reforms, or closing the stable door? *Journal of Corporate Finance* 13 (5): 929–958.

Gillan, S.L. and Panasian, C.A. (2015). On lawsuits, corporate governance, and directors' and officers' liability insurance. *Journal of Risk and Insurance* 82 (4): 793–822.

Goldman, E. and Slezak, S.L. (2006). An equilibrium model of incentive contracts in the presence of information manipulation. *Journal of Financial Economics* 80 (3): 603–626.

Grace, S.M. (2006). Strengthening investor confidence in Europe: U.S.-style securities class actions and the acquis communautaire. *Journal of Transnational Law & Policy* 15 (2): 281–304.

Graham, J.R., Li, S. and Qiu, J. (2008). Corporate misreporting and bank loan contracting. *Journal of Financial Economics* 89 (1): 44–61.

Griffith, S.J.L. and Alexandra D. (2013). The market for preclusion in merger litigation. *Vanderbilt Law Review* 66 (4): 1053–1140.

Gullifer, L. and Payne, J. (2015). *Corporate Finance Law: Principles and Policy*. Oxford: Hart Publishing.

Gurun, U.G., Stoffman, N. and Yonker, S.E. (2018). Trust busting: The effect of fraud on investor behavior. *Review of Financial Studies* 31 (4): 1341–1376.

Haslem, B. (2005). Managerial opportunism during corporate litigation. *Journal of Finance* 60 (4): 2013–2041.

Hass, L.H., Tarsalewska, M. and Zhan, F. (2016). Equity incentives and corporate fraud in China. *Journal of Business Ethics* 138 (4): 723–742.

Helland, E. (2006). Reputational penalties and the merits of class action securities litigation. *Journal of Law and Economics* 49 (2): 365–395.

Hennes, K.M., Leone, A.J. and Miller, B.P. (2008). The importance of distinguishing errors from irregularities in restatement research: The case of restatements and CEO/CFO turnover. *The Accounting Review* 83 (6): 1487–1519.

Hermalin, B.E. and Weisbach, M.S. (1998). Endogenously chosen boards of directors and their monitoring of the CEO. *American Economic Review* 88 (1): 96–118.

Hertzel, M.G. and Smith, J.K. (1993). Industry effects of interfirm lawsuits: Evidence from Pennzoil v. Texaco. *Journal of Law, Economics, & Organization* 9 (2): 425–444.

Hribar, P. and Jenkins, N.T. (2004). The effect of accounting restatements on earnings revisions and the estimated cost of capital. *Review of Accounting Studies* 9 (2-3): 337–356.

Huang, X., Rui, Y., Shen, J. and Tian, G.Y. (2017). U.S. class action lawsuits targeting foreign firms: The country spillover effect. *Journal of Corporate Finance* 45 (Supplement C): 378–400.

Humphery-Jenner, M.L. (2012). Internal and external discipline following securities class actions. *Journal of Financial Intermediation* 21 (1): 151–179.

Iliev, P. (2010). The effect of SOX section 404: Costs, earnings quality, and stock prices. *The Journal of Finance* 65 (3): 1163–1196.

Jackson, H.E. and Roe, M.J. (2009). Public and private enforcement of securities laws: Resource-based evidence. *Journal of Financial Economics* 93 (2): 207–238.

Jacobs, A.S. (1973). What is a misleading statement or omission under Rule 10b-5? *Fordham Law Review* 42 (2): 243–290.

Jenner-Humphery, M. (2013). Strong financial laws without strong enforcement: Is good law always better than no law? *Journal of Empirical Legal Studies* 10 (2): 288–324.

Jensen, M.C. and Meckling, W.H. (1976). Theory of the Firm: Managerial Behavior, Agency Costs and Ownership Structure. *Journal of Financial Economics* 3 (4): 305–360.

Jensen, M.C. and Ruback, R.S. (1983). The market for corporate control: The scientific evidence. *Journal of Financial Economics* 11: 5–50.

Jia, C., Ding, S., Li, Y. and Wu, Z. (2009). Fraud, enforcement action, and the role of corporate governance: evidence from China. *Journal of Business Ethics* 90 (4), 561–576.

Johnson, M.F., Nelson, K.K., Pritchard, A.C., 2000. In Re Silicon Graphics Inc.: Shareholder Wealth Effects Resulting from the Interpretation of the Private Securities Litigation Reform Act's Pleading Standard. *Southern California Law Review* 73, 773–810.

Johnson, S.A., Ryan, J.H.E. and Tian, Y.S. (2009). Managerial incentives and corporate fraud: The sources of incentives matter. *Review of Finance* 13 (1), 115–145.

Johnson, W.C., Xie, W. and Yi, S. (2014). Corporate fraud and the value of reputations in the product market. *Journal of Corporate Finance* 25 (Supplement C): 16–39.

Jones, M. (2011). *Creative Accounting, Fraud and International Accounting Scandals*. Chichester: Wiley.

Jones, R. and Yan, W. (2010). Executive compensation, earnings management and shareholder litigation. *Review of Quantitative Finance & Accounting* 35 (1): 1–20.

Karpoff, J.M. (2011). Does reputation work to discipline corporate misconduct? In *The Oxford Handbook of Corporate Reputation* (eds. M.L. Barnett and T.G. Pollock), 361–382. Oxford: Oxford University Press.

Karpoff, J.M., Koester, A., Lee, D.S. and Martin, G.S. (2017). Proxies and databases in financial misconduct research. *The Accounting Review* 92 (6): 129–163.

Karpoff, J.M., Lee, D.S. and Martin, G.S. (2008a). The cost to firms of cooking the books. *Journal of Financial and Quantitative Analysis* 43 (3): 581–612.

Karpoff, J.M., Lee, D.S. and Martin, G.S. (2008b). The consequences to managers for financial misrepresentation. *Journal of Financial Economics* 88 (2): 193–215.

Karpoff, J.M., Lee, D.S. and Vendrzyk, V.P. (1999). Defense procurement fraud, penalties, and contractor influence. *Journal of Political Economy* 107 (4): 809–842.

Karpoff, J.M. and Lott, J.R. Jr. (1993). The reputational penalty firms bear from committing criminal fraud. *Journal of Law and Economics* 36: 757–802.

——— (1999). On the determinants and importance of punitive damage awards. *Journal of Accounting and Economics* 42: 527–573.

Karpoff, J.M., Lott, J.R., Jr. and Wehrly, E.W. (2005). The reputational penalties for environmental violations: Empirical evidence. *Journal of Law and Economics* 48 (2): 653–675.

Karpoff, J.M. and Lou, X. (2010). Short sellers and financial misconduct. *The Journal of Finance* 65 (5): 1879–1913.

Kedia, S. and Philippon, T. (2009). The economics of fraudulent accounting. *The Review of Financial Studies* 22 (6): 2169–2199.

Kedia, S. and Rajgopal, S. (2011). Do the SEC's enforcement preferences affect corporate misconduct? *Journal of Accounting and Economics* 51 (3): 259–278.

Kennedy, J.E. (1977). Securities class and derivative actions in the United States District Court for the Northern District of Texas: An empirical study. *Houston Law Review* 14 (4): 769–811.

Khanna, V., Kim, E.H. and Lu, Y. (2015). CEO connectedness and corporate fraud. *The Journal of Finance* 70 (3): 1203–1252.

Kim, I. and Skinner, D.J. (2012). Measuring securities litigation risk. *Journal of Accounting and Economics* 53 (1–2): 290–310.

Klausner, M., Hegland, J. and Goforth, M. (2013). How protective is D&O insurance in securities class actions? – an update. *PLUS Journal* 26 (5): 1–4.

Komai, A. and Richardson, G. (2014). A history of financial regulation in the USA from the beginning until today: 1789 to 2011. In *Handbook of Financial Data and Risk Information I:*

Principles and Context (eds. B. Nichols, D. Krishna, M.S. Brose and M.D. Flood), 385–425. Cambridge: Cambridge University Press.

Kravet, T. and Shevlin, T. (2010). Accounting restatements and information risk. *Review of Accounting Studies* 15: 264–294.

Krishnan, C.N.V., Masulis, R.W., Thomas, R.S. and Thompson, R.B. (2014). Jurisdictional effects in M&A litigation. *Journal of Empirical Legal Studies* 11 (1): 132–158.

Kuang, Y.F. and Lee, G. (2017). Corporate fraud and external social connectedness of independent directors. *Journal of Corporate Finance* 45: 401–427.

La Porta, R., Lopez-De-Silanes, F. and Shleifer, A. (2006). What works in securities laws? *The Journal of Finance* 61 (1): 1–32.

——— (2008). The economic consequences of legal origins. *Journal of Economic Literature* 46 (2): 285–332.

La Porta, R., Lopez-de-Silanes, F., Shleifer, A. and Vishny, R.W. (1998). Law and finance. *Journal of Political Economy* 106 (6): 1113–1155.

Laux, V. and Stocken, P.C. (2012). Managerial reporting, overoptimism, and litigation risk. *Journal of Accounting and Economics* 53(3): 577–592.

Lee, C. (2011). New evidence on what happens to CEOs after they retire. *Journal of Corporate Finance* 17 (3): 474–482.

Lehman, C.R. and Okcabol, F. (2005). Accounting for crime. *Critical Perspectives on Accounting* 16 (5): 613–639.

Lennox, C., Lisowsky, P. and Pittman, J. (2013). Tax aggressiveness and accounting fraud. *Journal of Accounting Research* 51 (4): 739–778.

Li, X., Sun, S.X., Chen, K., Fung, T. and Wang, H. (2015). Design theory for market surveillance systems. *Journal of Management Information Systems* 32 (2): 278–313.

Lin, C., Officer, M.S., Wang, R. and Zou, H. (2013). Directors' and officers' liability insurance and loan spreads. *Journal of Financial Economics* 110 (1): 37–60.

Linck, J.S., Netter, J.M. and Yang, T. (2009). The effects and unintended consequences of the Sarbanes–Oxley Act on the supply and demand for directors. *Review of Financial Studies* 22 (8): 3287–3328.

Liu, C., Aharony, J., Richardson, G. and Yawson, A. (2016). Corporate litigation and changes in CEO reputation: guidance from US federal court lawsuits. *Journal of Contemporary Accounting & Economics* 12 (1), 15–34.

Liu, X. (2016). Corruption culture and corporate misconduct. *Journal of Financial Economics* 122 (2): 307–327.

Loewenstein, M. (1999). Shareholder derivative litigation and corporate governance. *Delaware Journal of Corporate Law* 24 (1): 1.

Lowry, M. and Shu, S. (2002). Litigation risk and IPO underpricing. *Journal of Financial Economics* 65 (3): 309–335.

Manahov, V. (2016). Front-running scalping strategies and market manipulation: Why does high-frequency trading need stricter regulation? *Financial Review* 51 (3): 363–402.

Marcel, J.J. and Cowen, A.P. (2014). Cleaning house or jumping ship? Understanding board upheaval following financial fraud. *Strategic Management Journal* 35 (6): 926–937.

Markham, J.W. (1988). Front-running – insider trading under the Commodity Exchange Act. *Catholic University Law Review* 38 (1): 69–128.

McTier, B.C. and Wald, J.K. (2011). The causes and consequences of securities class action litigation. *Journal of Corporate Finance* 17 (3): 649–665.

Meurer, M. (2003). Controlling opportunistic and anti-competitive intellectual property litigation. *Boston College Law Review* 44: 509–544.

Mitchell, L.E. (2009). Innocent shareholder: An essay on compensation and deterrence in securities class-action lawsuits. *Wisconsin Law Review* 2009 (2): 243–296.

Mitra, S., Jaggi, B. and Hossain, M. (2013). Internal control weaknesses and accounting conservatism: Evidence from the post-Sarbanes–Oxley period. *Journal of Accounting, Auditing & Finance* 28 (2): 152–191.

Murphy, D.L., Shrieves, R.E. and Tibbs, S.L. (2009). Understanding the penalties associated with corporate misconduct: An empirical examination of earnings and risk. *Journal of Financial and Quantitative Analysis* 44 (1): 55–83.

Neupane, S., Rhee, S.G., Vithanage, K. and Veeraraghavan, M. (2017). Trade-based manipulation: Beyond the prosecuted cases. *Journal of Corporate Finance* 42: 115–130.

Niehaus, G. and Roth, G. (1999). Insider trading, equity issues, and CEO turnover in firms subject to securities class action. *Financial Management* 28 (4): 52–72.

Nourayi, M.M. (1994). Stock price responses to the SEC's enforcement actions. *Journal of Accounting and Public Policy* 13 (4), 333–347.

O'Connor, J.P.J., Priem, R.L., Coombs, J.E. and Gilley, K.M. (2006). Do CEO stock options prevent or promote fraudulent financial reporting? *Academy of Management Journal* 49 (3): 483–500.

Palmrose, Z.-V., Richardson, V.J. and Scholz, S. (2004). Determinants of market reactions to restatement announcements. *Journal of Accounting and Economics* 37 (1): 59–89.

Palmrose, Z.-V. and Scholz, S. (2004). The circumstances and legal consequences of non-GAAP reporting: Evidence from restatements. *Contemporary Accounting Research* 21 (1): 139–180.

Peng, L. and Roell, A. (2014). Managerial incentives and stock price manipulation. *The Journal of Finance* 69 (2): 487–526.

Perino, M. (2012). Institutional activism through litigation: An empirical analysis of public pension fund participation in securities class actions. *Journal of Empirical Legal Studies* 9 (2): 368–392.

Persons, O. (2006). The effects of fraud and lawsuit revelation on U.S. executive turnover and compensation. *Journal of Business Ethics* 64 (4): 405–419.

Piotroski, J. and Srinivasan, S. (2013). Regulation and bonding: The Sarbanes–Oxley Act and the flow of international listings. Working Paper.

Posner, R.A. (2005). Intellectual property: The law and economics approach. *The Journal of Economic Perspectives* 19 (2): 57–73.

Pukthuanthong, K., Turtle, H., Walker, T. and Wang, J. (2017). Litigation risk and institutional monitoring. *Journal of Corporate Finance* 45: 342–359.

Putniņš, T.J. (2012). Market manipulation: A survey. *Journal of Economic Surveys* 26 (5): 952–967.

Roberts, J. (2013). Financial Services Act 2012: A new UK financial regulatory framework. In *Harvard Law School Forum on Corporate Governance and Financial Regulation* (ed. N. Noked).

Rockness, H. and Rockness, J. (2005). Legislated ethics: From Enron to Sarbanes–Oxley, the impact on corporate America. *Journal of Business Ethics* 57 (1): 31–54.

Romano, R. (1991). The shareholder suit: Litigation without foundation? *Journal of Law, Economics, & Organization* 7 (1): 55–87.

––––––– (2004). The Sarbanes–Oxley Act and the making of quack corporate governance. *Yale Law Journal* 114: 1521–1612.

Rubin, G.T. (2018). Investors warned of cryptocurrency 'pump-and-dump' schemes. *The Wall Street Journal,* February 15, 2018.

Schrand, C.M. and Zechman, S.L.C. (2012). Executive overconfidence and the slippery slope to financial misreporting. *Journal of Accounting and Economics* 53 (1): 311–329.

Scopino, G. (2015). The (questionable) legality of high-speed pinging and front running in the futures market. *Connecticut Law Review* 47 (3): 607–698.

SEC, Securities and Exchange Commission (2003). SEC Charges Parmalat with Financial Fraud Accounting and Auditing Enforcement Release No. 1936/December. Litigation Release No. 18527.

Shivdasani, A. (1993). Board composition, ownership structure, and hostile takeovers. *Journal of Accounting and Economics* 16 (1): 167–198.

Skinner, D.J. (1994). Why firms voluntarily disclose bad news. *Journal of Accounting Research* 32 (1): 38–60.

Soltani, B. (2014). The anatomy of corporate fraud: A comparative analysis of high profile American and European corporate scandals. *Journal of Business Ethics* 120 (2): 251–274.

Spier, K.E. (2007). Chapter 4 Litigation. In *Handbook of Law and Economics* (eds A.M. Polinsky and S. Shavell), 259–342. Amsterdam: Elsevier.

Srinivasan, S. (2005). Consequences of financial reporting failure for outside directors: Evidence from accounting restatements and audit committee members. *Journal of Accounting Research* 43 (2): 291–334.

Stuart, T. and Wang, Y. (2016). Who cooks the books in China, and does it pay? Evidence from private, high-technology firms. *Strategic Management Journal* 37 (13): 2658–2676.

Sun, P., Hu, H.W. and Hillman, A.J. (2016). The dark side of board political capital: enabling blockholder rent appropriation. *Academy of Management Journal* 59 (5): 1801–1822.

Tanimura, J.K. and Okamoto, M.G. (2013). Reputational penalties in Japan: Evidence from corporate scandals. *Asian Economic Journal* 27 (1): 39–57.

Teoh, S.H., Welch, I. and Wong, T.J. (1998a). Earnings management and the underperformance of seasoned equity offerings. *Journal of Financial Economics* 50 (1): 63–99.

––––––– (1998b). Earnings management and the long-run market performance of initial public offerings. *The Journal of Finance* 53 (6): 1935–1974.

Thompson, R.B. and Sale, H.A. (2003). Securities fraud as corporate governance: Reflections upon federalism. *Vanderbilt Law Review* 2003 (3): 859–910.

Uzun, H., Szewczyk, S.H. and Varma, R. (2004). Board composition and corporate fraud. *Financial Analysts Journal* 60 (3): 33–43.

Wang, T.Y. (2013). Corporate securities fraud: Insights from a new empirical framework. *The Journal of Law, Economics, and Organization* 29 (3): 535–568.

Wang, T.Y., Winton, A. and Yu, X. (2010). Corporate fraud and business conditions: Evidence from IPOs. *The Journal of Finance* 65 (6): 2255–2292.

Wang, Z., Chen, M.-H., Chin, C.L. and Zheng, Q. (2017). Managerial ability, political connections, and fraudulent financial reporting in China. *Journal of Accounting and Public Policy* 36 (2): 141–162.

Warren, M.G.I. (2012). The U.S. securities fraud class action: An unlikely export to the European Union. *Brooklyn Journal of International Law* 37 (3): 1075–1114.

Withanawasam, R.M., Whigham, P.A. and Crack, T.F. (2013). Characterising Trader Manipulation in a Limit-Order Driven Market. *Mathematics and Computers in Simulation* 93: 43–52.

Yermack, D. (1996). Higher market valuation of companies with a small board of directors. *Journal of Financial Economics* 40 (2): 185–211.

Young, M.R. (2000). *Accounting Irregularities and Financial Fraud*. San Diego: Harcourt.

Yu, F. and Yu, X. (2011). Corporate lobbying and fraud detection. *Journal of Financial & Quantitative Analysis* 46 (6): 1865–1891.

Yuan, Q. and Zhang, Y. (2015). Do banks price litigation risk in debt contracting? Evidence from class action lawsuits. *Journal of Business Finance & Accounting* 42 (9/10): 1310–1340.

Zhang, I.X. (2007). Economic consequences of the Sarbanes-Oxley Act of 2002. *Journal of Accounting and Economics* 44 (1-2): 74–115.

Zhao, Y. and Chen, K.H. (2008). Staggered Boards and Earnings Management. *The Accounting Review* 83 (5): 1347–1381.

Chapter 5

Insider Trading and Market Manipulation

Jonathan A. Batten
Royal Melbourne Institute of Technology (RMIT)

Igor Lončarski
University of Ljubljana

Peter G. Szilagyi
Central European University

5.1 Introduction

Insider trading refers to the use of private information to trade assets, whereas market manipulation involves attempting to cause the asset price to be above, or below, its expected equilibrium.[1] To achieve this end the price manipulator may engage in complex trading strategies or simply misrepresent information to other market participants. The intention from both practices is to make a financial gain from disruption of the proper functioning of markets. While these practices occur across many industries, media attention in recent years has focused on the activities of financial intermediaries, given the financial scale and scope of the reported activities.

There are several financial crimes of which insider trading and market manipulation are part. Others include fraud,[2] electronic crime including cybercrime, money laundering, bribery, and corruption.[3] These crimes are universally condemned, and a rich suite of regulations and regulatory bodies are present at a national level to prevent, identify and prosecute these crimes.

Table 5.1 provides an example of the scope of regulation using the case of the United States of America (US), with the Securities and Exchange Commission (SEC) providing the centrepiece for regulatory enforcement. Note the layered regulatory structure that comprises specific statutes designed to capture certain practices, further statutes that clarify process, and those that establish agencies designed to monitor and affect the legislation. In the United Kingdom the Financial Conduct Authority (FCA)[4] is the key authority with similar agencies operating in other countries.[5]

At an international level there is general guidance on what constitutes acceptable practice. The recent Principle 29, on effective banking supervision, by the Bank for International Settlements (BIS, 2016: 29) highlights the importance of monitoring the abuse of financial services and argues that

> '[the banking] supervisor determines that banks have adequate policies and processes, including strict customer due diligence rules to promote high ethical and professional standards in the financial sector and prevent the bank from being used, intentionally or unintentionally, for criminal activities.'

In addition, there is also guidance arising from key international institutions, such as the UN Global Compact, which asks for a 'shared set of values and principles, which will give a human face to the global market' to help ensure that its basic activities—dealing with markets, commerce, technology, and finance—will move

---

[1] Section 12(1)(a)(ii) of the UK Market Abuse Regulation terms this an abnormal or artificial price level.

[2] A spectacular recent example is the reputed US$1 billion fraud perpetrated by officials at various banks in Moldovia: www.ft.com/content/b582ad2c-c424-11e5-b3b1-7b2481276e45.

[3] See the Global Fraud Survey (2018) for further details on the scale and scope of these activities worldwide: www.ey.com/Publication/vwLUAssets/EY_Global_Fraud_Survey_2018_report/$FILE/EY%20GLOBAL%20 FIDS%20FRAUD%20SURVEY%202018.pdf.

[4] The Financial Conduct Authority (FCA) is responsible for protecting consumers, financial markets and promoting competition and 'is the conduct regulator for 59,000 financial services firms and financial markets in the UK and the prudential regulator for over 18,000 of those firms': www.fca.org.uk/about/ the-fca.

[5] See the list of regulators provided by the Bank for International Settlements: https://www.bis.org/ regauth.htm.

Table 5.1 The network of regulation and agencies involved in the detection, prevention and investigation of financial crime in the US.

US statutes and regulations

Section 32(a) of the Securities Exchange Act of 1934 (Exchange Act).
Section 24 of the Securities Act of 1933 (Securities Act).
Sarbanes–Oxley Act of 2002.
Mail and wire fraud statutes (18 U.S.C. §§ 1341, 1343).
Misapplication and embezzlement statute (18 U.S.C. § 656).
Criminal False Claims Act (18 U.S.C. § 287).
Internal Revenue Code (§§ 7201, 7206(1)).
Computer Fraud and Abuse Act (18 U.S.C. § 1030(a)(4)).
False Statements Statute (18 U.S.C. § 1001).
Major Fraud Act (18 U.S.C. § 1031).

Provisions that impose civil liability for fraud

Civil False Claims Act (31 U.S.C. §§ 3729-3733).
Sections 11, 12(a), and 17(a) of the Securities Act.
Sections 9, 10(b), 14, 16(b), and 18 of the Exchange Act.
Securities and Exchange Commission (SEC) Rules 10b-5 and 14a-9.
Commodity Futures Trading Commission (CFTC) Rule 180.1.
Financial Institutions Reform, Recovery, and Enforcement Act of 1989.

US agencies involved in the detection, prevention and investigation of financial crime

Department of Justice (DOJ), including the US Attorney's Office in each federal district and the Federal Bureau of Investigation (FBI).
Securities and Exchange Commission (SEC).
Commodity Futures Trading Commission (CFTC).
Non-governmental self-regulatory organisations (SROs) such as the Financial Industry Regulatory Authority (FINRA).
US Department of the Treasury, including the Internal Revenue Service (IRS).
Federal Trade Commission (FTC).

Source: Based on data from Zornow et al. (2017). Note also those regulations that exist within the European Union including Regulation (EU) No 596/2014 of the European Parliament and of the Council of 16 April 2014 on market abuse (market abuse regulation) and repealing Directive 2003/6/EC of the European Parliament and of the Council and Commission Directives 2003/124/EC, 2003/125/EC and 2004/72/EC, as well as specific national directives. Also, see the Council on Foreign Relations discussion on the US regulatory system: https://www.cfr.org/backgrounder/us-financial-regulatory-system and Cumming, Dai and Johan (2018) on the impact of markets of the implementation of the Dodd–Frank Act.

forward in ways that benefit economies and societies around the world (UN Global Compact, 2013 and 2015).

Better and more strict enforcement of law aimed at preventing financial market abuse has been shown to generate significant economic benefits as well as receiving widespread and popular support (Ernst and Young, 2018). For example, Bhattacharya and Daouk (2002) report reductions in the cost of equity capital due to the significant increase in worldwide restrictions on insider trading that began in the 1990s, while Aitken et al. (2015b) show that more detailed exchange trading rules and surveillance over time and across markets significantly reduces the number of suspected cases of insider trading. Overall, preventing market abuse encourages investment, both domestically and internationally, and thereby assists long-term economic growth and wealth creation.

What is novel now is the widespread use of technology, as well as the types of trading that expand the range of criminal possibilities. Recent attention has been directed to high frequency and algorithmic trading (see Coombs, 2016), which may provide benefits in the form of added liquidity and reduced-price dislocation (Aitken et al., 2015a), but also potential harms given that prices may be easily manipulated (Angel and McCabe 2013, Angel 2014, Angel et al., 2015 and Cooper at al. 2016). A recent example of the potential impact of high-frequency trading was the arrest and subsequent conviction of Navinder Sarao, a London-based day trader who used an automated trading program to manipulate the S&P 500 futures contracts on the Chicago Mercantile Exchange (CME) using techniques called spoofing and layering (see Stafford and Mackenzie, 2015). As noted by these authors, these trading techniques are difficult to distinguish from legitimate trading due to the role of algorithmic trading in many exchange-based markets, such as products trading on the CME.

It is worthy of mention that the pre-release of sensitive price information clearly has economic value and can be used by high-frequency traders and their trading systems to generate profits. Recently, Angel and McCabe (2018) considered the ethical issues associated with the recent practice by Thomson Reuters of selling the University of Michigan's Consumer Sentiment Index to computerized trading firms two seconds before releasing its data to its other paying clients. This practice remains legal, although clearly it provides a select group of market participants with an information advantage.

The scale and scope of financial crime is enormous and has significant impacts on the global economy as well as the lives of those involved. In a presentation to The World Economic Forum, Craig (2018) argued that financial crime proceeds (i.e. the amount of money from criminal activities being laundered through the financial system) totalled at least $2.4 trillion annually, While this figure represents a broad perspective of financial crime, the impact of financial misconduct, including market manipulation and insider trading, are economically significant and have now transcended simple zero-sum games typically associated with fraud where a gain for one is simply a loss for another.

While criminal losses may be allocated very broadly, these crimes are not victimless, with significant damage to the social and regulatory fabric as well as to market reputation. The effective collapse of the international short-term lending market associated with the London Interbank Offer Rate (LIBOR) scandal is one such recent example, with the Wheatley Review estimating LIBOR price manipulation affected a financial market whose contracts range in value from US$202 to US$333 trillion.[6]

Detection of market manipulation and insider trading is possible in exchange-traded funds, such as stock markets, using sophisticated search algorithms that target anomalous trading as well as patterns of trading (Hawke, 2016; Ehret, 2017). This more detailed analysis has moved beyond earlier analyses of accounting data for detecting manipulation and assessing the reliability of accounting earnings (Beneish, 1999; Dechow et al., 2011) to actual trading data, termed high-frequency data. Identifying such distortions in over-the-counter (OTC) markets is more difficult, since price, trade, and volume information at such a high-frequency is not readily available given that it is not occurring on a single exchange. As noted by the International Compliance Society,

> 'Due to the often complex nature of financial services, detecting and preventing fraud within the financial sector poses an almost insurmountable challenge. The threats are both domestic and international. They may come from within the organisation or outside it. Increasingly, internal and external fraudsters combine to commit significant fraudulent acts'.[7]

Thus, identification of key aspects of financial crime has shifted to incentivizing whistle-blowers (see Culiberg and Mihelič, 2016), which provides 'enhanced protection and financial rewards'.[8] For example, under the Dodd–Frank whistle-blower programme there are bounty provisions, which provide monetary rewards of between 10 and 30% of any cash collected if the information provided leads to a successful enforcement action and monetary penalties exceeding $1 million. These incentives have had considerable success. For example, Lee (2017) notes that since financial incentives have been offered to whistleblowers, the probability of accounting fraud was reduced by 7% between 2001 and 2010. Nonetheless, the rewards to whistleblowers, often those involved in the original crime but who have received immunity from prosecution for their testimony, has attracted criticism (Rapp, 2007; Rapp, 2012). To put these payments in perspective, the US SEC awarded more than $111 million to 34 whistleblowers in 2016. (SEC, 2017: 1).

The OECD (2018) has also recently highlighted the importance of the media and investigative journalism in combating financial crime. This owes much to the success of the Panama Papers investigation, by the International Consortium of Investigative Journalists (ICIJ) into tax evasion and bribery.[9]

---

[6] See Wheatley Report Table C1 (2012).

[7] ICA: https://www.int-comp.org/careers/a-career-in-financial-crime-prevention/what-is-financial-crime/.

[8] The Dodd-Frank Wall Street Reform and Consumer Protection Act of 2010 amended the Securities Exchange Act of 1934 (Exchange Act) by adopting Section 21F, entitled 'Securities Whistleblower Incentives and Protection.'

[9] https://panamapapers.icij.org/graphs/ and the ICIJ, Paradise Papers: Secrets of the Global Elite, www.icij .org/investigations/paradise-papers/.

Dealing with financial crime, broadly defined, is an important component of a corporation's risk management strategy and several authors have identified the importance of improving internal process. Key regulators, such as the SEC also highlight the importance of improving process in firms. As noted by Hawke (2016),

> 'The high percentage of cases that ultimately settle, and low recidivism rates, insider trading enforcement is also among the most visible of the (SEC) Division's programs. It should come as no surprise that the SEC seeks to optimize the technology that it uses to conduct investigations and to rethink and reinvent the methods, tactics, and strategies that it uses to identify and investigate suspicious trading activity. Given the reputational risk associated with even being investigated for insider trading, traders and compliance professionals should seek to better understand the SEC's 'trader-based approach' to insider trading enforcement'.

The 'trader-based' approach, refers to the examination of microstructure trading data to identify patterns between and among individual and institutional traders.

Overall, while the identification and successful prosecution of these crimes remains important with considerable regulatory effort and expense directed to this purpose, much more needs to be undertaken to prevent these crimes from occurring. That is, it is not just a national, industry, or firm-based problem, but also one that must be effected at the individual level. Others, including Batten, Lončarski and Szilagyi (2017) in their discussion of the LIBOR scandal, argue that greater attention should be paid to the role of the individual and the importance of instilling and promoting individual ethical principles and standards as well as more effective compliance at the organization level. These themes are discussed in the final section on the management of risks.

5.2   Regulatory Framework on Insider Trading and Market Manipulation

Goshen and Parchomovsky (2006) note that as custodians and intermediators of the nation's savings, financial market participants – both individuals and corporations – are subject to regulatory scrutiny, which falls into three broad categories: (i) disclosure duties, which reduce the costs of gathering information; (ii) restrictions on fraud and manipulation, which lower the costs of verifying information; and (iii) restrictions on insider trading that would undermine the investment made in gathering and verifying information. A taxonomy of market manipulation techniques is provided in the surveys by Putniņš (2012) and by Pirrong (2017), while Cumming Johan and Peter (2018) review the recent literature on financial market institutions, governance, agency costs, and financial market misconduct.

In an economic sense, price manipulation artificially leads to an erroneous equilibrium that in turn may trigger adjustments to demand and supply. However, insider trading pre-empts the price adjustment process that occurs in response to new information, thereby allowing an abnormal profit to be made by the insider. Profit taking by the insider relies upon the broader market eventually adjusting their prices to reflect the new information once it is known publicly. Nonetheless, in most jurisdictions it is not essential for successful prosecution for the insider to profit from these trades, since the initial act of trading signals intent to use the private information. With market manipulation, it is not intended to extract an economic rent from private information, but instead, to force the price to be above or below the correct market equilibrium. As will be discussed later on, given the scale and scope of some financial markets, successfully changing the price from its true equilibrium invariably involves collusion between some, but not necessarily all, market participants.

There may be subtle differences in the application of law associated with insider trading and market manipulation, although the types of acts considered are similar. For example, Table 5.2 lists a series of white-collar crimes investigated by the Federal Bureau of Investigation (FBI) in the US including the falsification of financial information, self-dealing by corporate insiders, kickbacks, and fraud. Some examples of these crimes are also provided. The FCA and European Commission regulation EU596/2014 on market abuse considers the following examples of insider trading and market manipulation and clarify by example aspects of the FBI list:[10]

a. Insider trading occurs when prior to the official publication of certain price sensitive information, a trader learns from an insider the nature of the information and takes a position (possibly leveraged through futures or options) expecting to profit when the information is released. These positions may involve either buying or selling an asset.

b. Front running/pre-positioning involves taking an advantage of an expected price movement associated with a client order that the agent buys or sells beforehand. A detailed discussion of this activity in the Indian stock markets is provided by Chaturvedula et al. (2015).

c. In the context of a takeover, an offeror or potential offeror taking a bet on financial contract, such as an option that should increase or decrease in value once news of the takeover is made public.

d. Price squeezes occur regularly in markets due to demand and supply shocks. However, as the FCA notes, 'Market tightness, is not of itself likely to be abusive . . . In addition, having a significant influence over the demand and supply of an asset is not in itself abusive.'[11] What is important is intention and whether the parties act to mitigate the consequences of their positions. One of the most famous market squeezes involved the Hunt brothers' cornering of the silver market, which involved stockpiling up to two thirds of the world's silver inventory. Nonetheless as Christopher (2016) points out, the case highlights the difficulty in distinguishing market manipulation from normal market trading.

What are the characteristics of those people charged with insider trading? In an early empirical study investigating the characteristics of 452 persons successfully prosecuted for insider trading in the US, Szockyj and Geis (2002) differentiated between insiders charged with civil versus criminal offences. First, there were more civil than criminal prosecutions partly due to the difficulty in establishing, as required in criminal prosecutions, that the offender, beyond reasonable doubt, knowingly and

---

[10] https://www.handbook.fca.org.uk/handbook/MAR/1/3.html: MAR 1.3.2G03/07/2016
[11] https://www.handbook.fca.org.uk/handbook/MAR/1/6.html

Table 5.2 Examples of white-collar crime investigated by the U.S. Federal Bureau of Investigation.

1. Falsification of financial information

- False accounting entries and/or misrepresentations of financial condition

  The examples include:

  - Enron (2001), where executives misrepresented earnings and balance sheet items in order to boost performance.[12]
  - Worldcom (2002), where executives recorded expenses as investments and inflated profits (instead of showing the net loss).[13]

- Fraudulent trades designed to inflate profits or hide losses

  The examples include:

  - Guinness (1986), where 'the Guinness Four' manipulated the Guinness stock price on London Stock Exchange in order to facilitate the takeover of a larger drinks firm Distillers.[14]
  - Lehman Brothers (2008), where executives used the repurchase agreements with the non-independent party to misrepresent the company's net leverage position.[15]

- Illicit transactions designed to evade regulatory oversight

  The examples include:

  - Deutsche Bank (2015), where employees were involved in the so-called mirror trading schemes in which the same entity sells and buys the same asset using companies at different locations, thus evading taxes by moving asset to offshore centres.[16]
  - UBS (2007 onward), where the bank systematically assisted nationals of many countries to evade taxes.[17]

2. Self-dealing by corporate insiders

- Insider trading (trading based on material, non-public information)

  The examples include:

  - Drexel Burnham Lambert (1986), a case that saw Dennis B. Levine, a banker at DBL, Ivan F. Boesky, a client of DBL, as well as Michael Milken, charged and convicted on several counts of insider trading and financial fraud.[18]
  - Martha Stewart (2001), an US household 'brand' and personality, was found guilty of the abuse and profiting of insider information related to biotech company ImClone.[19]

---

[12] www.theguardian.com/business/2006/jul/06/corporatefraud.enron

[13] www.theguardian.com/business/2002/aug/09/corporatefraud.worldcom2

[14] www.nytimes.com/1987/01/15/business/guinness-ousts-head-in-scandal.html

[15] https://dealbook.nytimes.com/2010/03/12/the-british-origins-of-lehmans-accounting-gimmick

[16] www.ft.com/content/5bc8008a-e722-11e6-967b-c88452263daf

[17] www.ft.com/content/fd4608f6-1b5e-11e7-a266-12672483791a

[18] www.nytimes.com/1990/02/14/business/the-collapse-of-drexel-burnham-lambert-key-events-for-drexel-burnham-lambert.html

[19] https://money.cnn.com/2018/05/31/news/companies/trump-martha-stewart-pardon/index.html

Table 5.2   (Continued)

- ■ Raj Rajaratnam (2011), once considered as one of the Wall Street's savviest investors according to New York Times, was charged of insider trading for swapping inside stock tips with corporate insiders and other traders.[20]

- Kickbacks

  The examples include:

  - ■ Amaya CEO (2016), where David Baazov and some other insiders were paid kickbacks in various forms in exchange for privileged insiders' information.[21]

- Misuse of corporate property for personal gain

  The examples include:

  - ■ Polly Peck (1990), where Asil Nadir was found guilty of stealing from the company, which went bankrupt in light of heavy indebtedness.[22]
  - ■ Tyco (2002), where the two executives embezzled funds and misrepresented the company's profits.[23]

- Individual tax violations related to self-dealing[24]

3. Fraud in connection with an otherwise legitimately operated mutual hedge fund

- Late trading
- Certain market timing schemes

  The most famous examples include:

  - ■ The mutual funds scandal (2003), where the New York attorney general Eliot Spitzer charged four mutual fund companies, a New Jersey hedge fund and several other fund and bank entities of illicit practice of late trading and market timing at the expense of fund investors.[25]

- Falsification of net asset values[26]

Source: https://www.fbi.gov/investigate/white-collar-crime

wilfully violated the law. Second, the median trading profit was also lower for civil versus criminal prosecutions (median of US$25,800 versus US$50,000). And third, not surprisingly, securities professionals were the group mostly likely to be charged with criminal offences, whereas the civil offenders where mostly business associates, colleagues, and family members. Finally, insider traders were mostly male, and were corporate officers and directors, and as Szockyj and Geis (2002) noted had 'considerable investment in their public persona'.

---

[20] https://dealbook.nytimes.com/2011/05/11/rajaratnam-found-guilty/

[21] www.theglobeandmail.com/report-on-business/former-amaya-ceo-was-involved-in-complex-kickback-scheme-watchdog-says/article31761550/

[22] www.bbc.com/news/uk-19161940

[23] http://edition.cnn.com/2002/BUSINESS/asia/09/12/us.tyco/

[24] https://www.irs.gov/pub/irs-tege/eotopicq85.pdf

[25] https://money.cnn.com/magazines/fortune/fortune_archive/2003/11/24/353794/index.htm

[26] https://www.sec.gov/fast-answers/answersnavhtm.html

Given the low average payoff to insider trading, it seems puzzling that those with a significant investment in their 'public persona' would risk the social backlash from a conviction for insider trading. A famous case that illustrates this point is when Martha Stewart, who created a multibillion homewares empire, was accused of 'insider trading after she sold four thousand ImClone shares one day before that firm's stock price plummeted'.[27] The subsequent scandal caused the share price of Martha Stewarts publicly listed firm Omnimedia to 'fall more than 70 percent...and washed away more than a quarter of her net worth. Before the scandal, Stewart had an estimated net worth of $650 million.'[28]

In a more recent study Kallunki et al. (2018) show that insiders' willingness to engage in informed insider trading is a function of wealth and income, although it differs for those selling versus those buying stocks. Kallunki et al. (2018) conclude that this asymmetric finding is consistent with 'reputational and legal risk associated with being detected for trading on private information is significantly higher for insider sales, compared to purchases'.

Market manipulation relies on interpretation by the courts in deciding whether a transaction is abusive or not, whereas acting on the information of an insider is more easily discerned, given the sequential trail of the insider's actions. In financial markets where trading occurs electronically, an insider trading can be identified through a forensic examination of the trading record. For example, the purchase by the insider of an option should cause the price to move in a manner that is inconsistent with other news in the market. This transaction could signal the entry of an insider to the market with further investigation by the regulator on the potential relationships between the various stakeholders (e.g. between the trader and corporate stakeholders with access to private information, including corporate officers and board members).

To better understand the processes involved in market manipulation, Ledgerwood and Carpenter (2012) decomposed the process into three stages: (i) The cause or the trigger: The price-making trades used to provide false information into the market about the value of the asset traded and the subsequent directional price movement; (ii) The effect or the target: The price-taking positions held by the trader that benefits from the directional price movement caused by the trigger; and (iii) the 'nexus' or the linkage between the trigger and target – in this case, the price that is directionally moved to execute the price-based manipulation.

Their point is that uneconomic bids and offers constitute transactional fraud, and clearly differ from outright fraud (for example, simply stealing the proceeds of an asset sale), or the creation of an artificial price, which is not manipulation of existing prices. By separating the analysis of manipulation into these three elements, Ledgerwood and Carpenter (2012) provide a framework to better understand the motives of a trader. For example, Batten, Lončarski and Szilagyi (2015) show that insiders made losing trades to cover their tracks to avoid unnecessary detection by regulators. That is the insider, or manipulator, is in effect making a cost-benefit decision based on the

---

potential profits versus the costs of achieving these benefits, including accounting for the costs of detection.

In response to the many technological challenges associated with monitoring these crimes and especially the impacts of internet-based attacks on financial agents and institutions,[29] Clayton (2018) explained how the US SEC has established a new Cyber Unit to address these various issues. This unit focuses its efforts on the following key areas:

1. Hacking to obtain material, non-public information and trading on that information.
2. Market manipulation schemes involving false information spread through electronic and social media.
3. Violations involving distributed ledger technology and initial coin offerings (ICOs).
4. Misconduct perpetrated using the dark web.
5. Intrusions into online retail brokerage accounts.
6. Cyber-related threats to trading platforms and other critical market infrastructure.[30]

5.3 Recent Examples of Market Manipulation and Insider Trading

There is a rich literature documenting the manipulation of prices in financial markets such as stock markets (e.g. Allen and Gale, 1992), including those where regulatory oversight might be compromised (see Chaturvedula et al. 2015). There are also several telling examples in the commodity (Pirrong, 2017) and precious metals markets, such as the previously mentioned manipulation of the silver price by the Hunt Brothers in the 1970s (see Pirrong, 1993 and 1995)). A more recent academic study of the gold and silver markets, however, shows no statistical evidence of price fixing (Batten, Lucey and Peat, 2016), despite subsequent regulatory penalties imposed on those involved. This serves to highlight the limitations of statistical techniques used to detect anomalous price trading.

The more recent study by Griffin and Shams (2018) investigated potential manipulation of the VIX volatility index, which is traded as options and futures on the Chicago Board Options Exchange (CBOE). This example highlights both the complexity of trading involved with potential price manipulation in modern financial markets (interconnected by derivatives as well as cash-based products), as well as the difficulty in its determination. The VIX is popularly known as the 'fear index' since it is based on the implied volatility, derived using a Black and Scholes (1973) option pricing model, of the Standard & Poor's 500 Stock Index (S&P 500 Index). If the index increases then market volatility is expected to rise, with the reverse also true. If one assumes that the other inputs to the option pricing model (time to maturity, interest rates, and moneyness) are constant, then the call and put prices will increase if volatility increases, or decrease if volatility decreases.

---

[29] See also www.pwc.com/financialcrime and financial crime in funds transfer systems: actions to counter an emerging international threat for a discussion of the cyber heist against the Bangladesh Central Bank.
[30] See www.sec.gov/news/press-release/2017-176 and discussion by Clayton (2018).

It is well known that around the time when option and futures contracts are settled, there may often be significant price movements in the underlying asset (e.g. Griffin and Shams, 2018). There is also an extensive literature highlighting the important information role that options provide to their underlying assets (e.g. Amin and Lee, 1997; Du and Fung, 2018). These information flows may be multidirectional and encompass a suite of cash based on derivative products, with the same or similar underlying basis. For example, Antonakakis at al. (2016) show that spot and futures stock volatility spillovers between the UK and US markets are bidirectional in nature and are affected by similar macroeconomic events. A more recent example is the study by Du, Fung and Loveland (2018) that shows that information contained in option trades prior to Federal Open Market Committee (FOMC) rate change announcements can predict bank stock returns. The authors conclude that the options markets can therefore act as a source of informed trading.

However, when exactly is informed trading manipulation? In the Griffin and Shams (2018) study, the authors show that at the settlement time of the VIX, volume spikes on S&P 500 Index (SPX) options occurred, but only in out-of-the-money options used to calculate the VIX. Thus, it appeared that traders were buying these options, not as informed traders, but to cause the settlement price of the VIX to be higher than would otherwise have been the case. Griffin and Shams (2018) investigated alternative explanations of hedging and coordinated liquidity trading but suggested the abnormal increases in volume were more consistent with market manipulation.

A recent list of important events (including prosecutions) on insider trading and manipulation in financial markets is provided in Table 5.3. There are two outstanding examples in the table. The first involves the announcement in 2015 by the U.S. Federal Reserve that it will impose fines totalling more than $1.8 billion against six major banking organizations for their 'unsafe and unsound practices in the foreign exchange (FX) markets'. The fines were for $342 million each for UBS

Table 5.3   List of recent events in financial markets linked to financial crime.

- 2017: April 10, Bank of England implicated in London Interbank Offered Rate (LIBOR) manipulation scandal.
- 2017: March Barclays CEO Jes Staley reprimanded by board for trying to uncover the identity of a whistle-blower.
- 2016: September, manipulation by Deutsche Bank AG of the silver price.
- 2015: May 20, the US Federal Reserve announces imposition of fines totalling more than $1.8 billion against six major banking organizations for their unsafe and unsound practices in the foreign exchange (FX) markets.
- 2015: Kamay and Hill charged for insider trading in the AUD–USD (the only insider trading case in over-the-counter (OTC) foreign exchange market).
- 2013: June, Bloomberg reports that major banks have been front running client orders and rigging the foreign exchange (FX) benchmark rates.
- 2012: Credit Suisse (amongst others) fined for helping customers avoid taxes.
- 2010: 'Flash Crash' of the Standard & Poor's 500 stock index.
- 2008: LIBOR scandal financial institutions were accused of fixing LIBOR.

Sources: Based on data from www.reuters.com/article/us-deutsche-bank-settlement-silver-idUSKBN12H2HB.

AG, Barclays Bank PLC, Citigroup Inc., and JPMorgan Chase & Co.; $274 million for Royal Bank of Scotland PLC (RBS); and $205 million for Bank of America Corporation. The total amount paid in fines by financial intermediaries involved in recent scandals was more than US$10 billion,[31] with a detailed timeline of events detailed in McGeever (2017).[32]

This scandal involved the prosecuted banks front running client orders in the lead-up to a key foreign exchange market rate fix on WM/Reuters. It had always been assumed that the size of the spot foreign exchange market, which trades US$5.3 trillion per day, according to the Bank for International Settlements (BIS) foreign exchange survey, would provide sufficient liquidity and prevent manipulation. However, as also noted by the BIS, this market is also highly concentrated with several dealers dominating global turnover. Thus, if these dealers colluded it would be easily possible – despite the market size – to force at least temporarily the spot exchange rate up or down to the desired level.

The second example, in terms of the scale of potential impacts, remains the most important example of recent financial market manipulation. This involved manipulation of the London Interbank Offered Rate (LIBOR) and the subsequent scandal that unfolded in financial markets after the Global Financial Crisis (GFC) from 2007 to 2009. As noted earlier, the Wheatley Report stated that the total value of financial contracts affected was more than US$300 trillion.[33]

LIBOR is the price used to set various floating rate financial contracts and loans and is set by the average of rates provided by a select group of banks and released to other market participants at 11 a.m. London time. Barclays Bank was fined for £59.5 million by the Financial Services Authority (FSA) in June 2012 for breaches under the Financial Services and Markets Act 2000, mostly between 2005 and 2009. Barclays was also fined for $360 million by various US authorities for tampering and false reporting of the EURIBOR and LIBOR during 2005 to 2009.

Numerous studies have subsequently investigated the actions of several banks to set the LIBOR rate including Kregel (2012) Vasudev and Guerrero (2014), Ashton and Christophers (2015) and Braml (2016). These authors note that the misreporting involved was of two types: first, for personal gain, since those involved received incentive-based compensation, and second for broader corporate interests, with the conduct encouraged by senior managers. The British Bankers Association (BBA) has historically managed the LIBOR setting process. However, in response to the LIBOR scandal the US Federal Reserve Bank of New York introduced new reference rates aimed at replacing LIBOR on financial contracts.[34] The regulatory response to the LIBOR scandal is explained in Janin and Stamegna (2016) and Yeoh (2016).

---

[31] Fines, exceeding US$6 billion, were levied on the various banks involved in the LIBOR and related foreign exchange scandals: www.abc.net.au/news/2015-05-21/us-britain-fine-top-banks-nearly-6-bn-for-forex-libor-abuses/6485510

[32] www.reuters.com/article/global-currencies-scandal/timeline-the-global-fx-rigging-scandal-idUSL5N1F14VV.

[33] See Appendix 1 Use of LIBOR in Financial Contracts from the Wheatley Report Table C1.

[34] See: www.newyorkfed.org/markets/opolicy/operating_policy_180403 and www.bba.org.uk/about-us/.

5.4 Conclusions

The International Compliance Association (ICA) highlights the importance of organization culture in preventing various forms of financial crime. They argue that 'correctly motivated, employees remain honest and become the most effective front-line defence against the fraudster'. Nonetheless, for a firm's employees to do so, they must believe that their institution is also honest and ethical, with all stakeholders being treated with respect and discipline and that achieving high ethical standards is a common objective within the organization.[35]

The previous examples of insider trading and market manipulation highlight the importance of greater transparency as well as corporate and individual accountability (Seyfert, 2016). They also demonstrate that compliance cannot simply replace a foundation in ethics in financial markets and in the corporation. It is noteworthy that while the examples provided may appear distinct, international concerns over regulatory arbitrage have meant that there has been a worldwide convergence of key national regulation, although the penalties may differ between countries. Thus, the examples provided are relevant to a broader audience beyond the national perspectives, or markets, in which they occurred.

One key feature of this discussion is that we distinguish between insider trading and market manipulation that has occurred in over-the-counter (OTC) financial markets, as well as exchange traded markets. Interest rate products such as bonds and bills, and foreign exchange spot and forward trading typically occurs in OTC markets. Derivative products, whose values depend upon market products traded in OTC markets, typically trade in exchange-traded markets, such as the various exchanges associated with the Chicago Mercantile Exchange (CME) Group. In addition, there is stock exchange trading in markets such as the New York Stock Exchange (NYSE) or the Nasdaq.

The specific examples discussed in this paper of market manipulation highlights the limits to national legislation making such schemes illegal. Historically, successful identification and prosecution of these illegal trading schemes has relied either on sophisticated market surveillance of trading behaviour, or the mandatory reporting by financial market participants or exchanges of suspicious activity. Despite some reported success of the deterring effect on crime of whistle-blowing legislation (e.g. Wilde, 2017), such oversight and surveillance and a reliance on self-reporting by industry has had mixed success worldwide. It is clear that individual responsibility and the encouragement of better moral and ethical standards cannot be ignored.

To provide additional insights into the processes and linkages between these various examples of market behaviour, we apply the framework of ethical behaviour described in Batten, Lončarski and Szilagyi (2017). While most corporate ethical codes reflect national regulation, with processes designed to enforce compliance to these rules, the Batten, Lončarski and Szilagyi interdependent model described above

---

[35] See: www.int-comp.org/careers/a-career-in-financial-crime-prevention/what-is-financial-crime/.

highlights the importance of a bottom-up approach to ensure ethical individual and organizational behaviour. This process allows a set of core ethical values to facilitate individual and corporate expression, beyond simple compliance.

We conclude that top-down, external approaches to preventing financial crimes such as insider trading and market manipulation cannot alone succeed. What is needed is more inclusive approach that enables the propagation of ethical behaviour, not only in terms of ethical (and legal) codes of conduct, but also in terms of embedding ethics in the culture of the individual and corporation. These perspectives support the position of Batten, Lončarski and Szilagyi that the legal, ethical and moral structures surrounding financial markets should be interdependent and inclusive, while still allowing for individual and corporate expression. This approach in effect sees ethical policy as being at the nexus of individual and national–international guidance.

References

Aitken, M., Cumming, D. and Zhan, F. (2015a). High frequency trading and end-of-day price dislocation. *Journal of Banking & Finance* 59: 330–349.

Aitken, M., Cumming, D. and Zhan, F. (2015b). Exchange trading rules, surveillance and suspected insider trading. *Journal of Corporate Finance* 34: 311–330.

Allen, F. and Gale, D. (1992). Stock-price manipulation. *The Review of Financial Studies* 5(3): 503–529.

Amin, K.I. and Lee, C.M.C. (1997). Option trading, price discovery, and earnings news dissemination. *Contemporary Accounting Research* 14 (2): 153–192.

Angel, J.J. (2014). When finance meets physics: The impact of the speed of light on financial markets and their regulation. *Financial Review* 49: 271–281.

Angel, J.J., Harris, L. and Spatt, C. (2015). Equity trading in the 21st century: An update. *Quarterly Journal of Finance* 5(1): 1–39.

Angel, J.J. and McCabe, D. (2013). Fairness in financial markets: The case of high frequency trading. *Journal of Business Ethics* 112(4): 585–595.

Angel, J.J. and McCabe, D.M. (2018) Insider trading 2.0? The ethics of information sales. *Journal of Business Ethics* 147(4): 747–760.

Antonakakis, N., Floros, C. and Kizys, R. (2016). Dynamic spillover effects in futures markets: UK and US evidence. *International Review of Financial Analysis* 48: 406–418.

Ashton, P. and Christophers, B. (2015). On arbitration, arbitrage and arbitrariness in financial markets and their governance: Unpacking LIBOR and the LIBOR scandal. *Economy and Society* 44(2): 188–217.

Bhattacharya, U. and Daouk, H. (2002). The world price of insider trading. *Journal of Finance* 57(1) (Feb.): 75–108.

Batten, J.A., Lončarski, I. and Szilagyi, PG. (2017). Financial market Manipulation, whistleblowing and the common good: Evidence from the LIBOR scandal (May 8, 2017). Available at SSRN: https://ssrn.com/abstract=2964917 or http://dx.doi.org/10.2139/ssrn.2964917.

Batten, J.A., Lončarski, I. and Szilagyi, P.G. (2015). When do insiders trade? Opportunistic versus strategic behaviour (May 23, 2015). Available at SSRN: https://ssrn.com/abstract=2653576 or http://dx.doi.org/10.2139/ssrn.2653576.

Batten, J.A., Lucey, B.M. and Peat, M. (2016). Gold and silver manipulation: What can be empirically verified? *Economic Modelling* 56: 168–176.

Beneish, M.D. (1999). The Detection of Earnings Manipulation. *Financial Analysts Journal* 55(5): 24–36.

Black, F. and Scholes, M. (1973) The pricing of options and corporate liabilities. *Journal of Political Economy* 81 (3): 637–657.

Braml, H. (2016). The manipulation of LIBOR and related interest rates. *Studies in Economics and Finance* 33(1): 106–125.

Chaturvedula, C., Bang, N.P., Rastogi, N. and Kumar, S. (2015). Price manipulation, front running and bulk trades: Evidence from India. *Emerging Markets Review* 23: 26–45.

Christopher, B. (2016). How the Hunt Brothers cornered the silver market and then lost it all. Published Aug 4, 2016: https://priceonomics.com/how-the-hunt-brothers-cornered-the-silver-market/.

Clayton, J. (2018). Testimony before the Financial Services and General Government Subcommittee of the Senate Committee on Appropriations. June 5, 2018. U.S. Securities and Exchange Commission: www.sec.gov/news/testimony/testimony-financial-services-and-general-government-subcommittee-senate-committee.

Coombs, N. (2016). What is an algorithm? Financial regulation in the era of high-frequency trading. *Economy and Society* 45(2): 278–302.

Cooper, R., Davis, M. and Van Vliet, B. (2016). The mysterious ethics of high-frequency trading. *Business Ethics Quarterly* 26(1): 1–22.

Craig, D. (2018). Why we need to talk about financial crime. World Economic Forum, January. www.weforum.org/agenda/2018/01/we-need-to-talk-about-financial-crime/.

Culiberg, B. and Mihelič, K.K. (2016). The evolution of whistleblowing studies: A critical review and research agenda. *Journal of Business Ethics*: 1–17.

Cumming, D., Dai, N. and Johan, S. (2018). Dodd-Franking the hedge funds. *Journal of Banking & Finance*: https://doi.org/10.1016/j.jbankfin.2017.09.012.

Cumming, D., Johan, S. and Peter, R. (2018). Developments in financial institutions, governance, agency costs, and misconduct. *Journal of International Financial Markets, Institutions and Money*, 54: 1–14.

Dechow, P.M., Ge, W., Larson, C.R. and Sloan, G. (2011). Predicting material accounting misstatements. *Contemporary Accounting Research* 28(1): 17–82.

Du, B. and Fung, S. (2018). Directional information effects of options trading: Evidence from the banking industry. *Journal of International Financial Markets, Institutions and Money* 56: 149–168.

Du, B., Fung, S. and Loveland, R. (2018). The informational role of options markets: Evidence from FOMC announcements. *Journal of Banking and Finance* 92: 237–256.

Ehret, T. (2017). SEC's advanced data analytics helps detect even the smallest illicit market activity, *Reuters: July* 1, 2017: www.reuters.com/article/bc-finreg-data-analytics-idUSKBN19L28C.

Ernst and Young (2018). Integrity in the spotlight – The future of compliance: 15th Global Fraud Survey: www.ey.com/Publication/vwLUAssets/EY_Global_Fraud_Survey_2018_report/$FILE/EY%20GLOBAL%20FIDS%20FRAUD%20SURVEY%202018.pdf.

Goshen, Z. and Parchomovsky, G. (2006). The Essential Role of Securities Regulation. *Duke Law Journal* 55(4): 711–782.

Griffin, J.M. and Shams, A. (2018). Manipulation in the VIX? *Review of Financial Studies* 31(4):1377–1417.

Hawke, D. (2016). The SEC's 'Trader-Based' Approach to Insider Trading Enforcement. September 13, 2016: www.arnoldporter.com/en/perspectives/publications/2016/09/the-secs-trader-based-approach-to-insider.

Janin, S. and Stamegna, C. (2016). Regulating global finance: The EU benchmarks regulation as a 'benchmark'? a political reading? *Law and Economics Yearly Review*: 58–81.

Kallunki, J., Kallunki, J-P., Nilsson, H. and Puhakka, M. (2018). Do an insider's wealth and income matter in the decision to engage in insider trading? *Journal of Financial Economics* 130(1): 135–165.

Kregel, J. (2012). The Libor Scandal: The fix is in-the Bank of England did it. Levy Economics Institute of Bard College. Policy Note 2012/9. ISSN 2166-028X.

Ledgerwood, S.D. and Carpenter P.R. (2012.) A framework for the analysis of market manipulation. *Review of Law and Economics* 8(1): 253–295.

Lee, H. (2017). Does the threat of whistleblowing reduce accounting fraud? (October 25, 2017). Available at SSRN: https://ssrn.com/abstract=3059231.

OECD (2018) The role of the media and investigative journalism in combating corruption: www.oecd.org/corruption/The-role-of-media-and-investigative-journalism-in-combating-corruption.htm.

McGeever, J. (2017). The global FX rigging scandal. Reuters: January 12, 4:07am. https://www.reuters.com/article/global-currencies-scandal/timeline-the-global-fx-rigging-scandal-idUSL5N1F14VV.

Pirrong, S.C. (1993). Manipulation of the commodity futures market delivery process. *Journal of Business* 66: 335–370.

Pirrong, S.C. (1995). Mixed manipulation strategies in commodity futures markets. *Journal of Futures Markets* 15(1): 13–39.

Pirrong, C. (2017). The economics of commodity market manipulation: A survey. *Journal of Commodity Markets* 5: 1–17.

Putniņš, T.J. (2012). Market manipulation: A survey. *Journal of Economic Surveys* 26(5): 952–967.

Rapp, G.C. (2007). Beyond protection: Invigorating incentives for Sarbanes–Oxley corporate and securities fraud whistleblowers. *Boston University Law Review* 87: 92–156.

Rapp, G.C. (2012). States of pay: Emerging trends in state whistleblower bounty schemes. *South Texas Law Review* 54: 53–79.

(SEC) Securities and Exchange Commission (2017) 2016 annual report to congress on the Dodd–Frank Whistleblower Program: www.sec.gov/files/owb-annual-report-2016.pdf.

Seyfert, R. (2016). Bugs, predations or manipulations? Incompatible epistemic regimes of high-frequency trading. *Economy and Society* 45(2): 251–277.

Stafford, P. and Mackenzie, M. (2015). Flash crash: Trading terms and manipulation techniques explained. *The Financial Times* (April 22, 2015): www.ft.com/content/a1114d60-e8d0-11e4-87fe-00144feab7de.

Szockyj, E. and Geis, G. (2002). Insider trading patterns and analysis. *Journal of Criminal Justice* 30(4): 273–286.

UN Global Compact (2013). Architects of a better world: Building the post-2015 business engagement architecture. New York: United Nations Global Compact.

UN Global Compact (2015). www.unglobalcompact.org.

Vasudev, P.M. and Guerrero, D.R. (2014). Corporate governance in banks – A view through the LIBOR lens. *Journal of Banking Regulation* 15(3): 325–336.

Wheatley, M. (2012). The Wheatley Review of LIBOR: Final Report (September). HM Treasury, London. URL: https://www.gov.uk/government/publications/the-wheatley-review.

Wilde, J.H. (2017). The deterrent effect of employee whistleblowing on firms' financial misreporting and tax aggressiveness. *The Accounting Review* 92(5): 247–280.

Yeoh, P. (2016). Libor benchmark: Practice, crime and reforms. *Journal of Financial Crime* 23(4): 1140–1153.

Zornow, D.M., Strauber, J.E. and Merzel, D. (2017). Financial Crime in the Unites States: Overview. Skadden, Arps, Slate, Meagher & Flom LLP. March 1, 2017.

Chapter 6

Financial Fraud and Reputational Capital

Jonathan M. Karpoff*
University of Washington

> 'I predict that in the years ahead Enron, not Sept. 11, will come to be seen as the greater turning point in U.S. society.'
>   – Paul Krugman, 'The Great Divide,' *The New York Times*, January 29, 2002.

---

* Much of this chapter, particularly in sections 6.2–6.5, is from Section 4 of Amiram et al. (2018) (Reprinted/ adapted by permission from Springer Nature, *Review of Accounting Studies*, 'Financial reporting fraud and other forms of misconduct: a multidisciplinary review of the literature,' Amiram et al., 2018.) I thank Carol Alexander, Douglas Cumming, and Quentin Dupont for helpful discussions and comments.

6.1   Financial Frauds in the 2000s

Paul Krugman's prediction may have seemed overblown at the time, and certainly seems so now. But it highlights a shift in popular awareness of financial fraud that persists to this day. Many frauds are splashy – e.g. HealthSouth Inc.'s CEO and CFOs made up $1.4 billion in reported earnings from 1996 to 2002, and in 2005, Tyco's CEO and CFO were convicted of stealing $600 million from the company. But few frauds were as deep-rooted, pervasive, and impactful as Enron's. Enron's fraud included both complex financial manoeuvring (e.g. hiding its debt via 'special purpose entities') and simple fabrication of numbers (e.g. its valuation of a failed venture with Block-buster). It toppled the 'It' company of the turn of the century. Within six short weeks of declaring a financial restatement on 16 October 2001, Enron – a company that had oozed wealth, smarts, and power – declared bankruptcy. Thousands of employees lost both their jobs and retirement savings. The scandal shook many peoples' trust in the economy and fed a popular cynicism toward business that permeates many aspects of our politics and culture. Combined with news of WorldCom's financial scandal in June 2002, Enron also set the political stage for the Sarbanes–Oxley Act of 2002, the most sweeping set of new business regulations in the United States since the 1930s.

Financial frauds continue to dominate news headlines. In March 2018, Theranos' founder Elizabeth Holmes was charged with 'massive fraud' involving misleading reports to investors about the company's technology, operations, and cash flows. In April 2018, Wells Fargo was fined $1 billion for misleading practices that affected millions of its customers. The financial press now runs frequent articles describing frauds and Ponzi schemes involving cryptocurrencies.

Frauds are newsworthy, partly because everyone likes a good crime story. Frauds unjustly enrich some people and harm many others, so a fraudster's comeuppance makes a good story. But financial fraud is newsworthy and an important public policy concern for a more fundamental reason: it undermines investors' trust. As Dupont and Karpoff (2020) argue, some level of trust is required for all economic exchange and financial transactions. Without some degree of trust, investors are unwilling to participate in financial markets (e.g. see Giannetti and Wang 2016). Without trust, large-scale enterprise via the corporate form would break down, as investors would be unwilling to invest in activities over which managers have day-to-day control (Mayer 2008). In theoretical models, economists have long realized the importance of trust as a foundation for contracting, exchange, and production.[1] But only recently have researchers begun to explore empirically how trust is formed and the consequences when trust is violated. In this chapter I explore and summarize one important area of this empirical research – the role of reputational capital.

---

[1] For example, Klein and Leffler (1981) and Shapiro (1983) develop models in which reputation – and reputation alone – encourages good behaviour and disciplines bad behaviour. In these models, individuals or firms develop reputations for honest dealing. Good reputations are valuable because they yield favourable terms of contract with customers, employees, suppliers, and investors. As a consequence, firms can invest in reputation, just as they might invest in machinery, R&D, or human capital.

Merriam-webster.com defines 'reputation' as one's 'overall quality or character as seen or judged by people in general.' In the finance literature, however, the term has acquired a more specific meaning. In particular, *reputational capital* is the present value of the improvement in net cash flow and lower cost of capital that arises when the firm's counterparties trust that the firm will uphold its explicit and implicit contracts, and will not act opportunistically to their counterparties' detriment. Viewed this way, reputation is a capital asset that a person or firm can invest in and build. The value of a firm's reputational capital is the present value of the surpluses earned when the firm's counterparties believe that it will uphold its end of its explicit and implicit contracts, i.e. that it will not act opportunistically to the detriment of its counterparties.

This definition of reputation and reputational capital yields powerful insights into the forces that encourage honest dealing and build trust (e.g. see Dupont and Karpoff 2020). A challenge for empirical research – to examine how and when reputation is built, and how and when it builds trust and disciplines misconduct – is that it is difficult to measure a firm's reputational capital. Reputational capital can account for a large portion of a firm's value, but it is not booked on the firm's financial statements and is conceptually difficult to separate from the firm's cash flows in general.[2] This is where research on financial misconduct yields another benefit. Financial fraud allows researchers to finesse the measurement problem by examining the counterexamples in which trust is broken and the value of a firm's reputational capital changes, that is, when firms and managers lie, cheat, and steal. Just like physicists can infer the importance and influence of dark matter by examining its effects, financial researchers can infer the importance and influence of reputational capital by examining instances in which it changes, e.g. when fraud is revealed. This approach does not yield direct measures of a firm's reputational capital, but it allows us to infer whether, where, and to what extent reputation works to build trust by enforcing explicit and implicit contracts.

As a brief illustration, consider the Enron scandal again. Enron's fraud highlights a monumental failure of the system of checks and balances on managers' activities that encourage investors to trust that their hard-earned dollars will be invested carefully. But Enron's fraud illustrates not only how the system broke down, but also, how it worked. No one can justify Enron's executives' greed and mendacity. But once investors, customers, and suppliers found out about the fraud, they rapidly changed their willingness to do business with the firm. Enron had many legitimate businesses and

---

[2] These measurement problems have not stopped researchers from trying to measure the stock of a firm's reputational capital, variously using surveys (e.g. Pevzner, Xie, and Xin 2015; Bargeron, Lehn, and Smith 2015), CSR-based rankings (Deng, Kang, and Low 2013), or firms' written materials (e.g. Guiso, Sapienza, and Zingales 2015). As Dupont and Karpoff (2020) discuss, researchers recently have constructed insightful measures of firm culture that also are plausibly related to reputational capital. These measures use information on managers' personal backgrounds, behaviour, and values (e.g. Cline, Walkling, and Yore 2018), an area's or individual's religion (e.g. Stulz and Williamson 2003), geographic commonalities (e.g. Parsons, Sulaeman, and Titman 2018), political affiliations (e.g. Hutton, Jiang, and Kumar 2015), and networks (e.g., Khanna, Kim, and Lu 2015).

was not a complete house of cards. But once people found out that Enron's managers were willing to sacrifice the firm's reputation for short-term gain, even the firm's legitimate activities suffered. For example, some of Enron's counterparties were electric utilities. These utilities had contracted to purchase electricity and had to trust that Enron would hold up its end of its deals to deliver electricity when it promised. After the scandal broke, many former customers went elsewhere because they no longer trusted Enron. This – and not the financial misconduct in and of itself – is the main reason Enron's value dropped so quickly and the firm declared bankruptcy so quickly after it reported restated earnings in October 2001. Enron and its senior managers were the targets of long-running investigations and lawsuits by the US Securities and Exchange Commission (SEC), Department of Justice (DOJ), and shareholders. Its top executives faced criminal sanctions. But the most immediate and targeted impact on the firm was not through the legal system, but rather, through the market impacts on Enron's operations and value. Enron's counterparties are the ones who imposed the largest financial penalties on Enron for its fraud. Furthermore, they did this not out of any conscious effort to impose penalties on Enron. Rather, they stopped doing business with Enron to protect themselves because they no longer trusted Enron to hold up its end of their contracts.

Enron is but one example of a strong pattern that emerges from recent research on financial fraud. Most firms that are caught cooking the books do not go bankrupt like Enron did, but they do suffer large losses in reputational capital. These losses reflect decreases in these firms' future earnings and increases in their costs of capital. For financial misconduct, the reputational losses dwarf the penalties imposed by regulators and through private securities lawsuits. The consequences to culpable managers and directors are less direct, but the large majority of directly culpable managers lose their jobs and face serious personal consequences. In short, reputational capital plays a large and important role in disciplining financial misconduct. From this evidence, we can infer that reputation plays an equally important role in helping to build the trust that encourages investors to participate in the financial system.

Although reputational effects discipline financial frauds heavily, it is equally important to point out that reputational losses are not automatic and do not penalize all types of corporate misconduct. Some managers and firms seem to escape serious reputational consequences for financial misconduct. Reputational penalties for financial misconduct appear to be smaller for firms outside of the US (e.g. Armour, Mayer, and Polo 2017; Chen et al. 2016). Even within the US, evidence indicates that some types of misconduct do not trigger meaningful reputational penalties, including foreign bribery, environmental violations, and misconduct that most directly impacts third parties. The rest of this chapter presents this evidence and the economic forces behind it.

6.2   The Effects of Fraud Revelation on Firm Value and Reputational Capital

6.2.1   Market Value Losses When Financial Misconduct Is Revealed

Many papers report that share values decrease, on average, upon news that suggests the possibility of financial misconduct, including earnings restatements, securities-related lawsuits, and regulatory enforcement actions for financial misrepresentation.[3] The point estimates of the loss in share values, however, vary widely. On the high end, Karpoff, Lee, and Martin (2008a) report a one-day average abnormal return of -25.2% for firms subject to SEC and DOJ enforcement for financial misrepresentation, and Beneish (1999b) finds a total cumulative loss of over 20% during a three-day window around announcements of GAAP violations (SEC AAERs and news media revelations). Other samples yield smaller estimates of loss. For example, Gande and Lewis (2009) report an average three-day abnormal return of -4.7% for firms targeted in securities class-action lawsuits. Dechow, Sloan, and Sweeney (1996) find an average one-day abnormal stock return of -8.8% for firms subject to an SEC Accounting and Auditing Enforcement Release (AAER), and Burns and Kedia (2006) report an average three-day abnormal stock return of -8.8% for a sample of financial restatement announcements.

Below, I show that the wide variation in point estimates partly reflects the fact that different studies use different proxies and data sources to compile samples of financial misconduct. These samples also differ by the extent to which their events reflect relatively benign errors or more serious frauds. For example, Hennes, Leone, and Miller (2008) calculate that the average abnormal stock return for a subset of reporting errors in the GAO database is -1.93%, compared to -13.64% for a subset of restatements in the GAO database that represent more serious irregularities. Karpoff et al. (2017) show that the events in several popular databases that are associated with fraud charges, as brought by the SEC or DOJ, have much more negative average stock returns than the events unassociated with fraud charges.

6.2.2   Spillover Effects

The revelation of financial misconduct affects not only the target firm, but also its industry peer firms. Goldman, Peyer, and Stefanescu (2012) find that the spillover effect is negative, as the revelation of misconduct at one firm is associated with small decreases in the share values of its industry peer firms. Choi et al. (2018) find that such spillover effects occur only at the beginning of industry-specific waves of revelations of misconduct, and that they reflect the increased likelihood that the industry peer firms also will be discovered committing financial misconduct. In addition, Beatty, Liao, and Wu (2013) and Li (2016) find that the revelation of misconduct also has a spillover effect on peer firms' investment, R&D expenditure, advertising, and

---

[3] Studies that find share value losses associated with earnings restatements include those by Anderson and Yohn (2002); Hribar and Jenkins (2004); Palmrose, Richardson, and Scholz (2004); Agrawal and Chadha (2005); Akhigbe, Kudla, and Madura (2005); Burns and Kedia (2006); Desai, Hogan, and Wilkins (2006); Hennes, Leone, and Miller (2008); Kravet and Shevlin (2010); and Chava, Huang and Johnson (2017). For share price reactions to securities-related lawsuits, see Kellogg (1984); Bohn and Choi (1996); Francis, Philbrick, and Schipper (1994); Ferris and Pritchard (2001); Griffin, Grundfest, and Perino (2004); Romano (1991); Bhagat, Bizjak, and Coles (1998); and Gande and Lewis (2009). For share price reactions to regulatory enforcement actions for financial misconduct, see Feroz, Park, and Pastena (1991); Dechow, Sloan, and Sweeney (1996); Beneish (1999b); Ozbas (2007); Karpoff, Lee, and Martin (2008a); and Karpoff and Lou (2010). Some papers use news stories or key word searches to identify samples of financial misconduct, e.g., Karpoff and Lott (1993); Davidson, Worrell, and Lee (1994); Bernile and Jarrell (2009); and Tanimura and Okamoto (2010). See also Yu (2013) for a survey.

pricing policies. Thus, the revelation of misconduct appears to convey information about industry peer firms' likelihood of misconduct, and also to affect these peer firms' operating decisions.

6.2.3   Reputational Losses for Financial Misconduct

Despite heterogeneity in the samples and point estimates, nearly all the available evidence indicates that share values fall, on average, upon news of financial misconduct. In reasonably efficient markets, share prices reflect investors' expected values of future cash flows to equity, changing when expectations change. This implies that changes in share values upon the revelation of the firm's misconduct provide a measure of investors' expectations of the losses faced by the firm. The losses can include direct costs, such as regulatory fines, class-action settlements, and increased legal expenses. They also likely include a decline in share value as investors realize they had been relying on incorrect financial information to forecast the firm's future cash flows, that is, a reversal of the share price inflation attributable to the incorrect financials. The losses can also include lost reputation, that is, the loss in value if the firm faces a higher cost of capital, lower sales, or higher operating costs as the revelation of misconduct changes the terms by which counterparties are willing to do business with the firm.

Several papers have attempted to isolate the portion of the total loss in share values that is attributable to each of these types of penalties. In samples that include both financial and other types of misconduct, Karpoff and Lott (1993) and Alexander (1999) estimate that very little of firms' total losses in share values – as little as 7% – is attributable to direct costs such as fines and legal settlements, and that most of the loss in share values represents lost reputation. In a sample consisting only of financial statement misconduct, Karpoff, Lee, and Martin (2008a) estimate that 25% of the loss in share values represents the reversal of the artificial price inflation that accompanies such misconduct. Another 9% represents such direct costs as legal fines and penalties, and the remaining 66% represents lost reputational capital. Consistent with this view, Beneish (1999b) finds that only a small portion of firms' losses around the announcements of GAAP violations is attributable to settlement costs.

Information about financial misconduct and its consequences typically is conveyed to investors via a long sequence of events that can stretch out over multiple years. Karpoff, Lee, and Martin (2008a), for example, report that the average time from the initial announcement of financial misconduct in their sample to the last SEC enforcement activity related to the misconduct exceeds 50 months. It can therefore be challenging to identify the value impact of news of the misconduct and to partition this impact into direct costs and reputational losses.

Armour, Mayer, and Polo (2017) exploit a setting that addresses this concern. In the UK, enforcement activities for possible violations of financial regulation and listing rules undertaken by the Financial Services Authority (FSA) and the London Stock Exchange (LSE) involve only one public announcement. News about an investigation is announced only after misconduct has been established, and the announcement includes complete information on any legal penalties. Furthermore, private securities class-action lawsuits are virtually non-existent in the UK, so the sole announcement contains complete information about the firm's legal penalties. This setting facilitates a precise breakdown of the loss in share value from news of regulatory enforcement into the portion that represents legal penalties. Armour, Mayer, and Polo (2017) find relatively small total losses to firms when their misconduct is revealed (-1.68%). Still, they find that reputational losses average nine times the losses that are attributable to legal penalties.

Overall, the evidence indicates that firms can temporarily inflate their share values by misrepresenting their earnings and assets. When the misrepresentation is detected, however, firm value decreases by much more than the original share price inflation. Some of the additional decline is due to legal penalties and other direct costs when the misconduct is uncovered. But the largest decline is due to lost reputational capital.

6.2.4   Direct Measures of Lost Reputational Capital

The measures of reputational loss summarized above are estimates of the residual market value loss after tallying the other sources of lost value. A problem with this approach is that the other sources of loss may be poorly measured. Karpoff, Lee and Martin (2008a) report, for example, that different methods to measure the artificial share price inflation all generate large estimates of reputational loss, but the point estimates vary.

An alternative approach is to examine directly whether the revelation of financial misconduct is associated with an increase in firm costs or a decrease in firm revenues. Hribar and Jenkins (2004) and Kravet and Shevlin (2010), for example, find that the cost of equity capital increases for firms that misrepresent earnings, and Chava, et al. (2010) find that the cost of equity capital increases following a securities class-action lawsuit. Graham, Li and Qiu (2008) and Chava, Huang, and Johnson (2017) find that restating firms face higher borrowing costs and tighter nonprice terms of their loan contracts, especially for firms that restate due to fraud. Yuan and Zhang (2015) estimate that interest rate spreads increase 19% for firms targeted by class-action lawsuits and that lenders also tighten nonprice terms of these loans.

The increase in firms' cost of capital appears to affect real investment activity, as Autore et al. (2014) and Yuan and Zhang (2016) find that firms that are targets of securities-related lawsuits subsequently reduce their external financing and investment activity. The revelation of misconduct may also affect firms' current operations, as Palmrose et al. (2004) show that analysts forecast lower future earnings for restating companies, and Murphy, Shrieves, and Tibbs (2009) find that misconduct firms experience both a higher cost of capital and a decrease in cash flows from operations. Barber and Darrough (1996); Karpoff, Lee, and Vendryck (1999); and Johnson, Xie, and Yi (2014) document wide-ranging operational losses for firms targeted by lawsuits related to product market frauds, as these firms experience higher operating costs and lower sales to large customers. It is not clear, however, whether these results would extend to samples that contain only financial misconduct.

Another open question is whether the residual and direct approaches to measuring reputational loss yield similar measures of reputational loss for individual firms, in addition to yielding similar inferences from sample averages. Two papers make headway on this question. For product market frauds, Johnson, Xie, and Yi (2014) show that their measures of reputational loss using stock price reactions to news of misconduct and changes in subsequent operating performance are positively correlated. Haslem, Hutton, and Smith (2017) use both the residual and direct approaches to support their inference that reputational losses are significant for securities-related lawsuits but not for several other types of lawsuits. Nonetheless, the exact pathways by which misconduct firms suffer reputational losses are only partly understood.

6.2.5   Do Misconduct Firms Always Lose Reputational Capital?

A central feature of models of reputational capital is that firms lose reputation only if the firm's counterparties change the terms with which they are willing to do business with the firm. I think it is unlikely that investors and firm counterparties *intend* to impose penalties on the offending firm. Rather, they are simply protecting their own interests by requiring a premium to do business with firms that are less trustworthy than previously believed. Firms that defraud customers, for example, experience large reputational losses because customers – acting in their own self-interest – go elsewhere. Similarly, firms that lose investors' trust by misreporting their financials face a higher cost of capital, as investors require a higher risk premium to invest in the firm.

This raises an important question: do the firm's counterparties care about and react to *any* indication of firm misconduct, even if it does not affect them directly? Or do they care only about misconduct that affects them directly? For example, suppose a firm is caught dumping toxic waste into a river. We would expect firm value to decline to reflect any expected legal consequences, such as EPA fines. But does the firm's pollution directly affect its contracting with investors and customers? That is, does the firm's willingness to push social norms and violate the law with regard to environmental safety cause investors to believe the firm's financial statements are more likely to be in error or cause customers to believe the firm is more likely to cheat them?

Some researchers argue that firm or managerial misconduct of any kind reflects a culture of corruption that affects all of the firm's counterparties. For example, Porter and Van der Linde (1995) argue that environmental polluters will suffer bad reputations that lead to lower sales, even if the pollution does not directly affect the firm's customers. This line of argument implies that any indication of illegal or unethical behavior can motivate a firm's counterparties to change the terms of their contracting with the firm, even if the misconduct does not directly affect them.

A preponderance of available evidence, however, does not support this view. Karpoff and Lott (1993); Alexander (1999); Karpoff, Lott, and Wehrly (2005); Murphy, Shrieves, and Tibbs (2009); and Karpoff, Lee, and Martin (2017) show that losses in reputational capital are negligible for misconduct that affects third parties, such as environmental violations, foreign bribery, and third-party regulatory violations. Examining a large sample of lawsuits related to several types of corporate misconduct, Haslem, Hutton, and Smith (2017) find evidence of reputational losses for securities-related lawsuits but not for lawsuits related to such other types of misconduct as civil rights, personal injury, or intellectual property violations.

Cline, Walkling, and Yore (2018) report evidence that points to a specific channel by which reputational penalties are imposed. Like Davidson, Dey, and Smith (2015) and Griffin, Kruger, and Maturana (2017), they show that there is a positive relation between a manager's personal indiscretions and the likelihood of misconduct at the firm level. They show, however, that managerial indiscretions affect firm value and operations only when they directly influence the firm's contracting with counterparties, for example, only when the manager's behaviour increases a strategic partner's concern that the manager will cheat on the strategic partner relationship. These empirical results indicate that the role of reputation is more complex than a blanket admonition that firms should 'follow the Golden Rule' or 'do well by doing right.' Reputational capital appears to discipline misconduct that directly affects a firm's counterparties but not other types of misconduct. This, in turn, implies that firm culture matters for firm value and operations primarily when it facilitates low-cost contracting with the firm's counterparties, including investors, employees, suppliers, and customers.

A related question is whether reputational capital works in similar ways in different institutional settings around the world. For example, Armour, Mayer, and Polo (2017) and de Batz (2018) find that reputational losses for financial misconduct are much smaller for firms in the UK. and France, respectively, than for US firms. Chen et al. (2016) find that managers of firms in China that commit fraud frequently do not lose their jobs, contrary to evidence from the US that managers that face sanctions for financial misrepresentation tend to lose their jobs (Karpoff, Lee, and Martin 2008b). It seems likely that reputational impacts vary widely depending on the specific legal, institutional, and cultural characteristics of the country and market in which the firm operates.

6.2.6   Rebuilding Reputational Capital

If reputation is an asset, firms can invest in it. Researchers have documented changes consistent with the notion that some firms reinvest in reputational capital when it is diminished following financial misconduct. Farber (2005) reports that firms change the composition of their boards following a restatement, and Wilson (2008) shows that restating firms that change their CEO or auditor recover their reporting credibility more quickly than firms that do not make these changes. Marciukaityte et al. (2006) find that firms increase the fraction of outside directors on their boards and on their audit, compensation, and nominating committees following a broad range of misconduct events. Chakravarthy, DeHaan, and Rajgopal (2014) and Chava, Huang, and Johnson (2017) find that firms that restate their financials pursue a wide variety of reputation-rebuilding investments that target both financial and nonfinancial stakeholders. Activities that target investors include improving governance and internal control systems, changing executives, increasing board independence, reorganizing the firm, and repurchasing stock. Most of these papers also find that firms' reputation-rebuilding activities are associated with improvements in firm value or performance, consistent with the view that firms make reputation-rebuilding investments when they have positive net present value. Chava, Huang, and Johnson (2017), however, find that reputational damage can be long-lasting and not easily reversed, as restating firms experience higher bank loan rates for at least six years after their restatements, even if they invest in reputation rebuilding activities.

Although reputational investments can have positive net present value, we would not expect them always to. For example, Klein and Leffler (1981) examine theoretically the conditions under which reputational investments will not arise to assure performance quality. An underexplored question in the literature is whether and under what conditions firms that lose reputation optimally choose *not* to reinvest in it, and whether such firms optimally liquidate or settle into a new market niche in which they offer low quality assurance in their contracting with investors, suppliers, and customers.

6.3   The Effects of Fraud Revelation on Shareholders and Managers

6.3.1   Should Shareholders Pay? Do Managers Pay?

La Porta, Lopez-de-Silanes, and Shleifer (2006) examine securities law enforcement around the world and conclude that private enforcement, for example, via securities class-action lawsuits, is associated with financial market development.[4] Nonetheless, critics of securities class-action lawsuits argue that a firm's shareholders should not be held financially responsible for financial misconduct that is perpetrated by managers (Arlen and Carney 1992). This argument can be extended to all penalties imposed on a firm for financial misconduct, including those imposed by regulators. Shareholders, according to this argument, are victimized twice – once by the cheating managers and again when the firm suffers direct or reputational penalties when the misconduct is revealed.[5]

This criticism raises three related questions. First, do firm-level penalties victimize shareholders twice? Second, does this imply that firm-level penalties are inefficient? Third, do the individual perpetrators suffer personal consequences for financial misconduct, or do they tend to get off without penalty?

6.3.2   Do Shareholders Pay Twice?

Regarding the first question, it is useful to use Jensen and Meckling's (1976) characterization of the firm as a nexus of contracts. The firm does not make decisions, but rather people do. And while we talk as if the firm suffers a penalty, the incidence of the penalty falls upon specific individuals. This perspective is the basis for the argument that firms should not be penalized for misconduct, as the firm does not commit misconduct. Rather, individual managers engage in the misconduct.

---

[4] For a counterargument and evidence that public enforcement via agencies such as the SEC are important for financial market development, see Jackson and Roe (2009).

[5] For a discussion of the legal perspective of this criticism, specifically whether penalties and class actions' monetary outcomes serve their compensatory role, see Amiram et al. (2018).

Viewed this way, it might seem that at least some shareholders are victimized twice. Anyone who purchases stock before the misconduct is revealed pays inflated prices, and all shareholders pay when the firm has to make legal payments or suffers reputational losses. A further complication is that the extent to which any individual shareholder pays depends on when she buys or sells shares. Shareholders who pay the most are those who buy while the stock price is artificially inflated by the false financial reports and who continue to hold until the misconduct is revealed and penalized. Shareholders who sell while the firm's price is inflated by the misconduct, in contrast, can benefit.

The argument that a firm's misconduct victimizes shareholders twice implies that assessing penalties on the firm, rather than solely on managers, can exacerbate the agency problem and provide too little misconduct deterrence. This is because the costs of getting caught are diffused among the firm's many stakeholders, rather than concentrated on the managers who are responsible for the misconduct.

6.3.3   Are Firm-Level Penalties Efficient?

Might firm-level penalties nonetheless be an efficient form of deterrence? The answer is yes, provided that the firm has a comparative advantage in monitoring and disciplining managers. Suppose, for example, it is very costly for an outside monitor, such as the SEC, to detect misconduct but relatively easy to construct internal reporting and monitoring systems to do so. It could then be efficient to expend resources internally to monitor managers and deter misconduct.[6]

This is how the prospect of penalties at firm level can induce an efficient investment of resources to monitor and deter misconduct. Since shareholders bear the direct and reputational costs that are imposed on the firm, they have incentive to invest optimally in internal monitoring and detection. So while shareholders are victimized when managers engage in misconduct and the firm pays a penalty, the expected costs of any potential misconduct are priced into the shares they purchase, and shareholders are incentivized to invest optimally in monitoring and governance processes to deter misconduct. As observed by Demsetz (1983) when discussing agency costs, the value of the firm is net of the expected costs from monitoring and penalties, just as it is net of the expected costs of labour and utilities. Indeed, the value of any idea that grows into a firm is net of all such expected costs.

6.3.4   Consequences for Managers and Directors

This efficiency argument for firm-level penalties requires that managers internalize the expected costs of their misconduct. One potentially important consequence is that a manager who engages in misconduct loses his or her job. Indeed, it is reasonable to conjecture that the threat of job loss is a primary avenue by which the firm's internal governance deters managers from engaging in misconduct that could

---

[6] For an overview of the debate over the optimal mix of individual and firm-level penalties, see Arlen and Carney (1992), Polinsky and Shavell (1994), Arlen and Kraakman (1997), and Jackson and Roe (2009).

be costly for shareholders. Despite such conjectures, early research yielded mixed results on whether managers who were caught in misconduct lost their jobs. While most findings suggested that they do (e.g. Feroz, Park, and Pastena 1991; Alexander 1999, 2007; Desai, Hogan, and Wilkins 2006; Arthaud-Day et al. 2006; Agrawal and Cooper 2016), others implied they do not (e.g. Beneish 1999b; Agrawal, Jaffe, and Karpoff 1999).

Karpoff, Lee, and Martin (2008b) argue that previous findings were mixed because the tests were poorly specified. For example, the Agrawal, Jaffe, and Karpoff (1999) sample is based on events that typically post-date the actual revelation of misconduct. As a result, many actual forced CEO turnovers are inaccurately categorized as occurring *before* the misconduct was uncovered and thus are not counted as forced turnovers in their tests. Karpoff, Lee, and Martin (2008b) use detailed case histories of financial misrepresentation prosecuted by the SEC to pinpoint when the misconduct was uncovered and find that more than 90% of the managers who are named as culpable are replaced. Further evidence indicates that sizable minorities of these managers face criminal charges and jail sentences. These results indicate that internal governance processes do, in fact, frequently discipline managers who are caught engaging in financial misconduct. Consistent with this interpretation, Hazarika, Karpoff, and Nahata (2012) find that managers who aggressively manage earnings are significantly more likely to be forced out of the firm, even if their earnings management does not trigger regulatory enforcement.[7]

The personal consequences to directors who serve on the boards of firms that experience financial misconduct, in contrast, are less clear. Individual directors are frequently named as defendants in securities-related lawsuits (Brochet and Srinivasan 2014). But Black, Cheffrins, and Klausner (2006) show that independent directors rarely are held personally responsible for misconduct in such lawsuits and argue that the major threat to directors is 'the time, aggravation, and potential harm to reputation that a lawsuit can entail, not direct financial loss' (p. 1056). Agrawal, Jaffe, and Karpoff (1999) find that directors do not experience a high rate of turnover following the revelation of misconduct at their companies, and Helland (2006) does not detect a decrease in these directors' other board seats. Srinivasan (2005), however, finds that outside directors, particularly those serving on the audit committee, experience high turnover rates when their firms restate earnings. Fich and Shivdasani (2007) find that outside directors do not experience high turnover rates at firms that are targeted by class-action lawsuits for financial misconduct, but they lose board seats in other companies.

---

[7] Griffin, Kruger, and Maturana (2019) document a seeming counterexample to these results, as they find that many bank managers who were associated with fraudulent residential mortgage-backed security offerings did not suffer large career consequences. One explanation for this finding is that the RMBS-related frauds examined in this study imposes only small reputational costs on the issuing banks. Cline, Walkling, and Yore (2018) find that, in general, managerial indiscretions are associated with large consequences only when they disrupt the firm's relationships with important counterparties. Another counterexample is examined by Chen, et al. (2016), regarding CEO turnover around financial misconduct in Chinese firms. As discussed elsewhere in this chapter, there is relatively little evidence on these types of reputational effects in non-US markets.

Cai, Garner, and Walkling (2009) find that directors of firms facing lawsuits receive slightly lower support in subsequent director elections, but the effect is very small and has no significant effect on directors' re-election or compensation. Brochet and Srinivasan (2014), however, find that the individual directors who are named as defendants in securities-related lawsuits receive significantly more negative votes in director elections and are more likely to leave the sued firms.

Some of these tests regarding directors may suffer from specification problems similar to those discussed above regarding managerial turnover. I infer that managers frequently experience significant personal costs when caught engaging in financial misconduct but the personal costs to directors are smaller and less clear. An important caveat to this literature, however, is that it does not establish whether the penalties imposed on managers and directors are socially optimal. Optimality depends not only on the size and cost of the penalty but also the social cost of the misconduct and the probability of detection.

6.4   Why Do Managers Do It? Motives and Constraints

The evidence summarized in Section 6.2 indicates financial misconduct can result in large share value and reputational losses. Section 6.3 indicates that managers caught committing misconduct frequently risk job dismissal, civil penalties, and even jail time. Given the risks, why do managers sometimes engage in misconduct?

We would expect managers to misrepresent their companies' financial statements when their expected private benefits exceed their expected private costs. Researchers have examined four broad areas of potential benefit: managers' desire to (1) increase their own compensation, (2) attract new external financing, (3) meet certain earnings thresholds, and (4) relieve financial distress. The expected costs are affected by how managers are monitored and constrained in their decision-making. These constraints are determined by the firm's governance, ownership structure, transparency, and external monitoring.[8]

6.4.1   Motives for Financial Misconduct

Compensation: There is some support for the notion that managers manipulate earnings to boost their compensation. Bergstresser and Philippon (2006) find that the use of discretionary accruals to manage earnings increases with the CEO's stock-based compensation. Burns and Kedia (2006) find that the likelihood of an earnings restatement increases with the sensitivity of the CEO's option portfolio to the firm's stock price. Denis, Hanouna, and Sarin (2006) detect a positive relation between option intensity and fraud allegations for firms facing class-action suits. Other compensation-related motives that are correlated with financial misconduct include stock appreciation rights (Beneish 1999b) and tournament-related CEO pay (Haß, Müller, and Vergauwe 2015). Wang, Winton, and Yu (2010) find that misconduct increases with

---

[8] Amiram et al. (2018, Section 3.2) point out another consideration in managers' motives to engage in misconduct: overconfidence and personal attitudes toward social norms.

executives' short-term compensation incentives, particularly when investors expect high performance.

Not all findings, however, indicate that managers' compensation drives their decisions to cook the books. As one example, Erickson, Hanlon, and Maydew (2006) report evidence inconsistent with an association between misconduct and executive equity incentives in their sample of AAERs. Johnson, Ryan, and Tian (2007) conclude that the likelihood of misconduct in their sample of AAERs is positively related to managers' unrestricted stock holdings but unrelated to managers' holdings of restricted stock, vested stock options, and unvested options. Armstrong et al. (2013) propose that prior findings are mixed because financial misreporting affects both a manager's wealth and her portfolio risk. Consistent with this argument, they find that misreporting is most strongly associated with the sensitivity of the manager's wealth to portfolio risk. Complicating this line of inquiry is that researchers have used a wide variety of equity incentive measures. I am not aware of a systematic examination of whether misconduct is associated with a broad-based measure of equity incentives, or with only some such measures.

New financing: Another motive for financial misconduct is to inflate a firm's earnings and asset values to gain new external financing at favourable terms. Consistent with this hypothesis, Dechow, Sloan, and Sweeney (1996) find that the violation periods referenced in AAERs frequently cover periods during which firms issue new securities.[9] Efendi, Srivastava, and Swanson (2007) find that earnings restatements also frequently cover periods during which firms issue new securities. Richardson, Tuna, and Wu (2003) find that restating firms have high debt levels and are subject to abnormally high earnings growth expectations and infer that managers' prime motive to manipulate earnings is to attract low cost external financing.

Earnings thresholds: Managers also may manipulate earnings when they have pressure to meet earnings thresholds, such as analysts' earnings forecasts. For example, Schilit (2010) warns that managers are tempted to manipulate earnings, especially during the inevitable decline in growth that all fast-growth firms experience. Consistent with this view, Richardson, Tuna, and Wu (2002) show that earnings restatements are often filed by firms that had recorded a consecutive string of abnormal earnings increases before engaging in the aggressive accounting policies that resulted in the restatement.

Robb (1998) finds that managers of financial institutions increasingly manipulate earnings through loan loss reserves as analysts' earnings forecasts converge, suggesting that managers work to meet analysts' forecasts, particularly when analysts agree. Degeorge, Patel, and Zeckhauser (2000) consider three behavioural thresholds of earnings management: reporting positive profits, sustaining recent performance, and meeting analyst expectations. They conclude that the predominant goal of managers who manipulate the books is to report positive earnings. This conclusion is supported by Payne and Robb (2000), who report that managers use discretionary accruals to meet analysts' expectations when expected performance is below market

---

[9] Beneish (1999b), however, does not find evidence that AAERs are associated with periods of external financing.

expectations, with a goal of preventing negative earnings surprises. Similar to Robb (1998), they also find that the tendency to use discretionary accruals increases as the dispersion of analysts' forecasts decreases.

Financial distress: Maksimovic and Titman (1991) construct a model in which managers' incentives to engage in misconduct increase as the firm's expected performance declines. The core idea is that poorly performing firms and managers have less to lose from the risk of getting caught; that is, they have less reputational capital. This idea has been applied to managers' decisions to misrepresent their financial statements as well. Loebbecke, Eining, and Willingham (1989) find that 19% of their sample of firms that engaged in misconduct were experiencing solvency problems. Beneish (1999b), however, does not find evidence that misconduct that prompts AAERs is motivated by a desire to avoid debt covenant violations.

6.4.2   Constraints on Financial Misconduct

Firm governance: Several papers find that the likelihood of financial misrepresentation is affected by the quality of firm governance. The exact features that matter, however, remain unsettled. For example, Beasley (1996) finds that firms cited in AAERs have significantly lower percentages of independent board members, and Klein (2002) finds a negative relation between board independence and the size of firms' abnormal accruals. Uzun, Szewczyk, and Varma (2004) find that financial and nonfinancial misconduct relates negatively to the number of independent directors on the board as well as on the audit and compensation committees. Gerety and Lehn (1997), in contrast, find that the incidence of disclosure violations is unrelated to board independence – as well as to board size, the presence of an audit committee, a classified board, the existence of an accounting-based incentive plan, and whether the auditor was one of the Big 8 auditing firms. Agrawal and Chadha (2005) also find that the probability of earnings restatements is unrelated to overall board independence but the probability is lower in companies whose boards or audit committees have an independent director with financial expertise.

Ownership structure: The incidence of misrepresentation also can be affected by the firm's ownership structure. Alexander and Cohen (1999), for example, find that corporate crime is less frequent when managers have large shareholdings. Gerety and Lehn (1997) find that misconduct relates negatively to board ownership, and Cornett, Marcus, and Tehranian (2008) find that institutional ownership and institutional investor representation on the board reduce the use of discretionary accruals in earnings management. However, Denis, Hanouna, and Sarin (2006) conclude that institutional and block ownership also exacerbates the option-based incentive to engage in misconduct. The most striking finding related to ownership structure is Anderson, Martin, and Reeb's (2015) discovery that financial misconduct is much more likely in firms controlled by the founders' family members. Agrawal and Chadha (2005) also find that restatements are more likely among companies in which the CEO belongs to the founding family.

Transparency: Financial misconduct is more likely when it is costly for outsiders to monitor the firm's operations and managers. Kedia and Philippon (2009) show theoretically that imperfect information creates incentives for low-productivity firms to over-invest, which leads to an increased likelihood of financial reporting violations. Povel, Singh, and Winton (2007) develop a model in which financial misrepresentation peaks toward the end of a boom period, particularly when monitoring costs decrease, only to be revealed during the following bust.[10] Wang, Winton, and Yu (2010) find that misconduct relates to investors' expectations and monitoring costs in a sample of IPO firms. Gerety and Lehn (1997) find that the incidence of disclosure violations relates positively to a proxy for the cost of valuing the firm's assets, and Dechow et al. (2007) find that the likelihood that a firm will have a material earnings misstatement increases with its accruals and its use of off-balance-sheet financing, such as operating leases. All of these findings are consistent with the view that financial transparency relates negatively to the incidence of financial misconduct.

External monitoring: The incidence of misrepresentation can vary over time because laws and regulations change. Since 1990, the US Congress has enacted or authorized five major changes in the regulation of financial misconduct. These include the Securities Enforcement and Penny Stock Reform Act of 1990, the implementation of the US Sentencing Commission Guidelines for crimes by organizations in November 1991, the Private Securities Litigation Reform Act of 1995, the Sarbanes–Oxley Act of 2002, and the Dodd–Frank Act of 2010. To the extent that these laws have changed the penalties or regulatory oversight for financial misrepresentation, they could also change the incidence of such misrepresentation. Cohen, Dey, and Lys (2005) report that earnings management rose steadily in the years preceding Sarbanes–Oxley's passage, primarily in poorly performing industries, and significantly immediately afterwards.

Misconduct, or its discovery and punishment, also can be affected by the nature and intensity of regulatory oversight. For example, Choi et al. (2018) find that SEC enforcement actions for financial misrepresentation follow industry-specific enforcement waves that are partly explained by the SEC's enforcement budget. Yu and Yu (2011) find that firms with high political lobbying expenses are less likely to face charges for financial misconduct. Kedia and Rajgopal (2011) find that firms are less likely to announce financial restatements if they are located close to an SEC office or in areas that have attracted past SEC enforcement activity. They also suggest that firms located close to an SEC regional office are more likely to be targeted by an SEC enforcement action, but Parsons, Sulaeman, and Titman (2018) find that this result disappears when controlling for other geographic characteristics.

6.5   Proxies and Databases Used to Identify Samples of Financial Statement Misconduct

Researchers use different proxies and data sources to collect samples to study financial misconduct. Early researchers compiled samples of financial statement misconduct from primary sources, such as keyword searches of financial press databases

---

[10] In the Povel et al. (2007) model, the combination of managers' incentives to commit fraud and investors' incentives to monitor yields nonmonotonic relations between fraud, investor beliefs, and monitoring costs. See also Hertzberg (2006), who develops a model in which positive investor beliefs generate greater managerial incentives to commit fraud.

(e.g. Davidson, Worrell, and Lee 1994) or SEC filings (e.g. Palmrose, Richardson, and Scholz 2004). Over the past 10 years, however, the large majority of papers that examine financial misconduct are based on samples drawn from one or more of four electronically available databases: the Government Accountability Office (GAO) and Audit Analytics (AA) databases of restatement announcements, the Stanford Securities Class Action Clearinghouse (SCAC) database of securities class-action lawsuits, and the Securities and Exchange Commission's (SEC's) Accounting and Auditing Enforcement Releases, most recently as compiled by the University of California-Berkeley's Center for Financial Reporting and Management (CFRM).

Karpoff et al. (2017) examine the GAO, AA, SCAC, and CFRM data sources and demonstrate that empirical results are frequently sensitive to the choice of proxy and database. In simple tests that examine changes in such outcome variables as return on assets and equity issues around the revelation of misconduct, they show that the replication rate is only 42% when the misconduct events from one randomly chosen alternative database are replaced by the misconduct events identified by another randomly chosen alternative database. These results suggest that a researcher's choice of a proxy and database to identify a sample of financial statement misconduct events can affect the empirical inferences.

The main reason different databases yield different results is that each captures a different subset of information about an instance of misconduct. A firm's financial misconduct typically is revealed to the public via a complex sequence of announcements that spread out over multiple years. Some instances of misconduct involve one or more earnings restatements, others involve class action lawsuits, others involve various regulatory actions, and still others have various combinations of these types of events. Each database captures only one of these many types of announcement. So samples constructed from restatement announcements do not have large overlap with samples constructed from, say, class-action lawsuits.

As an analogy, suppose the sequence of announcements by which investors learn about each instance of misconduct is like a novel. Class-action lawsuits sample from the front chapters, restatement announcements sample from the middle chapters, and regulatory actions (such as AAERs) sample from the end of the book. Researchers drawing a sample of, say, restatement announcements will compile a sample of middle chapters and ignore the beginnings and ends of the novels in their samples. This poses no problem if each chapter contains a fairly complete narrative of the whole story or if the research question pertains only to a specific part of the narrative. As Karpoff et al. (2017) show, however, each of the various announcements pertaining to an instance of misconduct contains information that is important for many research questions and that is not available in the other announcements related to the misconduct. Using stock price reactions to measure information content, they show that the events identified by any one of these popular databases capture only a small portion of the value-relevant information that informs how a researcher classifies and interprets the results from empirical tests. Because each database focuses on a different subset of information events that convey information about financial misconduct, each database tends to identify different dates upon which investors learn of misconduct. Karpoff et al. (2017) show that the differences can be substantial, thus having large impacts on inferences from event studies or studies that examine changes in firm characteristics around the revelation of misconduct. To return to the novel analogy, each chapter does not contain a fairly complete narrative of the whole story, and most research questions do not pertain only to a specific part of the narrative.

Researchers work to offset the gaps in their data, sometimes by combining events from multiple data sources, running separate tests using samples from different databases, or hand-collecting data to expand the scope and inclusiveness of their data (e.g. Beneish, Marshall, and Yang 2017). Future researchers using these databases will need to continue to such efforts. The most important single lesson is that each proxy and database used to identify misconduct events represents only a small part of the total sequence of events by which investors learn about the full scale of the misconduct, the periods over which it occurred, and its consequences. For many research questions about financial misconduct, this partial coverage of each database will be an important characteristic to manage. Karpoff et al. (2017) include a list of specific suggestions for researchers seeking to use these databases.

6.6   Conclusion: Reputation, Enforcement, and Culture

The evidence summarized in this chapter indicates that reputational capital serves as a powerful disciplining force for some types of fraud, particularly financial fraud, but not for other types of misconduct, such as foreign bribery and environmental violations. By what other mechanisms are managers and firms disciplined for misconduct? And what other forces work to build trust in financial contracting?

Dupont and Karpoff (2020) summarize previous attempts to answer these questions and propose a framework, the Trust Triangle, to organize and synthesize this prior work. The idea of the Trust Triangle is that trust is formed by the ex-ante belief that one's counterparty will suffer ex-post consequences for opportunistic or fraudulent behaviour. It is the ex-ante belief that the counterparty's net ex-post benefits of cheating are negative that builds trust and facilitates contracting and exchange. The ex-post consequences, in turn, can accrue through three broad channels. The first channel is the prospect of third-party enforcement through legal institutions. The second channel is the prospect of losing reputational capital, as documented in this chapter. If the first channel is about third-party enforcement, the reputational channel can be thought of as second-party (or related-party) enforcement. The third channel is the prospect of violating one's social, cultural, or personal norms and standard of integrity. This channel represents a person's incentives to behave honestly and perform as promised even in the absence of third- party or second-party consequences for opportunistic behaviour, and can be thought of as first-party enforcement.

The Trust Triangle provides a framework to synthesize several seemingly unrelated areas of research into financial misconduct. For example, the law and finance literature (e.g. La Porta et al. 1998) examines the role of legal and regulatory institutions in building trust, and their effects on firm values and operations, as well as overall financial and economic development. Researchers have also made gains in understanding the connections between social and cultural influences and the incidence of financial fraud (e.g. Liu, 2016; Parsons, Sulaeman, and Titman 2018). Clearly, in areas for which the reputational channel is weak – as with foreign bribery or environmental violations in the US, or possibly financial misconduct outside of the US – deterrence must rely on the other legs of the Trust Triangle, i.e. legal and cultural incentives and enforcement. A promising direction for future research is to explore the ways in which legal, reputational, and cultural mechanisms work as substitutes, or complements, in disciplining misconduct and encouraging the formation of ex-ante trust that forms the basis of exchange and production activities in different settings around the world.

References

Agrawal, A, Jaffe, J.F. and Karpoff, J.M. (1999). Management turnover and governances changes following the revelation of a fraud. *Journal of Law and Economics* 42: 23–56.

Agrawal, A. and Chadha, S. (2005). Corporate governance and accounting scandals. *Journal of Law and Economics* 48: 371–709.

Agrawal, A. and Cooper, T. (2016). Corporate governance consequences of accounting scandals: Evidence from top management, CFO and auditor turnover. *Quarterly Journal of Finance* 7(1).

Alexander, C.R. (1999). On the nature of the reputational penalty for corporate crime: Evidence. *The Journal of Law and Economics* 42: 489–526.

Alexander, C.R., and Cohen, M.A. (1999). Why do corporations become criminals? Ownership, hidden actions, and crime as an agency cost. *Journal of Corporate Finance* 5(1): 1–34.

Amiram, D., Bozanic, Z., Cox, J.D., Dupont, Q., Karpoff, J.M. and Sloan, R. (2018) Financial reporting fraud and other forms of misconduct: A multidisciplinary review of the literature. *Review of Accounting Studies* 23: 732–783.

Amiram, D., Bozanic, Z., and Rouen, E. (2015). Financial statement errors: Evidence from the distributional properties of financial statement numbers. *Review of Accounting Studies* 20: 1540–1593.

Arlen, J.H., and Carney, W. (1992). Vicarious Liability for Fraud on Securities Markets: Theory and Evidence. *University of Illinois Law Review*, 691.

Arlen J.H., and Kraakman, R. (1997). Controlling corporate misconduct: An analysis of corporate liability regimes. *New York University Law Review* 72, 687–779.

Armstrong, C.S., Larcker, D.F., Ormazabal, G. and Taylor, D.J. (2013). The relation between equity incentives and misreporting: The role of risk-taking incentives. *Journal of Financial Economics* 109: 327–350.

Anderson, R., Martin, G.S. and Reeb, D. (2015). Founders and financial misrepresentation. Temple University working paper.

Anderson, K. and Yohn, T. (2002). The effect of 10k restatements on firm value, information asymmetries, and investors' reliance on earnings. Working paper.

Armour, J., Mayer, C. and Polo, A. (2017). Regulatory sanctions and reputational damage in financial markets. *Journal of Financial and Quantitative Analysis* 52(4): 1429–1448.

Arthaud-Day, M., Trevis Certo, S.T., Dalton, C. and Dalton, D. (2006). A changing of the guard: Executive and director turnover following corporate financial restatements. *The Academy of Management Journal* 49: 1119–1136.

Autore, D., Hottom, I., Peterson, D. and Smith A.H. (2014). The effects of securities litigation on external financing. *Journal of Corporate Finance* 27: 231–250.

Barber, B.M. and Darrough, M.N. (1996). Product reliability and firm value: The experience of American and Japanese automakers, 1973–1992. *Journal of Political Economy*, 1084–1099.

Bargeron, L., Lehn, K. and Smith, J. (2015). Employee-Management Trust and M&A activity. *Journal of Corporate Finance* 35: 389–406.

Beasley, M.S. (1996). An empirical analysis of the relation between the board of director composition and financial statement fraud. *The Accounting Review* 71: 443–465.

Beatty, A., Liao, S. and Yu, J. (2013). The spillover effect of fraudulent financial reporting on peer firms' investments. *Journal of Accounting and Economics* 55(2): 183–205.

Beneish, M.D. (1999a). The detection of earnings manipulation. *Financial Analysts' Journal* 55(5): 24–36.

Beneish, M.D. (1999b). Incentives and penalties related to earnings overstatements that violate GAAP. *The Accounting Review* 425–457.

Beneish, M.D., Marshall, C.D. and Yang, J. (2017). Explaining CEO retention in misreporting firms. *Journal of Financial Economics* 123: 512–535.

Bergstresser, D. and Philippon, T. (2006). CEO incentives and earnings management. *Journal of Financial Economics* 80(3): 511–529.

Bhagat, S., Bizjak, J. and Coles, J.L. (1998). The shareholder wealth implications of corporate lawsuits. *Financial Management* 27: 5–27.

Black, B.S., Cheffins, B.R. and Klausner, M. (2006). Outside director liability. *Stanford Law Review* 58: 1055–1159.

Brav, A. and Heaton, J.B. (2016). Event studies in securities litigation: Low power, confounding effects, and bias. *Washington University Law Review* 93: 583–614.

Brochet, F. and Srinivasan, S. (2014). Accountability of independent directors: Evidence from firms subject to securities litigation. *Journal of Financial Economics* 111(2): 430–449.

Burns, N. and Kedia, S. (2006). The impact of performance-based compensation on misreporting. *Journal of Financial Economics* 79: 35–67.

Cai, J., Garner, J. and Walkling, R. (2009). Electing directors. *The Journal of Finance* 64(5): 2389–2421.

Chakravarthy, J., DeHaan, E. and Rajgopal, S. (2014). Reputation repair after a serious restatement. *The Accounting Review* 89: 1329–1363.

Chava, S., Cheng, C.S.A., Huang, H.H. and Lobo, G.J. (2010). Implication of securities class actions for cost of equity capital. *International Journal of Law and Management* 52(2): 144–161.

Chava, S., Huang, K. and Johnson, S.A. (2018). The dynamics of borrower reputation following financial misreporting. *Management Science* 64(10): 4775–4797.

Chen, J., Cumming, D., Hou, W. and Lee, E. (2016). CEO accountability for corporate fraud: Evidence from the split share structure reform in China. *Journal of Business Ethics* 138: 787–806.

Choi, H., Karpoff, J.M., Lou, X. and Martin, J. (2018). Enforcement waves and spillovers. University of Washington working paper. Available at https://ssrn.com/abstract=3526555.

Cline, B.N., Walkling, R.A. and Yore, A.S. (2018). The consequences of managerial indiscretions: Sex, lies, and firm value. *Journal of Financial Economics* 127(2): 389–415.

Cohen, D.A., Dey, A. and Lys, T.Z. (2008). Real and accrual-based earnings management in the pre- and post-Sarbanes–Oxley periods. *The Accounting Review* 83(3): 757–787.

Cornett, M.M., Marcus, A.J. and Tehranian, H. (2008). Corporate governance and pay-for-performance: The impact of earnings management. *Journal of Financial Economics* 87(2): 357–373.

Davidson, R., Dey, A. and Smith, A. (2015). Executives' "off-the-job" behavior, corporate culture, and financial reporting risk. *Journal of Financial Economics* 117(1): 5–28.

Davidson, W.N., Worrell, D.L. and Lee, C.I. (1994). Stock market reactions to announced corporate illegalities. *Journal of Business Ethics* 13: 979–987.

de Batz, Laure (2018). Financial impact of regulatory sanctions on French listed companies, Available at https://ssrn.com/abstract=3167132.

Dechow, P.M., Sloan, R.G. and Sweeney, A.P. (1996). Causes and consequences of earnings manipulation: An analysis of firms subject to enforcement actions by the SEC. *Contemporary Accounting Research* 13: 1–36.

Dechow, P.M., Ge, W., Larson, C.R. and Sloan, R.G. (2011). Predicting material accounting misstatements. *Contemporary Accounting Research* 28(1): 17–82.

Degeorge, F., Zeckhauser, R.J. and Patel, J. (2000). Earnings management to exceed thresholds. *The Journal of Business* 72(1): 1–33.

Demsetz, H. (1983). The structure of ownership and the theory of the firm. *The Journal of Law and Economics* 26(2), 375–390.

Deng, X., Kang, J-K. and Low, B.S. (2013). Corporate social responsibility and stakeholder value maximization: Evidence from mergers. *Journal of Financial Economics* 110: 87–109.

Denis, D.J., Hanouna, P. and Sarin, A. (2006). Is there a dark side to incentive compensation? *Journal of Corporate Finance* 12(3), 467–488.

Desai, H., Hogan, C. and Wilkins, M. (2006). The reputational penalty for aggressive accounting: Earnings restatements and management turnover. *The Accounting Review* 81: 83–112.

Dupont, Q. and Karpoff, J.M. (2020). The trust triangle: Three related areas of empirical finance research. *Journal of Business Ethics*, forthcoming. Available at https://ssrn.com/abstract=3105693.

Efendi, J., Srivastava, A. and Swanson, E.P. (2007). Why do corporate managers misstate financial statements? The role of option compensation and other factors. *Journal of Financial Economics* 85(3): 667–708.

Erickson, M., Hanlon, M. and Maydew, E.L. (2006). Is there a link between executive equity incentives and accounting fraud? *Journal of Accounting Research* 44(1): 113–143.

Farber, D.B. (2005). Restoring trust after fraud: Does corporate governance matter? *The Accounting Review* 80: 539–561.

Feroz, E.H., Park, K. and Pastena, V.S. (1991). The financial and market effects of the SEC's accounting and auditing enforcement releases. *Journal of Accounting Research*, 29:107–142.

Ferris, S.P. and Pritchard, A.C. (2001). Stock price reactions to securities fraud class actions under the Private Securities Litigation Reform Act. *The University of Michigan Law and Economics Research Paper*.

Fich, E.M. and Shivdasani, A. (2007). Financial fraud, director reputation, and shareholder wealth, *Journal of Financial Economics* 86: 306–336.

Gande, A. and Lewis, C.M. (2009). Shareholder-initiated class action lawsuits: Shareholder wealth effects and industry spillovers. *Journal of Financial and Quantitative Analysis* 44: 823–850.

Gerety, M. and Lehn, K. (1997). The causes and consequences of accounting fraud. *Managerial and Decision Economics* 18(7): 587–599.

Giannetti, M. and Wang, T.Y. (2016). Corporate scandals and household stock market participation. *The Journal of Finance* 71: 2591–2636.

Goldman, E., Peyer, U. and Stefanescu, I. (2012). Financial misrepresentation and its impact on rivals. *Financial Management* 41(4): 915–945.

Griffin, J.M., Kruger, S. and Maturana, G. (2017). Do personal ethics influence corporate ethics? (July 26, 2017). 'Personal Infidelity and Professional Conduct in 4 Settings'. *Proceedings of the National Academy of Sciences* (PNAS) 116 (33): 16268-16273 (2019). Available at SSRN: https://ssrn.com/abstract=2745062 or http://dx.doi.org/10.2139/ssrn.2745062.

Griffin, J.M., Kruger, S.A. and Maturana, G. (2019). Do labor markets discipline? Evidence from RMBS bankers. *Journal of Financial Economics* 133(3): 726–750.

Graham, J.R., Li, S. and Qiu, J. (2008). Corporate misreporting and bank loan contracting. *Journal of Financial Economics* 89: 44–61.

Griffin, P.A., Grundfest, J.A. and Perino, M.A. (2004). Stock price response to news of securities fraud litigation: An analysis of sequential and conditional information. *Abacus* 40: 21–48.

Guiso, L., Sapienza, P. and Zingales, L. (2015). The value of corporate culture. *Journal of Financial Economics* 117(1): 60–76.

Haß, L.H., Müller, M.A. and Vergauwe, S. (2015). Tournament incentives and corporate fraud. *Journal of Corporate Finance* 34: 251–267.

Haslem, B., Hutton, I. and Smith, A.H. (2017). How much do corporate defendants really lose? A new verdict on the reputation loss induced by corporate litigation. *Financial Management* 46(2): 323–358.

Hazarika, S., Karpoff, J.M. and Nahata, R. (2012) Internal corporate governance, CEO turnover, and earnings management. *Journal of Financial Economics* 104: 44–69.

Helland, Eric (2006). Reputational penalties and the merits of class action securities litigation. *Journal of Law & Economics* 49: 365–395.

Hennes, K.M., Leone, A.J. and Miller, B.P. (2008). The importance of distinguishing errors from irregularities in restatement research: The case of restatements and CEO/CFO turnover. *The Accounting Review* 83: 1487–1519.

Jackson, H.E. and M.J. Roe (2009). Public and private enforcement of securities laws: Resource-based evidence. *Journal of Financial Economics* 93(2): 207–238.

Hribar, P. and Jenkins, N.T. (2004). The effect of accounting restatements on earnings revisions and the estimated cost of capital. *Review of Accounting Studies* 9: 337–356.

Hutton, I., Jiang, D. and Kumar, A. (2015). Political values, culture, and corporate litigation. *Management Science* 61(12): 2905–2925.

Jensen, M.C. and Meckling, W.H. (1976). Theory of the firm: Managerial behavior, agency cost and ownership structure. *Journal of Financial Economics* 3: 305–360.

Johnson, S.A., Ryan, H.E. and Tian, Y.S. (2009). Managerial incentives and corporate fraud: The sources of incentives matter. *Review of Finance* 13(1): 115–145.

Johnson, W.C., Xie, W. and Yi, S. (2014). Corporate fraud and the value of reputations in the product market. *Journal of Corporate Finance* 25: 16–39.

Karpoff, J.M., Koester, A., Lee, D.S. and Martin, G.S. (2017). Proxies and databases in financial misconduct research. *The Accounting Review* 92(6): 129–163.

Karpoff, J.M., Lee, D.S. and Martin, G.S. (2008a). The cost to firms of cooking the books. *Journal of Financial & Quantitative Analysis* 43: 581–611.

Karpoff, J.M., Lee, D.S., and Martin, G.S. (2008b). The consequences to managers for financial misrepresentation. *Journal of Financial Economics* 88: 193–215.

Karpoff, J.M., Lee, D.S. and Martin, G.S. (2017). Foreign bribery: Incentives and enforcement (April 7, 2017). Available at SSRN: https://ssrn.com/abstract=1573222 or http://dx.doi.org/10.2139/ssrn.1573222.

Karpoff, J.M., Lee, D.S., and Vendrzyk, V.P. (1999). Defense procurement fraud, penalties, and contractor influence. *Journal of Political Economy* 107: 809–842.

Karpoff, J.M. and Lott, J.R. Jr. (1993). The reputational penalty firms bear from committing criminal fraud. *Journal of Law and Economics* 36: 757–802.

Karpoff, J.M., Lott, J.R. and Wehrly, E.W. (2005). The reputational penalties for environmental violations: Empirical evidence. *Journal of Law and Economics* 48: 653–675.

Karpoff, J.M. and Lou, X. (2010). Short sellers and financial misconduct. *The Journal of Finance* 65: 1879–1913.

Klein, A. (2002). Audit committee, board of director characteristics, and earnings management. *Journal of Accounting and Economics* 33(3): August 2002: 375–400. Available at SSRN: https://ssrn.com/abstract=316695

Klein, B. and Leffler, K.B. (1981). The role of market forces in assuring contractual performance. *The Journal of Political Economy* 89: 615–641.

Kedia, S. and Philippon, T. (2009). The economics of fraudulent accounting. *Review of Financial Studies* 22(6): 2169–2199.

Kedia, S. and Rajgopal, S. (2011). Do the SEC's enforcement preferences affect corporate misconduct? *Journal of Accounting and Economics* 51(3): 259–278.

Kellogg, R.L. (1984). Accounting activities, security prices, and class action lawsuits. *Journal of Accounting and Economics* 6: 185–204.

Khanna, V., Kim, E. and Lu, Y. (2015). CEO connectedness and corporate fraud. *The Journal of Finance* 70(3), 1203–1252.

Kravet, T. and Shevlin, T. (2010). Accounting restatements and information risk. *Review of Accounting Studies* 15: 264–294.

La Porta, R., Lopez-de-Silanes, F., Shleifer, A. and Vishny, R.W. (1998). Law and finance. *Journal of Political Economy* 106(6): 1113–1155.

La Porta, R., Lopez-de-Silanes, F. and Shleifer, A. (2006). What works in securities laws? *The Journal of Finance* 61(1): 1–32.

Li, V. (2016). Do false financial statements distort peer firms' decisions? *The Accounting Review* 91(1): 251–278.

Liu, X. (2016). Corruption culture and corporate misconduct. *Journal of Financial Economics* 122(2). 307–327.

Loebbecke, J.K., Eining, M.M. and Willingham, J.J. (1989). Auditor's experience with material irregularities: frequency, nature, and detectability. *Auditing: A Journal of Practice & Theory* 9 (1): Fall, 1–28.

Maksimovic, V. and Titman, S. (1991). Financial policy and reputation for product quality. *The Review of Financial Studies* 4: 175–200.

Marciukaityte, D., Szewczyk, S.H., Uzun, H. and Varma, R. (2006). Governance and perfor-mance changes after accusations of corporate fraud. *Financial Analysts Journal* 62: 32–41.

Mayer, C. (2008). Trust in financial markets. *European Financial Management* 14: 617–632.

Murphy, D.L., Shrieves, R.E. and Tibbs, S.L. (2009). Understanding the penalties associated with corporate misconduct: An empirical examination of earnings and risk. *Journal of Financial & Quantitative Analysis* 44: 55–83.

Palmrose, Z., Richardson, V.J., and Scholz, S. (2004). Determinants of market reactions to restatement announcements. *Journal of Accounting and Economics* 37: 59–89.

Parsons, C.A., Sulaeman, J. and Titman, S. (2018). The geography of financial misconduct. *The Journal of Finance* 73(5): 2087–2137. Available at https://doi.org/10.1111/jofi.12704.

Payne, J.L. and Robb, S.W.G. (2000). Earnings management: The effect of ex ante earnings expectations. *Journal of Accounting, Auditing and Finance*, 15: Fall 2000. Available at SSRN: https://ssrn.com/abstract=257687.

Pevzner, M., Xie, F. and Xin, X. (2015). When firms talk, do investors listen? The role of trust in stock market reactions to corporate earnings announcements. *Journal of Financial Economics* 117(1): 190–223.

Polinsky, M. and Shavell, S. (1994). Should liability be based on the harm to the victim or the gain to the injurer? *Journal of Law, Economics, & Organization* 10(2): 427–437.

Porter, M. and van der Linde, C. (1995). Toward a new conception of the environment–competitiveness relationship. *Journal of Economic Perspectives* 9: 97–118.

Povel, P., Singh, R. and Winton, A. (2007). Booms, busts, and fraud. *Review of Financial Studies* 20(4): 1219–1254.

Richardson, S.A., Tuna, A.I. and Wu, M. (2003). Predicting earnings management: The case of earnings restatements. Available at SSRN: https://ssrn.com/abstract=338681.

Robb, S.W. (1998). The effect of analysts' forecasts on earnings management in financial institu-tions. *Journal of Financial Research* 21(3): 315–331.

Romano, R. (1991). The shareholder suit: Litigation without foundation? *Journal of Law, Economics, and Organization* 7: 55.

Schilit, H. (2010). *Financial Shenanigans: How to Detect Accounting Gimmicks and Fraud in Financial Reports.* New York: McGraw-Hill. (p. 318).

Shapiro, C. (1983). Premiums for high quality products as returns to reputations. *Quarterly Journal of Economics* 98: 659–679.

Srinivasan, S. (2005). Consequences of financial reporting failure for outside directors: Evidence from accounting restatements and audit committee members. *Journal of Accounting Research* 43: 291–334.

Stulz, R.M. and Williamson, R. (2003). Culture, openness, and finance. *Journal of Financial Economics* 70(3): 313–349.

Tanimura, J.K. and Okamoto, G.M. (2013). Reputational penalties in Japan: Evidence from corporate scandals. *Asian Economic Journal* 27: 39–57.

Uzun, H., Szewczyk, S.H. and Varma, R. (2004). Board composition and corporate fraud. *Financial Analysts Journal* 60(3): 33–43.

Wang, T.Y., Winton, A. and Yu, X. (2010). Corporate fraud and business conditions: Evidence from IPOs. *The Journal of Finance* 65(6): 2255–2292.

Wilson, W.M. (2008). An empirical analysis of the decline in the information content of earnings following restatements. *The Accounting Review* 83: 519–548.

Yu, X. (2013). Securities fraud and corporate finance: Recent developments. *Managerial and Decision Economics* 34(7/8): 439–450.

Yu, F. and Yu, X. (2011). Corporate lobbying and fraud detection. *Journal of Financial and Quantitative Analysis* 46(6): 1865–1891.

Yuan, Q. and Zhang, Y. (2016), The real effects of corporate fraud: evidence from class action lawsuits. *Accounting & Finance* 56: 879–911.

Yuan, Q. and Zhang, Y. (2015). Do banks price litigation risk in debt contracting? Evidence from class action lawsuits. *Journal of Business Finance & Accounting* 42: 1310–1340.

Part II

How and Where Does Misconduct Occur?

Chapter 7

Manipulative and Collusive Practices in FX Markets

Alexis Stenfors
University of Portsmouth

7.1 Introduction

Until recently, the global foreign exchange (FX) markets were subject to surprisingly few allegations of manipulative or collusive practices in comparison to, say, the equity and commodity markets. This relatively clean bill of health was radically changed in June 2013, when three Bloomberg journalists published an article with the headline 'Traders Said to Rig Currency Rates to Profit Off Clients' (Vaughan, Finch and Choudhury, 2013). It strongly suggested that there was a widespread culture involving traders manipulating and colluding in the FX market – to the detriment of the banks' clients and other market participants.

Partly attaching itself to the LIBOR scandal, involving manipulation of interest rate benchmarks, the revelations of a 'Forex scandal' in a closely related area of the financial markets initiated a rapid process of whistleblowing, regulatory investigations, lawsuits, financial settlements, and criminal proceedings that is still ongoing. In 2014, the UK Financial Conduct Authority (FCA) fined Citi, HSBC, JP Morgan Chase, RBS and UBS an unprecedented £1.1 billion in total for 'FX failings' in their G10 FX spot businesses (FCA 2014a).[1] Simultaneously, total penalties of $1.4 billion were imposed upon the same banks by the Commodity Futures Trading Commission (CFTC), whereas the Office of the Comptroller of the Currency (OCC) additionally fined Bank of America, Citi and JP Morgan Chase $950 million (CFTC 2014a; OCC 2014). In May 2015, Bank of America, Barclays, Citi, JP Morgan Chase, RBS and UBS were fined a further $5.7 billion in the US, some of which pleaded guilty of felony (Freifeld, Henry and Slater 2015). According to the FBI, the conduct, which had taken place at banks, which more or less dominated the global FX market, amounted to criminality 'on a massive scale' (Chon, Binham, and Noonan 2015). Barclays also agreed a £284 million settlement with the FCA, and in 2017 Deutsche Bank, BNP, and Credit Suisse were fined over $600 million by US authorities (FCA 2015; Federal Reserve 2017; DFS 2017a,b). So far, the total fines imposed upon banks by authorities exceed $10 billion.

Transcripts hitherto made public by financial regulators reveal that the manipulative and collusive practices mainly concerned the most liquid and actively traded currency pairs traded by the banks' G10 FX spot desks. In some cases, however, emerging market currencies were also affected. It was also reported that the behaviour was systematic, and often very similar across the FX desks at the banks involved. However, the manipulation was not always done single-handedly. On numerous occasions, schemes involving sharing of confidential bank information, such as client orders and bid–ask spreads, and outright collusion between the competing banks were also prominent.

Given the vast scale, the revelations have since influenced the regulatory reform process and induced wide-ranging changes in the internal practices of banks involved in market-making of FX-related instruments. In light of these developments, which is still ongoing at the time of writing, the outline of the chapter is as follows. Section 7.2 describes the different types of order banks typically receive from their clients in the FX market, and how they relate to manipulative practices. Section 7.3 summarises some structural aspects, which make the FX market unique. Importantly, these also sustained the widely and long-held perception that the market was relatively immune to manipulative and collusive practices. Section 7.4 discusses the various types of misconduct in more detail, with emphasis on those at the heart of the regulatory

---

[1] Emerging market currencies are often traded on separate desks to the so-called 'G10' currencies, which typically include: the US dollar, the euro, the Japanese yen, the British pound sterling, the Swiss franc, the Australian dollar, the New Zealand dollar, the Canadian dollar, the Swedish krona, the Norwegian krone and the Danish krone.

findings. Section 7.5 concludes by reflecting upon the obligatory and voluntary changes made in FX trading areas in recent years.

7.2   Different Types of FX Order

Although there are numerous definitions, the consensus view is that to prove that attempted price manipulation has taken place, two elements need to be determined: (1) an intent to influence the market price in a direction that is inconsistent with market forces, and (2) an act to further that intent.[2] In the settlement agreements mentioned in this chapter, both elements have been established through trade data and communication records handed over to the regulators. The regulatory investigations show that manipulative and collusive practices in FX markets predominantly have involved large banks. More specifically, the misconduct has been linked to the liquidity provision role of market-making banks via different types of client orders. Several forms of manipulative tactics appear in the transcripts released by regulators. Theoretically, they could be regarded as forms of 'trade-based manipulation' (Allen and Gale 1992). However, before examining them in more detail, it is useful to outline the different types of orders banks typically receive from their clients in the FX market.

The intention of submitting a *market order* is to execute a transaction immediately at the current best bid–ask spread. A market order could also be submitted 'at best', for instance, if the amount exceeds the volume offered at the current best bid–ask spread. It is well established among market participants and in the market microstructure literature that order flow affects exchanges rates (Lyons 1997; Evans and Lyons 2002). As a market order contains information about the likely future direction of the market, a market buy [sell] order is, ceteris paribus, more likely to result in a higher [lower] price – at least in the short run (Daniélsson, Luo, and Payne 2012; Evans and Lyons 2005; King and Rime 2010; Payne 2003). Using this logic, a trader could, therefore, at least temporarily, cause an increase [decrease] in the price by deliberately submitting a large market buy [sell] order, as a large order is more likely to be perceived as information-rich by others. If the market price rises [falls] accordingly, the trader could then attempt to profit from the manipulative trading strategy by submitting a market sell [buy] order to reverse the position. 'Front running' involves trading in front of a large customer order to benefit from the likely price movement the order is likely to generate as a result of being executed in the market. However, as we shall see later, front running can also be applied to other types of orders.[3]

Clients not only submit FX market orders to banks but also *limit orders*. Traditional models in the market microstructure literature largely saw limit orders as passive orders by uninformed traders (Glosten 1994; Seppi 1997; Daniélsson and Payne 2012). However, more recently, and in line with market wisdom, limit

---

[2] An actual outcome of the manipulated price (or a resulting profit or loss) is not a necessary condition (CFTC 2014b).
[3] See, for instance, FINMA (2014) and DFS (2017b).

orders have become seen as information-rich and therefore treated as active strate-gies (Foucault, 1999; Foucault, Kadan and Kandel 2005; Rosu 2009). A limit order submission changes the information content of the limit order book, regardless whether it is submitted from a client to a bank, from a bank to an interdealer bro-ker or from a market participant to an electronic trading platform (Stenfors and Susai 2018b). Consequently, similar logic can be applied to trade-based manipu-lation concerning limit orders as to market orders. For instance, clients in the FX market frequently leave *stop-loss orders* and *take-profit orders* to market makers throughout the day, overnight or 'until cancelled'. By instructing the bank to buy or sell a specific amount of a currency at a specific price, the client can rest assured that the loss is limited or the profit is guaranteed should the market price reach a predefined level. 'Triggering a stop-loss' involves intentional buying [selling] activ-ity by a bank to push the market price higher [lower] so that the client order gets triggered.

There are also limit orders that lack a pre-defined price level. *Fix orders* are executed at an agreed-upon time in the future. As with financial derivatives, the execution or settlement price of a fix order ultimately depends on the benchmark fixing used. There are a number of FX benchmarks around the world, some of which are directly used for derivatives contracts. However, two of the most widely used FX benchmarks is the WM/Reuters 4 p.m. fix and the 1:15 p.m. ECB fix. These are used for a range of purposes, including valuation of assets and liabilities in foreign cur-rencies and portfolios held by pension funds and asset managers. The WM/Reuters 4 p.m. fix, in particular, has gained the status of an 'official' London closing rate for many currency pairs. For instance, by acting as a benchmark for $11 trillion worth of index funds, it generates a large number client orders around this particular time of the day. The WM/Reuters 4 p.m. fix is based on actual FX trading by market par-ticipants just before and just after the time of fixing (the 'fixing window'). Before February 2015, the fixing window was 60 seconds. A bank accepting a client buy [sell] order for a specific amount at the fix rate agrees to sell [buy] that amount at the fix rate, regardless where the market price is after that. Consequently, banks offset client buy and sell orders and are supposed to manage the remaining risk through buying and selling in the FX spot market. 'Banging the close' (concerning a fix order) involves a strategy whereby a trader attempts to influence the underlying price, typi-cally very close to the time of fixing, to profit from the fix order. The logic is similar to manipulating the market, which underpins the benchmark for a derivatives posi-tion. As the value of a derivative depends on the outcome of the fixing, the payoff is directly affected by the manipulation of the underlying market (Jarrow, 1994; Pir-rong, 2017).

7.3   The Unique FX Market Structure

Manipulative practices are not a new phenomenon in FX markets. However, several factors can be attributed to them being perceived as virtually immune to manipu-lation and collusion by the wider public, including policymakers and academics, up until the Forex scandal broke in 2013. In this respect, five important aspects are notable.

First, with a daily turnover of around $5.067 trillion, the over-the-counter (OTC) FX market is comfortably the largest in the world.[4] The market typically operates with zero commissions and often extremely tight (and seemingly competitive) bid–ask spreads. Even during episodes of volatility and stress, the market liquidity tends to be very good. 'I'm sceptical of the ability of traders to manipulate the major currencies in a meaningful way given the massive size of this market [. . .] Governments themselves often have a difficult time moving foreign-exchange markets through their interventions,' an academic is quoted having said in the Bloomberg article in 2013 (Vaughan, Finch, and Choudhury 2013). This view broadly captured the perception of FX markets from the outside at the time. In this respect, parallels can be drawn to the LIBOR scandal. The vast turnover of LIBOR-indexed derivatives contracts, coupled with its function as a benchmark for mortgages, bonds and loans, and usage in monetary policy assessments and methodologies related to tax, accounting and risk, served to mask its susceptibility to manipulation for a long time (Stenfors and Lindo, 2018). As Stenfors (2018) argues, these factors contributed to the belief that manipulative attempts in the FX market would render themselves to be unsuccessful. Put simply, it is less likely that an investigation is launched into a market that, absent central bank intervention, appears to be driven by market forces; and that is sufficiently efficient and robust to withstand price manipulation.

Second, financial institutions and dealers working for these are regulated. However, in contrast to securities markets, the global FX market, itself, is overwhelmingly unregulated. Thus, claims of what could constitute attempts of manipulation have fallen under the umbrella of unfair or unethical trading practices, but strictly speaking not illegal or in breach of any regulation. This does not mean that FX trading is entirely self-regulated by its millions of market participants and end users. Instead, informal rules relating to trading etiquette evolve from discussions, meetings, and interaction between the market-making banks, often in dialogue with central banks. Since 1975, the International Code of Conduct and Practice for the Financial Markets ('the Model Code'), although adopted on a voluntary basis, serves as an industry standard for the global FX market. The Model Code is published by the ACI ('Association Cambiste Internationale' or the Financial Markets Association), which, since 1955, serves as the trade organization for bank (including central bank) dealers in FX and money markets around the world. According to the 2009 edition of the Model Code (ACI 2009), 'honour, honesty and integrity' should be core principles underpinning trading practices. However, apart from issues relating to sharing of confidential information, the 86-page handbook contains limited guidance about manipulation and collusive practices. In fact, the term 'manipulation' is only mentioned once and even then not directly in relation to standard trade manipulation: 'the sudden temporary withdrawal of a specific credit limit or limits in a tactical manipulation to mislead the market is

---

[4] FX spot transactions (agreements to exchange sums of currency at an agreed-on exchange rate on a value date that is generally in two bank business days' time) make up approximately 33% of the FX market. FX forwards (agreements to exchange sums of currency at an agreed-on exchange rate on a value date that will be in more than two bank business days' time) stand for 14% and FX swaps (a combination of a spot and forward transaction done simultaneously but in the opposite direction) for 47%. The remaining turnover is largely made up by currency swaps and FX options.

bad practice and strongly discouraged.' 'Front running' is only brought up concerning dealing for a personal account, and whereas a section is devoted to 'stop-loss orders', it contains nothing suggesting dealers could intentionally attempt to trigger stop-loss orders submitted by clients. The enforcement mechanism as outlined by the 2009 Model Code is also lax. Should a dispute arise if 'an institution has breached the letter or spirit of The Model Code', the firm should 'seek to settle this amicably with the other party.' Only (on the extremely rare occasion) when this avenue had been exhausted, the issue should be brought to the attention of ACI's Committee for Professionalism. Thus, given the vital role of the ACI, it is only logical that behavioural issues related to FX trading were dealt with internally within the bank, or externally on a trader-to-trader, bank-to-bank or bank-to-customer basis in the spirit of self-regulation – before the revelations of widespread misconduct in 2013.

Third, the FX market is mainly OTC and therefore opaque and relationship-based. It is also subject to conflicts of interest. The exchange-traded FX derivatives market (consisting of FX futures and FX options) is minuscule with a daily turnover of $0.115 trillion (BIS 2016) when compared to the $5.067 trillion-a-day OTC FX market. The latter is decentralized and requires a different kind of coordination than, say, the stock market. Furthermore, there is no exchange or institution gathering and providing real-time price and volume data to the public. Importantly, prices in all OTC markets (including FX) depend on the relationships between the counterparties involved in the trading and market-making process. Traditionally, the liquidity provision has been conducted by market-makers in banks, who quote prices on a range of currency pairs to clients on demand. To enable this, competing market-makers also quote prices to each other. Ultimately, banks cannot lend money or sell currencies unless they can access liquidity themselves. The commitment to provide liquidity to each other (i.e. to quote two-way prices to in a range of currency pairs to other market-making banks) rests upon a voluntary but long-standing convention. The Model Code encourages such mutual trading relationships by stating that 'bilateral reciprocal dealing relationships are common in the OTC markets and often extend to unwritten understandings between Dealers to quote firm two-way dealing prices.' Furthermore, they are seen as 'a logical development in the OTC markets and play an important role in providing support and liquidity' (ACI, 2015). Historically, such conventions have included the 'price' for market liquidity, namely appropriate bid–ask spreads for different currency pairs and, in the case of FX swaps and FX forwards, for different maturities. For instance, according to surveys among FX spot dealers in Hong Kong, New York, Singapore, and Tokyo during the late 1990s, an overwhelming majority claimed that the 'market convention' was the primary driver opting for a particular interbank bid–ask spread (Cheung and Wong 2000; Cheung and Chinn 2001). Using data from 2005 to 2016, Stenfors (2018) finds that such bid–ask spread conventions may also play an essential role in FX swap markets. Conventions have also extended to volume-based market liquidity, such as standardized matrices for reasonable interbank trading amounts, and even unwritten understandings of the typical length of time a two-way price can be expected to be valid (Stenfors and Susai 2018a). With reciprocity being central to the liquidity provision, mutual understandings, even among competitors, have therefore been natural in the FX markets. This, in turn, suggests some form of communication among competing banks regarding certain aspects of the price determination process – something that inevitably poses problems from an antitrust perspective. Furthermore, by acting as principals and agents at the same time (and FX traders often performing the roles simultaneously), the market-maker versus market-taker role often becomes less than straightforward. The net 'inventory' held by an FX trader/desk/bank is difficult to define. Put simply: a bank can, technically, sell all its shares in a company or holdings in a specific commodity. It cannot, however, have zero exposure to currency. Conflicts of interest are inevitable outcomes of this. If one individual simultaneously performs the function of customer order flow trader, market maker and proprietary trader, establishing evidence of, for instance, front running or triggering of stop-losses becomes difficult.

Fourth, Pirrong (2017) defines price manipulation as 'intentional conduct that causes market prices to diverge from their competitive level (or, in the case of imperfectly competitive markets, exacerbates divergences between market prices and their competitive level).' Here, too, FX and money markets are different from stock markets. Throughout history, they have been subject to state-endorsed attempts via central bank decisions to deliberately move the market prices away from what could be regarded as their 'competitive level'.[5] Short-term money market instruments have an inherent link to the state and a natural 'anchor' in the official central bank interest rate. It is therefore plausible to assume that prices of financial instruments which depend on the monopoly price set by central banks are more difficult to manipulate than others. Likewise, such prices (even though traded in the open market) are more likely to observe price stickiness. Thus, without any communication between them, competing firms might 'harmonize' their quotes around this anchor (Stenfors 2018). This behaviour is more likely to apply to the short-term FX swap market, where prices are highly dependent on the monetary policy decisions by the respective central banks issuing the two currencies involved. However, the FX spot market also has a long history of central bank intervention in the price determination process. Direct state intervention into the price determination process not only exists in markets where the central bank operates under a fixed exchange rate regime. Even central banks without explicit exchange rate targets (Bank of Japan, Federal Reserve, and others) have occasionally intervened in the market processes, often with a justification that the volatility is unduly high or that the exchange rate is 'mispriced' from a long-term fundamental perspective.[6] Thus, whereas 'FX manipulation' is a relatively new term in the academic literature or the press, 'currency manipulation' is an old phenomenon. However, even though central bank intervention would not constitute market manipulation, it could partly explain why speculation with the intent to move the market price hitherto has been more 'tolerated' in the FX markets than in many other markets – and therefore been less investigated.[7]

---

[5] Although a currency intervention is normally undertaken by a central bank, the jurisdiction lies with the respective government (Vitale, 2006).

[6] According to the Federal Reserve (2007), 'U.S. foreign exchange intervention is used as a device to signal a desired exchange rate movement.'

[7] IMF prohibits currency manipulation for the purpose of gaining unfair trade advantage.

Fifth, when comparing the exchange-traded stock market with the OTC FX market, the latter is undoubtedly less susceptible to *some* forms of financial market misconduct (for a detailed synthesis on misconduct in exchange-traded markets, see Cumming, Dannhauser, and Johan 2015). For instance, the fundamental drivers of prices are different. Publicly announced macroeconomic data releases and central bank statements are perceived as more critical determinants for exchange rate movements than non-public information. The same goes for proprietary research reports by financial analysts or macroeconomists. Whereas both could be valuable and ultimately have a market impact, equity markets are considerably more sensitive to stock recommendations than FX markets to FX strategy reports. Thus, claims of insider trading or trading ahead of research reports are extremely rare in FX markets. Exceptions include highly publicized (but denied) allegations of FX insider dealing involving central bank officials (see, for instance, Wilson 2012) or alleged (but unconfirmed) FX dealing ahead of leaked macroeconomic data releases (see Bruce, Schomberg, and Graham 2017). Similar logic could be applied to possible dissemination of false and misleading information. The FX market is by no means free from market-moving rumours. However, they are, on balance, more easily verifiable. Furthermore, neither being classified as securities nor easily defined in terms of 'inventory', some forms of misconduct are less applicable to FX transactions – such as 'corners', 'squeezes', 'parking', and 'warehousing'.

In sum, whereas the FX market has never been immune to manipulative and collusive practices, a range of unique characteristics provide essential clues in explaining why widespread misconduct was allowed to go undetected, and unpunished, for such a long time. They are also important when reflecting upon the effectiveness and challenges facing regulators, lawmakers and compliance officers in establishing robust rulebooks in the markets going forward.

7.4   Examples of Manipulative and Collusive Practices in FX Markets

7.4.1   Front Running

Front running involves trading in front of a large customer order to benefit from the price movement the order is likely to generate as a result of being executed in the market.

Let us assume that the €/$ FX spot market is trading at 1.2500–1.2505. Assume also that the current bid–ask spread is only good for a relatively small amount (e.g. €10 million). Now suppose a client requests a bank to buy €1 billion 'at best'. Both the client and the bank are fully aware that the unusually large buy order is likely to cause the FX price to go up, and that the average fill will be higher than 1.2505. An example of front running would be the following. First, the bank buys €100 million for its proprietary account at an average rate of 1.2510. After that, the bank buys €1 billion for the client at an average price of 1.2535. Finally, the bank sells the €100 million from its proprietary account at 1.2530. The profit to the bank from front running is $200,000 (20 pips of €100 million).[8] The client is worse off, as the best rate would have been lower than 1.2535 had the bank not engaged in front running.

---

[8] Following the market convention, 1 pip is the 4th decimal in the €/$ FX market.

A core issue with front running in FX markets is the fact that traders often act as both principals and agents. If a client submits a market order to buy [sell] a large amount from a bank at best, the client expects the trader to buy [sell] from other market participants, as well as possibly use some of the inventory already held. Either way, the client would expect the best possible fill. However, FX transactions are not exchange-traded. Consequently, it is virtually impossible for the client to find out whether any of the initial trades that were executed at a lower [higher] price were added to the trader's inventory or included in the customer order fill.

In the numerous settlements between banks and the UK and the US regulators in 2014 and 2015, front running is not brought up as a specific failing. By contrast, however, the Swiss Financial Market Supervisory Authority FINMA (2014) refers to it several times in its investigation and subsequent fine imposed to UBS of Sfr134 million. A year later, FINMA (2015) issued industry bans for between one and five years against six FX and precious metals traders (including the heads of global FX trading and global FX spot trading) for, among other things, engaging in front running. The following extracts (using direct quotations) from electronic group chats, released by the Swiss regulator, show evidence of front running by UBS traders:

UBS trader: *'the day of intervention, i was front running EVERY SINGLE ODA and I mean EVERY haha'*.
UBS trader: *'I was front running EVERY single offer in usdjpy and eurjpy.'*
UBS trader: *'I was using my management book to front-run an order.'*
UBS trader: *'I made 150k Front Running the try styff.'*
UBS trader: *'thanks vm my friend [. . .] you can front run this as you like, up to you'* .
UBS trader: *'call me a legend! Front run legend.'*
UBS trader A to UBS trader B (internal chat): *'the thing is we are not allowed to front run an-ymore, compliance is on our asses'*.

Several observations are notable from the conversations. First, front running appears to have taken place frequently in the FX market (note the usage of 'EVERY') and also by experienced traders ('my management book'). Second, the misconduct seems to have been prevalent not only in the major currency markets ('usdjpy' and 'eurjpy' refers to $/¥ and €/¥) but also in emerging markets ('try' or 'TRY' is the currency code for the Turkish lira). Third, front running was very profitable for the bank ('150k', i.e. $150,000). Fourth, the casual and sometimes bragging language used (e.g. 'up to you', 'legend') suggests that traders were relatively unconcerned about the activity – until internal investigations involving the compliance department began taking place.

In 2017, the US Department of Financial Services (DFS) fined Credit Suisse $135 million for 'unlawful, unsafe and unsound' FX trading conduct. The consent order also included front running, whereby the bank had designed an in-house trading algorithm to front run both limit orders and stop-loss orders (DFS 2017b).

Being a form of market manipulation, front running is prohibited in most regulated securities markets. However, being both largely unregulated and difficult to enforce, the practice is not explicitly illegal in the global FX market. However, on

20 July 2016, two FX spot traders at HSBC, Stuart Scott and Mark Johnsson, were charged with conspiring to defraud a client through front running. According to the complaint, a client had left an order with HSBC to buy approximately £/$2.25 billion on 7 December 2011. Rather than executing the order 'at best', HSBC and the client agreed to execute the order using the 3 p.m. fixing in London (for fix orders, see Section 7.4.3). However, the traders did not simply execute the order for the client at 3 p.m. Instead, they bought pound sterling for HSBC's proprietary accounts beforehand and held on to this position until they executed the client trade. They then aggressively bought on behalf of the client, causing a spike in the £/$ FX spot price at precisely 3 p.m. As a result of front running the order, the traders generated profits of $8 million at the expense of the client (DOJ 2016). In this first criminal FX front-running case, the FBI Assistant Director in Charge Paul Abbate said: 'These individuals are accused of defrauding clients by misusing confidential information to manipulate currency prices for the benefit of the bank and themselves'. Mark Johnsson (found guilty in October 2017) argued in his defence that there were no regulatory, bank or market policies prohibiting front running and that it was 'common practice' (Hurtado and Nguyen 2017). (At the time of writing, Scott is fighting extradition and Johnson has not yet been sentenced). Further, in January 2018, the former Head of FX Trading at Barclays New York was criminally charged for allegedly front-running a large client trade. According to the indictment, the scheme also involved a form of derivatives manipulation – namely the suppression of volatility in order to influence the price of FX options (DOJ 2018).

7.4.2 Triggering Stop-Loss Orders

Clients in the FX market frequently leave stop-loss and take-profit orders to market makers throughout the day, overnight or 'until cancelled'. By instructing the bank to buy or sell a specific amount of a currency at a specific price, the client can rest assured that the loss is limited or the profit is guaranteed should the market price reach a predefined level.

Like in the FX market in general, clients neither pay fees for giving such orders nor commissions should they be executed. Instead, the banks benefit in other ways from providing this service. For salespeople, it is a way to maintain a dealing relationship. Furthermore, the lifetime of stop-loss and take-profit orders can be relatively long if they are submitted far from the current market price or if the volatility is low. A substantial in-house order book can, therefore, provide valuable (and confidential) information about the balance between supply and demand in the market, as well indications with regards to the sensitivity of the market to specific price levels. If the market is illiquid, a stop-loss order might also enable a trader with the opposite position or market view to offset risk without having to pay the current bid–ask t the order reach the predefined level. Suppose the €/$ FX spot market is trading at 1.2530–1.2535 and that a client has left a stop-loss order to sell €100 million at 1.2500. If the market price falls to 1.2500–1.2505, the stop-loss is triggered, and the bank buys €100 million from the client at 1.2500. If the trader watching the order is keen to buy €100 million at the time, s/he is not required to pay the full bid–ask spread, i.e. 1.2505.

Triggering a stop-loss involves intentional selling [buying] activity to push the market price lower [higher] so that the order gets triggered. Suppose, again, the €/$ FX spot market is trading at 1.2530–1.2535 and that a client has left a stop-loss order to sell €100 million at 1.2500. An example of triggering a stop-loss order would be the following. First, the bank sells €10 million for its proprietary account at 1.2530. Then, the bank sells another €10 million at 1.2527, another €10 million at 1.2523, etc., until the market price falls to 1.2500–1.2505 as a result of the intense selling activity. Assume that the bank manages to sell €100 million for its proprietary account at an average rate of 1.2515. However, as the FX spot market price now has reached the predefined stop-loss level of 1.2500, the bank can buy €100 million at 1.2500 from the client to cover its position. The profit to the bank from triggering the stop-loss order is $150,000 (15 pips of €100 million). In this case, the client is worse off as the stop-loss order is triggered as a result of the bank's deliberate selling activity induced by the order itself, rather than market forces. Without the bank's selling activity, the stop-loss order might not have been triggered at all. Alternatively, the process might have been slower, giving the client time to cancel or revise the order.

There is an apparent conflict of interest with such orders in the FX market. On the one hand, the bank (or trader) accepting the stop-loss order on behalf of the client acts as an agent. On the other hand, the same bank (or trader), though its role as principal, can influence the price by actively trading in the same market on a proprietary basis. If the market is resilient, the price might quickly return to its original level. In the example above, suppose the €/$ FX spot price, immediately after the client has sold €100 million at 1.2500 to the bank, rises to 1.2520. Problematically, as the market price *de facto* had reached the level at which the stop-loss was supposed to be triggered, the client would face a challenge in arguing otherwise.

Attempts to trigger clients' stop-loss orders featured in all FX-related Final Notices issued by the FCA (2014b,c,d,e,f) in November 2014 when it fined Citi, HSBC, JP Morgan Chase, RBS, and UBS £1.1 billion in total for their FX spot practices. Examples of conversation extracts (using direct quotations) released by the UK financial regulator read:

HSBC trader: *"love them [the stop-loss orders] . . . free money'* and *'we love the orders . . . always make money on them'.*
UBS trader: *'i had stops for years but they got sick of my butchering'.*
UBS trader: *'just jamming a little stop here'.*
HSBC trader: *'just about to slam some stops'.*
HSBC trader: *'going to go for broke at this stop. . . it is either going to end in massive glory or tears'.*

Several observations are notable from the conversations. The casual language used (e.g. 'jamming' or 'slam') suggests that the activity was relatively common. Furthermore, triggering of stop-loss orders appears to have been highly profitable for the bank (e.g. 'free money', 'love the orders'), but loss-making for the clients (e.g. 'butchering'). Despite the obvious risk involved from the trader's perspective (in this case of not being able to trigger a stop-loss order despite intense buying or selling activity), the risks sometimes seem to have been outweighed by the rewards (e.g. 'going to go for broke at this stop').

7.4.3 'Banging the Close'

Whereas a stop-loss order only gets executed should a predefined price level be reached before the order is cancelled, a fix order will be executed at a predefined point of time irrespective of the price level. 'Banging the close' (concerning a fix order) involves a strategy whereby a trader attempts to influence the underlying price, typically very close to the time of fixing, to profit from the fix order.

Suppose the €/$ FX spot market is trading at 1.2530–1.2535 at 3:45 p.m. and that a client has a left an order to a bank to sell €100 million at the WM/Reuters 4 p.m. fix. The WM/Reuters 4 p.m. fix is based on actual FX trading by market participants just before and just after the time of fixing (the 'fixing window'). Before February 2015, the fixing window was 60 seconds. By accepting the fix order, the bank guarantees that the client order will be executed at the fix rate. An example of 'banging the close' would be the following. First, just before the fixing window, the bank sells €50 million for its proprietary account at an average rate of 1.2520. Then, during the fixing window, the bank sells a further €50 million for its proprietary account at an average rate of 1.2510. Consequently, let us assume that the average rate traded in the €/$ FX spot market between 3:50 p.m. and 4:01 p.m. is 1.2510. Thus, the €/$ FX spot 4 p.m. fix settles at 1.2510 on that day. The profit to the bank from 'banging the close' is $50,000 (10 pips of €50 million). The client is worse off as the manipulative tactic caused the FX spot price to be lower than it had otherwise been at that particular time of the day. Without the bank's aggressive selling before the fixing window, the fixing might have been higher and thus in the client's favour.

Attempts to manipulate the WM/Reuters 4 p.m. fix and other frequently used FX benchmarks feature in several of the settlements between banks and the FCA. Sometimes, it was done in collusion with other banks in chat rooms.[9] For instance, the following scenario took place on the FX spot desk at HSBC on one day during the period for which it was fined by the FCA (2014c). The conversation shown in Table 7.1 between traders at different banks (using direct quotations) illustrates the collusive behaviour.

Table 7.2 shows HSBC's £/$ FX spot trading activity during half an hour before and within the fixing window.

As can be seen, HSBC sold £70 million between 3:32:00 p.m. and 3:59:00 p.m. that day, which caused the £/$ FX spot rate to fall significantly. Then, during the fixing window, the bank sold another £311 million in total. The selling caused the WM/Reuters 4 p.m. fix rate to settle at a fairly low rate (1.6003) ultimately. According to the findings by the UK financial regulator, HSBC netted $162,000 in profits from £/$ FX spot fix orders on that day. Notably, during the crucial fixing window, HSBC accounted for 51% of the turnover in the £/$ FX spot market.

---

[9] Electronic messaging services (e.g. chat rooms) allow market participants to communicate internally (with other market participants in the firm) and externally (with clients and traders at other banks).

Table 7.1   Manipulation of the WM/Reuters 4 p.m. fix (conversations).

Time	Conversation extract	Author's explanation
3:25 p.m.	HSBC has orders to sell £400 million against US dollars at the 4 p.m. fix, and Bank A has sell orders worth £150 million. *'Let's go,'* HSBC tells Bank A. *'Yeah baby.'*	HSBC and Bank A both have substantial £/$ sell orders from clients, and have an incentive to push the fix lower at 4 p.m. The conversation shows evidence of intended manipulation as well as collusion between the two competitors.
3:28 p.m.	*'Hopefully a few more get same way and we can team whack it,'* Bank A says. HSBC asks Bank C to do some *'digging'* to see if anyone else has orders in the same direction.	By now, three banks are in collusion. Bank C is encouraged to find what kind of fix orders other banks have. This conversation also suggests that some banks might be willing to share confidential information.
3:34 p.m.	Bank C has sell orders worth £83 million.	
3:36 p.m.	Bank A now has sell orders worth £170 million and Bank B has £40 million in the same direction. Bank D steps into the conversation and exclaims: *'Bash the fck out of it.'*	Five banks are in collusion. The trader at Bank D proposes that they should sell £/$ spot aggressively in the FX spot market.
3:42 p.m.	Bank A warns HSBC that Bank E is *'building'* in the opposite direction to them and will be buying at the fix.	A member of conspiracy finds out, and consequently warns HSBC, that a sixth bank (Bank E) has the opposite incentive. Moreover, Bank E is supposedly trying to increase its fix orders (referred to as 'building' or 'building ammo'). Banks with large fix order books have more market power, and also a greater incentive to attempt to influence the fix.
3:43 p.m.	Bank A tells HSBC, *'[I have] taken him [Bank E] out . . . so shud have giot rid of main buyer for u . . . im stilla seller of 90 [million] . . . gives us a chance.'*	Bank A has succeeded to 'neutralize' the bank with an opposite incentive, presumably through order matching (sometimes referred to as 'clearing the decks' or 'taking out the filth').

Source: Based on data from FCA (2014c).

7.4.4   Collusion and Sharing of Confidential Information

In the settlement agreement between the FCA and HSBC (and a series of other banks), the regulator pointed out several specific failings in respect the bank's FX spot trading business (FCA 2014c). Traders at HSBC had attempted to trigger clients' stop-loss orders and to manipulate the WM/Reuters 4 p.m. fix rate. Both manipulative practices were for HSBC's benefit and to the potential detriment of clients and other market participants. However, as illustrated in Section 7.4.3, the manipulation of the fix rate

Table 7.2   Manipulation of the WM/Reuters 4 p.m. fix (trading activity and FX spot movement).

Time	HSBC's £/$ FX spot trading activity	£/$ FX spot
3:32:00 p.m. –3:59:00 p.m.	HSBC sells £/$ 70 million	£/$ FX spot falls from 1.6044 to 1.6009
3:59:01 p.m. –3:59:05 p.m.	HSBC sells £/$ 101 million	£/$ FX spot falls to 1.6000
3:59:06 p.m. –4:01:00 p.m.	HSBC sells £/$ 210 million	
WM/Reuters 4 p.m. fix		1.6003

Source: Based on data from FCA (2014c).

had also been in collusion with traders at other banks. Furthermore, with regards to both stop-loss orders and fix orders, traders had shared confidential information with traders at other banks. As the regulator pointed out, this included information about the orders and specific client identities. The clients typically were significant market participants and included central banks, large corporates, pension funds, and hedge funds. Put together, this gave a group of traders at competing banks more insight about potentially market-moving information than they would have had absent collusion.

The abuse of market power through collusive practices could deprive end users of active price competition, resulting in higher prices. This issue has been brought up in several other settlement agreements (see, for instance, OCC, 2014; Federal Reserve, 2017), where communication between market-making banks not only involved coordinated market manipulation and disclosing of confidential client information, but also sharing of proprietary bank information such as FX bid–ask spreads. Furthermore, at BNP, the collusive conduct also involved the creation of fake trades intended to manipulate prices, and the determination of (wider) bid–ask spreads to customers in some currency pairs (DFS 2017a).

The susceptibility of financial markets to bid–ask spread conspiracies was highlighted more than two decades ago in relation to stocks traded on NASDAQ (Christie and Schultz 1994a,b). From an antitrust perspective, the bid–ask spread is treated as a 'price component', and such conduct might, therefore, be considered a price-fixing conspiracy and in breach of competition law (New York Southern District Court 2015). There are no commissions involved in buying and selling directly with an FX trading desk. Instead, trading both as market-makers *and* market-takers, banks make their profits from the bid–ask spread and price movements. This, coupled with reciprocal (but largely informal) arrangements in terms of liquidity provision between banks, makes the interbank market vulnerable to a bid–ask spread determination process that lacks competition at all times. Stenfors (2018) shows how bid–ask spread conventions in FX swap markets, in particular, can be harmful to end users without necessarily raising immediate concerns from antitrust authorities. Nonetheless, a violation of Section One of the Sherman Antitrust Act is specifically included in an indictment issued in May 2018, which *inter alia* alleges that a group of FX traders at various banks coordinated their bid-ask spreads for emerging market currency pairs (New York Southern District Court 2018).

7.4.5 Spoofing

Spoofing involves placing 'fictitious' limit orders in the market with the intent to influence other traders' perception of the prevailing state of the market and is also regarded as a manipulative tactic. Let us assume that the €/$ FX spot market is 1.2500–1.2505 on an electronic trading platform. Suppose also that this platform consists of just two orders: a limit buy order of €10 million at 1.2500 by Trader A and a limit sell order of €10 million at 1.2505 by Trader B. An example of spoofing would involve the following. Trader C submits a sell order of €3 million at 1.2506, a sell order of €2 million at 1.2507 and a sell order of €5 million at 1.2508. The traders having submitted their orders at 1.2500 and 1.2505, respectively, now see that the balance of buy versus sell orders has changed in the market. Although the new limit orders are placed outside the current best bid–ask spread, the limit order book on the sell-side has doubled. This indicates that there are more sellers than buyers in the market at this particular moment in time. Consequently, Trader A, having submitted the limit buy order at 1.2500, is led to believe that s/he might be picked off. To reduce the 'free-option risk', Trader A revises the buy order to 1.2497. Moreover, Trader B, having submitted the limit sell order at 1.2505, is led to believe that other sellers might jump the queue. To reduce the 'non-execution risk', Trader B revises the sell order to 1.2502. Then, in quick succession, Trader C cancels the three spoof orders and buys €10 million at 1.2502. Trader C profits $3,000 from spoofing (3 pips of €10 million). The three orders are 'spoof orders', as they are intended to be cancelled rather than executed.

Limit order submissions involve a trade-off between the appropriate size and the level of price aggressiveness (Lo and Sapp 2010). A relatively large and aggressive limit order might be interpreted as information-rich, acting to trigger order cancellations by traders on the other side of the order book or front running by traders on the same side of the order book – reducing the likelihood of being filled. Following this logic, it is easy to see how limit orders have the ability to affect both price-based and volume-based liquidity measures (Bjønnes, Rime, and Solheim 2005; Daniélsson and Payne 2012), which, consequently, makes limit order submissions essential ingredients in trading strategies. A trader intending to execute a large amount knows that the transaction price will depend on the liquidity, regarding price and volume, offered by other market participants. The other market participants, in turn, will adjust the liquidity provided depending on information received from the market. In the hypothetical example above, the spoof orders contained (misleading) information about the volume on the sell-side of the limit order book. Spoofing tactics involve the intent to create a false impression or the state of the market. Put differently, it is about creating an 'illusion of liquidity' with the purpose to influence other market participants' perception of (future) market price.

The 2010 Dodd–Frank Act explicitly makes spoofing a criminal act (defined as 'bidding or offering with the intent to cancel the bid or offer before execution') in the commodities and futures markets. The convictions and regulatory settlements so far suggest that markets highly populated with algorithmic limit orders could be particularly susceptible to manipulative trading tactics such as spoofing (CFTC 2018). Most other jurisdictions have not yet followed, perhaps as the manipulative practice already could be covered under fraud legislation (Quereé 2016). The Global FX Code

(BIS 2017) loosely covers spoofing by stating that 'Market Participants should not request transactions or create orders with the intention of disrupting market functioning or hindering the price discovery process, including undertaking actions designed to result in a false impression of market price, depth, or liquidity'. Thus, whereas manipulative trading tactics involving spoofing might not (yet) be illegal, they are widely considered to be unethical.

7.4.6   Market Abuse via Electronic Trading Platforms

In 2016, 43% of the FX turnover was voice-executed. The other 57% was electronic trading and split between direct (e.g. single bank platforms such as Barclay's BARX, Deutsche Bank's Autobahn and Citi's Velocity) and indirect (e.g. EBS, Reuters Matching and other ECNs) (BIS 2016). The revelations since 2013 surrounding widespread misconduct in the FX markets have overwhelmingly concerned human traders. More recently, however, banks' execution methodologies on such platforms have resulted in controversies and regulatory settlements too.

In November 2015, Barclays was fined an additional $150 million for its use of a 'Last Look' system on its electronic trading platform BARX (DFS 2015). The Last Look system enabled Barclays to put customer orders on hold – between acceptance and executing them. During this time interval (often measured in milliseconds), the bank would compare the price at the time of order acceptance and order execution. But doing so, it could use it defensively to reject 'toxic order flow' by high-frequency traders. However, the system was extended to adopting it to filter customer orders and, if the price moved against the bank beyond a certain threshold, Barclays would reject the trade. Thus, according to the New York State Department of Financial Services, it had used the electronic platform to distinguish which customer traders would be potentially (un)profitable for the bank. In 2017, BNP Paribas and Credit Suisse were fined for similar misconduct (DFS 2017a,b). Furthermore, the Department of Financial Services found that Credit Suisse had used a computer algorithm on its electronic platform and designed it to front-run clients' limit and stop-loss orders.

Algorithmic FX trading has increased dramatically since the early 2000s, particularly in the spot market. Following the revelations of widespread manipulation and collusion, this trend is unlikely to reverse. Indeed, a shift towards electronic trading is increasingly encouraged also as a means to minimize the likelihood of human misconduct. As a result, trading tactics involving limit orders on electronic platforms are likely to come under greater scrutiny – most notably spoofing. It is, for obvious reasons, very challenging for jurors and lawmakers to determine whether orders have been submitted without the intention of becoming executed. This issue is particularly complicated in markets, which have seen an influx of algorithmic and high-frequency traders – including the OTC FX spot market. For instance, using a data set from the Electronic Broking Services (EBS) from 8–13 September 2010 containing 1,419,630 €/$ FX spot orders, Stenfors and Susai (2018a) find that 99.43% of the orders were limit, rather than market, orders. Compared to over €1.8 trillion worth of limit orders submitted, actual transactions 'only' amounted to €11.9 billion (0.66%). Furthermore, with a median limit order lifetime of a mere 2.5 seconds, it could be argued that the 'liquidity' on such electronic trading platforms is almost entirely made up of limit order submissions which ultimately become limit order cancellations.

The share of algorithmic trading on EBS, together with Reuters Matching (the most widely used platform used by market-making banks) increased from 2% in 2004 to around 70% in 2013 (Moore, Schrimpf, and Sushko 2016). This highlights how trading algorithms involving ultra-frequent limit order submission can be used to 'take the pulse of the market' (sometimes referred to as 'pinging'), i.e. to extract information about the limit order book content by analysing how other (human or algorithmic) traders respond to a *change* in the limit order book (Stenfors and Susai 2019, 2020). Whereas this phenomenon, in itself, does not suggest the prevalence of spoofing (following the 2010 Dodd–Frank Act definition), it could nonetheless serve to create a 'false impression of market price, depth, or liquidity' as per The Global FX Code.

7.5   The Reform Process

Historically, the buying and selling of currencies have not been treated as a regulated activity. Instead, restrictions on FX trading (if at all) have been more closely linked to the macroeconomic matters, such as exchange rate regimes and capital flows. However, the Forex scandal has revealed that the FX market is considerably more susceptible to manipulative and collusive practices than previously thought – and in ways not too dissimilar from other financial markets. Whereas the FX trading activity itself has managed to escape regulation, the main players (financial institutions and dealers working for these) have not. The examples of behavioural misconduct referred to in this chapter have involved principal–agent issues and sharing of confidential information. Consequently, the reform processes induced by regulatory agencies and the industry itself have focused on imposing stricter communication rules between traders, salespeople and the banks' clients, as well as between competing traders at market-making banks.

Together with several other financial benchmarks such as LIBOR, the WM/Reuters 4 p.m. fix has since been brought under regulatory control. Under the new regulation, the FCA is able to bring criminal prosecution for benchmark manipulation. This acts as a deterrent against misconduct in the future. Moreover, the window for calculating the fix has been extended from one to five minutes and includes a more extensive range of price sources (FEMR 2015). By default, the new mechanism makes manipulative attempts in relation to fix orders more costly and less likely to succeed.

The vast majority of reforms in the FX market remain dependent on voluntary participation by the financial institutions themselves. A first version of the new Global FX Code, published by the Bank for International Settlements in 2016 (and the complete, updated version in 2017) sets out to strengthen code of conduct standards and principles in FX markets (BIS 2017). The Global FX Code is not legally binding, but there is a strong expectation that banks will follow the rules and guidelines. For instance, in comparison with the previous ACI Model Codes, it spells out the inherent conflict of interest more clearly that might result in front running. The Model Code also requests banks to disclose whether they act as an agent 'without taking on market risk in connection with the order' or as a principal 'taking on one or more risks in connection with an order' when executing an order on behalf of a client. When executing the order, the bank has some discretion, but 'should exercise this discretion reasonably, fairly, and in such a way that is not designed or intended to disadvantage the Client'. Central banks and financial regulators have endorsed such changes to the Model Code.[10]

Having been fined over $10 billion in total during the last few years, there have also been numerous changes initiated from within the banks themselves. These include more robust compliance and conduct risk control frameworks, and stricter Chinese walls – especially with regards to benchmark-related orders and fixings (FCA 2016a). The FX market remains remarkably concentrated, with the top-5 banks capturing a market share of around 45% and the top-12 banks close to 70% in 2016 (Moore, Schrimpf, and Sushko 2016). More stringent rules regarding communication that could involve sharing of confidential information have been introduced, such as bans on using mobile phones and multi-bank electronic chat rooms (see, for instance, Verlaine and Finch 2014; Martin and Stafford 2015; Finch, Detrixhe, and Choudhury 2016). Anecdotal evidence also suggests that surveillance of traders' behaviour has increased considerably and that 'anything that could be seen as a red flag' is brought to the attention of compliance officers.

However, challenges remain. For instance, recent cases show that forms of misconduct also can take place on electronic trading platforms, and therefore be more associated with algorithmic, rather than human, trading. In February 2018, the Bank of England and the FCA issued a joint statement proposing to bring algorithmic trading in the wholesale markets under their supervision (Bank of England 2018a; FCA 2018). According to the Bank of England (2018b), new rules will apply 'to all algorithmic trading activities of a firm including in respect of unregulated financial instruments such as spot foreign exchange (FX).' Indeed, FX spot trading, which merely involves the buying of one currency and the selling of another, is unlike any financial instrument. The vast majority of FX-related instruments are exempt from the 2010 Dodd–Frank Act. Likewise, the FX market is not totally covered by the EU-wide Market Abuse Regime (MAR), effective from 3 July 2016, and the Markets in Financial Instruments Directive (MiFID II) from 3 January 2018. The definition of a financial instrument is broader under MAR, and includes instruments traded on trading venues and derivatives linked to these. However, according to the FCA (2016a), FX spot is seen as a regulated activity only 'in certain circumstances, for example where spot FX manipulation impacts an FX derivative or where spot FX trading is an ancillary activity to regulated business.'

As outlined in Section 7.3 of this chapter, the FX market is unique in many ways. It is also a market where the definition of terms such as 'instrument' and 'derivative' has been less than straightforward. An FX spot transaction is normally settled after two business days, and any contract settling thereafter could, in principle, be regarded as a derivative. However, FX forwards and FX swaps (which account for more than half of the FX market) settling within seven days are not classified as derivatives in some jurisdictions (Norton Rose Fulbright, 2014). To make

---

[10] According to the FCA (2016b): 'We welcome in particular the recognition that even where a dealer sets out that it is acting as principal, it still has important responsibilities to its clients when using its discretion on their behalf'.

matters more complicated, the vast majority of FX swaps settle not only within seven days but also often *before* spot. Thus, considering how integrated the FX spot, FX forward and FX swap markets are, uncertainty is likely to remain – at least for a while (see, for instance, Golden, 2016). Furthermore, every FX transaction affects two currencies and, therefore, automatically more than one jurisdiction. The issue related to the jurisdiction has been particularly evident with regards to the criminal changes imposed by US authorities on non-US residents working for non-US financial institutions. Here, the prosecution has taken the stance that FX manipulation, while conducted abroad, is 'felt' in the US (Ring 2017). Nonetheless, it is clear that the reforms induced by authorities and the industry significantly reduce opportunities for manipulative and collusive practices in FX markets. Overall, they are underpinned by a desire to make the FX market fairer and more professional. Perhaps most importantly, they have succeeded in setting more specific behavioural principles for FX markets – similar to the principles that have underpinned regulated security markets for several decades.

References

ACI (2009). The Model Code: The International Code of Conduct and Practice for the Financial Markets, Version April 2009.

ACI (2015). The Model Code: The International Code of Conduct and Practice for the Financial Markets, Version February 2015.

Allen, F. and Gale, F. (1992). Stock-price manipulation. *The Review of Financial Studies* 5 (3): 502–529.

Bank of England (2018a). Algorithmic trading. Consultation paper CP5/18, February. Available at: www.bankofengland.co.uk/-/media/boe/files/prudential-regulation/consultation-paper/2018/cp518.pdf?la=en&hash=89AB31B883DF430E36387BACCC93F15FC7A75A4A.

Bank of England (2018b). Algorithmic Trading. Supervisory statement 5/18, 15 June. Available at: www.bankofengland.co.uk/prudential-regulation/publication/2018/algorithmic-trading-ss.

BIS (2016). Triennial Central Bank Survey – Foreign exchange turnover in April 2016, September 2016. Available at: www.bis.org/publ/rpfx16fx.pdf.

BIS (2017). FX Global Code: A set of global principles of good practice in the foreign exchange market. Available at: www.globalfxc.org/docs/fx_global.pdf.

Bjønnes, G.H., Rime, D. and Solheim, H.O.A. (2005). Liquidity provision in the overnight foreign exchange market. *Journal of International Money and Finance* 24 (2): 175–196.

Bruce, A., Schomberg, W. and Graham, P. (2017). Unusual sterling moves often precede UK data releases – analysis. *Reuters*, 14 March. Available at: https://uk.reuters.com/article/uk-britain-forex-data/unusual-sterling-moves-often-precede-uk-data-releases-analysis-idUKKBN16L1ZU.

CFTC (2014a). CFTC Orders five banks to pay over $1.4 billion in penalties for attempted manipulation of foreign exchange benchmark rates. Press release, 12 November. Available at: http://www.cftc.gov/PressRoom/PressReleases/pr7056-14.

CFTC (2014b). In the Matter of: JPMorgan Chase Bank, N.A. Respondent, CFTC Docket No. 15–04, 11 November. Available at: www.cftc.gov/idc/groups/public/@lrenforcementactions/documents/legalpleading/enfjpmorganorder111114.pdf.

CFTC (2018). CFTC files eight anti-spoofing enforcement actions against three banks (Deutsche Bank, HSBC & UBS) & six individuals. Press release, 29 January. Available at: www.cftc.gov/PressRoom/PressReleases/pr7681-18.

Cheung, Y.-W. and Chinn, M.D. (2001). Currency traders and exchange rate dynamics: a survey of the US market. *Journal of International Money and Finance* 20: 439–471.

Cheung, Y.-W. and Wong, C.Y.-P. (2000). A survey of market practitioners' views on exchange rate dynamics. *Journal of International Economics*, 51: 401–419.

Chon, G., Binham, C. and Noonan, L. (2015). Six banks fined $5.6bn over rigging of foreign exchange markets. *Financial Times*, 20 May. Available at: www.ft.com/cms/s/0/23fa681c-fe73-11e4-be9f-00144feabdc0.html#slide0.

Christie, W. and Schultz, P. (1994a). Why did NASDAQ market makers avoid odd-eight quotes? *Journal of Finance* 49: 1813–1840.

Christie, W. and Schultz, P. (1994b). Why did NASDAQ market makers stop avoiding odd-eight quotes? *Journal of Finance* 49: 1841–1860.

Cumming, D., Dannhauser, R. and Johan, S. (2015). Financial market misconduct and agency conflicts: A synthesis and future directions. *Journal of Corporate Finance* 34: 150–168.

Daníelsson, J., Luo, J. and Payne, R. (2012). Exchange rate determination and inter-market order flow effects. *The European Journal of Finance* 18 (9): 823–840.

Daníelsson, J. and Payne, R. (2012). Liquidity determination in an order-driven market. *The European Journal of Finance* 18 (9): 799–821.

DFS (2015). NYDFS announces Barclays to pay additional $150 million penalty, terminate employee for automated, electronic trading misconduct. Press release, 18 November. Available at: https://www.dfs.ny.gov/reports_and_publications/press_releases/pr1511181.

DFS (2017a). DFS fines BNP Paribas $350 million for illegal, unsafe and unsound conduct in connection with BNPP's foreign exchange trading business. Press release, 24 May. Available at: https://dfs.ny.gov/reports_and_publications/press_releases/pr1705241.

DFS (2017b). DFS fines Credit Suisse AG $135 million for illegal, unsafe and unsound conduct in its foreign exchange trading business. Press release, 13 November. Available at: https://dfs.ny.gov/reports_and_publications/press_releases/pr1711131.

DOJ (2016). Global head of HSBC's foreign exchange cash-trading desks arrested for orchestrating multimillion-dollar front running scheme. Press release, 20 July. Available at: www.justice.gov/opa/pr/global-head-hsbc-s-foreign-exchange-cash-trading-desks-arrested-orchestrating-multimillion.

DOJ (2018). Former head of Barclays New York foreign exchange operation indicted for orchestrating multimillion-dollar front-running scheme. Press release, 16 January. Available at: www.justice.gov/opa/pr/former-head-barclays-new-york-foreign-exchange-operation-indicted-orchestrating-multimillion.

Evans, M. and Lyons, R. (2002). Order flow and exchange rate dynamics. *Journal of Political Economy* 110: 170–180.

Evans, M. and Lyons, R. (2005) Meese-Rogoff redux: Micro-based exchange-rate forecasting. *American Economic Review Papers and Proceedings* 95 (2): 405–414.

FCA (2014a). FCA fines five banks £1.1 billion for FX failings and announces industry-wide remediation programme. Press release, 12 November. Available at: www.fca.org.uk/ news/press-releases/fca-fines-five-banks-%C2%A311-billion-fx-failings-and-announces-industry-wide.

FCA (2014b). Final Notice: Citibank, N.A., 11 November. Available at: www.fca.org.uk/publication/ final-notices/final-notice-citi-bank.pdf.

FCA (2014c). Final Notice: HSBC Bank plc, 11 November. Available at: www.fca.org.uk/publi-cation/final-notices/final-notice-hsbc.pdf.

FCA (2014d). Final Notice: JPMorgan Chase Bank N.A., 11 November. Available at: www.fca .org.uk/publication/final-notices/final-notice-jpm.pdf.

FCA (2014e). Final Notice: The Royal Bank of Scotland plc, 11 November. Available at: www.fca.org.uk/publication/final-notices/final-notice-rbs.pdf.

FCA (2014f). Final Notice: UBS AG, 11 November. Available at: www.fca.org.uk/publication/ final-notices/final-notice-ubs.pdf.

FCA (2015). Final Notice: Barclays Bank PLC, 20 May. Available at: www.fca.org.uk/publication/ final-notices/barclays-bank-plc-may-15.pdf.

FCA (2016a). FX remediation programme: our next steps, Press release, 28 July. Available at: www.fca.org.uk/news/news-stories/fx-remediation-programme-our-next-steps.

FCA (2016b). FCA welcomes a significant milestone in the development of standards in FX markets through the publication of the BIS Global FX Code. Statement, 26 May. Available at: www.fca.org.uk/news/statements/fca-welcomes-significant-milestone-development-stand-ards-fx-markets-through.

FCA (2018). Algorithmic trading compliance in wholesale markets. February. Available at: www.fca.org.uk/publication/multi-firm-reviews/algorithmic-trading-compliance-wholesale-markets.pdf.

Federal Reserve (2007). US foreign exchange intervention, May. Available at: www.newyorkfed. org/aboutthefed/fedpoint/fed44.html.

Federal Reserve (2017). Federal Reserve announces two enforcement actions against Deutsche Bank AG that will require bank to pay a combined $156.6 million in civil money penal-ties. Press release, 20 April. Available at: www.federalreserve.gov/newsevents/pressreleases/ enforcement20170420a.htm.

FEMR (2015). Fair and Effective Markets Review. Final report, June 2015.

Finch, G., Detrixhe, J. and Choudhury, A. (2016). Spies who chased terrorists join banks to hunt for rogue traders. *Bloomberg*, 16 February. Available at: www.bloomberg.com/news/ articles/2016-02-16/spies-who-chased-terrorists-join-banks-to-hunt-for-rogue-traders.

FINMA (2014). Foreign exchange trading at UBS AG: investigation conducted by FINMA. Report, 12 November. Available at: www.finma.ch/en/news/2014/11/mm-ubs-devisenhandel-20141112/.

FINMA (2015). Foreign exchange manipulation: FINMA issues six industry bans. Press release, 17 December. Available at: www.finma.ch/en/news/2015/12/20151217-mm-devisenhandel/.

Foucault, T. (1999). Order flow composition and trading costs in a dynamic limit order market. *Journal of Financial Markets* 2: 99–134.

Foucault, T., Kadan, O. and Kandel, E. (2005). Limit order book as a market for liquidity. *Review of Financial Studies* 18 (4): 1171–1217.

Freifeld, K., Henry, D. and Slater, S. (2016). Global banks admit guilt in forex probe, fined nearly $6 billion. *Reuters*, 20 May. Available at: www.reuters.com/article/us-banks-forex-settlement/global-banks-admit-guilt-in-forex-probe-fined-nearly-6-billion-idUSK-BN0O50CQ20150520.

Glosten, L.R. (1994). Is the electronic open limit order book inevitable? *Journal of Finance* 49: 1127–1161.

Golden, P. (2016). More clarity needed on impact of MAR on spot *FX. Euromoney*, 4 August. Available at: www.euromoney.com/article/b12kpl59bb140d/more-clarity-needed-on-impact-of-mar-on-spot-fx.

Hurtado, P. and Nguyen, L. (2017). Ex-HSBC trader says client got 'fair' price in currency deal. *Bloomberg*, 11 October. Available at: www.bloomberg.com/news/articles/2017-10-11/ex-hsbc-trader-says-client-got-fair-deal-in-currency-purchase.

Jarrow, R.A. (1994). Derivatives securities markets, market manipulation, bubbles, and option pricing theory. *Journal of Financial and Quantitative Analysis* 29: 241–246.

King, M.R. and Rime, D. (2010). The $4 trillion question: What explains FX growth since the 2007 survey? *BIS Quarterly Review*, December 2010.

Lo, I. and Sapp, S.G. (2010). Order aggressiveness and quantity: How are they determined in a limit order market? *Journal of International Financial Markets, Institutions and Money* 20: 213–237.

Lyons, R. (1997.) A simultaneous trade model of the foreign exchange hot potato. *Journal of International Economics* 42: 275–298.

Martin, K. and Stafford, P. (2015). Good times fade away: compliance holds sway in forex trading. *Financial Times*, 22 May. Available at: www.ft.com/cms/s/0/09016bca-005b-11e5-a908-00144feabdc0.html#slide0.

Moore, M., Schrimpf, A. and Sushko, V. (2016). Downsized FX markets: causes and implications. *BIS Quarterly Review*, December.

New York Southern District Court (2015). Case No. 1:13-cv-07789, Haverhill Retirement System v. Barclays Bank PLC et al., Document 481.

New York Southern District Court (2018). case No. 18-cr-00333, United States of America v. Akshay Aiyer.

Norton Rose Fulbright (2014). 10 things you should know – Regulation in the FX markets. June. Available at: www.nortonrosefulbright.com/knowledge/publications/117779/10-things-you-should-know-regulation-in-the-fx-markets.

OCC (2014). OCC fines three banks $950 million for FX trading improprieties. *Press release,* 12 November. Available at: www.occ.treas.gov/news-issuances/news-releases/2014/nr-occ-2014-157.html.

Payne, R. (2003). Informed trade in spot foreign exchange markets: an empirical investigation. *Journal of International Economics* 61 (2): 307–329.

Pirrong, C. (2017). The economics of commodity market manipulation: A survey. *Journal of Commodity Markets* 5: 1–17.

Quereé, N. (2016). 'Spoofing' is not a crime, but should it be? *The Times,* 8 December. Available at: www.thetimes.co.uk/article/spoofing-is-not-a-crime-but-should-it-be-5hq8pw875.

Ring, S. (2017). Ex-HSBC FX trader Scott loses U.K. bid to block extradition. *Bloomberg,* 26 October. Available at: www.bloomberg.com/news/articles/2017-10-26/ex-hsbc-trader-scott-to-be-extradited-to-u-s-to-face-charges.

Rosu, I. (2009). A dynamic model of the limit order book. *Review of Financial Studies* 22 (11): 4601–4641.

Seppi, D. (1997). Liquidity provision with limit orders and a strategic specialist. *Review of Financial Studies* 10: 103–150.

Stenfors, A. (2018). Bid–Ask spread determination in the FX swap market: Competition, collusion or a convention? *Journal of International Financial Markets Institutions and Money* 54: 78–97.

Stenfors, A. and Lindo, D. (2018); Libor 1986–2021: the making and unmaking of 'the world's most important price'. *Distinktion: Journal of Social Theory* 19 (2): 2018: 172–190.

Stenfors, A. and Susai, M. (2018a). High-frequency trading, liquidity withdrawal, and the breakdown of conventions in foreign exchange markets. *Journal of Economic Issues* 52 (2): 385–395.

Stenfors, A. and Susai, M. (2018b). The impact of strategic limit order submissions on foreign exchange market liquidity. Working paper, University of Portsmouth and Nagasaki University.

Stenfors, A. and Susai, M. (2019). Liquidity withdrawal in the FX spot market: A cross-country study using high-frequency data. *Journal of International Financial Markets, Institutions and Money* 59: 36–57.

Stenfors, A. and Susai, M. (2020). Spoofing and pinging in foreign exchange markets. *Journal of International Financial Markets, Institutions and Money* (forthcoming).

Vaughan, L., Finch, G. and Choudhury, A. (2013). Traders said to rig currency rates to profit off clients. *Bloomberg,* 12 June. Available at: www.bloomberg.com/news/articles/2013-06-11/traders-said-to-rig-currency-rates-to-profit-off-clients.

Verlaine, J. and Finch, G. (2014). Biggest banks said to overhaul FX trading after scandals. *Bloomberg*, 16 September. Available at: www.bloomberg.com/news/articles/2014-09-15/ biggest-banks-said-to-overhaul-fx-trading-after-scandals.

Vitale, P. (2006). A market microstructure analysis of foreign exchange intervention. ECB Working Paper Series, No. 629.

Wilson, H. (2012). Swiss National Bank chief Philipp Hildebrand resigns over wife's currency trade. *The Telegraph*, 9 January. Available at: www.telegraph.co.uk/finance/newsbysector/ banksandfinance/9003630/Swiss-National-Bank-chief-Philipp-Hildebrand-resigns-over-wifes-currency-trade.html.

Chapter 8

Fraud and Manipulation within Cryptocurrency Markets

David Twomey
University College London and Coinstrats

Andrew Mann
University College London and Coinstrats

8.1　Introduction

Digital currencies are electronic representations of value that include a broad range of common payment systems, such as gift cards, air miles, and mobile coupons. **Virtual currencies** are a subset of digital currencies which, rather than being denominated in fiat currency, (government backed currency, e.g. USD, GBP), use their own unit of account. Examples include those within online games or internet-based currencies. **Cryptocurrencies** are a type of virtual currency (and therefore a digital currency) but rely on techniques from cryptography for security, which allow them to function without a centralized authority, such as a central bank, government, or private company.[1] (See Figure 8.1.) The rise of cryptocurrencies was led by the introduction of bitcoin in 2008, which was one of the first to use a decentralized public ledger, known as a **blockchain**, to record transactions without the use of a trusted central authority.

In general, in this chapter, each financial instrument we discuss we refer to as a cryptocurrency. A cryptocurrency is in fact quite a narrow, albeit recognizable, description of a subset of an umbrella class of **cryptoassets**, a nomenclature appearing increasingly in regulatory frameworks. There is no single agreed definition of a cryptoasset, but in general they are cryptographically secured digital representations

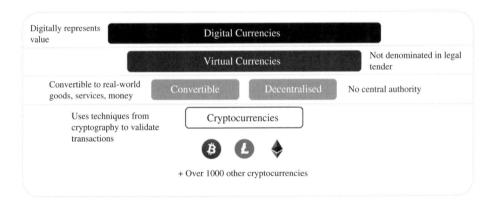

Figure 8.1　Cryptocurrencies as a subset of a broader category of digital currencies.

---

[1] Cryptography is the study of techniques for private communication in the presence of third parties called adversaries.

of value or contractual rights which can be stored, transferred or traded electronically. They are powered by a form of **Distributed Ledger Technology** (DLT). The different types of DLT are beyond the scope of this chapter, but DLT can be thought of as an umbrella of technological solutions which facilitate the distribution of records or information (the kind you might find on accounting ledgers), among all those who use it, either privately or publicly.[2]

The Bitcoin blockchain was the first fully functional DLT, used and maintained by a network of communicating nodes which run the client software.[3] Over time, many other projects have emerged. The level of innovation in these projects varies greatly: some are near clones of bitcoin or other cryptoassets and simply feature different parameter values (e.g. transaction speed, currency supply, and issuance scheme); however, some have emerged which, while sharing some familiar concepts, provide novel and innovative features that represent substantial differences.

Producing a universal taxonomy of all these new and emerging cryptoassets has proven difficult. However, recent published reports by the Financial Conduct Authority (FCA) and European Banking Association (EBA) settle on a similar framework, splitting cryptoassets into three categories as shown in Figure 8.2. The way a cryptoasset is used, or its features, mean it could fall under more than one category. For example, although bitcoin was initially intended as a means of exchange (exchange token), most current users of bitcoin hold it for investment purposes (security token).

This framework also identifies the three main use cases of cryptoassets:

1. As a means of exchange to enable the buying or selling of goods and services, or to facilitate regulated payment services.
2. For investment, by gaining direct exposure by holding and trading cryptoassets, or indirect exposure by holding and trading financial instruments which reference cryptoassets.
3. To support capital raising and/or the creation of decentralized networks through **Initial Coin Offerings** (ICOs).

ICOs, (or token sales), involve raising funds from the public by issuing project-specific exchange, security or utility tokens in exchange for an existing cryptoasset or fiat currency. They can be viewed as an alternative to traditional capital raising instruments and individuals and firms typically buy ICO tokens as an investment, to secure access to a specific service, or to gain other rights attached to a token. While ICOs are beyond the scope of this chapter, they present their own regulatory challenges: recent

---

[2] Thake, Max (2018) *What's the difference between blockchain and DLT?* Available at : https://bit.ly/2ETIxpv.
[3] A node is any device that connects to the Bitcoin network.

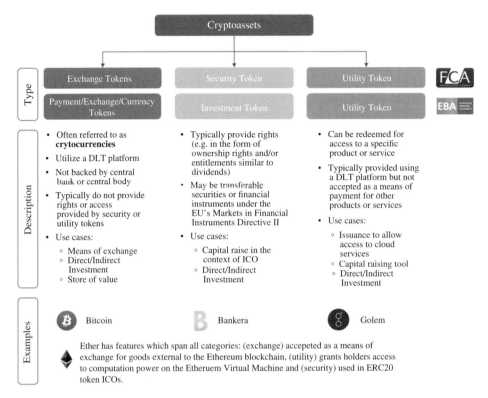

Figure 8.2   Taxonomy of cryptoassets as described by FCA and EBA reports published in Oct 2018 and Jan 2019, respectively.[4,5]

research identified that in 2017, 78% of ICO-initiated projects that achieved market capitalization over $50 million were scams.[6]

Crypto tokens are typically obtained via one of three methods: (1) participating in the transaction validation process (e.g. 'mining'), which yields crypto as a reward for expending resources; (2) receiving directly from another crypto holder; (3) investing directly in an ICO; or (4), purchasing through a **crypto exchange**.

Crypto exchanges form a fundamental part of the ecosystem as they offer a secondary market in which crypto can be bought or sold in exchange for either fiat currency or other crypto tokens. They are also the main target of a lot of the manipulations we examine, since they provide financial markets (which can be manipulated),

[4] Financial Conduct Authority (FCA) (Oct 2018) *Cryptoassets Taskforce: Final Report.* Available at: https://bit.ly/2GvY4x0.

[5] European Banking Authority (EBA) (Jan 2019) *Report with advice for the European Commission on crypto-assets,* see: https://bit.ly/2TUUb7I.

[6] Bloomberg research commissioned by SATIS Group, an ICO advisory firm, (11th July 2018), *Cryptoasset Market Coverage Initiation- Network Creation,* see https://bit.ly/2GvKFVK.

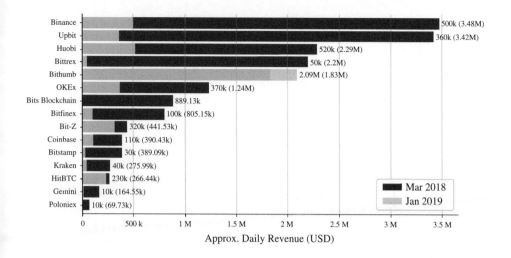

Figure 8.3   Comparative 2018 vs. 2019 daily crypto exchange revenue estimated with CoinMarketCap reported 24hr volume and fees listed on each exchange's website. Although trade volume has dropped considerably in 2019, top exchanges still maintain good revenues.

and often become single stores of immense value (which can be hacked and stolen from). As shown in Figure 8.3, it is typical to see millions of dollars' worth of crypto traded every 24 hours; this volume is required to be stored in exchange accounts. For example, Bittrex, a US-based crypto exchange holds $233.5 million worth of crypto tokens in one Ethereum wallet address.[7]

The market price and traded volume of the 2000+ crypto tokens currently listed on exchanges combine to form an asset class with a market capitalization (market price multiplied by the number of existing currency units) of $121bn.[8] While still relatively small compared to traditional asset classes, the growth of the crypto market in recent years has drawn the attention of traders and investors who look to profit from buying and selling units of cryptocurrency. Many traditional financial institutions, predominantly hedge funds, are reported to be moving into the area; partly attracted by the high volatility of prices (Chan, et al., 2017), and recent price rises.[9]

The first major exchange, Mt. Gox, originally designed in 2007 as an exchange for fantasy trading cards, was launched in 2010 allowing users to trade bitcoins and grew to handle most global bitcoin trading.[10] Due to several technical issues throughout its existence, (as detailed later in Section 8.6), bitcoins were being removed over a prolonged period by an unknown entity. The loss of bitcoins caused Mt. Gox to

---

[7] As measured on 16 February 2019 using the Bittrex's Ethereum public hot-wallet address: 0xfbb1b73c4f0bda4f67dca266ce6ef42f520fbb98.
[8] As measured on 11 February 2019 from coinmarketcap.com.
[9] Financial Times, (26 Sep 2017), *'Crypto' hedge funds spring up in crowded field,* see: http://bit.ly/2Cjzads.
[10] Mt. Gox was appropriately short for 'Magic the Gathering Online eXchange'.

collapse in 2013 and then file for bankruptcy in 2014. Despite Mt. Gox's failure, replacements quickly emerged and running a crypto exchange proved a lucrative business: the top 10 exchanges in 2017 we estimated to be generating as much as $3 million in fees per day during 2017. Today there are over 200 exchanges operating globally, with $19bn transacted over a typical 24hr period.[11]

One of the most important, often missed, factors of exchange trading is that a significant portion of trading occurs separately from the blockchain. Although normal cryptocurrency transactions are blockchain-based, i.e. if you were to send a friend some bitcoin from your wallet to theirs, you would be able to view this transaction on the public blockchain once completed with a provided transaction hash. However, trades on an exchange platform are done simply by updating a user's account balance within the service's database. As such, when an exchange trade is completed, you are not actually sending crypto to another person, (or vice versa), you are relying on the exchange to reflect this update within their internal records. The primary reason for this, in general, is that blockchains are too slow to handle the frequency and volume of exchange trades.

To be able to trade, users must have funds in their exchange account. To fund an account with crypto, a user transfers their crypto into the exchange's designated blockchain wallet, and the quantity received by the exchange is credited to the individual user's trading account in their internal system. The wallet addresses that an exchange gives you to deposit into are not your addresses. The exchange is holding your crypto for you, and they can do whatever they want with it: you do not technically have complete ownership of the crypto until you choose to withdraw it. On some exchanges, known as 'banked exchanges', fiat currency can be used as funding via a transfer to the exchange's bank account. Exchanges that do not accept fiat currency deposits and withdrawals are referred to as unbanked, since they do not (usually) possess a traditional banking license to facilitate this process. Whether crypto or fiat, once a deposit is completed, the user is then able to trade with other users of that exchange.

Withdrawals of cryptocurrencies or fiat are done in a similar way to how they are deposited. When you withdraw crypto, you are not sent crypto from 'your' addresses either, but rather from other addresses in the exchange's wallet and, often, your withdrawal will be part of the same transaction as other people's withdrawals.

Almost all crypto exchanges use a limit order book to facilitate trading. A limit order book represents the list of orders that an exchange uses to record the interest of buyers and sellers of a crypto-to-crypto or crypto-to-fiat instrument. At each price level, the number of shares being offered and demanded is recorded.

The two most basic types of order on a typical exchange are 'limit' and 'market' orders. **Limit orders** are those which indicate a price and quantity at which a trader is willing to buy (bid) or sell (ask) an asset (in this context, a particular crypto), and these are recorded in the order book. Traders who hold inventory and simultaneously post limit orders to both buy and sell are referred to as market makers. Market makers

---

[11] As taken from https://coinmarketcap.com/exchanges/volume/24-hour/ on 15 Feb 2019.

are important in providing liquidity and are compensated for the risk of holding assets through the spread (difference between bid and ask orders they post).

A **market order** does not specify a price, but a quantity and direction (buy or sell). Market orders are matched with limit orders from the opposite side of the order book. For example, a market order to buy one bitcoin would be filled from limit sell orders, starting from the lowest price level, (known as the 'best ask'). If the quantity of the market order is greater than that of the before combined volume of limit sell orders at that price level, the order is partially filled at that price level and the next best price is used to fill the remaining quantity. The matching process continues until the entire order has been filled. Figure 8.4 gives a visual representation of an order book (on the left-hand side) with price on the x-axis and buy/sell limit order cumulative volume on the y-axis. The most recently filled orders are shown under 'trade history' (on the right-hand side) and list the price and quantity at which trades have been executed.

Other types of order include stop orders that specify a 'stop price', which if hit, triggers the placement of a pre-specified limit or market order. Stop orders can help traders protect profits, limit losses or initiate new positions but (as seen in Section 8.5) may unknowingly magnify the effect of market manipulation.

Most cryptocurrencies are cross-listed assets, i.e. traded on multiple exchanges. This results in a global price determined by multiple exchanges simultaneously, leading to inter-exchange dynamics and price discovery implications (Brandvold, et al., 2015). Each exchange will have its own price for a cryptocurrency, which may vary depending on factors such as local demand, exchange reputability and trading fee structure. If prices between two exchanges diverge enough, variants of exchange arbitrage (buying on the cheaper exchange, and selling on the more expensive exchange) tailored specifically to cryptocurrency markets, will be likely to cause the prices to converge, where possible. Due to this fragmented global nature of the market, manipulation occurring on one exchange in one region of the world may affect the price of a cryptocurrency on other exchanges around the world.

The purpose of this chapter is to provide an overview of the many alleged manipulations occurring within crypto trading markets. Firstly, in Section 8.2 we attempt to document and explain the reasons why the cryptocurrency markets are an attractive target for manipulation. Next, we discuss each manipulation in detail: Section 8.3

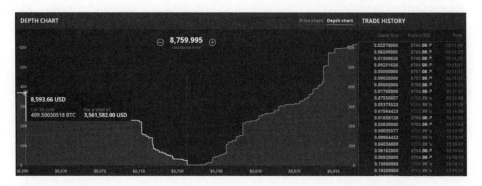

Figure 8.4   Example limit order book as seen on one cryptocurrency exchange.

introduces 'pump and dumps' where influential entities target and manipulate the price of certain cryptos; in 8.4 we discuss the alleged historic inflation of trading volume by certain exchanges; 8.5 examines the combination of a DDoS attack with specific trading patterns to achieve profits by manipulating exchange market activity;[12] 8.6 and 8.7 review hacks and flash crashes within crypto; 8.8 examines two order book-based manipulations known as quote stuffing and quote spoofing, which are designed to mislead or slow other traders; and 8.9 introduces the concept of a stablecoin and looks at the history and ongoing controversy of Tether, the largest stablecoin. Finally, 8.10 discusses the latest trends and how they might affect the propensity for fraud and regulation.

8.2   Why Do Fraud and Manipulation Occur in Cryptocurrency Markets?

Almost every fraud or manipulation we discuss in this chapter is derived from approaches seen elsewhere, often in traditional financial markets, which, while used historically without sanctions, would today be quickly reprimanded, given tighter modern regulation and accountability. In cryptocurrencies, however, their use remains prominent to this day (with the exception of inflated trading volume, which was stopped in early 2017). The occurrence of each manipulation covered in this chapter is linked to one or more of the reasons below.

8.2.1   Lack of Consistent Regulation

Many regulators around the globe have been cautious about imposing potentially restrictive regulation on the areas of cryptocurrencies, cryptocurrency trading, and related blockchain technology. Even for those seeking to be proactive, correct regulation has posed considerable challenges, as summarized in Pieters and Vivanco, 2017. Simply providing a coherent definition of *what* a cryptocurrency is (and thus an appropriate regulatory framework) has proved challenging, with different jurisdictions providing varying classifications – including as a currency, commodity, or payment system. In certain cases, authorities within the same country have classified cryptocurrencies in different ways, depending on their own area of oversight (Sotiropoulou and Guegan, 2017). Where stances have been taken, they range considerably, from permissive to hostile; a summary of the rapidly evolving regional differences can be seen in other existing work (Chohan, 2017).

Whatever stance a regional regulator takes regarding cryptocurrencies, it may be circumvented due to the ability of cryptocurrency to be accessed and transacted globally: participants (especially trading exchanges) can choose to operate within the jurisdiction most amicable to their objectives (Sotiropoulou and Guegan, 2017). In 2017, it was found that 78% of North American-based exchanges held a government

---

[12] A Distributed Denial of Service (DDoS) event is an attempt by an attacker to overwhelm a network target with a large volume of incoming messages (network traffic).

license/authorization, compared to only 15% of the exchanges in Asia-Pacific (Hileman and Rauchs, 2017). In addition to an exchange's decision as to which jurisdiction they prefer to reside under, traders may also take similar considerations into account when deciding within which exchange to trade. Consequently, it has been observed that exchanges that do not require identity validation exhibit statistically different price dynamics than those that do require identity validation (Pieters and Vivanco, 2017).

8.2.2   Relative Anonymity

There is a high level of anonymity for participants in crypto markets when compared to other financial markets. Many traditional financial exchanges are required to enforce Know-Your-Customer (KYC) and Anti-Money-Laundering (AML) procedures, which include the detailed records of traders using their exchanges. Some cryptocurrency exchanges do enforce KYC and AML procedures; however, some do not. As such, cryptocurrency trading exchanges may be able to identify the suspicious trades or accounts but may not be able to link this to real-world individuals and prevent them from attempting manipulations again through different accounts.

The onboarding requirements of several leading exchanges in 2018 were reviewed by the New York State Office of the Attorney General, (henceforth referred to as the OAG report).[13] The report found large variation in the information required to confirm a user's identity. Most require customers to submit some form of government-issued identification, especially for fiat trading. However, others require little more than an email address to begin trading crypto only. Given that this review only encompassed the largest crypto exchanges, these limited KYC procedures are likely to be similar or worse at smaller venues.

Most exchanges claim to stop customers from unauthorized jurisdictions from accessing their platform by monitoring IP addresses.[14] However, the OAG report raised questions regarding the ability to enforce this. To evade such monitoring, users can mask their IP addresses using a virtual private network (VPN), which routes activity through a third-party network and obfuscates the location of a log-in. For IP monitoring to be effective, platforms must take reasonable steps to unmask or block customers that attempt to access their site via known VPN connections, yet only two of the ten surveyed, (Bitstamp and Poloniex), purported to limit VPN access.

Furthermore, whereas many traditional financial markets have monitored locations for electronic communication relating to certain price movements, the majority of the discussion of cryptocurrency markets happens publicly on social media – popular platforms include Twitter and Reddit – where it is common for people to use an alias unconnected to their real-life identity.

---

[13] New York State Office of the Attorney General (OAG), (18 Sep 2018), *Virtual Markets Integrity Initiative*, see: https://on.ny.gov/2QJIMGJ.

[14] An IP address acts as a unique identifier assigned to a computer connected to the internet, allowing a website operator to monitor the computers that connect to its site. Among other uses, monitoring IP addresses allows a website operator to determine the approximate geographic location of users and track suspicious behaviour coming from a particular computer connection.

8.2.3   Low Barriers to Entry

Barriers to entry for cryptocurrency trading are extremely low. While real-time (live) data streams and direct market access are often costly in traditional financial markets, in cryptocurrency markets these are provided for free: either by the exchanges themselves or by public data providers.[15] Many participants enter cryptocurrency trading with no real prior trading experience, often in search of quick profits. This produces two effects:

1. Inexperienced/naïve market participants may be more prone to being manipulated; for example, believing spoofed order book data/fake volume and fictitious statements about certain cryptocurrencies on social media.
2. Inexperienced/naïve market participants may engage in certain forms of manipulation without realizing what they are doing. For example, traders participating in pump and dump groups may not be aware that they are actively manipulating the price.

8.2.4   Exchange Standards and Sophistication

Traditional stock exchanges, such as the NYSE or NASDAQ, are subject to extensive disclosure obligations regarding their ownership, operation, and rules. In contrast, anyone can set up a cryptocurrency exchange. For example, in the US, crypto asset platforms are currently not registered as trading venues under federal securities laws.

The ability of anyone to set up a trading venue increases the likelihood of technical vulnerabilities; such vulnerabilities can be exploited through DDoS attacks (see Section 8.5) and hacks (see Section 8.6).

There are several well-understood security practices that exchanges would be expected to adopt, yet many do not or do not enable it by default. Firstly, two-factor authentication is a data security measure that requires a user to input both a password and an additional piece of information in order to log in to an account. The additional piece of information is often a code sent to a phone, or a random number generated by an app or a token. Two-factor authentication helps protect an account even if a password is compromised. Most of the largest exchanges offer two-factor authentication; indeed all exchanges surveyed in the OAG's report do, but none by default.

In theory, crypto exchanges should keep a high percentage of the crypto assets in their possession in so-called 'cold storage'. Using cold storage is a security practice wherein the private keys to crypto are kept off the internet and thus not susceptible to hacking – in contrast to so-called 'hot storage', where keys are stored on a networked device. Several exchanges keep an alarming amount of crypto in their hot-wallets.[16] The OAG report highlighted that some participating exchanges did not provide a meaningful response to the question of cold storage usage.

---

[15] For example, see coinmarketcap.com or cryptocompare.com.
[16] Medium, (8 Aug 2018), *Which crypto exchange is putting your funds most at risk?*, see https://bit.ly/2lkzgK5

In an attempt to convince users of the safety of their funds held with the exchange, exchanges commonly perform security audits; 60% of large exchanges have their security audit performed by external parties; however, 65% of smaller exchanges have been found to perform their audits internally (Hileman and Rauchs, 2017), and may not provide details on the procedure of the audit.

Many crypto exchanges have no formal policies governing automated trading, market manipulation, and abusive trading. Some claim to monitor trading behaviour and have strategies to limit 'message rates' submitted to exchanges (high message rates are often a marker of an abusive trading system), or to suspend or block traders that submitted an excessive number of small orders in a given time frame (e.g. quote stuffing as discussed in Section 8.8.1). The OAG report identifies that *the industry has yet to implement serious market surveillance capacities, akin to detect and punish suspicious trading activity*'.

8.3   Pump and Dumps

The first manipulation we examine is known as a 'pump and dump'. In general, a pump and dump scheme is an approach which involves an entity accumulating a large amount of a target asset, typically one with low market capitalization and a low unit price, and subsequently promoting its purchase as an opportunity for substantial future returns, (in traditional pump and dumps, promotions may claim to have inside information of future events that are expected to cause price increases). The promotion is designed to create a significant buying demand which increases the price (i.e. the 'pump'). The promotion continues, and while others are still trying to enter, the initial position is fully unwound for a considerable profit. The promotion is then halted, and the price then crashes (i.e. the 'dump') often incurring significant losses for those slow to react.[17]

Within cryptocurrency markets, a variation of the above has become popular. Groups are formed on social chat platforms where low market capitalization cryptocurrencies are selected and advertised by administrators. Members of the group then engage in intensive purchasing within a short time span (within a couple of minutes). The group's mutual buying pressure causes a sudden rise in price. Unlike in more traditional markets, where those purchasing are doing so on false information (being duped by the promoter), members in these cryptocurrency groups are aware of what is occurring and are willing to participate in the belief they can sell to others who have been slower to act on the information.

Numerous cryptocurrency pump and dump groups have been established with member counts ranging into the tens of thousands. The groups are advertised widely within the cryptocurrency social media ecosystem – across Twitter, Slack, Discord, and Reddit – to attract new members. Most pump and dump groups follow a similar process: the coordinating entity sends out one (or many) messages advertising the time and trading exchange upon which the 'pump' will occur, but not which

---

[17] SEC, (25 June 2013), *Fast Answers: 'Pump and Dumps' and Market Manipulations*, see https://bit.ly/2ENzPue

cryptocurrency is being chosen. At the specified time, the coordinating entity informs the group of which target cryptocurrency to buy. People are willing to complete a purchase, (even at a premium compared to a few minutes before), based on their belief they can sell at a higher price while the cryptocurrency is being pumped. If members do make money, it is likely that they have done so at the expense of someone else in the group who has been slower at buying into the cryptocurrency. Some groups have tried to address this by prolonging price increases. One mechanism to do this is encouraging their members to promote the chosen cryptocurrency on social media platforms after it has been announced.

Groups are either free or cost a one-off or monthly fee to join. Those that cost money claim to offer better information or premium services, (including the release of information in advance of its dissemination to related free groups). Groups are also commonly locked so that only the coordinating entity can post. This avoids their notifications being lost in the noise of other messages. It also prevents any members who have grievances over losing money from communicating them with other members. The coordinating entities usually provide screenshots of previous pump events to show the price increases achieved historically.

There are historical examples of the price rising in the minutes before a cryptocurrency is announced. It has been suggested that this is the coordinating entity accumulating a large position in the chosen cryptocurrency before the announcement. They then place sell orders further up the order book, so any market orders placed in the frenzy caused by the pump event hit their sell orders. As the members are entering positions, the coordinating entity may be exiting their position.

Telegram is the most common mobile chat platform that groups are formed on, due to its high level of anonymity and encryption. This coupled with the relative anonymity of markets as discussed in Section 8.2.2, means it is difficult to identify perpetrators. Furthermore, with over 1000 cryptocurrencies, many of which have market capitalizations under $100,000, it is possible for the coordinating entities to own a substantial share of a cryptocurrency before commencing any pump and dump (Dierksmeier, 2016); the ability for anyone to coordinate an event, and the demand by traders looking for a quick profit, suggest this manipulation is also made possible by the low barriers to entry, see Section 8.2.3.

In the literature, Xu and Livshits (2018) are one of the first to provide a detailed study of pump-and-dump activities in cryptocurrency markets. They investigate 220 pump-and-dump activities organized in Telegram channels and construct a model which can predict the likelihood of a given coin pump prior to the event. This information is converted into a sample trading strategy where, given the exchange and time of a pump (information usually disseminated prior to a Telegram-coordinated event), the most likely coin to be pumped can be found from features such as market capitalization and recent return/volatility profiles.

While it is difficult to decipher true 'pump and dumps' without insider knowledge of such a scheme, we are able to present a case study which successfully identifies one clear example which occurred in July 2017. We were able to discover this post hoc by linking a free Telegram group's historically time-stamped messages to publicly available market data during the same period.

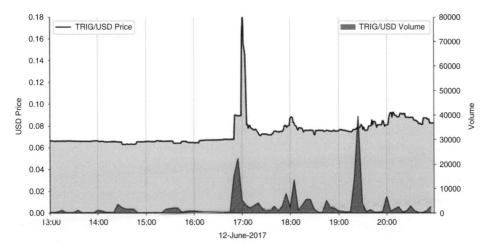

Figure 8.5 **TRIG/USD price and volume during pump and dump event. Just before 17:00 a spike in volume causes the price to rapidly increase from below $0.08 to $0.18 in a matter of seconds. This is quickly followed by a sharp decline back to the earlier price level. Trading volume after the event does increase, but with a dampened effect on the price.**

8.3.1 Case Studies

On 12 July 2017, one Telegram group coordinated a pump event. Updates were given on their Telegram channel throughout the day, counting down to the pre-specified event time, and providing provisional instructions to members in the group. At 5 p.m., the chosen cryptocurrency was announced, one called Triggers (ticker: TRIG). Figure 8.5 shows the price evolution during the event. When the announcement was made the TRIG/USD price was $0.089. Once the announcement was made, trading volume increased within seconds, causing a sharp jump in the price. The price hit a high of $0.18 momentarily, before declining rapidly; subsequent volatility ensued before the price returned to its pre-announcement region. Consequently, the market capitalization of TRIG grew 102.2%, a change of millions of dollars.

It should be noted that although TRIG was chosen as a target, its development team would have had no involvement or knowledge of what was happening. Its price and trading volume have increased significantly since then, so it is unlikely to be the target of such an event again.

8.4 Inflated Trading Volume

The next manipulation we cover no longer occurs, but previously had a big impact on the perception of the global cryptocurrency trading ecosystem. Prior to January 2017, Chinese cryptocurrency exchanges dominated bitcoin cryptocurrency trading volume, with December 2016 data showing they held 98.3% of global volume. However, it has been *alleged* that the volumes reported by certain Chinese exchanges at the time were in fact misleading and not an accurate representation of legitimate market activity. This belief was reinforced by the sudden and dramatic drop of trading volume in January 2017, following the increased involvement of the People's Bank of China (PBoC), China's central bank, which initiated the removal of mechanisms enabling the potential inflation of trading volume.

Trading data from the exchange further arouses suspicion due to counter-intuitive findings. In a study of cryptocurrency exchange dynamics using data between November 2016 and January 2017 (Dimpfl, 2017), it was found that Chinese exchanges exhibited the highest market liquidity when examined on a trading volume basis. However, when liquidity was instead measured via bid–ask spread, they displayed the lowest liquidity.[18] These differing results are surprising as given a normally functioning trading market, both factors should indicate a similar level of liquidity.

One motivation for claiming large trading volume is that it implies a better environment for trading. Exchanges with larger trading volume *should* have smaller bid–ask spreads and more depth in the order book; a favourable environment for traders.[19] Large volumes also act as a statement of trust in a certain exchange – something that is important in a market which has historically had a bad record of exchange closures and hacks. To the average trader, all of these characteristics are important and, as a result, may influence their decision on who they trade with. Finally, large volumes and high market share may be important factors when a particular exchange is seeking funding from investors.

Of the overarching motivations for manipulation detailed in Section 8.2, a combination of exchange standards and sophistication (8.2.4) and a lack of consistent regulation (8.2.1) made this manipulation possible. Throughout the period it was alleged to have been undertaken, there was little regulation/regulatory guidance preventing it from happening. It is likely that once one exchange started doing it, other exchanges followed so as not to lose their share of perceived market volume.

There are a variety of ways in which trading volume could have been inflated. These include:

- **Zero trading fees:** A trading fee is one which an exchange charges to execute a market or limit order on their platform. Starting in September 2013, many Chinese exchanges announced the introduction of zero fee trading. Whereas the announcement originally came from one exchange, others followed to ensure they remained competitive. Star Xu, CEO of OKCoin, acknowledged that zero fee trading distorts trading volume by a *'large multiplier, maybe 5 times, maybe 10'*.[20] Note that trading exchange transactions are different from blockchain transactions, which do have to pay a fee.

- **Incentivizing large trading volume:** Although many of these exchanges had zero fee trading, exchanges charged certain fees for withdrawals. Tiered withdrawal fee systems were used, charging users less the more trading they had conducted. As such, this incentivized traders to increase their trading volume.

---

[18] Bid–ask (buy–sell) spread is the amount by which the lowest sell order exceeds the highest buy order.
[19] Order book depth provides an indication of the liquidity and depth for that security or currency. The higher the number of buy and sell orders at each price, the higher the depth of the market.
[20] Coindesk, (26 Mar 2014), *OKCoin CEO on Expansion and China's Competitive Edge*, see http://bit.ly/2GbP23M.

- **Wash trading:** In the pursuit of inflating their own trading volume without taking on the risk of price changes, an individual trader could decide to set up two separate accounts, and by carefully placing orders, trade against themselves repeatedly. Zero fee trading enables this to occur with no loss of funds. This would inflate their own traded volumes, allowing for better withdrawal fees and, as a result, inflate the overall volumes of the exchange. Periods of high trading volume have been observed without considerable changes in the price, a potential indication of wash trading.[21]
- **Margin trading:** Many exchanges offer leveraged trading enabling users to trade in volumes 10 or 20 times their base capital.[22] Some exchanges are alleged to have offered naked short selling, whereby bitcoins could be short-sold without borrowing them in the first place.[23] This effectively allows bitcoins to be created from nothing.

As well as structuring their exchanges in a way that may encourage users to trade more, there are also allegations that exchanges were pursuing their own methods to further inflate trading volume. Bobby Lee, CEO of BTC-China, states: *'We've known for a while that other Chinese bitcoin exchanges have been faking data. We've seen our trading volumes drop off heavily while others have, supposedly, witnessed massive surges.'*[24] The former OKCoin CTO, Changpeng Zhao, alleged that OKCoin *'artificially inflates its volume through the use of bots that engage in self-trading'.*[25]

8.4.1 Case Study: January 2017 and PBoC Involvement

On 7 January 2017, news broke of interactions between the PBoC and the major Chinese exchanges. Among other things, including advising against offline marketing, and reiterating the need for KYC and AML laws, the PBoC had instructed the participating Chinese exchanges to stop inflating trading volume. By 12 January 2017, these exchanges halted margin trading. Reported trading volume (on the three major Chinese exchanges) dropped from an average of 8,382,983 bitcoins traded per day in the week before, to an average of 1,578,801 bitcoins traded per day in the week after: a decline of over 80%. On 24 January 2017, the exchanges introduced trading fees of 0.2% per transaction, preventing wash trading and strategies employed by users to inflate their personal trading volume.[26] Their reported trading volume dropped from

---

[21] Coindesk, (13 Jan 2017), *China's Bitcoin Exchanges Quietly Made Policy Updates Overnight*, see http://bit.ly/2nX5rm9

[22] Leveraging a position involves putting down collateral, known as a margin, to take on a position that is larger in value. For example, if the maximum leverage on a BTC-USD currency pair was 100:1, for each $1 of margin posted, you could trade the equivalent of $100 of BTC. As such, trading on leverage magnifies potential gains or losses from price movements.

[23] Naked short selling is short selling a financial instrument without first borrowing the instrument, or ensuring it can be borrowed, as conventionally done in a short sale repurchase (repo) agreement.

[24] Coindesk, (28 Jan 2014), *The Reality of Chinese Bitcoin Trading Volumes*, see http://bit.ly/2G9Icff.

[25] Coindesk, (30 May 2015), *Former Exec Hits Back at OKCoin Amid Contract Dispute*, see http://bit.ly/2EG2qAm.

[26] Steemit, (22 Jan 2017), *OKCoin, Huobi & BTCC will start charging trading fees from 24 January*, see http://bit.ly/2BY9ZkP.

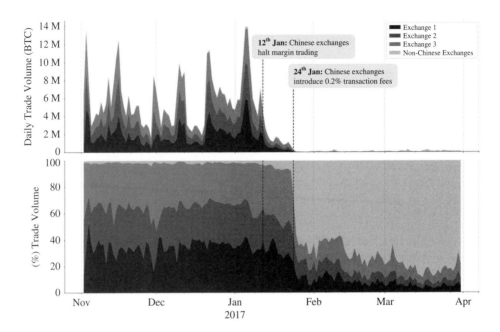

Figure 8.6   Global bitcoin trading volume.

an average of 1,096,092 bitcoins traded per day in the week before, to an average of 48,617 bitcoins traded per day in the week after; a further decline of over 95%, (of the remaining 20% volume).

Figure 8.6 shows that, by February 2017, the three major Chinese exchanges' joint trading volume was 0.5% of what had been reported in December 2016 and accounted for 32.2% of global trading volume.[27] While a dramatic decline in trading volume is observed, it should be noted that the PBoC's activity would also have dampened many traders' enthusiasm about trading cryptocurrencies, causing many to decide to rein back their trading activities while uncertainty was still present.

8.5   Exchange DDoS Attacks

A Distributed Denial-of-Service attack (DDoS) is an attempt by an attacker to overwhelm a network target with a large volume of incoming messages (network traffic). To the victim, a DDoS attack will appear to originate from numerous separate sources. However, these sources are a linked collection of 'zombie computers', known as a *Botnet*, which is remotely controlled by an underlying attacker (Gregory, 2014). DDoS attacks are illegal and intended to disrupt the normal functionality of the target and prevent normal legitimate usage (Loukas and Oke, 2009). Often, the individual

---

[27] Based on data obtained from Bitcoinity, see: https://data.bitcoinity.org/markets/volume/5y?c=e&r=day&t=b.

zombies, or *Bots*, are malware-infected machines whose owners are completely unaware of their participation in an attack. Typical targets of DDoS attacks include the servers of e-commerce websites, news websites, banks, and government websites.

Timed DDoS attacks can be launched on trading exchange servers in combination with specific trading activity to create a price manipulation strategy which, if successful, can be both quick and extremely lucrative (Feder, et al., 2016). Essentially, the approach is to disrupt normal market trading, preventing other market participants from submitting buy or sell orders, and creating an unfair advantage for the perpetrator.

The general form of the strategy deployed in cryptocurrency markets can be split into three steps:

1. **Initial sell order**: A large sell market order is placed on the exchange by the attacker just as the DDoS commences.
2. **Sustained DDoS attack**: The attacker initiates the DDoS attack preventing others from engaging in new trading. The large order to sell at the market price is filled with existing bid volume in the order book which creates downward pressure on that exchange's market price as the buy volume is reduced. As no new buy orders arrive, the price continues to drop to fill the large sell order. This creates a cascading effect as stop-losses positions begin to trigger, causing a further downward price spiral.
3. **Position accumulation**: The attacker stops the DDoS attack and buys a large position for a favourable (low) price.

Relative anonymity (8.2.2) is a key factor enabling these attacks. It is unlikely the true identity of the perpetrator of a DDoS attack will be discovered. Exchange standards and sophistication (8.2.4) may also play a part as the infrastructure of unprepared exchanges may not be able to mitigate an attack. It should be noted some exchanges use DDoS protection services. As the attacks require some technical understanding, low barriers to entry do not apply in this case. Furthermore, as the attacks require participation in an activity that is already well known to be illegal, the lack of consistent regulation of cryptocurrency markets is unlikely to be a contributory factor.

Historically, DDoS attacks have been launched on a wide range of services in the cryptocurrency ecosystem. Examples include cryptocurrency-based gambling sites and mining pools (Vasek, et al., 2014). However, previous studies in the literature have shown that exchanges have been targeted by DDoS attacks far more than on any other cryptocurrency service, especially in recent years.

DDoS attacks are usually reported on an exchange's Twitter feed, as this is one of the few ways to learn, from an external perspective, whether a DDoS incident has occurred. Scraping of the historical tweets of the current largest 30 cryptocurrency exchanges, (by bitcoin traded volume; ranked by coinmarketcap.com), shows that these DDoS-related attacks remain a problem.[28] Figure 8.7 shows the increase

---

[28] Data taken from coinmarketcap.com on 20 November 2017.

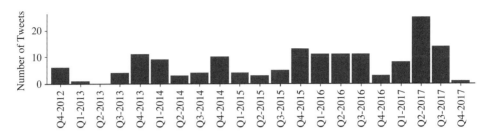

Figure 8.7 Twitter reported DDoS incidents across the 30 largest global cryptocurrency exchanges.

of tweets reporting DDoS-related incidents. We built a timeline of each exchange's tweet history which included the word 'DDoS' and then manually selected those referring to an attempted attack.

There are several studies in the literature examining cryptocurrency exchange DDoS attacks. Most existing work focuses on DDoS attacks of the now-defunct Mt. Gox exchange, since, shortly after filing for bankruptcy in early 2014, a detailed trade history of transactions was made public.

Vasek, et al., 2014, examine the prevalence and impact of DDoS attacks on various cryptocurrency services, such as exchanges, mining pools, and online wallets. Using social-media/forum posts mentioning DDoS attacks between May 2011–Oct 2013, (142 DDoS attacks on 40 Bitcoin services in total), they found that cryptocurrency exchanges were the most targeted cryptocurrency service, (41% of all occurrences). In further examinations of Mt. Gox DDoS attacks, it has been observed that several attacks follow shortly after a fall from a new peak in an exchange rate, which is *'consistent with the modus operandi of blocking exchanges in order to slow down a panicked sell-off'* (Vasek, et al., 2014). In the (slight) majority of cases, a decrease in transaction volume in the week following a DDoS, compared to the week prior, is observed.

(Feder, et al., 2016) used Mt. Gox leaked trading data spanning Apr 2011–Nov 2013, in combination with online sources reporting DDoS attacks at the time, to compare the impact of DDoS attacks against other types of shocks such as self-inflicted technical outages and pressure from regulators.[29] They found evidence that DDoS attacks had more serious effects than other types of shocks. In days following a DDoS attack, the skewness and kurtosis of trading volume fell by 56% and 28% respectively.[30] In other words, the distribution of daily transaction volume shifts, so that fewer extremely large transactions take place after shocks occur.

---

[29] *bitcointalk.org*, Reddit's bitcoin sub-forum and public announcements by Mt. Gox.
[30] Skewness is a measure of a distribution's lack of symmetry (where 0 represents a perfect symmetry). Kurtosis is the degree of excess *peakedness* of a distribution, where a positive number represents the excess from Gaussian.

8.5.1 Case Study

To illustrate the disruptive effect of DDoS attacks, we examine an attack, occurring on 7 May 2017, which targeted a well-known cryptocurrency exchange called Kraken. The attack had a dramatic effect on the liquidity and traded price of ether: the (average) traded price of ETH/USD fell from $88.7 to $45.8 within an hour, a 47% drop before the event was reported publicly by Kraken. The attack was confirmed by their Twitter feed which reported the incident at 22:57 (UTC): *'Site under heavy DDoS. We are working to mitigate the attack.'*

Figure 8.8 shows the average traded price and total traded volume of ETH/USD aggregated to 10-minute windows.

While it is difficult to truly know the motivation for such a DDoS attack, analysis of the price impact, as shown in Figure 8.9, on different traded currency pairs on Kraken before, during, and after the DDoS attack, appears to link suspicious trading

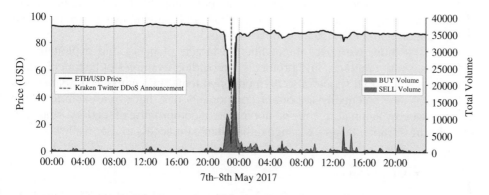

Figure 8.8 Kraken DDOS event – ETH/USD trade price plotted with accompanying volume. Prior to the DDoS announcement by Kraken, there is a spike in trade volume and a sharp crash in the ETH/USD price.

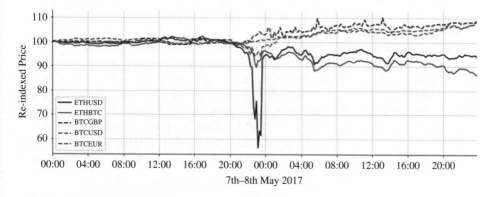

Figure 8.9 Kraken price impact during the DDOS event. ETH Kraken traded pairs are affected by a dramatic drop in price, whereas BTC pairs show a much smaller reaction and quickly return to pre-DDoS levels.

activity to the ETH/USD pair in particular. Bitcoin-based pairs were almost unaffected during the attack and other non-USD based ether pairs moved in a more reactive and lagged manner.

8.6 Hacks and Exploitations

The types of manipulation we now consider are hacks of cryptocurrency exchanges and exploitations of both smart contracts and cryptocurrency protocols themselves. It should be noted that we have been careful in certain areas of this section to use the term *exploit* rather than *hack*. We use exploitation to refer to taking advantage of unintended design flaws in a smart contract or cryptocurrency protocol, and hacks more generally as gaining unauthorized access to a private system or network.[31] The reason for this separation of terms is as follows. Smart contracts are meant to outline their terms within their code completely. The question then arises, does executing a smart contract in a format allowed by its code, but unintended by its original author, constitute hacking? This is a point of much debate and is the motivation for us to refer to exploitation rather than hacking in these cases.

In this section, we cover three different targets of hacks and exploitations – exchanges, smart contracts, and protocols – providing examples of historical occurrences in each case. It should also be mentioned that, although DDOS attacks, (see section 8.5), are potentially important components of a hack, we exclude DDOS attacks since, by their nature, they do not involve a compromise of security – their aim is to slow or disrupt a target exchange rather than gain access to user wallets.

8.6.1 Exchange Hacks

The 2017 surge in cryptocurrencies prices has made exchanges popular targets for criminals since they handle and store large amount of cryptocurrency (Hileman and Rauchs, 2017). In general, cyber hacks present a considerable risk for exchanges, highlighted by the fact that in 2013 it was found that 45% of exchanges had failed. In addition, they are also exposed to regulation risk, which is the risk of changes in regulation by local or regional authorities which may limit or prevent their business activities (Moore and Christin, 2013).

Almost all cryptocurrency exchanges require users to transfer their cryptocurrency into the exchange's ownership before the user can trade them through their exchange account. To do this, the cryptocurrencies are transferred to the exchange's blockchain wallet by the user. Therefore, exchanges are tasked with protecting large amounts of cryptocurrency owned by their users. As large amounts are being stored in one location, this makes exchanges highly lucrative targets for hackers.

If an attacker can find some way to take control of an exchange's servers, or any other valid approach, they may be able to transfer the cryptocurrencies owned by

---

[31] A smart contract is pre-written logic (specified in programming code) that is stored on a blockchain and run by participating computers. An example smart contract could hold funds making them inaccessible until a certain date or other condition is met.

users of that exchange into their ownership. In some cases, withdrawal may not be a viable option, but attackers can still profit by, prior to the attack, accumulating a large quantity of a specific cryptocurrency that has low trade volume and a small order book.[32] The attackers then use compromised accounts to submit large numbers of buy orders at an unreasonably high price (e.g. 10,000x the last traded price) and make a huge profit by matching these orders with their own sell orders using the cryptocurrency they previously purchased at a much cheaper price.[33]

Historically, cryptocurrency exchange hacks have been allowed to occur for numerous reasons which include incompetence/naivety, inside jobs, or purely because of the sophistication of the attack (some speculate that some attacks are being carried out by government-backed operations).[34] In **Table 8.1**, we examine the 6 largest exchange hacks which have occurred in the short history of cryptocurrency. The size of each attack is assessed by calculating the USD-equivalent value of the stolen tokens at the prevailing market rate at the time of the attack.

To date, the largest reported cryptocurrency exchange hack occurred in January 2018 when nearly $500M of NEM coins were stolen from the exchange Coincheck. It is not known how the attack was accomplished. Coincheck claimed it was not an inside job but admitted that its own sloppy security practices were to blame for the breach.[35] Rather than storing its customers' assets in offline wallets, the assets were stored in hot wallets that were connected to the internet. Coincheck also reportedly failed to protect the wallets with standard multi-signature security protocols.

Interestingly, because blockchain transactions for NEM are all public, Coincheck were able to identify and publish the 11 wallet addresses where all the 523 million stolen coins ended up. All the funds seem to have been funnelled through

Table 8.1   Largest reported cryptocurrency exchange hacks since 2011.

Rank		Exchange	Date	Approx. Amount Stolen
1	◈	Coincheck	**Jan 2018**	**~$500 Million**
2	MTGOX	Mt. Gox	**Feb 2014**	**~$460 Million**
3	BITGRAIL	BitGrail	**Feb 2018**	**~$187 Million**
4	◢	Bitfinex	**Aug 2016**	**~$77 Million**
5	ⓩ	Zaif	**Sep 2018**	**~$60 Million**
6	⑱	NiceHash	**Dec 2017**	**~$60 Million**

---

[32] Often, exchanges enforce higher security controls (e.g. two-factor authentication, IP whitelisting, email confirmation), or size limits on withdrawals. By default, API keys, which allow users to trade programmatically with funds/tokens from their account, do not have withdrawal permission enabled. This can mean that in many cases, even if a user's account is compromised, withdrawal is not possible.

[33] Medium, (14th Jul 2018), *A Thorough Investigation of the 'Binance Hack' – Anthony Xie*, see https://bit.ly/2OQtbrC.

[34] Cointelegraph, (23rd Aug 2018), *Kaspersky Lab: North Korea Hacks Cryptocurrency Exchange With 'First' macOS Malware*, see https://bit.ly/2Jf0sGL.

[35] Fortune, (31st Jan 2018), *How to steal $500 Million in Cryptocurrency*, see https://bit.ly/2O5h0C3.

one address which can be viewed within the NEM block explorer.[36] Since the attack, 6 of the 11 wallets have begun moving small amounts (between 1 and 10,000 NEM) and the other 5 moving larger amounts (300,000 to 20 million NEM). In response to the attack, the NEM development team created a new tagging system designed to alert crypto exchanges when an account has been tagged for stolen funds, thus making it difficult for the hacker(s) to convert them into other cryptocurrencies or fiat.[37]

One of the highest profile hacks within the cryptocurrency ecosystem remains that of the exchange Mt. Gox, which at the time handled the majority of global bitcoin trading volume. The hack culminated in Mt. Gox's collapse in 2014, with a total of over 600,000 bitcoins being stolen (valued then at ~$460 million). From subsequently released Mt. Gox logs it appears that, starting in 2011, the number of bitcoins Mt. Gox thought they held was overstated; it is believed a hacker was slowly syphoning off bitcoins over this period. It is still not known how the hacker was able to access the bitcoins.

In (Gandal, et al., 2018), researchers claim to have discovered suspicious trading activity occurring between February and November 2013 on Mt. Gox. The activity was deemed suspicious due to irregularities in how the trades were logged in the Mt. Gox database when compared to other trading activity. This activity had a significant impact on the bitcoin price. The price rose on 80% of days where suspicious activity was detected. In comparison, it only rose on 55% of days where suspicious activity was not detected. The authors believed that this activity was the cause of the price rise experienced by bitcoin during this time – a period where bitcoin experienced what many describe as a price bubble going from $150 to above $1000 in two months. The subsequent price decline seen in 2014 – described as the bubble bursting – was likely to have been caused by the uncertainty surrounding the collapse of Mt. Gox. The motivation of this suspicious trading activity is not known and not necessarily the work of a hacker. It has been speculated that this activity was conducted by someone internal to Mt. Gox attempting to recover funds previously lost to a hacker.

Recently, a Russian national was arrested on suspicion of laundering a considerable number of bitcoins. The bitcoins appear to be sourced from a number of different exchange thefts that occurred over the period 2011–2014, including a previous Mt. Gox hack. It should be noted the person arrested was the alleged money launderer and not the original hacker. Interested readers can find an information visualization of how bitcoins linked with particular attacks have since moved around the Bitcoin ecosystem online.[38]

The Italian exchange BitGrail was hacked in early February 2018, with an alleged 17 million Nano tokens stolen, representing approximately $187 million

---

[36] The wallet address is NC4C6PSUW5CLTDT5SXAGJDQJGZNESKFK5MCN77OG and can be viewed at http://explorer.nemchina.com/#/s_account?account=NC4C6PSUW5CLTDT5SXAGJDQJGZNESKFK 5MCN77OG.

[37] Cointelegraph, (2 Mar 2018), *Stolen Coincheck NEM Found in Exchanges in Canada, Japan, Law Enforcement to be Told,* see: https://bit.ly/2Aulfnf.

[38] Wizsec, (27 Jul 2017), *Breaking open the Mt. Gox case,* see: http://bit.ly/2Erbk5t.

in value at the time. There remains some confusion over the attack and whether the blame lies with BitGrail funder Francesco Firano, the Nano development team or the hackers.[39] Nano blockchain data appear to indicate that the hackers may have initiated the unauthorized attack weeks before it was reported as a hack, which prompted some accusations of an inside job.[40] However, these accusations prompted Firano to respond by claiming the timestamps of the transactions on the NEM blockchain explorer are inaccurate: *'they* [the public] *don't have the complete data (it is only available to us and law enforcement authorities). And secondly, we cannot rely on the official explorer developed and managed by the Nano dev (proved flawed), which is, to this day, the only way to determine the date of the transactions.'[41]*

In August of 2016, the cryptocurrency exchange Bitfinex reported a loss of over $77 million dollars' worth of bitcoin. An initial investigation by the exchange failed to reveal the cause of the alleged hack. Then, in October of the same year, the FBI began an investigation after a Bitfinex user reported that over a million dollars' worth of bitcoin was removed from his account during the attack. Despite the FBI's involvement, no further information has been revealed to the press to date.[42] However, more questions around Bitfinex arose in June 2018, when researchers at University of Texas discovered that entities associated with Bitfinex or traders with Bitfinex accounts may have artificially ballooned the price of bitcoin to record-breaking heights in 2017 (Griffin and Shams, 2018).

In September 2018, Japanese exchange Zaif (operated by the Tech Bureau) was hacked resulting in a reported loss of 6.7 billion yen (~$60 million). The security breach was first noticed at around 17:00 on 14 September 2018, upon which time the firm suspended asset withdrawals and deposits. Hackers had gained access to the exchange's hot wallets, even after the Financial Services Agency (FSA) had issued a business improvement order in March 2018 focused on anti-money laundering and security. An investigation found that 5,966 bitcoins had been taken, together with Bitcoin cash and MonaCoin, although the exact number stolen of the latter two coins is unknown. The scale of this hack was around 3x larger than Zaif's own asset reserve, forcing the exchange to look for bailout options. A listed Japanese firm named Fisco agreed to invest $44.5 million for a major share of Zaif.[43]

Slovenian-based cryptocurrency mining pool NiceHash, which also functions as a marketplace, was hacked on the 6 December 2017 for ~4,700 bitcoin. It was revealed an employee's computer was compromised, allowing the hackers to access the NiceHash marketplace. Bitcoin was then siphoned off from the firm's account and

---

[39] Investopedia, (6 July 2018), *The Largest Cryptocurrency Hacks So Far This Year,* see: https://bit.ly/2SkEq9H.

[40] CoinIQ, (Jun 2018), *30+ Cryptocurrency Exchange Hacks, A Comprehensive List,* see https://bit.ly/2Pmju3H.

[41] Cointelegraph, (13 Feb 2018), *'It's Impossible to Refund the Stolen Amount': Interview with BitGrail's Francesco Firano,* see: https://bit.ly/2Asibba.

[42] CoinIQ, (Jun 2018), *30+ Cryptocurrency Exchange Hacks, A Comprehensive List,* see https://bit.ly/2Pmju3H.

[43] A full report (in Japanese) is available at https://bit.ly/2PQ1ICi.

directed to another wallet address where the hackers subsequently emptied all funds from that wallet as of 23 December 2017.[44] NiceHash had promised users that their funds would be reimbursed, with payments occurring on a monthly basis. According to local media, as of 15 October 2018, the firm has paid back ~60% of the losses, less than a year on since the attack occurred.[45]

Exchange hacks are very detrimental for the cryptocurrency ecosystem, especially given the systemic importance of exchanges. As well as generating wide-reaching news articles, hacks can have considerable indirect effects on cryptocurrency markets; not only are individual victims affected by having their funds stolen, news of a hack can cause market prices to plunge. Depending on the scale of an individual attack, the impact can spread to the entire cryptocurrency market via contagion with uncertainty and fear driving prices down.

Figure 8.10 gives a visual representation of the most notable exchange hacks since 2011. The size of each bubble in the plot indicates the amount stolen, and its position on the y-axis measures the subsequent 5-day change in market price (in percentage terms).

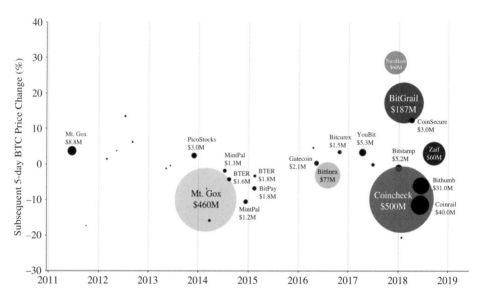

Figure 8.10 Historical timeline of notable exchange hacks. The size of each bubble indicates the (USD-equivalent) amount stolen. The position on the y-axis indicates the approximate change in the global BTC/USD price.[46]

---

[44] This target wallet address can be viewed at: www.blockchain.com/btc/address/1EnJHhq8Jq8vDuZA5a hVh6H4t6jh1mB4rq.

[45] NiceHash, (30 Jul 2018), *Seventh reimbursement of the Repayment program*, see: https://bit.ly/2PUGBPP.

[46] The day of each hack was taken, where possible, as the first public report of the incident – either by the exchange itself or a notable cryptocurrency news site such as coindesk.com. Daily data for the global BTCUSD price was obtained from https://www.coindesk.com/price/.

8.6.2 Smart Contract Exploits

Traditional legal contracts, which may outline the terms of a specific agreement, are usually enforceable by law. Smart contracts, on the other hand, are agreements written in code and enforced by the ecosystem in which they run. Interested parties can interact with a smart contract – hosted on a particular blockchain – by executing predefined functions for that smart contract.

Creation of verifiably secure smart contracts poses a number of challenges, which potentially opens such contracts up to exploitation. Firstly, in an attempt to be transparent, smart contract writers are encouraged to publish human readable versions of their code. This allows anyone to view its intentions (you may want to see what a software plans to do with your money before you send it). However, it also allows those attempting to use the software for nefarious purposes to search for vulnerabilities. Secondly, once a smart contract has been deployed and it has started to be used, it cannot easily be changed because it is embedded within the blockchain. Finally, although there are attempts to outline good practices, there are limited guidelines for what makes good smart contract code.[47]

An example of such an exploit involves some of the earliest software built on the Ethereum ecosystem, viz. the *Decentralized Autonomous Organization* (DAO). The DAO was intended to be a decentralized (i.e. crowd-run) venture capital fund. To be properly decentralized, with no one party in control, actions the DAO could take were written in its programming code. It was intended that participants would vote to take certain actions allowed by the code – e.g. potentially allocating funds to different projects vying for funding.

The DAO received funds (intended for later allocation) through one of the earliest token sales on the Ethereum ecosystem. Funds were sent to the system by those wishing to participate, and in return, they received a share of anticipated profits and the ability to vote on decisions. The software stored the funds that it had received. By the time that the funding phase ended on 28 May, approximately 12 million ether, (valued then in total at approximately $150,000,000), was contributed by over 10,000 participating Ethereum addresses.[48]

Before any funding could be allocated, an attack managed to drain considerable funds, preventing further progress of the project. On Friday, 17 June, the first public report of the attack appeared as a post by a concerned user on Reddit.[49] An attacker, using a known but yet to be fixed vulnerability in the DAO's code, was slowly draining funds from the DAO. Approximately 3.6 million ether were stolen by the attacker, which was around 1/3 of the total amount held by the DAO. The market price of ether reacted quickly to news of the attack, dropping from $20 to $13. Those selling were worried the vulnerability demonstrated the potential insecurity of the Ethereum network. Furthermore, if the ether taken in the attack were to be sold, it would undoubtedly reduce the price significantly.

---

[47] Consensys, (Accessed 26 Oct 2018), *Smart Contract Best Practices*, see https://bit.ly/2JjcbnH.

[48] The cryptocurrency is actually termed ether and the blockchain is termed Ethereum, however Ethereum is sometimes used to describe both protocol and cryptocurrency.

[49] Reddit, (17 Jun 2016), *I think The DAO is getting drained right now, Ethereum*, see https://bit.ly/2D8fZrX.

Luckily (for those who had funds in the DAO) as an unintended consequence of how the DAO was designed, the stolen funds could not be accessed by the attacker for 28 days. This gave the development team and community a chance to attempt to make changes to retrieve the stolen funds. After much debate, a hard fork was introduced to the Ethereum network which returned the funds stolen to an account accessible to original DAO investors; meaning they could claim back their original investment. A by-product of this change resulted in a version of the Ethereum blockchain called 'Ethereum Classic' which did not have this change implemented.

Over a year after the DAO exploit, the SEC published a report on whether the DAO – given its design – violated federal securities law. They ultimately determined not to pursue action against the creators of the DAO, but used the report to reiterate the need for compliance with suitable laws, stating *'the automation of certain functions through this technology, "smart contracts", or computer code does not remove conduct from the purview of the U.S federal securities law'.*[50] Those interested in further details on the DAO, how it was attacked and the resulting conflict of beliefs in the community are encouraged to read Mehar, et al., 2017.

8.6.3   Protocol Exploitation

The last type of exploit we examine is known as protocol exploitation. Protocol refers to the underlying rules of a cryptocurrency's software which govern its processes. A protocol exploit is possible when an exploitable attack vector is found in the mechanism by which a particular cryptocurrency operates.

One famous and early example of a protocol exploit is the Bitcoin protocol attack of August 2010, which worked by finding and exploiting an integer overflow bug which could not detect when a Bitcoin transaction output summed to over 184 billion bitcoins.[51] The bug meant that the Bitcoin network assumed there was only a very small amount of bitcoin in the transaction, and so accepted it (as part of block #74638). Fortunately, the issue was noticed and discussed publicly, and within hours a fix was deployed which, upon acceptance, saw the transaction removed from the future version of the blockchain. More detail can be found in a bitcointalk.org thread.[52]

8.7   Flash Crashes

This section investigates flash crashes and their link to market manipulation and fraud. We provide examples of historical flash crashes and focus on a detailed investigation of the Ethereum flash crash of 21 June 2017 on the cryptocurrency exchange GDAX.

---

[50] Forbes, (31 Jul 2017), *Digital Coins And Tokens Are Just Another Kind Of Security,* see https://bit.ly/2Av3TXc.

[51] In computer programming, an integer overflow occurs when an arithmetic operation attempts to create a numeric value that is outside of the range that can be represented with a given number of bits – either larger than the maximum or lower than the minimum representable value.

[52] Bitcointalk (15 Aug 2010), *Strange block 74638,* see https://bit.ly/2O6NrA9.

A flash crash can be defined as an extreme price fluctuation on the minute/sub-minute time scale – that is, a very large negative price movement followed almost immediately by an equally large price recovery. Cryptocurrency markets exhibit large daily volatility on a regular basis, underpinned by an immature infrastructure and frequent speculation. For this reason, large positive or negative returns are more common in cryptocurrency markets than traditional markets.

To ensure a fair comparison of flash crashes (extreme events) across different assets with vastly differing volatility dynamics, we impose a restriction to be considered where the price fluctuation must have breached three standard deviations from the mean, (i.e. the three-sigma rule). The definition of a flash crash should therefore depend on which market is being analysed and consider the following characteristics:

- The duration of the flash crash.
- The relative deviation from the mean return.
- The market's role in the wider economy (conventional or digital).

To help contextualize market differences, we visualize the daily returns of each asset as listed in Figure 8.11 to demonstrate the differences between traditional and digital assets. The chart shows ether has much fatter tails, (and often shows movements of a magnitude which are considered as flash crashes in traditional markets), than the DJIA or Gold Futures, thus justifying the need to contextualize the severity of a flash crash event on a market-by-market basis.

Most academic work surrounding flash crashes has focused on the 6 May 2010 crash on the DJIA. This is due to its importance in the world economy as it briefly wiped over $1 trillion in value from the US economy, affecting global firms from pension funds to state-owned businesses.

There is much debate on the exact cause of the 6 May 2010 flash crash. Kirilenko, et al., (2011) examined trade data at the time of the event and ruled out the role of High Frequency Trading (HFT) in causing the crash, given HFT trading patterns did not change either before or during the crash. Madhavan (2011) suggest that the

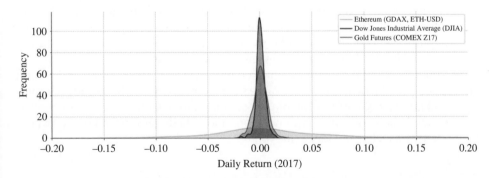

Figure 8.11   A comparison of daily returns from ETH/USD, the Dow Jones Industrial Average and COMEX Gold Futures. Ethereum has much fatter tails (i.e. a higher standard deviation) than the DJIA or COMEX meaning the severity of a market movement needs to be much larger in magnitude to justify the term 'flash crash'.

fragmentation of markets over several different exchanges creates a thinning effect of the limit order book and so makes liquidity shocks more prominent. Increased occurrences of liquidity shocks in turn increase the likelihood of flash crashes.

Traders who use market orders to fill their trades are liquidity takers and referred to as 'informed' as they are assumed to know something about the impending direction of the market, as this form of trading means you want to buy/sell immediately at the best ask/bid, (see Section 8.8 for more details on trading the limit order book). The order flow of informed traders is often called 'toxic flow' and in the literature, measures of order book toxicity have been explored as a leading indicator of flash crashes.[53]

Easley, et al., (1996) build a model around the concept of informed and uninformed traders by modelling their activity as an information arrival process. They propose a metric termed the Probability of Informed Trading (PIN), which is formulated as the ratio of orders occurring from informed traders against the total order flow.

This concept is taken further by Easley, et al., (1996), who create an adaptive metric that is supposedly more useful and not as difficult to estimate, called Volume Synchronized Probability of Informed Trading (VPIN), which is a common proxy of order book toxicity. An important part of VPIN is that the measure is calculated in volume time rather than trade time, meaning VPIN is linked to the time it takes to fill a set volume quantity. Easley et al. suggest that it is intuitive to compare periods of equal volume, (or information content in this context), which addresses trade frequency clustering, having the effect of smoothing out information bursts. Aslan, et al., (2011) suggest that VPIN is an effective leading volatility indicator and demonstrate this with analysis of the 6 May 2010 DJIA flash crash. However, Jonathan Heusser applied the technique to the 2013 bitcoin crash and found it to yield weaker results, (although the parameters were not optimized), leaving open the question: Is toxicity a useful factor in analysing cryptocurrency markets?[54]

In traditional markets, flash crashes may be induced by fraud and manipulation techniques such as spoofing, (see Section 8.8: order book based manipulations), as was the case in DJIA 2010.[55] However, aside from spoofing, market participants in cryptocurrency markets can, potentially, place very large market orders which may consume the order book and trigger stop-loss orders and margin calls. This will deepen the sell-off, possibly setting off a free-fall in prices. Once the price has fallen by an appropriate level the manipulators buy back into the market and, having sold high and bought at a lower price, they can profit from the manipulation. This form of manipulation can be accomplished in cryptocurrency markets more easily than it can in traditional markets, due to the large skew of ownership towards early adopters, (e.g. 1000 people own 40% of bitcoin, where they can organize between themselves a coordinated trade), or simply high-net-worth individuals, (as the market cap of cryptocurrencies was relatively low at the time).[56]

---

[53] Toxic to the uninformed trader (i.e. the market maker who places orders with limit orders).
[54] Heusser, J. (13 Oct 2013), *Order Flow Toxicity of the Bitcoin April Crash*, see https://bit.ly/2OR9QXq.
[55] FT (10 Nov 2016) 'Flash crash' trader Navinder Sarao pleads guilty to spoofing.
[56] Bloomberg (4 Dec 2017) *The Bitcoin Whales: 1,000 People Who Own 40 Percent of the Market*, see https://bit.ly/2D5saWi.

Some theories as to the real motive behind the Ethereum flash crash of 2017 on GDAX revolve around a fat-fingered (errored) trade which had nothing to do with market manipulation, whereas others propose that someone deliberately placed a large market order intended to put pressure on an already fragile cryptocurrency market.[57] It is still an open question as to whether the crash was a malicious attack or simply a mistake. Detailed literature focusing on flash crashes in cryptocurrency is all but non-existent; however, in general, flash crashes are caused by fragmented markets, low liquidity and a rapid increase in sell-side volume, which are all factors often present in cryptocurrency markets.

Many flash crashes have been observed in conventional markets in the past – most notably on 6 May 2010 when a $4.1 billion trade was placed on the New York Stock Exchange (NYSE) which resulted in the Dow Jones Industrial Average (DJIA) losing ~1000 points and then recovering within the space of 15 minutes. Other markets such as the S&P500 and Nasdaq also experienced similar price volatility as a result.

The 2010 flash crash on the E-mini S&P 500 futures contract was traced back to Navinder Singh Sarao, a trader who had used spoofing algorithms to modify $200 million worth of trades, approximately 19,000 times, moments before the flash crash.

There are many more examples of crashes in the cryptocurrency markets such as 10 April 2013 bitcoin crash, when a large trade volume lag at the Mt. Gox exchange sent the market plummeting over 60% within the day.[58] However, this cannot be defined as a flash crash as the event occurred over a number of hours, which does not constitute a 'very rapid' decline in price within the scope of cryptocurrency markets. **Table 8.2** summarizes the most notable recent flash crashes.

It can be seen from Table 8.2 that the duration and peak-to-trough magnitude of each flash crash are very different, especially when comparing conventional markets (DJIA, Gold) to cryptocurrency markets (ether). A 'deep' volatile fall (as stated in the definition of a flash crash) depends on what market is encountering the event. The 1.6% move in the price of Gold Futures within 60 seconds[59] in 2017 constitutes a contextually deep crash as this market is one of the most liquid in the world, whereas

Table 8.2   Recent notable flash crashes.

Date	Market	Peak-to-Trough (Magnitude)	Peak-to-Trough (Duration)	Reason
6 May 2010	DJIA	9%	~4 minutes	Market manipulation
26 June 2017	Gold Futures	1.6%	~8 seconds	$2bn market order
22 June 2017	Ether	99.97%	~1.5 seconds	Million-dollar market order

---

[57] CNBC (22 Jun 2017) *Ethereum price crashed from $319 to 10 cents on GDAX after huge trade,* see https://bit.ly/2PXaoYc.

[58] Forbes (11 Apr 2013) *An Illustrated History of Bitcoin Crashes,* see https://bit.ly/2zoO3S4.

[59] Bloomberg (26 June 2017) *Gold Plunges After 1.8 Million Ounces Were Traded in One Minute,* see https://bit.ly/2O6VNrp.

a change of 1.6% in cryptocurrency markets would not be classified as a crash but simply market noise. Crashes in cryptocurrency markets can be much deeper – for example ether's flash crash lost 99.97% of its value within seconds of a large market sell order being placed, before the price recovered. This magnitude of movement is unheard of in conventional markets.

8.7.1   GDAX-ETH/USD Flash Crash

On 21 June 2017, a $12.5 million market sell order was placed on the GDAX exchange at 12:30pm Pacific Time (PT), which triggered a flash crash on ETHUSD.[60] This massive order, (~14.5% of the GDAX 21-day average daily volume), which accounted for 39,300 ETH, removed a large chunk of liquidity from the order book, incurring a 29.4% price move, from $317.81 to $224.48, immediately.

The movement resulted in approximately 800 stop-loss orders and margin-funding liquidations. The volume of sell orders, (from stop-loss activation and margin calls), overwhelmed the market's available liquidity, causing further extreme downward movement. The price of ETH fell momentarily to $0.10, accounting for a 99.97% loss from trading prices seconds before.[61]

This event occurred over a period of approximately 10 seconds where the price went from $317.81 to $0.10 and recovered back to $302. Figure 8.12 shows the price movement over the period.

Interestingly, we can see bids in the order book starting at 10 cents and asks at $74 in the GDAX final update on their blog.[62] The spread quoted at $73.9 at the time of this snapshot exhibits an extreme market inefficiency which automated traders subsequently traded away, recovering the price to $302. However, it can be seen that

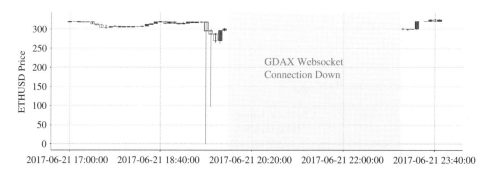

Figure 8.12   Five-minute candlestick representation of the GDAX ETH/USD traded price during the 21 June 2017 flash crash. Within a five-minute window, the traded price quickly drops from above $300 to just $0.10 and quickly reverts.

---

[60] Bloomberg (30 Jun 2017) *The 45-Millisecond Ether Flash Crash Prompts Safeguard Effort*, see https://bit .ly/2PXmeS9.
[61] GDAX Blog (21 June 2017) *ETH-USD Trading Update*, see https://bit.ly/2OQAQWQ.
[62] GDAX Blog (30 Jun 2017) *ETH-USD Trading Update 3, What Happened and What's Next?*, see https:// bit.ly/2OQAQWQ.

there were approximately 24,000 ETH filled at 15 cents and under, for a total price of around $2600; if these fills were from a single user they would have made nearly $7.8 million from the flash crash.[63]

After an investigation by GDAX, it was decided that all profitable trades during the time of the flash crash would be honoured. GDAX went a step further with an official announcement on their blog, stating:

> For customers who had buy orders filled — we are honoring all executed orders and no trades will be reversed. For affected customers who had margin calls or stop loss orders executed – we are crediting you using company funds.

This unusual act restored faith in GDAX's reputation as one of the most trusted cryptocurrency exchanges – they were not required to refund customers because no system errors were uncovered. The exchange stated their reasons for these actions were that they:

> . . .view this as an opportunity to demonstrate our long-term commitment to our customers and belief in the future of this industry.

The total cost to GDAX because of the flash crash is still unknown.

Although the ETHUSD flash crash of 2017 has seen no legal action, its ties to a possible market manipulation are clear. Price movements of this extreme magnitude cause many to speculate whether any wrongdoing was the central cause of such an event, (e.g. the large market order was intended to crash the market), or whether the event was caused by a large trade amount being entered accidently. The reason is still unknown to this day, although the cause is well documented (as in the above case study).

Conventional markets deal with unstable trading using systems such as circuit breakers, which would freeze trading should a market move by a large percentage in a very short period of time. GDAX stated that they were looking into how these measures could be integrated, although at the time of writing no action had been taken.[64]

This event on GDAX clearly highlights the effectiveness of regulation in conventional markets, which suggests that, if measures proposed after the 2010 flash crash on the DJIA had been implemented on GDAX, the flash crash on ETHUSD in 2017 would probably have been avoided. However, the onus is on the leading exchanges such as GDAX to develop market-stabilization systems to prevent such an event recurring.

8.8   Order Book-Based Manipulations

The next two approaches that we examine are based on manipulation of the order book. We introduced the concept of an order book in Section 8.1 and explained the difference between a market and limit order. In a typical market, there are a wide

---

[63] Trade fills can be found through GDAX's API and can be found at: https://api.gdax.com/products/eth-usd/trades?after=6326581&limit=18.

[64] GDAX Blog (30 Jun 2017) *ETH-USD Trading Update 3, What Happened and What's Next?*, see https://bit.ly/2OQAQWQ.

array of participants, each with their own motivations and behaviour. 'Quote stuffing' and 'Order spoofing' are two order book manipulations, using limit orders, which are designed to provide the manipulator with an unfair advantage. Both are quite sophisticated manipulations developed from traditional financial markets and intend to distort or influence the true price of a currency pair.

8.8.1   Quote Stuffing

Quote stuffing is an algorithmic trading strategy which involves rapidly placing and cancelling limit orders. During a quote stuffing event, high quote volatility is observed over a very short period where short-lived quote updates often follow specific patterns. One variation we focus on here creates new best bid or best ask prices, which are quickly cancelled. There are a number of reasons why this form of quote stuffing may be engaged in, as outlined in Tse, et al. (2012). Quote stuffing creates a false mid-price – the mid-price is the average of the current best bid and ask prices and is often used by algorithmic traders and traditional traders in benchmarking the trade execution and market price of an asset; manipulation of the mid-price can give an impression of rising or falling prices, and may manipulate others into trading if they are looking for mid-price related signals. Furthermore, quote stuffing may generate high volumes of inconsequential market data updates, potentially slowing and confusing the responses of other competing algorithms and traders, (in a similar way to a DDoS attack slowing a website server); this is especially important for high-frequency trading, where speed is a critical factor.

It should be noted that quote stuffing has also been observed in traditional markets, as identified by Tse, et al. (2012). Exchange standards and sophistication (8.2.4) within cryptocurrency markets may be a contributory factor to quote stuffing. Many cryptocurrency exchanges may not have the analytical systems set up to catch its occurrence. Furthermore, they may not see it as a priority to do so when other manipulations have a more dramatic effect.

To illustrate the effect of quote stuffing, we examined some order book BTC/EUR data from a prominent cryptocurrency exchange over a 10-week period in 2017. By recording real-time market updates which are broadcast publicly from their servers, we were able to reconstruct the historical state of the BTC/EUR order book and track placed and cancelled orders. Using the approach as described in Bogoev and Karam (2016), we identified periods of quote stuffing using the *D-ratio*. The *D-ratio* is a ratio between the start-to-end change and the sum of all incremental changes observed in a particular window of order book updates. More specifically, the in-bid *D-ratio* (for detecting stuffing occurring on the bid side of the order book) is defined as:

$$D = \frac{\dfrac{\sum_{i=2}^{j}|B_i - B_{i-1}|}{|B_j - B_1|}}{\dfrac{\sum_{i=2}^{j}|A_i - A_{i-1}|}{|A_j - A_1|}}$$

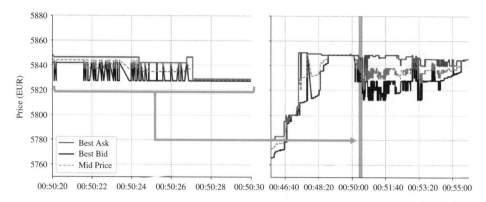

Figure 8.13 BTC/EUR (a) 10-second snapshot (b) 10-minute snapshot best bids.

where the numerator is the absolute sum of the incremental changes in best bid price during a period considered, divided by the absolute change in best bid prices from start to end of the window. The denominator is the same, but for the ask price. Essentially, the formula measures whether there is a lot of temporary movement in best bid prices without much overall movement, compared to the ask price. Appropriate approaches exist in Bogoev and Karam (2016) to detect in-ask stuffing, and stuffing on both sides of the book, but a full description is omitted here for brevity.

In our research, we calculate the *D-ratio* for each time window (chosen as 10-seconds) over the entire dataset. The windows are then ordered based on their *D-ratio*, creating a distribution of observed *D-ratios*. The methodology aims to capture windows of data that contain characteristics associated with quote stuffing events: repeated and small changes in best bid or ask, which are rapidly reversed, combined with little actual change in best bid or ask between the start and end of the window. The higher the *D-ratio,* the higher the likelihood a specific type of quote stuffing is taking place. Unfortunately, it is difficult to define in simple terms how frequently quote stuffing occurs since a *D-ratio* 'cut-off', defining what *is* and *is not* quote stuffing is somewhat arbitrary and therefore is chosen as a percentile of the *D-ratio* distribution.

As such, we opt to show one example time window that exhibits a high *D-ratio* as an example. Figure 8.13 (a) shows an example of a 10-second window containing bid-stuffing, and (b) gives a lower-frequency (10-minute) picture surrounding the identified quote stuffing event. It is observed that fleeting orders are being placed to alter the best bid, before being cancelled almost instantaneously. The ask price during this event is relatively static.

8.8.2 Order Spoofing

Order spoofing is another type of order book manipulation where limit orders are placed into the limit order book to deceive other market participants, such as normal traders and algorithmic trading bots, into believing that there is more demand or supply. Usually, these 'spoof' orders are comparatively large in quantity to create the impression of a large imbalance. However, what separates spoof orders from standard large limit orders is that the entity placing the orders intends to cancel them before they can be executed against. After a spoof order is placed, if successful, the market moves, based on its belief that the imbalance is real. This allows the entity placing the spoof order to manipulate the price; potentially to execute a trade on the opposite side of the book. Figure 8.14 gives a demonstration of the process undertaken.

Numerous examples occur where a large buy or sell limit order is placed, discussed on social media and then removed. Trader IDs, which would need to be supplied by the exchanges, would shed further proof that an individual event can be classified as 'order spoofing', and on whether the participating trader is filling orders on the other side of the book.

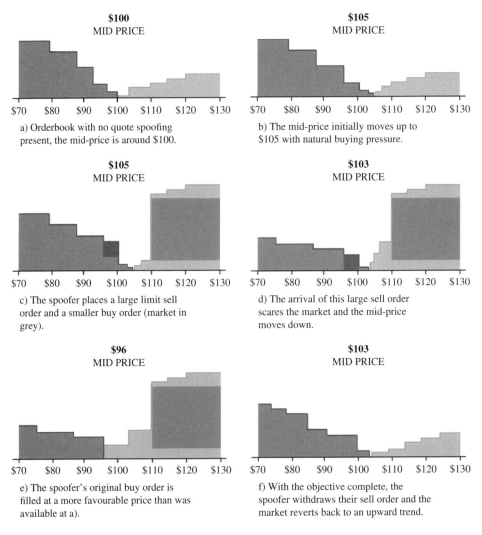

Figure 8.14   Illustrative example of order spoofing process

Existing literature investigating order spoofing occurring in any financial market is relatively sparse. However, it has been documented that many targeted financial assets have certain shared attributes, including higher return volatility, lower market capitalizations, and lower price level (Jung Lee, et al., 2013). All these attributes are common among cryptocurrencies, and those that do not have a low (unit) price level, have had this in the past. As such, the distribution of cryptocurrency ownership is skewed (Moore and Christin, 2013). Early investors have the potential to own large percentages of the total amounts available. As with quote stuffing, low exchange standards and sophistication (Section 8.2.4) may also enable this manipulation, as it may not be a priority to catch.

8.9   Stablecoins and Tether

A **stablecoin** is a type of price-stable cryptocurrency whose price is pegged to an asset, such as gold or a fiat currency. The majority of existing stablecoins use some form of collateralization; however, others are emerging that use algorithms which expand or contract the issuance scheme depending on the traded price of the coin.[65] Fiat-collateralized stablecoins require a certain amount of collateral to be deposited against which (stable)coins are issued, typically using a 1:1 ratio. Although this is a relatively straightforward currency issuance process, it requires a central party, acting as a custodian, who guarantees the issuance and redeemability of the stablecoin.

Unlike other cryptocurrencies, a stablecoin is designed to have little risk of suddenly changing in value. It is engineered explicitly not to provide any return. The idea is that if you bought $2,500 worth of stablecoins a year ago, you would have roughly $2,500 today. There is a demand for stablecoins from both exchanges and investors as they both provide an effective hedge against cryptocurrency volatility as well as facilitating dollar-like transactions without a banking connection, something many crypto-exchanges have difficulty obtaining or keeping (Griffin and Shams, 2018).

The story of stablecoin use and adoption to date is primarily one about Tether. **Tether** (denoted USDT), is currently the 8th largest crypto globally and largest stablecoin in existence.[66] In fact, Tether accounts for more crypto transaction volume than USD. Even with the emergence of some new entrants, it still accounts for approximately 98–99% of all stablecoin trading volume.[67]

As Tether explain on their website: *"Tether converts cash into digital currency, to anchor or 'tether' the value of the coin to the price of national currencies like the US dollar, the Euro, and the Yen."*[68]As such, the price of one USDT is pegged to $1, and so a current market capitalization of $2 billion indicates approximately 2 billion USDT tokens are in circulation. This quantity can also be verified from blockchain transactions. New USDT tokens are issued from one Tether wallet address on the Omni Layer (formerly Mastercoin), a platform that enables the creation of new assets

---

[65] For example, see https://basis.io or https://carbon.money.
[66] When measured via coinmarketcap.com on 23 Oct 2018.
[67] www.blockchain.com/ru/static/pdf/StablecoinsReportFinal.pdf.
[68] Tether.to (Accessed 25 Oct 2018) Homepage, see https://bit.ly/2D4d1og.

on the Bitcoin blockchain.[69] Every Omni transaction, and therefore every Tether transaction, is recorded in a Bitcoin transaction sharing the same transaction hash.[70] New tokens are purportedly issued upon new USD deposits and, since Tether claims to be fully-collateralized, this implies that Tether holds collateral of $2 billion in its bank accounts.

On paper, Tether proves to be an extremely successful example of a stablecoin project; however, its history has been plagued with controversy. To better understand these issues and shed light on the allegations of misconduct and suspicious activity, we first examine Tether's history. Following this, we examine some of the criticism put forward, including new research published in June 2018, which finds evidence of Tether being used for cryptocurrency price manipulation. Finally, we highlight the important role Tether plays in cryptocurrency market prices and discuss the ramifications of hypothetical wrongdoing.

8.9.1 Tether Historical Timeline

Table 8.3 provides a summary of important events in Tether and Bitfinex's history between 2012–2018, including key legal announcements and Tether market capitalisation milestones.

Table 8.3   A timeline of key events in Tether and Bitfinex's history.[71,72,73]

2012		–	IFinex, the eventual parent company of Tether (and Bitfinex) is founded in Hong Kong.
2013		–	Bitfinex is incorporated. Phil Potter runs the company alongside CEO Jan Ludovicus van der Velde and CFO Giancarlo Devasini.
2014	Jul	–	Realcoin is announced, built on top of Bitcoin with a protocol called Mastercoin (now called Omnicoin).
	Sep	–	Bitfinex operators (Potter and Devasini) set up Tether Ltd. in the British Virgin Islands but tell the public that Bitfinex and Tether are separate.
	Nov	–	Realcoin rebrands to Tether and announces several partners including Bitfinex.
2015	Feb	–	Tether begins trading under the symbol USDT, but currency circulation remains relatively low.
2016	May	–	Tether market capitalization rises to $7 million.
2017	Feb	–	Tether market capitalization hits $25 million.
	Mar	–	Wells Fargo ends its banking relationship with Tether, issuing a statement that *'all international wires to Tether have been blocked . . . As such, we do not expect the supply of tethers to increases substantially until these constraints have been lifted'*.

---

[69] The wallet address is *3MbYQMMmSkC3AgWkj9FMo5LsPTW1zBTwXL,* and a full history of issuances can be viewed at www.omniexplorer.info/address/*3MbYQMMmSkC3AgWkj9FMo5LsPTW1zBTwXL.*

[70] Tether Whitepaper (Jun 2016) *Tether: Fiat currencies on the Bitcoin blockchain,* see https://bit.ly/2EIroAh.

[71] Bitcoin Magazine (7 Feb 2018) *Warning Signs? A Timeline of Tether and Bitfinex Events,* see https://bit.ly/2RcJ7RN.

[72] Medium (22 Aug 2018) *Is the Price of Bitcoin Based on Anything at All?,* see https://bit.ly/2yHhcTl.

[73] Amy Castor (17 Jan 2019) *The curious case of Tether a complete timeline of events,* see https://bit.ly/2NbOj7E.

Table 8.3   (Continued)

	Apr	–	Tether market capitalization reaches $50 million.
		–	Bitfinex files a lawsuit against Wells Fargo for interrupting its banking transfers (eventually withdrawn in 2017).
		–	A pseudonymous character Bitfinex'ed appears online, accusing Bitfinex of creating Tether out of thin air to pay off debts.
	May	–	Bitfinex and Tether hire Friedman LLP to complete an external audit.
	Sep	–	Tether market capitalization expands exponentially to $440 million.
		–	Tether Ltd. publishes a memo from Friedman LLP affirming that Tether is fully backed. However, this does not constitute an official audit.
	Nov	–	Bitfinex and Tether are shown to be run by the same individuals via leaked documents dubbed the 'Paradise Papers'.
		–	Tether is hacked and 31 million USDT are moved from the Tether treasury wallet and sent to an unauthorized Bitcoin address – a hard fork is initiated to prevent those funds from being spent.
	Dec	–	The Commodity Futures Trading Commission (CFTC) send subpoenas to Bitfinex and Tether, but the actual documents are not made public. (To date, no charges have been filed).
2018	Jan	–	Tether parts ways with auditor Friedman LLP, blaming the accounting firm's overcomplicated procedures for what is a *'relatively simple balance sheet of Tether'*.
		–	Bloomberg reports on the CTFC subpoena of Tether and Bitfinex.
		–	Tether issues more than $850 million tether, more than any previous month.
	Jun	–	Tether releases a report it had commissioned from law firm Freeh Sporkin and Sullivan (FFS) attesting that 'Tether's unencumbered assets exceed the balance of fully-backed USD Tethers in circulation as of June 1st, 2018'.
	Aug	–	Tether market capitalization hits $3 billion.
	Oct	–	Bitfinex temporarily suspends all cash deposits four days after reports claiming the exchange is banking at HSBC under the name 'Global Trading Solutions' amid Tether insolvency woes.
		–	Bitfinex publishes three wallet addresses (BTC, ETH, and EOS) to prove the exchange is still solvent.
		–	Rumours claiming Tether is insolvent sees its pegging slip to $0.92, and $0.85 on Kraken.
		–	Tether appears to be holding reserves at Bahamas' Deltec Bank.
		–	Tether 'redeemed a significant amount of USDT' and burns 500 million USDT representing these redemptions. The remaining 446 million USDT is held in treasury for 'preparatory measures for future USDT issuances'.
	Nov	–	Tether provides an attestation letter from Deltec confirming its banking partner and showing proof of ~$1.8 billion which fully backs Tether, although the letter has an incomprehensible signature.
		–	Bloomberg report US federal prosecutors have 'homed in on suspicions that a tangled web involving Bitcoin, Tether, and crypto exchange Bitfinex might have been used to illegally move process'.
		–	Tether announces that customers can redeem USDT for USD again.
	Dec	–	Tether has issued over 1 billion USDT in 2018.

8.9.2   Tether Controversy and Criticism

Key events in Tether's history have raised concerns over its conduct. The fact that Bitfinex and Tether are run and operated by the same individuals immediately produces potential conflicts of interest: Tether and Bitfinex are issuers of a cryptocurrency on their own and other platforms, with a direct stake in its performance. A recent report commissioned by the NY Attorney General points out that running these multiple lines of business would be *'restricted or carefully monitored in a traditional trading environment'*, a safeguard which is currently not present in cryptocurrency markets.[74]

Many sceptics have questioned the reality of the US dollar peg and the token's redeemability. Some other have even accused Tether of cryptocurrency price manipulation. We now examine each of these claims in turn.

There has been very little transparency provided by either Bitfinex or Tether regarding the preservation of Tether's US dollar peg. Only days after Tether announced it had dissolved its relationship with auditors Friedman LLP in December 2017, it issued $600 million worth of tokens, raising its market capitalization by nearly half. Some, particularly in the blogosphere and press, have expressed scepticism that Bitfinex/Tether really have this kind of collateral.[75,76] Nonetheless, cryptocurrency exchanges and investors have largely rejected such concerns, and widely use Tether in transactions.

The September 2017 memo from Friedman LLP and the June 2018 commissioned report of Freeh Sporkin and Sullivan (FSS) go some way in demonstrating Tether is fully collateralized, but both fall short of a full audit. For example, FSS's report includes important caveats stating that *'FSS makes no representation regarding the sufficiency of the information provided to FSS'* and *'FSS is not an accounting firm and did not perform the above review and confirmations using Generally Accepted Accounting Principles'*.[77]

Some concede that the information provided in the reports may accurately confirm that Tether reserves matched that of circulating USDT on the date of examination. However, they raise different concerns regarding the way in which the funds were raised, and highlight the importance of the order of transactions. Without disclosing the order of transactions, it is theoretically possible for Tether to issue new tokens out of thin air, use these tokens to buy other cryptocurrency, sell that cryptocurrency, and used the proceeds to create its reserves. In February 2018, the blogger Bitfinex'ed illustrates a scenario where Tether first issues several million Tether to buy other cryptocurrencies on Tether-supported exchanges, transfers these to other exchanges such as GDAX, liquidates the cryptocurrency and then funnels the (now fiat), currency back to Tether-owned bank accounts. Bitfinex'ed backs up this scenario with

---

[74] New York State Office of the Attorney General (18 Sep 2018) *Virtual Markets Integrity Initiative*, see https://bit.ly/2RhOG37.

[75] See *https://twitter.com/bitfinexed* and *https://medium.com/@bitfinexed*.

[76] New York Times (21 Nov 2017) *Warning Signs About Another Giant Bitcoin Exchange*, see https://bit.ly/2z2qecU.

[77] Medium (22 Aug 2018) *Is the Price of Bitcoin Based on Anything at All?*, see https://bit.ly/2yHhcTl.

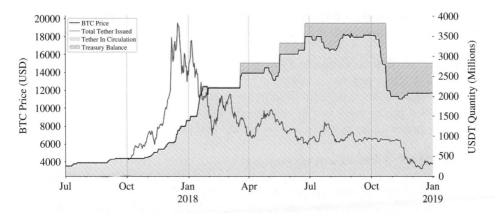

Figure 8.15 **Tether issuance plotted against BTCUSD price as quoted on Coinmarketcap .com. Tether can issue tokens but hold them in a treasury wallet; these tokens are considered not in circulation and excluded from its market capitalization.**

suspicious trading activity on Bitfinex and GDAX, saying 'when GDAX goes down, the volume on Bitfinex dries up dramatically . . . until GDAX comes back online'. They summarize: *'[Bitfinex] Pump on Tether exchanges while simultaneously having large sell orders on GDAX/Bitstamp/Gemini and then immediately transfer the funds back to their main account'.*[78]

Figure 8.15, constructed using Tether historical transactions recorded on the Omni Protocol, highlights the dramatically increasing rate at which new Tether was issued throughout 2017 and 2018. The figure also shows that very little Tether has ever been removed entirely. Tether are often moved to the Tether treasury wallet and kept as 'preparatory measures for future USDT' and thus not redeemed completely.[79] In September 2018, there had only ever been one Tether redemption transaction (30 million tokens were redeemed on 31 January 2018). This means that, on a net basis, Tether should have taken in more deposits than withdrawals. This said, on 24 October, Tether did destroy 500 million USDT from the Tether treasury wallet after a growing accumulation throughout 2018.

In December 2017, Bloomberg published an article wherein Oguz Serdar, a USDT user who relied on cryptocurrency to pay contractors, claimed that in early November he tried to cash out $1 million of Tether through Tether Ltd., but was refused and *'instead recommended in an email that he try to sell on one of the exchange partners it lists on its website'.*[80] Tether defended this decision, explaining that Serdar was flagged as suspicious and that they were not permitted to do business with him

---

[78] Medium (8 Feb 2018), @Bitfinexed, *Bitfinex and Tether is unauditable: Why they will never do a real audit*, see https://bit.ly/2PkSFN9.
[79] Tether.to (Accessed 26 Oct 2018), *Upcoming USDT Redemption – October 24, 2018*, see https://bit.ly/2SieKuF.
[80] Bloomberg (5 Dec 2017), *There's an $814 Million Mystery Near the Heart of the Biggest Bitcoin Exchange*, see https://bit.ly/2PmkogB.

until he completed their KYC process. Within Tether's terms of service, it is stated: 'Tether must and does at all times reserve the right to refuse to issue or redeem Tether tokens'.[81]

In June 2018, John Griffin and Aman Shams published their research examining the timing of Tether purchases following market downturns. They were able to establish that entities associated with Bitfinex were successfully using Tether to purchase bitcoin when prices were falling and reverse the trend of the market. These effects were only present after negative bitcoin returns and periods following the circulation of new Tether.

They asserted that 50% of bitcoin's and 64% of other top cryptocurrencies' price rises were due to well-timed, heavy Tether transactions. Patterns they found in publicly available trading data supported the hypothesis that Tether is used to support and manipulate cryptocurrency prices. The authors also mention that negative end-of-month price pressure on bitcoin only during months with large Tether issuance supports a month-end need for dollar reserves related to Tether.

Without the existence of USD/BTC and other fiat-to-crypto trading pairs, the price of Tether would be an entirely self-referential process, with the price of Tether always equal to itself. As these markets do exist on banked exchanges, Tether's global market price is expected to move away from one dollar given a change in the price of bitcoin (or any other cryptocurrency) in fiat markets, without an accompanying one in Tether markets. When Tether is consistently reported to be worth a dollar, implicitly, the price of bitcoin in Tether on unbanked exchanges is the same as the price of bitcoin in dollars on banked exchanges. However, there is no obvious mechanism for keeping the two values at parity.

Professor Rosa Abrantes-Metz finds this parity something extremely puzzling, because there is no reason for their prices to stay matched. Tether does not have a built-in (i.e. blockchain-encoded) stability mechanism and so, 'If things trade freely, the only way to keep parity is for someone to actively intervene in the markets', but who, or how, is unknown.[82]

Generally, USD and Tether trade on different exchanges and are therefore not visibly connected. Kraken is among very few markets worldwide that let investors trade USD for Tether and vice versa. In effect, Kraken should play a large role in establishing Tether's price.

In June 2018, Bloomberg published an investigation claiming the normal economics of supply and demand do not always appear to apply for USD/USDT. 'Counter to basic trade economics, large and frequent trade volumes appeared to have less influence on price than small trade volumes'– a clear indicator of market manipulation.

The distribution of Tether trade volumes showed an unusual pattern with the third most common Tether trade size 13,076.389 Tethers, an oddly specific number. Former Federal Reserve bank examiner Mark Williams's theory is that this could be a sign of wash trading as the software would look for orders with a unique size and trade

---

[81] Tether.to/legal (Accessed 25 Oct 2018), see https://bit.ly/2D5NKKn.
[82] Bloomberg (29 Jun 2018) *Crypto Coin Tether Defies Logic on Kraken's Market, Raising Red Flags*, see https://bit.ly/2qbPA44.

against that. Williams explains *'Many of the trade amounts are frequently occurring to the fifth decimal point, a unique identifier which increases the probability it is being generated by the same person or entity'*.[83],[84]

8.9.3   Tether's Significance in Cryptocurrency Global Markets

Tether is a systemically important part of the cryptocurrency ecosystem. The global published price of a cryptocurrency, e.g. bitcoin is generally a volume-weighted average of its price on all the markets on which it is traded. Since three times as much bitcoin trading takes place in Tether than in USD, this means that the published price is based three times as much on Tether trades as on dollar trades.

However, this volume-weighted method also applies to the quoted price of Tether itself. Just like any other coin or token, Tether's global price is a weighted average of all the available markets by volume. Since virtually all Tether trading occurs in markets where it is traded against bitcoin and other cryptocurrencies, the only way to arrive at a dollar price is by dividing its price in cryptocurrency by the price of that cryptocurrency in dollars. Similarly, the dollar prices of most cryptocurrencies are themselves derived from trades with other cryptocurrencies, primarily Tether. *'The price of crypto is derived largely from trades in Tether, the price of which is derived from trades in crypto, the price of which is derived largely from trades in Tether.'* This has large implications for cryptocurrency price discovery.[85]

As Wang Chu Wei, a researcher at the University of Queensland explains, *'If Tether was in fact able to issue tokens not backed by fiat reserves then effectively, they would be printing USD in the cryptocurrency ecosystem . . . . If that was the case, Tether Limited's role/power would not be dissimilar to that of a central bank; i.e. the ability to increase money supply and boost asset prices.'*[86]

In a worse-case scenario where Tether collapses, the ramifications for cryptocurrencies are concerning. Before Tether tokens began flooding the market at the start of 2017, bitcoin was priced at less than $1,000. Professor Sarit Markovich, who researches cryptocurrency at Northwestern University, has stated that *'If there's a panic in the market, we're going to go to the same price we had before and we're going to see it across all cryptos.'*

8.10   Summary and Conclusions

The purpose of this chapter was to provide the reader with a non-exhaustive survey of manipulations which have often occurred, or are alleged to have occurred, in cryptocurrency markets. We began with a general introduction to cryptocurrencies,

---

[83] Bloomberg (29 Jun 2018) *Crypto Coin Tether Defies Logic on Kraken's Market, Raising Red Flags*, see https://bit.ly/2qbPA44.

[84] Wash trading involves taking both sides of a transaction for the express purpose of feeding misleading information to the market.

[85] Medium (22 Aug 2018) *Is the Price of Bitcoin Based on Anything at All?*, see https://bit.ly/2yHhcTl.

[86] Medium (22 Aug 2018) *Is the Price of Bitcoin Based on Anything at All?*, see https://bit.ly/2yHhcTl.

the nature of their transactions, and the cryptocurrency exchanges upon which large volumes of cryptocurrency are traded. Section 8.2 then gave an idea of why manipulations are prominent in cryptocurrencies. Throughout the remainder of the chapter, we attempted to link back to these reasons. Often it is clear that one reason alone is not sufficient to motivate/facilitate manipulation and we, therefore, rely on a combination of reasons to explain them. In the subsequent subsections, we surveyed a variety of manipulations ranging from social-based manipulations to more technical and complex ones.

Although the first manipulation, a **pump and dump** event, occurs within traditional financial markets, we focused our investigation on a cryptocurrency-adapted version. This modification involves groups on social media coordinating buying pressure for a particular cryptocurrency; we included a case study with a real example of a coordinated pump and dump event in 2017, and analysed the event's effect on both the price and trading volume.

Next, we discussed a manipulation – **inflated trading volume** – allegedly employed by Chinese trading exchanges in an effort to give themselves an elevated image to different interested parties, and we saw that its eventual prevention in January 2017 caused an astonishing reduction in trading volume. The rapid series of regulatory-influenced events, which prompted such a change, emphasises that cryptocurrency markets are an extremely fast-evolving environment; opportunities to profit from different legitimate strategies come and go, as do the opportunities for manipulation. The work here has documented some of the most relevant instances of manipulation at the time of writing, but further down the line – even a year or two – numerous manipulations may or may not continue to occur; especially with increased regulatory scrutiny.

Our next two manipulations, **exchange DDoS attacks** and **hacks,** which are illegal wherever undertaken, tend to be deployed in the cryptocurrency markets rather than more traditional financial markets, due to what the manipulators deem as an unrivalled risk–return payoff: the potential return in cryptocurrency far outweighs the chance of being caught, in part because of the high level of anonymity in cryptocurrency markets.

The next manipulation, **flash crashes**, was the only one that may not always be intentional. Although flash crashes may be the result of manipulations such as a carefully executed DDoS attack, they can also be accidental. The fragmentation of trading across many venues and the low liquidity seen on a number of smaller exchanges, cultivates an environment where large sell orders may trigger stop losses which further propagate downwards price movement.

Section 8.8 looked at two order book-based manipulations, **quote stuffing** and **order spoofing,** which are examples of strategies which have been recorded a number of times in equities, commodities, and other more established markets, repurposed and deployed in cryptocurrency markets.

We finished our survey off with a slightly different, but important, section on the role of stablecoins, and more specifically the controversy concerning Tether, the largest stablecoin. At the time of writing, no allegation of misconduct by Tether or related parties has been substantiated. However, closer examination does highlight the importance Tether has on the cryptocurrency market in general.

After our discussion of the vast array of manipulations within cryptocurrencies, two questions may be raised:

1. What is the impact of the manipulations covered on normal cryptocurrency market participants?
2. Why does participation within cryptocurrency markets continue to grow while manipulations such as these are occurring so freely?

In addressing the impacts (1) it is best to consider each manipulation separately:

- The documented near-instantaneous pump and dump groups appear primarily to redistribute money between those actively participating. Those that buy can quickly flip the targeted asset at a mark-up to later participants in the group, who end up buying at a premium and losing out. To other market participants, the price spike may at most become a nuisance when examining, or training models on, historical data.
- The inflated trading volume was well documented and discounted by the majority of market participants who were well aware of who was engaging in it; many reporting websites refused to report on trading volumes of the culprit exchanges.
- As documented above, exchange DDoS attacks have the potential to cause large short-term price deviations. A successfully executed DDoS attack has the potential to cause stop-losses to execute at below true market prices and also cause margin traders to be forced from their positions.
- Hacks arguably have the largest potential impact of the manipulations covered. If market participants are over-invested in one exchange, (e.g. if a market participant has all their cryptocurrency stored with one trading exchange), or one particular cryptocurrency, they are at risk of losing funds through the failure of that exchange or cryptocurrency.
- Order spoofing may scare traders, (and trading bots) into making rash, wrongly-informed decisions; however, once it is understood what order spoofing is and that it occurs commonly in cryptocurrency markets, it can increasingly be ignored. Quote stuffing may only manipulate other similar trading bots, and due to the speed in which it occurs, manual traders may be completely unaware of and unaffected by the effects of it.

Although certainly not without impact, the number of participants engaging in manipulative strategies are insubstantial compared to those following legitimate short, medium, and long-term trading and investment strategies.

We now look at addressing the second question raised (2). Indeed, despite the presence of the manipulations we document here, the enthusiasm of participants to remain in the markets, and for new traders and investors to enter, has only grown in recent times. We hypothesize that this is because of the potentially meteoric returns cryptocurrency markets can offer: people are happy to overlook the potential risks of manipulations. In 2017, the values of the two largest cryptocurrencies (by market capitalization), bitcoin and ether's, grew approximately 1,411% and 8,500% respectively. These price rises can be paired with a sizeable increase in mainstream interest, including a growing body of inexperienced market participants with little understanding of the blockchain protocol underlying the cryptocurrencies which they trade, and of the exchange trading and direct peer-to-peer markets for cryptocurrencies. It is expected that with the recent boom in interest, further regulatory scrutiny will follow. In 2018, market prices reversed and by October 2018 the market capitalization had fallen to approximately $200 billion but cryptocurrencies look set to stay.

In 2018, the New York State Office of the Attorney General (OAG) sent letters to 13 cryptocurrency exchanges to gather data for a 40-page report eventually published in September 2018.[87] Within the report, several key shortcomings of exchanges were cited including a lack of ability to combat market abuse real-time and prevent wash trading. They also highlighted that conflicts are rampant, with exchanges engaging in several business lines and that there was no 'rhyme or reason' to the listing of new currencies on their platforms. In other words, creators of worthless cryptocurrencies can simply bribe exchanges to feature their coin.

Many exchanges were quick to respond to the report. Coinbase's Mike Lempres (their CPO), was largely welcoming of the report but disagreed with some aspects; in particular, that Coinbase (GDAX) were engaging in proprietary trading.[88] Kraken, one of four exchanges that refused to provide information for the report, explained that since they do not operate in New York they were not obligated to participate.[89] However, the OAG noted that *"In announcing the company's decision not to participate, Kraken declared that market manipulation 'doesn't matter to most crypto traders' even while admitting that 'scams are rampant' in the industry."* Based on the investigation, the OAG referred Binance, Gate.io, and Kraken to the Department of Financial Services (NYDFS) for potential violation of New York's virtual currency regulations. At the time of writing, no formal charges have been brought against any exchange.

Practically all the problems the OAG listed can be linked to the discussion in 8.2 explaining why fraud and manipulation are rife in cryptocurrency markets, and the report's conclusion points toward a clear need for increased regulation. However, regulators wishing to remove manipulative practices like those documented here need to be careful when doing so, not to alter the wider characteristics that make cryptocurrency markets a unique and attractive environment to the many legitimate traders and investors.

Furthermore, as mentioned in Section 8.1, cryptocurrencies are cross-listed assets (i.e. identical products which can be traded in multiple locations) and so, although many 'banked' exchanges such as Coinbase will maintain traditional banking relationships and comply with local KYC and AML requirements, they will be linked to unbanked exchanges where it is easier to manipulate the market.[90] This makes effective regulation difficult and is one of the reasons the SEC continues to reject cryptocurrency ETF proposals.[91]

---

[87] New York State Office of the Attorney General (18 Sep 2018) *Virtual Markets Integrity Initiative*, see https://bit.ly/2RhOG37.
[88] Coinbase Blog (19 Sep 2018), *Correcting the record: Coinbase does not engage in proprietary trading*, see https://bit.ly/2OPK99p.
[89] Binance, Kraken, Gate.io and Huobi.
[90] Maintain relationships with traditional finance sources which facilitate fiat deposits/withdrawals.
[91] CoinDesk, (22 Aug 2018), SEC Rejects 9 Bitcoin ETF Proposals, see https://bit.ly/2ORp6DC.

References

Aslan, H., Easley, D., Hvidkjaer, S. and O'Hara, M. (2011). The characteristics of informed trading: Implications for asset pricing. *Journal of Emprical Finance* 18(5): 782–801.

Bogoev, D. and Karam, A. (2016). Detection of algorithmic trading. *Physica A: Statistical Mechanics and its Applications* 484: 168–181.

Brandvold, M., Molnar, P., Vagstad, K. and Valstad, O. (2015). Price discovery on bitcoin exchanges. *Journal of International Finance Markets, Institutions and Money* 36: 18–35.

Chan, S., Chu, S., Nadarajah, J. and Osterrieder, J. (2017). A statistical analysis of cryptocurrencies. *Journal of Risk and Financial Management* 10(2): 12.

Chohan, U. (2017). Assessing the differences in bitcoin and other cryptocurrency legality across national jurisdictions. *SSRN*.

Dierksmeier, C. (2016). Cryptocurrencies and business ethics. *Journal of Business Ethics* 152(1): 1–14.

Dimpfl, T. (2017). Bitcoin market microstructure. *SSRN*.

Easley, D., Kiefer, N., O'Hara, M. and Paperman, J. (1996). Liquidity, information, and infrequently traded stocks. *Journal of Finance* 51(4):1405–1436.

Easley, D., Lopez de Prado, M. and O'Hara, M. (2011). The microstructure of the 'flash crash': Flow toxicity, liquidity crashes and the probability of informed trading. *The Journal of Portfolio Management* 37(2): 118–128.

Feder, A., Gandal, N., Hamrick J.T. and Moore, T. (2016). The impact of DDoS and other security shocks on Bitcoin currency exchanges: Evidence from Mt. Gox. *Workshop on the Economics of Information Security (WEIS)* 3(2):137–144.

Gandal, N., Hamrick, J.T., Moore, T. and Oberman, T. (2018). Price manipulation in the Bitcoin ecosytem. *Journal of Monetary Economics Volume* 95: 86–96.

Gregory, P. (2014). *CISSP Guide to Security Essentials* (2nd edn.). Boston: Cengage Learning.

Griffin, J. and Shams, A. (2018). Is Bitcoin really un-tethered? *SSRN*.

Hileman, G. and Rauchs, M. (2017). *Global Cryptocurrency Benchmarking Survey*. Cambridge: Cambridge Centre for Alternative Finance.

Jung Lee, E., Shik Eom, K. and Suh Park, K. (2013). Microstructure-based manipulation: Strategic behaviour and performance of spoofing traders. *Journal of Financial Markets* 16(2): 227–252.

Kirilenko, A., Samadi, M., Kyle, A. and Tuzun, T. (2011). The flash crash: The impact of high frequency trading on an electronic market. *SSRN*.

Loukas, G. and Oke, G. (2009). Protection against denial of service attacks: A survey. *The Computer Journal* 53(7): 1020–1037.

Madhavan, A. (2011). Exchange-traded funds, market structure and the flash crash. *SSRN*.

Mehar, M., Shier, C., Giambattista, A. et al. (2017). Understanding a revolutionary and flawed grand experiment in blockchain: The DAO attack. *SSRN*.

Moore, T. and Christin, N. (2013). Beware the middleman: Empirical analysis of Bitcoin exchange risk. *International Conference on Financial Cryptography and Data Security,* 25–33.

Pieters, G. and Vivanco, S. (2017). Financial regulations and price inconsistencies across bit-coin markets. *Information Economics and Policy* 39: 1–14.

Sotiropoulou, A. and Guegan, D. (2017). Bitcoin and the challenges for financial regulation. *Capital Markets Law Journal* 12(4): 466–479.

Tse, J., Lin, X. and Vincent, D. (2012). *AES Analysis, High Frequency Trading – Measurement, Detection and Response*. Credit Suisse, AES Analysis.

Vasek, M., Thornton, M. and Moore, T. (2014). Empirical analysis of denial-of-service attacks in the Bitcoin ecosystem. *Lecure Notes in Computer Science*.8438: 57–71.

Xu, J. and Livshits, B. (2019). The anatomy of a cryptocurrency pump-and-dump scheme. *Proceedings of the 28th USENIX Security Symposium,* 1606–1625.

Chapter 9
The Integrity of Closing Prices

Ryan J. Davies
Babson College

9.1 Why Closing Prices Matter

The integrity of closing prices matters. Closing prices are used to determine mutual fund net asset value (NAV), option and futures final settlement values, variation margin, mark-to-market and daily settlement for futures, forwards, and other derivative contracts. Closing prices are also used for benchmarking institutional and broker trade execution and for determining fund manager remuneration. Some crossing networks use closing prices as the benchmark price. Closing prices are also used in the pricing of seasoned equity offerings and in the pricing of mergers and acquisitions. Exchange listing requirements typically specify minimum closing prices over a given period. Closing index values and index rebalancing decisions are based on closing prices of constituent stocks. Some momentum-based strategies and technical analysis-based strategies are influenced by closing prices, particularly when those prices exceed or fall below key threshold values. Finally, there is some evidence that end-of-day manipulation can reorient corporate managers to become more short-term focused and can worsen certain traditional corporate finance outcomes. For example, firms that experience end-of-day manipulation appear to file less patents subsequently (see Cumming, Ji, and Peter 2016), and are more likely to have mergers and acquisition deals withdrawn (see Cumming, Ji, Johan, and Tarsalewska 2016).

Given the importance of closing prices, it is essential to understand how to detect financial market misconduct that reduces closing price integrity, and design markets and regulation that deter such behaviour. Detection can be challenging and only a small fraction of closing price manipulation is prosecuted. Comerton-Forde and Putniņš (2014) estimate that one percent of closing prices are manipulated, using an approach whereby they jointly estimate the probability of being detected and the process by which violations occur. Often researchers can only infer whether manipulation occurred based on changing in underlying market conditions. For example, Comerton-Forde and Putniņš (2011) examine the effects of closing price manipulation and find that manipulation is associated with large increases in day-end returns, return reversals, trading activity and bid–ask spreads.

In this chapter, I examine three research themes related to the potential manipulation of closing prices. First, I examine the incentives for mutual fund and hedge fund managers to inflate the closing prices of their existing holdings by trading near the close on the last trading day of key performance measurement periods, such as the end of the quarter and the end of the year. Second, I examine how other financial intermediaries reacted to a well-documented alleged manipulation in which a portfolio manager repeatedly used 'bang-the-close' trades to influence the settlement prices of commodity futures contracts. Third, I examine potential manipulation of closing stock prices on equity option expiration dates. The chapter concludes with a discussion of regulatory implications and recent market design issues.

9.2   Painting the Tape and Portfolio Pumping

'Painting the tape' or 'leaning for the tape' is often used to describe when mutual fund or hedge fund managers purchase securities that they already hold with the intention of inflating the end-of-quarter price to improve their relative performance.[1] This behaviour is also referred to as portfolio pumping and net asset value (NAV) inflation.[2] These trades occur near the market close with the goal of triggering a short-term price impact that increases the closing prices used to calculate end-of-quarter reported NAV. The short-term price impact typically unwinds at the opening of the next day, and as such, fund managers are effectively increasing the returns of the ending quarter

---

[1] In other contexts, the term 'painting the tape' is used to refer to a series of transactions designed to give the impression of activity or price movement.

[2] Painting the tape is not to be confused with 'window dressing', which is characterized by purchasing recent 'winners' and selling recent 'losers' prior to the end of quarters, so that reported mutual fund holdings look more favourable to investors. Lynch, Puckett, and Yan (2014) use trade data to distinguish between window dressing, institutional tax-loss selling, and risk shifting at year-ends. Sias and Starks (1997), Agarwal, Gay, and Ling (2014), Lakonishok, et al. (1991), and Ng and Wang (2004) also study window dressing and end-of-year risk adjustments.

at the expense of the next quarter. Quarterly returns are reported to fund investors in their quarterly statements and often are used to determine fund performance rankings. These returns are used by rating agencies and regulators, and used by retirement investment committees with a fiduciary responsibility to monitor and evaluate available fund choices. Fund manager remuneration is also often determined, in part, by end-of-year fund return performance.

The empirical evidence that portfolio pumping occurs is quite strong. Carhart, et al. (2002) find that 80% of funds beat the S&P on the last trading day of the year (62% for other quarter-end dates), but only 37% (40% other quarters) do so on the first trading day of a new year. They find that the difference is greater for small-cap funds, and that end-of-year performance is more pronounced for better historical performers. Bernhardt and Davies (2005) argue that Carhart, et al. (2002) may actually be underestimating the effect. Using net flows to mutual funds as an explanatory variable in a time-series regression framework, Bernhardt and Davies (2005) provide evidence that 'painting the tape' may be so widespread that its effect is reflected in the overall index. Specifically, daily returns of the equally weighted index on the last trading day of a quarter greatly exceed the daily returns on the first trading day of the succeeding quarter, and this return difference rises with the share of total equity held by mutual funds. As such, empirical studies such as Carhart et al. (2002) that benchmark price inflation relative to the index are likely to underestimate the true impact of painting the tape. As further evidence of painting the tape (as well as window dressing), Brown et al. (2017) find that active funds underperform the market and other passive benchmarks only in the first month of a quarter.

End-of-quarter and end-of-year return patterns may be driven by other factors as well, such as the impact of tax loss selling and window dressing. The pattern may extend to end-of-months, as McConnell and Xu (2008) find a turn-of-the-month returns pattern has persisted in US markets over the period 1926–2005, and find similar patterns in 31 out of 35 countries examined. They argue that these patterns cannot be explained by the performance-flow incentives of fund managers alone.

Direct evidence of portfolio pumping is obtained from institutional trade data. Gallagher, Gardner, and Swan (2009) use daily trading data of a set of active fund managers in Australia to provide direct evidence of 'painting the tape' at the end of quarters and show that such gaming behaviour is more likely to occur in smaller, illiquid stocks, momentum stocks, and stocks in which the fund is overweight. Hu et al. (2014) examine US-based institutional trade data provided by Abel Noser Solutions and argue that year-end price inflation may be caused more by depressed selling, rather than excessive buying by investment managers. Conditional on buying at year-end, they find that institutions tend to buy stocks in which they already have large positions.

Portfolio pumping may help explain some of the other puzzling empirical anomalies for mutual funds and hedge funds. For instance, Bernhardt and Davies (2009) develop a model of portfolio pumping that incorporates three well-known obser-vations: (i) past fund performance influences subsequent net fund flows, (ii) fund manager compensation rises with total assets under management, and (iii) trading has short-term price impacts. These observations provide fund managers the incen-tive to mark up their holdings at quarter-end through aggressive trading of stocks they already hold. Fund managers' incentives to distort investment of new cash inflows toward stocks in which the fund has larger positions leads to the empiri-cally observed short-run persistence and long-run reversal in fund performance. The intuition is that funds with greater past performance will have more cash inflows, providing them with more ability to engage in end-of-quarter trading, which leads to greater reported performance and greater inflows the next quarter. In the model, the benefits of portfolio pumping are not sustainable long-term, since each subse-quent quarter, the fund will start with a greater deficit as the price impact of the end-of-quarter trades decay, requiring the fund to inflate subsequent returns by even more. Eventually, the fund will not be able to 'paint the tape' enough to overcome the performance deficit, leading to a reversal in performance. The model provides a possible reason for why funds appear to exhibit clairvoyant stock selection and yet under-perform long term.

Mutual fund incentives to 'paint the tape' are driven by the tournament-like investment behaviour in the fund management industry, with cash inflows going to winners. Sirri and Tufano (1998) examine the flow of funds into mutual funds in response to performance and show that flows go disproportionately into winners (i.e. the performance-flow relationship is convex). Berk and Green (2004) develop a model to show that the observed flow-performance relationship can arise *endogenously* in rational markets, even when performance is not persistent and active managers, with varying skill levels, underperform passive benchmarks on average.

In the model of Bernhardt and Davies (2009), the response of fund flow to past fund performance is exogenous. Given the convex performance-flow relationship, mutual funds with the *best* recent performance are the most likely to have both the incentive and the capacity (new funds) to engage in painting the tape behaviour. This feature is consistent with the patterns observed in US markets by Carhart, et al. (2002) and Duong and Meschke (2016), and in Korean markets by Lee, Baek, and Park (2014). In these markets, portfolio pumping appears motivated by the flow-performance rela-tionship. In contrast, Shackleton et al. (2020) argue that end-of-quarter price inflation is larger for the worst-performing fund managers in China because of the threat of replacement and dismissal for poor performance. Similarly, Gallagher, Gardner, and Swan (2009) focuses on institutional, wholesale funds in Australia that lack a strong performance-flow relationship. These institutional funds have professional trustees that will dismiss poorly performing fund managers, and as such, poor-performing managers appear more likely to engage in gaming trades, presumably to protect their jobs.

Hedge fund managers may have an additional incentive to inflate end-of-year portfolio values since their performance incentive fees are directly tied to fund values at certain key measurement points. Ben-David et al. (2013) show that hedge funds also engage in portfolio pumping trades, particularly for illiquid stocks. Agarwal, Daniel, and Naik (2011) show that hedge funds tend to have higher December returns if they have high incentives and more opportunities to inflate returns. They argue that a hedge fund's incentive to inflate its returns depends on: (i) the asymmetric call-option-like payoff of its incentive fees; (ii) its flow-performance sensitivity and current performance ranking; and (iii) its penalties for poor performance, including lockup and restriction periods. Similarly, they argue that a hedge fund has more opportunities to inflate returns when its returns are more volatile, thereby allowing it to hide returns management, and when it has higher exposure to liquidity risk, thereby allowing it to paint the tape more effectively.

Mutual fund and hedge fund managers are financial intermediaries acting on behalf of their investors. By engaging in NAV inflation, they impose direct and indirect costs on investors, largely to increase their own compensation. In the next section, I examine a specific example of how financial intermediaries reacted to a long-term scheme to inflate commodity futures settlement prices using 'bang-the-close' trades.

9.3 'Bang-the-Close' Manipulation: The Response of Financial Intermediaries

Atanasov, Davies, and Merrick (2015a) study the response of NYMEX floor traders to an alleged manipulation, whereby a hedge fund portfolio manager (PM) submitted large 'bang-the-close' buy orders for platinum and palladium futures contracts over a 7-month period (November 2007 to May 2008). Detailed court records allow them to examine whether the floor traders, acting as financial intermediaries, mitigated or magnified the alleged manipulative scheme.[3] In this case, court transcripts outline the PM's desire to purchase these contracts at the highest possible prices, thereby triggering 'buy signals' through new highs in the futures daily settlement prices. The PM had a major financial motive to increase these prices as his fund held large net long positions in platinum and palladium – worth almost a billion dollars at the peak of this period. Higher fund returns would result in higher compensation for the PM and would also attract fund inflows, leading to higher fund management fees.

At the time of the alleged manipulation, platinum and palladium futures contracts were traded via open outcry on the NYMEX floor and via the Globex electronic limit order book. While most trading had migrated to the electronic platform, about 20% of trading volume still occurred on the floor. The platinum open outcry session ran from 8:20 a.m. to 1:05 p.m., and the palladium open outcry session ran from 8:30 a.m. to 1:00 p.m. Electronic trading for both platinum and palladium occurred in a near 24-hour session from 6 p.m. to 5:15 p.m. the next day. The daily settlement price for the futures contracts was based on the volume-weighted average price of all NYMEX floor and Globex transactions during a two-minute closing period (1:03 p.m.–1:05 p.m. for platinum; 12:58 p.m. –1 p.m. for palladium).

Theoretical models predict that tacit collusion can persist in a transparent market with repeated interaction by a small number of similar participants and high barriers

---

[3] See: In Re: Platinum & Palladium Commodities Litigation, No. 10-cv-3617, 2011. WL 4048780 (United States District Court, Southern District of New York, Sept. 13, 2011).

to entry (see, for example, Ivaldi et al. 2003).[4] At the time of the alleged manipulation, there were less than a dozen NYMEX floor traders remaining in these markets. These traders interacted with each other on a daily basis in a highly visible manner. Market frictions limited the ability of non-floor participants to interact with floor trades. Under these conditions, Atanasov, Davies and Merrick (2015a) find evidence that, in response to the bang-the-close trades, the floor traders appear to have extracted significant rents through non-competitive pricing and behaved in a manner consistent with tacit (implicit) collusion.

The PM directed his orders to the NYMEX floor rather than the more liquid, parallel electronic market. Over time, these trades became predictable and contained no fundamental market information. Irrespective of the PM's motives, competition among NYMEX floor traders should have limited the price impacts of his repetitive bang-the-close trades to a normal 'size and immediacy' mark-up. Empirical evidence suggests otherwise. The PM trades had price impact both because the trades received higher prices on the floor and because floor trading enabled him to trade in higher quantities (and thereby influence the weighted settlement price by more). Importantly, the floor traders had hand-held devices that allowed them to trade directly on the electronic order book, allowing them to unwind positions at the walk-the-book price with very little risk. Floor trading rules allowed the floor traders to specify the quantity they wished to trade, so that they did not need to sell the entire position requested by the PM. The PM directed his futures commission merchant's floor broker to execute his orders at very close to (possibly even slightly after) the official market close. As a consequence, the floor traders who were counterparty to the PM's trades needed to unwind their short positions on the electronic book after the closing settlement period. Observed intraday trading patterns were consistent with this hypothesis, with trade volumes in the two-minute window immediately after the floor close higher during the alleged manipulation period than during the non-manipulation period.

Atanasov, Davies and Merrick (2015a) develop counterfactual futures contract pricing benchmarks to separate the share of estimated damages caused by the non-competitive behaviour of floor traders from the share caused by the direct impacts of the PM's bang-the-close trades. These benchmarks are constructed using data from trades and orders on the parallel Globex electronic platform. Through this approach, damages can be attributed properly across the multiple market participants.

The decomposition of the impact of the bang-the-close trades is illustrated by considering three cases. In the first case, they consider the proportion of the PM's

---

[4] Friedman (1971) shows that collusion may be a possible equilibrium outcome if the future costs to each player of deserting the equilibrium exceed the immediate gains. Dutta and Madhavan (1997) develop a game-theoretic model to show that, when order flow access is restricted, implicit collusion can arise even from non-cooperative behaviour among dealers. In experimental settings, Cason (2000) shows that dealers can tacitly collude to widen spreads, even without any direct communication, and Kluger and Wyatt (2002) find that the ability for dealers to internalize order flow allows them to coordinate on a less competitive equilibrium. Back and Zender (1993) show that collusive strategies can be self-reinforcing in uniform-price divisible-goods auctions. Khwaja and Mian (2005) find instances in which stockbrokers in Pakistan, acting as financial intermediaries, colluded to trade among themselves to raise prices artificially in a 'pump and dump' price manipulation scheme. These brokers traded for their own advantage at the expense of outside investors.

order that could have been executed immediately on the Globex electronic limit order book by walking-the-book. This 'smoking gun' evidence compares prices for the PM's exchange floor-filled orders to the concurrent volume-weighted average price for tradeable depth on the Globex platform. The difference between the walk-the-book price and the price obtained on the floor reflects non-competitive pricing on the floor. In the second case, they hold constant the mark-up obtained on the floor but now consider the impact of the ability of the PM to trade larger volumes on the floor than available on the electronic limit order book. Specifically, $\Theta^{PM} > \Theta^{WTB}$, where Θ^{PM} is defined as the PM's trade volume on floor during the closing period as a share of the total trade volume on both the floor and Globex during the closing period; and Θ^{WTB} is defined as the available walk-the-book depth at the close divided by the sum of the closing period volume on Globex, the available walk-the-book depth at the close, and the closing period floor trades not involving the PM. Finally, in the third case, they examine the excess price impact on the residual portion of the PM volume, over and above the mark-up on the quantity of the PM's trades immediately available on the electronic limit order book. Figure 9.1 illustrates this final decomposition.

The PM submitted large trades at the close almost every day. To investigate how the floor brokers reacted over time, the alleged manipulation period was split into halves. In a competitive market, one would expect that the floor brokers and other traders on the floor would reduce the price impact of these trades over time. The opposite was observed: the PM's bang-the-close trades had greater price impacts and received worse prices in the second half of the alleged manipulation period. During the second half of the alleged manipulation period, floor traders executed the PM's platinum futures contract buy orders at prices that were 40–80 ticks above competitive benchmarks. This pattern is consistent with tacit (implicit) collusion. The observed impact is much larger than the conjecture of Pirrong (1996) that the effect on prices from cooperation by floor traders (or locals) in a typical open outcry market may be limited to one or two ticks.

Atanasov, Davies, and Merrick (2015a) estimate the potential profits of the floor brokers using two approaches. The first approach estimates profits based on the floor brokers executing only the immediately available walk-the-book portion of the PM's trades. Under these assumptions, the floor traders are estimated to have achieved a profit of $1 million that is close to risk-free. The second approach estimates profits assuming that the floor brokers executed the volume exceeding the walk-the-book portion by participating in half of the volume of buyer-initiated trades on Globex post-close. Under these assumptions, the floor traders are estimated to have achieved a profit of roughly $6 million with minimal risk. Regulators and exchange operators often presume that competitive forces will limit the ability of prices to deviate from fair values. But this example highlights that the inflated contract settlement prices resulting from an alleged manipulative scheme can be facilitated and magnified by the actions of other financial intermediaries. As such, these parties also share part of the blame for the resulting damages.

Unlike 'painting the tape', which is intended to have a short-term price impact, 'banging the close' manipulation is often intended to trigger longer-term follow-on impacts. While Atanasov, Davies, and Merrick (2015a) are able to decompose the

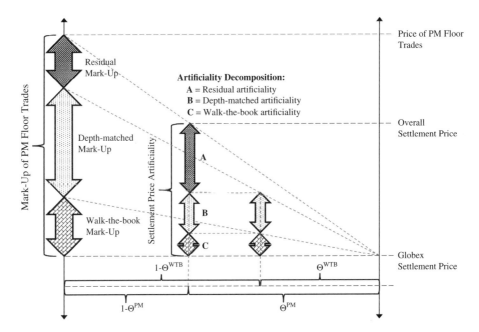

Figure 9.1   Decomposition of Settlement Price Artificiality when the number of contracts traded for the PM on the floor exceeds the available walk-the-book depth on Globex, $\Theta^{PM} > \Theta^{WTB}$, and there exists an additional mark-up for the contracts that cannot be immediately executed on Globex (Residual Mark-Up > 0). The residual settlement price artificiality can be attributed to both the ability of the PM to execute larger volume on the floor than Globex and to the additional price impact of this larger volume. The figure assumes that, excluding trades involving the PM as counterparty, the average price of floor trades executed during the 2-minute closing period is equal to the Globex Settlement Price.

Source: Figure is a modified version of figure 1c in the following article: Atanasov, V., Davies, R.J., Merrick, J.J. (2015). Financial intermediaries in the midst of market manipulation: Did they protect the fool or help the knave?, *Journal of Corporate Finance* 34, 218.

short-term reaction of other market participants to the bang-the-close orders, it is more challenging to determine the long-term second-order effects from the manipulation. Court records suggest that the PM intended for his trades to cause the price to cross key technical levels, triggering trades by other market participants that use technical analysis and/or momentum-based strategies. Anecdotal evidence suggests that the rise in platinum and palladium prices during this period may have been largely driven by other macro trends and not the PM's trades, but additional analysis would be needed to attribute these effects.

The fragmentation of order flow across two alternative trading channels enabled the PM's trades to have a greater price impact. Off-the-floor futures market participants did not, or could not, place limit orders on the floor to take advantage of the mispricing. This observation provides guidance for the design and regulation of today's markets, in which fragmentation can occur through both barriers to access and differences in latency.

At the time, the settlement price mechanism for platinum and palladium futures contracts used a volume-weighted average price across the two markets. This mechanism appears to have enabled the alleged manipulation to occur. Subsequent to this case, the mechanism was changed such that only Globex trades would be used in the determination of the settlement price.

With the rise of electronic trading of commodities futures, the settlement price mechanisms for other products have also changed. For instance, the method for determining the settlement price for corn futures on the Chicago Board of Trade changed in June 2012. Prior to the change, the settlement price was based solely on a weighted average of floor trade prices during the last minute of floor trading. After the change, the price of both floor trades and electronic trades, occurring during the last minute of floor trading, were included in the calculation. Onur and Reiffen (2018) examine how trading behaviour, and the incentives to bang-the-close, changed in response to the new 'blended settlement' methodology for corn futures. They provide some evidence that manipulation decreased after reducing the importance of floor trading, as measured in terms of less price reversals and in terms of price movements more closely resembling a random walk.

Bang-the-close trades have been studied in other contexts as well. In the context of foreign exchange 'fix' orders, Saakvitne (2016) develops an equilibrium model of trading behaviour and benchmark prices. This model shows that bang-the-close trading can arise naturally as a solution to an optimal order execution problem for dealers that receive fix orders that are benchmarked against a price at a certain time. Similarly, Baldauf, Frei, and Mollner (2018) develop a model of an agency broker executing a large trade for a client, where performance is benchmarked to a reference price, such as the closing price. Their model shows that the broker has the incentive to time their trades over the day in a manner that impacts the reference price. These papers highlight how principal–agent problems can arise when closing prices are used as reference prices to evaluate broker performance.

In the next section, I discuss how trading patterns in a security that underlies a soon-to-expire derivative contract can also raise concerns about potential manipulation. The issue is complex, since the hedging trades of financial intermediaries, such as market makers, may be difficult to disentangle from intentional manipulation.

9.4   Stock Price Pinning on Option Expiration Dates

In option markets, 'pinning' occurs when the underlying stock price closes at, or near to, an option strike price on an option expiration date. Pinning causes both call and put options at this strike price to expire worthlessly, which has led some market participants to believe that pinning is often caused by the manipulation of stock prices.[5] Ni, Pearson, and Poteshman (2005) show that closing stock prices do tend to cluster

---

[5] Edmunds et al. (1984) provides an early study of stock pinning on option expiration. More generally, the interaction between stock prices and options has been studied by Klemkosky (1978), Sorescu (2000), and others. The issue of pinning is related to a growing, much larger literature that shows that *non-fundamental* (or technical) factors have become more important in determining security prices.

at option strike prices on option expiration dates. They are, however, largely unable to resolve whether the pinning is caused by deliberate manipulation or as a natural by-product of market maker delta hedging. The importance and frequency of stock pinning has likely increased over time, corresponding to the dramatic increase in exchange-traded option trading volumes.

Before proceeding, consider the following explanation for why delta hedging can lead to stock pinning. Delta-hedging agents, such as market makers, must frequently rebalance their portfolios in order to maintain their delta hedge. As the price of the underlying asset changes, the delta of an option position changes. Recall that the rate of change in delta with respect to the price of the underlying asset is called *gamma*. The gamma of a long (bought) call or put option position is always positive. As the underlying share price rises, agents with a *written* option contract will need to purchase additional shares to maintain their hedge. This action corresponds to buying more shares to hedge a written call option position and reducing the number of shares sold short to hedge a written put option position. A high gamma indicates that delta is highly sensitive to the price of the underlying asset.

As expiration approaches, the delta of an out-of-the-money call option approaches zero and the delta of an in-the-money call option approaches one. When a call option is trading close to at-the-money, its delta will tend to remain close to 0.50 until the final day of trading; as the final closing price on expiration becomes clearer, its delta will converge rapidly toward either zero (out-of-the-money) or one (in-the-money). A similar pattern exists for put options, with the delta of a near at-the-money put option converging rapidly toward either minus one (in-the-money) or zero (out-of-the-money) at expiration. In both cases, a short-life option trading near at-the-money will have a high gamma and will require active rebalancing to remain hedged. Furthermore, the delta of an in-the-money (out-of-the-money) call option and the delta of an out-of-the-money (in-the-money) put option both increase (decrease) as expiration approaches.

Stock price pinning can occur as a natural by-product of delta hedging on expiration dates when two conditions occur: (i) only a subset of agents actively delta hedge their option positions; and (ii) this group of agents has a net *bought* option position (i.e. their positions have a net positive gamma). To see why, first suppose that the stock is trading below the nearest strike price. As time passes, as long as the share price remains below the strike price, these delta-hedging (positive gamma) agents will rebalance their hedge by purchasing additional shares. If their share purchases have sufficient price impact, their purchases will drive the share price toward the strike. Next, suppose that the stock is trading above the nearest strike price. Now delta-hedging (positive gamma) agents will rebalance their hedge by selling shares as expiration approaches; again, the price impact of these sales will tend to drive the share price towards the strike price.

Because optimal delta hedging is a more complex trading strategy that can incur substantial transaction costs, it is reasonable to suppose that only market makers and some sophisticated institutional investors will typically engage in it. Prior research (see, for example, Lakonishok, et al. 2007) finds that the most common option position for retail traders is a net written call option, which suggests that other, more sophisticated, investors are likely to have an offsetting net bought call option position.

If so, the tendency of delta-hedging agents to have a net bought option position could lead to a greater tendency for a stock to be pinned.

The unconditional likelihood that delta-hedging leads to a particular stock pinning at a strike price depends on many factors. These factors include: (i) the coarseness of the option strike price grid, (ii) the volatility of the stock price, (iii) the average trade volume and open interest in the options (both in an absolute sense and relative to equity trade volume), (iv) the average net gamma position of market makers and institutional traders in nearby and distant contracts, and (v) the price impact of equity trades. At a given time, the conditional likelihood of pinning also depends on the distance from current stock price to the closest strike price, which acts like a 'magnet'.

Krishnan and Nelken (2001), Avellaneda and Lipkin (2003), and Avellaneda, Kasyan, and Lipkin (2012) develop mathematical models of stock pinning. The key feature of these models is how the price impact of trading is determined. Krishnan and Nelken (2001) model the stock dynamics assuming that the ex-ante likelihood of pinning is determined by a random variable (formally, they use a Brownian-bridge framework). Avellaneda and Lipkin (2003) model the effect of option market maker hedging trades on the underlying stock price. They allow pinning to be determined endogenously by the hedging trades, based on linear price impact function, incorporating an exogenous price elasticity of demand. Avellaneda, Kasyan, and Lipkin (2012) extend the model of Avellaneda and Lipkin (2003) to incorporate non-linear price impact functions. Ultimately, these models highlight the importance of the magnet effect of strike prices. A reduction in the coarseness of the strike price grid increases the likelihood that a stock will trade at prices close enough to a strike price to be pinned, while, at the same time, the strength of each magnet is likely reduced by spreading open interest across more strike prices.

In a series of regulatory decisions, options exchanges have been allowed to increase the number of stocks with options at a finer strike grid. More strikes appears to make pinning more likely since stock prices will be more likely to be in the range of a strike price near expiration. Does doubling the number of strikes cause the likelihood of pinning to double? It depends on how it impacts the strength of the magnets. More strike prices increase the likelihood that the nearest strike is closer to the current price (increasing the magnet strength), but at the same time, more strike prices may lead to less outstanding contracts at each strike (reducing the magnet strength). The optimal coarseness of the strike price grid for exchange-traded options is an important decision for regulators and exchange operators.

Delta hedging does not eliminate all risk. It is difficult for market makers to hedge their positions in options that are close to at-the-money near expiration. Small changes in the price of the underlying stock can cause the delta of these options to go from almost one to almost zero very quickly (i.e. their gamma is very high). Some traders may elect to exercise their options when it is not expected (particularly during the last few days prior to expiration), leaving the other side of the trade with an unexpected delivery. A market maker with a written option position faces the risk that the option is exercised unexpectedly *after* the market closes on the last day of trading prior to expiration. Since after-hours equity trading, particularly on Friday, is often highly illiquid, the market maker may be unable to close the unexpected position over the weekend, exposing them to considerable price risk. This risk suggests that optimal delta-hedging trades might continue after hours on expiration dates. As such, after-hours trading patterns may depend on the deadline for option exercise decisions and their settlement. Weekly options typically expire on Friday evening, whereas serial options typically expire on Saturday. While this distinction appears to have received little attention, the later expiration time may increase the possibility of a late, unfavourable delivery.

Determining whether the effect is due to market maker delta hedging or intentional manipulation depends critically on understanding the net position of market participants that use delta hedging. Ni, Pearson, and Poteshman (2005) studied the period 1996 to 2002, during which time US equity option trading occurred only on the Chicago Board Options Exchange (CBOE). Their data set included complete information on option market maker positions. Unfortunately, market maker positions are much harder to identify today. As of July 2018, equity options are publicly traded on 16 exchanges in the US, each with their own open-close data. Not only does the open-close data not typically include confidential market maker position information, the fragmentation of order flow, along with the possibility that offsetting market maker positions could be taken on another venue, makes it difficult to develop proxies for market maker positions. It is also complicated by a blurring of who is a market maker in option markets, as sophisticated high frequency traders also engage in market making activities, in part to due to the market-taker fee structure on many option exchanges.

Stivers and Sun (2013) examine stock return patterns during option expiration weeks for S&P 100 constituent stocks. They argue that delta-hedging rebalancing by market makers leads to predictable weekly patterns in returns. Specifically, the tendency for market makers to have a net long position in call options leads them to have short equity positions. These short positions are unwound as expiration approaches, which causes higher weekly returns during option expiration weeks. To examine the role of high frequency trading in pinning, Figueiredo, Mishra, and Jain (2017) use Nasdaq Totalview-ITCH data to examine intraday trading behaviour near the market close on option expiration dates. Non-HFT limit order submissions appear to be clustered near round number strike prices, whereas the HFTs appear to submit fleeting orders that are inside or outside the round number prices.

A closely related widespread belief among traders is that stocks are manipulated such that they close at the 'max pain' price on option expiration dates. Max pain is commonly defined as the stock price that causes the most outstanding written options to expire 'out-of-the-money' (i.e. to be worthless). Despite being widely discussed within the trading community, the academic literature has been largely silent on max pain and other forms of manipulation focused on option expiration. This silence appears to be related to the difficulty in identifying manipulation and measuring its effects.

To the extent that market participants believe in stock pinning and max pain, these beliefs can become self-fulfilling as traders begin to trade in anticipation of the stock closing at the nearest strike or max pain price. With the introduction of weekly options, additional strikes, and an expansion in the number of stocks with listed options, these option expiration date effects could occur on more days and for more securities.[6] Interestingly, the magnet effect of a strike price could do some of the manipulator's work for them – the manipulator would simply need to push the stock price in the direction of the desired strike and the magnet effect would do the rest.

9.5   Conclusion: Lessons for the Regulation and Design of Financial Markets

This chapter has examined three main research themes related to the manipulation of closing prices. In all three cases, the economic consequences of closing price manipulation are potentially very large. An artificially high mutual fund NAV results in a transfer of wealth from new investors to existing investors in the fund. Improper price signals from futures contracts can distort management decisions and lead to an inefficient allocation of resources. The manipulation of the prices used for the settlement of derivatives can reduce the effectiveness of derivatives as a hedging instrument.

The issues raised in this chapter have implications for the design of markets and for the design of fund manager performance-based contracts. A natural question is whether the adoption of a certain market closing mechanism can prevent or reduce closing price manipulation. Unfortunately, there does not appear to be an easy solution. Some exchanges have adopted closing call auctions to increase transparency and liquidity at the close.[7] These call auctions, however, may also be manipulated. There is a complex interaction between the closing call auction and trading of the limit order book immediately prior to the close. A determined manipulator can find ways to abuse indicative quotes, indicative order imbalances, and specialized order types (e.g. market-on-close).

Cordi, Foley, and Putniņš (2015) study the introduction of closing batch mechanisms in 20 markets. They divide the mechanisms broadly into those with closing call auctions that occur after continuous trade ends, and those with on-close facilities that operate in parallel to continuous trading, with limitations on new orders based on imbalances during the pre-close period. Both mechanisms appear to improve closing price efficiency relative to using the last trade. Cordi, Foley, and Putniņš (2015) argue that the on-close facility lowers trading costs and improves price stability and informational efficiency. Call auctions cause spreads to increase because order flow is drawn away from the continuous market. In general, neither mechanism has a significant effect on the prevalence of closing price manipulation. Overall, they argue for a closing batch mechanism that has randomized closing times and extensions if volatility thresholds are breached. As well, they argue the mechanism should prevent traders from altering their orders during the pre-close time and should not display indicative closing prices.

---

[6] Zhang, Chen, and Cai (2015) examine the impact of introduction of weekly options in 2010 on stock price pinning. They find that pinning tends to occur less frequently with weekly options, due in part because of their lower trading volumes during the period studied (June 2010–December 2012).

[7] The efficiency of call auction mechanisms has been studied by Pagano and Schwartz (2003), Hillion and Suominen (2004), Chang et al. (2008), Pagano, Peng, and Schwartz (2013), and Kandel, Rindi, and Bosetti (2012).

Another natural question is whether the reporting of mutual fund performance, and the associated incentive structure for fund managers and other financial intermediaries, should be changed. Again, the answer is not clear. Most mutual fund investors already have easy access to daily mutual fund prices. Limited attention causes them to focus disproportionately on quarterly returns and their behavioural biases cause them to chase returns by investing in past top performers. Net asset values could be determined based on a weighted average of trade prices over a window of time (e.g. last five minutes of trading day), but these prices would also be subject to the potential for manipulation. Clearly, the compensation structure for hedge fund performance, combined with limited transparency, is also fertile ground for potential manipulation. Hedge fund investors, however, are typically sophisticated investors who should be able to perform their own oversight.

Goetzmann et al. (2007) propose that a 'manipulation-proof' measure for evaluating a fund manager's performance that accounts for non-normal returns distributions and avoids rewarding 'information-free' trading. This measure resembles the average of a power utility function and is based on the fund's return history. By focusing on the entire return history, rather than the fund value at a particular date, this measure should reduce incentives for portfolio pumping. While this 'manipulation-proof' measure is highly cited in the academic literature, anecdotal evidence suggests that it has not been widely adopted in the finance industry.

Both opening and closing prices can be subject to manipulation. In general, closing price manipulation is typically trade-based, whereas opening price manipulation is typically quote or order-based. As after-hours trading becomes more common and trading becomes increasing fragmented, the distinction between opening and closing mechanisms has become blurred. As such, lessons from the literature on market opening mechanisms are relevant to this discussion of the integrity of closing prices.[8] Biais, Hillion, and Spatt (1999), Cao, Ghysels, and Hatheway (2000), Davies (2003), and Lescourret (2017) study price discovery and 'gaming behaviour' during preopening sessions. Bellia et al. (2017) find that high frequency traders are able to extract valuable information during the preopening of Paris Euronext, allowing them to profit at the opening auction. Biais, Bisière, and Pouget (2014) use an experimental setting to examine how price discovery at the market opening depends on whether preopening orders are binding and whether the preopening time is deterministic or random. They highlight some of the trade-offs in market design, such as noting that a random opening time may reduce manipulation, while increasing the cost of valuable 'preplay communication'. It is difficult to know, however, the extent to which their conclusions would apply outside of their highly stylized experimental setting.

Hauser, Kamara, and Shurki (2012) show that the introduction of a random market opening time on the Tel-Aviv Stock Exchange improved price discovery and reduced excess volatility, especially on option expiration dates. Hauser, Kedar-Levy, and Milo (2018) study the parallel preopening sessions for stock and options on the

---

[8] Other market openings, such as those after trading halts, or in the case of initial public offerings, may also be subject to manipulation but are beyond the scope of this chapter. See, for instance, Kuk, Liu, and Pham (2016) for a discussion of the preopening periods for IPOs.

Tel-Aviv Stock Exchange. As a proxy for mispricing at the opening, they measure the percentage gap between the at-the-money option-implied index and the indicative index. They find evidence that this gap is significantly larger on option expiration dates, which combined with subsequent reversals during trading hours, is suggestive of manipulation of these dates.

From a regulatory and legal perspective, it can be difficult to distinguish between legitimate trading behaviour and illegal fraud and manipulation. Typically, enforcement requires more than one-off trading because everyone has an Alternative Plausible Explanation (APE). Hence, enforcement of regulation is only possible (or more likely) with a clear pattern of repeat behaviour. End-of-day manipulation may be easier to detect and enforce since it often occurs in a regular pattern (e.g. option expiration, end-of-quarter). That said, legitimate explanations for some of these patterns are still possible. Mutual funds have the incentive to trade at the close to reduce tracking error and to reduce their trading costs. Market makers, faced with inventory constraints, may rationally respond to repetitive manipulative trades by increasing their price impact. Option market makers must delta hedge to manage their risk exposure.

Davies and Sirri (2018) summarize many of the economic and regulatory issues facing US trading markets today. They highlight that a particular regulatory challenge is determining how different trading venues interact with each other, with regards to order protection rules, best execution requirements, market linkages, market access fees and minimum tick sizes, and pre- and post-trade transparency. As the earlier example of 'bang-the-close' trades in platinum and palladium futures contracts highlighted, market frictions can enable manipulative trades to persist and have greater impact. A manipulator could elect to trade in venues with lower liquidity (and higher price elasticity) to maximize the impact of their trades on closing prices. Today, traditional market making, performed by specialists or other dedicated human market makers with affirmative obligations, has been largely replaced by high frequency trading. Fleeting quotes mean that trade execution costs can only be predicted on a probabilistic basis. In such an environment, reference prices, such as closing prices, may be difficult to establish and manipulation of these prices can be difficult to detect and enforce.

Traditionally, derivative markets and equity markets have operated under different sets of rules, governed by different regulatory organizations. Markets have become increasingly interconnected, and as such, regulatory environments need to be designed to detect and prevent financial market misconduct that occurs across different markets and financial products.

There is some evidence that regulation can curtail manipulation and make the effect of manipulation on markets less severe.[9] In Europe, the 2003 Market Abuse Directive (MAD)[10] sought to implement an EU-wide market abuse regime. The subsequent LIBOR benchmark manipulation scandal and the development of new trading

---

[9] For instance, Cumming, Johan, and Li (2011) find that exchange trading rules for market manipulation, insider trading, and broker-agency conflict can have significant impacts on liquidity.

[10] Directive 2003/6/EC of the European Parliament and of the Council of 28 January 2003 on insider dealing and market manipulation (market abuse).

platforms highlighted the need to update MAD with more robust legislation. This need led to publishing in 2014 of the Market Abuse Regulation (MAR)[11] and the Directive on Criminal Sanctions for Market Abuse (CSMAD)[12], which, in combination, are known as MAD II. These new regulations were implemented into national law by the EU Member States in July 2016. Notably, the UK and Denmark opted out of the CSMAD. These regulations are intended to be consistent with the new Markets in Financial Instruments Directive (MiFID II). Among other things, MAR introduced offences related to the manipulation of benchmarks and commodities, as well as cross-market manipulation and the manipulation of opening and closing prices. The expanded scope of these regulations highlight the importance of closing and settlement prices to the proper functioning of financial markets.

From their study of alleged manipulation of commodity futures markets, Atanasov, Davies, and Merrick (2015b) highlight six regulatory implications:

1. The mechanism used to determine the settlement (or closing) price can magnify the impact of the bang-the-close trades.
2. Tacit collusion can occur in an environment with frequent, repeated interaction by a small number of similar participants in a transparent market with barriers to entry.
3. Market access plays a role in preventing market manipulation.
4. Participants may not be fully forthcoming about possible misconduct.
5. Timely, accountable enforcement of exchange rules can be lacking.
6. Counterparties to manipulative trades can be responsible for a significant share of the total artificiality in prices caused by the manipulation scheme.

These findings have implications for the determination of LIBOR, foreign exchange rates, and other interest rate benchmarks. For example, in the $5.3 trillion/day foreign exchange (FX) market, the WM/ Reuters currency benchmarks are set at regular times by interbank trades occurring in a 1-minute interval (2 minutes for less active currencies). These interbank trades represent only a subset of FX trades and are conducted by a small group of participants, in a repeated process that is not easily accessible by outsiders. Dealers in this market, acting in the role of a financial intermediary, are alleged to have colluded to move these currency rates in anticipation of the settlement of customer orders. Many of the economic incentives of these FX dealers are similar to those of the floor traders studied by Atanasov, Davies, and Merrick (2015a).

Barclays Bank, UBS, Rabobank, RBS, Deutsche Bank, JP Morgan, and other major money centre banks, have been fined, or are under investigation, for their role in apparent collusion to set daily LIBOR fixings over an extended period of time. Total fines and settlements have exceeded $9 billion to date and are expected to rise further.[13] Gandhi et al. (2017) estimate manipulation of LIBOR could have increased

---

[11] Regulation (EU) No 596/2014 of the European Parliament and of the Council of 16 April 2014 on market abuse (market abuse regulation).

[12] Directive 2014/57/EU of the European Parliament and of the Council of 16 April 2014 on criminal sanctions for market abuse (market abuse directive).

[13] 'HSBC to pay $100 million to end Libor rigging lawsuit in US' (by Jonathan Stempel), Reuters, March 29, 2018. https://www.reuters.com/article/us-hsbc-libor-settlement/hsbc-to-pay-100-million-to-end-libor-rigging-lawsuit-in-u-s-idUSKBN1H6009.

the market value of panel banks by over \$22 billion. Abrantes-Metz et al. (2012) find statistical evidence of patterns in LIBOR rate submissions that appear inconsistent with those expected to occur under conditions of market competition. In response to the LIBOR scandal, the oversight of the LIBOR rate setting process was transferred from the British Banking Association (BBA) to the Financial Services Authority (FSA). Under the new system, the individual submissions of panel banks are published with a three month lag, thereby reducing the *immediate* transparency of submissions and the ability of participants to enforce a collusive equilibrium.

In contrast to some of the changes to LIBOR, Aspris et al. (2017) examine changes to the London 'fix' intended to reduce potential manipulative conduct by *increasing* transparency. They find that increased transparency improved market quality for the gold and silver fix, in terms of less information leakage, higher quoted depth, and lower transaction costs and volatility. They did not find similar effects for the less liquid platinum and palladium contracts. These results are interesting in light of models that suggest that transparency may increase implicit collusion, as it allows a small number of participants to enforce a collusive equilibrium in a repetitive setting, as evidence in Atanasov, Davies, and Merrick (2015a) supported.

Equity markets and option markets have become increasingly dependent on each other. In the past, option prices were assumed to be *derivative* from the underlying equity prices. Today, option markets have grown to sufficient size that the 'tail is wagging the dog': trade in options can and does influence underlying equity prices. For some widely held stocks (e.g. Alphabet Inc.), the average daily trading in option contracts can represent a number of shares exceeding 25% or more of the average daily trade volume of the underlying equity.[14] Furthermore, for many of these names, the total open interest across option contracts, in terms of shares represented, *far exceeds* the typical daily trade volume in the shares.

The potential gains from manipulation of the underlying equity on option expiration are substantial. If a market maker or another trader has a large outstanding option position, the cost of moving the underlying stock price could be much smaller than the resulting gains from the options.[15] In part, this phenomenon arises from the embedded leverage in options. All else equal, this type of manipulation should be easier when the stock is relatively illiquid (trades have high price impact), but the option has low implied volatility (options are cheaper, allowing for a larger option position).

The embedded leverage in options also manifests itself in products tied to option volatility. Because of the manner in which these products are settled, they are also subject to possible manipulation. Griffin and Shams (2018) find price and volume patterns in S&P 500 Index (SPX) options consistent with strategic trading with the apparent goal of influencing the settlement value of the CBOE Volatility Index (VIX).

---

[14] For example, in July 2018 the average daily option volume in Apple Inc. (AAPL) options on the CBOE alone (just one of several US-based option trading venues) was 63,435 contracts. These contracts represent 6.3 million shares (100 shares/contract), which is about a quarter of AAPL's average daily trade volume of about 24 million.

[15] Jarrow, Fung, and Tsai (2018) provide some evidence consistent with cross-market manipulation between index futures and index options in Taiwan.

Their analysis leverages the feature that only some options are used in the VIX calculation and that some options have a higher and discontinuous influence on VIX. These 'influential' options are more likely to exhibit abnormal trading near VIX settlement, consistent with market manipulation. Empirical evidence does not support alternative explanations such as hedging and coordinated liquidity trading. Overall, these results highlight the importance of the settlement procedure and how manipulation may be more likely to occur when price elasticities differ across different, interconnected contracts.

New concerns related to VIX and settlement prices have arisen because of large losses incurred by investors in XIV, the VelocityShares Daily Inverse VIX Short-Term ETN (exchange-traded note).[16] As an ETN, XIV was a debt instrument issued by Credit Suisse, with a value inversely related to the S&P 500 VIX Short-Term Futures Index. The XIV prospectus disclosed that Credit Suisse expected to hedge its exposure to XIV by trading VIX futures (and other related derivatives) and noted that such hedging activities might adversely affect the level of the underlying index.[17] At the close of equity trading at 4 p.m. on 5 February 2018, XIV was worth $99 per share. After the market close, VIX futures spiked dramatically, as much as 96%. Between 4:10 p.m. and 5:09 p.m., the Intraday Indicative Value of XIV was not updated from its last reported value of approximately $24.70. At 5:10 p.m., the Intraday Indicative Value of XIV was updated to $4.22 per share, reflecting the large spike in the VIX futures. Overall, this spike led to a drop of 97% in the value of the XIV from its prior closing value on 1 February, when it had been worth approximately $1.6 billion. This fall was sufficiently large that it triggered an acceleration event, enabling Credit Suisse to announce the next day its intention to close the ETN to prevent further losses. Regardless of whether Credit Suisse is found to be legally at fault for these losses, this case raises many concerns: (i) the demise of XIV was driven by a single spike in prices, which appears extreme relative to prices before and after; (ii) the hedging program of Credit Suisse was not aligned with the interests of the XIV investors and likely magnified the losses sustained by those investors; (iii) the XIV product and its hedging program may not have been well understood by investors; and (iv) during the market dislocation, Intraday Indicative Values of XIV were not updated every 15 seconds, as was typical (Janus Index and Calculation Services LLC was responsible for providing estimates of the notes value).

The settlement process for options (and other derivatives) impacts the ease with which manipulation can occur. For instance, manipulation incentives may be different if an option contract is cash settled or has physical delivery at expiration. With cash settlement, the manipulator only needs to influence the price of the underlying security at expiration, at which point the manipulator settles in cash the value of the option based on this price. By contrast, with physical delivery, the manipulator may receive (or deliver) the underlying asset – the unwinding of the resulting position will cause the price to move against the manipulative trades, reducing the value of the

---

[16] For details see: Chahal v. Credit Suisse Group AG et al., US District Court, Southern District of New York, 1:18-cv-02268-AT-SN. May 14, 2018.

[17] See details here: www.sec.gov/Archives/edgar/data/1053092/000095010318000969/dp85741_424b2-vix48.htm.

manipulation. This phenomenon is sometimes known as the challenge of 'burying the corpse' after the manipulation.

Regulation of trade-based manipulation tends to focus on the *intent* of the trader. The examples highlighted in this chapter highlight that it can be very difficult to identify intent. Automated rule-based trading algorithms that do not have direct human intervention magnify these challenges. Trading programs based on artificial intelligence and machine learning could execute trades near the market close that appear manipulative but arise from 'innocent' optimization routines. Interestingly, Aitken, Cumming, and Zhan (2015) provide empirical evidence that the presence of high frequency trading (HFT) has helped mitigate the frequency and severity of suspected end-of-day price manipulation. Of course, high frequency trading firms also have the capacity to engage in manipulation. In 2012, the high frequency trading firm Optiver Holding reached a $14 million settlement with the CFTC in relation to allegations that Optiver, two of its subsidiaries, and three employees attempted manipulation of crude oil, heating oil, and gasoline futures on the NYMEX. The traders were alleged to have used bang-the-close trades in at least 19 instances during March 2007 to manipulate the settlement prices of crude and distillate oil futures contracts.[18] The settlement prevented the company from trading oil futures in the three minutes prior to the market close for two years.

To the extent that HFT may be a 'force for good', it is also important to note that high frequency and low latency trading, combined with market fragmentation, have dramatically increased the sheer quantity of reported trades and quotes, and as such, it has become increasingly challenging in practical terms to detect and infer the intent of potential manipulative trades. To enforce trading rules in such an environment, regulators need to invest in computer surveillance technology and update regulations to reflect these new realities. The integrity of closing prices depends on it.

References

Abrantes-Metz, R.M., Kraten, M., Metz, A.D. and Seow, G.S. (2012). Libor manipulation? *Journal of Banking and Finance* 36(1): 136–150.

Agarwal, V., Daniel, N.D. and Naik, N.Y. (2011). Do hedge funds manage their reported returns?, *Review of Financial Studies* 10(1): 3281–3320.

Agarwal, V., Gay, G.D. and Ling, L. (2014). Window dressing in mutual funds. *Review of Financial Studies* 27(11): 3133–3170.

Aitken, M., Cumming, D. and Zhan, F. (2015). High frequency trading and end-of-day price distortion. *Journal of Banking and Finance* 59: 330–349.

Aspris, A., Foley, S., Gratton, F. and O'Neill, P. (2017). Transparency in commodities markets. Working paper, University of Sydney.

Atanasov, V., Davies, R.J. and Merrick, J.J. (2015a). Financial intermediaries in the midst of market manipulation: Did they protect the fool or help the knave? *Journal of Corporate Finance* 34: 210–234.

---

[18] See CFTC v. Optiver US LLC et al, US District Court, Southern District of New York, No. 08-06560.

Atanasov, V., Davies, R.J. and Merrick, J.J. (2015b). How well do futures markets limit manipulation?, *Review of Financial Regulation Studies*, Center for the Study of Financial Regulation, Summer, *No.* 15, p. 3–4.

Avellaneda, M., Kasyan, G. and Lipkin, M.D. (2012). Mathematical models for stock pinning near option expiration dates. *Communications on Pure and Applied Mathematics* 65(7): 949–974.

Avellaneda, M. and Lipkin, M.D. (2003). A market-induced mechanism for stock pinning. *Quantitative Finance* 3(6): 417–425.

Back, K. and Zender, J.F. (1993). Auctions for divisible goods: On the rationale for the Treasury experiment. *Review of Financial Studies* 6(4): 733–764.

Baldauf, M., Frei, C. and Mollner, J. (2018). Contracting for financial execution. Working paper, University of British Columbia.

Bellia, M., Pelizzon, L., Subrahmanyam, M.G., Uno, J. and Yuferove, D. (2017). *Coming early to the party: High frequency traders in the pre-opening phase and the opening auction of NYSE Euronext Paris*. Working paper, New York University.

Ben-David, I., Franzoni, F., Landier, A. and Moussawi, R. (2013). Do hedge funds manipulate stock prices? *Journal of Finance* 68(6): 2383–2434.

Berk, J. and Green, R. (2004). Mutual fund flows and performance in rational markets. *Journal of Political Economy* 112: 1269–1295.

Bernhardt, D. and Davies, R.J. (2005). Painting the tape: Aggregate evidence. *Economics Letters* 89(3): 306–311.

Bernhardt, D. and Davies, R.J. (2009). Smart fund managers? Stupid money? *Canadian Journal of Economics* 42(2): 719–748.

Biais, B., Bisière, C. and Pouget, S. (2014). Equilibrium discovery and preopening mechanisms in an experimental market. *Management Science* 60(3): 753–769.

Biais, B., Hillion, P. and Spatt, C. (1999). Price discovery and learning during the preopening period in the Paris Bourse. *Journal of Political Economy* 107(6): 1218–1248.

Brown, S.J., Sotes-Paladino, J., Wang, J. and Yao, Y. (2017). Starting on the wrong foot: Seasonality in mutual fund performance. *Journal of Banking and Finance* 82: 133–150.

Cao, C., Ghysels, E. and Hatheway, F. (2000). Price discovery without trading: evidence from the Nasdaq pre-opening. *Journal of Finance* 55(3): 1339–1365.

Carhart, M., Kaniel, R., Musto, D. and Reed, A. (2002). Leaning for the tape: Evidence of gaming behavior in equity mutual funds. *Journal of Finance* 5(2): 661–693.

Cason, T.N. (2000). The opportunity for conspiracy in asset markets organized with dealer intermediaries. *Review of Financial Studies* 13(2): 385–416.

CFTC v. Optiver US LLC et al. No. 08-cv-06560-LAP, 2012 (United States District Court, Southern District of New York, April 19, 2012).

Chang, R.P., Rhee, S.G., Stone, G.R. and Tang, N. (2008). How does the call market method affect price efficiency? Evidence from the Singapore Stock Market. *Journal of Banking and Finance* 32: 2205–2219.

Comerton-Forde, C. and Putniņš, T.J. (2011). Measuring closing price manipulation. *Journal of Financial Intermediation* 20(2): 135–158.

Comerton-Forde, C. and Putniņš, T.J. (2014). Stock price manipulation: Prevalence and determinants. *Review of Finance* 18(1): 23–66.

Cordi, N., Foley, S. and Putniņš, T.J. (2015). Is there an optimal closing mechanism? Working paper, University of Sydney.

Cumming, D., Ji, S., Johan, S. and Tarsalewska, M. (2016). Manipulation and M&As. Working paper, York University.

Cumming, D., Ji, S. and Peter, R. (2016). Market Manipulation and Innovation. Working paper, York University.

Cumming, D., Johan, S. and Li, D. (2011). Exchange trading rules and stock market liquidity. *Journal of Financial Economics* 99(3): 65–671.

Davies, R.J. (2003). The Toronto Stock Exchange preopening session, *Journal of Financial Markets* 6(4): 491–516.

Davies, R.J. and Sirri, E. (2018). The Economics of Trading Markets. In *Securities Market Issues for the 21st Century* (eds. M.B. Fox, L.R. Glosten, E.F. Greene, M.S. Patel). Columbia University, 149–220.

Duong, T.X. and Meschke, F. (2016). The rise and fall of portfolio pumping among U.S. mutual funds. Working paper, Iowa State University.

Dutta, P.K. and Madhavan, A. (1997). Competition and collusion in dealer markets. *Journal of Finance* 52(1): 245–276.

Edmunds, J.C., Platt, H.D. and Platt, M.A. (1984). Price fluctuations of underlying shares as listed options expire. *Akron Business and Economic Review* 15(3): 33–39.

Figueiredo, A., Mishra, S. and Jain P. (2017). Order book characteristics and stock price pinning on options expiration. Working paper, University of Memphis.

Friedman, J. (1971). A non-cooperative equilibrium for supergames. *Review of Economic Studies* 38(1): 1–12.

Gallagher, D., Gardner, P. and Swan, P.L. (2009). Portfolio pumping: An examination of investment manager quarter-end trading and impact on performance. *Pacific-Basin Finance Journal* 17(1): 1–27.

Gandhi, P., Golez, B., Jackwerth, J.C. and Plazzi, A. (2017). Financial market misconduct and public enforcement: The case of LIBOR manipulation. *Swiss Finance Institute Research Paper Series* No. 17–53.

Goetzmann, W., Ingersoll, J., Spiegel, M. and Welch, I. (2007). Portfolio performance manipulation and manipulation-proof performance measures. *Review of Financial Studies* 20(5): 1503–1546.

Griffin, J.M. and Shams, A. (2018). Manipulation in the VIX? *Review of Financial Studies* 31(4): 1377–1417.

Hauser, S., Kamara, A. and Shurki, I. (2012). The effects of randomizing the opening time on the performance of a stock market under stress. *Journal of Financial Markets* 15(4): 392–415.

Hauser, S., Kedar-Levy, H. and Milo, O. (2018). Price discovery during parallel stocks and options preopening: Information distortion and hints of manipulation. Working paper, Ben-Gurion University of the Negev.

Hillion, P. and Suominen, M. (2004). The manipulation of closing prices. *Journal of Financial Markets* 7(4): 351–375.

Hu, G., McLean, R., Pontiff, J. and Wang, Q. (2014). The year-end trading activities of institutional investors: evidence from daily trades. *Review of Financial Studies* 27(5): 1593–1614.

In Re: Platinum & Palladium Commodities Litigation, No. 10-cv-3617, 2011. WL 4048780 (United States District Court, Southern District of New York, Sept. 13, 2011).

Ivaldi, M., Jullien, B., Rey, P., Seabright, P. and Tirole, J. (2003). The economics of tacit collusion. Final Report for DG Competition, European Commission.

Jarrow, R., Fung, S. qne Tsai, S.-C. (2018). An empirical investigation of large trader market manipulation in derivatives markets. *Review of Derivatives Research* 21: 331–374.

Kandel, E., Rindi, B. and Bosetti, L. (2012). The effect of a closing call auction on market quality and trading strategies. *Journal of Financial Intermediation* 21(1): 23–49.

Khwaja, A.J. and Mian, A. (2005). Unchecked intermediaries: Price manipulation in an emerging stock market. *Journal of Financial Economics* 78(1): 203–241.

Klemkosky, R. C. (1978). The impact of option expirations on stock prices. *Journal of Financial and Quantitative Analysis* 13(3): 507–518.

Kluger, B.D. and Wyatt, S.B. (2002). Preferencing, internalization or order flow, and tacit collusion: Evidence from experiments. *Journal of Financial and Quantitative Analysis* 37(3): 449–469.

Krishnan, H. and Nelken, I. (2001). The effect of stock pinning upon option prices. *RISK Magazine*. December.

Kuk, J., Liu, W.-M. and Pham, P.K. (2016). Strategic order submission and cancellation in pre-opening periods: The case of IPO firms. Working paper, Australian National University.

Lakonishok, J., Lee, L., Pearson, N.D. and Poteshman, A.M. (2007). Option market activity. *Review of Financial Studies* 20(3): 813–857.

Lakonishok, J., Shleifer, A., Thaler, R. and Vishny, R. (1991). Window dressing by pension fund managers. *American Economic Review* 81(2): 227–231.

Lee, J., Baek, K. and Park, Y.S. (2014). What drives portfolio pumping in the Korean Equity Fund Market? *Asia-Pacific Journal of Financial Studies* 43(2): 297–315.

Lescourret, L. (2017). Cold case file? inventory risk and information sharing during the pre-1997 NASDAQ. *European Financial Management* 23(4): 761–806.

Lynch, A., Puckett, A. and Yan, X. (2014). Institutions and the turn-of-the-year effect: Evidence from actual institutional trades. *Journal of Banking and Finance* 49: 56–68.

McConnell, J.J. and Xu, W. (2008). Equity returns at the turn of the month. *Financial Analysts Journal* 64(2): 49–64.

Ng, L. and Wang, Q. (2004). Institutional trading and the turn-of-the-year effect. *Journal of Financial Economics* 74(2): 343–366.

Ni, S.X., Pearson, N.D. and Poteshman, A.M. (2005). Stock price clustering on option expiration dates. *Journal of Financial Economics* 78(1): 49–87.

Onur, E. and Reiffen, D. (2018). The effect of settlement rules on the incentive to bang the close. *Journal of Futures Markets* 38(8): 841–864.

Pagano, M.S., Peng, L. and Schwartz, R.A. (2013). A call auction's impact on price formation and order routing: Evidence from the NASDAQ stock market. *Journal of Financial Markets* 16(2): 331–361.

Pagano, M.S. and Schwartz, R.A. (2003). A closing call's impact on market quality at Euronext Paris. *Journal of Financial Economics* 68(3): 439–484.

Pirrong, C. (1996). Market liquidity and depth on computerized and open outcry trading systems: A comparison of DTB and LIFFE bund contracts. *Journal of Futures Markets* 16(5): 519–543.

Saakvitne, J. (2016). 'Banging the close': Price manipulation or optimal execution?, Working paper, BI Norwegian Business School.

Shackleton, M., Yan, J. and Yao, Y. (2020). NAV Inflation and Impact on Performance in China. *European Financial Management* 26(1): 118-142.

Sias, R.W. and Starks, L.T. (1997). Institutions and individuals at the turn-of-the-year. *Journal of Finance* 52(4): 1543–1562.

Sirri, E. and Tufano, P. (1998). Costly search and mutual fund flows. *Journal of Finance* 53(5): 1589–1622.

Sorescu, S.M. (2000). The effect of options on stock prices: 1973 to 1995. *Journal of Finance* 55(1): 487–514.

Stivers, C.T. and Sun, L. (2013). Returns and option activity over the option-expiration week for S&P 100 stocks. *Journal of Banking and Finance* 37: 4226–4240.

Zhang, G., Chen, H. and Cai, F. (2015). Weekly options on stock pinning. *Journal of Business and Economic Studies* 21(1): 62–73.

Chapter 10
A Trader's Perspective on Market Abuse Regulations

Sam Baker

SJB Capital Limited

10.1 Introduction

This is a personal account of a trading journey which started in 2005 when I developed a passion to understand the information that drives financial market prices in a certain direction, and execute trades accordingly. I examine market abuse regulations from my perspective as a trader, describing them to those not so familiar with the markets with as much detail as possible. I explain, using plenty of practical examples, how these market abuses might be used to gain an edge and profit the executor of the trade, and how these abuses of the market would affect the trading process of a trader witnessing the market abuse. I explore two case studies in detail. Both try to find an edge in the market by using clever order management and executing techniques, one of which is currently deemed legal and another which has resulted in a conviction and fine. I describe how major exchanges are complying with the new market regulations to stop abuse, and how they are working with market participants to make sure that the rules are understood and adhered to. I will share what my company is doing to comply at business entity level and at trader level and conclude with discussions on limitation on regulations from governing bodies and rules set by exchanges.

The focus of this chapter is the European Market Abuse Regulation (MAR) which is a directive covering all European exchanges which came into force in July 2016. This standard was introduced to modify the existing legislation governing market abuse and brought with it a broader scope of regulation and focus on identifying and eliminating abusive behaviour in all sectors of the financial markets, creating a legal obligation to have trade surveillance and submit reports on an exchange, trading firm and individual trader level. In the UK this is overseen by the Financial Conduct Authority (FCA) and in Europe by the European Securities and Markets Authority (ESMA).

During the last few years Europe has implemented some of its most far-reaching financial services regulations. There has been a period of unprecedented regulatory change, increased oversight and tighter scrutiny. Increased regulatory focus since the financial crisis of 2008 has led to a more concentrated global regularity force. Swathes of regulation[1] have been introduced to govern previously untouched areas of the financial markets and to increase scrutiny on those areas seen to pose the most risk to financial stability.

As a trader operating pre-2008 there were very few documented cases of market abuse and very few investigations taking place. We were, after all, living in a globalized free marketplace where markets moved, sometimes orderly, sometimes irrationally, but you placed a trade, took a chance and there were winners and losers. After the financial crisis in 2008, governments around the world realized that the way the financial world was operated, and to a lesser extent self-regulated, had to change.[2]

My first proprietary trading house role was working with seasoned London International Financial Futures and Options Exchange (LIFFE) floor traders who specialized in short-term interest rate futures. Specifically, the firm focused on EURIBOR (European interbank offered rate) futures and short sterling futures (UK interest rate market strongly linked to LIBOR, the London interbank offered rate) benchmarks of where the markets believe interest rates will be priced in Europe and the UK, respectively, at certain points in the future. Financial institutions, banks pension funds, insurance companies, investment houses and governments would look at the market perception of where rates would be and react to those prices accordingly to hedge any exposures

---

[1] Dodd–Frank Act, 2010; Market Abuse Regulation, 2016; MiFID II, 2018; BASEL III, 2019.

[2] The monumental policies laid out by the Dodd–Frank act, Basel II and MIFID II are beyond the scope of this chapter but will be scrutinized throughout this book. All are designed to reduce systematic risk in financial markets by implementing a number of transparency measures, as well as improving investor protection and controlling trading venues, notably the exchanges where trades are executed.

they might have to interest rates moving either up or down. There are a large number of events that can move the price of an interest rate futures contract within the UK or the eurozone, far too many to list here. At the start of my path as a trader, however, I was armed with just the basics of fundamental analysis, i.e. macro-economic news, macro-economic data, central banker's opinion, political shocks, and the regular release of the LIBOR fixings.

LIBOR was announced every Thursday at 10 a.m. It was an average of the interest rates estimated by each of the leading banks in London that it would be charged if the bank were to borrow from the other banks. It is the primary benchmark, along with EURIBOR, for short-term interest rates around the world, and how it was set in the present would have a knock-on effect on the rate in the future. A very big deal was made of the LIBOR announcement because, as per the efficient market hypothesis, the price of every asset reflects all known information about it at any one time. So putting theory into practice we would all be waiting with bated breath for the weekly LIBOR figure to be announced so we could use it to reprice the short sterling yield curve accordingly. Higher than anticipated LIBOR would indicate rate increases in the future and give us as traders the signal to sell the short sterling contract. A lower than anticipated LIBOR would indicate possible rate decreases in the future and therefore we would be seeking to buy short sterling futures. We would get the information in audio format from what is known in the industry as a 'squawk', a desk of researchers whose job it is to keep their eagle eyes scanned overall the newswires – Bloomberg, Reuters, Market News International, Dow Jones news, and all the commercial news stations, to then squawk the news over a PA system as quickly as it is read, so that traders can react to the data or news as quickly as possible. By using a squawk, traders could be fully focused on the markets, not having to read the data to then jump back to reading the market and possibly missing the market move.

So, there I am – a young trader ready to make his mark in the world of financial futures. The big release of the day is imminent, my palms are sweaty, and I am nervous with anticipation – realizing that making the right decision will make me a great deal of profit if I'm quick enough to disseminate the data and trade with speed and accuracy. The clock strikes 10 a.m., the squawk is as quick as it can be, and I react to place a trade on the short sterling market which is directly related to the pricing of LIBOR. But . . . nothing happens. It's as if the market knows the information already – 10 a.m. on Thursday is when *I* get the LIBOR rate fixings for that week – but someone else obviously gets them before me.

This was way back in 2005/2006 and since then, as mentioned earlier in this book, it has come to light that LIBOR at that time was rigged. My gut feeling and the feeling of the majority of market participants at the time was right – someone was getting the data early and the market was moving prior to its release. On 27 July 2012, the *Financial Times* published an article by a former trader which stated that LIBOR manipulation had been commonplace since at least 1991.[3]

---

[3] Keenan, Douglas (27 July 2012) My thwarted attempt to tell of lie or shenanigans. *Financial Times*: https://www.ft.com/content/dc5f49c2-d67b-11e1-ba60-00144feabdc0.

Banks were falsely inflating or deflating their rates to profit from trades or to give the impression that they were more creditworthy than they were. There have been multiple agencies around the world that have sought to bring justice against those involved in the LIBOR fixings over the years, most of which are already well documented in this book. What stands out for me is the release of a transcript of a conversation that happened on 19 August 2007 between Royal Bank Of Scotland trader Tan Chi Minh and Deutsche Bank's Mark Wong:

Tan: '. . . it's just amazing how LIBOR fixing can make you that much money or lose it. It's a cartel now in London'.
Wong: '. . . must be damn difficult to trade man, especially if you are not in the loop'.[4]

Well, Mr Wong was right, it is extremely difficult to trade when the playing field isn't level and the market is being abused by traders' at large institutions that are rigging the data to their benefit week in, week out, and trading on that information days before the rest of the world sees it.

10.2   Getting the Trading Edge

Since my time starting out as a short-term interest rate trader I have since developed into a multi-asset multi-exchange macro trader, trading a very diverse portfolio of financial futures, commodity futures, agricultural futures and energy futures. Alongside my own personal trading I have been recruiting, teaching, mentoring, and managing university graduates who want to follow a similar path into futures trading on the world's leading exchanges: CME, ICE, EUREX. My time as a trader and trainer has placed me well to understand why markets do get abused.

Trading is all about the edge. How do we define what the 'edge' is as a trader? For some it could be detailed technical analysis, the ability to read a chart, study where the price has been, or how it's got to the current point and where it will be going in the short, medium, or long term. For others, it could be the ability to disseminate fundamental information about an asset class, reading between the lines in a forensic manner, trying to find a piece of the puzzle that unlocks the holy grail of price discovery. Or, rather than constant in-depth analysis of the information, a trader could merely have the fastest trigger finger when it comes to reacting to information that is released. A trader could simply watch the order flow through the market and try and gain an edge from spotting simple patterns between prices using the order book, order flow, or the size as a reason to trade.

---

[4] Can, Andrei. 25 September 2012. RBS instant messages show LIBOR rates skewed for traders. *Bloomberg*: https://www.bloomberg.com/news/articles/2012-09-25/rbs-instant-messages-show-libor-rates-skewed-for-traders.

Now, having traded for many years, and having trained over a hundred traders, I can tell you that all the above ways to gain an edge in the futures market are very hard indeed. There are thousands of participants all over the world looking at all the very same information you are, the same technical analysis chart, reading the same fundamental information, reacting at the same time when data is released, and looking at the same price action as you are. The competition is tough, but the rewards are not only financially uncapped; as a trader you get the instant feedback of knowing all your hard work in preparing and executing your trade was essentially right.

The high-profile cases of the LIBOR and EURIBOR traders show a clear case of greed as a motivation. Christian Bittar, recently jailed for over five years and four months for his part in trying to rig EURIBOR, was once one of Deutsche Bank's most profitable traders. At one point he earned £47 million in commission in a single year, on top of his £130,000 basic salary. Judge Gledhill said, "Greed alone does not provide an answer to Bittar's actions and that he had been motivated at least in part by the satisfaction of being able to beat the system undetected."[5] This beating of the system, undetected as described by Judge Gledhill, is the ultimate edge and will be the focus of much of this chapter.

There was an another incident of a junior trader in the company I worked for trying to gain an edge by attempting to game the matching algorithm of one of the exchanges that we traded on at the time. A matching algorithm is used by a trading exchange, ICE, CME, etc., to determine which market participant gets allocated a fill of their order of contracts when a bid or an offer is traded at the best market price. There are two order allocation matching algorithms used by exchanges: first-in first-out (FIFO), and pro-rata.

It is best to explain the pro-rata order allocation with an example. In this instance the market is bid at 5.5 for 100 contracts, this bid is made of five participants each wanting to buy 20 lots at that price:

$$20 + 20 + 20 + 20 + 20 = 100$$

A limit sell order at the price of 5.5 for 60 lots is entered and gets matched with the bid working at 5.5; it is the matching algorithm's job to determine who gets their orders completed on that bid and for how many contracts.

In this instance there are 5 participants each with 20 contracts working on the bid, and only 60 contracts have been sold. So, who gets allocated the 60 contracts that have traded out of the 100 contracts that are on the bid?

This is where the matching algorithm comes in. It's the algorithm's function to determine that there is an even allocation of contracts over those 5 market participants' working orders on the bid, in this instance the algorithm would allocate each

[5] Barney Thompson (July 19, 2018) Two former star traders jailed in EURIBOR rigging case. *Financial Times*: https://www.ft.com/content/3f15a63c-8b4e-11e8-b18d-0181731a0340.

of the 5 participants 60% of their order working on the bid, i.e. 15 contracts. The percentage allocation can be adjusted by the exchange at any time, but this example is based on the current calculation used by the CME.

All large exchanges use either a matching algorithm to allocate order distribution or a FIFO Q-based order allocation system. In the example we used previously, the 60 contracts that were sold at 5.5 would be split to the first 3 orders of 20 lots to be places on the bid, first in the market and then first out when the price trades.

The trader in question had worked out that they could split their order working on the bid or the offer on an exchange using the pro-rata matching algorithm into multiple orders to gain advantage over the matching algorithm. This would increase their share of any contracts trading where they had an order.

For instance, if the market was 5.5 bid and there was still 100 on the bid, made of 4 orders of 20 contracts, but the final 20 being made of 20 orders of 1 contract but by the same participant, the order was split from 1 order seen by the exchange to 20 individual orders:

$$20 + 20 + 20 + 20 + 20(1+1+1+1+1+1+1+1+1+1+1+1+1+1+1+1+1+1+1+1)$$
$$= 100.$$

Then when the order to sell 60 lots is entered and gets matched with the bid at 5.5, the matching algorithm would naturally have to give out a fill to all those orders for 1 contract because 60% of 1 contract would have to be a 1 contract; the algorithm cannot deliver an order smaller than 1. So instead of getting a fair distribution as intended to be delivered by the exchange, the trader in question managed to get a complete fill of 20 contracts rather than their fair share, which would have been 15 had they placed 1 order for 20 contracts. This would leave the other participants' working orders on the bid at 5.5 with a reduced order allocation. It was a very simple and accessible way to gain an edge for the trader over other market participants; receiving more than their fair share of contract allocation would lead to greater profit potential but had consequences.

In the above example, the trader in question was contacted by the exchange for persistent order splitting and given a warning: should this practice continue he would be banned from trading on the exchange and fined. This was an easy piece of self-regulation on the exchange's part, as order splitting is very clear, defined, measured, and simple to stop.

My close encounter with a market abuser was caught early on and the lesson was learnt company wide. Order splitting hasn't been defined in the new Market Abuse Regulation (MAR) laid out for the financial markets. The rules set by the exchanges are clear, orders should be placed for the correct number of contracts only at any price with no exceptions. There was an obvious advantage to order split that enticed the trader, but no way another market participant could tell that the offence was taking place. Luckily the exchange policed the market and the offender was stopped.

The next part or the chapter will look at the market abuse regulations, how they are executed, and how they affect trader's decisions.

10.3   A Typical Trader's Market Window

In order to successfully explain the number of abuses laid out in MAR I will first of all show an example of a typical trader's market window which gives us the information we need to enter a trade and to understand how abusers operate.

An example of a typical trader's market window is depicted in Figure 10.2. The market window has been broken up into two sections. The sidebar on the left and the live market on the right, which changes in real time as the buy and sell orders enter the market.

Figure 10.1   Sidebar.

First we describe the sidebar, which is shown in Figure 10.1 above.

1. The numerical pad is used to input the quantity of contracts to be traded.
2. The position window highlights whether the position held is long or short and in what amount. If the trader is long it is highlighted dark grey, and short is grey. In this instance the trader is long 10 contracts.
3. This number below the position window tells us how many contracts have traded in that trading session at that time in that market viewed. At the time of capture the market highlighted had traded 6023 contracts.
4. The grey 0.02 highlights how many prices up or down the market has moved from its settlement price the day before. In this instance it has moved up 2 prices. Dark grey highlights a move up and grey highlights a move down.
5. Dark grey, grey, and light grey X buttons delete certain orders in that market window, all buy orders will be removed by the grey X, all sell orders by the light grey X, and all orders in the market window by the dark grey X.

The live market: the seven columns are broken down as follows:

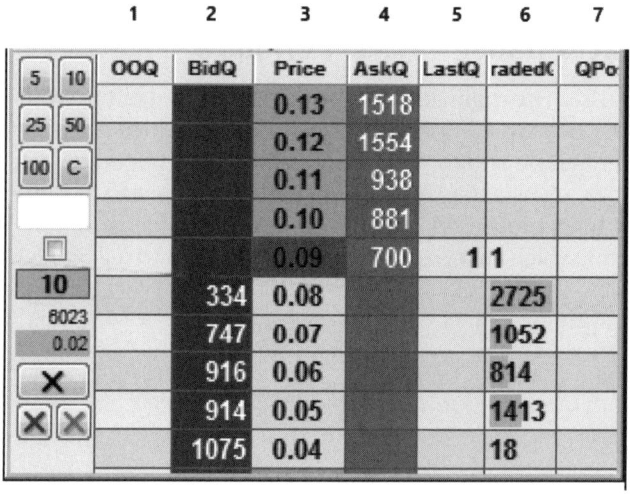

		1	2	3	4	5	6	7
		OOQ	BidQ	Price	AskQ	LastQ	radedC	QPo
5	10			0.13	1518			
25	50			0.12	1554			
100	C			0.11	938			
				0.10	881			
	☐			0.09	700	1	1	
10			334	0.08			2725	
8023			747	0.07			1052	
0.02			916	0.06			814	
✕			914	0.05			1413	
✕	✕		1075	0.04			18	

Figure 10.2   A trader's window of the order book.

1. **OOQ** – Own order quantity. When placing an order, it will highlight how many contracts you are bidding or offering at that price. For instance, should an order to buy 20 contracts at the price of 0.08 be placed it will show the number 20 in Blue (buy) in the OOQ column next to the price 0.08.
2. **BidQ** – Bid column. This shows all the contracts working on the bids for the entire depth of the market. It is a good measure of liquidity on the buy side and shows the best price at which the contract can be bought immediately.
3. **Price** – The market price. This shows the best price which can be lifted immediately. At 0.09, have a bid – 0.08 – or offer – 0.09 – worked at market or have a sell order filled straight away – at 0.08.
4. **Ask/offer column.** This shows all the contracts working on the ask/offer for the entire depth of the market which is a good measure of liquidity on the sell side and shows the best price at which the contract can be sold immediately.
5. **LastQ** – Last traded quantity column. The number shown in this column is the last manned contract that have either been bought at the offer price or sold at the bid price.
6. **Traded quantity at price column.** The number that we see in the left sidebar is broken down here to how many contracts have been traded at each price.
7. **Q position.** This is the trading software best guess of where the own order is in the queue of contracts on either the bid or the offer that is being worked.

10.4   Wash Trades

Wash trades are defined by compliance departments the world over as:

'Entering into arrangements for the sale or purchase of a financial instrument where there is no change of beneficial interest or market risk'

In simplistic terms: trading with yourself or another party in a *prearranged* trade at a price agreed prior to the trade.

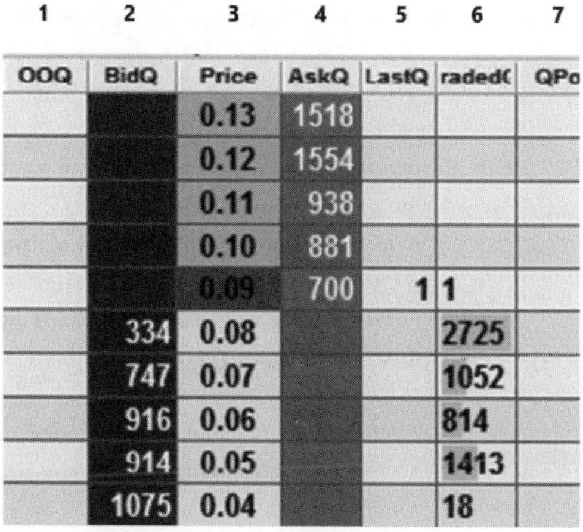

1	2	3	4	5	6	7

OOQ	BidQ	Price	AskQ	LastQ	radedC	QPo
		0.13	1518			
		0.12	1554			
		0.11	938			
		0.10	881			
		0.09	700	1	1	
	334	0.08			2725	
	747	0.07			1052	
	916	0.06			814	
	914	0.05			1413	
	1075	0.04			18	

Figure 10.3   Market window example 1.

Before I start to explain the reason why a trader might benefit from wash trading, and how it affects other market participants and their trading process, I will show you what it looks like visually using a market window which displays all the live information a trader sees when viewing the market prior to trading.

Figure 10.3 is the same as the one used in Section 10.3 with all the same characteristics; we only need to use the second section of the market window with 7 columns of market information in this example.

In column 2, the bid quantity, there is an order for 334 lots at a price of 0.08. This number of contracts is small compared to the bid of 747 contracts at the price below at 0.07 and the offer above of 700 contracts at 0.09. To explain a wash trade, we shall assume that the bid at 0.08 is 1 order of 334 contracts.

Into the market comes a sell order which hits the bid at 0.08 for the full 334 contracts; the order has been fully filled. In this instance, to be deemed a wash trade, the owner of the bid of 334 contracts at 0.08 would have had to have sold 334 contracts to themselves, or prearranged with another counterparty to sell those 334 contracts to them. It is not stipulated in MAR that an order needs to be fully filled or partially filled by either party that is participating in wash trading, but it removes ambiguity when looking to convict someone of wash trading if the whole of the order is completed.

The reason a trader might look to wash trade could be to pass financial transactions from one account to another, possibly moving a profitable trade to a jurisdiction that has more advantageous taxation laws or moving a position to a company that had are better profit split term when it came to calculate a trader's bonus. An individual trader could have volume targets that they might need to meet so would wash trade with themselves to artificially inflate their volume. A trading company may gain a rebate from a clearer or exchange, based on many trades they did in a specific market. It may be a viable financial option to create false volumes by trading with itself to reach targets set out.

From the perspective of a trader viewing that sort of activity, the wash trades create price and volume distortion. For instance, if a price was to trade 10 times the average amount for no reason but for wash trading, it will give a trader more of a reason to focus on that price due to heightened activity, distracting them from the process of identifying trades where market conditions are more transparent. The integrity of what is happening at that price will always be the subject of question – why was so much volume traded and what does that mean for price discovery or the quest to find an edge?

In December 2017, the Chicago mercantile exchange brought and settled disciplinary action against Brandon Elsasser for purportedly engaging in wash sales and trading fee credits for his employer under CME administered incentive program. According to CME, Elasser placed matching buy and sell orders on Globex in Eurodollar futures (US short-term interest rates) for the same beneficial owner with the expectation that trades would match between June 2014 and July 2015. Elsasser agreed to pay a fine of US $40,000 to resolve the CME's disciplinary action and agreed to a 20-business day all CME group trading access plan. Elasser previously settled charges by the commodity futures trading commission's related to this incident by agreeing to pay a fine of US $200,000.[6]

10.5   High Ticking/Low Ticking – Momentum Ignition

I would describe the offence of high/low ticking as reckless order behaviour to influence market direction, influencing and changing the perception of the market's behaviour when viewed in the future or trying to influence the market's closing price.

Trading compliance describes it as entering orders to trade or a series of orders to trade or executing transactions, likely to start or exasperate a trend, and to encourage other participants to accelerate or extend the trend to create an opportunity to close out or open a position in a favourable price.

We will refer to Figure 10.4 for our example. The Market is bid at 0.08 with a bid quantity of 334 contracts and offered at 0.09 with 700 contracts working on the

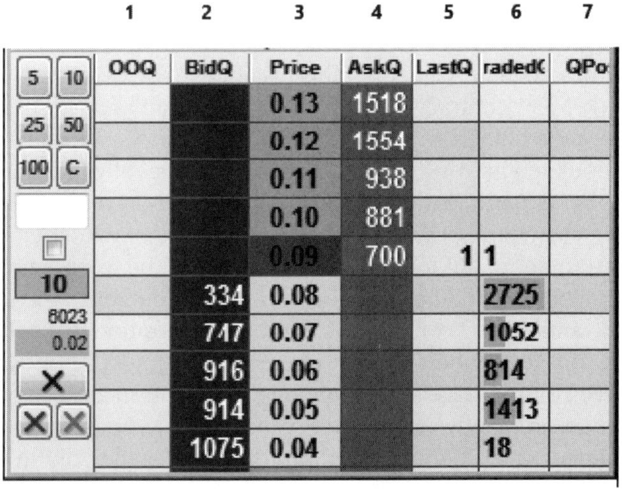

| | | 1 | 2 | 3 | 4 | 5 | 6 | 7 |
		OOQ	BidQ	Price	AskQ	LastQ	radedC	QPo
5	10			0.13	1518			
25	50			0.12	1554			
100	C			0.11	938			
				0.10	881			
□				0.09	700	1	1	
10			334	0.08			2725	
8023			747	0.07			1052	
0.02			916	0.06			814	
X			914	0.05			1413	
X	X		1075	0.04			18	

Figure 10.4   Market window example 2.

---

[6] Trader Sanctioned by CME for Wash Sales to Generate Credits Under Exchange incentive Program, Rosenman, Katten, 17 December 2017: https://www.lexology.com/library/detail.aspx?g=6d93fe79-657c-42d6-ad79-29e53a67ebc8.

offer, moving to column 5, Last Q, we can see that the last traded quantity is 1 contract bought at the price of 0.09. Column 6, Traded Quantity, tells us that this is the only contract to have traded there as the total traded quantity at the price of 0.09 is 1 contract, the smallest amounts that can be traded. This could be a perfectly innocent transaction, in this case a participant in the market may just want to buy 1 contract at a price of 0.09. We shall look at this suspiciously, however, and question if that market participant really did want to buy 1 contract at 0.09, or did they really want to high tick the market and encourage other participants to accelerate or extend the trend higher.

Should this be a case of market abuse and a trader placed this order for other participants to extend the trend beyond this new high at 0.09, they would have been looking, one would have thought, primarily to have set off market stop orders. These are order types that trigger when a price trades in a contract. For instance, if a short position was held in this market and a stop was put in the price of 0.09 to enter the market if the market traded 0.09, as soon as the 1 lot was high ticked the stop would go into the market, possibly triggering more trading at 0.09 and igniting momentum for more buyers to buy, which could in turn take that price to higher highs. The market abuser in question may have a long position in this contract and is looking to close out for profit needing buyers to buy at 0.09, or the price is near to where they want to sell so beginning the trend will get to the trade entry they desire.

If a trader had a position short at 0.08 with a very close market stop at 0.09, there would be frustration and a financial loss should the market stop trigger due to the market being high ticked. In this particular instance it looks like if you want to buy the market, the most efficient way to do so would be to place a bid at 0.08 where the volume of 334 is less than half of what is on the offer, 700 waiting for the bid to trade until market conditions change and the price at 0.09 needs to be bought. A trader wouldn't be rushing to buy at the contract high of the day when no other volumes traded there under normal circumstances. This high ticking will show up permanently when looking at the contract using a charting package and using technical analysis to identify a trade, in this instance the price of 0.09 will be showing as the high of the trading session at the time of that 1 lot trading. Technically speaking, the market has traded at 0.09, but we know that in this scenario it is because a market abuser has high ticked the price. Our expectations of this price in the future returning to the high will be influenced by the fact that it appears to have traded there legitimately before; the basis of technical analysis is looking where prices have been to determine where prices will be in the future.

One of the most famous instances of high ticking arose when oil prices first reached $100 per barrel on 2 January 2008. Richard Arens, an independent trader on the New York mercantile exchange (NYMEX) shot to fame after a lifetime of obscurity, thanks to determination to print the golden hundred-dollars-a-barrel trade ticket. Arens, who was trading the commodity on a particularly bullish day in the backdrop of a cold winter and tensions running high in the Middle East – which had been naturally sending the oil market up throughout the day – was biding his time knowing what he wanted to do. When the price got close to the historic hundred dollars mark he released a series of orders buying the few contracts he could until the price reached $100. It's questionable in this instance whether Arens wanted to start or exasperate the trend and encourage other participants to accelerate or extend the trend; he was rumoured to have lost approximately $600 on his trade once it had been closed but did get a lot of press coverage for his actions, which looks like the real reason for this trade.[7]

The US commodity futures trading commission ordered UBS to pay $15 million penalty for attempted manipulation in the precious metals futures market. The order found that from January 2008 through to at least 2 December 2013, UBS, by and through the acts of certain precious metals traders on the spot desk, traded in a manner to trigger customer stop loss orders. The alleged offences took place on precious metals futures contracts traded on the commodity exchange (COMEX), including gold and silver. The order found on occasions between December 2009 through 2 February 2012, one of the traders placed orders and executed trades to attempt to manipulate the price of precious metals futures contracts in order to trigger customer stop loss orders and obtain a profit on proprietary trading. This was a clear violation of the commodity exchange act and was self-reported by UBS, leading to a more lenient penalty for internal transparency. It's not clear whether the customers of UBS were given any compensation for the acts of abuse committed by those traders at UBS.[8]

10.6   Spoofing

Spoofing is arguably the largest component of MAR; it's certainly the one element that has had the most convictions around the world and the regulation that is under the most scrutiny by countries and regularity bodies, as well as exchanges and traders themselves. In a post-financial crisis world, the industry wants to enhance the integrity of the financial system and support open, transparent, and competitive markets, and this simply cannot be done if there are persistent market abusers trying to gain an edge by fooling other participants with their activity, in particular the disruptive trading practices which shall be explored.

One of the many descriptions of spoofing – and there are many due to the nature of translating the abuse – is as follows. The entering of orders which are withdrawn before execution, thus having the effect, or which are likely to have the effect, of giving a misleading impression that there is a demand for or supply of a financial instrument or a related spot commodity contract at that price.[9] Loosely put, placing orders with no intention of executing them to deceive market participants. There are many things to consider when trying to determine whether an order in the market is a spoof or not, and all centre around the market participant's intent:

- Was the order that was placed done so to entice other market participants to trade when they otherwise wouldn't?
- Was the order placed to affect a price rather than to change position?
- The order that was entered was done so with the intent to cancel or modify the order for execution or to avoid execution completely.

---

[7] Oil trader wins fame with $100-a-barrel trade, Brodie, Sophie, 4 January 2008: https://www.telegraph .co.uk/finance/newsbysector/energy/2781988/Oil-trader-wins-fame-with-100-a-barrel-trade.html.

[8] CFCT Orders UBS to Pay $15 million Penalty for Attempted Manipulation and Spoofing in the Precious Metals Futures Market, Holden, Dennis, 29 Jan 2018: https://www.cftc.gov/PressRoom/PressReleases/ pr7683-18.

[9] Local Compliance.

- The market participant is trying to disrupt the orderly conduct of trading, fair executions of transactions or create misleading market conditions.
- Was the intent to place user-defined strategy orders in a manner intended to deceive or unfairly disadvantage other market participants?[10]

Figure 10.5 shows an example of what I would consider to be a potential spoof order – the bid in column 2 for 3249 contracts at a price of 162.00 is significantly larger than the offer above for 213 contacts and the average volume of contracts on any of the bid quantity or offer quantity by a multiple of 10. To establish if the order is in fact a spoof order we will use the above questions as a guide when investigating

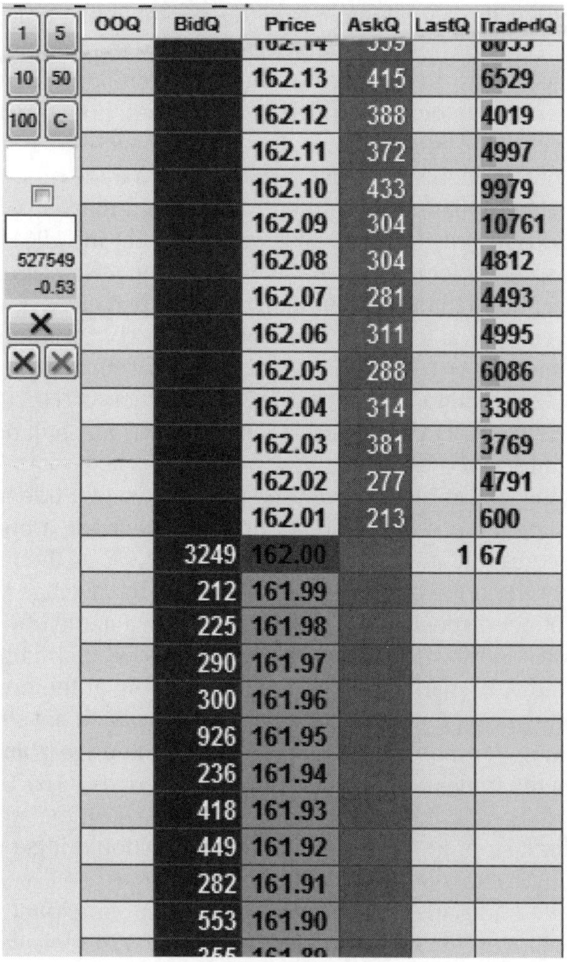

1 5	OOQ	BidQ	Price	AskQ	LastQ	TradedQ
			162.14	555		6055
10 50			162.13	415		6529
100 C			162.12	388		4019
			162.11	372		4997
☐			162.10	433		9979
			162.09	304		10761
527549			162.08	304		4812
-0.53			162.07	281		4493
✗			162.06	311		4995
✗ ✗			162.05	288		6086
			162.04	314		3308
			162.03	381		3769
			162.02	277		4791
			162.01	213		600
		3249	162.00		1	67
		212	161.99			
		225	161.98			
		290	161.97			
		300	161.96			
		926	161.95			
		236	161.94			
		418	161.93			
		449	161.92			
		282	161.91			
		553	161.90			
		355	161.89			

Figure 10.5   Spoof study example.

---

[10] FIA (Futures Industry Association) Guidelines, Market Conduct Fundamentals, https://training.fia.org/market-conduct-fundamentals.

whether it is genuine market activity or not. Before jumping to the conclusion that the order is market abuse, we need to consider the market participant's previous behaviour, including historic patterns of activity – have orders been placed and completed that are like the one highlighted on the bid at 162.00? We also need to consider order entry and cancellation activity in the market previously, and any other related markets or contracts, for instance does the market participant need to hedge his exposure by completing this order. Market conditions need to be judged in the impacted market where the order was placed and in any related market. Characteristics of the order need to be scrutinized, the size of the order relative to the market at time the order was placed, the size of the order relative to the position that the alleged abuser has in the market, the duration of order exposure (time order is left in the market) and the total number of orders the participant has in the market at that time.

There are examples of this type of order every day in multiple markets and it is part of a trader's job to ascertain whether these are genuine orders, and if they are real orders with genuine intent to be filled in the market, how the order can be used to benefit trade process. Alternatively, if it is an order with no genuine intent to be filled, it's important to not only consider that as part of a trade process but also to flag up with an internal compliance department, as part of a market participant's duty to report any suspicious activity to the local governing body, the UK FCA.

The potential spoof order in column 2 for 3249 contracts at a price of 162.00 is in the German 10-year bond future, the Bund. It could be perceived as a rogue order due to its relative size compared to those orders on both the bid column on prices below 162.00 (212 contracts at 161.99, 225 contracts at 161.98), and on the offer column on prices 162.01, 213 contracts and above 277 contracts at 162.02. The order was in fact genuine and was fully completed at the price, but we shall discuss its possible merits as a potential spoof order.

If we look at this bid at 162.00 from the perspective of a trader looking to trade the market, assuming the order is genuine, how do they trade around it? They could certainly be enticed to buy in front of the order at 162.01, as the perception is there is a huge buy order the price below which is 10 times the average bid volume or ask volume in the contract. Executing a trade is very much a game of risk versus reward; in this case we assume the risk is very low buying above such large order because, as a trader, you know all market participants are looking at the order thinking there is a very strong buy bias in that contract – is a market participant showing their hand and know something you don't, which will result in the price going up? So a trader decides to take on the trade, buying 10 contracts at a price of 162.01 and looking for a gain of 5 prices for profit. It is a short-term trade, based on the large bid at 162.00, the trader sets a limit stop on the large bid order, and should it get below 1000 contracts, the stop will be executed to limit the loss to 1 price.

Shortly after the trader makes the trade, the market participant working their bid order at 162.00 removes it from the market; instead of 3249 lots working on the bid there are now only 249 – the other 3000 contracts was a spoof order. The result of the order being pulled would shock the market into reacting based on the new order information; the traders that came to the same trading conclusion of buying a price above the big order, as the market was perceived to have a bid bias, would be rushing to sell the 249 lots left on the bid exit their long position for a loss. The instant result of that bid not being genuine is a quick loss for the short-term trader basing trades around the order size; for traders with long positions the perception may change of a market that is very bid to being more neutral, positions and strategies may need to be examined. The integrity of the market comes into question.

If the authorities were to convict this market participant, we shall call them Trader X, for a breach of market abuse regulations: this would be disruptive for trading practices – or spoofing. Using the guidelines previously mentioned, which are taken from the Futures Industry Association (FIA), we can say with some certainty that Trader X was trying to entice others to trade when they otherwise wouldn't, as the trader placed their trade solely based on the information that there was a strong bid of 10 times the average amount at 162.00. Was Trader X trying to affect a price rather than to change position? We would need to know the position prior to this order going into the market; in this instance, there was no position in the bond market so it's fair to say it was the price that was trying to be affected. The order was clearly entered with the intent to cancel or modify the order before execution, or to avoid execution already and disrupt the orderly conduct of trading, thus creating misleading market conditions which deceived or unfairly disadvantaged other market participants.

To be able to convict Trader X for what appears to be a clear example of spoofing, in the above context, regulators would investigate their previous behaviour in the market. Does Trader X regularly put in orders of that size and cancel them before they get completed, and if they do what is the next order or trade done once the order has been cancelled? In removing the order for 3000 contracts at 162.00, does the market then move lower to a point where Trader X is working a bid to buy the Bund at a better price before the market goes in their favour? Does Trader X place big orders, then when removing them take an opposing position, removing the bid at 162.00 then selling to go short to profit from changing market participants sentiment based on the large bid order. It is important to understand what Trader X is trying to gain from placing a spoof order in the Bund; it has the clear characteristics initially of a spoof purely due to its size in relation to the other orders in the market. As a trader you won't know everyone's position relative to every order placed in the market, not only in the market you are looking at but every other market that is related. In our scenario Trader X could quite easily be working a bid to buy an alternative government bond to gain the same market exposure, or they could have had their order completed in another market first, which led to the order being cancelled at 162.00. Or simply be short selling the market looking to take profit.

All the factors highlighted in our scenario with Trader X need to be considered by each local regulator when investigating disruptive trading practices in the financial markets by way of spoofing. Traders see orders that look deceptive every day; from their perspective there may be an emotional attachment to the order as it might be trying to send the market against their position. A trader is looking for a reason other than an incorrect trade decision to blame losses, so using a market manipulator can be an easy way out.

Should the orders in the market get filled, which they mostly do, then there is no doubt that the order is genuine and was intended to be executed; however, should the order be removed prior to being executed traders fully understand that market conditions change hour by hour, minute by minute, and even second by second, and that all market participants place genuine orders based on the trading conditions and parameters at that moment in time, which is subject to change based on market fluc-tuations in price and change in market rhetoric.

It would be a strange trading environment if every order that was placed on the market was final and never subject to change; as this will never be the case, all orders could be subject to scrutiny under MAR. As a trader you must keep the integrity of the marketplace, placing genuine orders that wish to be executed at the time of placing, which aren't seen to mislead other participants. Should market conditions change when removing your order, it won't have a large impact on market direction or percep-tion. Participants like Trader X who find their trading edge through misleading other market participants with their order activity have no place in a market and deserve to feel the full force of the authorities for breaching regulations – removing trading privileges, imposing hefty financial penalties, and potentially a prison sentence.

While a lot of attention is being given to the landmark case of the owner of New Jersey-based Panther energy trading, Michael Coscia, and the resulting conviction for spoofing in which a three-year prison sentence was handed down for market manipu-lation, there is another case that also stands out.

On 22 March 2017 an ex-DBS Vickers trader named Dennis Tey Thean Yang was sen-tenced to 16 weeks in prison for spoofing the securities market in the first case brought jointly by the monetary authority of Singapore and white-collar crime police. According to court papers, Tey sought to manipulate prices of contracts for difference (CFDs). After purchasing the CFDs he would make false orders in the underlying securities which he would then delete. Tey used three securities and two CFD accounts opened in the names of his parents and client to facilitate this market abuse, entering 465 orders through the securities account and 325 trades for the CFD accounts between 24 October 2012 to 8 January 2013 to make a total profit of $30,239.[11] Mr Tey would have thought he had genuinely found a trading edge as he was placing the position in one market and using orders in related markets to affect the price in his favour without taking the risk.

This was clear market abuse and the gains for Tey were in the tens of thousands as opposed to millions in the case of Michael Coscia, however the message is clear: if you try to gain your edge through market manipulation you risk going to jail.

The market abuse regulation that we have been looking into covers all European exchanges and creates a legal obligation to have trade surveillance by all parties as well as the responsibility to report any suspected wrongdoing. This differs from the US regime where there is no legal requirement to survey and report suspicious activity but exchanges in the US place an obligation on the trader to report abuse, and while there is no law you can still be prosecuted.

10.7 Layering

Very similar to the offence of spoofing, layering is the act of submitting multiple orders to trade away from the market price to influence the market direction in favour of the trader's position. Once the position has been executed in either the contract

---

[11] Ex-DBS Vickers trader Dennis Tey gets 16 weeks' Jail for spoofing Singapore stock market, Leong, Grace, 22 March 2017, https://www.straitstimes.com/business/companies-markets/ex-dbs-vickers-trader-dennis-tey-gets-16-weeks-jail-for-spoofing.

where the layering is taking place or a related market, all the orders are removed without being executed. The only real difference to spoofing is that layering is a *multiple* number of orders trying to reinforce a market's direction using the bid or ask volume depth.

Figure 10.6 shows a market window with the characteristics of layering, as was the case in Figure 10.5 with the instance of spoofing this wasn't market abuse but a genuine set of orders which were executed. For this scenario to be explained we will describe as if market abuse was taking place.

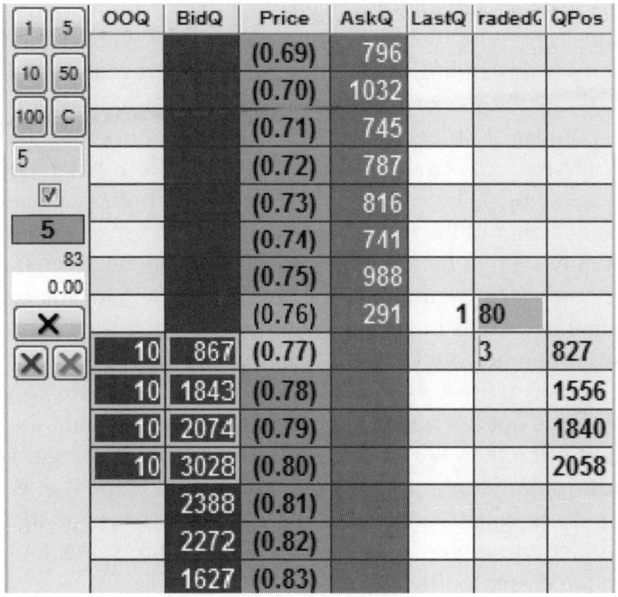

OOQ	BidQ	Price	AskQ	LastQ	radedC	QPos
		(0.69)	796			
		(0.70)	1032			
		(0.71)	745			
		(0.72)	787			
		(0.73)	816			
		(0.74)	741			
		(0.75)	988			
		(0.76)	291	1	80	
10	867	(0.77)			3	827
10	1843	(0.78)				1556
10	2074	(0.79)				1840
10	3028	(0.80)				2058
	2388	(0.81)				
	2272	(0.82)				
	1627	(0.83)				

(Left panel controls: 1, 5, 10, 50, 100, C, 5, [✓], 5, 83, 0.00, X, X X)

Figure 10.6   Layering example.

In Figure 10.6 the market is bid for 867 contracts at a price of 77 and offered at 76 for 291 contracts, the bid of 867 contracts is in line with the average volume on the depth of offer, if we take an average of the contracts at each price from 75–69 it will be a similar number of contracts to that on the bid at 77. What makes this stand out as possible layering are the prices on the bid in the BidQ column at 78 and below, the bid volume jumps up from a reasonable 867 contracts at the price of 78 to over double, 1843 contracts at a price of 79, and almost 4 times the amount at 80, 3028 contracts. A market participant would most certainly have the perception that this contract would have a bid bias based on the larger than average buy orders in the Bid column, in this example there are working orders to buy the market alongside the large bid orders.

As we are looking at this market order setup as a case of market abuse, we will question why the orders are in the market and what the perpetrator intends to achieve by having them in the market. The trader in question shall be Trader Z: they have placed these orders for one of two reasons, both of which to gain an unfair advantage over other market participants. In layering orders below the market price of 77, Trader Z has given the perception that there is a strong bid bias in that market enticing others to trade; traders would buy based on those orders in the market or would exit any short positions. Trader Z would hope the result of the layering will either push the market up in their favour, so they can exit a long position for profit. Alternatively, once the market has moved up they can execute sell orders to put on an initial position and then delete the bid orders to change market sentiment and catch out the other market participants.

Layering, as opposed to spoofing on its own, carries much more weight as a form of market manipulation as the use of multiple orders over multiple prices enhances the perception of market direction. Trader Z is placing defined strategy orders in a manner intended to deceive or unfairly disadvantage other market participants, enticing others to trade when they otherwise wouldn't, entering an order with intent to cancel before execution and create misleading market conditions. The example in Figure 10.6 was highlighted because of the size of orders on the bid relative to the market average order volume and the number of orders in the depth of the market on the bid side.

Most spoofing prosecutions that have led to convictions have regularly cited layering as well as spoofing as the cause of market abuse, both of which give an unfair advantage to the executer of the trades by deceiving other market participants. While spoofing is generally seen to be a market order that is uncharacteristically large relative to the other orders in the market, the market participant that places the order can always argue that there is intent for the order to be completed, as it is exposed to being filled should another market participant want to trade for that amount at that price. Trader Z has no market exposure or risk in placing their orders from the 78 bid and below, as it is not the best bid working at market; should the price trade out at 77 and the best price then be 78, Trader Z could move his large bid down further removing market risk but continuing the deception that the market is heavily bid. It's this lack of market risk which makes layering so tempting for a market abuser and at the same time difficult to regulate, as the market conditions inevitably change when market prices move closer to the layering orders.

10.8   Smoking

The final subcategory of spoofing in the market abuse regulations is another act which tries to disrupt the orderly conduct of trading and the fair execution of transactions, or the creation of misleading market conditions, and is known as smoking. This is the act of posting an order to trade, which then attracts other market participants employing traditional trading techniques to work orders either on the bid or the offer where the offending order is placed. The market abuser then rapidly reverses his order onto less generous terms, generally from bid to offer or offer to bid, hoping to execute profitability against the incoming flow or slow traders whose orders were behind theirs. This is also known as 'flipping the price'.

Figure 10.7 is an example of how a market is set up for a possible smoking offence. We can see in the BidQ column a bid price at 0.06 for 29,262 lots. I have the benefit of my trading software being able to tell me what different orders market participants are working at that price. Overlapping the TradedQ column we see a list of numbers that show the number of contracts each market participant is working on the bid. We can see the top the majority of the bid is made from one order for 29,191 contracts with six small orders completing the total quantity of 29,262 lots. The theory being for the offence of smoking that this market participant who has ownership of that large order of 29,191 contracts can quickly remove the bid, and whilst doing so reverse the order onto the offer side, completing the orders of those other participants left on the bid side and moving the market to look like it is more offered than bid.

Figure 10.8 shows what the market would be like after the abuse had taken place: a relatively small amount traded at the price 0.06 as we can see in the TradedQ column – 123 contracts, from where the market was heavily bid at 0.06 for 29,262 contracts, to now being offered for 29,955 contracts. At the end of the market window you can see the order breakdown. The bulk of the offer at 0.06 is comprised of one very large order of 29,887 contracts and two small orders 67 and 1; this is a large order based on the liquidity of the depth of market in this contract and it's a third of the size of the bid and half of that of the offer above at 0.07. In this instance, like in the other examples, we will assume that there is no wrongdoing but with such a large share of the total liquidity at that market participant's disposal, one could rightly ask questions on the reasons for moving the size of order so quickly from the bid side to the offer.

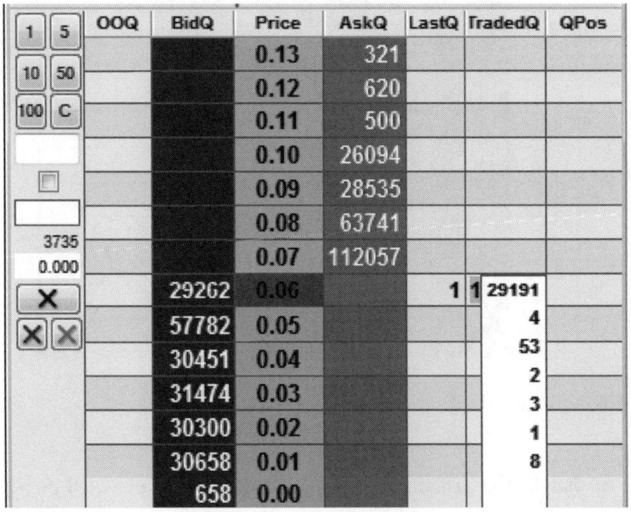

		OOQ	BidQ	Price	AskQ	LastQ	TradedQ	QPos
1	5			0.13	321			
10	50			0.12	620			
100	C			0.11	500			
				0.10	26094			
				0.09	28535			
				0.08	63741			
3735				0.07	112057			
0.000			29262	0.06		1	1	29191
X			57782	0.05				4
X	X		30451	0.04				53
			31474	0.03				2
			30300	0.02				3
			30658	0.01				1
			658	0.00				8

Figure 10.7   Smoking example 1.

The reason a market participant may look to commit this type of market abuse would primarily be to build a position in a certain direction once a trading strategy had been identified, should a trader believe the price of the market should be going lower they would want to build a short position. As in Figure 10.7, where we see a large bid at 0.06 for 29,262 contracts, the aim of the market abuser would be to entice others to join on that bid due to the large volume giving the perception that the market is strongly bid and could possibly be going higher. In smoking/flipping the bid to the offer, a trader would hope to catch all the slower reacting market participants who didn't remove their bids in time and have them completed by the large order which has taken the price from heavily bid to heavily offered; the executor of the smoking now has a short position in the market and a reason to keep the market heavily offered so they can profit from the short.

It is difficult to trade in a market that has continual smoking/flipping taking place, as it disrupts the orderly conduct of trading and creates misleading market conditions. If a short position which appears to be onside, as in Figure 10.8 when the offer is 29,955 contracts, it is reassuring that the trade is the right one and the market may be going down in the position's favour. However, if within an instant the position is turned offside and the market is heavily bid like in Figure 10.7, a market participant may join the bid to get out of the position for no loss or gain, only to have the market turned around again to heavily offered but with the position flattened by the smoker.

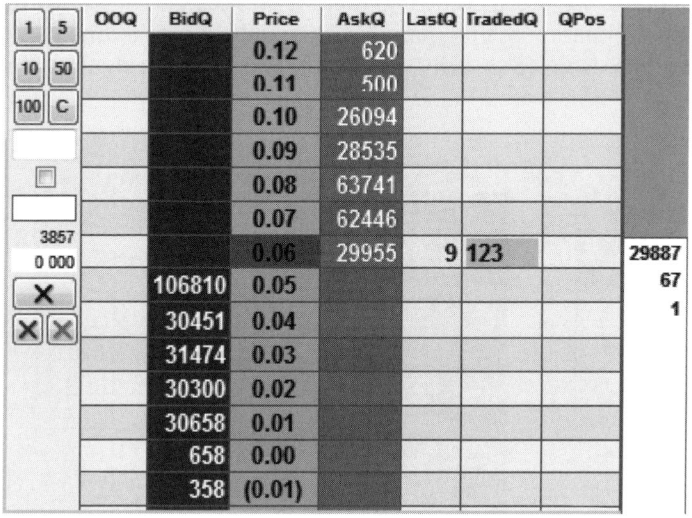

		OOQ	BidQ	Price	AskQ	LastQ	TradedQ	QPos	
1 · 5				0.12	620				
10 · 50				0.11	500				
100 · C				0.10	26094				
				0.09	28535				
☐				0.08	63741				
				0.07	62446				
3857 / 0 000				0.06	29955	9	123		29887
✕			106810	0.05					67
✕ ✕			30451	0.04					1
			31474	0.03					
			30300	0.02					
			30658	0.01					
			658	0.00					
			358	(0.01)					

Figure 10.8   Smoking example 2.

Following the frustration of being caught by the market smoker/flipper, the original position may want to be placed again by offering at market, adding to the volume at a price of 0.06 and assisting the market abuser by making the market look more offered. One can easily be caught several times in the smoking process, as it is often a technique that is used to affect price action through confusion. If a trader initially thought the market was sell, for example at 0.06, but the price flips from offer to bid and then bid to offer several times, there is going to be doubt created in the trader's mind as to where the market abuser will want to push the price next, resulting in an unwillingness to hold a position in the market.

As with all forms of spoofing, layering and smoking, the market participant placing the orders which could be presumed as market abuse will always have the argument that they are providing liquidity to the market and the orders are genuine and have a possibility of getting filled. It is down to the regulators and exchanges to decide whether these orders are to disrupt the orderly practice of trading.

10.9   Case Study: Paul Rotter a.k.a. 'The Flipper'

As a trader in pre-financial crisis fixed-income markets, one of the standout memories would have been the legend of The Flipper. If a market participant was trading the short-term interest rates of the eurozone and UK, these markets were known as the 'short end' due to their estimation of interest rates from three months to roughly three years into the future, i.e. of a short duration. Market participants also had to understand what the 'long end' was doing, the long end being government bonds with a duration of expiry 10 years and further into the future. For guidance in the European market, traders would look at the 10-year German Bund and the 10-year gilt, to give an idea how to price the UK short-term interest rate market. The movement on these 10-year bonds were far larger than the movements on the interest rates markets that we were trading, due to the length of duration of the debt. Essentially the market was trying to price the 10-year average of yield for that government debt obligation using all information out at that time for that particular jurisdiction. Most of the big moves in the Bund could be explained: updated macroeconomic information, a continuation of the trend or trend reversal, a political event or a bond auction. Some moves, however, were down to the work of The Flipper.

Like most lessons in trading, you have to learn for yourself, and I remember trying to base my trades in the short-term interest rate market based on movements in the Bund, placing a trade that would, for example, require the Bund to go up. The Bund would look heavily bid, I'd be patting myself on the back, as the market was going my way and my position was onside. Then, all of a sudden, from looking heavily bid the Bund price had been flipped, not just from bid to offer but combined with the layers of strong bids removed and then hit from bid to offer, moving the Bund down several prices and moving my once onside position to offside, forcing me to rethink my strategy. In my own trading world, on a small scale, I was falling foul of The Flipper.

Paul Rotter, with his not-so-flattering nickname, has been infamous in the world of electronic trading for many years, and happily used as a scapegoat for traders' losses when trading European short-term interest rates and government bonds. In the earlier stages of my trading career, when he was most active, he was blamed for pretty much everything in the markets, such was his presence in everyday trading – a true pantomime villain in the serious world of financial futures trading.

At his peak, Rotter was rumoured to be the largest volume trader of European government debt futures on the EUREX exchange, which included the 2-year bond called the SCHATZ, the 5-year bond called the BOBL, and the 10-year bond called the BUND. His trading strategy is called scalping – this is where a trader tries to make gains in the markets by trading the small incremental moves in price. It is very volume intense; a trader is looking to trade every price almost on the bid and the offer making the most of the markets liquidity.

Using the earlier example of a market with a potential spoof, Figure 10.9 illustrates how a scalper would be looking to work bids at the price of 162.00 all the way down to 161.90 and at the offer price of 162.02 all the way up to 162.13 with an order size dependent on their risk parameters. For this example, we will assume the scalper is working 10 contracts at each price. A scalper will be monitoring the order flow and price movements intensely and trying to work their position and orders in the most profitable way. If the bid trades at 162.00 and the position is long-10

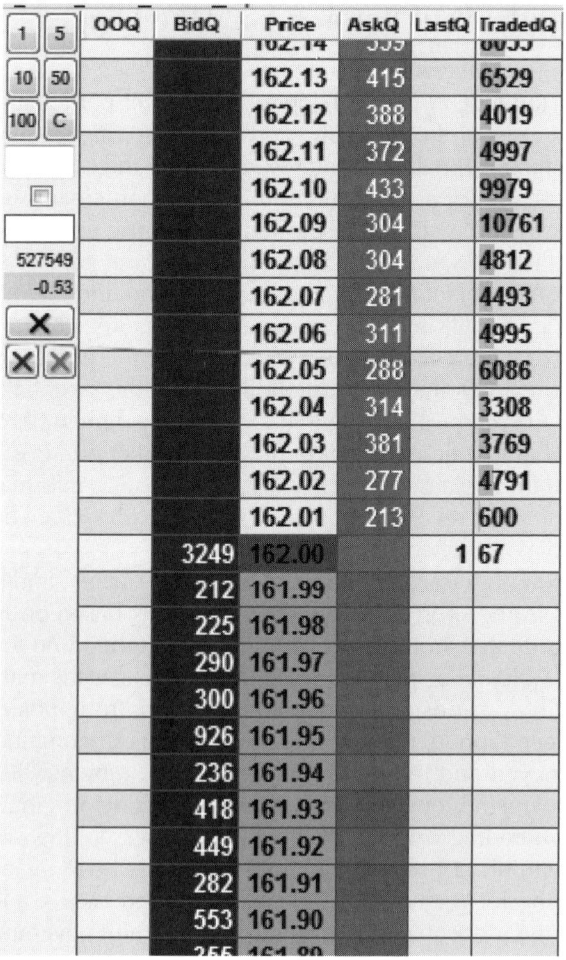

		OOQ	BidQ	Price	AskQ	LastQ	TradedQ
1	5			162.14	359		6053
10	50			162.13	415		6529
100	C			162.12	388		4019
				162.11	372		4997
	□			162.10	433		9979
				162.09	304		10761
527549				162.08	304		4812
-0.53				162.07	281		4493
✕				162.06	311		4995
✕	✕			162.05	288		6086
				162.04	314		3308
				162.03	381		3769
				162.02	277		4791
				162.01	213		600
			3249	162.00		1	67
			212	161.99			
			225	161.98			
			290	161.97			
			300	161.96			
			926	161.95			
			236	161.94			
			418	161.93			
			449	161.92			
			282	161.91			
			553	161.90			
			255	161.89			

Figure 10.9   The Bund.

contracts an offer will go in immediately at the price above 162.01 to take 1 price of profit; should the bid at 162.00 be sold into and look to go from bid to offer then the trader would look to take that position for no loss and possibly reverse the position to go short, knowing that they have an early bid working at 161.99 to exit the position for profit. This is a very brief description of scalping based on the market price of the Bund in Figure 10.9, but what is key to understand is that process must be repeated and orders moved or executed at every price. To provide some sort of context, in the left sidebar of Figure 10.9 you can see the number of traded lots of over half a million contracts. To effectively scalp the Bund contract, which most days trade between 500,000 and 2 million contracts, you need to be running the above scenario a huge amount of times throughout the day, based on trade volume at price and market movements. Rotter was doing this not only in the Bund but the related markets of the Schatz and BOBL.

According to an interview printed in 2015 in the magazine *Trader Daily*, 'Flipping Out' by Imogen Rose-Smith, Rotter began his career as an apprentice on the bond desk of a German bank in Frankfurt. Desperate to trade, he borrowed from a corporate credit card to buy options which didn't go too well, leading Rotter to take a job in Frankfurt office of Daiwa securities, where he worked his way up on the trading desk and within two months was trading the Bund in five lots. By the time he left the bank in 1996 to join the Dublin-based Midas trading house Rotter was already the biggest single trader in German debt futures on the DTB, Germany's precursor to the EUREX exchange. Rotter and his unique style of scalping and intense order management with the ability to adopt the flipper's position from one side of the book to the other gave him enough confidence to form Greenhouse Capital Management in 1998. Within three months the firm had made $6.5 million and was beginning to ruffle some feathers. A former managing director with Midas and the man who hired Rotter recalls, 'Paul sometimes played a controversial role, some traders didn't like it because it changed his position so quickly'. In 2001, Rotter formed Rotter Invest and eventually moved his operation to Zug, Switzerland, an affluent town that is home to its fair share of traders in a country known for its privacy and security in the financial world.[12]

The actions of Paul Rotter in the government debt market does leave a question mark over the legality of whether it was indeed a genuine trading strategy or an attempt to game other market participants using disruptive trading practices for his own profit. The article by Rose-Smith cites traders saying, 'You would see giant orders on one side of the market that would flip and go the other way', 'The flipper does so much volume in the Bund, the BOBL and the Schatz that he is able to influence the whole yield curve and catch people out', and 'The flipper *is* the market'.

As described in previous pages what is being alleged here is a clear case of layering, a version of spoofing where a participant submits multiple large orders to trade away from the market price to influence the market direction in favour of the trader's positions. The price of the government debt would be influenced by large orders on the bid side driving the price and possible position higher, when the position is exited and possibly reversed, Rotter could then continue this order process driving the price and position lower. Combined with layering the market, there would be an element of smoking involved, posting orders to trade to attract other market participants that are then rapidly reversed onto less generous terms catching out the incoming flow of orders to trade against.

We saw in Figure 10.6, the example that we used for layering, that should a single market participant be working the majority of the contracts above the average amount on the bid or offer – in this case approximately 850 at prices 78 to 83 – they could be doing so to give other market participants the impression the market was going bid, enticing buy orders from traders using a strong bid volume as a reason to trade. All the while, the owner of those above-average bids is actually working sell orders on the offer which are completed by those in the belief the market is going up. Once the sell orders have been completed the bids from the price of 78 down to 83 could be removed from

---

[12] Flipping Out, Rose-Smith, Imogen (April 2015) *Trader monthly*: https://largecaplinks.files.wordpress .com/2015/04/paul-rotter-trader-monthly.pdf.

the market, changing the perception of the market being very bid. In the case of The Flipper, he would then perhaps hit the bid at 77 sending that price offered and putting the same volume of contracts that were working on the bid from 78 to 83 on the offer side at prices 76 to 69, reversing market sentiment from strongly bid to strongly offered.

Rotter admits to handling large volumes on both sides of the order book but insists he was not trading inappropriately. His trading style can be described as aggressive scalping; this when done on a massive scale could arguably benefit the market. Rotter goes on to say in the article, 'I am a kind of market maker who provides liquidity with many orders in different markets, when I'm active I am permanently involved in market transactions through fields of both sides and different contracts.' Rotter's defence being that he never pulls orders quickly but rather 'leaves an order working for a couple of minutes.'

This is the grey area that regulators must argue to convict a market abuser: trying to decipher whether orders are intended to be completed or being used to disrupt trading practices. Whilst an order is in the market it is there to be traded with, and the market participant is opening themselves up to risk of being filled on the order by placing the order anywhere on the bid or offer. It can always be argued that the trader who placed the order at that point in time wanted the contracts to be completed, and if the order wasn't completed, it was up to the participant to move the order due to the nature of a trader's need to be dynamic in their strategy, both with orders and market view. A market is never static for long, so how can the orders be for those trading it?

The existence of Paul Rotter in the trading world is so well documented and his trading techniques so controversial that one would have thought regulators would have had to scrutinize his trading techniques in the European debt market on the EUREX exchange, concluding that he is, and was, placing orders in the Bund, BOBL and Schatz with the full intention to execute these orders. The argument for Rotter being a market abuser and at risk of prosecution by the European securities and markets authority can be viewed as follows:

- The act of placing several bids or offers of larger quantities than the market average and moving them up or down with the market to influence the price.
- Enticing others to trade when they otherwise wouldn't.
- Having the intention to cancel or modify the orders before execution, which creates misleading market conditions.
- Placing user-defined strategies in a manner intended to deceive or unfairly disadvantage other participants.

All are breaches of the rules set out in the market abuse regulations and the Dodd–Frank act in the US and should lead to conviction and penalties.

The case for The Flipper's innocence is that only he knew his overall position in all the related European debt markets, what orders he needed at any one time, and which orders needed to be quickly removed to adjust the position to mitigate risk and remain profitable. Due to the size of the positions and orders, I doubt they could be perceived as market abuse, as there would be no other barometer to compare against; after all, he was the biggest single volume market participant on the EUREX exchange claiming to trade up to 180,000 contracts per day on the BUND, roughly 10% of market share. Rotter was providing liquidity by showing many contracts in a very liquid market widely traded by the biggest banks and hedge funds around the world who, if they wanted to, could buy or sell into the government debt market in large size with minimal price impact. Should the large orders get completed, Rotter's strategy was to get out of those positions for profit, sometimes take a loss, or hedge that position in a related market. The orders were always placed with the intent to be completed; the strategy that came after the removal was purely based on position.

Paul Rotter and his aggressive scalping trading style led to an infamous reputation in the trading world and a lot of hard feelings for those who will always continue to question The Flipper and his strategy. Possibly also after reading this chapter you may question the strategy. One thing is for certain, with earnings rumoured to be at $7 million a month in his prime, the strategy worked very well for Rotter, and provided a very profitable edge.

10.10   The Innocent and the Guilty

Paul Rotter, as it stands, is one of the most successful traders to trade the European Debt market on EUREX, executing a hard-to-match strategy in unrivalled quantity and risk for many years. On the other end of the spectrum you have Michael Coscia, the first trader to be jailed for the act of spoofing. This case was a landmark victory for regulators and opened the gate for further prosecutions for market abuse, sending a signal to market participants that market abuse will no longer be tolerated. We will look at an example of corcias account of spoofing taken from the court report and see how it differs to that of Rotter.

The testimony presented at trial explained that the relevant conduct began in August 2011, lasted about 10 weeks, and followed a very particular pattern. When he wanted to purchase, Coscia would begin by placing a small order, requesting to trade at a price below the current market price. He then would place large volume orders, known as quote orders, on the other side of the market. A small order could be as small as 5 futures contracts, whereas a large order would represent as many as 50 or more futures contracts. The large orders were generally placed in increments that quickly approach the price of the small orders.

Coscia's specific trading activity in copper futures helps to clarify this dynamic. During one round of trading, he placed a small sell order at a price of 32755, which was, at that time, higher than the current market price. Large orders where then placed on the opposite side of the market (the buy side) at steadily growing prices, which started at 32740, then increased to 32745, and increased again to 32750. These buy orders created the illusion of market movement, swelling the perceived value of any given futures contract (by fostering the illusion of demand) and allowing Coscia to sell his current contract at the desired price of 32755 – a price equilibrium that he created.

Having sold the five contracts for 32755, Coscia now needed to buy the contracts at a lower price in order to make a profit. Accordingly, he first placed an order to buy 5 copper futures contracts for 32750, which was below the price that he had just created. Second, he placed large volume orders on the opposite side of the market (the sell side), which totalled 184 contracts. These contracts were priced at 32770, and then 32765, which created downward momentum on the price of copper futures by fostering the appearance of abundant supply at increment the decreasing prices. The desired evaluation of the contract was almost immediately achieved, allowing Coscia to buy his small orders at the artificially deflated price of 32750. The large orders were then immediately cancelled. The whole process outlined above took place in approximately two-thirds of a second, and was repeated tens of thousands of times, resulting in over 450,000 large orders, and earning Coscia $1.4 million. All told, the trial evidence suggested that this process allowed Coscia to buy low and sell high in a market artificially distorted by his actions.

Coscia was using two programs to run his trading strategy which were introduced as evidence in court regarding his intent to cancel the large orders prior to their execution. The programs are called 'flash trader' designed by Jeremiah Park who testified that Coscia asked that the programs act like a decoy, which would be used to pump the market. Park interpreted this direction as a desire to get a reaction from the other algorithms. In particular, he noted that the large volume orders were designed specifically to avoid being filled and accordingly would be cancelled in three particular circumstances: (i) Based on the passage of time (usually merely seconds); (ii) The partial filling of the large orders; or (iii) Complete filling of the small orders.

John Redmond, a director of compliance for Intercontinental exchange, Inc. (ICE) testified that Coscia would place a small buy or sell order in the market, and then immediately after that, he would place a series of much larger opposite orders in the market, progressively improving price levels towards the previous order that he placed. That small initial order would trade, and then the large order would have been cancelled and be replaced by a small order, and the large orders in the opposite direction will have previously taken place. Redmond further testified that Coscia placed 24,814 large orders between August and October 2011, although he only traded on 0.5% of those orders. During the same period, he placed 6782 small orders on the Intercontinental exchange, and approximately 52% of those orders were filled, meaning that the small orders were a hundred times more likely to be filled than the large volume orders. Mr Redmond made clear that this was highly unusual, Coscia's order to fill ratio (i.e. the average size of the order he showed to the market divided by the average size of the orders filled) was approximately 1600% whereas other traders generally presented ratios of between 91% and 264%.[13]

There is a clear case of market abuse by Michael Coscia, as algorithms were programmed and used to find an edge in the copper market (Coscia implemented his scheme over multiple markets) by enticing others to trade when they otherwise wouldn't, using orders to affect price rather than change position, entering orders with the intent to cancel before execution, and disrupting the orderly conduct of trading. This differs from the approach taken by Paul Rotter, who manually enters all those orders himself and looks to change position regularly based on orders completed over multiple related markets. Coscia asserts that the statute of spoofing laid out by the Dodd–Frank act and defined in section 4C of the Commodity Exchange Act is vague and his provision is not interpreted by the CFCT rule, only non-binding

---

[13] United States of America v. Michael Coscia, case number 16 – 3017 decided: August 7, 2017: https://caselaw.findlaw.com/us-7th-circuit/1869999.html.

guidance issued in 2013. The guidance laid out by the CFCT provides several examples of spoofing activity and states that the commission intends to distinguish between legitimate trading and spoofing by evaluating the facts and circumstances of each particular case, including a person's trading practices and patterns. Coscia argued that the guidance does not provide the clarity participants in the commodity market need.

The fact, however, quite clearly shows that the non-spoof orders that Coscia's algorithmic trading program entered into the market were 100 times more likely to be completed, and the larger orders were never intended to be matched. One can only assume the same metric has been applied to the market activity of The Flipper during his period as the largest single trader on the EUREX market, with the result of order to fill ratio being in line with the market average between 91% and 264%, as highlighted by the prosecution in the US v. Michael Coscia case.

10.11   What Are Exchanges Doing to Prevent Market Abuse?

The two largest exchanges, CME Group and ICE, are bound by the laws laid out in the US Dodd–Frank Act and the Market Abuse Regulation in Europe. They have a duty to ensure orderly trading practices on their exchanges by constantly monitoring activity and holding violators accountable for their actions.

10.11.1   CME Group

CME have broken their market regulation department into six teams, Market surveillance, Investigations, Data Investigations, Enforcement, Strategic and systems, and Regulatory Outreach.

The Market surveillance team is responsible for detecting and preventing market manipulation by monitoring the price relationship between underlying physical and future market prices and reviewing positions held by participants to ensure fair and orderly trading of exchange contracts.

Investigations are responsible for detecting and investigating trade practice violations, such as wash trades, non-competitive trades, money passes and suspected acts of spoofing though data analysis, reviewing documentary evidence, and, where necessary, interviewing suspected market abusers.

Data investigations reveals anomalies in trade records sent from clearer's trade records that help reconstruct trades, and detect and prevent market abuses.

Enforcement try and resolve any matter through the CME disciplinary process which always looks for a settlement between parties involved in market abuse. Should a settlement not be reached, then the case will be taken to the Probable Cause Committee for the issuance of charges, and they will prosecute the charges issued against the alleged violator before the business conduct committee.

The strategic and systems team develop and manage the proprietary systems that support the market regulation team and deliver internal training on market regulation within CME.

Finally, the Regulatory Outreach team provides market participants with education needs to prevent rule violations and meet compliance needs. Each unit works closely together to make sure all exchanges under the CME banner have their integrity protected.[14]

10.11.2   ICE

ICE works with regulators and policymakers around the world to ensure supervision, compliance, and reliable operation of markets. As a catalyst in the development of transparent, global markets, ICE works proactively to maintain the confidence of participants and the integrity of markets.

ICE Futures Europe is a London-based Recognized Investment Exchange, supervised by the UK Financial Conduct Authority (FCA). US-linked contracts, including WTI crude oil, are subject to further oversight by the Commodity Futures Trading Commission (CFTC). ICE Futures Europe Market Supervision is responsible for the monitoring and regulation of all trading activity for ICE's European futures markets. Operating around-the-clock, the team provides both front-line trading and back office support and generates daily settlement prices.[15]

Major exchanges take instances of abuse very seriously, after the financial crisis fingers were pointed not just at Investment banks that were making outrageous gambles in the subprime debt market, but all those involved at any point in financial transactions were to be held accountable for the integrity of the market. If exchanges are not policing the participants in their marketplace then they are as much to blame for instances of market abuse as those committing the violation.

10.12   What Are Trading Companies Doing to Prevent Abuse?

The company I have worked with for the past 13 years, is the largest privately owned financial futures trading company in Europe with over 400 traders working over 13 locations worldwide. The company has been focusing on training and educating all employees on Exchange Rules and Regulations for many years. This has been accomplished through both the training programme junior traders receive during their initial training with office managers, as well as through a semi-annual review and signoff of the bespoke Internal Guide to Exchange Rules and Regulations. The semi-annual review is a compulsory online test on market and exchange regulations taken by all market participants – without a 100% pass mark the individual isn't allowed to continue to trade on the live market.

As a company, it has been important to be proactive in the area of market compliance, not only through their training and education programmes, but additionally with investment in compliance monitoring systems which monitor all trading activity by in-house traders. This bespoke tool allows the internal compliance department to identify any activity which could be viewed as potential market manipulation and allows discussions to be had with trades before activity is flagged with exchanges and authorities. This has been a very successful addition to the compliance department. A trader was highlighted internally with suspected spoofing activity and warned that the

---

[14] https://www.cmegroup.com/market-regulation/market-surveillance.html.
[15] https://www.theice.com/futures-europe/regulation.

style of trading could be perceived as market abuse even if it was not the intention; the trader was unaware he was in a breach of market abuse regulation and changed his strategy going forward.

It has been vital to the companies continued growth and close working relationship with the world's leading exchanges that not only current rules are adhered to but preparation is made in advance of a change or adjustment of those rules. With the responsibility put on the individual to make sure they are complying with market regulations, by providing a condensed document regarding acceptable market behaviours traders can trade with the confidence that their activity complies with generally accepted market behaviours.

10.13   Will There Be an End to Market Abuse?

The majority of participants want the market to be run as efficiently and transparently as possible, so trading can be undertaken without anyone looking to abuse your position or orders. As we have seen in the case studies in this chapter, there are those market participants that wish to use instances of market abuse as their edge, from fixing prices as in the LIBOR case, to sending out spoof orders to gain advantageous fills in the gold market. These market abusers have one thing in common, they want to trade risk free.

As traders we take on risk every time we place a trade. It is hard to say a trade is risk free, as the very nature of the financial markets carries the possibility of a piece of information coming out at any time which changes the very dynamic of the market where the position is held. A central banker that changes their mind on where the economy is headed, a president placing tariffs on an agricultural market, natural disasters affecting commodity supply – the list is endless. Those who want to circumnavigate that risk will inevitably look to cheat the market somehow, leading to a breach of MAR.

The case study of Paul Rotter highlights the possible limitations of prosecutions for spoofing and the ambiguity of the description of the offence. Rotter will always argue – as Coscia did – that every order he placed in the European debt market was there to be traded with and how the market perceived those orders was not his problem. As rumoured to be the largest volume participant trading on the exchange it would be very bad for business should Rotter be prosecuted for market abuse, causing a loss of fees charged for trading on the exchange – not that this would be the reason for his non-conviction.

When there are financial rewards at stake and many market participants to police, there will always be those who look to gain an edge through market abuse. It will be up to the exchanges, clearers, regulators, and other market participants to find them, and prosecutors to find a clear way to define the abuse and make sure the sentence outweighs any gains, for market abuse to be eradicated.

Part III

Who Are These Scoundrels?

Chapter 11

Misconduct in Banking: Governance and the Board of Directors

Duc Duy Nguyen
King's College London

Jens Hagendorff
University of Edinburgh

Arman Eshraghi
Cardiff University

11.1 Introduction

The reputation of banks for professional and ethical conduct has come under pressure. Over recent years, regulators have taken out a record number of enforcement actions against banks that require banks to take corrective measures against identified cases of misconduct. For example, JPMorgan faced several recent enforcement actions related to credit card fraud, money laundering, and internal accounting controls.[1] Likewise, Wells Fargo received a high-profile enforcement action in 2018 over a misconduct case that involved the opening of millions of bank and credit card accounts without the consent of its customers. Box 1 provides some detail on this case. In this and other cases, regulators view a lack of effective monitoring of senior management by the board as one of the causes of misconduct.

Illustrative Example: The Wells Fargo Account Fraud Case

September 2016: Press reports indicate that Wells Fargo (WFC) charged consumers unauthorized fees and opened up to 3.5 million retail customer accounts without their clients' consent between 2011 and 2015. While initial reports blame individual WFC branch workers, the focus later shifted to senior management pressuring branch staff to open as many accounts as possible.

29 September 2016: John Stumpf, then CEO of WFC, testifies in front of the House Finance Committee. In the hearing, Congressman Randy Neugebauer raises concerns over whether WFC's board was sufficiently objective when monitoring senior executives. It was revealed that, although Mr Jumpf had been aware of problems related to consumer accounts in 2013, the board was not informed until two years later. This allegedly highlighted an overly comfortable relationship between the board and the senior management at WFC.

2 February 2018: Regulators issue a formal cease-and-desist order against WFC. Well Fargo's stock plummeted nearly 10% (the equivalent of $2.5 billion and significantly greater than the $1 billion fine levied by regulators).

- In the enforcement docket, the OCC (WFC's main regulator) emphasizes the need to improve oversight of WFC's senior executives: *'The Board shall submit a written plan to further enhance the Board's effectiveness in carrying out its oversight and governance of WFC, [. . .] including holding senior management accountable for implementing and maintaining the Firm's strategy in accordance with Board direction.'*
- On the same date, the Board of Governors of the Federal Reserve System sends a formal letter to WFC's board of directors, stating that *'WFC's board's performance of this oversight role did not meet our*

---

[1] 'OCC to hit JPMorgan Chase With Enforcement Actions', Dow Jones, 14 January 2013.

supervisory expectations.' The letter also emphasizes the need to improve communications between the board and senior executives: *'The board should have received more detailed and concrete plans from senior management on such a critical issue.'*

20 April 2018: WFC agrees to pay $500 million in penalties to each the OCC and the Consumer Financial Protection Bureau (CFPB). More importantly, the bank also submitted to an unprecedented order that gives the OCC the right to remove WFC's senior executives or board members at the discretion of the OCC.

In some ways, the recent surge in bank misconduct cases is surprising. By most accounts, oversight and monitoring of CEO decision-making has improved markedly in recent years. Data from RiskMetrics show that eight out of ten US bank board members were classified as independent in 2012, up from around half in 2000. With increasing levels of independence, one would expect bank boards to be more effective in preventing misconduct. However, far from a declining trend, the number of yearly enforcement actions has increased from 5 to 28 between 2010 and 2012. The apparent contradiction between progressively more independent bank boards on the one hand and an increasing number of regulatory enforcement actions against banks on the other hand is illustrated by Figure 11.1.

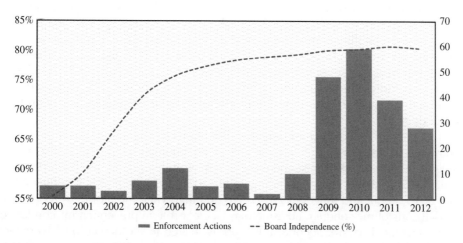

Figure 11.1   The percentage of directors classified as independent on US banks and the number of enforcement actions received by US banks.
Source: Authors' calculations based on data from RiskMetrics and SNL Financial.

One explanation for the rise in bank misconduct cases is that true board independence is difficult to achieve and not accurately reflected in established measures of board independence (e.g. see Coles et al. 2014; Lee et al. 2014). Established matters of board independence, that result from the rules of public exchanges on which firms list their stocks, view a director as independent if she or he is not a (former) employee, is not related to a (former) employee, and does not have other financial dealings with the firm.

However, this type of board independence can be undermined if CEOs exert intangible influence over independent directors. One way in which a CEO could yield intangible influence is by capturing the board through director appointments (Khanna et al. 2015). Since the CEO is typically involved in the process of recommending directors to the board, directors appointed during the tenure of the current CEO have an incentive to return the favour (Coles et al. 2014; Khanna et al. 2015). Under these circumstances, independent directors may reciprocate the CEO's requests and agree to side with the CEO to support, engage in, or conceal wrongdoing. Therefore, only directors appointed before the current CEO's tenure are free from this type of intangible influence and are therefore capable of objectively monitoring the CEO. In this chapter, we propose a new measure of the quality of board monitoring as the fraction of directors who are appointed before the current CEO takes office.

To identify cases of bank misconduct, we employ a large data set of regulatory enforcement actions issued by the three US supervisory bodies – the Federal Reserve Board (FRB), the Federal Deposit Insurance Corporation (FDIC), and the Office of the Comptroller of the Currency (OCC) – against banks that engage in unsafe, unsound and illegal banking practices which violate laws. We find that banks are less likely to engage in misconduct as the fraction of directors who have been appointed before the CEO increases.

To illustrate this point, banks where all directors have been appointed before the CEO takes office have a 27% lower probability of committing misconduct and a 35% higher probability of detection (conditional upon misconduct having occurred) than a bank where all directors have been appointed under the current CEO. This finding is robust to a set of variables that control for bank, board, and CEO characteristics, including the proportion of independent directors on boards. Importantly, traditional measures of board monitoring have little or no power to explain bank misconduct.

This chapter makes two important contributions to ongoing discussions. First, it contributes to debates on the determinants and economics of corporate misconduct. Previous work has linked misconduct to a lack of monitoring by the board (Khanna et al. 2015), outside investors (Wang et al. 2010) or various other parties (Dyck et al. 2010; Kedia and Rajgopal 2011). We find that while monitoring is required to deter all sorts of misconduct, advising plays a clear role in preventing misconduct of a more technical nature. Second, this work is related to the debate on governance and risk-taking in the banking industry (Ellul and Yerramilli 2013; Minton et al. 2014). Relative to other bank risk measures studied in the literature, enforcement actions provide a suitable identification of the effectiveness of internal governance. This is because enforcement actions provide an unambiguous external indicator of undesirable conduct in the industry.

11.2   Literature Review

There is a growing body of literature on the drivers of and the impediments to professional misconduct. While studying misconduct cases in detail may require significant contextual knowledge about the particular profession or discipline in question, one can draw some general lessons from existing research. For example, studies have linked professional misconduct to misconduct in earlier life, such as cheating at school and college (Simkin and McLeod 2010; Sims 1993). Another important question is concerned with the impediments to the detection of misconduct. In other words, why do whistleblowers come forward relatively rarely? Biaggio et al. (1998) argue this is mainly due to three obstacles: (i) reluctance to take action against colleagues and institutions where there are ties of loyalty, (ii) avoiding the personal costs of taking action, and (iii) insufficient understanding about the misconduct in question.

The focus of this chapter is on the banking profession. Misconduct cases are costly to bank investors with the fines imposed often outweighed by substantial reputational losses for offending banks. There are also concerns that repeated instances of misconduct erode public confidence in the safety and soundness of the banking sector as a whole. What banks can do to prevent misconduct is therefore an important question. Arguably, a bank's board of directors, in its capacity to monitor and advise the CEO (Adams and Ferreira 2007; Fama and Jensen 1983), should play a key role in the implementation and oversight of controls to mitigate the risk of misconduct.

Bank boards that are more independent in the sense that they are not psychologically captured by the CEO should be more willing to monitor the CEO than less independent boards. This type of board independence is therefore likely to prevent misconduct. This is grounded in social influence theory, which posits that individuals rely on principles of reciprocity, a nearly universal code of moral conduct, when making decisions (Gouldner 1960). Theory suggests that most people exhibit a psychological aversion to over-benefiting or under-benefiting from social relationships (Fehr and Schmidt 1999).

As the CEO is typically involved in appointing and recommending directors to the board, directors appointed by the CEO tend to feel indebted to her and thus have a natural tendency to return the favour (Coles et al. 2014; Khanna et al. 2015). Consequently, these directors are averse to monitoring the CEO, which creates an environment conducive to misconduct, makes detection of misconduct difficult, and reduces a CEO's expected costs of committing misconduct. Therefore, one can expect that directors appointed before the current CEO are psychologically independent and in a position to objectively monitor the CEO in a way that prevents wrongdoing. As a result, we measure a board's *Monitoring Quality* using the fraction of the board appointed before the current CEO.

The second plausible expectation relates board advising to bank misconduct. While early studies suggest that boards monitor and give advice to the CEO (e.g. Mace 1971), the focus of much subsequent study has been on the monitoring role of the board. Coles et al. (2012), Field et al. (2013), and Dass et al. (2014) highlight the role of board advice for firms. Therefore, better board advice should prevent corporate misconduct. For instance, some misconduct cases may occur because the CEO is unaware of the illegality of a certain activity (Khanna et al. 2015). In banks, some CEOs may lack the technical expertise to successfully oversee regulatory provisioning and reserve requirements – and breaches of either could result in regulatory enforcement actions. Therefore, a board with a higher capability to give advice to the CEO will facilitate more informed decision-making and thus lower the instances of misconduct.

In this context, director connections can be used as an indicator of board advising. Fama and Jensen (1983) argue that connections are a signal of director quality. In a competitive labour market, only high-quality directors receive additional board seats. In addition, better-connected directors are likely to have had experience with a variety of issues that firms face, and they can also lever their network to access better information (e.g. Coles et al. 2012; Field et al. 2013). To this end, a board's *Advising Quality* can be measured using the total number of directors to whom board members on the board are collectively connected, scaled by board size.

11.3   Research Design

11.3.1   Data

We gather data on regulatory enforcement actions issued by the three main US banking supervisory authorities (FDIC, FRB, and OCC) for the period 2000–2013 from SNL Financial.[2] Our sample encompasses all severe enforcement actions, including (i) formal agreements, (ii) cease and desist orders, and (ii) prompt corrective actions.

Formal (written) agreements are agreements between the bank and the regulator that set out details on how to correct conditions that provide the basis for the agreement. *Cease and desist orders* prohibit the bank from engaging in certain banking activities. They also require the bank to take corrective actions to improve on areas that provide the basis for the order. *Prompt corrective actions* are imposed on undercapitalized banks. They require the bank to restore adequate levels of capital and demand submission of a capital restoration plan within a predetermined period.

Next, we obtain bank accounting data from the FR Y–9C reports for the period of 1999 to 2012. We then merge FR Y–9C report data to market data obtained from Center for Research in Securities Price (CRSP), corporate governance data from BoardEx,[3] and enforcement actions data from SNL Financial. If there are multiple enforcement actions related to a single case of misconduct, we group them together so that only one case is identified. Our final sample contains 4,072 bank-year observations of 533 unique banks and 244 enforcement actions.

---

[2] Enforcement is a key tool that regulators use to ensure that banks maintain safe and sound practices (Delis and Staikouras 2011). Typically, regulators conduct on-site examinations to ensure that bank operations are consistent with sound banking practices. The regulator will issue an enforcement action when there is *substantial* evidence of misconduct. Therefore, one advantage of using regulatory enforcement actions to identify banks that engage in misconduct is that there is a low chance of misidentifying banks engaged in misconduct.

[3] BoardEx provides biographic data of more than 60,000 unique directors serving at over 70,000 private, public and not-for-profit companies.

Table 11.1   Time distribution of banks receiving enforcement actions.
This table reports the number of regulatory enforcement actions in our sample over the period 2000–2013. We also display the number of enforcement actions in our sample as a percentage of all enforcement actions issued against listed US banks. We also report the total assets of banks receiving enforcement actions in our sample as a percentage of the total assets of all listed US banks that receive enforcement actions.

Year	# Enforcement Actions in our sample	% Enforcement Actions in our sample	% Total assets of banks in our sample that receive Enforcement Actions
2000	5	55.56%	98.48%
2001	5	41.67%	84.34%
2002	3	37.50%	65.24%
2003	7	70.00%	96.61%
2004	12	80.00%	99.01%
2005	5	50.00%	92.77%
2006	6	66.67%	99.24%
2007	2	50.00%	99.67%
2008	10	62.50%	98.62%
2009	48	82.76%	93.49%
2010	59	88.06%	95.18%
2011	39	90.70%	99.60%
2012	28	90.32%	99.85%
2013	15	83.33%	99.82%
TOTAL	**244**	**78.71%**	**94.42%**

Table 11.1 provides descriptive statistics on the enforcement action sample. It shows that enforcement actions were taken against banks in every year with a surge following the 2007 global financial crisis. The table also shows that our sample is comprehensive. That is, our sample contains nearly 80% of all enforcement actions issued against the listed US banks during our sampling period.

11.3.2   Empirical Design

Empirical research on corporate misconduct faces an inherent challenge, namely that misconduct is not observed until it has been detected. This means the outcome we observe is the product of two processes: the commission of misconduct and the detection of misconduct. As long as detection is not perfect, we do not observe every instance of misconduct that has been committed. To address this partial observability problem, we follow Wang (2013) and Wang et al. (2010) and use the bivariate probit model.

The theoretical foundation of this model is drawn from Becker's (1968) economic approach to crime. The model implies that an individual's probability of committing fraud increases with the expected payoffs and decreases with its expected cost (from getting detected and penalized). Thus, the probability committing misconduct is determined by two sets of variables. The first set is derived from the expected benefit of committing fraud. The second set of variables is related to the expected cost of committing fraud, which essentially depends on the probability of detection.

In addition, there are factors that are related to both the probability to commit misconduct and to detect misconduct, for example, a board of directors that is not willing to monitor the CEO, and therefore should be included in both equations. However, there are factors that affect the likelihood that misconduct is detected but not a bank's incentives to commit wrongdoing. Likewise, there are factors that incentivize misconduct but do not affect the likelihood that misconduct is detected. The bivariate probit model relies on this intuition to separate fraud detection from commission processes.

The bivariate model can be estimated using the maximum likelihood method. According to Poirier (1980), an important feature of this approach is that $X_{M,it}$ and $X_{D,it}$ do not contain the same set of variables such that there is at least one vector that has one or more variables absent in the other vector (see also Wang 2013; Wang et al. 2010).

11.3.3 Variables

Monitoring Quality. We capture board monitoring quality using the number of board members appointed before the current CEO takes office. We refer to such members as 'non-captured' board members.[4] We define the variable as:

$$Monitoring\,Quality = \frac{\#\,non-captured\,board\,members}{Board\,size - 1}$$

The denominator is the total number of directors sitting on the board less the CEO as she always sits on the board in our sample. This variable ranges from 0 to 1, with higher values indicating a board that is not captured by the CEO and thus is more willing to independently monitor the CEO. The average *Monitoring Quality* in our sample is 0.54.

Advising Quality. We use the number of directors to whom existing board members of a given bank are connected to proxy for the ability of the board to advise the CEO. Following Coles et al. (2012), we define the variable as:

$$Advising\ Quality = \frac{\#\,directors\ to\ whom\ board\ members\ are\ connected}{Board\ size}$$

For each board member of a given bank, we count the number of directors in other firms that this member is connected to by serving as co-directors. We then sum across all board members of this bank and then divide this sum by the size of the

---

[4] To construct this variable, we compare the start of the employment date of the board member and date the CEO takes office. Should a CEO step down and then gets reappointed at a later stage, we do not reset tenure to zero but add on the pre-departure tenure.

board to obtain *Advising Quality*. The average *Advising Quality* in our sample is 1.81. The correlation between *Monitoring Quality* and *Advising Quality* is 0.01 confirming that the two are distinct measures that proxy for different board functions.

In addition to the main variables, we employ two sets of control variables to estimate the bivariate model. One set is designed to explain the commission of misconduct and the other for detection of misconduct. The variables are chosen based on the existing theoretical and empirical work in the corporate fraud literature (Wang 2013; Wang et al. 2010).

Commission of Misconduct Regressions

Our baseline regression for the commission of unobserved misconduct is as follows:

$$M_{it}^{*} = \mathbf{X}_{M,it}\beta_M + \mathbf{X}_{MD,it}\gamma_M + \mu_{it}$$

$\mathbf{X}_{M,\,it}$ contains a set of variables that previous studies have shown to influence a bank's incentives to commit wrongdoing but not the likelihood that the wrongdoing is detected. $\mathbf{X}_{MD,\,it}$ contains a set of factors that affect the bank's incentives to commit wrongdoing and the likelihood of detection. $\mathbf{X}_{M,\,it}$ includes the bank's ROA (earnings before interest and tax divided by total assets), leverage (total liabilities divided by total assets) and investor beliefs about the industry growth prospects. Wang et al. (2010) show that investor beliefs about the industry growth prospects have a nonlinear effect on corporate misconduct. We measure this using the median charter value of all listed banks in a given year (Industry charter value) and include Industry charter value and (Industry charter value)^2 in $\mathbf{X}_{M,\,it}$.

$\mathbf{X}_{MD,\,it}$ contains various bank, board, CEO, and regulator variables that could influence a bank's incentives to commit wrongdoing, as well as the likelihood of detection. First, we control for bank size using the natural logarithm of the book value of total assets (Ln(Assets)). Furthermore, we control for a bank's growth prospect using the ratio of market value of equity divided by the book value of equity (Charter value) and the percentage of change in bank assets over the prior year (Asset growth). Finally, we include a bank's risk-weighted assets to total assets to control for its portfolio risk.

Board characteristics: We control for traditional measures of board monitoring quality, including the number of directors on the board (Board size) and the fraction of independent directors (Board independence). We also control for the ratio of independent directors with prior experience as a CFO or a finance director (Board financial expertise) since the prior literature shows that directors with relevant expertise could offer advice to the CEO and could therefore play an important advising role (Agrawal and Chadha, 2005). Finally, we control for the quality of director networks using a board's exposure to misconduct, defined as the aggregate connections board members have with firms that were involved in a misconduct case committed within the past 10 years.[5]

---

[5] We use a database of accounting fraud cases, namely, the SEC's Accounting and Auditing Enforcement Releases (AAERs). The database provides detailed information on more than 1,300 cases of accounting misconduct involving banks and non-financials between 1982 and 2013. These frauds are often committed by firms with weak operating performance and cash flows.

CEO characteristics: We control for the number of years the CEO has served in the current position (Ln(CEO tenure)) and whether the CEO also chairs the board (CEO is chair) in all specifications in this chapter. Controlling for CEO tenure is important to show that our results based on the measure of monitoring quality are not driven by CEO tenure.

Regulators: We control for the main regulator that supervises the bank. We include two dummies: OCC (equals 1 if the bank is overseen by the OCC) and FRB (equals 1 if the bank is overseen by the FRB).

Detection of Misconduct Regressions

$$D_{it}^* = \mathbf{X}_{MD,it}\delta_D + \mathbf{X}_{D,it}\beta_D + v_{it}$$

There are also certain factors that trigger the detection of misconduct while being unrelated to the causes of banks committing misconduct. This is true for factors that cannot be anticipated by the CEO at the time when misconduct is committed. For example, a sudden drop in performance is difficult to predict for CEOs, but this performance drop may trigger additional regulatory scrutiny of banks and thus contribute to misconduct being detected. We identify a vector $\mathbf{X}_{D,it}$ which includes variables that affect detection but are exogenous to a bank's ex ante incentives to commit wrongdoing. Following Wang (2013), we include Abnormal ROA, Adverse stock return, Abnormal return volatility and Abnormal stock turnover in this vector.

To capture Abnormal ROA performance relative to recent past performance, we compute the residuals (ε_{it}) from the following model for each bank: $ROA_{it} = \beta_0 + \beta_1 ROA_{it-1} + \beta_2 ROA_{it-2} + \varepsilon_{it}$. Adverse stock return is a dummy variable that equals 1 if the bank's stock return is in the bottom 10% of all the bank-year return observations in the CRSP database. In addition, the bank's stock return volatility and stock turnover could also trigger detection by regulators. We measure Abnormal return volatility as the demeaned standard deviation of daily stock returns in a given year and Abnormal stock turnover as the demeaned daily stock turnover in a given year.

Finally, we include year dummies in all regression specifications in the chapter to control for the general economic environment. Table 11.2 provides summary statistics for the variables that we use in our analysis.

11.4   Empirical Results

11.4.1   Main Results

Table 11.3 reports our bivariate probit estimation regression results. Odd-numbered columns report prediction results for banks committing misconduct [P(M=1)]; even-numbered columns show the prediction results for banks that were detected to have committed misconduct, conditional upon misconduct having been committed [P(D=1|M=1)].

The coefficients of our key variables of interest, *Monitoring Quality* and *Advising Quality*, are statistically significant. Effective board monitoring and advising are thus

Table 11.2 Descriptive statistics.

For each variable, the p-value of the difference between banks with misconduct and without misconduct are calculated. ***, **, and * indicate significance at the 1, 5 and 10% level, respectively.

	N	Mean	Median	Std.	p.1	p.99	Misconduct? Yes	Misconduct? No
Key governance measures								
Monitoring Quality	4072	0.544	0.545	0.314	0.000	1.000	0.462	0.548***
Advising Quality	4072	1.815	0.000	3.802	0.000	18.263	1.788	2.338**
Bank-specific characteristics								
ROA (%)	4072	0.580	0.857	1.278	−5.225	2.197	−0.572	0.639***
Leverage	4072	0.906	0.909	0.029	0.815	0.966	0.918	0.905***
Industry charter value	4072	1.503	1.312	0.613	0.787	2.591	1.169	1.169***
Ln(Assets)	4072	21.692	21.328	1.699	19.090	27.298	22.067	21.673***
Asset growth	4072	0.102	0.066	0.190	−0.172	0.789	0.037	0.106***
Portfolio risk	4072	0.728	0.739	0.142	0.314	1.023	0.740	0.727
Charter value	4072	1.503	1.384	0.924	0.139	4.366	1.070	1.526***
Loans	4072	0.666	0.685	0.143	0.135	0.904	0.673	0.666
Non-performing loans	4072	0.002	0.000	0.008	0.000	0.036	0.005	0.002***
Tier–1 capital	4072	0.089	0.086	0.023	0.041	0.161	0.081	0.089
Corporate governance measures								
Board size	4072	11.598	11.000	3.528	6.000	23.000	11.035	11.626**
Board independence	4072	0.765	0.800	0.138	0.364	0.933	0.772	0.765
Board financial expertise	4072	0.040	0.000	0.077	0.000	0.333	0.050	0.040*
Exposure to misconduct	4072	0.147	0.000	0.569	0.000	3.000	0.172	0.146
Ln (Board age)	4072	4.125	4.126	0.064	3.957	4.288	4.136	4.125**

(continued)

Table 11.2 (Continued)

	N	Mean	Median	Std.	p.1	p.99	Misconduct? Yes	Misconduct? No
CEO characteristics and incentives								
Ln (CEO tenure)	4072	1.916	1.988	0.793	0.095	3.395	2.053	1.909**
CEO is chair	4072	0.490	0.000	0.500	0.000	1.000	0.485	0.490
Detection of misconduct								
Abnormal ROA	3018	0.000	0.217	1.164	-4.864	2.302	-0.960	0.055***
Adverse stock return	3018	0.045	0.000	0.207	0.000	1.000	0.197	0.037***
Abnormal stock volatility	3018	0.000	-0.009	0.063	-0.124	0.219	0.043	-0.002***
Abnormal stock turnover	3018	0.000	-0.024	0.740	-1.765	2.484	0.282	-0.014***

Table 11.3   Bivariate probit model estimation for board effectiveness and bank misconduct.
Columns (1) and (3) report the estimated relations between *Monitoring Quality* and *Advising Quality* and the commission of misconduct (M=1), and Columns (2) and (4) report the relations between *Monitoring Quality* and *Advising Quality* and detection, given misconduct (D=1|M=1). Standard errors are clustered at the bank level. The sample covers the period 1999–2012. *t-Statistics* are reported in parentheses. ***, **, and * indicate significance at the 1, 5 and 10% level, respectively.

	P(M=1)	P(D=1|M=1)	P(M=1)	P(D=1|M=1)
	(1)	(2)	(3)	(4)
Monitoring Quality	−1.180***	2.187**		
	(−3.212)	(2.044)		
Advising Quality			−0.131***	0.087***
			(−3.839)	(3.360)
ROA	−0.003		0.203**	
	(−0.058)		(2.264)	
Leverage	9.440***		10.789**	
	(2.925)		(2.386)	
Industry Charter Value	−4.923***		−10.326***	
	(−3.111)		(−4.205)	
(Industry Charter Value)^2	1.594***		3.191***	
	(3.014)		(3.650)	
Ln (Assets)	−0.108	0.873***	0.234***	0.097*
	(−1.254)	(3.890)	(3.066)	(1.815)
Asset growth	−0.224	−2.528*	−0.020	−1.555***
	(−0.347)	(−1.793)	(−0.038)	(−3.917)
Portfolio risk	1.259*	−0.321	0.803	0.819
	(1.955)	(−0.208)	(0.907)	(1.169)
Charter value	−0.305***	0.372	−0.354***	0.044
	(−2.968)	(1.535)	(−3.679)	(0.532)
Loans	−1.872**	5.728**	1.016	−0.270
	(−2.255)	(2.490)	(1.364)	(−0.408)
Non-performing loans	10.526	−26.039*	18.607	−12.635**
	(0.976)	(−1.766)	(1.550)	(−2.479)
Tier-1 capital	−2.253	11.234	−6.645	−0.574
	(−0.541)	(1.075)	(−1.338)	(−0.189)
Board size	0.038	−0.204***	−0.018	−0.031
	(1.437)	(−2.594)	(−0.310)	(−1.452)
Board independence	0.241	−0.297	−1.107	0.360
	(0.372)	(−0.185)	(−0.643)	(0.594)
Board financial expertise	0.900	−2.084	0.606	−0.025
	(1.315)	(−1.232)	(0.685)	(−0.043)
Exposure to misconduct	0.391**	−1.209***	0.318*	−0.347***
	(2.115)	(−3.453)	(1.851)	(−3.200)
Ln (Board age)	3.243***	−2.876	−0.215	2.255**
	(2.951)	(−0.849)	(−0.140)	(2.504)
Ln (CEO tenure)	−0.133	0.335	0.414***	0.048
	(−1.023)	(1.048)	(4.067)	(0.619)

(continued)

Table 11.3   (Continued)

	P(M=1)	P(D=1|M=1)	P(M=1)	P(D=1|M=1)
	(1)	(2)	(3)	(4)
CEO is chair	0.510***	−1.610**	0.910***	−0.314***
	(2.942)	(−2.546)	(3.729)	(−2.709)
Abnormal ROA		−0.574***		−0.359***
		(−2.925)		(−5.499)
Adverse stock return		0.584		0.559***
		(1.189)		(3.062)
Abnormal stock volatility		3.544*		3.761***
		(1.725)		(3.644)
Abnormal stock turnover		−0.128		−0.091
		(−0.790)		(−1.474)
Observations	3004	3004	3004	3004
Prob>Chi²	0.000	0.000	0.000	0.000
Log likelihood	−497	−497	−491	−491

associated with fewer cases of committed misconduct and more cases of detected misconduct. The results are economically significant. The estimated coefficient of *Monitoring Quality* suggests that a bank with all directors appointed before the CEO taking office (*Monitoring Quality* = 1) has a 27% lower probability of wrongdoing commission and a 35% higher probability of detection than a bank with no director appointed before the CEO taking office (*Monitoring Quality* = 0). A one-standard-deviation increase in *Advising Quality* is associated with 11% lower probability of wrongdoing and 7% higher probability of detection. The estimated effects of board monitoring and advising on the probability that banks receive an enforcement action are graphically depicted in Figure 11.2.

The control variables have the expected signs. Most interestingly, board independence does not enter significantly. This indicates that the current standard for director independence, which mostly focuses on the absence of economic ties between directors and a firm, fails to pick up unobserved aspects of boardroom governance. We also find that banks with greater exposure to firms that have engaged in misconduct have a higher likelihood of committing misconduct and a lower likelihood of misconduct detection. This confirms that network quality plays an important role in preventing misconduct.

The variables excluded from the detection equation but included in the commission equation (*Abnormal ROA, Adverse stock return* and *Abnormal stock volatility*) show the expected signs and are statistically significant. Likewise, the variables excluded from the commission equation are also individually and jointly significant.

11.4.2   Results for Different Classes of Enforcement Actions

While we find that effective boards reduce wrongdoing, it is unclear whether this reduction holds for different types of misconduct. For instance, effective board advising could be particularly relevant in reducing technical types of misconduct where

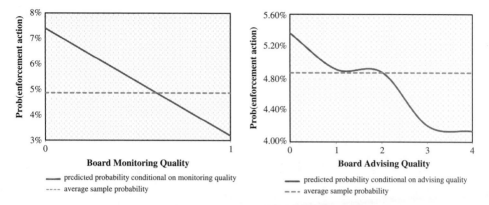

Figure 11.2 The estimated effects of board monitoring and board advising on the probability that banks receive an enforcement action.

Source: Authors' calculations. Dotted lines show the unconditional probability that an enforcement action will occur which is around 5% in our sample of 4,000 bank-year observations. Solid lines show the probability of enforcement actions conditional on board monitoring quality (left) and conditional on advising quality (right). The estimations are based on the model presented in Table 11.3.

advising via the board will be particularly important to inform CEO decision-making. To verify this, we classify enforcement actions according to how technical the underlying violation is. We classify misconduct cases as technical if the enforcement action has been caused by violations of requirements concerning capital adequacy and liquidity, asset quality, lending, provisions and reserves. They will be classified as non-technical if the enforcement actions are related to failures of the bank's internal control and audit systems, risk management systems, anti-money laundering systems, etc. Non-technical misconduct cases also include breaches of the requirements concerning the competency of the senior management team and the board of directors as well as violations of various laws, such as consumer compliance programmes and the Equal Credit Opportunity Act (ECOA), etc.[6]

Consistent with our expectation, Table 11.4 shows that *Advising Quality* reduces technical types of misconduct (such as violations of capital requirements or substandard asset quality) but has no measurable effect on non-technical types of misconduct. Thus, consistent with previous literature (Coles et al. 2012; Field et al. 2013), our results indicate that board advising matters more when the demand for director advice is high. On the other hand, *Monitoring Quality* matters to both types of misconduct.

---

[6] While we cannot rule out that certain technical and non-technical types of misconduct could be functional to each other in some cases, we can demonstrate that these two types of misconduct capture largely unrelated types of behaviour. We find the correlation between the two types to be 0.02 (not statistically significant). To further ensure that our results are not driven by cases in which both types of enforcement actions occur, we exclude banks that receive both types of enforcement actions during our sample period. This test does not alter our main findings.

Table 11.4 Board effectiveness and bank misconduct: split-sample tests.

Odd-numbered columns report the estimated relations between *Monitoring Quality* and *Advising Quality* and the commission of misconduct (M=1), and even-numbered columns report the relations between *Monitoring Quality* and *Advising Quality* and detection, given misconduct (D=1|M=1). We split the enforcement actions sample into technical enforcement actions and non-technical enforcement actions. *Technical misconduct* are enforcement actions taken for violations of capital adequacy and liquidity, asset quality, lending, provisions and reserves. *Non-technical misconduct* are enforcement actions related to failures of the bank's internal control and audit systems, risk management systems, anti-money laundering systems etc. This also includes breaches of the requirements concerning the competency of the senior management team and the board of directors as well as violations of various laws such as consumer compliance programs, Federal Trade Commission Act (FTCA), Equal Credit Opportunities Act (ECOA) etc. Standard errors are clustered at the bank level. The sample covers the period 1999–2012. *t-Statistics* are reported in parentheses. ***, **, and * indicate significance at the 1, 5 and 10% level, respectively.

	P(M=1)	P(D=1|M=1)	P(M=1)	P(D=1|M=1)	P(M=1)	P(D=1|M=1)	P(M=1)	P(D=1|M=1)
	Technical misconduct				**Non-technical misconduct**			
	(violations of capital, liquidity requirements, etc.)				(internal control failures, money laundering, etc.)			
	(1)	(2)	(3)	(4)	(5)	(6)	(7)	(8)
Monitoring Quality	−1.165***	4.308**			−0.782**	1.255**		
	(−3.174)	(2.510)			(−2.341)	(2.501)		
Advising Quality			−0.074**	0.338***			−0.037	0.477
			(−2.156)	(3.011)			(−1.601)	(1.146)
Other controls	Yes	Yes	Yes	Yes	Yes	Yes	Yes	Yes
Observations	3004	3004	3004	3004	3004	3004	3004	3004
Log likelihood	−251	−251	−251	−251	−256	−256	−208	−208
Prob > Chi²	0.000	0.000	0.000	0.000	0.000	0.000	0.000	0.000

11.4.3   Does Better Board Quality Alleviate Shareholder Wealth Losses?

In the previous sections, we showed that effective boards reduce the likelihood of bank misconduct. We now test whether effective boards also reduce the *severity* of misconduct. We capture the severity of misconduct using the abnormal stock price reaction to the announcement of misconduct (e.g. Cumming et al., 2015). Since high-quality boards are more effective at preventing misconduct, detected cases of misconduct are likely to be less severe. Further, effective boards are more likely to take corrective action, such as disciplining the CEO and 'fixing' the issues after wrongdoing has been detected. Thus, investors may be more positive about misconduct when the current board exhibits high monitoring or advising quality. Thus, we also include contemporaneous measures of monitoring and advising in our analysis.

We use event study methodology to test these hypotheses. We define the event day as the earliest trading day when the news of the enforcement action is made public. This yields a sample of 206 announcements. We then estimate a market model using a value-weighted CRSP stock index as a market index from 46 to 146 days before the announcement of an enforcement action. We construct cumulative abnormal returns (CARs) as the sum of the prediction errors of the market model. We find that the average CARs over a three-day $[-1, +1]$ event window is -3.50%, (significant at the 1% level). This shows that regulatory enforcement actions significantly damage shareholder wealth.

Table 11.5 displays the multivariate regression results. The dependent variables are CARs of three-day window $[-1, +1]$. Columns (1) and (2) show that the announcement returns are positively related to measures of Monitoring Quality when wrongdoing is committed $(t-1)$ as well as when it is detected (t). CARs are on average 6% higher when the board has all directors appointed before the CEO compared to when none are appointed before the CEO, implying that effective board monitoring reduces the severity of the misconduct. Further, investors expect an effective board to take action to help the bank recovers from the misconduct. Finally, Columns (3) and (4) show that Advising Quality does not enter the regression significantly.

11.5   Conclusion

This chapter has focused on two key functions of bank boards, monitoring and advising, and finds that both functions are effective in reducing the probability that banks receive enforcement actions from regulators. Further analyses reveal that while board monitoring reduces all categories of misconduct, board advising reduces misconduct of a more technical nature. Furthermore, effective boards also mitigate the severity of misconduct.

Our study has important implications. The Financial Stability Board (2014) places bank boards at the core of effective risk management and emphasizes 'heightened expectations' of its role in risk management and the prevention of misconduct. In line with this view, our study illustrates that board governance matters in banking. Regulators and investors are right to expect more effective board governance in the banking sector going forward. In particular, conventional board measures such as board independence and financial expertise have no measurable effect on bank misconduct

Table 11.5　Do effective boards alleviate shareholder wealth losses when misconduct becomes public?

This table reports the multivariate regression analyses of stock market reactions to the announcements of banks receiving an enforcement action. The dependent variables of all models are CARs for a three-day window [−1, +1] (%). All models include year dummies. t-*Statistics* are reported in parentheses. ***, **, and * indicate significance at the 1, 5 and 10% level, respectively.

| | CARs [−1, +1] % | | | |
	(1)	(2)	(3)	(4)
Monitoring Quality$_{t-1}$	6.237**			
	(2.127)			
Monitoring Quality$_t$		5.927**		
		(2.507)		
Advising Quality$_{t-1}$			−0.134	
			(−0.786)	
Advising Quality$_t$				−0.145
				(−0.752)
ROA	0.626*	0.491	0.595	0.621*
	(1.713)	(1.365)	(1.639)	(1.701)
Leverage	−10.245	−15.323	−10.124	−13.629
	(−0.330)	(−0.502)	(−0.328)	(−0.435)
Ln(Assets)	−0.109	0.061	−0.097	0.130
	(−0.260)	(0.146)	(−0.233)	(0.251)
Asset growth	−3.055	−2.795	−3.341	−2.746
	(−0.530)	(−0.493)	(−0.577)	(−0.477)
Portfolio risk	0.734	1.313	0.678	0.819
	(0.083)	(0.151)	(0.077)	(0.093)
Charter value	0.363	0.492	0.280	0.340
	(0.563)	(0.775)	(0.434)	(0.530)
Loans	−4.683	−3.531	−3.890	−4.137
	(−0.587)	(−0.450)	(−0.488)	(−0.520)
Non-performing loans	6.167	14.100	4.250	8.097
	(0.175)	(0.406)	(0.121)	(0.229)
Tier-1 capital	−0.997	−6.661	−2.642	−4.411
	(−0.030)	(−0.204)	(−0.079)	(−0.131)
Board size	0.458**	0.379*	0.449**	0.447**
	(2.113)	(1.759)	(2.051)	(2.037)
Board independence	5.802	3.956	5.092	5.574
	(1.112)	(0.766)	(0.975)	(1.067)
Board financial expertise	2.837	3.257	2.416	2.414
	(0.455)	(0.531)	(0.388)	(0.387)
Exposure to misconduct	−0.670	−0.398	−0.033	−0.734
	(−0.655)	(−0.395)	(−0.025)	(−0.719)
Ln (Board age)	10.751	10.903	12.208	12.077
	(1.123)	(1.159)	(1.268)	(1.256)
Ln (CEO tenure)	−0.419	0.993	−0.079	−0.078

Table 11.5   (Continued)

	CARs [−1, +1] %			
	(1)	**(2)**	**(3)**	**(4)**
	(−0.651)	(1.175)	(−1.045)	(−1.031)
CEO is chair	0.785	0.302	1.025	1.001
	(0.560)	(0.217)	(0.722)	(0.705)
Constant	−41.393	−46.007	−47.340	−48.467
	(−0.780)	(−0.884)	(−0.896)	(−0.915)
Observations	206	206	206	206
R-squared	0.216	0.225	0.197	0.193

being committed or detected. By contrast, the board metrics we study in this chapter related to monitoring and advising are important predictors of misconduct. Our findings demonstrate that governance metrics revolving around CEO connections warrant more attention from regulators, investors and governance activists.

References

Adams, R.B. and Ferreira, D. (2007). A theory of friendly boards. *Journal of Finance* 62: 116–150.

Agrawal, A. and Chadha, S. (2005). Corporate governance and accounting scandals. *The Journal of Law and Economics* 48: 371–406.

Becker, G.S. (1968). Crime and punishment: An economic approach. *Journal of Political Economy* 76: 169–217.

Biaggio, M., Duffy, R. and Staffelbach, D.F. (1998). Obstacles to addressing professional misconduct. *Clinical Psychology Review* 18: 273–285.

Coles, J.L., Daniel, N.D. and Naveen, L. (2012). Board advising. Working paper.

Coles, J.L., Daniel, N.D. and Naveen, L. (2014). Co-opted boards. *Review of Financial Studies* 27(6): 1751–1796.

Cumming, D.J., Leung, T.Y. and Rui, O.M. (2015). Gender diversity and securities fraud. *Academy of Management Journal* 58: 1572–1593.

Dass N., Kini O., Nanda V., Onal, B. and Wang, J. (2014). Board expertise: Do directors from related industries help bridge the information gap? *Review of Financial Studies* 27(5): 1533–1592.

Delis, M.D. and Staikouras, P. (2011). Supervisory effectiveness and bank risk. *Review of Finance* 15: 511–543.

Dyck, A., Morse, A. and Zingales, L. (2010). Who blows the whistle on corporate fraud? *Journal of Finance* 65(6): 2213–2253.

Ellul, A. and Yerramilli, V. (2013). Strong risk controls, lower risk: Evidence from US bank holding companies. *Journal of Finance* 68(5): 1757–1803.

Fama, E.F. and Jensen, M.C. (1983). Separation of ownership and control. *Journal of Law and Economics* 26(2): 301–325.

Fehr, E. and Schmidt, K.M. (1999). A theory of fairness, competition and cooperation. *Quarterly Journal of Economics* 114(3): 817–868.

Field, L., Lowry, M. and Mkrtchyan, A. (2013). Are busy boards detrimental? *Journal of Financial Economics* 109(1): 63–82.

Financial Stability Board. (2014). Guidance on supervisory interaction with financial institutions on risk culture. April 7 2014, http://www.financialstabilityboard.org/wp-content/uploads/140407.pdf.

Gouldner, A.W. (1960). The norm of reciprocity: A preliminary statement. *American Sociology Review* 25(2): 161–178.

Kedia, S. and Rajgopal, S. (2011). Do the SEC's enforcement preferences affect corporate misconduct? *Journal of Accounting and Economics* 51(3): 259–278.

Khanna, V.S., Kim, E.H. and Lu, Y. (2015). CEO connectedness and corporate frauds. *Journal of Finance* 70: 1203–1252.

Lee, J., Lee, K.J. and Nagarajan, N.J. (2014). Birds of a feather: Value implications of political alignment between top management and directors. *Journal of Financial Economics* 112: 232–250.

Mace, M. (1971). *Directors, Myth, and Reality*. Boston: Harvard Business School Press.

Minton, B.A., Taillard, J.P. and Williamson, R. (2014). Financial expertise of the board, risk taking and performance: Evidence from bank holding companies. *Journal of Financial and Quantitative Analysis* 49 (2): 351–380.

Poirier, D.J. (1980). Partial observability in bivariate probit models. *Journal of Econometrics* 12: 209–217.

Simkin, M.G. and McLeod, A. (2010). Why do college students cheat? *Journal of Business Ethics* 94: 441–453.

Sims, R.L. 1993. The relationship between academic dishonesty and unethical business practices. *Journal of Education for Business* 68: 207–211.

Wang, T.Y. (2013). Corporate securities fraud: Insights from a new empirical framework. *Journal of Law, Economics and Organization* 29: 535–568.

Wang, T.Y., Winton, A. and Yu, X. (2010). Corporate fraud and business conditions: Evidence from IPOs. *Journal of Finance* 65: 2255–2292.

Chapter 12

Misconduct and Fraud by Investment Managers

Stephen G. Dimmock
Nanyang Technological University

Joseph D. Farizo
University of Richmond

William C. Gerken*
University of Kentucky

12.1   Introduction

Fraud and misconduct by investment managers is an important and justified concern for investors. During the period 2001–2016 the Security and Exchange Commission (SEC) successfully prosecuted 981 cases of fraud committed by investment managers,

* We thank Carol Alexander and Douglas Cumming. ChangHwan Choi and Qiping Huang provided outstanding research assistance.

which collectively caused more than $40 billion in direct losses. In addition, these frauds also cause indirect harm; Gurun, Stoffman, and Yonker (2018) show that fraud by investment managers has significant spillover effects, resulting in reduced stock market participation and investment even by those not directly victimized. Further, this harm is not limited to a single category of investment manager. Zitzewitz (2006) estimates that the mutual fund late trading scandal cost shareholders $400 million per year from 1998 to 2003. Hedge funds, with their non-traditional holdings and less regulatory scrutiny, have also suffered from fraud. Capco (2003) finds that nearly half of hedge fund failures are due to fraud, mainly from misappropriation of investor funds and misrepresentation of investments.[1] Practitioners also recognize the potential harm from fraud and misconduct by investment managers (e.g. Scharfman 2009; Swensen 2000). This issue has become increasingly relevant in recent years, as investors have shifted away from direct holdings and into indirect investments through investment managers (e.g. see French 2008, Table I).

Despite the significant economic consequences of fraud by investment managers, academics have produced relatively little research on this topic until recently. In part, this is because detailed data on investment managers and fraud has only recently become publicly available in a format that permits rigorous academic study. Indeed, one of the purposes of this chapter is to detail the available data and to stimulate research in the area by making available the data used in the present study (https://doi.org/10.13023/nsjd-rk62). In addition to stimulating research in this area, our results provide useful information for regulators and policymakers concerned with preventing fraud and provide guidance for investors when selecting investment managers.

In this chapter, we provide a systematic examination of all detected fraud cases committed by registered investment advisors during the period 2001–2016. We document the type and extent of fraud and show the relation between fraud and various characteristics that investment management firms disclose in their Form ADV filings. These firm characteristics fall into three categories. First, firms with prior regulatory, civil law, or criminal violations are significantly more likely to subsequently commit fraud. Although these prior violations are frequently for minor issues, they have strong predictive power. Second, conflicts-of-interest predict fraud; fraud is significantly more likely to occur at firms that buy securities from or sell securities to their clients. Third, there is a strong relation between monitoring and fraud. Firms with a dedicated Chief Compliance Officer, an indicator of the strength of internal monitoring, are less likely to commit fraud. External monitoring by clients is also important; firms with large clients are less likely to commit fraud, but firms whose clients are primarily themselves agents are more likely to commit fraud. These results are consistent with the findings of Dimmock and Gerken (2012) and suggest the prior paper captured long lived predictive factors.

The economic magnitude of the predictability of fraud is large. An investor who avoided the 5% of firms with the highest predicted risk of fraud, would successfully avoid 27.1% of fraud cases and 28.6% of the dollar losses from fraud. We conduct

---

[1] Capco (2003) finds that 54% of hedge fund failures are caused by operational issues, and 46% are caused by operational issues that can be classified as forms of fraud.

K-fold cross-validation tests, and show that these results are robust in out-of-sample data. As an additional test of the predictive ability of the data, we divide the sample into newly initiated fraud cases and continued fraud cases (cases that were initiated in a previous year but continue into the subsequent year). We find that our model can successfully predict 29.8% of newly initiated frauds.

We further divide the sample of frauds into firm-wide frauds, committed by the firm's senior executives, and rogue employee fraud, committed by non-executive employees without the knowledge of senior executives. We find that rogue employee fraud is much more predictable – avoiding the 5% of firms with the highest fraud risk would allow an investor to avoid 61.8% of rogue employee frauds. Firm-wide fraud is less predictable, but our model continues to successfully predict an economically meaningful proportion of such fraud.

The final empirical results presented in this chapter are a true out-of-sample test of the predictability of investment manager fraud. Dimmock and Gerken (2012) predict fraud using mandatory disclosures made by investment managers during the period 2001–2006. We take the coefficient estimates from Dimmock and Gerken (2012) and use these to predict fraud detected post-publication. The results show that the model continues to perform well out-of-sample, although not as well as during the in-sample period.

12.2   Related Research

This chapter is closely related to Dimmock and Gerken (2012) who use Form ADV data for the years 2001 to 2006 to predict fraud by investment managers. They find that disclosures of prior misconduct, conflicts of interest, and monitoring all have power to predict fraud. Using their model, an investor who avoided the 5% of firms with the highest fraud risk would have avoided 29.4% of fraud cases and $4 billion in losses. Other studies that predict fraud by investment managers include Zitzewitz (2006) and Bollen and Pool (2012). Zitzewitz (2006) examines mutual fund late trading, and shows it can be predicted based on fund-level correlations between daily mutual fund flows and market returns. Bollen and Pool (2012) show that suspicious patterns in the reported returns of hedge funds can predict hedge fund fraud. Gregoriou and Lhabitant (2009) provide a case study of the infamous Ponzi scheme committed by Bernie Madoff, highlighting operational red flags that hinted at the potential for fraud.

Instead of predicting fraud, Gurun, Stoffman, and Yonker (2018) focus on how fraud by investment managers affects investor behaviour. They find that fraud results in investors withdrawing assets from investment managers. However, this effect is mitigated by trust building activities. Gurun et al. also highlight an important spillover effect from fraud by investment managers: In addition to direct losses financial losses, fraud causes a decline in trust that results in reduced stock market participation, which has potentially large welfare losses due to forgone investment opportunities.

The mutual fund late trading scandal motivated multiple academic studies of fraud by investment managers. Houge and Wellman (2005), Choi and Kahan (2007),

Chapman-Davies, Parwada, and Tan (2014), and Wu (2017) examine investors' reactions to the revelation of mutual fund scandals, and find that the fund families implicated in these scandals suffered large outflows. Goetzmann, Ivković, and Rouwenhorst (2001) and Zitzewitz (2003) propose pricing methods that prevent the possibility of late-trading arbitrage.

Another branch of the literature on fraud by investment managers examines return misreporting by hedge funds.[2] Bollen and Pool (2008) find evidence of conditional return smoothing in the returns reported by hedge funds; hedge funds appear to quickly report positive returns, but smooth out the reporting of bad returns over multiple months. Bollen and Pool (2009) show the returns reported by hedge funds exhibit a strong discontinuity around zero; hedge funds are nearly twice as likely to report a small positive return as a small negative return. Further, this discontinuity does not occur in the months when the hedge fund is audited. Agarwal, Daniel, and Naik (2011) show that hedge funds report significantly higher returns in the last month of their fiscal year (i.e. the month when the hedge fund manager's annual incentive fee is calculated). Ben-David et al. (2013) show that hedge funds manipulate stock prices at quarter ends, and this is affected by incentive fees and relative performance considerations. Cici, Kempf, and Puetz (2016) show direct evidence of valuation misreporting by hedge funds. They compare the individual stock valuations reported by hedge funds in their 13F filings with the stock prices in the CRSP database, and find that 7% of all equity positions reported by hedge funds are misvalued.[3] Further, stock value misreporting is correlated with hedge funds' incentives to misreport, and with the return misreporting patterns documented by Bollen and Pool (2009) and Agarwal, Daniel, and Naik (2011).

Following the discovery of these patterns of return misreporting by hedge funds, various authors studied different mechanisms that can reduce misreporting. Cumming and Dai (2010a, 2010b) show that across-country variation in legal restrictions on hedge fund is related to return misreporting, and Cumming and Dai (2009) show that hedge fund regulation is related to capital flows. Cumming, Dai, and Johan (2015) show that hedge funds subject to Delaware state law are different than funds incorporated in other states. Dimmock and Gerken (2016) use changes in hedge fund registration requirements in the US to evaluate how regulatory oversight affects return misreporting. They find that return misreporting decreased following a mandatory registration requirement, but then increased again following the reversal of this requirement. A later study, Honigsberg (2019), independently replicates the finding of Dimmock and Gerken (2016). Cassar and Gerakos (2011) show that stronger internal control systems by hedge fund managers reduce the occurrence of return misreporting. Jylhä (2011) shows that misreporting is significantly greater when hedge fund managers have stronger financial incentives to misreport. Clifford, Ellis, and Gerken (2017) study the relation between hedge fund fraud and boards of directors. They find that hedge funds with independent directors on their boards are significantly less likely to engage in fraud, and the economic magnitudes of this effect are large. Finally,

---

[2] Agarwal, Mullally, and Naik (2015, Section 3.3) provide an excellent review of studies on operational risk and fraud in hedge funds.

[3] Form 13F is a quarterly report to the SEC of an institutional investment manager's equity assets under management of at least $100 million in value.

in a cross-country study Kang, Kim, and Oh (2016) examine the relation between national cultures and return manipulation by hedge funds, and find more manipulation in cultures with greater individualism, masculinity, and power distance.

Brown et al. (2008, 2009) examine the relation between information disclosed in Form ADV filings and operational risk of hedge funds. Brown et al. define operational risk as any fund managed by an advisor who has disclosed any past legal or regulatory violation (committed either by the hedge fund adviser itself, any non-hedge fund advisory part of the firm, or by any affiliated firm). They show that this measure of operational risk is correlated with various organizational features of the hedge fund adviser. They also show their measure of operational risk is correlated with fund performance and survival, but is not correlated with hedge fund flows. Brown et al. (2012) find similar results using due diligence reports rather than Form ADV disclosures.

This chapter is also related to a recent, but growing literature on misconduct by individual financial advisors employed by investment advisory firms. Charoenwong, Kwan, and Umar (2019) provide evidence that the identity of the regulator influences misconduct committed by individual advisors at regulated firms. Dimmock, Gerken, and Graham (2018) show there are peer effects in misconduct by financial advisors; individual advisors are significantly more likely to commit misconduct if they are exposed to co-workers who commit misconduct. Egan, Matvos, and Seru (2019a) explore how misconduct affects the labour market for financial advisors. They find that misconduct frequently results in financial advisors being fired, but many are subsequently rehired and certain firms seem to specialize in misconduct. Egan, Matvos, and Seru (2019b) study gender differences in the punishment for misconduct by financial advisors, finding that women are more likely to be fired and less likely to be rehired following misconduct. Dimmock, Gerken, and Van Alfen (2017) study exogenous shocks to financial advisors' wealth caused by real estate price changes during the financial crisis, and find that advisors are significantly more likely to commit misconduct following a negative wealth shock.

12.3 The Investment Advisers Act of 1940 and Mandatory Disclosures

Our data about investment managers come primarily from mandatory disclosures required by the Investment Advisers Act of 1940 (IAA).[4] The IAA authorizes the SEC to regulate investment advisers, and requires investment advisers to comply with detailed anti-fraud provisions, to register with the SEC, and to disclose certain information.

The IAA requires advisers to register with the SEC if the adviser has 15 or more US clients and more than a certain level of assets under management (AUM). The level of AUM requiring registration was increased from $25 million to $100 million on 1 January 2012. Advisers not required to register with the SEC are generally required to register with state regulators (for further information on registration requirements see Charoenwong, Kwan, and Umar 2019). The IAA defines an investment adviser as an individual or legal entity that is compensated for providing advice regarding

---

[4] For a detailed explanation of the Investment Advisers Act of 1940 and its provisions, see https://www.sec.gov/divisions/investment/iaregulation/memoia.htm.

investment securities. Historically, some hedge fund advisers avoided the registration requirement by counting each fund as a client, rather than counting the fund's investors. In 2004, the SEC passed Rule IA-2333 requiring hedge funds to count investors instead of funds for the purpose of determining whether registration was necessary. In 2006, a Federal Court overruled Rule IA-2333 and some hedge funds deregistered. The Dodd–Frank Act included a provision requiring hedge fund advisors to count investors and not funds, forcing many hedge fund advisors to register starting in 2011 (see Cumming, Dai, and Johan, 2017 for further discussion of the effects of Dodd–Frank on hedge funds).

Registration with the SEC requires an investment advisor to comply with strict record-keeping requirements, prohibits certain types of fees, and imposes some other restrictions on behaviours. Most importantly, for the purposes of this chapter, registered investment advisors are required to disclose certain information by filing Form ADV.[5] Registered investment advisors must file Form ADV at least annually, but must also refile if there are any material changes to the disclosed information. Form ADV reports a large amount of information about the investment advisor's business, conflicts of interest, and past legal and regulatory violations.

12.4   Data

In this chapter, we employ two primary types of data: SEC filings regarding investment fraud by US registered investment advisors and disclosures made by these investment advisors in their Form ADV filing. We combine the two data sources by matching on the firms' Central Registration Depository (CRD) number;[6] if the CRD number is not available in the SEC fraud filings, we match using full legal names.

12.4.1   Investment Fraud

We collect investment fraud data by searching two sources on the SEC's enforcement action website: administrative proceedings[7] and litigation releases[8] for the period 1 August 2001 to 31 December 2016. We mechanically search the filings for phrases related to 'fraud' and 'investment adviser' (or 'investment advisor'). From these subset of documents, we then identify by hand all case filings that involve violations of the anti-fraud provisions in the Investment Advisers Act of 1940. We do not include types of fraud or misconduct committed by an investment advisor that do not directly affect investment advisor clients (e.g. defrauding brokerage clients), nor do we include misconduct that potentially benefits the investment advisor's clients (e.g. insider trading).

Many fraud cases occur over multiple years and are often detected years after initiation. In our sample, we read all legal filings for each fraud case and identify

---

[5] There are six distinct versions of Form ADV over our sample period. While the vast majority of disclosures are the same throughout, Form ADV has expanded reporting for certain types of information (e.g. AUM by clientele).

[6] The CRD number is a unique identification number that identifies an investment management firm. It is similar to the permco variable in CRSP.

[7] See https://www.sec.gov/litigation/admin.shtml.

[8] See https://www.sec.gov/litigation/litreleases.shtml.

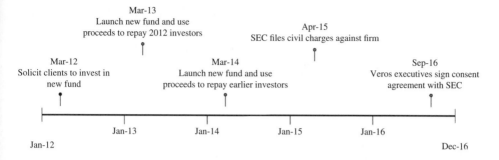

Figure 12.1   Timeline for fraud committed by Veros Partners.

the period when fraud occurred. We then assign the fraud case to the year(s) when it was committed, not the year when it was detected. To illustrate, Figure 12.1 shows an example of one fraud case. In 2012, Veros Partners solicited clients to invest in a new fund that would provide short-term operating loans to farmers; Veros made loans to farmers, but the loans were not repaid. In the spring of 2013 and again in the spring of 2014, Veros solicited clients to invest in a new fund that would provide short-term financing for farmers, but instead used the proceeds to repay investors in the earlier funds (and to pay Veros managers undisclosed 'success fees'). The SEC filed civil charges against Veros and its management in April 2015. In September of 2016, the SEC signed a consent agreement in which the Veros management team agreed to sanctions and repayment. A criminal trial was scheduled for February 2017. We classify this as a single fraud case occurring in 2013 and 2014, with detection occurring in 2015.

The SEC administrative proceedings and litigation releases include investment fraud committed by both registered and unregistered investment advisors. Although our empirical tests use only the sample of registered advisors, Panel A of Table 12.1 summarizes fraud by both registered and unregistered advisors. There are 639 fraud cases committed by registered advisors and 342 cases by non-registered advisors. Columns (2) and (3) divide the fraud cases into 'firm-wide' versus 'rogue employee' fraud. Firm-wide frauds are either committed by senior executives or occur with their knowledge and, at the very least, implicit acceptance. Rogue employee frauds are committed by non-executive employees who evade their firms' internal control systems. The vast majority of fraud is firm-wide fraud, comprising 95.9% and 82.8% of cases at unregistered and registered advisors, respectively.

The final column of Panel A shows the aggregate losses to investors during this period were $45.6 billion, which almost certainly understates losses as we are unable to determine a dollar amount in 22.4% of the cases. Panel B of Table 12.1 summarizes the distribution of losses for fraud committed by registered advisors. The average loss was $78.8 million, with losses for firm-wide fraud substantially larger than for rogue employee fraud. Panel B also summarizes the duration of fraud cases. The median fraud persists for three years, but this is positively skewed as a small number of cases persist for over a decade.

Table 12.1 Summary of investment fraud.

This table summarizes cases of investment fraud committed by investment advisors between 1984 and 2016 as reported on SEC administrative proceedings and litigation releases filed from 2001 to 2016. 'Registered' denotes firms that file a Form ADV with the SEC. Firm-wide fraud is committed by high level executives, or at the very least, with the firms' implicit acceptance. Rogue employee fraud is committed by individuals who evade their firms' internal control systems and the firms do not knowingly benefit.

Panel A: Registered versus non-registered advisors

	Total	Firm-wide	Rogue employee	Investor losses ($ billions)
Non-registered	342	328	14	6.5
Registered	639	529	110	39.1
Total	981	857	124	45.6

Panel B: Fraud characteristics

		Investor losses ($ million)				Duration (years)		
	Obs.	Mean	Median	Max	Missing	Mean	Median	Max
Firm-wide	529	93.5	3.2	18,000.0	122	4.2	3.0	20.8
Rogue employee	110	11.7	1.3	300.0	21	4.0	3.0	15.0
Total	639	78.8	2.7	18,000.0	143	4.1	3.0	20.8

Figure 12.2 shows the number of *detected* fraud cases by year. For each year, the dark bars show the number of initiated frauds and the light bars show the number of ongoing frauds for the firms in the ADV sample. The figure includes only fraud cases that were ongoing during the sample period 2001–2016. Thus, the reported cases for the period 1984–2000 include only those frauds initiated prior to 2001 that continued into the sample period. The number of initiated frauds is stable early in the sample, but rises during the financially crisis and then declines. The number of ongoing frauds shows a similar pattern. The rise during the financial crisis suggests that investment advisors may be more likely to commit fraud when asset markets perform poorly. The decline in both initiated and ongoing fraud cases towards the end of the sample highlights an important feature of fraud data. Although it is possible that investment fraud has become much less frequent in recent years, another important factor is that fraud is detected with a significant lag. Thus, the low rates of fraud in 2014 onward likely reflect, at least in part, that recent frauds have not yet been detected rather than a decrease in the actual commission of fraud.

Table 12.2 summarizes the types of fraud committed by registered investment advisors. *Direct theft* occurs when an advisor directly steals money from clients (but does not include theft through related party transactions nor Ponzi schemes).

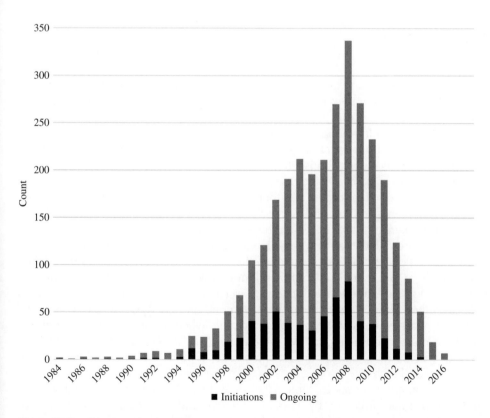

Figure 12.2   Fraud cases over time.

Table 12.2   Summary of fraud types.
This table summarizes the types of investment fraud committed by registered investment advisors between 1984 to 2016 as reported on SEC administrative proceedings and litigation releases filed from 2001 to 2016. Direct theft occurs when an investment advisor directly steals money from a client. Misrepresentation occurs when an advisor makes material misrepresentations to clients. Self-dealing occurs when an advisor siphons off clients' money through related party transactions. Overstating assets occurs when an advisor overstates the amount of assets under management to increase fees. A Ponzi scheme occurs when an advisor steals clients' money, and uses new investments to repay old investments. Mutual fund late trading occurs when an advisor allows some investors to transact shares after a fund's net asset value has been calculated. The numbers in parentheses exclude Bernie Madoff's 2008 Ponzi scheme.

	Number of cases	Percent of total cases	Investor losses ($ billions)	Percent of total losses	Average loss per case ($ millions)
Direct theft	212	33.2%	5.21	13.3% (24.7%)	24.56
Misrepresentation	161	25.2%	2.80	7.2% (13.3%)	17.39
Self-dealing	145	22.7%	0.87	2.2% (4.1%)	5.98
Overstate assets	49	7.7%	0.98	2.5% (4.7%)	20.04
Ponzi scheme	37	5.8%	27.5	70.3%	743.24
	(36)	(5.6%)	(9.50)	(45.0%)	(263.89)
Mutual fund late trading	35	5.5%	1.74	4.5% (8.3%)	49.8

Misrepresentation occurs when an advisor makes material misrepresentations to a client, and does not commit other acts that would fall under another category (all fraud involves an element of misrepresentation). This includes cases in which an advisor lies about assets under management or past returns, or lies about past misconduct (e.g. falsely denies prior sanctions by regulators). *Self-dealing* includes a wide-range of behaviours that involve transactions between clients and parties related to the investment advisor. Examples include front-running, in which the advisor purchases securities ahead of client orders and then resells them at slightly higher prices; trading between client accounts and a proprietary trading desk at prices unfavourable to the client; brokerage fraud, in which the advisor trades through an affiliated broker at terms that are unfavourable to the client and have not been adequately disclosed; and ex post allocation of trades, in which the advisor purchases securities but delays assigning them to a specific account, and instead waits to assign winners to the proprietary trading desk and losers to clients. *Overstating assets* occurs when an advisor overstates the value of assets under management, and charges advisory fees based on these inflated values. A *Ponzi scheme* occurs when an advisor uses investment inflows to meet investment outflows. *Mutual fund late trading* occurs when an advisor allows some investors to transact shares after a fund's net asset value has been calculated for the day.

The summary statistics in Table 12.2 show that *Direct theft* is the most common type of fraud, followed by *Misrepresentation* and *Self-dealing*, with *Overstate assets*, *Ponzi scheme*, and *Mutual fund late trading* being relatively less common. However, the losses per case are particularly large for *Ponzi scheme* and *Mutual fund late trading*. We also report in parentheses summary statistics that exclude the sizable Madoff Ponzi scheme which represents over 65% of total Ponzi scheme losses. The percentage of total losses and the average loss per case remain highest for Ponzi schemes, regardless of this exclusion.

12.4.2   Form ADV Data and Variables

The SEC website allows the public to view the information disclosed in an investment advisor's most recent Form ADV filing.[9] The SEC also provides access to monthly historical snapshots of Form ADV filings. These publicly available files do not include Schedules A, B, or C, or the DRP filings that detail past misconduct. Also, detailed data on free response fields such as the private fund information in Section 7.B. are also not available. For filings prior to November 2009, the snapshots include only a limited summary of select Form ADV variables (and no data of any type is available for filings prior to June 2006). For this study, we obtained the complete set of historical Form ADV variables through a Freedom of Information Act request. Another complication for researchers using these data is that Form ADV has been altered multiple times changing the mapping of variable names to form questions across different versions of the forms. To facilitate access to the complete Form ADV data for other researchers, we have made these data available at https://doi.org/10.13023/nsjd-rk62.

Following Dimmock and Gerken (2012) and Dimmock, Gerken, and Marietta-Westberg (2015), we use Form ADV data to construct an annual panel of registered investment advisors. Table 12.3 summarizes the Form ADV variables from each firm's first Form ADV filed from 2000 to 2015. Panel A summarizes the continuous variables and Panel B summarizes the binary variables.

Employee ownership is the percentage of the firm that is owned by employees and is calculated following the methodology in Dimmock, Gerken, and Marietta-Westberg (2015). This variable accounts for indirect employee ownership through trusts and pass-through entities. The majority of firms in the sample are wholly employee owned. We include this variable because ownership affects both the incentives and the oversight of the firm. Owners receive the benefits of committing fraud, but also bear the full reputational penalty if fraud is detected. More generally, employee ownership eliminates the principal–agent problem between the managers and owners (although the agency conflict between clients and the firm remains). *Firm age* (in years) is included in all regressions as a control for the firm's reputational capital that would be at risk if the firm committed fraud.

Assets under management (AUM) is the total market value of the assets managed by the advisory firm. AUM is highly skewed; in 2015, the largest 1% of advisors managed more than half of the industry's total AUM. *Average account size* is the firm's AUM divided by the number of clients. The definition of client includes both people and investment vehicles (i.e. an investment company with multiple investors is counted as a single client). *Average account size* is also highly skewed.

---

[9] The filings of individual firms are available at https://www.adviserinfo.sec.gov. Bulk downloads of some of the information in historical filings are available at https://www.sec.gov/help/foiadocsinvafoiahtm.html.

Table 12.3   Summary of investment advisory firms.

This table summarizes information from each firm's first Form ADV filing from 2000 to 2015. There are 24,536 unique firms in the sample. Employee ownership is the aggregate employee ownership of the firm. 'Percent client agents' is the percentage of clients that are agents for the owners of the assets. Past fraud equals one if the firm is identified as committing fraud in a previous SEC filing. Past affiliated fraud equals one if the firm's affiliates have been identified as committing fraud in a previous SEC filing. Past regulatory equals one if the firm reports past regulatory violations. Past civil or criminal equals one if the firm reports past civil or criminal violations. Referral fees equals one if the firm compensates any party for client referrals. Interest in transaction equals one if the firm recommends securities in which it has an ownership interest, serves as an underwriter, or has any other sales interest. Soft dollars equals one if the firm receives benefits other than execution from a broker-dealer in connection with clients' trades. Broker in firm equals one if the firm employs registered representatives of a broker-dealer. Investment Company Act equals one if the firm is registered under the Investment Company Act of 1940. Custody equals one if the firm has custody of clients' cash or securities. Dedicated CCO equals one if the chief compliance officer has no other job title. Hedge fund clients equals one if more than 75% of the firm's clients are hedge funds. The column 'Clean (Fraud)' summarizes firms in which a fraud is not committed (is committed) from first filing through December 2015. The symbols *, **, and *** denote significance at the 10%, 5%, and 1% levels based on Fisher's exact test.

Panel A: Firm characteristics

	Mean	SD	25th	50th	75th
Employee ownership	62.1%	38.6	15.0	87.5	92.5
Avg. acct. size ($ thousand)	65,285	610,636	158	895	24,115
Percent client agents	25.7%	34.8	0.0	10.0	35.0
Assets under mgmt. ($ million)	1,307	11,304	3	50	228
Firm age (years)	3.3	5.8	1	1	1

Panel B: Firm disclosures

	All	Clean	Fraud
Past fraud	0.1	0.1	1.3***
Past affiliated fraud	1.1%	1.1	2.6**
Past regulatory	9.8%	9.4	29.6***
Past civil or criminal	2.8%	2.6	11.3***
Referral fees	33.6%	33.2	50.0***
Interest in transaction	28.8%	28.5	46.5***
Soft dollars	51.1%	50.9	56.3**
Broker in firm	50.4%	50.2	60.1***
Investment Company Act	8.9%	8.7	17.2***
Custody	18.2%	18.2	17.9
Dedicated CCO	15.5%	15.6	11.7**
Hedge fund clients	10.7%	10.7	8.3*

Percent client agents is the percentage of the firm's clients that are agents rather than direct beneficiaries of the invested funds (e.g. pension funds or other investment advisors). All of these variables are related to monitoring and oversight. There is likely greater investor oversight when total AUM and AUM per client are higher. Clients who are themselves agents have weaker incentives, but possibly greater expertise, than principals.

Panel B of Table 12.3 summarizes the binary independent variables, and includes univariate significance tests comparing fraud firms and clean firms (firms that do not commit fraud during the sample period). The first group of variables measure disclosures of past misconduct. *Past fraud* identifies firms that a prior SEC filing identifies as having committed investment management fraud (it does not include other forms of fraud that did not affect the firm's investment advisory clients). *Past fraud* includes only fraud cases that have already been publicly identified and that have ended. *Past affiliated fraud* identifies firms that have an affiliated firm that has previously committed investment management fraud. (Affiliated firms are any firm that controls, is controlled by, or is under common control.) *Past regulatory* identifies firms that disclose past regulatory violations. *Past civil or criminal* identifies firms that disclose past civil or criminal violations. For the regulatory, civil, and criminal violations, we include disclosures related to the firm as well as disclosures related to employees of the firm. As shown by the paired *t*-test results, firms with past misconduct are more likely to subsequently commit fraud.

The next group of variables are disclosures of potential conflicts of interest. *Referral fees* identifies firms that pay a third party for referring clients to the firm. This practice creates a potential conflict of interest for the third party, and could facilitate the flow of funds to asset managers who commit fraud. *Interest in transaction* identifies firms that trade directly with their clients, or recommend securities in which the firm has an ownership or any other type of sales interest. *Soft dollars* identifies firms that receive research or other products or services from a broker in connection with clients' securities transactions. *Broker in firm* identifies firms that employ registered representatives of a broker-dealer. *Interest in transactions, Soft dollars*, and *Broker in firm* can all create conflicts of interest and provide mechanisms for self-dealing through related parties. The univariate *t*-tests show that firms with *Interest in transactions, Broker in firm*, and *Soft dollars* all have higher rates of fraud.

The final group of variables measure oversight and monitoring. *Investment Company Act* identifies firms that manage funds on behalf of an investment company registered under the Investment Company Act of 1940 (e.g. mutual funds); this Act requires certain disclosures and monitoring by independent directors, among other requirements. *Custody* identifies firms that have direct custody of their clients' assets. *Custody* facilitates many types of fraud, although firms with custody of clients' assets are subject to more stringent audit requirements, including at least one 'surprise' audit each year.[10] *Dedicated CCO* identifies firms whose Chief Compliance Officer (CCO)

---

[10] SEC Rule IA-2968 became effective on 12 March 2010 and enhanced the regulatory safeguards to prevent misconduct when the investment advisor and custodian are related parties, including requiring use of an auditor registered with and following the standards of the Professional Company Accounting Oversight Board (see Bedard, Cannon, and Schnader (2014) for more details).

has no other formal role at the firm. All registered investment advisors are required to designate a CCO, who is responsible for ensuring compliance with all regulatory requirements. At many firms, however, the CCO also holds other roles within the firm. *Hedge fund clients* identifies firms at which 75% or more of the clients are 'pooled investment vehicles (other than investment companies),' as this indicates a relatively sophisticated client base.

12.5   Predicting Fraud and Misconduct

In this section, we test whether it is possible to use the disclosure information summarized above to predict fraud by investment managers. The purpose of these regressions is to show variables that predict fraud; as such, these regressions provide potentially useful information to investors selecting asset managers or to regulators allocating monitoring resources. We do not claim that these regressions show causality. Investment managers jointly choose organizational structures and business practices along with the decision of whether to commit fraud. Thus, our results should not be interpreted to imply it would be desirable to change or prohibit practices that are correlated with misconduct.

As noted in the data section, our dependent variable is *detected* fraud. It is highly likely that there are undetected fraud cases committed by firms in our sample. Thus, any significant relation between an independent variable and fraud measures both that variable's relation with the actual commission of fraud and the variable's relation with the probability of detection conditional upon commission. Investment advisors who intend to commit fraud should select business practices that hinder the detection of fraud, which will bias towards zero the coefficient estimates in empirical tests.

This chapter provides novel insights into how undetected fraud affects predictive tests of fraud by investment managers, and builds heavily upon Dimmock and Gerken (2012), who ran predictive tests within the sample period 2001–2006. This current chapter includes a significantly longer time period, and includes fraud cases that occurred during the period 2001–2006 but were not detected until after the publication of Dimmock and Gerken (2012), allowing us to examine how the subsequent detection of these cases alters the inference in the earlier article. Additionally, it also allows for a true out-of-sample (post-publication) test of the models in Dimmock and Gerken (2012).

12.5.1   Predicting Fraud by Investment Managers

Panel A of Table 12.4 shows the results of probit regressions that predict fraud by investment managers. In Column (1), the sample is a cross-section of the investment management firms with one observation per firm. The independent variables are taken from each firm's first Form ADV filing, and the dependent variable equals one if the firm ever commits fraud during the sample period. In Columns (2)–(5), the sample is a panel of firm-year observations. The independent variables are based on the Form ADV data as of the firm's most recent filing before the beginning of the calendar year, and the dependent variable equals one if the firm commits fraud during the subsequent year. Columns (2) and (3) include all firm-years with valid data. Column (4) excludes firms with a prior history of fraud. Column (5) excludes firms that have, or are affiliated with another firm that has, any prior legal or regulatory violations. In Column (1), the reported standard errors are robust. In Columns (2)–(5), the reported standard errors are clustered by firm. The model χ^2 at the bottom of each column shows the significance of the overall model.

Past fraud and Past affiliated fraud are both insignificant predictors of future fraud. There are very few (surviving) firms with a history of past fraud, so the power for these coefficients is quite low. This finding is identical to that of Dimmock and Gerken (2012), who estimated a similar relation over a much shorter time period. Indeed, Panel A of Table 12.4 contains more than twice as many firm-year observations as in the earlier study. Despite the large expansion of the sample size, the results are similar. Given the similarity of the results, for the remaining independent variables we compare with the results of Dimmock and Gerken (2012) only for those results that differ.

Past regulatory and Past civil or criminal violations both have a strong positive relation with fraud. Such prior violations are likely indicative of poor internal controls, unethical management, or other underlying problems within a firm. Prior violations may also increase scrutiny by regulators and investors, increasing the rate of detection conditional upon the occurrence of fraud. Form ADV requires advisors to disclose their own past violations as well as all violations by affiliated firms; thus prior violations are generally higher for firms that are affiliated with more firms. Such affiliations may increase conflicts of interest or create a mechanism for fraudulent self-dealing, resulting in fraud.

Investment advisors that pay Referral fees to third parties for client recommendations have significantly higher rates of fraud. Referral fees represent a potential conflict of interest and may indicate a general lack of ethics in a firm. Fraudulent firms may also be more willing to pay referral fees because they may find acquiring clients relatively difficult, as they cannot survive standard due diligence procedures. Further, frauds such as Ponzi schemes require a constant inflow of investors, creating a strong incentive to pay for referrals.

The coefficient estimate on Interest in transaction is highly significant. Firms that trade directly with their own clients have higher rates of fraud. Trading directly with clients is an obvious conflict of interest and may indicate a lack of ethics. Client transactions also provide a mechanism for committing fraud. For example, front-running clients' trades or pump-and-dump schemes depend on trading directly with the client.

Soft dollars is not significantly related to fraud. The use of soft dollars is a potential conflict of interest, and soft dollar abuse can rise to the level of fraud. However, prior to the beginning of our sample period the SEC aggressively cracked down on soft dollar abuse, following a series of inspections in 1998 that found 28% of investment advisors misused soft dollars.[11] This result is suggestive that the regulatory changes made in response to the 1998 report were successful.

---

[11] For more details see https://www.sec.gov/news/studies/softdolr.htm#sweep.

Table 12.4   Predicting fraud.

The full sample consists of 128,468 firm-year observations. In the first column, the sample includes only each firm's first Form ADV filed during the sample period. In the remaining columns, the independent variables are taken from each firm's Form ADV filing for each year from 2000 to 2015. In the second and third columns, the full sample is included. In the fourth column, the sample excludes firms with a previously disclosed fraud. In the fifth column, the sample excludes all firms that disclose in Item 11 of Form ADV any type of prior legal or regulatory violation, either by the firm itself or an affiliated firm. Refer to Table 12.3 for variable definitions. Column (1) of Panel A shows the results of a cross-sectional probit regression predicting fraud. The dependent variable equals one if the firm commits fraud in any subsequent year through 2015. Standard errors are robust. Columns (2)–(5) show the results of pooled probit regressions predicting fraud. The dependent variable equals one if the firm commits fraud in the subsequent year. Standard errors are clustered by firm and year. In the interest of brevity, the constants are not reported. Standard errors are reported in square brackets. The symbols *, **, and *** denote significance at the 10%, 5%, and 1% levels, respectively. The columns in Panels B and C correspond to the columns in Panel A. Panel B shows the proportion of fraud that could be predicted within-sample. Panel C shows the results from k-fold cross-validation tests.

Panel A: Predictors of fraud

	Cross Section	Full sample	Full sample	No prior fraud	No prior violat.
Past fraud	0.213		0.136		
	[0.28]		[0.14]		
Past affiliated fraud	-0.209		-0.100	-0.099	
	[0.14]		[0.11]	[0.12]	
Past regulatory	0.318***	0.321***	0.323***	0.329***	
	[0.06]	[0.05]	[0.05]	[0.05]	
Past civil or criminal	0.310***	0.195***	0.205***	0.200***	
	[0.09]	[0.06]	[0.06]	[0.07]	
Referral fees	0.037	0.128***	0.130***	0.124**	0.134**
	[0.05]	[0.05]	[0.05]	[0.05]	[0.06]
Interest in transaction	0.239***	0.316***	0.317***	0.319***	0.361***
	[0.06]	[0.05]	[0.05]	[0.05]	[0.07]
Soft dollars	-0.067	-0.025	-0.023	-0.020	-0.013
	[0.05]	[0.04]	[0.04]	[0.04]	[0.05]
Broker in firm	0.203***	0.083	0.085	0.084	0.033
	[0.05]	[0.07]	[0.07]	[0.07]	[0.08]
ICA of 1940	0.117	0.122	0.126	0.139*	0.156*
	[0.07]	[0.08]	[0.08]	[0.08]	[0.09]
Custody	-0.103	-0.071	-0.070	-0.084*	-0.114
	[0.07]	[0.04]	[0.04]	[0.05]	[0.07]
Dedicated CCO	-0.048	-0.154***	-0.154***	-0.140**	-0.026
	[0.08]	[0.06]	[0.06]	[0.06]	[0.06]
Majority emp. owned	-0.053	-0.069	-0.075	-0.068	-0.077
	[0.05]	[0.07]	[0.07]	[0.07]	[0.07]

Table 12.4 (Continued)

	Cross Section	Full sample	Full sample	No prior fraud	No prior violat.
Log(avg. acct. size)	-0.061***	-0.080***	-0.080***	-0.075***	-0.037**
	[0.02]	[0.01]	[0.01]	[0.01]	[0.02]
Percent client agents	0.001	0.002***	0.002***	0.002***	0.002**
	[0.00]	[0.00]	[0.00]	[0.00]	[0.00]
Hedge fund clients	0.091	0.162*	0.163*	0.149*	0.153*
	[0.10]	[0.08]	[0.08]	[0.08]	[0.09]
Log(AUM)	0.082***	0.062***	0.062***	0.059***	0.009
	[0.02]	[0.02]	[0.02]	[0.02]	[0.02]
Log(firm age)	0.015	-0.062**	-0.062**	-0.062**	-0.071***
	[0.03]	[0.03]	[0.03]	[0.03]	[0.03]
Model chi-square	315.4***	279.1***	265.8***	258.6***	86.38***
Observations	15,848	128,468	128,468	127,646	102,704

Panel B: Within-sample predictions

	Cross Section	Full sample	Full sample	No prior fraud	No prior violat.
# Fraud	389	1,260	1,260	1,224	673
Fraud predicted	111	339	341	321	89
	28.5%	26.9%	27.1%	26.2%	13.2%
# Clean firms	15,459	127,208	127,208	126,422	102,031
Clean firm false pos.	772	6,360	6,360	6,321	5,101
	5.0%	5.0%	5.0%	5.0%	5.0%
Prop. $ losses avoided	28.8%	28.5%	28.6%	24.1%	13.5%

Panel C: K-fold cross-validation hold-out sample predictions

	Cross Section	Full sample	Full sample	No prior fraud	No prior violat.
Avg # fraud predicted	104.2	336.25	340.8	317.8	87.7
Avg % fraud predicted	26.8%	26.7%	27.0%	26.0%	13.0%
Stdv # fraud predicted	3.8	2.1	2.1	3.1	3.9
Min # fraud predicted	98	332	336	311	78
Max # fraud predicted	110	339	344	322	93
Avg # false positives	766.9	6,352.0	6,367.7	6,316.8	5,106.7
Avg % false positives	5.0%	5.0%	5.0%	5.0%	5.0%
Stdv false positives	33.2	54.6	69.1	80.8	114.3
Min # false positives	723	6,258	6,266	6,164	4,900
Max # false positives	852	6,482	6,482	6,471	5,288

Broker in firm is not significantly related to fraud (except in Column (1)). Trading through an affiliated brokerage firm enables certain types of fraud (e.g. ex post allocation of trades or front-running) and removes one possible source or external oversight. However, brokerages must register with the SEC and are subject to additional regulatory requirements (e.g. SEC and FINRA broker-dealer examinations and inspections) and auditing requirements, which may discourage the commission of fraud. Alternatively, it may be more difficult to detect fraud committed through an affiliated brokerage firm, reducing the detection of fraud rather than its occurrence.

There is a positive, albeit weak, relation between fraud and *Investment Company Act*. This result is mainly driven by the mutual fund late trading scandal, and the coefficient estimates are considerably smaller than in Dimmock and Gerken (2012), suggesting this finding may reflect past practices and may not be predictive of future misconduct.

Custody of client assets is negatively related to fraud. Although custody potentially facilitates fraud, it also increases regulatory scrutiny and comes with enhanced audit and regulatory requirements. There are two possible interpretations of this result. First, the increased audit requirements are sufficient to outweigh any effect through which custody facilitates fraud. Second, even with the increased audit requirements, custody allows fraudulent advisors to avoid detection, and thus the weakly negative relation reflects a difference in the detection rate. Dimmock and Gerken (2012) did not find a relation between *Custody* and fraud, and the regulatory requirements were made more stringent since the end of the sample used in that paper, suggesting that it is more likely that the enhanced regulatory requirements reduce the occurrence of fraud.

Dedicated CCO and *Majority employee owned* both measure types of internal governance. *Dedicated CCO*, indicating firms with a Chief Compliance Officer who has no other formal role, is negatively associated with fraud. This can be interpreted as a signal of how seriously a firm takes compliance issues, and is thus related to a reduced propensity to commit fraud. Alternatively, it is possible that *Dedicated CCO* causes a reduction in fraud via internal monitoring and oversight. *Majority employee owned* is not significantly related to fraud.

There is a negative relation between fraud and the logarithm of the average account size. This is consistent with monitoring and due diligence by large investors. Large investors have more resources for screening investment advisors, greater familiarity with best practices, and stronger incentives to monitor advisors. *Percent client agents*, on the other hand, is positively related with fraud. Clients who are agents (e.g. pension funds or charitable trusts), have weaker incentives to screen and monitor investment advisors relative to clients who invest their own funds. *Hedge fund clients* is not significantly related to fraud.

Neither *Log(AUM)* nor *Log(firm age)* are consistently associated with fraud. Dimmock and Gerken (2012) found a positive relation between fraud and *Log(AUM)*, but this relation appears to have been driven primarily by the mutual fund later trading scandal in the early part of the sample and does not persist in the later part of the sample.

12.5.2   Interpreting the Predictive Content of the Models

The χ^2 test results at the bottom of each column in Panel A of Table 12.4 show that the fraud prediction models are highly statistically significant. These results do not provide, however, the economic meaning of the predictability in an easily interpretable form. In this section, we examine the economic interpretation of the probit regression results. Figure 12.3 shows the receiver operating characteristic (ROC) curve for the probit regression in Column (3) of Table 12.4. Predicting fraud involves a trade-off between correctly identifying fraud cases (sensitivity) versus false positives from incorrectly classifying clean firms as fraudulent (1-specificity). The ROC curve visually displays this trade-off. The y-axis displays the proportion of fraud cases correctly predicted and the x-axis displays the proportion of false positives. If the model has no predictive power, and thus classifies fraud firms essentially at random, the ROC curve will be a 45-degree line. The ROC curve in Figure 12.3 rises steeply at first, indicating that a sizeable fraction of frauds can be predicted with a low false positive rate. The relatively flat slope in the upper right portion of the graph indicates that a small fraction of frauds are very difficult to detect.

As an alternative means of displaying the trade-off between predicting fraud versus false positives, Panel B of Table 12.4 summarizes the within-sample predictive performance of the model. Following Dechow et al. (2011), we select the cut-off point that produces a false positive rate of 5% and summarize the model's predictive

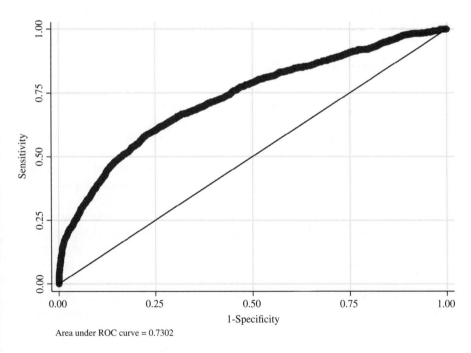

Area under ROC curve = 0.7302

Figure 12.3   Model diagnostic performance.

accuracy (i.e. we set the cut-off level by taking the predicted value from the probit regression such that 5% of clean firms have a predicted value equal or higher, and 95% of clean firms have a lower predicted value). We then summarize the number and proportion of fraudulent firms with a predicted value equal to or higher than the cut-off point.

In the full sample results, shown in Column (3), the model successfully predicts 27.1% of frauds with a false positive rate of 5%. In Column (4), in which the sample is limited to include only firms with no prior fraud cases, the model successfully predicts 26.2% of frauds. The predictive accuracy is substantially lower in Column (5), in which the sample is limited to exclude all firms with any prior legal or regulatory violation. In this restricted sample, the model predicts 13.2% of frauds with a false positive rate of 5%. This highlights the importance of past legal and regulatory disclosures in predicting fraud. Indeed, although only 19.8% of firm-year observations have a past violation, these firm-years contain 46.6% of fraud observations. The comparison between the final column and the earlier columns shows the importance of the mandatory disclosures in Form ADV. Although many of the disclosures are for minor issues, any prior misconduct is a strong predictor of future fraud.

The last row in Panel B shows the proportion of total dollar losses from fraud that could have been avoided based on the prediction model (assuming the investor avoided all firms with a predicted probability of committing fraud equal to or higher than the cut-off level that produces a 5% false positive rate). In all columns, the proportion of dollar losses avoided is similar to the proportion of fraud cases predicted. That is, the models seem to predict large and small fraud cases with equal accuracy. This differs from Dimmock and Gerken (2012) who found more accurate predictions for larger frauds.

12.5.3   K-Fold Cross-Validation Tests

A common concern for predictive models is overfitting – that the within-sample prediction rate overstates out-of-sample performance. In this section, we perform model assessment using k-fold cross-validation (see James, Witten, Hastie, and Tibshirani 2014, chapter 5) for an excellent introduction to both model assessment and k-fold cross-validation). For these tests, we randomly assign each firm to one of 10 groups. Importantly, we randomize at the firm (and not firm-year) level to avoid across-time dependence within firm observations. We then designate one of the groups as the hold-out sample, estimate the model using observations from the other nine groups, and use these coefficient estimates to predict fraud in the hold-out sample. We repeat this procedure for each of the 10 groups. We then repeat this procedure 20 times, resulting in 200 separate out-of-sample comparison groups, and report the average number of fraud cases successfully predicted.

The k-fold cross-validation results in Panel C of Table 12.4 show that the out-of-sample performance of the models is very similar to the in-sample performance. For the baseline model, shown in Column (3), on average we predict only 0.2 fewer frauds out-of-sample. The standard deviation of the number of frauds predicted, along with the minimum and maximum numbers, show the results are very stable across iterations of the cross-validation tests. Finally, the results at the bottom of the panel show that the false positive rate is not substantially larger out-of-sample than in-sample. Overall, these results support that the validity of the predictive models.

12.6   Predicting the Initiation vs. the Continuance of Fraud

In the baseline mode, the dependent variable includes frauds that are newly initiated in the next year, as well as frauds that were previously initiated and continue into the next year. Predicting fraud prior to initiation is potentially more valuable than predicting continued frauds. Additionally, ongoing fraud can alter the predictive ADV variables, obscuring the distinction between predicting new acts of fraud and detection of ongoing cases. Both are potentially interesting, but differentiating them could reveal offsetting effects (e.g. if some variable is positively related to initiation of fraud, but causes the fraud to be detected earlier, shorting its continuation). In this section, we separate newly initiated and continued fraud cases and estimate a sequential logit model of initiation and continuance of fraud (see Buis 2011) for further discussion of the sequential logit model).

Panel A of Table 12.5 presents the regression results. Column (1) predicts the initiation of fraud in the subsequent year, while Column (2) predicts whether a firm that had already initiated a fraud will continue this fraud case in the subsequent year. Standard errors are clustered by firm. In general, the coefficient estimates in Column (1) are larger than those presented in Table 12.4. In contrast, the coefficient estimates in Column (2) are smaller than those presented in Table 12.4. The overall pattern of results suggests that the Form ADV variables are better at predicting the initiation of fraud than at predicting which initiated fraud cases will continue. There is, however, a change in both sign and significance for *Past fraud* and *Past affiliated fraud* in Column (2) relative to the full model in Table 12.4. The negative coefficient on *Past Fraud* is consistent with past offenders having new instances of fraud detected sooner and thus being unable to continue the scheme, consistent with the firm's past actions attracting greater regulatory scrutiny. The positive and significant loading on *Past affiliated fraud* indicates that past instances of fraud at affiliated firms predict the continuance of fraud at a firm.

Panel B of Table 12.5 shows that at a false positive rate of 5% the model correctly predicts 29.8% of fraud cases initiated in the next year.[12] This is slightly higher than the baseline model prediction rate (27.1%), suggesting the Form ADV data can be used to predict the initiation of fraud and not just the continuation of previously initiated cases.

---

[12] We do not report the proportion of continued fraud cases predicted, because for continued frauds it is only possible to make predictions conditional upon knowing with certainty which firms were committing fraud in the prior year, which is not a reasonable assumption.

Table 12.5   Initiation versus continuance of fraud.
The sample consists of 129,465 firm-year observations. The independent variables are taken from each firm's Form ADV filings from 2000 through 2015. Panel A shows the results of a sequential logit regression predicting fraud. The first column shows estimates of the probability that a firm initiates a fraud in the subsequent year. The second column shows estimates of the probability that a firm with a pre-existing fraud continues that fraud into the subsequent year. Refer to Table 12.3 for variable definitions. In the interest of brevity, the constants are not reported. All significance tests are based on standard errors clustered by firm. Standard errors are reported in square brackets. The symbols *, **, and *** denote significance at the 10%, 5%, and 1% levels, respectively. Panel B shows the proportion of initiated fraud cases that could be predicted within-sample.

Panel A: Predicting initiation versus continuance of fraud

	Initiate	Continue
Past fraud	0.246	-0.801*
	[0.30]	[0.47]
Past affiliated fraud	-0.292	0.831***
	[0.20]	[0.29]
Past regulatory	0.803***	0.046
	[0.13]	[0.18]
Past civil or criminal	0.474***	-0.328
	[0.15]	[0.21]
Referral fees	0.374***	-0.266*
	[0.12]	[0.15]
Interest in transaction	0.821***	0.047
	[0.14]	[0.16]
Soft dollars	-0.039	0.078
	[0.12]	[0.14]
Broker in firm	0.258**	0.067
	[0.12]	[0.17]
Investment Company Act	0.220	-0.183
	[0.16]	[0.25]
Custody	-0.187	0.003
	[0.12]	[0.18]
Dedicated CCO	-0.431***	0.378**
	[0.13]	[0.19]
Majority emp. owned	-0.207*	0.129
	[0.12]	[0.17]
Log(avg. acct. size)	-0.208***	-0.034
	[0.03]	[0.04]
Percent client agents	0.005***	0.007**
	[0.00]	[0.00]
Hedge fund clients	0.386*	0.389
	[0.23]	[0.34]
Log(AUM)	0.175***	-0.001
	[0.03]	[0.04]
Log(firm age)	-0.140***	0.018
	[0.05]	[0.06]
Model chi-square	352.16***	291.11***

Table 12.5 (Continued)

Panel B: Within-sample predictions	Initiate
# Fraud	228
Fraud predicted	68
	29.8%
# Clean firms	129,237
Clean firm false positives	6,411
	5.0%

12.7   Firm-Wide Fraud vs. Fraud by a Rogue Employee

Investment management fraud can be 'firm-wide' as in the Madoff Ponzi scheme, where the firm's owners and senior managers were actively involved in perpetrating the fraud. In such cases, the same individuals who choose to commit fraud also choose the firm's organizational structure and business practices. Thus, firm-wide fraud may be correlated with practices that are deliberately chosen to enable fraud. Investment management fraud can also be committed by a rogue employee, who must evade the firm's oversight procedures and who cannot alter the firm's policies to enable the fraud. Thus, rogue employee fraud may be correlated with weak internal controls. In this section, we examine the distinction between these two types of frauds.

Panel A of Table 12.6 presents the results of a multinomial probit regression predicting fraud. The dependent variable in Column (1) is equal to one if the firm commits a firm-wide fraud in the subsequent year. The dependent variable in Column (2) is equal to one if a rogue employee commits fraud in the subsequent year. The coefficient estimates in both columns are generally similar with a few exceptions. *Past civil or criminal* is significant only for rogue employee fraud, suggesting that firms with prior civil violations or who hire criminals, likely have relatively weak internal control systems. Rogue employee fraud is significantly less common at *Majority employee owned* firms, which suggests managerial ownership improves monitoring incentives. *Percent client agent* has a significant positive relation with firm-wide fraud; this is likely an endogenous relation with fraudulent firms targeting a client base with reduced incentives for monitoring. Firm-wide fraud is significantly lower at older firms, consistent with the argument that reputational capital provides a disincentive for fraud.

Panel B of Table 12.6 shows the proportion of fraud cases that can be predicted at a false positive rate of 5%. Firm-wide fraud is considerably more difficult to predict; the model successfully predicts 20.5% of firm-wide frauds versus 61.8% of rogue employee frauds. With firm-wide fraud, the senior management can choose policies and procedures that decrease the probability that fraud is detected, and the fraud is unlikely to be detected by internal monitoring procedures. Thus, firm-wide fraud is more difficult to detect.

Table 12.6   Firm-wide versus rogue employee fraud.

The sample consists of 129,465 firm-year observations. The independent variables are taken from each firm's Form ADV filings from 2000 through 2015. Panel A shows the results of a multinomial probit regression predicting fraud. In the first column, the dependent variable equals one for firms that experience a firm-wide fraud in the subsequent year. In the second column, the dependent variable equals one for firms that experience a rogue employee fraud in the subsequent year. The excluded category is clean firms. Refer to Table 12.3 for variable definitions. In the interest of brevity, the constants are not reported. All significance tests are based on standard errors clustered by firm. Standard errors are reported in square brackets. The symbols *, **, and *** denote significance at the 10%, 5%, and 1% levels, respectively. The columns in Panel B correspond to the columns in Panel A. Panel B shows the proportion of fraud that could be predicted within-sample.

Panel A: Predicting firm wide versus rogue employee fraud

	Firm	Rogue
Past fraud	0.067	0.363
	[0.19]	[0.28]
Past affiliated fraud	-0.003	-0.063
	[0.10]	[0.22]
Past regulatory	0.425***	0.520***
	[0.08]	[0.15]
Past civil or criminal	0.150	0.433***
	[0.09]	[0.14]
Referral fees	0.139**	0.215
	[0.06]	[0.14]
Interest in transaction	0.453***	0.287*
	[0.07]	[0.17]
Soft dollars	0.005	-0.080
	[0.06]	[0.14]
Broker in firm	0.120*	0.252
	[0.06]	[0.16]
Investment Company Act	0.224**	0.158
	[0.09]	[0.18]
Custody	-0.072	-0.206
	[0.07]	[0.13]
Dedicated CCO	-0.113*	-0.154
	[0.07]	[0.16]
Majority emp. owned	-0.023	-0.294*
	[0.07]	[0.16]
Log(avg. acct. size)	-0.080***	-0.192***
	[0.02]	[0.03]
Percent client agents	0.003***	-0.001
	[0.00]	[0.00]
Hedge fund clients	0.181	-0.135
	[0.12]	[0.28]
Log(AUM)	0.049***	0.205***
	[0.02]	[0.04]
Log(firm age)	-0.099***	0.068
	[0.03]	[0.06]
Model chi-square	212.85***	198.81***

Table 12.6 (Continued)

Panel B: Within-sample predictions	Firm	Rogue
# Fraud	1,133	249
Fraud predicted	232	154
	20.5%	61.8%
# Clean firms	128,332	129,216
Clean firm false positives	6,404	6,404
	5.0%	5.0%

12.8   Out-of-Sample Prediction and Model Stability

The true test of a predictive model (and the value of its inputs – in this case the SEC's mandated disclosures via Form ADV) is its out-of-sample performance. In this chapter we revisit the tests of Dimmock and Gerken (2012), which allows us an opportunity to evaluate the out-of-sample performance of the models in that paper by applying the predictions to post-publication data. We graphically display this out-of-sample performance in Figure 12.4. This figure uses the model estimates from Column (3) of table 3 of Dimmock and Gerken (2012), which was estimated on fraud data for the period 2001–2006. For each year for the period 2001–2015, we show both the sensitivity (proportion of fraud cases correctly predicted) and 1-specificity (proportion of clean firms incorrectly labelled as fraud firms) for the model. The cut-off for classifying a firm as a fraud firm is set so that 1-specificity within sample is equal to 5%. The prediction sample for Figure 12.4 includes two types of out-of-sample fraud cases.

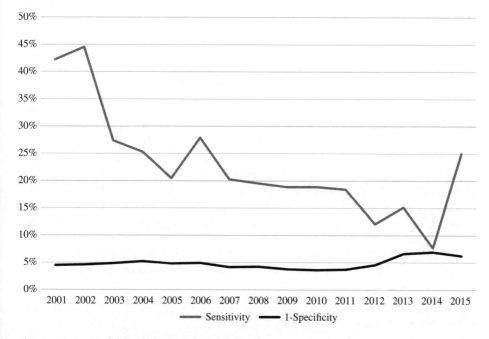

Figure 12.4   Model performance over time.

First, we use frauds that were initiated in the period 2001–2006, but which were not detected until after the data were collected for the 2012 article. Second, we use frauds that were initiated and detected after 2006. Before proceeding to discuss the results in Figure 12.4, it is worth revisiting the findings in Figure 12.2, which show the fraud cases in our sample by year. As Figure 12.2 shows, there are relatively few fraud cases in the later years of our sample, with particularly few cases in 2014 and 2015. This likely reflects the fact that fraud is detected with a lag, and thus the later years of the sample likely contain many fraud cases that have not yet been detected.

Figure 12.4 shows that the proportion of fraud cases correctly identified was highest in the early years of the estimation sample. This period had a large number of mutual fund late trading cases, which the model does an excellent job of predicting. Moving to the out-of-sample period, the model predicts approximately 20% of fraud cases during the period 2007–2011, and does so with a false prediction rate that is lower than 5% (fewer false predictions out-of-sample than in-sample). The model's out-of-sample performance becomes more volatile in the period 2012–2015 as the sample of fraud cases becomes smaller. Unfortunately, the time-series evidence is unable to disentangle alternative explanations for the relative drop in model performance. Model performance could decline post-publication because regulators (and investment managers) could shift behaviour (i.e. a form of the Lucas critique). Specifically, the SEC significantly increased access to Form ADV data in line with the suggestions of Dimmock and Gerken (2012), which could have increased the deterrence effects of these disclosures. Another confounding factor is that there were other significant regulatory changes due to the implementation of the Dodd–Frank Wall Street Reform and Consumer Protection Act during this period. The decrease in model power in the later years, due to fewer fraud observations, also means we cannot dismiss the possibility that the decrease is due simply to chance. Overall, the model continues to perform well out-of-sample, although apparently not as well as in-sample, suggesting that the mandated disclosures still contain useful information to predict fraudulent activity.

12.9   Policy Implications and Conclusions

Consistent with Dimmock and Gerken (2012), we find that mandatory disclosures related to past regulatory and legal violations, conflicts of interest, and monitoring are significant predictors of fraud by investment managers. Further, these variables can predict both the initiation and continuation of fraud, as well as firm-wide and rogue-employee fraud. The predictions perform well both in- and out-of-sample. The results clearly show that the mandatory disclosures made by investment managers contain useful and relevant information for the investing public. Until 2011, the SEC did not provide public access to historical Form ADV data through its website. Shortly after the initial public circulation of the working paper version of Dimmock and Gerken (2012), the SEC began to provide access to monthly snapshots of historical Form ADV data.[13] However, those publicly available files on the SEC website do not contain all

---

[13] See https://www.sec.gov/help/foiadocsinvafoiahtm.html or https://www.adviserinfo.sec.gov/IAPD/InvestmentAdviserData.aspx.

of the information provided in Form ADV filings, and these data are severely limited prior to 2010, reducing their usefulness to researchers.[14]

We believe that improving public access to comprehensive historical disclosures could increase the benefits these disclosures were meant to provide. Our models incorporate only a fraction of the data available through the Form ADV and its schedules. Future work could incorporate a richer set of variables based on recent research (e.g. Clifford, Ellis, and Gerken 2017, and Cumming, Leung, and Rui 2015 shows board characteristics – which are available via Form ADV Schedule A – are related to hedge fund fraud). Accordingly, in conjunction with writing this chapter, we have created a publicly available data set that contains the complete set of SEC Form ADV filings we obtained including the data used in our tests. These data are available at https://doi.org/10.13023/nsjd-rk62. It is our hope that easier data access will spur additional research on the topic of fraud by investment managers and provide investors with important information regarding their choice of investment manager.

This figure shows a simplified timeline of a Ponzi fraud committed by Veros Partners. Veros began operations in 2006. In March 2012, Veros initiated a Ponzi scheme in which clients were promised a high guaranteed rate of return for a 12-month investment. When repayment came due, Veros used the proceeds from new investments to repay outstanding amounts or convinced the client to 'roll over' their investment.

This figure shows fraud initiations (darker bars) and ongoing fraud cases (lighter bars) by calendar year for all detected cases disclosed in the SEC litigation releases or administrative proceedings for firms in the sample. The beginning and ending dates for each fraud case is disclosed in the SEC releases. The figure includes only fraud cases that were ongoing during the 2001–2016 sample period and were committed by firms filing Form ADV during the sample period. Thus, the reported cases for 1984–2000 include only those fraud cases initiated prior to 2001, but which continued into the sample period. Fraud cases initiated prior to 2001, but which were detected or discontinued prior to 2001 are not included.

This figure shows the receiver operating characteristic (ROC) curve for the probit mode specification from Column (3) of Table 12.4. The sample consists of 128,468 firm-year observations. The ROC curve plots the relation between the proportion of fraud detected and the proportion of false positives for all possible classification cut-points. The ROC curve is generated by taking each observation's estimated fraud probability and computing the sensitivity and specificity using that observation as a cut-point.

This figure shows model prediction statistics (sensitivity and specificity) by calendar year. The model uses the coefficient estimates from Column (3) of table 3 of Dimmock and Gerken (2012), who estimated a prediction model using data for the period 2001–2006. The inputs of the model are obtained from Form ADV filings for the period 2001–2015.

---

[14] Due to data requirements, the study is limited to US-based investment advisors. Nevertheless, the fraud predictors identified in this paper should provide useful information to investors and regulators in a global setting. However, further research in an international context would be valuable.

Appendix: Variable Definitions

Variable	Definition	Data source
Past fraud	The firm committed a previously detected fraud	SEC administrative proceeding or litigation release was filed for firm prior to firm-year observation
Past affiliated fraud	An affiliate of the firm committed a previously detected fraud	SEC administrative proceeding or litigation release was filed for affiliated firm prior to firm-year observation and Form ADV Schedule D Section 7.A reports fraud firm as affiliate
Past regulatory	Filed a regulatory disclosure reporting page (DRP)	One of more of: Items 11c1-3, 11d1-5, 11e-4
Past civil or criminal	Filed a criminal or civil DRP	One of more of: Items 11a1-2, 11b1-2, 11h1a, 11h1b, 11h1c, 11h2
Referral fees	Do you or any related person, directly or indirectly, compensate any person for client referrals?	Item 8f
Interest in transaction	Do you or any related person: buy (or sell) securities from advisory clients; recommend securities in which you have an ownership interest or serve as underwriter, general or managing partner or have any other sales interest?	One of more of: Items 8a1, 8a3, 8b2, 8b3
Soft dollars	Do you or any related person receive research or benefits other than execution from a broker-dealer or a third party in connection with client securities transactions?	Item 8e, Item 8g1 beginning in 2012
Broker in firm	Employs registered representatives of a broker-dealer	Item 5b240
Investment Company Act	Investment adviser (or sub-adviser) to an investment company registered under the Investment Company Act	Item 2a4
Custody	Do you or any related person have custody of any advisory clients' cash or securities?	One of more of: Items 9a1-2, 9b1-2
Dedicated CCO	CCO has no other stated role within firm	CCO on Schedule A has no other 'Title or Status'
Majority employee owned	Over 50% aggregate employee ownership	Imputed using Dimmock, Gerken, & Marietta-Westberg (2015) method

Variable	Definition	Data source
Log (avg. acct. size)	Logarithm of assets under management per client	Log (Item 5f2c/(Item 5f2f + 1) + 1)
Percent client agents	Percent of banking, mutual, pension, charitable, corporate, and government clients	Sum of items: 5d3, 5d4, 5d5, 5d7, 5d8, 5d9 imputed using Dimmock, Gerken, & Marietta-Westberg (2015) method
Hedge fund clients	Primarily hedge fund clients	Item 5d6 ≥ 75%
Log (AUM)	Logarithm of assets under management	Log (Item 5f2c + 1)
Log (firm age)	Logarithm of firm age in years	Log (years since date registered with the SEC)

References

Agarwal, V., Daniel, N.D. and Naik, N.Y. (2011). Do hedge funds manage their reported returns? *The Review of Financial Studies* 24 (10): 3281–3320.

Agarwal, V., Mullally, K.A. and Naik, N.Y. (2015). The economics and finance of hedge funds: A review of the academic literature. *Foundations and Trends in Finance* 10 (1): 1–111.

Bedard, J.C., Cannon, N. and Schnader, A.L. (2014). The changing face of auditor reporting in the broker-dealer industry. *Current Issues in Auditing* 8(1): A1–A11.

Ben-David, I., Franzoni, F., Landier, A. and Moussawi, R. (2013). Do hedge funds manipulate stock prices? *The Journal of Finance* 68 (6): 2383–2434.

Bollen, N.P.B. and Pool Veronika K. (2008). Conditional return smoothing in the hedge fund industry. *Journal of Financial and Quantitative Analysis* 43 (2): 267–298.

Bollen, N.P.B. and Pool, V.K. (2009). Do hedge fund managers misreport returns? Evidence from the pooled distribution. *The Journal of Finance* 64(5): 2257–2288.

Bollen, N.P.B. and Pool V.K. (2012). Suspicious patterns in hedge fund returns and the risk of fraud. *The Review of Financial Studies* 25(9): 2673–2702.

Brown, S., Goetzmann, W., Liang, B. and Schwarz, C. (2008). Mandatory disclosure and operational risk: Evidence from hedge fund registration. *The Journal of Finance* 63(6): 2785–2815.

Brown, S., Goetzmann, W., Liang, B. and Schwarz, C. (2009). Estimating operational risk for hedge funds: The ω-score. *Financial Analysts Journal* 65(1): 43–53.

Brown, S., Goetzmann, W., Liang, B. and Schwarz, C. (2012). Trust and delegation. *Journal of Financial Economics* 103(2): 221–234.

Buis, M.L. (2011). The consequences of unobserved heterogeneity in a sequential logit model. *Research in Social Stratification and Mobility* 29(3): 247–262.

Capco (2003). Understanding and Mitigating Operational Risk in Hedge Fund Investments. *White Paper, The Capital Markets Company, Ltd.*

Cassar, G. and Gerakos, J. (2011). Hedge funds: pricing controls and the smoothing of self-reported returns. *The Review of Financial Studies* 24(5): 1698–1734.

Chapman-Davies, A., Parwada, J.T. and Tan, KM.E. (2014). The impact of scandals on mutual fund performance, money flows and fees. Working paper, University of New South Wales.

Charoenwong, B., Kwan, A. and Umar, T. (2019). Who should regulate investment advisers? *American Economic Review* 109: 3681–3712.

Choi, S. and Kahan, M. (2007). The market penalty for mutual fund scandals. *Boston University Law Review.* 87: 1021.

Cici, G., Kempf, A. and Puetz, A. (2016). The valuation of hedge funds' equity positions. *Journal of Financial and Quantitative Analysis* 51(3): 1013–1037.

Clifford, C.P., Ellis, J.A. and Gerken, W.C. (2017). Hedge fund boards and the market for independent directors. *Journal of Financial and Quantitative Analysis,* forthcoming.

Cumming, D. and Dai, N. (2009). Capital flows and hedge fund regulation. *Journal of Empirical Legal Studies* 6(4): 848–873.

Cumming, D. and Dai, N. (2010a): A law and finance analysis of hedge funds. *Financial Management* 39(3): 997–1026.

Cumming, D. and Dai, N. (2010b). Hedge fund regulation and misreported returns. *European Financial Management* 16(5): 829–857.

Cumming, D., Dai, N. and Johan, S. (2017). Dodd–Franking the hedge funds. *Journal of Banking and Finance,* forthcoming.

Cumming, D., Dai, N. and Johan, S. (2015). Are hedge funds registered in Delaware different? *Journal of Corporate Finance* 35: 232–246.

Cumming, D., Leung, T.Y. and Rui, O. (2015). Gender diversity and securities fraud. *Academy of Management* 58(5): 1572–1593.

Dechow, P.M., Ge, W., Larson, C.R. and Sloan, R.G. (2011). Predicting material accounting misstatements. *Contemporary Accounting Research* 28): 17–82.

Dimmock, S.G. and Gerken, William C. (2012). Predicting fraud by investment managers. *Journal of Financial Economics* 105(1): 153–173.

Dimmock, S.G. and Gerken, W.C. (2016). Regulatory oversight and return misreporting by hedge funds. *Review of Finance* 20(2): 795–821.

Dimmock, S.G., Gerken, W.C. and Graham, N.P. (2018). Is fraud contagious? Co-worker influence on misconduct by financial advisors. *Journal of Finance* 73: 1417–1450.

Dimmock, S.G., Gerken, W.C. and Marietta-Westberg. J. (2015). What determines the allocation of managerial ownership within firms? Evidence from investment management firms. *Journal of Corporate Finance* 30: 44–64.

Dimmock, S.G., Gerken, W.C. and Van Alfen, T. (2019). Real estate shocks and financial advisor misconduct. Working paper, University of Kentucky.

Egan, M., Matvos, G. and Seru, A. (2019a). The Market for Financial Adviser Misconduct. *Journal of Political Economy* 127: 233–295.

Egan, M., Matvos, G. and Seru, A. (2019b). When Harry fired Sally: The double standard in punishing misconduct. Working paper, NBER.

French, K.R. Presidential address: The cost of active investing. *The Journal of Finance* 63(4): 1537–1573.

Goetzmann, W.N., Ivković, Z. and Rouwenhorst, K.G. (2001). Day trading international mutual funds: Evidence and policy solutions. *Journal of Financial and Quantitative Analysis* 36(3): 287–309.

Gregoriou, G.N. and Lhabitant, F-S. (2009). Madoff: A flock of red flags. *The Journal of Wealth Management* 12(1): 89–97.

Gurun, U.G., Stoffman, N. and Yonker, S.E. (2018). Trust busting: The effect of fraud on investor behavior. *Review of Financial Studies* 31: 1341–1376.

Honigsberg, C. (2019). Hedge fund regulation and fund governance: Evidence on the effects of mandatory disclosure rules. *Journal of Accounting Research* 57: 845–888.

Houge, T. and Wellman, J. (2005). Fallout from the mutual fund trading scandal. *Journal of Business Ethics* 62(2): 129–139.

James, G., Witten, D., Hastie, T. and Tibshirani, R. (2014). *An Introduction to Statistical Learning with Applications in R*. New York, NY: Springer.

Jylhä, P. (2011). Hedge fund return misreporting: incentives and effects. Working paper, Aalto University.

Kang, B.Uk., Kim, T.S. and Oh, D.J. (2016). National culture and return manipulation by hedge funds. Working paper, Hong Kong Polytechnic University.

Scharfman, J.A. (2009). *Hedge Fund Operational Due Diligence: Understanding the Risks*. Hoboken, NJ: Wiley

Swensen, D.F. (2000). *Pioneering Portfolio Management: An Unconventional Approach to Institutional Investment*. New York, NY: The Free Press.

Wu, K. (2017). The economic consequences of mutual fund advisory misconduct. Working paper, Cornell University.

Zitzewitz, E. (2003). Who cares about shareholders? Arbitrage-proofing mutual funds. *Journal of Law, Economics, and Organization* 19(2): 245–280.

Zitzewitz, E. (2006). How widespread was late trading in mutual funds? *American Economic Review* 96(2): 284–289.

Chapter 13

Options Backdating and Shareholders

Johan Sulaeman
National University of Singapore

Gennaro Bernile
University of Miami

13.1   Introduction

Employee stock option grants continue to be a popular compensation form. Around 8.5 million American workers hold stock options in their companies in 2014.[1] The National Center for Employee Ownership (NCEO) estimates that almost 20% of US employees earning more than $75,000 hold stock options. The majority of

---

[1] The National Center for Employee Ownership (NCEO) provides statistics on the stock and option ownership of US employees using information from the 2014 General Social Survey.

these options are granted by the companies, as they seek to link compensation to employee performance. Stock options provide employees with additional monetary incentive to work diligently to improve the company's performance and ultimately its stock price.

Companies typically issue these stock options as an at-the-money options award, in which the option exercise price is set as the stock price on the grant date. Somewhat surprisingly, a disproportionately high number of such option grants are followed by seemingly positive stock performance. The empirical pattern of favourable stock price patterns surrounding option grant dates is documented in multiple studies, including Yermack (1997), Aboody and Kasznik (2000), and Chauvin and Shenoy (2001).

While this favourable pattern can also be attributed to firms being able to fortuitously or skilfully time the option grants, Lie (2005) proposes the 'backdating hypothesis' to explain it. To provide favourable treatment to an employee, a company could grant stock options to the employee on one date, while providing documentation asserting that the options were granted at an earlier date when the stock price was lower (ex-post date). This backdating practice allows the employee to benefit from favourable upward stock price movement as the exercise price is lower than the current price (i.e. in-the-money option). This practice seems to be beneficial for all stakeholders, as the favourable ex-post date allows employees to receive more valuable in-the-money options, and companies to fictitiously report at-the-money stock options award for reporting purposes.

The publication of Lie (2005) is followed by coverage in the *Wall Street Journal*, starting from a story on 18 March 2006 that many consider to be the spark of what is eventually dubbed the 'backdating scandal'. By December 2006, at least 140 companies were under public scrutiny due to allegations that they engaged in illegal backdating of option grants.

Not having received direct disclosure of this practice, shareholders were deprived of a chance to approve or disapprove it and, as a result, reacted violently to news of such a practice. Stock prices of firms that were alleged to be involved in options backdating practice experienced negative abnormal returns around increased public exposure of such practice. Narayanan, Schipani, and Seyhun (2007) and Bernile and Jarrell (2009) document average abnormal returns of around negative 6–8% corresponding to these events.

While these practices are not typically public knowledge, institutional investors – particularly local ones – seem to anticipate the public disclosures of backdating practices. They display negative abnormal trading imbalances – i.e. their selling volumes are higher than their buying volumes – ahead of public disclosures. As a result, these investors seem to profit from these disclosures amid the corresponding negative abnormal returns.

13.2   Stock Return Patterns around Option Grants

In examining the timing of stock option awards to Fortune 500 CEOs between 1992 and 1994, Yermack (1997) identifies a striking pattern that companies issuing CEO option awards outperform the market by about 2%, which is not reversed afterwards. Yermack (1997) attributes this abnormal performance to managers receiving stock option awards ahead of issuing favourable corporate news that increases the stock price.

Surprisingly, Aboody and Kasznik (2000) find the same pattern around *scheduled* awards, suggesting that the effect in Yermack (1997) is not driven by the timing. Instead, they argue that this increase is driven by opportunistic voluntary disclosure decisions: delaying good news and rushing forward bad news. In particular, option grants typically follow lower earnings forecasts from both analysts and corporate managers.

In addition to the superior post-grant stock performance, Chauvin and Shenoy (2001) also observe inferior pre-grant performance. This V-shaped pattern is consistent with potential short-term manipulation of firm stock price to achieve the lowest price possible for the stock option exercise price. Using a larger dataset of 5,977 option awards from 1992 through 2002, Lie (2005) identified a strong V-shaped pattern around *unscheduled* awards: –3% abnormal returns before the awards, followed by +4% after the awards. The effect is much weaker around *scheduled* awards.

13.3   The Backdating Practice

Given the preponderance of stock pattern evidence above, Lie (2005) proposes a 'backdating' hypothesis to explain the documented return patterns. In particular, he argues that 'the awards might be timed ex post facto, whereby the grant date is set to be a date in the past on which the stock price was particularly low'.

It is important to note that this seemingly innocuous practice is not necessarily illegal. As Fried (2008) writes (p. 861):

> The backdating of stock option grants to lower the exercise price is not per se illegal. Firms generally have complete discretion over the setting of stock option exercise prices. They can use any exercise price-setting methodology they wish, including ones – such as hindsight backdating – that make options in-the-money.

However, companies accused of backdating could face potential legal problems as a direct consequence of such allegations. Conducting internal investigations of past option granting practices and correcting companies' historical financial records and tax returns requires time and resources, which may delay the public release of required financial statements. This delay could cause firms to run afoul of exchange rules.

The direct implication of this practice is that the company and its employees become potentially subject to the IRS for back taxes, penalties, and interest. The knock-on effect associated with correcting backdating options includes cooperating with investigations by outside regulatory agencies; dealing with class-action lawsuits and/or derivative actions by shareholders; paying make-whole bonuses to employees who received backdated options; and potentially violating debt covenants, forcing renegotiation, and/or payment of the resulting penalties.

Lastly, this practice also seems to run afoul of the fiduciary duty of the board of directors. The practice could have received board approval and been properly disclosed for financial reporting and tax purposes. However, most companies involved in the backdating scandal allegedly violated at least one of these disclosure requirements.

Heron and Lie (2009) estimate that 13.6% of all option grants to top executives during the period 1996–2005 were backdated or otherwise manipulated. Moreover, they estimate that almost 30% of publicly listed firms manipulated grants to top executives at some point between 1996 and 2005. These instances are more prevalent in option grants that were unscheduled and awarded at-the-money, and were more prevalent before 29 August 2002, when the Securities and Exchange Commission (SEC) imposed more stringent reporting regulations in which executives are required to report option grants they receive within two business days. Narayanan, Schipani and Seyhun (2007) report that this more stringent requirement seems to have curtailed the prevalence of late reporting, and consequently the V-shaped stock price pattern around the grant dates.

13.4   Media Coverage, Restatement, and Investigation

The potential prevalence of backdating practices received massive media exposure. The *Wall Street Journal* ran a front-page story 'The Perfect Payday' on 18 March 2006 that many consider to be the spark initiating the backdating scandal.[2] As of December 2006, at least 140 companies were under public scrutiny due to allegations that they engaged in *illegal* backdating of option grants. It is important to note that backdating can be legal if it receives board approval and is properly disclosed for reporting and tax purposes. However, most companies identified in the backdating scandal allegedly violated at least one of these requirements.

The public exposure of potential backdating is followed by various firm-level events. A large majority of firms have announced internal reviews of their past option granting practices. Conducting internal reviews requires paying fees to outside lawyers and accountants. The information of the actual costs of such reviews is sparse. Mercury Interactive disclosed the largest expense in this category, with total legal and accounting expenses amounting to $70 million, or 1.7% of its pre-scandal market capitalization. Given that Mercury is one of the first companies caught in the scandal (i.e. in July 2005) and arguably one whose backdating practices have proven to be pervasive over a 13-year period (1992–2004), this is likely to represent one of the highest amounts.

As a result of these internal investigations, almost one-third of identified firms reports finding a material weakness of their internal controls. Additionally, some firms choose to reclassify, cancel, or reprice the tainted options. A small fraction of firms announce that the recipients of tainted options, typically executives, forfeit those options or provide restitution of the corresponding ill-gotten gains. A larger portion of the firms announce repricing or changing the terms (vesting periods) of backdated options. In these cases, the repricing typically applies to options held by executive and directors, as well as rank-and-file employees. In relatively few cases, firms provide make-whole bonuses for the effect of correcting backdated options on the

---

[2] The first two backdating-related cases became public in November of 2004. At that point, publicly available filings showed the SEC had initiated informal inquiries of stock options granting practices at Nyfix Inc. and Analog Devices Inc.

compensation and personal tax liability of rank-and-file employees and executives/directors that unknowingly received tainted options.

Reclassifying backdated options to in-the-money status or issuing make-whole bonuses requires firms to amend historical financial records to recognize the resulting 'incremental' compensation expense. In all, more than two-thirds of identified firms explicitly quantifies the amount of historical earnings to be restated or announces the amount of (non-material) charges to be imputed to current earnings. Of those firms, the mean (median) cumulative effect is an earnings reduction of $122.4 (31.1) million, corresponding to 4.7% (2.3%) of the typical firm's pre-scandal market capitalization.

These restatements attract the interests of federal prosecutors (publicly observed in about 40% of the identified firms) as well as shareholders lawsuits (in about 60% of the cases). These restatements also increase the likelihood of delays in filing (restated) financial statements, resulting in warnings or notices of potential delisting from exchanges (in about 40% of the cases). Such legal difficulties can result in senior executives and/or directors parting with the company; this happens in about one-third of the cases.

In addition to these direct effects, the backdating scandal also has implications on the market of corporate control. There are two channels through which firms identified in this scandal become more likely to receive takeover offers. First, as we will discuss later, backdating accusations depress equity values – potentially significantly more than the direct costs described above – providing potential buyers with the opportunity to acquire these firms at discounted prices. Second, the incidence of backdating practices could indicate deeper agency issues. As such, these firms are more likely to become takeover targets to the extent that gains from improving governance structure are higher in these companies than in otherwise similar firms. In the span of a year since the public revelations of backdating issues, 12 firms with average pre-scandal market capitalization of $5.65 billion received takeover offers; all but one of those offers are all-cash. The resulting takeover rate of almost 10% is around double the highest such annual rate for public companies between 1980 and 2003.

13.5   Stock Market Reaction to Public Revelations of Backdating

The stock market reacts negatively to potential backdating incidences. In tracking the abnormal performance of firms (eventually) identified as having participated in backdating starting from February 2004, i.e. the initial circulation of Erik Lie's (2005) article, Bernile and Jarrell (2009) document an abnormal cumulative drop in firm value of more than 10%. This pattern is driven by significant drops around the emergence of early cases, articles from the *Wall Street Journal* (e.g. a story on November 11, 2005 quoting an early draft of Heron and Lie (2007), the front page article on March 18, 2006), and various firm-specific public exposures.

Narayanan, Schipani and Seyhun (2007) and Bernile and Jarrell (2009) report that the first public exposure is accompanied by substantial risk-adjusted returns in the order of negative 6% to 8%. In particular, Bernile and Jarrell (2009) report that the revelation is accompanied by an average abnormal return of around −2.5% in days (−1:1) around the public news. They also document a strong pre-event trend, in which these stocks underperform their benchmark portfolios/factors by almost −5% in the twenty trading days (−20:−2) preceding the event window. These drops in market valuations are not reversed following the first revelations, and are slightly larger than the direct costs associated with the reductions in restated earnings. Indeed, Narayanan, Schipani and Seyhun (2007) estimate the average market value loss to be almost $400 million per firm.

The gap between the direct loss and the market value loss is potentially related to concerns regarding agency and reputational issues beyond the backdating incidence. As these public revelations occur in waves, the first wave of revelations could have a knock-on effect on other firms that are not yet but eventually identified to have participated in backdating. Indeed, Bernile and Jarrell (2009) find that pre-event negative price movements occur earlier for firms identified at later dates.

The market reaction to the backdating scandal is not limited to firms that are publicly identified or investigated. Carow et al. (2009) develop a predictive model for these public identifications and identify other firms which could have been reasonably predicted to have backdating problems due to their similar characteristics to investigated firms, but are not actual subjects of publicly revealed investigations. These firms also experience negative stock price performance during the same period, similar to that of firms with publicly revealed investigations.

13.6   Investor Reaction to (and Anticipation of) Public Revelations

Bernile, Sulaeman, and Wang (2015) report that these pre-exposure drifts are driven by institutional investors, as their abnormal trading imbalances (i.e. buy minus sell) are significantly negative throughout the trading *month* prior to the first firm-specific revelations. These negative imbalances are larger for firms eventually subjected to investigations by Securities and Exchange Commission (SEC) or Department of Justice (DOJ), or eventually experienced shareholder lawsuits. Consistent with the price patterns in Bernile and Jarrell (2009), negative pre-exposure trading imbalances manifest earlier in event time for firms exposed at later dates. These pre-exposure institutional trades are profitable both over short and long horizons after the exposure.

Bernile, Sulaeman, and Wang (2015) also report that 'local' institutional investors drive the pre-exposure trading and profitability patterns above. Local investors display negative pre-exposure trading imbalances earlier in event time, particularly for firms exposed at later dates. Moreover, pre-exposure local trades consistently earn higher profits than similarly timed non-local ones. Bernile, Sulaeman, and Wang (2015) conclude that local institutional activities are more informed and timelier than the trading activities of non-local institutions, consistent with local investors being more likely to facilitate market efficiency.

Bernile, Sulaeman, and Wang (2015) also examine institutional trades *following* the arrival of public information. Specifically, after identifying high-backdating-risk firms following Carow et al. (2009), they examine whether revelations of public investigations spill over onto institutional trades on these stocks that are never implicated in the scandal. Bernile, Sulaeman, and Wang (2015) report three related results. First, independent of firms' actual involvement in the scandal, institutional abnormal trading imbalances on high-backdating-risk stocks become significantly negative, as the frequency of firms exposed engaged in option backdating practices double in the period June–August 2006 compared to the period March–May 2006. Second, this pattern is fairly short-lived: while stocks that are ultimately implicated continue to experience negative imbalances during the following six months, non-implicated high-risk stocks experience no abnormal imbalance over the same period. Third, local investors do not contribute to these negative spillovers. Non-local investors *alone* account for any negative spillover; they also earn negative abnormal profits on the corresponding trades.

Lastly, Bernile, Sulaeman, and Wang (2015) examine whether institutional trading acts as a destabilizing force following the public revelation of backdating issues. In particular, they examine whether the first arrival of firm-specific backdating news is followed by continuing negative trading imbalances. They find this to be the case, but again non-local institutions *alone* account for this pattern. These investors again earn negative abnormal profits on these 'late' trades.

Bernile, Sulaeman, and Wang (2015) conclude that institutional investors, particularly those located in the proximity of the scandal firms, seem to anticipate firm-specific exposures, which is consistent with the pre-revelation drift documented in Narayanan, Schipani, and Seyhun (2007) and Bernile and Jarrell (2009).

13.7 Other Types of Misbehaviour Related to Option Grants

The option grant backdating practice for top company executives is associated with several other types of corporate misbehaviour. Again, some of these practices are not illegal per se.

13.7.1 Forward Dating

Narayanan and Seyhun (2008) discuss another potential method that managers can use to inflate their option-based compensation. Imagine a situation in which a firm is experiencing a declining stock price, and therefore its managers cannot take advantage of the backdating strategy (as there is no lower stock price to be used as a fictitious at-the-money strike price). Narayanan and Seyhun (2008) define 'forward dating' as a response to this situation, in which the 'grant' date is chosen to be after the decision date as the stock price continues to fall. This strategy does not always benefit managers, as the stock price could continue to fall after the grant date is chosen, and therefore the grant date is not necessarily followed by rising stock prices. However, this strategy shares one trait with the backdating practice: the grant dates are preceded by declining stock prices.

13.7.2 Selective Disclosure

Some companies employ fixed award schedules. This practice should be effective in removing the possibility of backdating as the option grant date is fixed ex-ante, and therefore companies cannot arbitrarily backdate their employee option grants. Nevertheless, Aboody and Kasznik (2000) observe a V-shaped pattern around these scheduled option grants. They argue that this surprising finding is due to the practice of selective disclosure of information around the scheduled grant date. In particular, managers would delay issuing good news and rush forward bad news before the scheduled grant date. This would lower the market's expectation regarding the firm, and likely to lead to a lower stock price – and hence a lower exercise price for at-the-money employee options – at the fixed grant date. In support of this selective disclosure interpretation, Aboody and Kasznik (2000) document that these scheduled grants are typically preceded by lower earnings forecasts from both analysts and corporate managers.

13.7.3 Option Exercise Backdating

Dhaliwal, Erickson, and Heitzman (2009) report that some option *exercise* dates are backdated to days with low stock prices. This practice is favourable to employers as it allows parts of their compensation – i.e. the difference between the fictitious stock price and the actual stock price – to be taxed at the lower 'capital gain' rate, instead of the higher personal income rate. Dhaliwal et al. (2009) estimate that this practice generates average tax savings of $96,000.

13.7.4 Independent Director Backdating

Bebchuk, Grinstein, and Peyer (2010) find that independent directors also benefit from fortuitous option grants. Moreover, they find that the odds of option grants to CEOs being 'lucky' – i.e. the grant date corresponds to the lowest stock price for the month – were significantly higher when the independent directors of the firm also received option grants on the same date. More generally, Bizjak, Lemmon, and Whitby (2009) document a strong correlation between a firm's directors receiving option grants and the firm's CEO benefiting from option backdating practice. Moreover, Bizjak, Lemmon, and Whitby (2009) argue that board connections play an important role in the spread of the practice. In particular, they document that a firm's probability of being identified as using backdating increases by about one-third when the firm shares a board member with another firm that employs backdating.

13.8 Connections with Questionable Practices by Corporate Executives and Other Agents

The practice of option backdating is ethically questionable but may not be illegal per se. Its benefit to corporate agents involved in backdating is easily quantifiable (albeit potentially temporary), i.e. the difference between the stock price at the actual grant date and the price at the earlier, fictional date. This stands in stark contrast to the difficulty in estimating potential legal and reputational costs of such practice, particularly since its legality is unclear. As such, firms' decisions to adopt this practice are likely to be related to the relevant corporate agents' perception of the potential legal costs and reputational ramifications. These perceived penalties, particularly the latter, are likely to be driven by the prevailing social and ethical norms faced by these agents.

Norms tend to vary regionally, correlated with various local factors including religious adherences and practices, demographics, socioeconomic conditions, and education. Capturing these local norms are quite difficult, but one potential way of quantifying such norms is by observing the revealed preferences – i.e. misbehaviours – of local residents. Parsons, Sulaeman, and Titman (2018) take this approach, and examine local data on various misbehaviours that are unethical, but not necessarily illegal. Misbehaviours in the illegal category includes financial misconducts of corporate managers, misconducts committed by registered financial advisors, and corruption-related activities of elected public officials. Misbehaviours that are not necessarily illegal include cheating spouses, and doctors prescribing medication in conjunction with incentives from pharmaceutical companies.

Parsons, Sulaeman, and Titman (2018) document a high correlation between regional propensities of financial misconducts and backdating practices. Among the 20 largest US cities, the rank correlation of these two types of misbehaviour is 0.55. Given the potential overlaps of corporate agents committing these misbehaviours, this high correlation reflects the variation in corporate norms across US cities. However, the positive correlation is not limited only to corporate misbehaviours or only to misbehaviours that are potentially illegal. The rank correlations between backdating and non-corporate misbehaviours are consistently positive: 0.38 with local doctors' sensitivity to incentives from pharmaceutical companies, and 0.65 with the percentage of Ashley-Madison subscribers of the local over-18 population with access to the internet. Indeed, the regional propensity to commit backdating exhibits the highest average pairwise correlation with other regional misbehaviour propensities. In a principal component analysis of these regional propensities, backdating is the second most important contributor to the first component – only slightly behind financial misconduct. Overall, the propensity of local corporate agents committing option backdating seems to be a reflection of local norms and therefore could be a useful indicator of these difficult-to-quantify norms.

13.9 Conclusion

A disproportionately high number of stock option grants are followed by positive stock performance. This pattern is beneficial for corporate managers and employees receiving the stock option grants. While this favourable pattern can also be attributed to firms being able to fortuitously or skilfully time the option grants, Lie (2005) proposes the 'backdating hypothesis' to explain it. To provide favourable treatment to an employee, a company grants stock options to the employee on one date, while providing documentation asserting that the options were granted at an earlier date when the stock price was lower (ex-post date). This practice seems to be beneficial for all stakeholders, as the favourable ex-post date allows employees to receive more valuable in-the-money options, and companies to fictitiously report at-the-money stock options award.

However, not having received direct disclosure of this practice, shareholders were deprived of a chance to approve or disapprove such practice. As a result, shareholders react violently to the news of the occurrence of such practice. While these practices are not typically public knowledge, institutional investors – particularly local ones – seem to anticipate the public disclosures of backdating practices. They display negative abnormal trading imbalances – i.e. their selling volumes are higher than their buying volumes – ahead of public disclosures. As a result, these investors seem to profit from these disclosures amid the corresponding negative abnormal returns.

Beyond the direct negative implication of option backdating, i.e. the potential legal costs incurred by the firm, the negative returns associated with revelations of option backdating practices also reflect the indirect cost associated with the reputational penalty to the firms' managers, directors, and auditors. Additionally, these revelations also reflect the limitations of local and corporate norms that could have inhibited these ethically questionable but not necessarily illegal practices.

References

Aboody, D. and Kasznik, R. (2000). CEO stock option awards and the timing of corporate voluntary disclosures. *Journal of Accounting and Economics* 29: 73–100.

Bebchuk, L.A., Grinstein, Y. and Peyer, U. (2010). Lucky CEOs and lucky directors. *Journal of Finance* 65: 2363–2401.

Bernile, G. and Jarrell, G.A. (2009). The impact of the options backdating scandal on shareholders. *Journal of Accounting and Economics* 47: 2–26.

Bernile, G., Sulaeman, J. and Wang, Q. (2015). Institutional trading during a wave of corporate scandals: 'Perfect payday', *Journal of Corporate Finance* 34: 191–209.

Bizjak, J., Lemmon, M. and Whitby, R. (2009). Option backdating and board interlocks. *Review of Financial Studies* 22: 4821–4847.

Carow, K., Heron, R., Lie, E. and Neal, R. (2009). Option grant backdating investigations and capital market discipline. *Journal of Corporate Finance* 15: 562–572.

Chauvin K.W. and Shenoy, C. (2001). Stock price decreases prior to executive stock option grants. *Journal of Corporate Finance* 7: 53–76.

Dhaliwal, D., Erickson, M. and Heitzman, S. (2009). Taxes and the backdating of stock option exercise dates. *Journal of Accounting and Economics* 47: 27–49.

Fried, J.M. (2008). Option backdating and its implications. *Washington and Lee Law Review* 65: 853–886.

Heron, R.A. and Lie, E. (2007). Does backdating explain the stock price pattern around executive stock option grants? *Journal of Financial Economics* 83: 271–295.

Heron, R.A. and Lie, E. (2009). What fraction of stock option grants to top executives have been backdated or manipulated? *Management Science* 55: 513–525.

Lie, E. (2005). On the timing of CEO stock option awards. *Management Science* 51: 802–812.

Narayanan, M.P., Schipani, C. and Seyhun, H.N. (2007). The economic impact of backdating of executive stock options. *Michigan Law Review* 105: 1597–641.

Narayanan, M.P. and Seyhun, N.H. (2008). The dating game: Do managers designate option grant dates to increase their compensation? *Review of Financial Studies* 21: 1907–1945.

National Center for Employee Ownership, 2014, https://www.nceo.org/articles/widespread-employee-ownership-us.

Parsons, C. P., Sulaeman, J. and Titman, S. (2018). The geography of financial misconduct. *Journal of Finance*, forthcoming.

Wall Street Journal (2007). Options backdating scorecard, September, 2007.

Wall Street Journal (2006). Perfect payday, by C. Forelle and J. Bandler, March 18.

Wall Street Journal (2005). Authorities probe improper backdating of options – practice allows executives to bolster their stock gains; A highly beneficial pattern, by M. Maremont, November 11.

Yermack, D. (1997). Good timing: CEO stock option awards and company news announcements. *Journal of Finance* 52: 449–476.

Chapter 14

The Strategic Behaviour of Underwriters in Valuing IPOs

Stefano Paleari
University of Bergamo

Andrea Signori
Catholic University of Milan

Silvio Vismara
University of Bergamo
Ghent University

14.1   Valuing IPOs

An initial public offering (IPO) is the event in which a firm sells its shares to the public market for the very first time. This is done by listing on a stock exchange, in which two types of shares can be sold, namely primary and secondary shares. Primary shares are newly issued shares where capital is raised in exchange for a share of ownership in the company. This means that there is a capital inflow to the company's account and, at the same time, the firm's ownership structure is diluted since the equity stake owned by pre-IPO owners is reduced due to the issuance of new shares. Secondary shares are instead sold by pre-IPO shareholders. This means that the capital flows from market investors to the existing shareholders of the firm, whose balance sheet does not change because of this trade.

The main document associated with a public offer of shares is the prospectus, which is accompanied by a variety of agreements that, among others, include an arrangement setting out the responsibilities of the company and its directors for the prospectus, as well as the responsibilities of an investment bank for sponsoring and underwriting the offer. The underwriter ensures that the firm satisfies all regulatory requirements, such as filing with the appropriate regulatory bodies and depositing all fees, and makes all mandatory financial data available to the public. Underwriters are in contact with prospective investors, including institutional investors like mutual funds and insurance companies. Clearly, a firm conducting an IPO needs to have its equity valued before the listing, in order to determine a price range within which the shares will be offered to the public. The offer price, which is the price at which the shares will be sold, is usually set within this range. A high offer price would benefit both the issuing firm, because of the higher capital inflow, and the underwriter, because of its compensation scheme, which is usually defined as a proportion of the amount of capital raised. However, an excessively high price may undermine the success of an IPO, as investors may become reluctant to bid if the offer is too costly, thereby leaving the firm with unsold shares.

There are several methods to value a firm. The most widely used approaches are the discounted cash flow and the relative valuation method. The latter relies on the comparison of the firm with a number of publicly traded peers, typically belonging to the same industry and with similar characteristics, for which valuation multiples can be easily computed. In the absence of a publicly observable price, private peers that have been involved in equity transactions may also be selected.

Equity valuation using multiples is an approach based on the market valuation of companies that are thought to be comparable to the firm that needs to be priced. The idea is that the multiple of similar firms can be used as a driver for the valuation of a specific company. This implies that investors evaluate a company in the same way in which they evaluate comparable firms. For example, when using the price-to-earnings valuation multiple, the estimated value is obtained by multiplying the firm's earnings to the peers' average (or median) multiple. Thereby, the selection of the group of peers, which is at the underwriter's discretion, becomes crucial for the outcome of the valuation process. This is particularly relevant to our case, as the comparable method carries the risk of self-justifying an over- or undervaluation of firms in a certain industry.

Relative valuation methods have the advantage of being intuitive and simple to apply. However, they are accompanied by several concerns. The first issue is that the definition of a comparable firm is essentially a subjective one. The use of other firms in the industry as the control group is often not the solution because firms within the same industry can have very different business mixes, as well as risk and growth profiles, that make it difficult to find two identical companies. If the established selection criteria are too strict, few comparable firms can be identified, which leads to the pricing process being strongly affected by the valuation of a small number of firms. If, on the other hand, the selection criteria are too loose, the risk is to obtain a sample of firms that are not fully comparable with the one that is being evaluated. The correct selection of the peer group therefore requires the optimization of a trade-off between more and less strict selection criteria. Furthermore, given a certain peer group, different valuation estimates can be obtained simply because different types of accounting measures as a basis for the valuation multiples (e.g. book value of equity, earning before interests and taxes). Thus, the choice of which multiples have to be used in the valuation process is also critical. The most popular multiple used in practice is the price-to-earnings ratio. Earnings can be normalized for unusual or one-off items that can impact earnings abnormally. One way to normalize earnings is to use the average earnings over prior periods. A close variant of this approach is to estimate the average operating or net margin in prior periods and apply this margin to current revenues to arrive at normalized operating or net income. The price-to-earnings ratio, however, cannot be used for valuation purposes for firms with negative earnings. This is one of the reasons why most valuations do not rely exclusively on this ratio, but make use of other metrics, such as the price-to-book or enterprise value-based multiples.

14.2   The Underwriter's Incentives in the Valuation of IPOs

The IPO underpricing phenomenon has drawn considerable attention by academics, practitioners, and market participants in general. Underpricing is defined as the difference between the official closing price of the issuer's stock at the end of the first day of trading and the offer price at which shares are sold to IPO investors. This difference is, on average, positive, and has been approximately 14% of the offer price for US IPOs during 2001–2016.[1] This implies that the average investor who is allocated shares in an IPO gets a positive 14% return by selling her shares just after one day. Ritter (2011) argues that agency problems between issuers and underwriters have become increasingly important to understand underpricing.

From the issuer's perspective, underpricing is traditionally seen as one of the costs of going public, which explains why it is often referred to as 'money left on the table'. More precisely, it can be considered as an opportunity cost to an issuing firm because a positive first day return implies that the shares were sold to IPO investors at a lower valuation (i.e. underpriced) than the one recognized by the market once trading activity has begun. In other words, a deeper underpricing means that the issuing firm could have potentially raised a larger amount of money at the IPO.

---

[1] See Jay Ritter's website for updated IPO data (https://site.warrington.ufl.edu/ritter/ipo-data).

Maximizing IPO proceeds is sought after not only by the issuing firm, but also by its underwriter. An important part of the underwriter's remuneration comes from the investment banking fee, known as the gross spread, which is expressed as a percentage of IPO proceeds. Therefore, a higher offer price should make both issuers and underwriters happy. However, gross spread is not the only remuneration channel for underwriters, but there are at least two other important sources of profit. First, underwriters often give preference in favourable IPO allocations to rent-seeking investors, who pay commissions in excess of direct execution costs, known as soft dollars (Loughran and Ritter, 2002). Second, underwriters tend to allocate underpriced IPOs to corporate executives as a way of influencing their choice of investment banking decisions, a practice known as spinning (Liu and Ritter, 2010).[2] The necessary condition that enables underwriters to exercise their discretionary power in IPO allocations and engage in spinning practices is the presence of excess demand for shares, which is in turn stimulated by underpricing as long as the prospect of a positive first day return encourages investors to subscribe IPO shares. Therefore, the trade-off faced by underwriters when valuing IPOs can be modelled as follows: on one hand, gross spread generates the incentive to raise the offer price in order to maximize proceeds, thereby minimizing underpricing; on the other hand, the amount of profits arising from the soft dollars and spinning mechanisms increases with underpricing, which generates the incentive to propose a lower offer price than would be optimal for the issuer.

Valuing IPOs using the comparable firms methodology may be particularly suitable for underwriters to optimally solve their trade-off, due to the considerable degree of discretion associated with this valuation technique. Ultimately, the underwriter wants to maximize the difference between the offer price and the subsequent market price. This increases profits from the soft dollars and spinning channels. One way for underwriters to maximize this difference would be to lower the offer price. This, however, would cause a reduction in the profit arising from the gross spread. An alternative, more profitable way to maximize the above difference is therefore to induce a higher subsequent market price. This would guarantee a significant amount of profits from the gross spread, while simultaneously ensuring a certain level of underpricing, which would allow underwriters to obtain soft dollars and engage in spinning practices. Thus, by selecting comparable firms that justify a high valuation, the underwriter is able to increase the offer price while simultaneously presenting the IPO as conservatively valued, which may shift the demand of investors and result in a higher market price.

14.3 Literature Review

Kim and Ritter (1999) is the first paper to investigate the valuation of IPOs. They do so using a sample of US IPOs. As American IPO prospectuses do not reveal details about the pricing mechanisms, they compare the valuation of issuing firms with that

---

[2] The term 'spinning' originates from the idea that the shares can be immediately resold, or spun, by the subscriber.

of peers selected using different algorithms. They find that valuing IPOs on the basis of multiples such as the price-to-earnings, price-to-sales, enterprise value-to-sales, and enterprise value-to-operating cash flow ratios of comparable firms may lead to inaccurate estimates if historical numbers rather than forecasts are used. The reason for such large valuation errors is simple: within an industry, the variation in these ratios is so large that their predictive power becomes modest. In other words, among publicly traded firms in the same industry, price-earnings (P/E) ratios typically display such great variation that just about any price can be justified.

Kim and Ritter's paper served as a reference for following studies on the valuation of IPOs. Their contribution, however, is limited by the scarce disclosure of the valuation procedures in the prospectuses of US IPOs. In Europe, this information is instead often disclosed in IPO prospectuses. IPO value estimates by the underwriting investment bank are indeed often published in the IPO-prospectus, which is made available at the start of the public offering. The availability of this information allows to examine how IPOs are valued, and how this valuation affects the offer price. It can be expected that the accuracy of ex ante valuation by investment banks will differ from the valuation accuracy measured by academics, for several reasons. Value estimates by investment banks may be less accurate because academics are more objective than investment banks, who may be tempted to report valuations that justify a high price, for instance by choosing comparable firms with high multiples. On the other hand, value estimates by investment banks may be more accurate than value estimates by academics because investment banks have more information available for valuation. In any case, the disclosure of information about the valuation of firms going public makes it possible to assess how it is done.

The seminal studies using such real world estimations to investigate the different valuation approaches are those by Cassia, Paleari, and Vismara (2004) and by Deloof, De Maeseneire, and Inghelbrecht (2009). Cassia et al. (2004) study how underwriters value firms that went public on Italy's Nuovo Mercato during the period 1999–2002. They document that the most frequently used method was peer comparables. Deloof et al. (2009) compare the value estimates obtained by lead underwriters of Belgian IPOs for the offer price with the stock price over the first month of listing. They find that underwriters consciously underprice IPO shares by relying on a valuation method that tends to underestimate value. They also find that the use of price-earnings and price-cash flow multiples computed with forecasted earnings and cash flows for the year after the IPO leads to more accurate valuations than multiples using forecasted earnings and cash flows for the IPO year.

The limitation of these papers lies in the fact that they do not investigate how underwriters select the comparable firms. This is done by Paleari, Signori and Vismara (2014) and Vismara, Signori, and Paleari (2015). Using a large sample of firms going public in France and Italy, Paleari et al. (2014) develop empirical evidence that underwriters perform a biased selection of comparable firms for valuing the firms they are taking public. They find that peers published in IPO prospectuses show higher multiples than peers obtained using different selection methodologies, including the selections done by sell-side analysts or the list of peers proposed by websites of data providers. Specifically, they find that underwriters often excluded those comparable firms with the lowest multiples. Even when underwriters apply a discount to their value estimates to set the final offer price, the valuation of the IPO firm remains significantly higher than that of alternatively selected peers. As an example, the limited availability of publicly traded boat manufacturers leads the underwriter of Ferretti, an Italian yacht producer, to choose four comparable firms, two of which are luxury motor vehicles manufacturers (Ducati and Porsche) with very high valuation ratios.

Vismara et al. (2015) compare the selection of peer firms made by investment banks as underwriters at the IPO with that done shortly thereafter as analysts. Surprisingly, they find that 3 out of 7 comparable firms, on average, are changed. This is a large change, if we consider that analysts' reports are published few months after the IPO. A large proportion of the firms used as comparables for pricing the IPO are no longer used when assessing the firm as 'external' analyst. The peers published in the IPO prospectuses have higher valuations than those published in the post-IPO equity research reports of the same firm. They conclude that underwriters select comparable firms that make the issuer's shares look conservatively priced at the IPO, while this conflict of interest tends to fade afterwards. The upward bias in peer selection is larger for underwriters with greater market power, and lower for repeat players in the IPO market.

None of the above-mentioned papers explicitly address the role of industry. In particular, the characteristics of the industry in which an IPO firm operates shapes the degree of discretion enjoyed by underwriters in the selection of comparable firms. This, in turn, is likely to affect both the way in which the valuation process is carried out and its estimates. For instance, the selection of peers of a firm operating in the automotive industry is arguably a less ambiguous process that that of selecting peers of a technology firm, which may produce goods or deliver services that profoundly differentiate the firm from industry competitors. In this chapter, we fill this gap by taking an industry perspective to address how IPO underwriters value companies going public.

14.4   Sample, Data, and Methodology

14.4.1   Sample and Data

We use the population of IPOs in the period 1999–2013 on the three largest economies in Continental Europe, namely Euronext (which comprises the stock exchanges of Belgium, France, Netherlands, and Portugal), Germany, and Italy, from the EurIPO database.[3] We focus on Continental Europe because these markets are characterized by a higher level of disclosure of information about valuation techniques used by underwriters in the official IPO prospectuses. Despite the introduction of a Prospectus Directive (2003/71/EC) by the European Commission that established a harmonized format for IPO prospectuses, the level of disclosure varies considerably across

---

[3] For France, we use the French Paris Bourse stock exchange until the creation of Euronext (with the merger of the stock exchanges of Belgium, France, the Netherlands, and Portugal) on 27 January 2005. Afterwards, we consider Euronext in its entirety. See Vismara et al. (2012) for a detailed description of the EurIPO database.

countries.[4] For an IPO to be included in our sample, it has to report in the prospectus information about the methodologies used by the underwriter in the valuation process; 480 IPOs meet this criterion, 452 of which declare to be valued using the peer comparables approach. Of these 452 IPOs valued using comparable firms, only 370 make full disclosure of both the names of the peers selected by the underwriter and their multiples at the time of the valuation process. These 370 IPOs represent the core sample in this chapter, which will be matched with comparable firms from alternative selection criteria in the main empirical analyses.

Table 14.1 reports the distribution of the 480 IPOs across valuation methods, both at an aggregate level and by market where the firm went public. In terms of market distribution, the majority of our sample IPOs took place in Euronext (64.2%), while German offerings represent only a small proportion of the sample (3.3%), due to the considerably lesser propensity of German issuers to disclose information in the prospectus. In terms of valuation method, exactly one third of the IPOs were valued using comparable firms as the only valuation methodology, while the largest portion (56.9%) has been valued using both the comparable firms and the discounted cash flow (DCF) methods. In a few IPOs, underwriters have used either the DCF as a stand-alone methodology (5.8%) or the peer comparables approach together with the dividend discount model (DDM) (4%). The table also reveals some differences in the adoption rates of the valuation techniques across markets. While the pattern associated with Euronext is similar to that of the whole sample, Germany is characterized by a relatively higher percentage of IPOs valued using comparable firms only (62.5%), and in Italy the simultaneous use of comparable firms and DCF is by far the most common approach adopted by underwriters (85.3%).

Among IPOs that are valued using the comparable firms approach, there is considerable heterogeneity both in the number of peers and the type of multiples selected by the underwriter. Table 14.2 focuses on the 452 IPOs valued using this methodology, and reports information about the number of peer firms and multiples used in the valuation process, as reported in the official prospectus. Panel A reports statistics

Table 14.1 Valuation methods.
Valuation methods used by underwriters to value IPOs, as declared in official IPO prospectuses.

	All markets (480 IPOs)		Euronext (308 IPOs)		Germany (16 IPOs)		Italy (156 IPOs)	
	no.	%	no.	%	no.	%	no.	%
Comparables only	160	33.3	134	43.5	10	62.5	16	10.3
DCF only	28	5.8	17	5.5	4	25.0	7	4.5
Comparables & DCF	273	56.9	138	44.8	2	12.5	133	85.3
Comparables & DDM	19	4.0	19	6.2	0	0.0	0	0.0
Total	480	–	308	64.2	16	3.3	156	32.5

---

[4] The 'level of disclosure concerning price information' is defined in Article 8.1 of the Directive and item 5.3.1 of Annex III.

Table 14.2   IPOs valued using comparable firms.
The table reports the number of peer firms and multiples selected by underwriters to value IPOs, as reported in official IPO prospectuses. The table also reports the number and percentage of IPOs in which the underwriter used the multiple reported in the corresponding row in its valuation process. Panel A reports statistics for the whole sample and by market. Panel B refers to industries (1-digit SIC code), where technology firms are identified as in Loughran and Ritter (2004).

	All IPOs (452 IPOs)		Euronext (291 IPOs)		Germany (12 IPOs)		Italy (149 IPOs)	
Panel A. By market	mean	median	mean	median	mean	median	mean	median
No. peers	5.9	5.0	5.1	4.0	7.6	6.0	7.3	7.0
No. multiples	2.6	2.0	2.4	2.5	1.8	2.0	3.1	2.0
	no.	%	no.	%	no.	%	no.	%
EV/Sales	215	47.6	143	49.1	10	83.3	62	41.6
EV/EBITDA	203	44.9	84	28.9	4	33.3	115	77.2
EV/EBIT	142	31.4	93	32.0	2	16.7	47	31.5
P/E	329	72.8	215	73.9	4	33.3	110	73.8
P/CF	113	25.0	50	17.2	2	16.7	61	40.9
P/BV	127	28.1	57	19.6	4	33.3	66	44.3

	Technology (146 IPOs)		Manufacturing (138 IPOs)		Services (67 IPOs)	
Panel B. By industry	mean	median	mean	median	mean	median
No. peers	7.0	6.0	6.1	5.0	6.1	5.0
No. multiples	2.7	3.0	2.5	2.0	2.4	2.0
	no.	%	no.	%	no.	%
EV/Sales	91	62.3	47	34.1	37	55.2
EV/EBITDA	51	34.9	80	58.0	23	34.3
EV/EBIT	45	30.8	37	26.8	26	38.8
P/E	106	72.6	107	77.5	44	65.7
P/CF	43	29.5	33	23.9	13	19.4
P/BV	47	32.2	33	23.9	15	22.4

	Trade (43 IPOs)		Transportation & Communication (31 IPOs)		Other industries (27 IPOs)	
	mean	median	mean	median	mean	median
No. peers	3.5	3.0	4.2	4.0	4.2	4.0
No. multiples	2.7	2.0	2.9	3.0	1.9	2.0

Table 14.2   (Continued)

	no.	%	no.	%	no.	%
EV/Sales	18	41.9	13	41.9	9	33.3
EV/EBITDA	14	32.6	24	77.4	11	40.7
EV/EBIT	16	37.2	11	35.5	7	25.9
P/E	35	81.4	21	67.7	16	59.3
P/CF	15	34.9	9	29.0	0	0.0
P/BV	16	37.2	10	32.3	6	22.2

for the whole sample and by market. Aggregate figures document that underwriters select, on average, 5.9 comparable firms and 2.6 multiples to estimate the offer price. At a single market-level, German and Italian IPOs are associated with a larger number of comparable firms and a lower number of valuation multiples relative to Euronext. In terms of multiples, the most frequently adopted is the Price-to-Earnings (P/E) ratio, used to value 329 IPOs (72.8% of the sample), followed by the Enterprise Value-to-Sales (EV/Sales) and Enterprise Value-to-EBITDA (EV/EBITDA) ratios, which are used in slightly less than half of the IPOs. Other, less common multiples are the Enterprise Value-to-EBIT (EV/EBIT), Price-to-Cash Flow (P/CF), and Price-to-Book Value (P/BV), which are used to price approximately one fourth of the sample IPOs each. The predominance of the P/E ratio persists only among Euronext IPOs, while the EV/Sales and EV/EBITDA ratios are the most frequently adopted in the German and Italian markets, respectively.

Panel B reports the same statistics about comparable firms and multiples by industry, defined according to the 1-digit SIC code with the exception of technology firms, that are identified as in Loughran and Ritter (2004). The average technology IPO is valued by its underwriter using 7 comparable firms (6 in median), the highest number across the industries represented in our sample. This may indicate that the valuation of tech firms, which typically suffer to a greater extent from the presence of information asymmetry, is carried out with a larger group of peers in an attempt to reduce uncertainty about their valuation. The industry in which underwriters select the smallest group of comparable firms is trade, with 3.5 peers on average (3 in median), which is consistent with the previous argument about valuation uncertainty, as firms operating in the trade sector should be less exposed to such an issue. In terms of number of multiples, transportation and communication is the industry associated with the largest number (2.9 multiples, on average), followed by technology (2.7) and trade (2.7). The adoption rate of each valuation ratios is largely consistent with the aggregate evidence, as the P/E is predominant across all industries except transportation and communication, where the EV/EBITDA is the most frequently adopted. The P/E ratio also remains the leading multiple among technology firms (72.6%), despite the presence of a large number of firms going public with negative earnings (Aggarwal et al. 2009). However, the adoption rate of the EV/Sales is considerably higher than that associated with the whole sample (62.3% vs. 47.6%), suggesting that revenues are also frequently used as valuation base.

14.4.2   Alternative Selection Criteria of Comparable Firms

In this section, we compare match the valuation of comparable firms chosen by the investment banks as published in the official prospectus with that obtained by using alternative criteria to select peers. To this aim, we implement the same selection methodologies used by Paleari et al. (2014). These methodologies produce three algorithmic and two non-algorithmic alternative groups of peers, available for the whole final sample of 370 IPOs. Using algorithmic methods, we (i) take the list of comparable firms proposed by the Thomson One database, (ii) apply a propensity score-matching model, and (iii) execute an EV/Sales matching with a sample of public companies. First, we rely on reports from an external source of information by looking at the 'Company Analysis' section of Thomson One database, which proposes a pre-built set of peers matched on the base of industry (4-digit SIC code) and size. Second, we perform a propensity score-matching model to find up to 10 comparable firms from all Datastream equities available in each sample year. This methodology consists of estimating a score for both our sample firms and the candidate comparable firms, and then match the former with up to 10 firms having the closest predicted score. The score is estimated by means of a probit regression in which the dependent variable is a dummy equal to 1 for our sample of IPOs and 0 for the candidate comparable firms, and is estimated using firm size, profitability, industry, and country dummies as predictive variables. We adopt the common support criterion and discard any potential match with a score distance greater than 0.01 to improve matching accuracy. Third, we repeat a propensity score-matching model in which the score is the EV/Sales ratio, as in Bhojraj and Lee (2002). This technique is less constrained by industry membership.

We then use two alternative groups of comparable firms obtained from non-algorithmic selections, that are the peers selected by (iv) affiliated and (v) unaffiliated sell-side analysts published in the first post-IPO equity report released about the issuing firm. Analysts release research reports that provide stock recommendations (e.g. 'buy' or 'sell') together with a valuation section, which is often obtained from a group of comparable firms. The difference between affiliated and unaffiliated analysts is that the former are independent, while the latter are affiliated with the investment bank that is in charge of underwriting the IPO. It is often assumed that affiliated analysts are subject to a stronger conflict of interests than independent ones, with consequences on the performance of stock research (Cliff 2007). The source of the comparable firms selected by both types of analysts is Investext Investment Research. Due to unavailability of equity reports or lack of disclosure of the peers' names and/or the valuation multiples used, we are able to compare the underwriter's selection with that of affiliated and unaffiliated analysts for 130 out of 370 IPOs.

14.4.3   Valuation Bias and IPO Premium

We employ two measures to detect the strategic behaviour of underwriters in the selection of comparable firms when valuing IPOs, namely valuation bias and IPO premium. Following Paleari et al. (2014), valuation bias compares the valuation of peers selected by the underwriter with that of peers from alternative procedures, while IPO premium compares the valuation implied by the preliminary offer price of the firm going public with that of peers from alternative procedures. The difference between the two measures lies in the numerator: in valuation bias, it is the average across the comparables selected by the investment bank; in IPO premium, it is the multiple of the IPO firm calculated using the preliminary offer price set by the underwriter. In other words, the former compares the valuation of underwriter-selected peers with that of alternatively selected peers, and the latter compares the valuation of the IPO firm with that of alternatively selected peers. The difference between the two measures arises from the fact that underwriters typically set the offer price by applying a discount to their valuation estimates, in order to stimulate investor demand, reduce marketing expenses, and compensate buy-side investors. In both measures, the mean multiple associated with alternatively selected peers is the denominator. We then compute the natural logarithm of this ratio. Valuation bias and IPO premium are computed for each multiple M. The two aggregate measures of our interest are then defined as the average across the multiples used to value the IPO. In formulas:

$$valuation\ bias = \frac{1}{N}\sum_{j=1}^{N} ln\left(\frac{M_{(j)underwriter}}{M_{(j)peers,i}}\right)$$

$$IPO\ premium = \frac{1}{N}\sum_{j=1}^{N} ln\left(\frac{M_{(j)POP}}{M_{(j)peers,i}}\right)$$

where $M(j)$ represents each single multiple of the N used to value the IPO firm (i.e. EV/Sales, EV/EBITDA, EV/EBIT, P/E, P/BV, P/CF, with N varying from 1 to 6), and i represents alternative selection methodologies.

14.5   Results

14.5.1   Algorithmic Selections

In this section, we assess the strategic behaviour of underwriters in the selection of peers by comparing the valuation of underwriter-selected peers with that of peers obtained from alternative criteria. Table 14.3 reports the multiples of the comparable firms selected by the investment bank and published in the IPO prospectus, together with those of the peers obtained from the three algorithmic selection criteria, namely Thomson One, propensity score matching, and EV/Sales matching. Panel A shows the mean and median values for the whole sample, while Panels B and C report the evidence for the markets of Euronext and Italy. At a first glance, all the valuation multiples in Panel A that refer to the group of peers reported in prospectus are persistently higher than those of the peers obtained from algorithmic selections. This is a first indication of the fact that underwriters tend to select comparable firms with better valuations. This evidence holds across all multiples for the mean values, while there are a few exceptions in terms of median values. For instance, the average of the most commonly adopted multiple, namely the P/E, is equal to 29.9 for the peers in

Table 14.3   Valuation multiples: prospectus vs. algorithmic selection criteria.
The table reports the average and median values of the valuation multiples used by underwriters to value IPOs, as reported in official IPO prospectuses, as well as those obtained by the following alternative selection criteria for comparable firms: peers proposed by Thomson One database, propensity score matching on the Datastream population, EV/Sales matching following Bhojraj and Lee (2002) on the Datastream population. Panel A reports aggregate statistics, Panel B and C refer to firms going public in Euronext and Italy, respectively.

		Prospectus		Thomson ONE		Propensity score		EV/Sales matching	
Panel A. All markets	Obs	mean	median	mean	median	mean	median	mean	median
EV/Sales	198	4.1	2.6	2.5	2.0	1.9	1.6	2.0	1.7
EV/EBITDA	184	17.6	11.7	12.8	10.0	10.9	9.2	12.8	10.5
EV/EBIT	125	26.9	14.2	19.4	16.3	14.9	13.9	18.3	15.9
P/E	282	29.9	23.3	26.1	21.7	29.4	26.8	24.9	23.1
P/CF	85	27.4	12.3	20.0	15.2	12.5	10.8	19.6	18.0
P/BV	97	4.2	3.5	2.9	2.4	3.2	2.9	2.3	2.1
Panel B. Euronext									
EV/Sales	136	3.6	2.3	2.5	2.1	1.8	1.6	2.1	1.7
EV/EBITDA	73	14.9	11.6	13.2	9.9	11.9	9.2	13.4	9.8
EV/EBIT	83	24.0	13.4	19.5	16.2	14.5	13.7	17.8	15.9
P/E	191	28.4	21.7	27.1	22.3	29.4	28.0	24.3	20.9
P/CF	34	13.1	9.4	21.2	16.6	12.9	10.8	21.4	18.2
P/BV	45	3.1	2.5	2.9	2.4	3.4	3.0	2.4	2.2
Panel C. Italy									
EV/Sales	55	5.5	4.2	2.5	1.9	1.9	1.6	1.8	1.5
EV/EBITDA	107	20.1	12.3	12.4	10.0	10.0	9.2	12.4	10.6
EV/EBIT	41	37.1	15.1	19.1	16.5	16.3	14.8	19.5	15.8
P/E	88	33.4	27.3	24.3	20.6	29.4	24.2	26.0	24.5
P/CF	51	38.5	22.2	18.7	13.0	11.9	11.4	17.9	17.6
P/BV	50	5.3	4.5	2.9	2.4	2.8	2.6	2.2	2.0

prospectus, while it ranges from 24.9 (EV/Sales matching) to 29.4 (propensity score matching) for the peers obtained from algorithmic selections. Also, the mean value of the EV/Sales multiple is 4.1 compared to a range of 1.9 (propensity score matching) to 2.5 (Thomson One). At a single market-level, evidence in Panels B and C is largely consistent with that of the full sample. In particular, the multiples of the peers reported in the prospectus of Italian IPOs are further away from those of alternatively selected peers relative to Euronext. For instance, the gap in the P/E ratio becomes wider (33.4 in prospectus vs. a range of 24.3–29.4 for alternative selections).

Table 14.4 allows for the further investigation of this aspect by reporting the mean and median values of valuation bias between the multiples of the underwriter-selected peers and those of the alternatively selected peers, both at an aggregate and single multiple-level. A positive value of valuation bias indicates that the peers

Table 14.4 Valuation bias with respect to algorithmic selection criteria by market.
The table reports the average and median values of valuation bias, computed as the percentage logarithm of the ratio between the mean multiple associated with peers selected by the underwriter and those selected by the following alternative methodologies: peers proposed by Thomson One database, propensity score matching on the Datastream population, EV/Sales matching following Bhojraj and Lee (2002) on the Datastream population. Valuation bias is the cross-multiple average (first row), while single multiple-level valuation bias (labelled as the name of the multiple) is the average across IPOs in which a given multiple was used by the underwriter in the valuation process. Panel A reports aggregate statistics, Panel B and C refer to firms going public in Euronext and Italy, respectively. ***, **, and * indicate significance at the 1%, 5%, and 10% levels, respectively, of the unpaired t-test and Wilcoxon signed-rank test for the difference from zero.

		Thomson ONE		Propensity score		EV/Sales matching	
Panel A. All markets	**Obs**	**mean**	**median**	**mean**	**median**	**mean**	**median**
Val. bias	370	23.1***	21.5***	14.4***	4.6***	28.2***	20.8***
EV/Sales	198	30.4**	35.6***	36.1***	41.3***	52.0***	47.9***
EV/EBITDA	184	26.6***	22.2***	20.8***	17.2***	22.3***	14.0***
EV/EBIT	125	10.1**	−0.6	15.6**	−0.1	10.6**	0.2
P/E	282	18.5**	13.8**	−7.9	−10.4	15.1***	15.8***
P/CF	85	10.0	20.2	17.4**	15.0*	9.3**	16.1
P/BV	97	34.1***	33.1***	6.2	8.4	50.0***	49.8***
Panel B. Euronext							
Val. bias	229	15.8**	12.8**	10.7**	5.1**	20.0***	19.6***
EV/Sales	136	18.1**	31.3***	29.7***	45.9***	35.7***	30.2***
EV/EBITDA	73	18.1**	18.7**	16.9**	15.5**	14.9**	24.3***
EV/EBIT	83	5.0	−7.2	18.6**	2.3	9.1	0.5
P/E	191	9.8	5.4	−12.4*	−20.1**	8.9	11.8
P/CF	34	−55.6**	−49.4**	−11.9	−4.1	−45.6**	−43.5**
P/BV	45	8.2	4.4	−15.3**	−15.9**	15.0	−1.8
Panel C. Italy							
Val. bias	133	37.8***	32.0***	23.9***	16.5***	40.3***	24.2***
EV/Sales	55	67.0***	53.5***	59.1***	42.7***	86.1***	89.0***
EV/EBITDA	107	33.9***	22.7***	26.4***	19.7***	27.4***	11.7**
EV/EBIT	41	28.8***	13.7**	9.1	−5.1	20.7*	0.1
P/E	88	34.8***	33.3***	3.8	10.8	24.6***	22.3***
P/CF	51	61.6***	39.5***	47.3***	43.6***	43.9***	35.2***
P/BV	50	59.1***	61.2***	30.9***	47.8***	77.7***	72.1***

selected by the underwriters have a higher valuation relative to those selected using alternative methodologies. As reported in the first row of Panel A, there is a positive and significant cross-multiple valuation bias that ranges, on average, from 14.4% to 28.2%, depending on the benchmark. This bias tends to be less pronounced relative to peers selected using propensity score matching, and more pronounced relative to peers selected by the EV/Sales matching. Also, valuation bias varies substantially across the different multiples used to value the IPO firm, with EV-based ratios yielding the highest values of valuation bias. For instance, the average EV/Sales ratio of the peers published in prospectus is 52% higher than that of the peers obtained from the EV/Sales matching procedure. Panels B and C report the mean and median values of valuation bias by market. Consistent with the evidence reported in Table 14.3, valuation bias is more pronounced in Italy, where underwriters select comparable firms whose average valuation is 23.9–40.3% higher than that of alternatively selected peers. Valuation bias for Euronext IPOs is lower and ranges between 10.7% and 20%. At a single multiple-level, the evidence of greater bias in the presence of EV-based ratios is largely confirmed.

Table 14.5 illustrates how valuation bias varies based on the industry of IPO firms. Panels A, B, and C report the mean and median valuation bias for the three most represented industries, namely technology, manufacturing, and services. When valuing technology IPOs, the average valuation of the peers selected by underwriters is 24–56.8% higher than that of alternatively selected peers, depending on the benchmark. This range slightly narrows to 25.1–52.3% among services firms (Panel C), and markedly decreases to 3.9–20.9% among manufacturing firms (Panel B). Among the multiple-specific valuation bias, EV-based multiples keep being associated with the largest bias, but also the P/CF and P/BV ratios report statistically significant results mainly among technology and manufacturing firms.

The above documented evidence across industries provides support to the view that underwriters upwardly bias the selection of peers to a greater extent when firm characteristics provide them with a higher degree of discretion. In particular, technology and services firms are likely to face a larger pool of potential peers relative to the case of manufacturing firms. This is confirmed by the previously documented evidence about the number of peers published in the prospectus of technology and services firms (7 and 6.1 on average, see Table 14.2), the highest values across all industries. On the other hand, manufacturing firms are likely to have more unambiguous comparable firms. Overall, the evidence indicates that, when the issuing firm's industry allows underwriters to act with a higher degree of discretion, underwriters tend to cherry-pick comparable firms characterized by higher valuations.

We now assess the persistence of a positive valuation bias after considering the deliberate discount applied by underwriters to their fair value estimates. In other words, because underwriters typically set the offer price by applying a discount to the valuation of the comparable firms they select, this difference in valuation may disappear after accounting for such a discount. Figure 14.1 illustrates the average and median values of IPO premium, a modified version of the valuation bias in which the numerator is the multiple implied by the preliminary offer price of the IPO. The valuation implied by the preliminary offer price is benchmarked not only against that of alternatively selected peers, but also against that of the peers published in the prospectus (left-hand side), in order to assess the magnitude of such discount. The IPO premium relative to the peers published in prospectus is always negative, confirming that underwriters apply a discount to their valuation estimates. This discount varies across the type of multiple used, and ranges from 1.5% (P/E and P/CF) to 13.8% (EV/ EBITDA). The IPO premium turns instead positive when computed with respect to the groups of alternatively selected peers, indicating that, even after accounting for the

Table 14.5   Valuation bias with respect to algorithmic selection criteria by industry.
The table reports the average and median values of valuation bias, computed as the percentage logarithm of the ratio between the mean multiple associated with peers selected by the underwriter and by the following alternative selection methodologies: peers proposed by Thomson One database, propensity score matching on the Datastream population, EV/Sales matching following Bhojraj and Lee (2002) on the Datastream population. Valuation bias is the cross-multiple average (first row), while single multiple-level valuation bias (labelled as the name of the multiple) is the average across IPOs in which a given multiple was used by the underwriter in the valuation process. The table shows the three most represented industries of the sample. Panel A refers to Technology firms, Panel B to Manufacturing firms, and Panel C to services firms. Technology firms are identified as in Loughran and Ritter (2004). ***, **, and * indicate significance at the 1%, 5%, and 10% levels, respectively, of the unpaired t-test and Wilcoxon signed-rank test for the difference from zero.

Panel A. Technology	Obs	Thomson ONE mean	Thomson ONE median	Propensity score mean	Propensity score median	EV/Sales matching mean	EV/Sales matching median
Val. bias	146	29.3***	26.5***	24.0***	17.9***	56.8***	47.3***
EV/Sales	91	30.4***	31.9***	43.4***	46.2***	78.2***	80.7***
EV/EBITDA	51	51.5***	45.6***	24.6***	18.4***	64.1***	62.8***
EV/EBIT	45	40.0**	9.0*	31.7***	41.0***	40.5**	4.4
P/E	106	7.4**	5.3*	1.4	0.8	32.7***	30.2***
P/CF	43	41.6**	29.5**	41.5***	42.5***	80.4***	70.5***
P/BV	47	50.8***	41.3***	22.6***	23.2***	93.5***	86.2***
Panel B. Manufacturing							
Val. bias	138	20.9***	18.2***	5.1*	1.9	3.9	1.4
EV/Sales	47	40.0***	37.2***	31.3**	19.2**	18.9**	3.2
EV/EBITDA	80	15.7***	14.8**	13.4**	13.7**	7.4*	3.1
EV/EBIT	37	−1.1	−1.6	−4.6	−5.0	−3.3	−3.1
P/E	107	15.9**	5.1	1.4	0.8	3.9	5.9**
P/CF	33	10.9**	18.9**	18.0**	14.7***	6.9*	5.2*
P/BV	33	36.7***	38.8***	20.0***	14.8**	42.4***	40.6***
Panel C. Services							
Val. bias	67	25.1***	23.7***	37.1***	26.5***	52.3***	33.5***
EV/Sales	37	29.7***	29.7***	43.5***	39.0***	70.4***	39.9***
EV/EBITDA	23	31.6**	9.1*	36.2***	19.7***	34.2**	10.0*
EV/EBIT	26	−7.4	−11.5	26.5*	1.6	15.1*	1.0
P/E	44	31.5***	21.2***	1.4	0.8	35.7**	25.2**
P/CF	13	−11.2*	−41.2	19.8*	0.0	11.4*	4.6
P/BV	15	17.3*	19.6	1.8	1.7	41.3***	33.9***

underwriter's discount, the valuations of IPO firms remain significantly higher than those of the peers obtained from algorithmic selections. In particular, the premium is more pronounced relative to the peers obtained from the EV/Sales matching, ranging between 3.1% and 37.4%, and less pronounced relative to Thomson One's peers, where it ranges from 0.1% to 23%. In terms of valuation multiples, the use of the EV/Sales ratio is often associated with the largest premium.

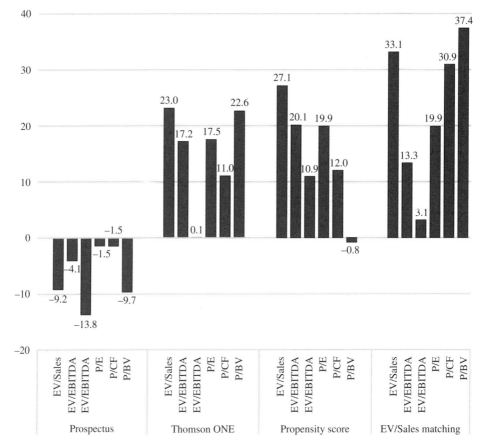

Figure 14.1 IPO premium.
The graph reports the average values of IPO premium, computed as the percentage logarithm of the ratio between the issuer's multiple implied by the preliminary offer price and the corresponding median multiple associated with the following alternative selection methodologies: peers proposed by Thomson One database, propensity score matching on the Datastream population, EV/Sales matching following Bhojraj and Lee (2002) on the Datastream population.

14.5.2 Affiliated and Unaffiliated Analysts

In this section, we assess the strategic behaviour of underwriters in the selection of peers by comparing their valuations with those of alternative peers obtained from non-algorithmic criteria, namely those published by affiliated and unaffiliated analysts in their first post-IPO equity report.

14.5.2.1 The Case of Geox
We start by presenting the case of the Geox IPO. Geox is an Italian shoe manufacturer that went public on the Milan stock exchange in December 2004. Figure 14.2 shows the lists of peer firms selected by (1) the lead underwriter, extracted from the IPO

(1) IPO prospectus selection by underwriter

	EV/EBITDA	P/E
Hennes & Mauritz	15,3x	26,8x
Coach	15,4x	30,1x
Inditex	14,0x	28,0x
Burberry	10,2x	20,7x
Tod's	12,0x	37,0x
Puma	11,9x	19,7x
Timberland	8,7x	17,3x

(2) Post-IPO equity report selection by affiliated analyst

	Cu. Price	EV	EV/Sales			EV/EBITDA			P/E		
			2004E	2005E	2006E	2004E	2005E	2006E	2004E	2005E	2006E
Footwear											
Tod's	€ 32.73	946	2.3	2.1	1.9	10.4	8.9	7.6	26.6	21.8	19.3
Timberland	$ 63.4	1932	1.3	1.2	1.2	7.6	7.0	6.6	15.0	13.4	12.1
Puma	€ 182.2	2700	1.8	1.6	1.4	7.0	6.3	5.8	11.6	10.4	9.7
Average footwear			**1.8**	**1.6**	**1.5**	**8.3**	**7.4**	**6.7**	**17.7**	**15.2**	**13.7**
Retailers											
Benetton	€ 9.8	2,243	1.3	1.3	1.3	7.1	6.7	6.2	14.1	12.7	11.5
Gap	$ 20.9	19,993	1.2	1.2	1.2	7.6	6.8	6.2	17.0	14.4	17.1
H&M	Skr 227.0	173,116	3.2	2.8	2.5	14.8	12.8	11.4	26.3	22.7	20.2
Inditex	€ 21.6	13,193	2.3	1.9	1.7	11.1	9.3	8.0	22.2	18.4	16.0
Next	£ 1620.0	4,518	1.6	1.4	1.3	8.9	8.1	7.4	14.2	12.8	11.7
Average Retailers			**1.9**	**1.7**	**1.6**	**9.9**	**8.8**	**7.8**	**18.8**	**16.2**	**15.3**
Luxury and Apparel											
Coach	$ 53.7	10,152	7.7	6.1	5.2	20.8	15.8	13.3	39.5	29.4	24.7
Hugo Boss	€ 25.5	1,805	1.6	1.5	1.4	10.2	9.6	8.8	20.4	18.6	17.8
Burberry	£ 404	1,861	2.6	2.4	2.2	9.8	8.8	8.3	18.3	16.3	14.6
Average L&A			**3.9**	**3.3**	**2.9**	**13.6**	**11.4**	**10.2**	**26.1**	**21.4**	**19.1**
Total Average			**2.4**	**2.1**	**1.9**	**10.5**	**9.1**	**8.2**	**20.5**	**17.4**	**15.9**

(3) Post-IPO equity report selection by unaffiliated analyst

	Rating	Mkt Cap (EURm)	2005E EV/Sales	2005E EV/EBITDA	2005E P/E
Puma	2	3 314	1.57	6.4	11.6
Burberry	2	2 934	2.16	8.6	17.9
Tod's	3	975	2.09	9.2	28.1
H&M	1	19 203	2.35	10.7	19.3
Inditex	2	12 703	1.79	8.6	17.3
Weighted average			**2.08**	**9.5**	**18.1**

Figure 14.2   The case of Geox.
The figure reports the lists of the peer firms and valuation multiples selected to value the Geox IPO by (1) the underwriter in the IPO prospectus, (2) the affiliated analyst and (3) an unaffiliated analyst in the respective research reports.

prospectus; (2) the affiliated analyst; and (3) an unaffiliated analyst, extracted from the respective equity research reports. The lead underwriter chose seven comparable firms (H&M, Coach, Inditex, Burberry, Tod's, Puma, and Timberland) and two valuation ratios (EV/EBITDA and P/E) to justify the offer price of the Geox shares at the time of the IPO. These comparable firms led to an average EV/EBITDA and P/E of 12.5 and 26.6 (unreported), respectively. In the equity report released less than two months after the IPO, the affiliated analyst published a larger group of peers composed of

11 firms. The majority of the newly added peers were publicly traded firms operating in the retail industry (Benetton, Gap, Next), whose market valuation was relatively low. As a result, the average EV/EBITDA and P/E ratios associated with this new selection of comparable firms was 10.5 and 20.5, respectively. This implied a 16% and 20% decrease relative to the same valuation ratios of the peers published in the official prospectus. Also, the average valuation of the comparable firms selected by the unaffiliated analyst was in line with that of the peers published by the affiliated analyst, although the number of comparable firms decreased to five. In particular, Coach, a US luxury manufacturer of handbags and accessories, characterized by the highest value of the EV/EBITDA ratio among the peers published in the IPO prospectus, was no longer considered. Overall, this example gives a good idea of the discretion in the choice of comparables.

14.5.2.2 Empirical Evidence

Table 14.6 reports the valuation multiples of the underwriter's and analysts' groups of peers for the subsample of 130 IPOs with available equity reports that make full disclosure of the peers' names and valuation multiples used. Again, Panel A shows the mean and median values for the whole sample, while Panels B and C report the evidence for the markets of Euronext and Italy. Similar to the previously documented evidence with respect to algorithmic selections, the valuation multiples in Panel A that refer to the group of peers reported in prospectus are persistently higher than those selected by affiliated and unaffiliated analysts, both for mean and median values. For instance, the average P/E is equal to 44.4 for the peers in prospectus, while it markedly decreases to 27.1 and 25.4 for those published by affiliated and unaffiliated analysts, respectively. At a single market-level, evidence in Panels B and C is largely consistent with that of the full sample.

Table 14.7 reports the mean and median values of valuation bias between the multiples of the underwriter-selected peers and those of affiliated and unaffiliated analysts, both at an aggregate and single multiple-level. As reported in the first row of Panel A, there is a positive and significant cross-multiple valuation bias. This indicates that the average valuation of the peers selected post-IPO by sell-side analysts, regardless of their affiliation with the underwriter, is persistently lower than that of the peers reported in the official prospectus. This bias tends to be more pronounced in correspondence of the peers selected by unaffiliated analysts, whose average valuation is 37.8% lower, compared to those selected by affiliated analysts, whose average valuation is 20.9% lower. The evidence is stronger in the presence of the most widely used multiples. For instance, the average EV/Sales ratio of the peers published in prospectus is 26.5% and 47.3% higher than that of the peers selected by affiliated and unaffiliated analysts, respectively. Panels B and C report the mean and median values of valuation bias by market. Consistent with the previously documented evidence, valuation bias is more pronounced (and more statistically significant) in Italy, where underwriters select comparable firms whose average valuation is 25.9 and 42.2% higher than that of affiliated and unaffiliated analysts.

Table 14.8 illustrates the cross-industry variation in valuation bias. When valuing technology IPOs, the average valuation of the peers selected by underwriters is 33.2%

Table 14.6   Valuation multiples: prospectus vs. affiliated and unaffiliated analysts.
The table reports the average and median values of the valuation multiples used by underwriters to value IPOs, as reported in official IPO prospectuses, as well as those selected by affiliated and unaffiliated analysts in their first post-IPO equity report. Panel A reports aggregate statistics, Panel B and C refer to firms going public in Euronext and Italy, respectively.

		Prospectus		Affiliated analyst		Unaffiliated analyst	
Panel A. All markets	Obs	mean	median	mean	median	mean	median
EV/Sales	58	15.1	7.9	5.4	4.1	3.4	2.2
EV/EBITDA	103	18.4	15.6	12.6	11.7	11.5	9.7
EV/EBIT	40	36.5	29.5	21.1	19.2	15.6	14.6
P/E	94	44.4	38.4	27.1	23.3	25.4	20.8
P/CF	32	43.0	33.1	28.9	20.0	19.0	16.5
P/BV	37	7.4	6.7	2.5	2.3	4.1	4.6
Panel B. Euronext							
EV/Sales	22	12.5	6.2	4.3	3.6	3.3	2.3
EV/EBITDA	27	13.6	13.1	11.2	10.9	12.1	10.5
EV/EBIT	18	23.5	23.1	8.9	9.0	14.4	13.0
P/E	32	53.3	41.1	38.6	31.2	30.0	22.4
P/CF	0	-	-	-	-	-	-
P/BV	3	3.6	3.3	-	-	4.8	4.8
Panel C. Italy							
EV/Sales	36	17.0	9.0	6.0	4.4	3.5	1.7
EV/EBITDA	76	20.0	16.5	13.0	12.0	11.3	9.1
EV/FBIT	22	47.4	34.9	26.8	24.0	17.3	18.5
P/E	62	41.2	37.4	22.7	20.3	21.3	20.6
P/CF	32	43.0	33.1	28.9	20.0	19.0	16.5
P/BV	34	7.9	7.1	2.5	2.3	4.0	3.9

and 61.5% higher than that of the peers selected by affiliated and unaffiliated analysts, respectively. The magnitude of the bias decreases to 22.4% and 33.5% among manufacturing IPOs (Panel B), and further decreases to 6% and 17.9% among services IPOs (Panel C). In terms of multiple-specific valuation bias, EV-based multiples are still those that account for the largest portion of the bias.

The cross-industry patterns of valuation bias documented in Table 14.8 slightly differ from those obtained by benchmarking the underwriter-selected peers with those obtained from algorithmic criteria. In particular, while technology and services IPOs resulted in the highest values of valuation bias relative to algorithmic selections, services IPOs are no longer associated with a considerable bias, arguably due to the lower number of observations with available data. Still, manufacturing firms also report positive and significant values of valuation bias, both for affiliated and unaffiliated analysts, that are robust across multiples. Therefore, while it is true that the strategic behaviour of underwriters is more pronounced when the issuing firm's industry provides them with a higher degree of discretion, the evidence is less unequivocal

Table 14.7   Valuation bias with respect to affiliated and unaffiliated analysts by market.
The table reports the average and median values of valuation bias, computed as the percentage logarithm of the ratio between the mean multiple associated with peers selected by the underwriter and by affiliated and unaffiliated analysts in the first post-IPO equity report. Valuation bias is the cross-multiple average (first row), while single multiple-level valuation bias (labelled as the name of the multiple) is the average across IPOs in which a given multiple was used by the underwriter in the valuation process. Panel A reports aggregate statistics, Panel B and C refer to firms going public in Euronext and Italy, respectively. ***, **, and * indicate significance at the 1%, 5%, and 10% levels, respectively, of the unpaired t-test and Wilcoxon signed-rank test for the difference from zero.

		Affiliated analyst		Unaffiliated analyst	
Panel A. All markets	Obs	mean	median	mean	median
Val. bias	130	20.9***	19.5***	37.8***	29.0***
EV/Sales	58	26.5***	13.5***	47.3***	39.5***
EV/EBITDA	103	21.8***	22.1***	37.2***	27.7***
EV/EBIT	40	23.9**	15.4*	43.2	22.3**
P/E	94	19.4***	24.0***	31.3***	28.4***
P/CF	32	11.7	12.4	91.4	115.3
P/BV	37	31.0*	25.1*	9.8	23.6
Panel B. Euronext					
Val. bias	61	15.0***	13.3***	31.2***	27.4***
EV/Sales	22	8.2	1.0	46.7***	48.4***
EV/EBITDA	27	17.1*	10.8	9.5	14.6
EV/EBIT	18	28.5**	24.4**	25.6*	22.3*
P/E	32	10.2	9.8	23.5**	23.6**
P/CF	0	-	-	-	-
P/BV	3	22.8	15.2	34.1	34.1
Panel C. Italy					
Val. bias	69	25.9***	26.3***	42.2***	41.7***
EV/Sales	36	38.3***	29.6***	57.1***	39.5***
EV/EBITDA	76	23.1***	22.4***	44.9***	31.3***
EV/EBIT	22	20.8*	12.3*	55.9**	45.1*
P/E	62	25.3***	25.5***	38.4***	30.9***
P/CF	32	11.7	12.4	91.4	115.3
P/BV	34	31.7**	37.3***	−1.3	9.8

when affiliated and unaffiliated analysts are used as benchmark. We shed further light on this point in the following section.

14.5.3   Underwriters' Selection of Comparable Firms Pre- vs. Post-IPO

In this section, we focus on the comparison between the selection of peers made by investment banks as underwriters at the IPO with that done shortly thereafter as (affiliated) analysts. Since the valuations of these two groups of peers are

Table 14.8   Valuation bias with respect to affiliated and unaffiliated analysts by industry.
The table reports the average and median values of valuation bias, computed as the percentage logarithm of the ratio between the mean multiple associated with peers selected by the underwriter and by affiliated and unaffiliated analysts in the first post-IPO equity report, for the three most represented industries of the sample. Valuation bias is the cross-multiple average (first row), while single multiple-level valuation bias (labelled as the name of the multiple) is the average across IPOs in which a given multiple was used by the underwriter in the valuation process. Panel A refers to Technology firms, Panel B to Manufacturing firms, and Panel C to services firms. Technology firms are identified as in Loughran and Ritter (2004). ***, **, and * indicate significance at the 1%, 5%, and 10% levels, respectively, of the unpaired t-test and Wilcoxon signed-rank test for the difference from zero.

		Affiliated analyst		Unaffiliated analyst	
Panel A. Technology	Obs	mean	median	mean	median
Val. bias	33	33.2***	11.5***	61.5***	45.8***
EV/Sales	22	45.8***	13.9***	83.5***	65.0***
EV/EBITDA	21	50.7***	22.4***	67.7***	25.4**
EV/EBIT	12	49.1**	15.5**	14.6**	4.2
P/E	21	16.9***	6.4*	56.5***	47.3**
P/CF	12	13.4**	9.7**	41.6**	35.3***
P/BV	12	19.3***	15.6***	37.7**	17.2**
Panel B. Manufacturing					
Val. bias	55	22.4***	18.8***	33.5***	26.6***
EV/Sales	18	18.6***	15.2***	35.7**	7.5**
EV/EBITDA	51	23.7***	20.2***	39.1***	25.8***
EV/EBIT	14	22.3**	13.9*	19.3**	11.2*
P/E	48	22.8***	20.8***	36.5***	21.6**
P/CF	8	24.1*	11.1*	18.4*	10.0
P/BV	8	11.7*	8.6	18.9**	13.3*
Panel C. Services					
Val. bias	13	6.0*	5.4	17.9***	16.6***
EV/Sales	8	10.8	4.0	26.9	18.1
EV/EBITDA	9	15.3*	3.2	57.1**	30.2*
EV/EBIT	6	13.3**	12.7**	23.6	14.3
P/E	4	1.8	1.3	24.1	16.1
P/CF	0	-	-	-	-
P/BV	4	3.0	0.7	7.2	3.3

quite different, resulting in a positive and significant valuation bias, we investigate the factors that explain this pattern. We do so by showing in Figure 14.3 the changes in the selection of comparable firms before and after the IPO (that is, by the underwriter in the official prospectus and by the affiliated analyst in the first post-IPO equity report). As reported in the upper graph, on average 6.7 peers are used to value IPOs both at the IPO and later as analyst. However, while both selections are made of 6.7 peers, 2.9 of them are replaced. This practice is

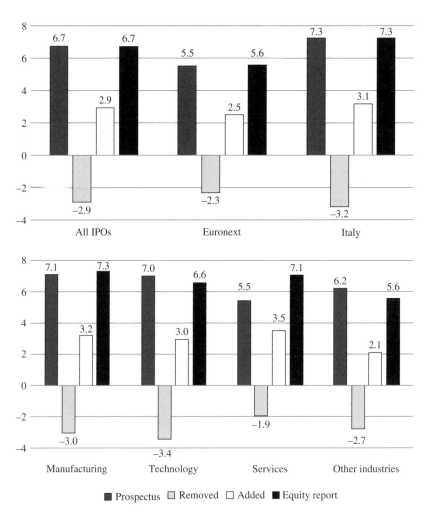

■ Prospectus ▨ Removed ☐ Added ■ Equity report

Figure 14.3   Underwriters' selection of comparable firms pre- vs. post-IPO.
Comparison of the peers selected by the underwriter at the IPO with those selected by an affiliated analyst post-IPO. The graph shows the average number of comparable firms selected at the
IPO, as reported in the official prospectus; comparable firms published in prospectus but not
included in the post-IPO equity research report (removed); comparable firms published in the
post-IPO report but not previously included in prospectus (added); comparable firms selected
as analyst in the first post-IPO equity report. The upper graph shows averages for the whole
sample and by market, the lower graph by industry.

more evident among Italian IPOs, where the average number of peers changed
is slightly higher than 3, than among Euronext IPOs, where this number is considerably lower than 3. The lower graph illustrates the patterns in the revision of
the groups of peers across industry. Manufacturing and technology IPOs are those
associated with both the most numerous selections of peers and the largest numbers of peers changed. Specifically, 3 peers are removed and 3.2 are added among

manufacturing IPOs, on average, and similar statistics are found among technology IPOs (3.4 removed, 3 added).

We now compare the valuation multiples of prospectus' peers that do not appear in the subsequent reports ('removed') with those 'added'. In the right-hand side of the table, statistical significance of the difference between the valuation multiples of the two groups is tested by means of the t-test and Wilcoxon signed-rank test. The above documented valuation bias suggests that, once the IPO is completed, affiliated analysts remove the peers with the highest valuation and add some more conservative peers that result in a lower overall valuation. Table 14.9 explicitly addresses this issue. The evidence reported in Panel A documents that removed peers have significantly higher valuations than added peers. The evidence is confirmed at a single market-level, although with lower levels of statistical significance, as documented in Panels B and C.

Table 14.9   Valuation multiples of added and removed peers by market.
The table reports the mean and median values of the valuation multiples of the peers that were not included in prospectus but were published in the equity report (added), and peers that were published in the prospectus but not included in the post-IPO equity research report (removed). Panel A reports aggregate statistics, Panel B and C refer to firms going public in Euronext and Italy, respectively. ***, **, and * indicate significance at the 1%, 5%, and 10% levels, respectively, of the t-test and Wilcoxon signed-rank test for the difference between the two groups.

	Added peers		Removed peers		Difference Re.-Ad.	
Panel A. All markets	mean	median	mean	median	mean	median
EV/Sales	9.1	7.7	19.9	16.2	10.8**	8.5*
EV/EBITDA	10.9	10.6	17.5	15.8	6.6***	5.2***
EV/EBIT	18.8	16.1	34.8	27.3	16.0*	11.2
P/E	24.5	22.8	43.2	40.9	18.7***	18.1***
P/CF	28.8	24.5	50.7	41.8	21.9	17.3
P/BV	2.0	1.8	8.9	8.4	6.9*	6.6*
Panel B. Euronext						
EV/Sales	7.7	2.6	26.8	4.7	19.1**	2.2
EV/EBITDA	10.6	8.9	13.0	9.3	2.4	0.4
EV/EBIT	14.0	11.1	26.6	18.5	12.6**	7.5*
P/E	35.7	23.4	35.0	27.2	−0.7	3.8
P/CF	34.2	22.0	27.7	16.2	−6.5	−5.8
P/BV	1.9	2.1	7.9	3.9	6.0	1.8
Panel C. Italy						
EV/Sales	9.9	1.8	15.2	4.2	5.3	2.4
EV/EBITDA	10.9	9.3	19.0	12.7	8.1	3.4
EV/EBIT	20.7	12.4	39.7	15.5	19.0***	3.1
P/E	22.0	19.6	44.6	29.1	22.6***	9.5*
P/CF	26.6	20.5	60.4	10.0	33.8**	−10.5
P/BV	2.2	2.6	10.5	4.5	8.3	1.9

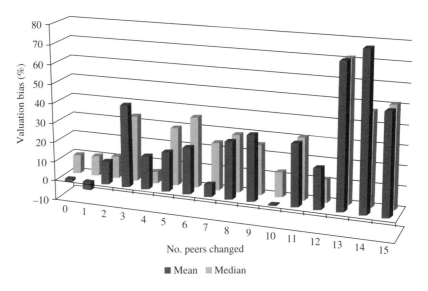

Figure 14.4   Number of peers changed and valuation bias.
The graph reports the mean and median values of valuation bias for each number of peers
changed, defined as the sum of peers published in prospectus but not included in the post-IPO
equity research report (removed) and those published in the post-IPO report but not previously
included in prospectus (added).

To further investigate whether the revision in the selection of comparable from
the prospectus to the first equity report is aimed at correcting the upward bias associated with the valuation of the initial selection of peers, Figure 14.4 illustrates how
valuation bias varies based on the number of peers changed from the pre- vs. post-
IPO groups of peers. The mean and median values of valuation bias are reported for
different numbers of changed peers, defined as the sum of removed and added peers.
Although the relationship is not strictly monotonic, the magnitude of the valuation
bias generally increases with the number of peers changed. In particular, the peak
in the average valuation bias is around 75% and is reached in correspondence of 14
peers changed, followed by approximately 70% associated with 13 peers changed.
This documents that underwriters revise their own prior selection of peers to a greater
extent when they need to considerably lower the valuation of the new group of peers.
They do so by removing peers with high valuations from the initial selection, and then
adding peers with low valuations to the new group.

14.5.4   Pre- vs. Post-IPO Selections and Industry Effects

We started from the idea that each industry provides underwriters with a different
degree of discretion in the selection of peers, as issuers in some industries face a less
ambiguous pool of potential peers than in others. We now assess the extent to which
this reflects in a revision of the selection of peers from the time of the publication of
the official prospectus to the release of the first post-IPO equity report. Table 14.10
compares the valuation multiples of removed and added peers by industry. Consistent

Table 14.10   Valuation multiples of added and removed peers by industry.
The table reports the mean and median values of the valuation multiples of the peers that were not included in prospectus but were published in the equity report (added), and peers that were published in the prospectus but not included in the post-IPO equity research report (removed), for the three most represented industries of the sample. Panel A refers to Technology firms, Panel B to Manufacturing firms, and Panel C to services firms. Technology firms are identified as in Loughran and Ritter (2004). ***, **, and * indicate significance at the 1%, 5%, and 10% levels, respectively, of the t-test and Wilcoxon signed-rank test for the difference between the two groups.

	Added peers		Removed peers		Difference Re.-Ad.	
Panel A. Manufacturing	mean	median	mean	median	mean	median
EV/Sales	4.8	3.0	6.8	2.4	2.0	−0.6
EV/EBITDA	9.2	8.0	14.1	12.6	4.9**	4.6**
EV/EBIT	14.5	11.6	16.7	15.4	2.2	3.8
P/E	20.2	17.9	29.8	28.8	9.5***	10.9***
P/CF	29.7	24.0	26.1	13.4	−3.6	−10.6**
P/BV	2.8	3.6	6.3	5.2	3.5	1.6
Panel B. Technology						
EV/Sales	17.5	13.8	32.3	19.6	14.8**	5.8**
EV/EBITDA	14.5	10.3	29.9	16.4	15.4**	6.1**
EV/EBIT	34.9	15.5	52.3	19.7	17.4**	4.2*
P/E	32.2	25.6	81.6	56.1	49.4***	30.5***
P/CF	22.0	18.3	48.0	20.6	26.0***	12.3***
P/BV	2.5	2.1	10.0	4.1	7.5*	2.0
Panel C. Services						
EV/Sales	4.2	4.0	15.0	5.0	10.7	1.0
EV/EBITDA	11.3	9.9	8.1	7.8	−3.2	−2.1
EV/EBIT	17.7	12.8	21.5	16.7	3.7*	3.9**
P/E	29.5	20.9	68.3	40.0	38.8***	19.1***
P/CF	-	-	-	-	-	-
P/BV	1.6	1.8	8.0	5.8	6.4**	4.0**

with the evidence documented so far, IPOs from the technology industry are associated with the largest and most significant differences between the valuations of removed and added peers. The difference in the P/E ratio is striking, as the average P/E of the added peers is 32.2 while that of the removed peers is as high as 81.6. Among manufacturing IPOs, the difference in the P/E ratio between the two groups of peers is still significant but is considerably lower (9.5). Together with the evidence that underwriters tend to substantially revise their own choices by replacing a large number of peers when valuing tech IPOs, the results indicate that this industry is the most exposed to the underwriters' strategic behaviour.

The industry diversification of the IPO firm, defined as its number of unique 2-digit SIC codes, is interpreted as a measure of the discretion of the underwriters in the choice of comparable firms. The idea is that more diversified issuers provide

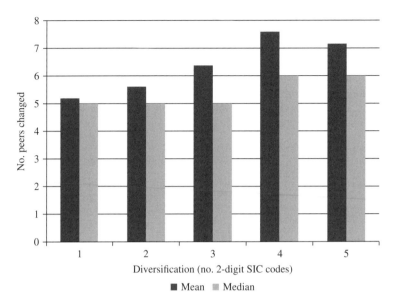

Figure 14.5   Firm diversification and number of peers changed.
The graph reports the mean and median values of the number of peers changed, defined as the sum of peers published in prospectus but not included in the post-IPO equity research report (removed) and those published in the post-IPO report but not previously included in prospectus (added), as a function of diversification, defined as a firm's number of unique 2-digit SIC codes.

underwriters with a higher degree of freedom in the selection of peers, while more focused issuers imply less ambiguity. We employ the same measure and investigate whether more diversified issuers experience greater revisions in the selection of peers from the official prospectus to the post-IPO equity report. Figure 14.5 illustrates the mean and median values of the number of peers changed, defined as the sum of removed and added peers, for different degrees of firm diversification. The graph clearly indicates that more diversified firms are subject to a larger number of replacements in the group of comparable firms before vs. after the IPO. In particular, the number of changed peers steadily increases from approximately 5 among firms with only one 2-digit SIC code to almost 8 among firms with four 2-digit SIC codes, and then decreases to approximately 7 for the most diversified firms. This provides further support to the view that the strategic behaviour of the underwriter is exacerbated in industries that leave them with more flexibility in the selection of peers.

14.6   Conclusions

In this chapter we shed light on the presence of possible strategic behaviour by underwriters in the valuation of IPOs by focusing on the most common valuation methodology, namely comparable firm multiples. Since this approach leaves underwriters with a considerable degree of discretion, we investigate whether they perform a strategic selection of comparable firms and valuation multiples, with the aim of justifying a higher valuation for the firm going public while simultaneously presenting it as conservatively priced with respect to these 'overvalued' peers. While disclosure of information about the valuation methods used by IPO underwriters to estimate the offer price is very limited in the United States, more information is available in Continental Europe, which makes it an ideal setting in which to pursue the objective of this study. We therefore address our research questions in a sample of recent IPOs occurring on the three largest exchanges in Continental Europe, namely Euronext, Germany, and Italy. In particular, we focus on the role played by industry member-ship. The idea is that the bias in the choice of comparable firms by underwriters is expected to increase when there is more discretion, and discretion is largely affected by the issuer's industry. Industries like technology and services, in which firms face a larger pool of potential peers, should be exposed to the underwriter's strategic behaviour to a greater extent than industries in which firms face a more unambigu-ous set of peers.

The evidence obtained from the comparison of the peers selected by underwriters with those picked by three alternative algorithmic criteria reveals that underwriter's peers have systematically higher valuations. This evidence persists even relative to the valuation of the firm going public measured at the offer price, i.e. after account-ing for the deliberate price discount applied by underwriters to the valuation of their peers. Then, by comparing the underwriter's selection of peers with that performed by affiliated and unaffiliated analysts after the IPO, we document the persistence of such valuation bias. In particular, a significant fraction of peers is replaced from the pro-spectus selection to the first post-IPO equity report released by an affiliated analyst, despite the limited time window between the two publications. Removed peers have significantly higher valuations than newly added peers, and valuation bias increases with the number of peers changed, confirming the strategic use of these replacements by underwriters.

We then find that all the above documented evidence is shaped by industry effects. In particular, valuation bias is more pronounced when the issuer operates in the tech-nology industry, as it faces a larger and more ambiguous pool of potential peers. On the other hand, valuation bias is lower in the manufacturing industry. Consistently, we find that the number of peers changed from the underwriter's selection at the IPO to that of affiliated analysts is larger in the technology industry. Also, the number of peers changed increases with an IPO firm's degree of diversification, which proxies for the underwriter's level of discretion in the selection of peers, and so does valuation bias.

References

Aggarwal, R., Bhagat, S. and Rangan, S. (2009). The Impact of fundamentals on IPO Valuation. *Financial Management* 38 (2): 253–284.

Bhojraj, S. and Lee, C. (2002). Who Is My Peer? A valuation-based approach to the selection of comparable firms. *Journal of Accounting Research* 40 (2): 407–439.

Cassia, L., Paleari, S. and Vismara, S. (2004). The valuation of firms listed on the Nuovo Mer-cato: the peer comparables approach. *Advances in Financial Economics* 10: 113–129.

Cliff, M.T. (2007). Do affiliated analysts mean what they say? *Financial Management* 36 (4): 5–29.

Deloof, M., De Maeseneire, W. and Inghelbrecht, K. (2009). How do investment banks value initial public offerings (IPOs)? *Journal of Business Finance & Accounting* 36 (1-2): 130-160.

Kim, M. and Ritter, J.R. (1999). Valuing IPOs. *Journal of Financial Economics* 53 (3): 409–438.

Liu, X. and Ritter, J. R. (2010). The economic consequences of IPO spinning. *Review of Financial Studies* 23 (5): 2024–2059.

Loughran, T. and Ritter, J.R. (2002). Why don't issuers get upset about leaving money on the table in IPOs? *Review of Financial Studies*, Vol. 15 (2): 413-444.

Loughran, T. and Ritter, J.R. (2004). Why has IPO underpricing changed over time? *Financial Management* 33 (3): 5–37.

Paleari, S., Signori, A. and Vismara, S. (2014) How do underwriters select peers when valuing IPOs? *Financial Management* 43 (4): 731–755.

Ritter, J.R. (2011) Equilibrium in the Initial Public Offerings market. *Annual Review of Financial Economics* 3 (1): 347–374.

Vismara, S., Signori, A. and Paleari, S. (2015) Changes in underwriters' selection of comparable firms pre- and post-IPO: Same bank, same company, different peers. *Journal of Corporate Finance* 34: 235–250.

Chapter 15

Governance of Financial Services Outsourcing: Managing Misconduct and Third-Party Risks

Joseph A. McCahery
Tilburg University

F. Alexander de Roode
Robeco

15.1 Introduction

Financial institutions have become highly reliant on outsourcing critical business processes to external service providers. Institutions are increasingly taking advantage of outsourcing to lower costs and acquire higher quality services to sustain their competitive advantage. By 2018, the financial services outsourcing market was estimated to be worth $130 billion and expected to increase approximately 7.5% annually.[1] Although the growth and expansion of outsourcing in past decades have increased productivity and, thus, benefited institutions, there is also evidence that outsourcing has generated new risks. Some of these risks also stem from the fact that more financial institutions are relying on a small group of vendors. For example, companies outsourcing cybersecurity functions can select from only a small number of third-party suppliers for IT-related tasks.

With the rapid spread of outsourcing in the financial services market, it is essential to establish a governance framework to limit agency problems and manage risk (see, e.g., Williamson (2002) for an overview of the related literature). Prior studies show that the optimal level of reliance on third parties is determined, on the one hand, by the institution's ability to manage the risks associated with outsourced activities and, on the other hand, by cost reduction (Mudambi and Tallman 2010). However, less is known about the mechanisms used to monitor and detect unobserved violations of contracts and possible misconduct. Indeed, recent IT and data security incidents have revealed the need for additional, more specialized detection methods to supplement the traditional due diligence and governance model (Mitts and Talley 2018).

The recent financial crisis exposed the limitations of the internal control and monitoring capabilities of some major financial institutions. Since the crisis, regulators have revised their guidelines for third-party relationships based on a framework that involves service provider selection, contractual terms, ongoing monitoring and termination (OCC 2013; Federal Reserve 2013). The premise underlying the revised guidelines is that institutions should strengthen their third-party risk management programs to mitigate the operational and legal risks to the firm. However, prior research raises the question of whether contractual governance alone can successfully manage outsourcing relationships, due to contractual complexity (Poppo and Zenger 2002; Schwartz and Scott 2003). Of course, contracts contain many control mechanisms that are associated with better outcomes in outsourcing relationships (Choudhury and Sabherwal 2003). However, there are very few studies on the extent to which financial institutions have implemented measures that have proved sufficient in third-party risk management.

To gain a better understanding of the governance of third-party relationships, we examine the contractual arrangements and governance mechanisms for selecting and managing service providers. For this chapter, we canvassed financial institutions themselves on their preferences and beliefs about the potential risks connected with third-party activities and the controls to monitor and manage these risks. By means of a survey, we documented the preferred characteristics of third-party suppliers and analyse the different techniques used to help identify the direct and indirect costs of service providers. In addition, in this chapter, we shed light on the broad range of

---

[1] 15 Must-Know Outsourcing Statistics (2020 Update). http://fortunly.com/statistics/outsourcing [Last retrieved: 2 February 2020].

misconduct risks in financial services outsourcing and the methods and processes to maintain an effective fraud risk management programme. While the focus here is on the behaviour of individual firms, identifying the differences in governance mechanisms and monitoring techniques allows us to provide evidence of the key measures involved in reducing operational risk and protecting against misconduct.

Two views regarding the governance of outsourcing activities are well known. The transaction costs view suggests that firms will always prefer to internalize business activities if the costs of market coordination are higher than the firm's production costs. When facing the decision to outsource, institutions must find a balance between the potential transaction and production costs that arise and the performance level of the outsourced process. One of the assumptions is that firms have the ability to specify and value contingent contracts that specify future contingencies and include ex-ante solutions. The second view leads us to expect that when financial intermediaries use outsourcing to improve the firm's business activities, they are likely to experience agency problems due to asymmetric information issues or misaligned interests. The most well-known methods to stem agency problems include incentivizing vendor performance in line with the institution's interests and monitoring vendor behaviour during each phase of the outsourcing process.

To address these two views, we examine the preferences of financial institutions for managing third-party functions. The challenge is to assess the extent to which transaction costs influence management's overall strategy for the projects most likely to be outsourced to a third party. Yet, due to the complexity of indirect costs, such as training and management of the vendor, we consider the factors that frequently provide the motivation for the outsourcing decision. Specifically, we focus on the cost effectiveness of outsourcing, the extent to which core business processes are outsourced and the specialized capacity of the vendor that is necessary for accomplishing the project.

Our examination of outsourcing can be summarized as follows. Most financial institutions mention IT and data management systems as the most frequently outsourced activities, together with traditional accounting and compliance processes as the next most common outsourced activities. In making the decision to outsource, we find that financial institutions place the most emphasis on the overall cost and competitive benefits of outsourcing. Moreover, institutions outsource for a variety of other important reasons, including access to specific knowledge, greater focus on core processes, scalability, and increased service-level performance. We show that the outsourced activities that pose the most risk are data management and core business processes. We further examine how and to what extent different types of risk affect the outsourcing relationship. We find that a number of factors, including frequent staff and senior management changes, will contribute to the increased likelihood of fraud.

Next, we study the governance mechanisms of outsourcing and the institution's ability to monitor third parties. We find that firms rely mainly on internal auditing and whistleblowing to uncover fraud in third-party relationships. Firms also use several specific actions to detect fraud: site visits and special investigative team monitoring are examples of techniques that firms employ to monitor fraud risk. Finally, we investigate contractual termination as a response to supplier misconduct. We find that vendor dependency and product complexity play a pronounced role in delaying the termination of the contract. Our results suggest that there are great difficulties associated with replacing a supplier, suggesting that well-designed contingency plans are important.

This chapter contributes to the literature on the risks arising from financial services outsourcing. A stream of literature finds that the link between the outsourcing level and risk is well established. Gonzalez et al. (2010) conclude, for example, that excessive dependence on the service provider is a major outsourcing risk. Other studies emphasize the major risks involved in outsourcing complex products or services (Ernst and Young 2015). We share with these papers that vendor dependency and product complexity can lead to excessive risk in third-party relationships. Our chapter also adds to the literature on fraud and misconduct in financial services outsourcing. Coram et al. (2008) find that firms with an internal audit function are more likely to detect fraud than are those without such a function. Our findings suggest not only that internal monitoring is the most preferred detection mechanism, but also that whistleblowing plays an important role in this context.

The remainder of the chapter is structured as follows. Section 15.2 discusses the theory on outsourcing and explains the theoretical governance mechanisms in outsourcing relationships. In Section 15.3, we introduce our survey data and look at the role of screening, contract clauses, monitoring and termination in outsourced service contracts. Section 15.4 examines the ability of financial institutions to monitor third-party vendors by focusing on fraud and misconduct risk and documents the strategies that can detect third parties engaged in such conduct or that can prevent them from doing so. Section 15.5 concludes.

15.2   The Four Components in Outsourcing

In this section, we provide a brief review of the theories motivating our analysis of the outsourcing process. We also discuss the main components of the governance of the outsourcing relationship between client and vendor.

15.2.1   Efficient Outsourcing

The concept of outsourcing has been thoroughly studied in the literature. Economists studying the theory of the firm explain that, under the stringent assumption of zero transaction costs, there is no economic rationale for undertaking a business process within the firm versus outsourcing it to a third-party service provider. One of the early insights is that, since transaction costs matter in most practical decisions, the choice to externalize the process depends on the expected costs of outsourcing. From the perspective of rational agents, we would expect that institutions would not only attach costs to the actual outsourcing but would also include indirect costs in the anticipated risks through a cost-benefit analysis (Coase 1937). To derive an efficient outcome for the firm, contractual complexity (i.e. contract detail) is a key feature (Williamson 1985; 1991). On the other hand, the complexity in financial services outsourcing implies that not every possible outcome and all associated risks can be anticipated in outsourcing agreements. Hence, the economic rationale for outsourcing can be understood as an equilibrium between the complexity and the associated costs to outsource a business process.

To align the incentives between financial institutions and service providers, traditional contractual mechanisms are widely adopted to mitigate opportunism (Lacity and Hirschheim 1993). Firms tend to include a variety of contractual provisions to align the interests of the service provider with those of the financial institution and to reduce the threat of opportunistic behaviour. Moreover, contracts can limit the dependence on service providers and discourage information asymmetries (Anderson 1985). Still, contracts may be incomplete in the sense that not all contingencies can be specified in the contract or verified by third parties. MacLeod (2000) suggests that parties can achieve their goals by drafting provisions that take into account the changing environment. Others suggest that relational governance and networked relationships may be a solution to the problems of complexity and contractual incompleteness (Poppo and Zenger 2002; Gulati 1995; Dyer 1997). An environment of trust, of course, is also central to the design of contracts that mediate the agency problems and create a successful long-term relationship between parties (Logan 2000; Babin, Bates, and Sohal 2017). Nevertheless, these findings raise the question of whether both parties will benefit from relational governance. In a more recent study, Gopal and Koka (2009) show that the benefits exist only if the transferred risks are sufficiently large.

A critical factor is the concept of asset specificity, which influences the complexity of the relationship between the financial institutions and the service providers (Dyer 1997). The concentration of skills and knowledge offered by a few vendors may leave institutions dependent on the supplier's expertise, which is often difficult to assess. The prior research shows that firms need to contractually specify these risks in order to achieve an efficient combination of insourcing and outsourcing. The advantage of this approach is that it reduces both the asymmetric information between the service provider and the financial institutions and the associated transaction costs. Such an approach has been shown to be particularly beneficial for long-term contracts with vendors.

Although our emphasis has been on how contractual arrangements may facilitate the performance of third-party suppliers, there is evidence that financial institutions focus mostly on the direct costs to acquire outsourcing activity and are less likely to take indirect costs into consideration (Ang and Straub 1998). Early studies document that most institutions consider the direct cost advantages more valuable than the level of perceived risks (Barthelemy 2001; Gewald, Wullenweber, and Weitzel 2006). From the perspective of cost-effectiveness, it is efficient for an institution to take the certain risks instead of mitigating or eliminating such risks altogether (Stulz 2015). On the other hand, some studies focus on contract provisions aimed at mitigating risk in order to protect the firms against supplier opportunism (Currie, Mitchell, and Abanishe 2008).

At the same time, regulators have investigated the contracts between financial institutions and service providers to shed light on the role of indirect costs. While regulators learn about indirect costs, it is difficult for institutions to specify these costs due to estimation problems. Furthermore, the discovery of indirect costs can be costly. One example is the misalignment of mortgage servicing by banks, which is done by a service provider. As service providers have no stake in the actual performance of the loans, a principle–agent conflict is introduced between the financial institution and the service provider (Levitin and Twomey 2011). Similarly, financial outsourcing introduces risk in mutual funds. Chen et al. (2013) show that financial institutions that outsource their asset management activities to advisory firms frequently underperform. Other related studies (e.g. Cumming, Schweinbacher, and Zhan 2015), however, find no performance differences associated with outsourcing. Debaere and Evans (2014) also establish that, after controlling for selection bias, the performance of outsourced mutual funds show no performance effects. In contrast, the literature on hedge fund outsourcing indicates that problem funds exhibit significant operational risk that is associated with external and internal conflicts of interest (Cumming, Dai, and Johan 2013).

As discussed above, regulators updated their guidelines after the financial collapse of 2007–2009 to ensure that parties have adequate control over the selection of third parties and a comprehensive set of monitoring mechanisms to manage operational risk and ensure business continuity (OCC 2013; Federal Reserve 2013). The following section discusses the four-factor model of third-party risk governance.

15.2.2   The Four-Factor Governance Model

The specific governance structure of financial services outsourcing comprises four factors:[2] screening, contracting, monitoring and control, and termination. Since agency costs are inherent to the outsourcing relationship, an adequate governance framework is needed to enhance the relationship between the parties. This framework can help attain the goals of the outsourcing project through increased revenue or reduced costs and strengthening the soundness and compliance management system.

15.2.2.1   Screening

In this section, we examine the evidence on the selection of third-party vendors. High levels of asymmetric information tend to prevent fair contracting between financial institutions and vendors. In this context, the industry trend is for service providers to offer more knowledge process outsourcing (Currie, Mitchell, and Abanishe 2008). The integration of knowledge processes will, in turn, increase the asset specificity. This may not only heighten the risk of outsourcing the activity, but also raise costs due to asymmetric information. To avoid adverse selection problems, institutions engage in extensive pre-contractual screening to identify higher-quality vendors.

---

[2] In 2005, the Basel Committee on Banking Supervision released a publication in which the Joint Forum's working group derived a set of principles for financial outsourcing. Similarly, the Federal Reserve Bank of New York released a report in 1999 on how to mitigate outsourcing risk with equivalent principles. On 30 October 2013, the Office of the Comptroller of the Currency provided updated guidance to US financial institutions, introducing a life-cycle approach to third-party risk management and requiring financial institutions to ensure that their risk management processes are commensurate with the level of risk and the complexity of their service provider relationships.

In contrast to the literature on financial contracts, there is little empirical research on vendor selection in financial services outsourcing. Prior work focuses on the costs of outsourcing and the costs associated with screening a supplier. For example, Ang and Straub (1998) find that the information systems (IS) outsourcing decisions of 243 US banks were driven mainly by production costs. While the trend in outsourcing lends support to the view that institutions need to reduce their costs to meet consumer demand for innovative products and better-quality service delivery, the complexity of outsourced processes may induce higher transactional costs (Williamson 1991). For example, innovations by vendors are typically harder to account for in the screening process. Moreover, the Basel Committee on Banking Supervision (2004) observed that financial institutions justify their outsourcing programs in terms of cost reduction and control of operating costs. With the renewed guidance on third-party risk management, regulators have increased the emphasis on the importance of screening for the integrity and reliance of external suppliers (OCC 2013).

Financial institutions can also limit information asymmetries by performing rigorous due diligence to evaluate the quality of the supplier's products and the prevalence of internal control weaknesses (see, e.g., Evans 2005; Cox and Pilbourne 2018). Previous work has emphasized the importance of the investment in due diligence in terms of performance payoffs (Brown et al. 2008). The challenge of due diligence involves investing in the scrutiny of the target firm's characteristics and the potential operational, legal, and financial risks. Such an evaluation, which may be performed internally or externally, includes benchmarking vendor activities against services delivered within the firm or by alternative service providers. Cumming and Zambelli (2016) show that the time spent and the role played by a particular agent performing the due diligence (i.e. internally, by fund managers) will have a significant effect on the performance of the target firm.

15.2.2.2   Contracting

Our discussion so far has focused on due diligence and screening of service providers. We now examine the contractual arrangements with suppliers. In theory, contracts are structured to mitigate agency problems that arise in the outsourcing of products and services. Indeed, a long-term relationship with a service provider is considered a highly effective structure for mitigating risks when large, specific investments are made. Supplier performance measures can contribute to reducing uncertainty about supplier behaviour (Lacity and Hirschheim 1993). In addition, contingent contracts with multiple providers of services can mitigate some of the monitoring issues and guard against the risks associated with unknown external contingencies (Basel Committee on Banking Supervision 2004).

Outsourcing contracts are typically divided into two components. On the one hand, the formal contract is of the plain vanilla form used in most outsourcing relations. On the other hand, the service-level agreement (SLA) serves to benchmark the output from the service provider (Geis 2009). Larger financial institutions are expected to benefit since they have lower costs for setting up in-house facilities to manage an outsourcing relationship and can better address the inherent risks in outsourced activities. That said, the SLA is the key mechanism for allocating the risks and incentives and providing coordination between the firm and the service provide. Overall, experience suggests that a well-designed SLA can alleviate some of the risks arising from cost overruns, variable supplier output, and opportunism (Klein 1992).

Additionally, service providers have incentives to standardize their outsourced tasks in order to benefit from economies of scale and lower costs (Ang and Staub 1998). The inclusion of innovation and incentive clauses can also help deter vendors from engaging in untrustworthy behaviour (Jap and Anderson 2003). The role of these measures is a crucial factor in managing third-party risk. However, until recently, there has been only limited evidence of their usage as best practice in outsourcing contracts.

While the focus on a variety of contractual methods is important for managing outsourcing relationships, the evidence shows that there are other arrangements, besides contractual mechanisms, that are relevant to managing vendor opportunism (Bahli and Rivard 2003). For example, Schlosser and Wagner (2011) find evidence that the governance of the outsourcing relationship is unrelated to contractual mechanisms. Experience shows that the service provider's performance is affected mainly by the quality of the outsourcing relation. In particular, Bapna et al. (2010) find – from a sample of 700 large IT outsourcing contracts during the period 1989–2009 – that the likelihood of failure is higher in the presence of intermediaries who both help define the scope of the contract and search for the appropriate service provider. Overall, the specific characteristics of the outsourcing relationship may call for a variety and range of relationship management and governance structures to create an effective and reliable transactional relationship with third-party suppliers.

15.2.2.3   Monitoring

As we've seen, a singular focus on complex contracts may play too limited a role to eliminate agency conflicts connected with outsourcing. Previous work has long recognized the uses of governance mechanisms to manage and expose third-party risks. Monitoring relates to the actual capacity of financial institutions to benchmark their outsourced activities. Given the increasing complexity and risk of third-party relationships, senior management's monitoring of third-party operations is considered of major importance for large banks (Gewald, Wüllenweber, and Weitzel 2006). However, the authority and accountability of institutions to monitor these risks depends on the incentives and actual capacity of firms to perform these functions. Empirical evidence confirms that the quantification of risk assessment can substantially improve matters.

To be sure, recent research finds that some financial institutions might be less able to manage, let alone exert influence over, the delivery of complex outsourced services (Krivin et al. 2013). There are several possible explanations for the difficulties of managing third-party suppliers. First, this seems to be more likely in cases where there are multiple tasks and objectives in an outsourcing agreement. For example, Fitoussi and Gurbaxani (2012), explicitly testing outsourcing contracts with multiple objectives and varying measurement costs, find that as the number of performance measures increases, the more likely it is that satisfaction with the outcome will decrease. Second, financial institutions may be less able to improve their monitoring to the extent that there are many performance measurements that are difficult to benchmark. Third, the costs associated with the monitoring of complex SLAs can deter institutions from engaging in detailed monitoring. This presumably helps to explain why many contracts are structured to rely solely on cost-related metrics to achieve their main outsourcing goals.

15.2.2.4 Termination

Termination is an important mechanism to limit potential hold-up problems. As we noted above, the outsourcing relationship may, due to asset specificity, lead a hold-up situation between the financial institution and service provider. The literature offers two perspectives on how to mitigate this risk. First, the hold-up problem can be addressed by ex-ante contracting, so that extensive contracting serves to curb potential threats and align interests. The alternative view, expressed by incomplete contract theory, attempts to mitigate the hold-up problem by assigning the rights of the outsourcing relationship ex post to exclude opportunistic behaviour (Grossman and Hart 1986; Segal 1999; Susarla, Subramanyman, and Karhade 2009). Susarla et al. (2009) propose that a hold-up problem may arise due to the complexity of the outsourcing relationship and contractual incompleteness. Other studies have offered different insights into the source of the hold-up problem. For example, Whitten, Chakrabarty, and Wakefield (2010) find that high switching costs of service providers decrease the willingness of the financial institution to acquire a new service provider and, therefore, play a crucial role in resolving hold-up problems. High switching costs will put serious pressure on firms to continue the outsourcing relationship rather than to terminate it in favour of other alternatives.

A crucial consideration influencing switching costs is the duration of the outsourcing contract. On the one hand, Jiang, Yao, and Feng (2008) argue that shortening the duration of the contract leads to better supplier monitoring and, hence, minimizes the likelihood of a hold-up problem. With short-term contracts, institutions can incentivize suppliers by contract renewal since suppliers may rely on renewal due to their initial investment costs. Kern, Willcocks, and van Heck (2002) also explain that hold-up problems are less likely to occur in competitive markets. Service providers often enter into contracts below their profit margin and, consequently, performance may suffer due to the provider's incapacity to innovate his services. As a result, both parties have incentives to terminate, which effectively solves the hold-up problem. As noted, competitive markets also promote contracts with multiple service providers, reducing potential hold-up problems. While such agreements could discourage vendor participation, the feasibility of such contracts is influenced mainly by the threat of termination and the superior bargaining power of financial institutions (Costello 2013).

15.2.3 Misconduct in Outsourcing and the Ability of Financial Institutions to Monitor

Regulators have always needed to focus on the role of misconduct in financial markets. For example, a number of large banks, such as Wells Fargo and J.P. Morgan, have been involved in high-profile misconduct cases for credit card and consumer loan fraud and money laundering. A central theme motivating regulators is that financial institutions are particularly prone to abuse that often results in uncertainty, losses to customers and investors, as well as potential shocks to the market (FCA 2013). One inherent challenge for regulators is the difficulty of determining the precise level of misconduct in financial markets (Carletti 2017). Addressing this challenge, Dyck, Morse, and Zingales (2014) estimate that, each year, about 15% of companies are engaged in fraud.

What about penalties to deter misconduct? Prior research shows that between 2009 and 2016, the cost of fines and settlements by banks in the US amounted to about $180 billion, while in Europe, regulators collected $20 billion in fines (European Parliament 2017). In terms of the impact, an assessment of conduct risk losses for 51 EU-wide banks carried out in 2016 reveals that the impact of the fines for misconduct would be amount to €71bn over a three-year period (ESRB 2017). This research shows that, although the penalties for fraud are substantial, they are unlikely to reduce the occurrence of fraud.

Theories on the role of regulation have focused on the deterrent effect of fines and the reputational damage from an investigation (Karpoff, Lee, and Martin 2008; Murphy, Shrieves and Tibbs 2009; Armour, Mayer, and Polo 2017). Besides the associated fines for misconduct, criminal penalties target individuals who have acted dishonestly toward investors (Coffee 2007; Jackson and Roe 2009). Following the financial crisis, regulators have shifted their emphasis to deal with misconduct issues that may result, for example, from misaligned incentives (IOSCO 2017).

Market misconduct is widely considered one of the underlying factors responsible for the 2007–2009 financial crisis. Post-crisis reforms have focused on three main areas (Carletti 2017). First, on the conduct side, guidelines for effective management processes were designed to provide a corrective mechanism to limit the opportunities for misconduct (FSB 2018). Second, regulators have sought to address enforcement deficiencies by imposing a variety of sanctioning devices, enforcement techniques, and penalties (Götz and Tröger 2017). Third, because of the misconduct resulting from the outsourcing of payment and settlement systems, cybersecurity, and customer data management, there have been ongoing efforts to step up coordination between different regulators and supervisors, making it easier to manage information-processing and monitoring for the detection of fraud and misconduct (Basel Committee on Banking Supervision 2018).

Note that substantial benefits arise from the implementation of better monitoring and enforcement practices to deter fraud and misconduct (Kedia and Rajgopal 2011). Indeed, there is evidence that high-level monitoring can lead to a 27% lower probability of banks committing misconduct and a 35% higher probability of detection, compared to institutions in which boards have little or no power to prevent misconduct (Nguyen, Hagendorff, and Eshraghi 2016).

15.3   The Interaction between Contracting and Monitoring

To date, little is known about the governance of outsourcing activities within financial institutions. In the absence of data on governance mechanisms at the institutional level, we use a survey to understand the variety of practices that financial institutions use to monitor sub-contractors' performance. In this section, we introduce the summary statistics of the data set. To more accurately assess the fraud risk management framework of institutions, we analyse the most common services outsourced, types of fraud risk, fraud prevention measures, and range of proactive fraud detection mechanisms.

15.3.1 Characterization of Financial Institutions

The data set used in this chapter was obtained from a survey of financial institutions taken in 2017. Our target group of respondents was a selection of employees at financial institutions and financial services firms. The survey focused on addressing the governance mechanism in three sections: financial outsourcing, monitoring, and misconduct in outsourcing. The survey questions were designed to test our hypotheses. The phrasing used in the survey was structured to avoid financial jargon, except if the questions addressed specific outsourcing issues or misconduct-related questions.

Table 15.1 reports the characteristics of our sample with the variables firm size and type.

Our sample contains two important types of financial institutions: financial services firms, and financial management institutions such as asset managers, insurance and banks. The financial services and investment management firms both acquire and deliver financial outsourcing services. This set-up allows us to view the outsourcing relationship from two perspectives.

To verify the degree of outsourcing, we asked respondents about the level of outsourcing in specific activities. Table 15.2 shows that most firms in our sample have outsourced both core and non-core business activities. Important core activities that are likely to be outsourced include IT-services, back office-related tasks, and accounting. Some of these core processes are associated with the risk management efforts of financial institutions. Other core business processes, such as research, data management, and payment processes, are less likely to be sourced from external suppliers.

Table 15.1 Sample characteristics.
This table provides information about firm size and type in our survey of 20 respondents. Smaller institutions make up around 50% of the sample; the remaining 50% is made up of medium-sized to large financial institutions.

Firm size	Total
Less than €100M	9
Between €100M and €500M	4
Between €500M and €1B	6
Over €1B	1

Firm Type	Total
Asset managers, Banks, Insurance institutions	11
Financial service firm	9

Table 15.2   Outsourced financial activities.

This table reports the percentage of activities that are outsourced among the financial institutions in our sample and the average score of the response. The second part of the table includes respondents' views on future outsourcing activities.

Activity	No outsourcing at all	Few minor activities	Most activities, except crucial components	All components are outsourced	Average score
Research	31%	46%	23%	0%	1.92
Data Management	29%	41%	18%	12%	2.12
IT systems	5%	21%	68%	5%	2.74
Recruitment	33%	44%	22%	0%	1.89
Compliance & Legal	32%	42%	21%	5%	2.00
Accounting	15%	50%	30%	5%	2.25
Payment processes	44%	33%	11%	11%	1.89
Facility management	27%	33%	13%	27%	2.40
Client Screening	40%	27%	20%	13%	2.07
Back office	35%	29%	29%	6%	2.06

	Outsourcing needed	Less outsourcing needed	Optimal level achieved	More outsourcing needed	Average Score
For Core Business processes	10%	20%	45%	25%	2.85
For Non-Core Business processes	0%	6%	12%	82%	3.76

Table 15.2 shows that respondents report that they use a broad range of vendors for their day-to-day operations. Likewise, facilities management is generally outsourced, reflecting an increasing trend over the last few years.

Table 15.2 shows each type of outsourced activity, the percentage that were not outsourced, and the percentage outsourced that involved all components or most activities, except for crucial components. Our results show that financial institutions are willing to further outsource core business activities. As can be seen, non-core business activities receive a higher average score than the core business score, and both average scores are higher than the average for the current level of outsourcing.

Our survey extends an earlier study by the European Central Bank (2004), which showed that banks rarely outsourced their core business processes. However, given the time elapsed since the ECB study, we expect that banks would be willing to

Table 15.3   Reasons for outsourcing.

In Table 15.3, we look at the reasons that financial institutions outsource. To get an overall ranking, we asked respondents to identify their top four reasons for outsourcing.

Rank	Reason
1.	Cost effectiveness of outsourcing
2.	Requirement of specific knowledge
3.	Focus on core business
4.	Scalability
5.	Improves service level
6.	Access to intellectual capital
7.	Internationalization
8.	Innovation

outsource more of their core activities because of cash-flow pressures. This is contrary to the KPMG 2015/2016 survey of banking systems, which reports that usage of in-house built core banking systems remains high. In terms of outsourcing a specific activity, a majority of institutions (78%) indicate that they would prefer to hire a supplier than to create a bespoke application in-house.

To further dissect the hypothesis of why institutions would require more outsourcing, we asked respondents about their reasons for outsourcing. Table 15.3 shows that cost remains one of the most important reasons for a firm to outsource an activity. Not surprisingly, most respondents indicated that outsourcing can also enhance growth in terms of both knowledge acquisition and an increased focus on the core business. These results show support for the literature on information system outsourcing, which views outsourcing as an opportunity to improve current levels of operations (Gonzalez, Gasco, and Llo 2010).

As noted, the underlying premise of outsourcing is that it is a cost-cutting mechanism. At this point, one might, of course, ask: Does this include both the direct and indirect costs (latest technology, best talent, and ability to refocus) associated with outsourcing the activity? (Kremic, Romic, and Tukel 2006) To be sure, while we were not able to disentangle direct from indirect costs, there is some evidence that firms, in general, are less able to fully capture indirect costs (Ang and Straub 1998). Our results also show that firms rank the requirement of specific knowledge and the focus on core business highly. From an efficiency perspective, these results are unsurprising since the acquisition of specific knowledge may be costly to insource or to develop and, hence, may cause a divergence in their business activities. Alternatively, this result raises a number of questions from a monitoring perspective. If the level of the services outsourced depends on the institution's ability to monitor, it is reasonable to assume that the service provider may be more likely to engage in misconduct.

Finally, what other factors are likely to influence the outsourcing decision? Scalability and improved service levels also appear to be important drivers. As expected, access to intellectual capital, internationalization, and innovation have little impact on the outsourcing decisions of financial institutions. Overall, these results portray a landscape in which institutions require specific knowledge of service providers, with a focus on the cost-efficient integration of the activities in their business model.

15.3.2   Risks in Outsourcing Services

We have established so far that institutions are likely to increase their outsourcing activity. To assess the specific risks in the outsourcing relationship, we asked respondents to identify the risk of outsourcing specific functions. The questionnaire asked respondents about the outsourcing risk in their sector generally and not necessarily at their own institution. Table 15.4 reports on the four categories of risk for each area.

Core business processes receive the most attention, as managers believe that misconduct in any of these crucial components is more likely to damage the institution's reputation and profitability. Another key area is data management. As we show above, data management is one of the leading areas outsourced, and managers consider it slightly more risky than core business processes. Surprisingly, the table shows that Cloud services, which are closely related to data management, are perceived as less risky. This result may be due simply to the slow adoption of Cloud services by financial institutions. We also find that areas more closely related to long-term profitability, such as research and strategic planning, are considered less risky for financial institutions to outsource.

Our interpretation of the results raises a question about managers' salient beliefs about financial services outsourcing. There is evidence that the perceived benefits have greater impact than the perceived risks on the decision to outsource. For example, Gewald and Dibbern (2009) surveyed the 200 largest German banks and found that the benefit of outsourcing is that it allows banks to refocus on their core competences. However, this is not the only possible explanation. Historical factors matter, as they have an impact on future outsourcing decisions of business processes, which we indeed find in some of our responses.

We next study the types of risks in outsourcing relationships. Table 15.5 shows the risks identified at the service provider and the consequences for institutions. As can be seen, multiple factors can cause risk at the service provider. Frequent staff changes and senior or middle management turnover are more likely to be important sources of fraud and misconduct. We also find support for earlier studies showing that product

Table 15.4   Areas of potential risks in financial institutions.
This table reports the respondents' assessment of outsourcing risk within their financial sector.

Areas	No risk at all	Some risk; not to crucial components	Moderate risk; also crucial components	Risky; critical components	Average Score
Core business processes	6%	33%	11%	50%	3.06
Data management	0%	16%	32%	53%	3.37
Cloud services	0%	28%	44%	28%	3.00
Compliance and legal	0%	26%	53%	21%	2.95
Research & strategic planning	5%	55%	30%	10%	2.45

Table 15.5   Risks in the outsourcing relationship.
This table reports the respondents' views on the risk associated with the service providers.

	Not at all	Not so likely	Likely	Strongly agree	Average Score
Risk at service provider					
Frequent changes in staff at vendor	0%	41%	47%	12%	2.71
Senior or middle management at vendor	6%	19%	56%	19%	2.88
Complexity of product	12%	35%	41%	12%	2.53
Risk at institutions					
Increased dependency on vendor	0%	29%	47%	24%	2.94
Monitoring ability of the service level agreement	6%	29%	29%	35%	2.94

complexity of core services and processes is a major risk in business processes outsourcing (Ernst and Young 2015).

The results in the lower section of Table 15.5 show that increased dependency on an external service provider can lead to additional risk. However, the reliance on third parties, such as IT vendors, may not have a negative impact on all institutions. As noted above, there are good business reasons that some financial institutions seek to strengthen third-party relationships –such as keeping up with technology and other competitive innovations. For example, traditional financial institutions are continuing to outsource their credit scoring, risk management, and customer services to financial service providers to increase their technical capabilities and innovative client services (Basel Committee on Banking Supervision 2018).

Conversely, the increasing reliance on suppliers for their innovative capacities raises possible strategic threats that could damage the financial institution's reputation and profitability. As noted, financial institutions with inadequate monitoring systems are considered more prone to fraud and misconduct risks. Equally, close monitoring of the service-level agreement lowers the ability of service providers to engage in fraud or misconduct. In addition, prior work shows that a comprehensive risk management program – which holds the institution's board and senior management ultimately responsible for managing the conduct of service providers – is likely to have a measurable impact on the ability of the firm to effectively deter and detect misconduct. Thus, if we want to mitigate risk, we should focus on those mechanisms that are likely to detect fraud in these relationships.

15.4   Governance Mechanisms to Detect Misconduct in Financial Outsourcing

As discussed in the previous section, theory suggests that institutions implement certain governance mechanisms to reduce the likelihood of misconduct. To empirically determine the extent to which governance mechanisms are created, we focus on the techniques used in third-party risk management.

15.4.1 Screening and Detection

We start by exploring the types of fraud that arise in the financial sector to understand the impact of vendor fraud relative to other types of fraud. Table 15.6 reports the responses on the types of fraud that emerge in the financial industry.

Our survey indicates that vendor, supplier, and procurement fraud are the leading types in the financial services industry. Prior evidence shows that managers are aware of the type of fraud involving the theft of personal, security, and credit card information, as in the 2006 case of unauthorized transfers from customer accounts by HSBC Electronic Data Processing India and the bank fraud committed by employees of Mphasis Ltd., involving the theft of Citibank customer accounts (Ramasastry 2006).

We next examine whether a particular governance mechanism has the potential to uncover misconduct. Table 15.7 shows that institutions rely on various methods to discover misconduct in outsourcing relationships.

Despite the differences in views on detection mechanisms, respondents rated internal monitoring as the single most effective mechanism to uncover misconduct. This is followed by whistleblowing, which is perceived as an effective fraud mitigation strategy. We can compare these findings to the study of Ernst and Young (2017), which found that 56% of employees surveyed indicated that they were uncomfortable reporting their concerns of possible violations or suspected wrongdoing. To date, little data are available on employees' incentives to use whistleblowing hotlines to identify fraud (Lee and Xiao 2018). Nonetheless, we show that the respondents are concerned about potential reputational consequences and social pressures that weaken their incentives to engage in whistleblowing (Dyck, Morse, and Zingales 2010). We interpret our finding as evidence of the reluctance of employees to expose misconduct and of the need for firms to have an effective procedure to increase incentives and support for whistleblowing. Interestingly, there are significant differences across industries in how informed employees are about their firm's whistleblowing hotline. In non-financial firms, the level is very low, with only 21% aware of the internal communication channel in the firm.

Table 15.6 Type of frauds that occurred in the financial sector.
This table reports respondents' awareness of fraud and misconduct in their financial sector.

	Aware	Not Aware
Physical assets	35%	65%
Vendor, supplier, or procurement fraud	63%	38%
Information theft	53%	47%
Management conflict of interest	67%	33%
Regulatory or compliance breach	73%	27%
Corruption and bribery	47%	53%
Internal financial fraud	50%	50%
Misappropriation of company funds	40%	60%
Intellectual Property theft	36%	64%
Market collusion	33%	67%

Table 15.7 Methods to uncover misconduct.
This table reports the respondents' views on their firms' methods to uncover misconduct.

	Not at all	Not so likely	Likely	Strongly agree	Don't know	Average score
General method						
Whistleblower	0%	20%	40%	30%	10%	3.11
External audit	0%	20%	45%	25%	10%	3.06
Internal audit	0%	25%	40%	30%	5%	3.05
Internal monitoring	5%	0%	60%	30%	5%	3.21
Specific actions						
On-site visits	0%	35%	53%	12%	0%	2.76
Special dedicated team monitoring SLA	0%	18%	47%	35%	0%	3.18
Issues in the outsourcing relation lead to re-evaluation of the entire service level of the vendor	0%	13%	73%	13%	0%	3.00

Next, we find that external audit scores are similar to those of internal audit for revealing misconduct in the outsourcing agreement. This result is counter to what is typically seen in the accounting literature (Corum, Ferguson, and Moroney 2008), in which firms that have an internal audit function are more likely to detect fraud than firms who outsource this function. Moreover, it is well known that external auditors pay attention only to financial reporting fraud (DeZoort and Harrison 2007). This suggests that an internal audit department, supported by other governance measures, is likely to be more effective in responding to fraud in outsourcing relationships. While regulations such as the Sarbanes–Oxley Act have also prohibited outsourcing certain internal audits to third-party service providers, it is not clear whether these restrictions have helped lower the risk of fraud (Prawitt, Sharp and Wood 2012). On the other hand, if the outsourced service or product is complex, this negatively effects the probability of detection overall.

To shed light on specific actions of institutions to reduce misconduct in outsourcing, we also found that onsite visits and special dedicated teams are effective methods for uncovering misconduct. This confirms our earlier analysis in Table 15.5, which showed a link between risk and the level of monitoring. Yet onsite visits receive less attention from institutions than do special dedicated teams. Significantly, our respondents expect that their institutions will fully evaluate, in light of the firm's contractual objectives, the conduct of the service provider in case of potential issues. Consistent with the earlier literature, we find evidence that management will take action against the service provider when the special dedicated team detects misconduct.

So far, we have looked at the measures that financial institutions employ to detect fraud. Next, we address the issue of termination in the case of vendor misconduct. Having established a relationship with a service provider to develop or acquire complex services, financial firms face significant challenges in arranging a contract with a new vendor. To limit this risk, firms are required to have a contingency plan to

Table 15.8   Termination in case of misconduct.
This table reports the actions that firms are willing to undertake when there is misconduct.

	Not at all	Not so likely	Likely	Strongly agree	Average Score
Actions					
Replace vendor with a competitor	0%	12%	35%	53%	3.41
Complicating factors in termination					
Complex outsourcing agreements	6%	29%	53%	12%	2.71
Complexity of product	0%	33%	60%	7%	2.73
Dependency on the outsourcing vendor	0%	27%	53%	20%	2.93

mitigate the risk in case of vendor termination and to ensure the transition to a new supplier (OCC 2013).

Table 15.8 shows that a large number of respondents are willing to terminate and replace a high-risk service provider. However, the dispersion regarding the variable of the re-evaluation of the service provider in the case of misconduct is much larger than in Table 15.7.

Table 15.8 indicates that multiple factors tend to dissuade the firm from opting for termination. A major factor is supplier dependency. For example, this may occur in cases in which a supplier provides an essential function or a network of services that can lead to supplier dependency. A second factor is the effect of product complexity, which may result in vendors taking advantage of the inconvenience of the firm moving to another supplier. Third, leaving one supplier and switching to a new service provider also involve both high monetary and non-monetary costs, which play a large role in the firm reconsidering its termination options. This is why firms more often seek a partial termination or renegotiate contract terms and personnel (Kimball 2010).

15.5   Conclusion

In this chapter, we examine the governance mechanisms of third-party relationships in financial institutions. Using survey data on institutions' outsourcing preferences, we study the key phases of outsourcing in both the governance framework and the externalities of the outsourcing relationship, such as misconduct and fraud. In line with the literature, we find that financial institutions outsource a substantial number of processes to third-party vendors. We find that cost is the key factor influencing the decision to outsource. There is also evidence that the requirement of specific knowledge and the focus on core business processes provide incentives for the firm to outsource. While this constitutes a higher level of risk for the institutions, our survey confirms that institutions indeed attach higher risk to outsourcing core business processes and data management activities.

To investigate the ability to monitor the financial institution's outsourcing relationships, our empirical investigation also looks at the types of fraud and misconduct risk in the financial services sector. We find that procurement vendor and supplier fraud is one of the most common forms of misconduct within financial institutions. Our evidence suggests that third-party risk is related to frequent staff and senior management changes at the service provider. However, financial institutions also employ various governance mechanisms to detect fraud and misconduct. Our evidence is consistent with firms employing a variety of governance mechanisms, some more promising than others, to maximize the chance of detecting misconduct. In terms of general methods, institutions reveal that external auditing is as likely to detect misconduct as internal audits. In addition, we also find that whistleblowing is a relevant measure to control misconduct. Overall, we find that the weakness in monitoring third parties is associated with contractual complexity that prevents firms from detecting non-compliance and misconduct by the service provider.

In sum, our analysis sheds light on the importance of third-party relationships regarding the risk of misconduct and fraud. This chapter contributes to the growing literature on the role played by corporate governance mechanisms in addressing operational risks in financial institutions. Our insights suggest that, as the outsourced activities have become more complex and sophisticated, conventional formal measures may prove ineffective in mitigating major risks, and traditional measures of monitoring and control are unlikely to deter and detect misconduct. Our research further suggests that monitoring of third-party relationships will remain crucial for financial institutions. The establishment of a strong corporate governance model is likely the most effective way to monitor to third-party performance and hinder misconduct.

References

Anderson E. (1985). The salesperson as outside agent or employee: A transaction cost perspective. *Management Science* 4: 234–254.

Ang, S. and Straub, D.W. (1998). Production and transaction economies and IS outsourcing: A study of the US banking industry. *MIS Quarterly* 22(4): 53–55.

Armour, J., Mayer, C. and Polo, A. (2017). Regulatory sanctions and reputational damage in financial markets. *Journal of Financial and Quantitative Analysis* 52(2): 1429–1448.

Babin, R., Bates, K. and Sohal, S. (2017). The role of trust in outsourcing: More important than the contract. *Journal of Strategic Contract and Negotiation* (3)1: 38–46.

Bahli, B. and Rivard, S. (2003). The information technology outsourcing risk: A transaction cost and agency theory-based perspective. *Journal of Information Technology* 18(3): 211–221.

Bapna, R., Gupta, A., Ray, G. and Singh, S. (2010). Analyzing IT outsourcing contract outcomes: The role of intermediaries. In *11th International Conference on Web Information System Engineering*.

Barthelemy, J. (2001). The hidden costs of IT outsourcing. *MIT Sloan Management Review* 42(3): 60–69.

Basel Committee on Banking Supervision (2004). The Joint Forum: Outsourcing in Financial Services. Bank for International Settlements.

Basel Committee on Banking Supervision (2018). Sound Practices: Implications of fFntech Development for Banks and Bank Supervisors. Bank for International Settlements.

Board of Governors of the Federal Reserve System (2013). Guidance on Managing Out-sourcing Risk.

Brown, S., Goetzmann, W., Liang, B. and Schwarz, C. (2008). Mandatory disclosure and operational risk: Evidence from hedge fund registration. *Journal of Finance* 63(3): 2785–2815.

Carletti, E. (2017). Fines for misconduct in the banking sector: What is the situation in the EU? In-depth Analysis for the European Parliament. PE 587.402.

Chen, J., Hong, H., Jiang, W. And Kubik, J.D. (2013). Outsourcing mutual fund management: Firm boundaries, incentives, and performance. *Journal of Finance* 68(2): 523–558.

Choudhury, V. and Sabherwal, S. (2003). Portfolios of control in outsourced software development projects. *Information Systems Research* 14(3): 291–314.

Coase, R.H. (1937). The nature of the firm. *Economia* 4(16): 386–405.

Coffee, J.C., Jr. (2007). Law and the market: The impact of enforcement. *University of Pennsylvania Law Review* 156(2): 230–311.

Corum, P., Ferguson, C. and Moroney, R. (2008). Internal audit, alternative internal audit structures and level of misappropriation of assets fraud. *Accounting and Finance* 48(4): 543–559.

Costello, A.M. (2013). Mitigating incentive conflicts in inter-firm relationships: Evidence from long-term supply contracts. *Journal of Accounting and Economics* 56(1): 19–39.

Cox, N. and Pilbourne, J. (2018). Outsourcing critical financial systems operations. *Journal of Business Continuity and Energy Planning* 11(3): 202–210.

Cumming, D., Dai, N. and Johan, S.A. (2013). *Hedge Fund Structure, Regulation, and Performance around the World*. New York: Oxford University Press.

Cumming, D.J. and Zambelli, S. (2016). Due diligence and investee performance. *European Finance Management* 23(2): 211–253.

Cumming, D.J., Schwienbacher, A. and Zhan, F. (2015). The scope of international mutual fund outsourcing: Fees, performance and risks. *Journal of International Financial Markets, Institutions and Money* 38: 185–199.

Currie W., Michell, V. and Abanishe, A. (2008). Knowledge process outsourcing in financial services: The vendor perspective. *European Management Journal* 26(2): 94–104.

Debaere, P.M. and Evans, R.B. (2014). Outsourcing vs. integration in the mutual fund industry: An incomplete contracting perspective. Working paper.

DeZoort, T. and Harrsion, P. (2007). The effects of fraud type and accountability pressure on auditors fraud detection responsibility and brainstorming performance. Working Paper.

Dyck, A., Morse, A. and Zingales, L. (2010). Who blows the whistle on corporate fraud? *Journal of Finance* 65(6): 2213–2253.

Dyck, A., Morse, A. and Zingales, L. (2014). How pervasive is corporate fraud? Working paper.

Dyer, J.H. (1997). Effective interim collaboration: How firms minimize transaction costs and maximise transaction value. *Strategic Management Journal* 18(7): 535–556.

Ernst and Young (2015). *Outsourcing in Europe: An in-depth review of drivers, risks and trends in the European outsourcing market*. New York: Ernst and Young.

Ernst and Young (2017). *Europe, Middle East, India and Africa Fraud Survey 2017*, New York: Ernst and Young. https://assets.ey.com/content/dam/ey-sites/ey-com/en_gl/topics/digital/ey-emeia-fraud-survey-2017.pdf. [Last retrieved: 2 February 2020].

European Central Bank (2004), Report On EU Banking Structures.

European Parliament (2017). Briefing: Fines for Misconduct in the Banking Sector—What Is the Situation in the EU?

European Systemic Risk Board (2015). Report on Misconduct Risk in the Banking Sector.

Evans, R. (2005). Outsourcing: The regulatory challenge for financial institutions. *Journal of international Compliance* 6(3): 52–57.

Federal Reserve Bank of New York (1999). Outsourcing Financial Services Activities: Industry Practices to Mitigate Risks.

Financial Conduct Authority (2013). FCA Risk Outlook 2013.

Financial Stability Board (2018). Strengthening Governance Frameworks to Mitigate Misconduct Risk.

Fitoussi, D. and Gurbaxani, V. (2012). Outsourcing contracts and performance measurement. *Information Systems Research* 23(1): 129–143.

Geis, G.S. (2009). The space between markets and hierarchies. *Virginia Law Review* 95: 99–153.

Gewald, H. and Dibbern, J. (2009). Risks and benefits of business process outsourcing: A study of transaction services in the German banking industry. *Information & Management* 46(4): 249–257.

Gewald, H., Wüllenweber, K. and Weitzel, T. (2006). The influence of perceived risks on banking managers' intention to outsource business processes – a study of the German banking and finance industry. *Journal of Electronic Commerce Research* 7(2): 78–96.

Gonzalez, R., Gasco, J. and Llopis, J. (2010). Information systems outsourcing reasons and risks: A new assessment. *Industrial Management & Data Systems* 110(2): 284–303.

Gopal, A. and Koka, B.R. (2009). When do vendors benefit from relational governance? Contracts, relational governance and vendor profitability in software development outsourcing. *ICIS 2009 Proceedings*.

Götz, M.R. and Tröger, T.H. (2017). Fines for Misconduct in the Banking sector—What Is the Situation in the EU? In-Depth Analysis for the European Parliament, PE 587.401.

Grossman S.J. and Hart, O.D. (1986). The costs and benefits of ownership: A theory of vertical integration. *Journal of Political Economy* 94(4): 691–719.

Gulati, R. (1995). Does familiarity breed trust? The implications of repeated ties for contractual choice in alliances. *Academy of Management Journal* 38(1): 85–112.

IOSCO (2017). IOSCO Task Force Report on Wholesale Market Misconduct.

Jackson, H. and Roe, M. (2009). Public and private enforcement of securities law: Resource-based evidence. *Journal of Financial Economics* 93(2): 207–238.

Jap, S.D. and Anderson, E. (2003), Safeguarding interorganizational performance and continuity under ex post opportunism. *Management Science* 49(12): 1684–1701.

Jiang, B., Yao,T. and Feng, B. (2008). Valuate outsourcing contracts from vendors' perspective: A real options approach. *Decision Sciences* 39(3): 383–405.

Karpoff, J. M., Lee, D.S. and Martin, G.S. (2008). The Consequences to Managers for Financial Misrepresentation. *Journal of Financial Economics* 88(2): 193–215.

Kedia, S. and Rajgopal, S. (2011). Does the SEC's Enforcement Preferences Affect Corporate Misconduct. *Journal of Accounting and Finance* 51(3): 259–278.

Kern, T., Willcocks, L.P. and van Heck, E. (2002). The winner's curse in IT outsourcing: Strategies for avoiding relational trauma. *California Management Review* 44(2): 47–69.

Kimball, G. (2010). *Outsourcing agreement, A Practical Guide*. Oxford: Oxford University Press.

Klein, B. (1992). Contracts and incentives. In: *Contract Economics* (eds. L. Werin and H. Wijkander) Oxford: Basil Blackwell.

KPMG (2016). *Banking Systems Survey 2015/2016: Technology challenges for Dutch banks in the digital era*. KPMG, London.

Kremic, T., Romic, W.O. and Tukel, O. (2006). Outsourcing decision support: A survey of benefits, risks, and decision factors. *Supply Chain Management* 11(2): 467–482.

Krivin, D., Samandari, H., Walsh, J. and Yueh, E. (2013). Managing third-party risk in a changing regulatory environment. *McKinsey Working Papers on Risk, Number 46*.

Lacity, M.C. and Hirschheim, R.A. (1993). *Information Systems Outsourcing: Myths, Metaphors and Realities*. New York, NY: Wiley.

Lee, G. and Xiao, X. (2018). Whistleblowing on accounting-related misconduct: A synthesis of the literature. *Journal of Accounting Literature* 41: 22–46.

Levitin, A.J. and Twomey, T. (2011). Mortgage servicing. *Yale Journal on Regulation* 28(1): 1–90.

Logan, M.S. (2000). Using agency theory to design successful outsourcing relationships. *International Journal of Logistics Management* 11(2): 21–32.

MacLeod, W.B. (2000). Complexity and contract. Working paper.

Mitts, J. and Talley, E. (2018). Informed trading and cybersecurity breaches. Working paper.

Mudambi, S.M. and Tallman, S. (2010). Make, buy or ally? Theoretical perspectives on knowledge process outsourcing through alliances. *Journal of Management Studies* 47(8): 1434–1456.

Murphy, D.L, Shrieves, R.E. and Tibbs, S.L. (2009). Understanding the penalties associated with corporate misconduct: An empirical examination of earnings and risk. *Journal of Financial and Quantitative Analysis* 44(1): 55–83.

Nguyen, D.D., Hagendorff, J. and Eshraghi, A. (2016). Can bank boards prevent misconduct? *Review of Finance* 20(1): 1–36.

Office of the Comptroller of the Currency (OCC) (2013). Third-Party Relationships: Risk Management Guidance Bulletin 2013-29.

Poppo, L. and Zenger, T. (2002). Do formal contracts and relational governance function as substitutes or complements? *Strategic Management Journal* 23(8): 707–725.

Prawitt, D.F., Sharp, N.Y. and Wood, D.A. (2012). Internal audit outsourcing and the risk of misleading or fraudulent financial reporting: Did Sarbanes-Oxley get it wrong? *Contemporary Accounting Research* 29(4): 1109–1136.

Ramasastry, A. (2006). Risk business? How multinationals outsourcing involving consumer data can lead to identity theft. http://supreme.findlaw.com/legal-commentary/risky-business-how-multinationals-outsourcing-involving-customer-data-can-lead-to-identity-theft-and-other-fraud.html. [Last retrieved: 2 February 2020]

Schlosser, F. and Wagner, H. (2011). Applying importance-performance analysis to IT outsourcing: A survey among financial institutions. *Proceedings of the 15th Pacific Asia Conference on Information Systems (PACIS)*.

Schwartz, A. and Scott, R.E. (2003). Contract theory and the limits of contract law. *Yale Law Journal* 113: 541–619.

Segal, I. (1999). Complexity and renegotiation: A foundation for incomplete contracts. *Review of Economic Studies* 66(1): 57–82.

Stulz, R. (2015). Risk-taking and risk-management by banks. *Journal of Applied Corporate Finance* 27(1): 8–18.

Susarla, A., Subramanyman, R. and Karhade, P. (2009). Contractual provisions to mitigate holdup: Evidence from information technology outsourcing. *Information Systems Research* 21(1): 1–19.

Whitten, D., Chakrabarty, S. and Wakefield, R. (2010). The strategic choice to continue outsourcing, switch vendors or backsource: Do switching costs matter? *Information & Management* 47(3): 167–175.

Williamson O.E. (1985). *The Economic Institutions of Capitalism*. New York: Free Press.

Williamson, O.E. (1991). Comparative economic organization: The analysis of discrete structural alternatives. *Administrative Science Quarterly* 36(2): 269–296.

Williamson, O.E. (2002). The theory of the firm as governance structure: From choice to contract. *Journal of Economic Perspectives* 16(3): 171–195.

Part IV

Detection and Surveillance of Financial Misconduct

Chapter 16

Identifying Security Market Manipulation

Mike Aitken
Rozetta Institute

Ann Leduc
Capital Markets Consulting

Shan Ji
Capital Markets Consulting

16.1 Introduction

Expert witnesses in jurisdictions using or applying Anglo-Saxon law are invariably required to act independently of the parties that hire and pay for them. Their primary obligation is to assist the Court in sorting the wheat from the chaff as they assess a series of arguments and counter-arguments, ultimately boiling down to whether the market for a security has been subject to the 'normal' – alternatively referred to as the 'free market' or 'genuine' – forces of demand and supply, or not. If one concludes the latter then it follows from legislation that the actions of the parties involved lead to a false and misleading appearance of either volume, price and the marketplace or all.

Notwithstanding this overriding obligation to assist the court, it is hard not to be influenced by the parties asking the questions/paying the bills, either implicitly or explicitly. While experienced expert witnesses tend to better understand their obligations, experts starting out often have difficulty resisting the pull of advocacy, leading them to get to appreciate the ramifications of failure to act in an independent manner when reminded of their obligations by a judge, a rather humiliating situation to experience.

This chapter explains how to use trading data to help identify prima facie evidence of market manipulation. While not all steps in the process that we outline are relevant to every case and the evidence does not conclusively identify manipulation (except for step 1), the outcomes do allow one to present a compelling case in the absence of a legitimate commercial explanation for the trading. To help avoid questions of conflict of interest, and in order to remain as objective as possible, this chapter outlines a procedure which allows the trading data tell the story. Although we acknowledge up front that parties can be convicted of market manipulation with no obvious impact on the trading data, simply because it was their intention to manipulate, direct evidence of the intention to manipulate is often difficult to adduce. This results in a great deal of reliance being placed on the impact of the manipulator's actions (typically represented by order placements, amendments, and cancellations as well as trades), on prices (a proxy for volatility), and/or volume (a proxy for liquidity), or a range of alternative proxies.

The procedure we implement in this chapter is based on many years of experience building algorithms to detect prima facie cases of market manipulation for the SMARTS real-time surveillance system. SMARTS is a system that is currently in use in more than 40 national exchanges and regulators and more than 200 brokers across 50 countries.[1] It is important to note at this stage that the specific algorithms identified in this chapter are not associated with any particular SMARTS client. We have no access to the algorithms used by any SMARTS clients and have developed an independent set of algorithms with which to identify manipulation.

For the purpose of our expert witness work, we have our own copy of the SMARTS market surveillance platform and the rules we have developed are those which we run against data in any case in which we are asked to participate. In this respect, it is important to appreciate that the client (whether they be the defence or

---

[1] Originally an offshoot of the CMCRC, SMARTS was sold to NASDAQ in 2010. See https://business.nasdaq.com/market-tech/marketplaces/market-surveillance.

the prosecution) have no say over either the algorithms we run or the parameters associated with the variables that form part of those algorithms.

In the following: Section 16.2 outlines the legislative underpinnings of our work, summarizing relevant laws and regulations from 7 jurisdictions including Australia, the UK, Hong Kong, Canada, Singapore, Malaysia, and New Zealand, all jurisdictions in which we have worked.[2] Section 16.3 then embeds the regulation into a discussion of trading activity, highlighting key elements that motivate the actions of surveillance departments. Section 16.4 outlines the specific rules which follow from this discussion and section 5 concludes by summarizing our key findings.

16.2 Background Legislation

16.2.1 Australia

Relevant legislation on market manipulation in Australia is contained in the Corporations act 2001 section 1041A. The section notes that a person cannot take part in or carry out (either directly or indirectly) one or more transactions likely to create or maintain an artificial price for a financial product. More details are supplied in section 1041B where a person is prohibited from creating or causing the creation of a 'false and misleading appearance' of active trading, market for, or price of, a security. As we will see later, other jurisdictions use different more detailed descriptions in place of the word market referring to the 'demand for and supply of' a financial product.

Section 1041B 2 (a) and (b) then outlines deemed manipulation as involving wash or prearranged trading. The former occurs when a party buys or sells to themselves or associated parties. The latter occurs when orders are placed by one party knowing by the nature of their timing (in close proximity) that there is a good chance they will trade with and associated party placing an opposite order for essentially the same or similar volume.

Section 1041C (a) then associates such trading with three purposes, being either to maintain, increase or depress price while section (b) appears to broaden the impact to causing volatility in the price of a financial product. This later condition is somewhat problematic as it would appear to encompass movements between the bid and ask prices. The problem of such a wide definition will be taken up in Section 16.3 below. Section 1041D then prohibits the communication of information of transactions that would create an artificial price, particularly where they receive a financial reward for so doing. Finally, section 1041E prohibits the making or dissemination of false and misleading statements for the purpose of inducing other parties to trade, which is outlined in more detail in section 1041F.

---

[2] See list of cases at https://capitalmarketsconsulting.com.au/engagements/ .

In all cases (except wash trading), a defence against such provisions is outlined in section 5.7.2 (g) of the ASX Market Integrity Rules[3] and a number of cases[4] where the concept of a legitimate commercial purpose is outlined.

16.2.2 UK

Relevant legislation on market manipulation in the UK is contained in the Financial Services and Markets Act 2000, Part 8, where section 118 deals with a more generic Market Abuse regime. Sections 5 and 7 of this section deal specifically with market manipulation where reference is made to the word 'abnormal' in addition to 'artificial price' at section 5(b). Section 7 makes the dissemination of information leading to a false and misleading appearance illegal, echoing notions from Australia that refer to the person knowing, or ought reasonably to have known, that the trading would cause the false and misleading appearance. The terms false and misleading are again used in 5(a) with the words 'supply or and demand for' being used in place of 'markets' as in Australia.

The UK legislation follows the EU Market Abuse Directive, articles 12 and 13, where a fair bit of emphasis is placed on the interaction between financial instruments, specifically prohibiting actions designed to create an artificial price in another financial instrument. The directive is more general than the UK legislation, nevertheless identifying in section 2 of Article 12 actions which would likely be considered as manipulative. These include a person who secures a dominant position in the demand for, and supply of, a security to fix a price or create what are referred to as 'unfair trading conditions'.

Other activities deemed to be manipulation are misleading investors as to price at the opening and closing of a market, the use of algorithmic trading to affect a false and misleading appearance as well as to prevent others from entering orders into a marketplace, the latter sometimes referred to as quote stuffing.

Another activity considered to be manipulative is disseminating information on a security while taking a position in that security so as to benefit from the information. In all cases, it is a defence against such charges if the person entering into the transaction established that it was for a legitimate commercial purpose or conforms with an accepted market practice, with the conditions for the latter being outlined in Article 13 section 2 including whether there is a substantial degree of transparency with respect to the transaction, it does not interfere with the free market forces of demand and supply and has a positive impact on liquidity and efficiency.

16.2.3 Hong Kong

Relevant legislation on market manipulation in Hong Kong is contained in the Securities and Futures (SFO) and sub legislation, Division 5, sections 274–278 (which defines each term) and sections 295–299 which formally identifies such behaviour as

---

[3] See https://www.legislation.gov.au/Details/F2018C00334/Html/Text#_Toc513191229.
[4] See North V Marra Developments *(1981) 148 CLR 42 9 December 1981, par 38*.

an offence. Section 274 deals with False Trading and, like other jurisdictions, notes that false and misleading appearance is caused by either active trading or interference with the market or the price of a security. Section 274 (3) also identifies false trading as occurring when an artificial price is created or maintained. Section 274 (5) then deems wash trading to be manipulation, except the extent that it is part of an off-market transaction. Subsection 274 (6) provides a defence based on the fact that there is more than one purpose and the actual purpose was not for the purpose of creating a false and misleading appearance.

Section 275 deals with price rigging and deals with wash trading that maintains, increases, reduces, stabilizes or causes fluctuations in a security's price either in HK or an overseas market. Section 276 prohibits disseminating information about illegal transactions, while section 277 constitutes a general provision not to provide false information to induce others to trade. In all cases, one thing a little different about the Hong Kong market is numerous provisions identifying defences to the prohibitions. Section 278 provides a general description of Stock Market Manipulation as occurring when a party increases, reduce, maintains, or stabilizes the prices of a security in Hong Kong (or a relevant overseas market) with the intention of inducing others to trade/not trade, subscribe/not subscribe for a given security.

16.2.4   Canada

Relevant legislation on market manipulation in Canada is contained in the Securities Act R.S.0 1990, section 5. The section of most relevance is section 126. Section 126 (1) (a) refers to a misleading appearance of trading activity or the creation of an artificial price. Section 126 (2) prohibits the dissemination of statements with are 'misleading or untrue'. The lack of specificity apparent in other jurisdiction's legislation is made up for in the Universal Market Integrity Rules (UMIR) of the Investment Industry Regulatory Authority of Canada, which is the practical surveillance authority for all markets in Canada. Policy 2.2, Parts 1–3 are the relevant provisions. In part 1 the rules refer to a 'fictitious trade' and, unlike the UK, refers specifically to a deemed 'manipulative and deceptive method'. Part 1 (c) also prohibits cornering the market in a security in order to dictate settlement terms. Part 2 then refers to creating a false and misleading appearance and specifically prohibits prearranged trading at (a), (b), and (e). Part 2 (f) also prohibits entering orders that are not intended to be executed, which seems to outlaw the practice of providing a simultaneous bid and ask in order to prevent parties, presumably other than market makers, from entering a bid/ask into a market as part of a strategy to disguise the precise motive for trading.[5] Wash trading is again prohibited as giving rise to a false and misleading appearance under section (i).

Part 3 deals with Artificial Pricing and notes a series of factors that would be taken into account in determining whether an artificial price had occurred. These include, but are not limited to, the preceding and succeeding trades, the change in the last

---

[5] A case in point are the circumstances associated with Australian Securities Commission v Nomura International PLC [1998] FCA 1570;89 FCR 301, where large orders of equal size were placed either side of the market in an apparent attempt to hide the trading parties true trading intentions.

trade price, bid and ask, the recent liquidity in the security, and the time when the order is entered and the instructions from the principal party. The latter almost certainly refers to orders entered late for small volumes which impact price and do not allow the market to respond. This will occur at the starting and closing auctions and the end of normal trading in a trading session.

16.2.5   Singapore

Relevant legislation on market manipulation in Singapore is contained in the Securities and Futures Act Part 12, in particular sections 196–204. Section 197 (1) refers to 'False Trading and Market Rigging' and outlaws creating a false and misleading appearance by active trading and through interfering with the market for and price of a security. Section 197 (2) then refers to actions which inflate, depress or maintain a price deemed through wash trading, and at 197 (3) deems wash trading and prearranged trading to be manipulation. Section 198 then prohibits parties from carrying out two or more transactions likely to induce others to subscribe for a security by raising, lowering, maintaining, or stabilizing the price of a security or an associated security.

Like all other jurisdictions, section 199 then prohibits the making of false and misleading statements, the purpose of which is to induce others to trade or which has the impact of raising, lowering, maintaining or stabilizing the price of a security. Similar to other jurisdictions (though not all), reference is made to making a statement known to be false or which the party ought to have known was false or misleading. The section also uses the same terms as used in the UMIR in Canada of 'Manipulative and Deceptive Devices' as a catch-all provision. Dissemination of information about illegal transactions is similarly outlawed under section 201, and there is a very specific provision under section 203 outlawing failure to live up to continuous disclosure obligations. As opposed to other jurisdictions that tend to account for all securities in general provisions, in Singapore futures are dealt with in Divisions 2 sections 205–212.

16.2.6   Malaysia

Relevant legislation on market manipulation in Malaysia is contained in the Securities Industry Act 1983 Part 9, Division 1 sections 84–88. Section 84 is very similar to the legislation in Singapore with the same subline, namely, 'False Trading and Market Rigging Transactions'. Under this provision Active Trading that gives rise to a false and misleading appearance is prohibited, as are actions that result in the false and misleading appearance of the market for, and price of, a security. Wash trading is prohibited under section 84 (2). Similar to Singapore, wash sales and prearranged trading are deemed to be manipulation under section 84 (3). A defence is outlined in subsection 4, although the defence does not this time refer to the transaction as being for legitimate commercial purposes but simply that it was not for the purpose of creating a false and misleading appearance.

Section 85 deals with the bylines 'Stock Market Manipulation' and introduces two new terms besides raising, lowering, maintaining, or stabilizing the price. The two terms are fixing and pegging. Again, this is a general provision not to do any of the above for the purpose of inducing others to trade, which is made more general at section 87. Section 86 prohibits false and misleading statements, similar to other jurisdictions, with section 88a providing a point of difference in that it contemplates civil action by parties that have lost out as a result of parties contravening section 86–88.

16.2.7   New Zealand

Relevant legislation on market manipulation in New Zealand is contained in the Financial Markets Conduct Act 2013, Subpart 3 sections 262–269. Section 262 deals with the provisions of misleading statement or information to induce others to trade. It adds as an offence inducing others to exercise or abstain from exercising a voting right. Section 265 deals with the false or misleading appearance of trading as a result of active trading or altering the demand and supply for a security or its price. Section 267 deals with deemed manipulation which again encompasses wash trading (267 (1)) and prearranged trading (267 (3)). While section 266 excludes short-selling and crossings and 268 provides a general defence if the transactions are in conformity with accepted market practice or for a proper purpose, section 269 makes contravention of these various provisions a criminal offence.

16.3   Attributes of Manipulation

Securities markets can be manipulated in a variety of ways. The most obvious method is for a trader to provide false or misleading information to the market in connection with a company or its securities. The false information induces others to trade, or not trade, when they wouldn't otherwise. In this case, it is the false information itself that leads to a market not subject to the genuine forces of demand and supply through affecting the demand, supply, and price of a company's securities.

Another approach is to trade in the securities in a way that gives the impression of positive (or negative) price-sensitive information impacting a marketplace, even though no such information, in fact, exists. A manipulator can alter the perception of demand and supply of a security by entering a significant amount of buy or sell orders on a public limit order book through wash trading or close to the close of trading with more limited volume. Either way, such actions give rise to an *artificial volume* or price. It is worth emphasizing that artificial volume is of little point unless it is used ultimately to constrain, lift, or reduce price.

There are numerous ways that a manipulator could engage in manipulative trading. This chapter cannot exhaustively cover all such means. However, several illustrative examples are now provided. For example, to artificially inflate the demand and price of a company's securities, a manipulator could place multiple orders on the buy side of the order book (but away from the best bid so as to avoid trading) to convey the impression of strong buying interest. This practice is called *layering*.[6] Layering the order book on the buy side can push up the price of a security, allowing

---

[6] See http://www.bailii.org/ew/cases/EWHC/Ch/2015/2401.html.

a manipulator to sell at a higher price than they might otherwise have expected. The alternative form of layering is for the manipulator to place multiple orders in large volume on both sides of the order book (at or away from the best bid and best ask) in order to constrain the price of the share within a narrow band. This practice is commonly referred as '*constraining the spread*', which conveys the impression of abundant liquidity and frenetic trading activity. Such a manipulator could also make a series of aggressive market orders several price steps above the best ask price, to convey the impression of strong buying interest. Again, this can push up the price of a security, allowing a manipulator to sell at a higher price than they would might otherwise have expected.

A manipulator who wishes to artificially hold the price of a company's securities within a stable range can place large limit orders on both sides of the order book but this can be very costly unless it is done through *wash trading*, more details of which are given below. The impact of the large orders are such that it becomes nearly impossible for the price of the share to move upwards or downwards, without very large orders corresponding orders by third parties, or unless the associated parties delete their limit orders. A manipulator may wish to do this when he has some ulterior reason for wanting to ensure that the price volatility of the securities in question is kept low (for example, if he wishes to use the securities as collateral for borrowing, and the lender examines price volatility in determining whether and how much to lend against such collateral).

Having placed such limit orders on both sides of the order book, a manipulator can then cause the price of the securities to rise, by suddenly deleting/amending or wash trading the limit orders on the sell side of the order book, or to fall, by suddenly deleting the limit orders on the buy side of the order book. In such a scenario, the manipulator's goal is that the sudden removal of significant orders on one side of the order book would convey to the market the impression of a significant change in buying (or selling) interest, which in turn can therefore be expected to have an impact on genuine supply and demand, as well as the price of the security.

16.3.1   How Traders Minimize the Resources Needed for Manipulative Trading

Many manipulative trading methods involve the manipulator using resources to generate artificial trading volume and to push up/down or maintain the price of the securities. For a manipulator to sustain such manipulation over a prolonged period of time, a substantial amount of resources is likely needed, and/or a strategy to minimize the extent of resources they need to deploy.

One method is for the manipulator to work with a group of associated traders so that they deal in *prearranged wash trades*. Thus, for example, when the manipulator wishes to have one associated trader place a series of buy orders in order to generate artificial trading volume, he could instruct another associated trader to place a corresponding series of sell orders. The manipulator is, in effect, simply trading with himself. There will be little net gain or loss to the group (other than minimal transaction or brokerage costs) from such an arrangement, regardless what price the buy orders executed at, if the corresponding sell orders are similarly executed. The cost associated with the buy orders could then be offset by the proceeds realized from the corresponding sell orders. Proceeds or gains from one member of the group can be repatriated to members of the group that sustain losses. Such activity is often deemed manipulation by the prevailing security codes of most markets.

Painting the tape (also called *marking the close* when it is at the end of trading) is an alternative method where a trader uses resources to affect the price of a security at particularly significant and strategic time. This is typically at the end of a trading session, particularly at day-, quarter- or year-ends, on option expiry days, on index rebalancing days, or in the period leading up to a corporate acquisition where the securities in question are intended to be used as consideration for the acquisition. While unusual movements at the end of a trading session (especially if there is a pattern of such alerts) are not the only way to spot manipulative behaviour, they are often an important clue. What happens when trading opens in the next trading session can be instructive. If the price reverses during the next trading interval, and particularly around the open, this is often serves as an indication that the movements of price in the prior trading session were artificial.

16.3.2   Difficulties in Determining Whether Trading Behaviour Is Manipulative

Firstly, on days when price-sensitive information is announced to a marketplace, it is often difficult to differentiate between trades that are the result of purposeful manipulators and trades that are the result of reacting to the new information. This requires that one carefully delineate between situations when new price sensitive information may be present, and situations when it is not. In the event of the former, the ability to conclude that manipulation has occurred is more challenging unless the price moves in the opposite direction to the price sensitive information.

It should be emphasized that the above difficulty does not apply to instances of wash trades, prearranged trades, and constraining price within a narrow band. Such trades and orders cannot be explained or justified even by the release of price sensitive information, and are therefore always indicative of manipulative intent, even if they occur on days when price-sensitive information has been released. The existence of price-sensitive information is not a reason for a person to trade with him/herself or with associated traders acting in concert, or to prearrange trades with such persons, or to hold the price of a stock within a band.

Secondly, a common defence that accused persons raise against charges of manipulation is that the impugned transaction(s) had a legitimate commercial purpose. Whether a transaction is for a legitimate commercial purpose or not can be inferred from several parameters associated with the trade – including whether one buys at the lowest possible price and sells at the highest possible price (see North v Marra[7]), with the lowest or highest price necessarily differing depending upon how anxious one is to trade. For passive traders, the best price to buy is the best bid price, and the best price to sell is the best ask price. Even for parties that wish to buy/sell

---

[7]   See https://jade.io/article/66955.

immediately, the lowest possible price is clearly the price on the other side of the bid-ask spread, depending upon whether one is buying or selling.

Where a trader buys at a price higher than one sells, or vice versa, over a sustained period, the circumstances are generally classified as 'uneconomic trading'. Where uneconomic trading is identified, the trader needs to be able to explain his actions in such circumstances. Some explanations might indicate that the trader's intention was not to manipulate, for example, where the release of unexpected price-sensitive information during a trading day changes a portfolio managers view of a stock. Other 'explanations' may confirm that the trader's intention was to manipulate, for example, where a portfolio manager pushes prices higher in order to benefit from a remuneration contract that pays off on the higher prices, or a senior manager pushes prices higher because the value of his remuneration package (in particular, his stock options) is based on the price of the company's shares.

Even in circumstances where traders are motivated by legitimate commercial purposes, professional traders need to be mindful of their general obligations to not bring the market into disrepute or cause disorderly trading. Indeed, each broker providing a Direct Market Access (DMA) facility is required to have in place automated algorithms that check client orders and reject orders that are likely to have that effect.

A third difficulty arises from the frequent assumption that parties that trade near the close on low order/trade volume are prima facie manipulators. However, low order/trade volume must always be seen in context of the average size orders of the particular trader over a prior period. In this sense, it is important to appreciate that small order/trade size is not in itself an indication of manipulation. It is the combination of unusual small order/trade volume and the proximity to the close of trading that would be of concern and then often a pattern of such orders.

An additional factor that needs to be considered in assessing the likelihood of manipulation is the minimum tick size in a stock; that is, the minimum distance between the best bid and ask price. Trading at either the ask or the bid when a security is trading at the minimum tick is very difficult, if not impossible, to classify as manipulation unless one is on both sides of the book. The only time manipulation might be considered is where the trade in question is the last traded price in the seconds leading up to the close, the minimum spread is out of line with the typical spread in that stock and was set earlier in the trading session by the alleged manipulator, and the trades before the trade in question were predominantly on the other side of the market. Even then, such activity will be mitigated if the price established in the subsequent closing auction is established at the same price by parties other than the party being accused of manipulation. Finally, even if the accused party has an order in the closing algorithm, a conclusion of manipulation will likely be sustainable only if there were few parties participating, the order was entered late in the auction period, and for a volume which is a major contributor to the closing price.

16.3.3 Surveillance Systems

Regulators have at their disposal a variety of tools to identify prima facie cases of manipulation, including rules guarding against any imbalance between volume and/

or price movements (legitimate or otherwise) at the end of a trading session without prior notification to the regulator. Of major concern are order volumes that alter the closing price at the end of a trading session, particularly a trading session where the price is likely to be used as a benchmark in third party contracts.

In consequence, surveillance algorithms typically look for significant changes in price on relatively small changes in volume at the end of a trading session and/or the number of times during a trading day that one ticks the price up/down (depending upon one's motivation) relative to one's total volume. They have tended to focus on changes in the prices of securities in the last 15 to 30 minutes of a trading session, particularly where they occur on very small volume.[8] Telltale signs of manipulative activity include traders leaving their trading late and moving the price beyond the best bid-ask prevailing in a marketplace. In the parlance of the market, such activities are called 'trade throughs'. While all 'trade throughs' are identified for the purpose of a pattern alert[9], in general only single 'trade throughs' that move the price through three price steps are the subject of closer scrutiny. Patterns of such circumstances are much more problematic.

To find these events, surveillance departments build alerts based on computer algorithms which involve the comparison of a point estimate of a metric[10] against a benchmark of that metric[11]. Typical alert metrics include volume per trade or change in traded price (something called a return). One might, for example, build an algorithm that identifies all changes in price over 30-minute periods during a trading day. The algorithm would then build a distribution of such changes around a mean, taking observations from the last 30 trading days for each security to develop the distribution. Note that a benchmark is generally based on prior trading in the same security, and is often time-of-day and day-of-the-week dependent, consistent with evidence of day and time of the week regularities from the academic literature[12]. In some instances, changes in returns on any particular security may be adjusted by changes in market/industry returns.

A much more pragmatic approach is to simply look for the number of price steps that an order moves the price. The larger the number of price steps the more aggressive the trade leading to questions as to why a party would want to be that aggressive. In general, the movement of three price steps at a point in time (or over time), particularly where it is close to the end of a trading session, is likely to be the source of some inquiry by a surveillance authority. A broker (acting as principal or agent) or a client trading using the DMA of a broker would need to be careful in

---

[8] The advent of High Frequency Trading has brought more focus on issues like layering and spoofing, which can occur throughout a trading day.

[9] A sequence of such alerts by the same client is regarded as much more of a problem than one or two occurrences.

[10] That is an estimate at a particular point in time, like the end of a trading session.

[11] Benchmarks are generally based on a distribution of the metric developed over a 'rolling window' covering the last 30 trading days, where the earliest trading day is dropped when the new trading day is entered.

[12] An Analysis of Intraday Patterns in Bid/Ask Spreads for NYSE Stocks, Thomas H. McInish and Robert A. Wood, *The Journal of Finance,* Vol. 47, No. 2 (Jun., 1992), pp. 753–764. Since this original publication, such intraday patterns have been identified in most world markets.

such circumstances and have a legitimate trading purpose in order to avoid causing disorderly trading.

One last element in algorithms used to identify possible manipulation is the reversion of price at the beginning of the next trading session. Combined with a movement of three or four price steps at or around the close of the previous trading session and smallish volume in the process of moving the price, a trader would need to have a very good reason for the trading. Typically, exchanges warn against just such practices and few professional traders would not be aware of the suspicion that such trading patterns would evoke, often leading to advance warning to surveillance departments of the likely trades.

16.4   Detection Algorithms

Based on the above attributes of market manipulation, the following 10 algorithms may assist in identifying unusual trading circumstances which are either deemed to be, or are indicative of, an intent to create a false or misleading appearance in respect of a security:

1. **Algorithm 1:** Does the trading result in wash trades (that is, where one party or alleged associated parties is the buyer and the seller)? If it does, then manipulation is deemed to have occurred as wash trading leads to a market place where traders are not independent of one another, which is a key assumption in genuine markets. This in turns leads to a market not subject to the genuine forces of demand and supply and therefore by definition a false and misleading marketplace. If such evidence is found, most of the subsequent price alerts are more an indication of how control of volume leads to control of price.

2. **Algorithm 2:** Does the order submission strategy lead to buy and sells which execute against each almost simultaneously for the same or similar volumes, consistent with prearranged trading? In the absence of client information in order to run algorithm 1, often surveillance departments run Algorithm 2 in order to identify coordinated behaviour by traders. The object of the algorithm is to establish the need for a more thorough examination of the relationship between traders that are the subject of such trading behaviour. In all likelihood, they will turn out to be a subset of 1.

3. **Algorithm 3:** Does the order submission strategy lead to substantial volumes of orders being placed on both sides of the book for long periods of time? This alert looks specifically for price stabilization. Given it is likely that no single account can hold the market constant for long without risking substantial resources, it is most often the consequence of a positive outcome from Algorithm 1.

4. **Algorithm 4:** Has there been price-sensitive information released during the trading day or at least before any suspicious trading activity was identified? While irrelevant as far as the first three alters are concerned, price sensitive information can explain price movements on particular days. It is usual to discount all price alerts on a particular day that are consistent with the nature of the information, namely that if the information is positive/negative, it will likely explain a positive/negative movement in price.

5. Algorithm 5: Does the weight of orders move from one side of the book to the other (in succession) with price moving in the direction of the imbalance (i.e. price goes up if there is a sudden imbalance on the buy side)? Assuming algorithm 3 fires, this alert looks for behaviour where the manipulator suddenly removes one side of the constraints identified in (3) above (by cancelling/editing or trading out the orders) allowing the price to move in one direction or other.

6. Algorithm 6: Does the order submission and trading result in a new best bid/ ask price for the day, particularly where it is within 15–20 minutes of the close? Assuming wash trades are not a factor in an alleged manipulation, the ability to offset losses from wash trades no longer exists and as a consequence manipulators need to be more circumspect about when they trade in order to minimize the amount of trading that must be done. Algorithm 6 looks for unusual trading activity close to the close.

7. Algorithm 7: Are the orders in the auction entered late such that they influence the auction price? The closing price algorithm is used as the benchmark price when it is run and supersedes the last traded price during continuous trading. This makes activity in the closing auction more relevant with this alert looking for very late entry of orders into the auction which affect the auction price.[13]

8. Algorithm 8: Does the instance found in algorithm 6 above lead to price reversal during the next trading session/morning? Algorithm 6 adds weight to 6 and 7 through observation that the price reverts to its pre algorithm 6 and 7 levels.

9. Algorithm 9: Does the trading show signs of aggression that is moving the price by three of more price steps in one direction? Sometimes described as 'breaking the market', which as a practical matter means altering the bid/ask spread, this alert looks for parties moving prices over very short periods. This will be done at the close in cases of parties with limited resources, or any time during the day with parties who wash trade or who trade in order to impact the price of a derivative or its related underlying security purchased/sold in a prior period.

10. Algorithm 10: Is the trading uneconomic? The norm for markets is to buy low, sell high. The difference is one's profit. Algorithm 10 looks for behaviours (usually on a daily basis) that shows the reverse, buying high and selling low. Without a price sensitive information announcement part way through the day that explains a change in trading strategy, this evidence leads one to question the motives of the traders and possibly to ask whether there are other motives for the trading. Wash sales, for example, may allow the losses that this algorithm identifies to be repatriated among the associated parties, highlighting a market not subject to the free market forces of demand and supply.

---

[13] This involves the creation of what is known as 'cross-market alerts' which look at trading in an underlying security executed in order to change the price of a derivative security and capture a profit from a position in the derivative (e.g. shares/warrants). The algorithms need to be run on the combined data feed of related markets.

Each of the rules above needs to be set up as a computer algorithm to be run against the data. For this purpose, we need to create variables of interest and parameters on each of the variables. For example, in running algorithm 9, notice that we have identified three price steps as parameters in the rule.

An important additional element of the process (to maximize independence) is to ensure that, when the data are handed over, no information of the parties involved is provided except where traders are known to be associated. Not knowing the client allows the algorithm to independently identify the client by their trading activity if indeed the algorithms/alerts are fired. For this purpose, the only information that should be provided is the trading period of interest and 3 to 6 months either side of the period of interest as part of establishing a benchmark period of trading during which no manipulative activity is alleged.

In building these 10 algorithms to measure the incidence of market manipulation, we have in fact gone a long way down the path of operationalizing the concept of *market fairness*, one of the two key concepts underlying the universal mandate of regulators (see Figure 16.1). That mandate is to ensure that markets and changes thereto face and pass the dual tests of fairness and efficiency, collectively known as market quality.

Defining fairness as the extent to which investors engage in prohibited trading behaviour, we therefore need to measure the incidence of insider trading, market manipulation, and broker–client conflict (e.g. front running) in order to measure fairness. Defining efficiency as minimizing the cost of trading while ensuring that prices reflect all available information leads us to measure transaction costs and price discovery as proxies for market efficiency.

Sample Statements of Objectives from World Regulators:

1. Protecting investors
2. Ensuring that markets are fair, efficient and transparent
3. Reducing systemic risk

ISOCO:	'. . . protecting investors, ensuring that markets are **fair, efficient** and transparent; reducing systemic risk. . . .'
SEC (US):	'protect investors, maintain **fair**, orderly, and **efficient** markets, and facilitate capital formation'
FSA (UK):	'promote **efficient**, orderly and **fair** markets'
FSA (Japan):	'. . . to ensure integrity (sic) of capital markets and protect investors'
ASIC (Australia):	'a **fair** and **efficient** market characterized by integrity and transparency and supporting confident and informed participation of investors and consumers'
OSC (Canada):	'To provide protection to investors from unfair, improper, or fraudulent practices and to foster **fair** and **efficient** capital markets and confidence in capital markets.'
MAS (Singapore):	'To promote **fair**, **efficient** and transparent markets . . .'

Figure 16.1　Key concepts associated with market quality.

Putting the two together in light of the universal mandate of regulators means that we verify the impact every time there is a market design change, in order to ascertain that the objective of a fair and efficient market structure is met. That requires us to measure the impact of the change on insider trading, market manipulation, broker-client conflict, transaction cost, and price discovery.

The algorithms described above can also be run across markets more generally and serve as one of the elements that can be used to enable evidence-based policymaking.

16.5 Conclusion

This chapter outlines how independent experts may build a toolkit of surveillance algorithms that they can run across data that are subject to the claim of market manipulation, in order to, at the very least, highlight trading that the accused manipulators need to explain to a Court as legitimate trading. The algorithms follow from legislation as was demonstrated by reference to the legislation from a number of markets that have been influenced by UK law. They require one to check for wash and prearranged trading as part of identifying artificial volume, i.e. volume which contravenes the assumption presumed in all securities markets that all traders are independent of one another. The legislation also refers to the possibility of parties constraining, increasing, or reducing prices.

In the absence of client level information, a surveillance analyst will look for evidence of unusual price movements, particularly in the lead-up to the close of the market where benchmark prices are created. This can be end of day, month, or quarter, with algorithms tailored to the three dates. In addition to individual alerts, it is important to look for pattern of alerts as part of discounting the claim of idiosyncratic behaviour.

As part of the process of evaluating the impact of alerts, the expert witness will also need to establish the impact of market and industry effects, compare the security in question to peers, and to market indices and compare price movements in related instruments (on different markets) by the same or related parties. The expert will also need to perform a detailed analysis of trading of the accused and other traders in relation to typical order size bands and average and median-sized trades. With this information, an independent expert is armed with the information necessary to make and assessment as to whether trading is subject to the free market forces of demand and supply, requiring traders to explain their actions to the court in order to avoid being convicted of market manipulation.

A collateral benefit of the work we have done as expert witnesses is an empirical estimate of the impact of market design changes, which are required to face, and pass, the dual test of fairness and efficiency. As one of the three elements of a fair market, the algorithms can be run pre- and post-market design changes (such as the change in a closing algorithm) to work out whether instances of market manipulation increase or decrease after the change.

Chapter 17

The Analytics of Financial Market Misconduct

Ai Deng
NERA Economic Consulting and John Hopkins University

Priyank Gandhi
Rutgers Business School*

* We would like to thank Carol Alexander and Douglas Cummings for the opportunity to contribute this chapter. All errors are our responsibility.

17.1 Introduction

Despite the considerable effort expended by regulators to detect financial market misconduct, observers note that the number of detected cases and the detection rate have largely decreased over time.[1] On one hand, this observation could imply that improved methods to detect misconduct have discouraged market participants to engage in such misconduct in the first place, or that compliance with existing laws and regulations has improved. On the other hand, this could also imply that offenders are becoming better aware of typical detection techniques, and adapt their methods to avoid detection for as long as possible.

Given offenders' ability to dynamically adapt their behaviour, there is a perennial need for novel methods to detect emerging methods of financial market misconduct. However, new empirical detection methods are not easy to develop. Therefore, we begin in this chapter by examining financial market misconduct through the lens of theory of finance, economics, and law. Theory can not only help guide empirical analysis once instances of misconduct are uncovered, but also yield insights into market conditions under which misconduct is more likely. Armed with this knowledge, regulators can potentially try to prevent such conditions from arising, or pay special attention when such conditions naturally arise in financial markets.

There is a very large stream of theoretical papers that can inform empirical techniques to detect and quantify financial market misconduct.[2] Of the extant literature, most relevant to us are papers on theory of economic regulation. This includes papers that study taxes, subsidies, and explicit laws that control all facets of economic activity. Important contributions include those by Stigler (1971), Posner (1974), Watts and Zimmerman (1978), Laffont and Tirole (1993), Dewatripont and Tirole (1994), Shleifer and Vishny (1994), Jolls, Sunstein, and Thaler (1998), Kothari (2001), Acharya (2009), and Brunnermeier, Crockett, Goodhart, Persaud, and Shin (2009), among others. A comprehensive review of this literature is beyond the scope of this chapter.

Becker (1968) provides an early important contribution on this topic. To understand the optimal amount of enforcement and regulation, Becker (1968) develops an economic model of crime. Becker's definition of crime includes activities that fall under the rubric of financial market misconduct. Becker framework can be used to understand conditions under which financial market misconduct is more or less likely. Three factors drive Becker's model: (a) the frequency of financial market misconduct, and the cost and benefits of such misconduct; (b) the expenditures on enforcement, which in turn influences the probability of being caught; and (c) the number of convictions and the punishments meted out for financial market misconduct.

---

[1] The statistic for detected cases and the detection rate are based on an analysis of cases of financial misstatements analysed by the SEC over 2000–2008. The SEC detected 77 instances of financial misstatement in 2003, but only 44 such cases in 2006. The average time between the initiation of misconduct and the date on which the SEC initiated an enforcement action has increased from 4.1 years in 2001 to 5.6 years in 2006. See Deloitte (2007) for further details. Note that detection rate may also be defined as the number of uncovered or detected cases as a percentage of all, detected or undetected, fraud cases. The latter is, of course, unobservable. For an attempt to quantify such a detection rate in the context of closing price manipulation, see Comerton-Forde and Putniņš (2015).

[2] The Royal Swedish Academy of Sciences recognized the importance of this topic when in 2014 they decided to award the Sveriges Riksbank Prize in Economic Sciences to Jean Tirole in part for his economic analysis of market power and regulation.

A brief outline of the essential part of Becker's model is as follows: Offenders engage in financial market misconduct each period by balancing the benefits from engaging in misconduct, against the probability of being caught, and the punishment received if convicted. For an offender, an increase in the benefit from misconduct, or a decrease in the probability of being caught increases the expected income from misconduct, and hence the incentives to engage in such misconduct. The model in Becker is much richer than the brief description presented here. For example, the model can take into account the influence of other variables, such as the existing wealth or income of an offender, on his or her proclivity to engage in misconduct.

Becker's (1968) model elegantly highlights circumstances under which instances of financial market misconduct are more likely. When enforcement and oversight is lax, financial market misconduct is more likely. Misconduct is also more likely if penalties are weak, or paid by the victim firms or their shareholders. Alternatively, draconian enforcement and overregulation reduces instance of financial market misconduct to nearly zero.

Coffee (2005) builds on Becker (1968) to investigate a puzzle: The US pursues financial misconduct cases with an enforcement intensity unmatched elsewhere in the world, which implies that, ceteris paribus, perpetrators have a higher probability of being caught. Yet, the US frequently suffers waves of financial market misconduct, that is not common in many other countries. Given Becker (1968)'s framework, one should (at least over time) expect to observe fewer instances of market misconduct.

That the US has higher enforcement intensity as compared to other countries is clear from Figure 17.1 based on Corlytic (2017). The figure indicates that US regulators hand out the heaviest fines, and account for a majority of enforcement actions and fines among all regulators in all countries in the period 2012–2017. US financial penalties in misconduct cases dwarf those imposed by other jurisdictions. In addition, US public enforcement is supplemented by vigorous private enforcement (such as class actions lawsuits) that extracts even greater penalties. This system has no true analogue anywhere else in the world. The US also criminalizes many instances of financial market misconduct whereas in many other countries misconduct cases are civil matters.[3]

Yet, periodically the US experiences a dramatic increase in the frequency of misconduct. One example is the plethora of financial misstatements in the US in the late 1990s and early 2000s that led to the passage of the Sarbanes–Oxley Act in 2002. The US General Accountability Office (GAO) estimates that during this period over 10% of all listed companies in the US announced at least one financial statement restatement. Others, such as Oxley (2003), have placed the number of financial statement restatements to be higher.

Some argue that asset bubbles, and their subsequent sudden deflation explains the frequent waves of financial market misconduct in the US These researchers suggest that financial market misconduct is more likely in bull (or bubble) markets, and when such bubbles subsequently burst, instances of financial market misconduct come to light.[4]

---

[3] For example, see Masters and McCrum (2012), which compares the insider trading laws in the US and the UK.

[4] Banner (1997) documents a link between bubbles and financial market misconduct over a 300 year period. He argues that the technology bubble explains the misconduct wave of the 1990s, and that the housing bubble explains the misconduct wave of 2007–2009.

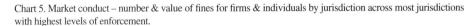

Chart 5. Market conduct – number & value of fines for firms & individuals by jurisdiction across most jurisdictions with highest levels of enforcement.

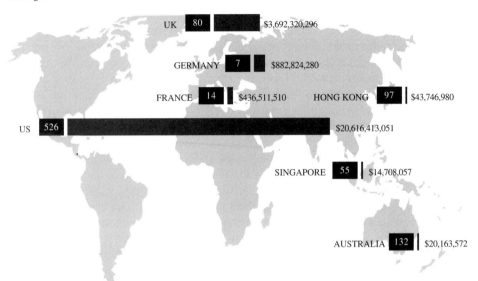

Figure 17.1   Number of cases and value of fines for cases of financial market misconduct.
Notes: In 2017, Coryltics, a consulting firm analysed number of cases and fines imposed by regulators in various countries for instances of financial market misconduct over a year period, 2012–2017. The figure plots the number of instances and dollar fines for offenders by country or region of jurisdiction. For more information visit their website at http://www.corlytics.org.

Coffee (2005) does not accept this as a complete explanation, and as a counter-example cites the case of UK and Europe which also experience bubbles, but do not experience misconduct cases as frequent or as egregious as the US. Instead, Coffee argues that dispersed share ownership in the US, which allows perpetrators to more easily capture the benefits of financial market misconduct, is to blame for the waves of misconduct. With dispersed ownership, management is practically in control, and agency problems are more severe. In such a system, corporate managers often tend to engage in financial market misconduct, and an easy way for them to do this is to manipulate financial statements. As proof, he points to the strong link between equity-based compensation contracts and incidence of misconduct. For example, Efendi, Srivastava, and Swanson (2007) compares firms that did or did not engage in misconduct in early 2000s. He finds that CEOs that hold more equity options are more likely to engage in misconduct. Equity-based option incentives increase the likelihood of engaging in financial market misconduct by 55%.

Coffee (2005) further suggests that in many countries (including the UK and Europe), share ownership is more concentrated. In most cases there is a controlling shareholder or shareholder group. Such concentrated ownership results in better control, reduces agency costs, obviates the need for equity-based compensation contracts to motivate management, and naturally results in a lower frequency of misconduct. In other words, controlling shareholders directly monitor management and do not rely on equity-based compensation, which lowers the benefits from misconduct for managers.

While controlling shareholders themselves can engage in financial market misconduct, the modus operandi of such misconduct is characteristically different. If controlling shareholders tend to engage in misconduct, they do so by exploiting the private benefits of control.[5] Regulators cannot easily discern when controlling shareholders capture private benefits, and even disagree on what these benefits are. In some emerging markets, practices allowing controlling shareholders to capture private benefits are legal.[6] Thus, concentrated ownership can account for lower frequency of what is commonly understood to be financial market misconduct in some countries.

The key message from Coffee (2005) is that factors other than those identified by Becker (1968) such as, ownership structures, corporate control, and agency problems can be used to understand most cases of financial market misconduct across countries.[7] More generally, Becker (1968) and Coffee (2005) can be used to construct a structural model to detect and quantify financial market misconduct.

This structural approach entails identifying economies or markets with traits that are more conducive to misconduct. The approach suggests that misconduct is more likely when perpetrators have a low probability of being caught, when penalties imposed on the offender are small, or when the expected benefits from engaging in financial market misconduct are high. Institutional features such as regulations, practice of enforcement actions, public and private intensity of enforcement, ownership structures, information asymmetry, and misaligned incentives (agency problems) can all influence proclivity to engage in misconduct. Once identified and suitably measured, these traits can then be used to empirically quantify the likelihood of misconduct in a particular market or country.[8]

---

[5] Private benefits of control is defined either as the 'psychic' value (Harris and Raviv 1988; Aghion and Bolton 1992), or the 'perquisites' value enjoyed from being in control (Jensen and Meckling 1976). Private benefits of control are not shared among all shareholders in proportion of the shares owned, but is enjoyed exclusively by the party in control. Dyck and Zingales (2004) estimate private benefits of control in 39 countries and find that on average it equals 14% of firm value. They also find that private benefits of control increases with concentrated ownership.

[6] For example, in some emerging markets, minority shareholders can be forced to tender their shares to controlling shareholders at below fair market value.

[7] Coffee's (2005) framework also explains why frequency of misconduct peaks during asset bubbles. In a bull market, investor attention is focused on returns or investment process, and they are less concerned about the benefits of misconduct, and how these benefits are captured by managers. This encourages some market participants to increasingly engage in misconduct.

[8] For example, traits identified in this section can be used in a Bayesian framework to empirically quantify the likelihood of misconduct. A well-known example of such an application comes from epidemiology. Public health officials know that the probability that a certain individual testing positive for a particular disease, actually has that disease (i.e., the 'posterior') depends on the accuracy of the medical screen is (the 'likelihood') and the prevalence of that particular disease is in the population to which the individual belongs (the 'prior'). In our case, structural traits and characteristics can inform the 'prior' probability of financial market misconduct.

This structural framework can be applied to many recent cases of financial market misconduct. For example, Gandhi et al. (2018) analyse the manipulation of the London Interbank Offer Rate (LIBOR), and show that weak enforcement and lack of penalties implied that the net benefits from manipulation for perpetrators were high.[9] Similarly, Corwin, Larocque, and Stegemoller (2017) show that the Global Analyst Research Settlement in 2003 increased enforcement, and lowered benefits for sell-side analysts acting on conflicts of interest at investment banks.[10]

17.2 Financial Economic Analysis

In this section, we begin by surveying empirical techniques developed and used by financial economists to detect and quantify financial market misconduct. Financial economists have investigated a wide and varied list of questions related to financial market misconduct in thousands of academic papers on the topic. Naturally, they have also employed a slew of empirical techniques to investigate these questions. At first sight, any sensible review of this vast literature seems impossible. However, our review finds that there *is* a common theme underlying all the empirical studies on financial market misconduct.

Any empirical study on financial market misconduct attempts to reveal the hidden behaviour and actions of agents. For this, it typically relies on comparing the value of some financial variable (such as prices, volumes, transactions, returns, etc.) generated via financial market misconduct, with the value of the exact same financial variable under the null hypothesis of no financial market misconduct. In other words, the primary tool used by financial economists to detect and quantify financial market misconduct is 'benchmarking', where actual observed financial variables are benchmarked to expected values of these variables. The differences between one empirical study on financial market misconduct and the next essentially boils down to the methodology used to generate the expected values of variables to which the observed values of variables can be compared or benchmarked. The exact methodology of generating expected values depends on the entities engaged in misconduct, the markets, the availability (or lack thereof) of data, and the exact nature of misconduct being analysed.

There are three common techniques used by financial economists to benchmark the observed values of variables with the expected values of these variables. The first and simplest approach is to compare the actual value of a financial variable to its historical or past values. A related strategy is to examine time series of financial variables for anomalous patterns. For example, one strategy is to exploit the assumptions of the efficient market hypothesis, which postulates that future asset returns should not be predictable. So if a decision, such as the decision to invest or not to invest in

---

[9] One of the authors (Ai Deng) consulted for the LIBOR-based Financial Instruments Antitrust Litigation. The discussion on LIBOR here draws exclusively from the academic literature.

[10] The structural model for financial market misconduct proposed here is similar to the structural screens of collusion used to detect market cartels that aim to restrict supply, boost prices, or rig bids. Structural theory for detecting cartels has been developed by Stigler (1964), Hay and Kelley (1974), Ayres (1987), and Harrington (2008) among others. Harrington (2008) also reviews the methodological issues and limitation of the structural approach to detect cartels.

an asset, correlates with its future returns, it could be indicative of financial market misconduct. Henceforth, we refer to this approach as 'Benchmarking to historical or past data.'

A second approach to detect and quantify financial market misconduct is to compare two proxies that capture the exact same financial variable. That is, in some cases, financial economists can find two measures of the same financial variable. In these studies, the hypothesis is that financial market misconduct is the only reason why one proxy deviates from another. We will refer to this approach as 'Benchmarking to an alternate proxy'.

Finally, researchers can compare the actual value of a financial variable of interest to its expected value constructed from a model. Such models can either be theoretical or statistical in nature. In these cases, the researcher has to rule out alternative explanations or potential other reasons for why actual values differ from model implied values. For example, perhaps the actual values differ from those implied by a theoretical model because the model does not successfully capture real world market frictions. Or perhaps, the actual differs from the values implied by statistical models because the model suffers from an omitted variable bias. We refer to this approach as 'Benchmarking to a model.'

Arguably, there is some overlap in these three approaches. For example, one could classify 'Benchmarking to historical or past data' as a special case of the 'Benchmarking to a model' approach. While we treat these three major approaches used by financial economists as distinct, most academic papers use not just one but multiple or a combination of these approaches to detect and quantify financial market misconduct. For example, a paper on financial market misconduct may benchmark data not only to a model, but also to an alternate proxy. In the next subsection, we review a broad range of papers to highlight how they have exploited the three approaches to 'Benchmarking' to detect and quantify financial market misconduct. In doing so, we do not attempt an exhaustive summary of the academic papers on this topic but pick a few important papers that elegantly highlight each of the benchmarking techniques described above. We focus on more recent academic papers that study the types of misconduct that are more widespread, or are considered especially egregious.

17.2.1   Benchmarking to Historical or Past Data

This is one of the simplest and by far the most common approach to detect and financial market misconduct, and a number of studies fall in this category. The most direct example of this approach is Ljungqvist, Malloy, and Marston (2009) who compare different versions of Thomson Financials I/B/E/S stock analyst recommendation data, which contain historical records of investment bank analyst recommendation regarding stock purchases and sales in the period 1993–2002. In the years prior to 2004, regulators investigated analysts working for investment banks for conflicts of interest. It appeared that the analysts working for investment banks were more optimistic in their recommendations related to firms who were clients of the investment banks. Perhaps, because the analysts were concerned that their bullish recommendations recorded in the historical database in I/B/E/S would be construed as misconduct, the authors of this study find that in many instances analysts logged in and changed, anonymized, added, or deleted recommendations to appear less bullish. Deleted recommendations were disproportionately strong buys; added recommendations were disproportionately holds and sells. Changes were disproportionately from buy to sell. Anonymizations were disproportionately strong buy recommendations of stocks that subsequently underperformed and were more likely for analysts who remained in the industry.[11]

Analysis of historical time series data can reveal anomalous trends and patterns that are consistent with and indicative of financial market misconduct. Christie and Schultz (1994, 1995) provide an excellent example. Using NASDAQ data Christie and Schultz (1994, 1995) find that NASDAQ market makers avoid quoting certain stocks in odd-eighths, which they interpret as evidence of collusion to keep minimum tick size higher. A higher tick size implies higher profit for the market maker. The fact that the incidence of odd-eighth quoting increased sharply on the exact day their study was publicized is consistent with the publicity related to their study causing the misconduct to collapse.

Heron and Lie (2007) provide a recent instance of how benchmarking to historical or past data can detect financial market misconduct. Their study relates to how executives back-dated their stock option grants in order to maximize their payoffs. To understand why executives may wish to backdate option grants, consider that the taxes that executives pay on their options grants are minimized when options are granted at-the-money, i.e. when the strike price equals the current market share price. However, options that are in-the-money, i.e. when the strike price is less than the current market share price, are more valuable for executives.

Ideally, executives would wish to receive at-the-money stock options on days when the stock price is low. That is, executives *can* arrange for options to be granted with low strike prices, so that they are granted at-the-money. An easy way to do this is to choose any day in the past when stock prices were low and claim to shareholders that options were granted on that day. This not only means that stock options are granted at-the-money at a low strike price, but also that stock options are now already in-the-money, and hence profitable for the executives to exercise. This practice is referred to as options backdating, and while not illegal per se in the US, results in options being granted at a more favourable term than that disclosed to shareholders, and is considered a form of financial market misconduct.

Heron and Lie (2007) present evidence for options backdating by analysing the correlation between stock options and future stock returns. Their study relies on the theory of market efficiency (Fama 1970). Market efficiency requires that the decision to grant stock prices should not be systematically and favourably correlated with future stock returns. That is, one should not find that the decision to grant executives stock options have significant economic and statistic positive correlation with future stock returns. However, Heron and Lie (2007) find that stock option grants are fortunately timed from the perspective of the executive. Stock prices tended to drop immediately before the option grant and rise soon afterwards. These correlations suggest that either when executives' private information suggested their stock

---

[11] After Ljungqvist, Malloy, and Marston (2009) circulated a working paper, Thomson Financial reversed many of the changes made to the 2004 version of the data, attributing them to computer error.

was undervalued, or that executives were choosing dates after the fact when stock price were low. Heron and Lie (2007) interpret this as evidence in favour of options backdating. They also find that the correlation between option grants and future stock returns declined sharply after the Securities and Exchange Commission (SEC) adopted a rule requiring grants to be disclosed within two days, effectively ending the window of opportunity for backdating of options.

A clever use of the benchmarking to historical data approach is Huang, Sialm, and Zhang (2011). Mutual funds are required to reveal their returns and their portfolio holdings periodically. Huang, Sialm, and Zhang (2011) compare the *actual* returns that a mutual fund reports at the end of period t to the *constructed* returns on the portfolio that the same mutual fund reported in period $t - 1$. The returns are adjusted for fees and commissions. They call the difference between the *actual* and *constructed* returns, the return gap. Ideally, if the mutual fund manager did not engage in any transactions that resulted in significant changes to its portfolio holdings between reporting dates, the *actual* and *constructed* returns should be identical, and the return gap should be close to zero. In other words, the return reported by the mutual fund at end of period t plus fees and commissions should equal the value-weighted return on the securities held at time $t - 1$. However, Huang, Sialm, and Zhang (2011) find that the return gap is almost always different from zero, indicating non-zero profit or loss generated on trades since the most recent holdings disclosure. That is, mutual funds actively trade stocks in between holding disclosure dates, which are hidden from their customers. Huang, Sialm, and Zhang (2011) find that such hidden trades often destroy investor wealth for some mutual funds.

The hidden actions analysed in Huang, Sialm, and Zhang (2011) are commonly referred to as window dressing. As described in the previous chapter, window dressing refers to actions taken by mutual fund managers, often near the end of a financial quarter or a financial year, right before issuing financial statements or reporting data to regulators, that aim to improve the performance of a firm on paper. For example, mutual fund managers can sell stocks with large losses or they can invest in securities that are considered less risky, right before they are required to disclose their portfolios publicly. Morey and O'Neal (2006) detect an example of window dressing by bond mutual fund managers in the US. They specifically analyse the historical data for mutual fund returns and find that bond mutual funds' returns are more correlated with lower-credit-quality bond returns than one would expect from their disclosed holdings. They also find that bond fund returns become more correlated with safer bonds around holdings disclosure dates. They conclude that bond funds engage in window dressing, i.e. bond mutual fund managers alter their holdings around disclosure dates to present a safer portfolio to shareholders.

While Huang, Sialm, and Zhang (2011) and Morey and O'Neal (2006) study the actions of mutual funds wishing to window dress and hide the true nature of risk and returns from their customers, Allen and Saunders (1992) find that commercial banks in the US systematically adjust the values of their assets and liabilities in order to appear safer or better, right before they report data to regulators. Allen and Saunders (1992) exploit the fact that at the end of each quarter, banks in the US are required to submit detailed income and balance sheet data to Federal bank regulators such as the Federal Reserve Bank, the Office of the Comptroller of Currency, and the Federal

Deposit Insurance Corporation. Both regulators and investors closely monitor this quarterly data to assess bank risk and performance. This increased investor and regulatory attention, however, gives bank managers an incentive to window dress their numbers to make them look better.

To detect if banks engage in window dressing, Allen and Saunders (1992) compare the end-of-quarter values for various variables to their monthly or quarterly averages for each bank in their sample. The key assumption is that it is more costly for banks to manipulate monthly or quarterly averages than it is for them to manipulate end-of-quarter data. The extent of window dressing is computed by subtracting the monthly average value from the end-of-quarter value for each financial variable of interest. The key result in Allen and Saunders (1992) is that banks tend to overstate the value of their assets and understate the value of their liabilities at the end of each quarter, in order to appear safer to regulators.

Yet another example of window dressing by a financial intermediary is provided by Agarwal, Daniel, and Naik (2009) who find that hedge funds inflate their reported returns at the end of the year, and that hedge fund returns during December are significantly higher than returns in other months during the year. Their results hold even after controlling for proxies for portfolio risk. To prove that this pattern is due to hedge funds managing their returns in an opportunistic fashion to earn higher fees, the authors further document that the December spike is greater either for funds with higher incentive fees (i.e. fees that kick in beyond a performance threshold) or for funds which have more opportunities to inflate their returns. It turns out that one method that hedge funds use to inflate December returns is to underreport their returns for months earlier in the year.

When analysing the historical time series data for a financial variable alone to detect financial market misconduct, one needs to carefully distinguish causation from correlation and understand alternative mechanisms that may cause or explain the results. One approach is to identify an exogenous change in the economic or institutional environment that affects the incentives of market participants to engage in misconduct, and to test if the time series patterns around such changes are consistent with the mechanism of misconduct.

Zitzewitz (2002) highlights this approach when he examines the effect of a change in SEC chairman on market participants' compliance with Regulation Fair Disclosure (Reg FD). He finds that a proxy for compliance with Reg FD increased sharply when the requirement for the disclosure becomes effective. However, most of this increase in compliance is reversed when Arthur Levitt, who was a proponent of Reg FD, is replaced as the SEC chairman by Laura Unger, who is an opponent of the disclosure requirement. Here, the research exploits the exogenous change in the regulator, or a possible exogenous change in the regulatory regime, to detect market participants compliance with regulations.

Another use of discontinuities to prove causation is provided by Keys et al. (2010). They test if banks' ability to securitize mortgage assets led them to relax their underwriting standards. In other words, if banks were no longer on the hook when borrowers defaulted due to securitization, they may have become less concerned with the credit risk of borrowers and their ability to repay the mortgage. The authors exploit the fact that while credit risk decreases continuously with borrower credit scores, the ease of securitizing a loan increases discontinuously at certain credit scores thresh-olds. The authors find that default probabilities are higher for loans that are just above score thresholds that were important for a loan's securitizability. This is consistent with banks using more relaxed underwriting criteria on non-credit score signals of borrower risk when a loan was more readily securitized, and thus its risk more readily transferable to a third party.

Recent work on earnings manipulation also exploits incentive discontinuities. For example, Burgstahler and Dichev (1997) argue that firms may be more likely to manipulate earnings around certain thresholds namely, zero, last year's earnings, or analysts' median expectations of earnings (Degeorge, Patel, and Zeckhauser 1999). They find that firms are especially likely to report earnings that just beat these thresh-olds and unlikely to report earnings that just miss these thresholds. They also show that firms that just beat thresholds rely disproportionately on components of earn-ings that are known to be easy to manipulate. Bhojraj et al. (2009) and Malenko and Grundfest (2014) confirm these findings in more recent data.

17.2.2   Benchmarking to Alternate Proxies

In a few cases, financial economists have been able to compare two proxies for the same financial variable to check if they are similar, in order to detect financial market misconduct. The assumption is that in the absence of financial market misconduct, the conclusions from the two measures should be closely related (or the same). If one meas-ure is very different from the other, and can be manipulated, then one suspects financial market misconduct, in the absence of other explanations. We review several papers that implement versions of this approach to detect and quantify financial market misconduct.

This approach was recently applied to examine the allegation that several banks manipulated a key barometer of their financial health – the London Interbank Offer Rate or the Libor. The Libor is computed by the British Bankers Association (the BBA) and it is a crucial interest rate that determines the price of several loans, fixed income derivatives, and financial instruments. To compute the Libor, the BBA asks several large banks based in the UK to report their borrowing costs.[12] The BBA then uses these borrowing data for individual banks to compute an average borrowing rate – the Libor. By construction, Libor reflects the rate at which investors are willing to lend money to an average large bank in the UK.[13]

Naturally, if banks do not report their true borrowing costs, the subsequent Libor computed from these data will underestimate or overestimate the true borrowing costs. Mollenkamp (2008) was the first to allege that many banks were misreport-ing their true borrowing costs to the BBA either to appear safer or in an attempt to manipulate Libor so as to benefit their trading books. Following these allegations in

---

[12] Specifically, the BBA asks each of the participating banks to reply to the following question, 'At what rate could you borrow funds, were you to do so by asking for and then accepting interbank offers in a reason-able market size just prior to 11 a.m. London time?'

[13] There are some nuances to how the Libor rate is computed. It is not just a simple, straightforward aver-age of the borrowing rates reported by the individual banks. For example, while computing Libor, the BBA drops outlier data. For other details regarding the Libor computation see https://www.theice.com/iba/libor.

the popular press, the early academic studies focused on testing for manipulation by comparing banks' reported Libor to other alternate proxies of their borrowing costs. For example, Abrantes-Metz et al. (2012) compare the Libor rates reported by banks to other short-term borrowing costs reported elsewhere or even their credit default swap rates (CDS) rates. Other studies that followed this approach of benchmarking Libor rates to alternate borrowing rates include Kuo, Skeie, and Vickery (2012) and Wong (2009).

However, the results from these earlier studies were either inconclusive or only weakly favoured manipulation by the banks. This is because two exact identical proxies for borrowing rates of banks do not exist. To see this, consider the fact that Libor reflects the interest rate that a large bank, say Royal Bank of Scotland (RBS), based in UK, would pay on an unspecified loan amount, for an unspecified maturity, which is borrowed without providing any collateral or security in the London interbank market. Comparing this rate, to say, the rate on a credit default swap (CDS) contract referencing RBS is not an apples-to-apples comparison.[14] This is because, while the CDS contract reflects the default risk of RBS, it is written for a specific notional amount ($5 million versus the unspecified amount for the interbank market), for a specific maturity (5 years versus unspecified maturity for the interbank market), with a specific collateral (100% cash collateral with mark-to-market values versus no collateral required for borrowing in the interbank market). Thus, while the early Libor case studies highlight how data for alternate proxies can be cleverly used to detect and quantify financial market misconduct, they also suggest that researchers should be careful when using alternate proxies, especially if there are important practical differences that affect these alternate proxies.

Instead of comparing data for two proxies for the exact same financial variables, investigators can also choose to compare data for the same variable for two separate entities. For example, researchers can compare data for two firms, two traders or brokers, or even data for two different venues or locations. Next, we present several examples of how this approach has been used to detect and quantify financial market misconduct.

Khwaja and Mian (2005) compare bank loan data for firms where the directors are politicians with bank loan data for firms where the directors are not politicians and have no political connections. They find that firms with politicians as directors are able to borrow 45% more from the banks and are 50% more likely to default. Further, in most cases the lending bank is a government-owned bank. There investigate two possible explanations for their results. Either the banks, especially government-owned banks, tend to favour firms where politicians (their 'owners') are directors, or that politicians tend to act as directors of firms that further social or developmental goals, which is also often a goal for government-owned banks. They provide several results that cast doubt on this latter, benign explanation for their results. For example, they show that banks with explicit social lending goals actually lend less to politically

---

[14] The CDS contract can be best thought of as a simple insurance contract on the event that a specific bank defaults on its debt. As an example, imagine that one buys a CDS contract on RBS defaulting by paying a fixed spread of say, 200 basis points per year for five years. If RBS does not default during this period of time, then no payments are due on the CDS contract. If RBS defaults, then the seller of the CDS contract has to pay the buyer of the CDS contract the difference between the par value of the bond and the post-default value of the bond (typically determined by a single auction mechanism) of a specific bond issued by RBS.

connected firms. Similarly, Faccio, Masulis, and McConnell (2006) find evidence of favouritism towards politically connected firms, specifically that they are more likely to receive government bailouts that are ultimately financed by the World Bank or International Monetary Fund. These studies compare data for firms with political connections to those without such connections to detect and quantify misconduct.

In another setting, Lin and McNichols (1998) and Michaely and Womack (1999) compare the stock recommendations issued by investment bank analysts for firms that are (or are not) clients of the investment bank. They find that analysts affiliated with investment banks issue more positive stock recommendations for firms for whom their employer bank also provides other services. This correlation could be partly driven by the fact that underwriters, who often bear the risk of failed offerings, can seek firms that on average have a strong upside potential. That their analysts subsequently issue strong positive opinions for these firms is, then, not surprising. However, this and several other alternative explanations were laid to rest when the issue of conflicts of interest in investment banks were uncovered by US regulators. As a result of these investigations, US regulators (the SEC, the NASD, and the NYSE) signed the Global Analyst Research Settlement with the 10 largest investment banks to ensure that they address and avoid any issues of conflict of interest within their businesses in the future. Corwin, Larocque, and Stegemoller (2017) show that the settlement did actually reduce conflicts of interest among the banks that were party to this settlement agreement.[15]

Lin and McNichols (1998) and Michaely and Womack (1999) essentially show how incentives of market participants (in this case investment bank analysts and underwriters) can potentially lead to financial market misconduct. Several other studies have analysed how market participants' incentives can lead them to engage in misconduct, and this is an area that seems ripe for future research. An interesting application is Liu and Ritter (2010) and Reuter (2006). Liu and Ritter (2010) examine the behaviour of CEOs who were revealed by a regulatory investigation to have received allocations of other firms' hot or underpriced IPOs from an investment bank. They show that CEOs who receive hot IPOs from an investment bank were more likely to have underpriced their own IPOs, and were less likely to switch their next offering away from the investment bank who provided them with the shares in the hot IPOs. In a similar setting, Reuter (2006) shows that mutual funds who do more brokerage business with an investment bank receive larger allocations of hot IPOs underwritten by that investment bank. The results in Liu and Ritter (2010) and Reuter (2006) indicate that underwriters use underpriced IPO shares to 'bribe' other firms' CEOs to win their business.[16]

---

[15] The Global Analyst Settlement was reached among the Securities and Exchange Commission, the National Stock Dealers Association, the New York Stock Exchange, the New York Attorney General, several state regulators, 10 Wall Street firms, and two individual analysts. The 10 investment banks were Bear Stearns, Credit Suisse, Goldman Sachs, Lehman Brothers, J.P. Morgan, Merrill Lynch, Morgan Stanley, Citigroup, UBS, and Piper Jaffray. More details regarding the settlement can be found at https://www.sec.gov/news/speech/factsheet.htm.

[16] Yet another example of incentives affecting outcomes and potentially leading to misconduct is provided by Reuter and Zitzewitz (2006). These authors compare the recommendations of personal financial magazines and find that personal finance magazines are more likely to recommend the funds of their advertisers. Their result holds even after controlling for funds' objective characteristics (e.g. past returns, expenses), the overall level of advertising, and past media mentions.

Conflicts of interest not only affect investment banks, but other financial intermediaries as well. Cici, Gibson, and Moussawi (2010) provide an example from the
fund management industry. They compare data for mutual funds run by firms that
also offer hedge funds with those that run only mutual funds. Hedge fund managers
typically earn incentive fees of 20% of funds performance (above some threshold),
while incentive fees for mutual funds are rare and comparatively small (Elton, Gruber,
and Blake 2003). Cici, Gibson, and Moussawi (2010) find that managers who manage both hedge and mutual funds favour their hedge funds because this generates a
larger compensation for themselves. Cici, Gibson, and Moussawi (2010) basically
analyse how shares from an underpriced IPO are allocated between a hedge fund
and a mutual funds run by the same manager. Their central result is that managers
tend to allocate shares from an underpriced (hot) IPO to their hedge fund to boost its
performance, instead of allocating such shares to the mutual fund.

Analysing incentives can also reveal why corporate executives do not always
act in their shareholders' best interests. Malmendier and Tate (2009) find that firms
with CEOs who win media awards suffer negative subsequent returns. They also find
that 'super-star' CEOs, i.e., those that are more highly compensated, recognized by
industry as exceptional, or those that engage in more outside activities earn negative
subsequent returns for their firms. This may be an instance of corporate executives
focus more on their personal development and recognition rather than on shareholder value maximization.

17.2.3   Benchmarking to a Model

Another way for researchers to detect and quantify financial market misconduct is to
compare the actual data to the predictions of a model. The nature of the model will
vary and will depend on the exact nature of the alleged misconduct and the market
being analysed. The model can either be theoretical or statistical in nature and we
review several case studies for each. When employing this approach, it is important to
rule out alternative explanations or potential other reasons for why actual values differ from model implied values. For example, perhaps actual values differ from those
implied by a theoretical model because the model does not adequately capture real
world market frictions. Or perhaps, the actual differs from the values implied by statistical models because the statistical models omitted a relevant explanatory variable
(i.e. an omitted variable bias).

One of the earliest examples of this approach is the model used by Beneish
(1999) to detect earnings manipulation. Beneish (1999) uses a data set of firms known
to manipulate earnings to build a statistical model to predict which firms are more
or less likely to manipulate earnings in the future. According to Beneish (1999), a set
of eight accounting variables, namely, receivables, gross margin, asset quality, sales
growth, depreciation, sales and general administrative expenses, leverage, and accruals, can be used to predict which firms are likely to manipulate earnings in the future.
He performs out-of-sample tests on his model by trying to identify manipulators in his
data set before they became publicly known. Beneish (1999) shows that his model
would have successfully identified at least half the manipulators before regulators or
other market participants.

Burns and Kedia (2006) build on this approach and add a new variable, namely, the compensation structure of the CEO. They find that the sensitivity of the CEO's option portfolio to stock price movements is significantly positively related to the propensity to misreport financial data. Other components of CEO pay, such as equity compensation, restricted stock allocation, long-term incentive payout, salary, and bonuses, have no significant impact on the propensity to engage in misconduct. The authors find that stock options affect the incentives to misreport because of their asymmetric payoff. That is, because stock options are immune to any subsequent downside risk, having an option portfolio that is sensitive to stock price movement creates an incentive for the CEO to engage in misconduct.

An example of a theoretical model that can be used to generate empirical predictions regarding fraudulent accounting is provided by Kedia and Philippon (2009). In their model, low productivity firms wish to mimic high quality, high productivity firms. One way for them to do so is to over-hire employees and overinvest in projects, in order to signal to the market that they have access to profitable projects and investment opportunities. The model reasonably suggests that high productivity firms generate strong cash flows, while low productivity firms engage in earnings manipulation to 'keep up appearances' of productivity. The theoretical model in Kedia and Philippon (2009) predicts that low-productivity firms hire and invest excessively, and managers, knowing that bad news is around the corner, tend to exercise their options early. The model provides testable implications regarding which managers tend to engage in misconduct and manipulate data, and these implications are borne out in the data.

The statistical or theoretical models can often be used to address some of the drawbacks of the benchmarking approaches outlined earlier. We noted the limitations and drawbacks of these approaches in each of the sections above. For example, recall the recent case of Libor manipulation discussed in the previous section. As we noted above, the early academic attempts to detect and quantify Libor manipulation focused on comparing the Libor bank borrowing rate with other proxies for bank borrowing costs. We also noted some limitations of such an approach. An alternative approach is to build either a statistical (or theoretical) model for Libor rates for individual banks, and then compare the actual data from a bank to the expected value from the model in order to detect and quantify financial market misconduct. This is the approach taken in Gandhi et al. (2018).[17]

Gandhi et al. (2018) first use a statistical model to quantify the incentives of banks to misreport their borrowing rates. For example, a manipulating bank may quote a higher borrowing rate (than the actual rate) if it believes that its actions are likely to increase Libor, and if its trading positions benefit from such an increase. Alternatively, a manipulating bank may quote a lower borrowing rate compared to the true rate, if it believes that such an action makes the bank appear safer. The reaction of a bank's equity price to changes in Libor rates and its own borrowing rate are used to quantify its incentives to manipulate Libor. Gandhi et al. (2018) then show that a bank's

---

[17] The model in Gandhi et al. (2018) is a statistical one. Snider and Youle (2010) provide a theoretical model to detect Libor manipulation. Specifically, they build a model of bank quote choices in the Libor survey. Their model predicts that if banks have incentives to affect the rate, one should observe that the quotes of the individual banks bunch around particular percentage points. They then take their model to the data and show that the empirical results line up with those from their model.

incentives, measured ex-ante, are likely to affect the data it provided to the BBA, from which Libor was subsequently computed. In other words, banks whose equity returns are likely to benefit from Libor rate increases were likely to subsequently submit a higher rate to the BBA. Since their statistical model allows them to control for a number of other factors, their result indicates that banks that are long (short) Libor attempt to nudge the rate higher (lower).

The approach in Gandhi et al. (2018) also allows them to produce a hypothetical true Libor rate that would be generated if none of the involved banks manipulated data. They compare the actual Libor to the hypothetical Libor generated by their statistical model to quantify losses from Libor manipulation and estimate it to be of the order of $10 billion over their entire sample.

Several other examples of statistical and theoretical models to detect and quantify financial market misconduct exist and a full review of these papers would require more space than available to us here. We highlight a few prominent examples. Cumming and Walz (2010) show that returns reported by venture capital and private equity firms can be biased. They analyse data from 221 private equity funds that are managed by 72 private equity management firms, in 5,040 entrepreneurial investee firms, spanning 33 years, and 39 countries. They compare actual unrealized returns, as reported to institutional investors, to the predicted unrealized returns based on the estimates of realized returns. They show that significant systematic biases exist in the reporting of unrealized investments to institutional investors, depending on the level of the earnings aggressiveness and disclosure indices in a country, as well as proxies for the degree of information asymmetry between institutional investment managers and venture capital and private equity fund managers.

Last but not the least, we highlight a novel approach to detecting and quantifying financial market misconduct in Bollen and Pool (2009). Instead of benchmarking data for individual returns, Bollen and Pool (2009) compare the entire distribution of returns generated by hedge funds to a return from a normal distribution to detect misconduct. In particular, Bollen and Pool (2009) find that hedge funds are much more likely to earn barely positive than barely negative returns. They further show that hedge funds that earn barely positive returns are likely to earn much lower future returns. Essentially, Bollen and Pool (2009) find a significant discontinuity in the pooled distribution of monthly hedge fund returns and that the number of small gains far exceeds the number of small losses. The discontinuity disappears when the fund is audited, suggesting it is not attributable to skilful loss avoidance. Interestingly, the incentives for manipulation are reinforced by the fact that missing a threshold takes on a special significance in an environment where other firms manipulate to avoid missing them. In this environment, missing a threshold causes investors to infer that a firm has exhausted its stock of deferred earnings.

17.3   Quantitative Techniques

In this section, we review the broader academic literature for empirical techniques developed by researchers in other disciplines, such as information management, operations research, machine learning, and law, to detect and quantify financial market misconduct.

17.3.1   The Principles of Fraud Detection

In fraud detection, the key goal is to correctly identify fraudulent activities, while simultaneously minimizing the incorrect identification of such activities. Thus, an efficient fraud detection technique maximizes the fraud catching rate, defined as the actual percentage of fraudulent transactions.[18] And it also tries to minimize the false alarm rate, defined as the percentage of transactions incorrectly identified as fraudulent, i.e. the false positives.

As discussed above, the primary tool used by financial economists to detect misconduct is benchmarking. Not surprisingly, benchmarking (and in particular anomalous data pattern recognition) is also at the heart of empirical methodologies used by researchers in other disciplines to detect and quantify financial fraud. A variety of statistical and machine learning techniques are used to identify anomalous patterns in the data and the exact technique deployed depends on the nature of fraudulent activity.

Broadly speaking, all statistical fraud (anomalous pattern) recognition techniques can be classified into two categories – supervised learning or unsupervised learning techniques.[19] A supervised learning technique is one which uses known examples of fraudulent and non-fraudulent records to construct predictive models. Researchers then use these models to estimate the likelihood that a new observation is fraudulent or not. In other words, a supervised learning technique uses known fraudulent and non-fraudulent observations to construct classification rules that can then be used to detect future fraud.[20]

To implement a supervised learning techniques, researchers need access to known fraudulent and non-fraudulent observations. When such data are available, supervised learning techniques can be very powerful.[21] At the same time, when data are unreliable (e.g. if observations are systematically 'mislabelled' as either fraudulent or not), supervised learning techniques can generate biased results. Supervised learning techniques, typically, can only be used to detect previously known types of fraud, unless the unknown types of fraud manifest them in a way that is recognizable by the system (Bolton and Hand 2002). Supervised learning techniques are unlikely to check evolving fraud techniques, and will not prevent a knowledgeable offender intent on fooling detection systems (Deloitte 2007). Another challenge of applying supervised learning techniques is that the data are typically highly unbalanced. Brause, Langsdorf, and Hepp (1999) show that only 0.2% of all credit card transactions can be confidently shown to be fraudulent. Hassibi et al. (2000) found that of 12 billion credit card transactions annually, only one out of every 1200 is fraudulent.[22]

---

[18] The fraud catching rate is also known in the literature as the true positive rate or the detection accuracy rate.

[19] There are also two additional categories – semi-supervised techniques and reinforcement learning techniques. See Zhou and Belkin (2014) for descriptions.

[20] When financial economists benchmark actual data to expected value from a statistical model, that is an example of using a supervised learning technique to detect and quantify financial market misconduct.

[21] In fact, in many other disciplines, such as image or speech recognition, supervised learning techniques is the dominant approach to identify patterns.

[22] For an approach that addresses sample imbalances, see Chawla et al. (2002).

Unsupervised learning techniques can be used when there are no prior data sets of fraudulent and non-fraudulent observations from which a model can be built. The basic idea behind unsupervised learning techniques is to directly examine and exploit the differences between observations. A very common unsupervised learning technique in fraud detection is outlier or anomaly detection. Unsupervised learning techniques allow researchers to identify instances of fraud which are dissimilar from the norm. These instances can then be flagged for close examination by human experts.

An example of an unsupervised technique is Benford's law. Benford's law (Hill 1995) states that the distribution of the first significant digits of numbers drawn from a wide variety of random distributions will (asymptotically) have a certain form. Until recently, this law was regarded as a mere mathematical curiosity with no apparent useful application. Nigrini and Mittermaier (1997) and Nigrini (1999) were one of the first to show that Benford's law can be used to detect accounting fraud. Their premise is that fabricating data which conform to Benford's law is difficult.

Regardless of the methodologies employed (i.e. supervised or unsupervised learning techniques) to detect financial fraud, a suspicion score is a helpful metric that allows researchers in this field to rank order observations based on how likely they are fraudulent. Depending on the context, suspicion scores can be computed for each observation, each customer, each account, each computer, and so on. The exact formulation of the suspicion scores can also vary across different types of fraud that are being detected.

17.3.2   Popular Supervised Learning Techniques for Fraud Detection

We list popular supervised and unsupervised techniques for fraud detection. Our approach is to list the technique, provide a brief description, and highlight an academic study that utilizes this technique.

17.3.2.1   Classification
Classification is the process of categorizing observations and ultimately predicting the category (i.e. fraudulent or non-fraudulent) of a new observation. In a typical supervised classification approach, statistical models are trained using both fraudulent and non-fraudulent data, and then each new observation is analysed and assigned to a category (Zhang and Zhou 2004). By definition, classification encompasses a large variety of statistical techniques. Classification is used to detect to detect credit card, health-care, insurance, and corporate fraud. Classification is hard to implement when category of observations cannot be easily defined or are uncertain. Some recent work addresses how classification can be used to detect fraud even when categories are not distinctly defined or if there are errors in modelling the first stage.[23]

17.3.2.2   Regression
Regression is probably the most well-known and widely used supervised learning technique. This standard technique is familiar to economists, and that it is also

---

[23] See e.g. Lachenbruch (1974), Chhikara and McKeon (1984), Provost and Fawcett (2001), among others.

used by researchers in other disciplines to detect fraud is not surprising. Traditional regression techniques are commonly used to detect credit card, agricultural crop and automobile insurance, and corporate fraud. Many empirical studies also use logistic regression and discriminant analysis to detect fraud (Agresti 2003; Duda, Hart, and Stork 2012; Sharma 1995; Viaene et al. (2002); Webb 2003). A prominent example is Spathis (2002), who uses data for 76 firms that did or did not manipulate financial statements to predict which firms are more likely to manipulate financial statements. He finds that 10 independent variables – the ratio of net profit to total assets ratio, the ratio of total debt to total assets, financial distress, the inventories to sales ratio, and the working capital to total assets ratio can predict if firms engage in financial statement manipulation. Companies with high inventories with respect to sales, high debt to total assets, low net profit to total assets, low working capital to total assets and high financial stress are more likely to manipulate data.

17.3.2.3   Neural Networks

Despite the considerable buzz that they have generated lately, neural networks are just another type of nonlinear regression. In fact, the logistic regression, familiar to most financial economists, can be thought of as a simple neural network. The neural network is a system that can be trained to recognize patterns in data that can be important for predicting an outcome.

Specifically, suppose one has identified a set of variables $x_1, x_2, ..., x_p$ (or features as they are often referred to in the neural network and the broader machine-learning literature) that can predict an outcome (in our case, whether a transaction is fraudulent or not). A simple neural network first combines these variables into an index using a set of pre-specified weights such as $Z = a + \sum_i [w_i x_i]$. Here, a is a constant, commonly referred to as the 'bias' and w_i are the weights or the importance of each variable x_i for the outcome. Next, a nonlinear transformation function is applied to the index of variables, Z. Logistic function is a typical choice, so that one gets $f(Z) = 1/(1 + e^{(-Z)})$. In the neural network literature f is referred to as the activation function.[24] The neural network system is designed in a way such that if a pattern is observed (say that a particular transaction is fraudulent), the overall value of the activation function would ideally exceed a pre-specified threshold.

Neural networks are flexible and allow for multiple variables and multiple sets of weights, as well as multiple nonlinear transformations of these variables. They can be layered, where the input to one layer is the output (or activation function) from another. Data can be analysed using any algebraic or non-parametric functional form. Properly designed, neural networks can discover unknown intercorrelations among observations. They are therefore particularly suited to cases where assumptions for other statistical techniques (such as linearity) are not valid.

---

[24] An increasingly more popular choice for the activation function is the rectified linear unit (RELU). See, e.g. Efron and Tibshirani (1991).

Neural networks also present challenges in terms of model design. In particular, because of the potentially large number of unknown parameters, 'training' a neural network typically requires a huge amount of reliable data. Brause, Langsdorf, and Hepp (1999) provides a detailed treatment of advantages and disadvantages of neural networks. Neural networks have been successfully used to detect financial fraud (Chen and Du 2009; Fanning, Cogger, and Srivastava 1995; Fanning and Cogger 1998; Odom and Sharda 1990; White 1989). For example, 'CARDWATCH' uses a neural network trained with past data for each customer to detect possible anomalies.

17.3.2.4 Decision Trees

Decision trees are used classify observations into mutually exclusive and exhaustive subgroups (i.e. fraudulent or non-fraudulent) based on attributes that best separate the sample. An example is Chye Koh and Kee Low (2004), who construct decision tree to predict financial statements fraud. Chye Koh and Kee Low (2004) find that a combination of six variables (quick assets to current liabilities, market value of equity to total assets, total liabilities to total assets, interest payments to earnings before interest and tax, net income to total assets, and retained earnings to total assets) can be used to separate firms that will or will not manipulate financial statements.

17.3.2.5 Hidden Markov Models

A Hidden Markov model (HMM) is a statistical model in which the system (or data) being modelled is assumed to be a Markov process with unobserved or hidden states.[25] HMMs are best explained with an example of how they can be used to detect credit card fraud. In an HMM, the state of a transaction is hidden or unknown to the observer. The observer, however, does see the sequence of operations or credit card transactions for a particular holder. An HMM is initially trained with the normal behaviour of a credit card holder. This trained model is then used to analyse each incoming transaction. If an incoming credit card transaction is not 'accepted' by the trained HMM, it is considered to be fraudulent. Srivastava et al. (2008) provide further details on how HMM can be used for fraud detection in the credit card industry.

17.3.3 Popular Unsupervised Learning Techniques for Fraud Detection

17.3.3.1 Outlier Detection

An outlier is an observation that deviates so much from other observations as to arouse suspicion that it is fraudulent (Hung and Cheung 1999). An outlier detection method measures the 'distance' between observations to detect those that are grossly different from or inconsistent with others (Han, Pei, and Kamber 2011). In a typical application, researchers build a distribution model from a given data set, and compare each new observation to this distribution to identify outliers. Alternatively, any new observation is compared to all prior observations to identify outliers. A prominent example is abnormal spending behaviour or frequency of transactions by a credit card user.

---

[25] The Markov process, in turn, is a stochastic process describing a sequence of possible events, in which the probability of each event depends only on the previous event.

Bolton and Hand (2002) discuss unsupervised credit card fraud detection methodologies using outlier detection.

17.3.3.2   Clustering

Clustering is used to divide objects into conceptually meaningful groups (or clusters), with objects in one group being similar to one another but very dissimilar to objects in other groups. Clustering is considered a kind of unsupervised classification methodology (Han, Pei, and Kamber 2011; Tan, Steinbach, and Kumar 2005). The most common clustering techniques are the K-nearest neighbour. The naive Bayes technique and self-organizing map techniques can also be thought of specific clustering techniques. Yue et al. (2007) and Zhang and Zhou (2004) discuss how clustering is used to detect financial fraud.

17.3.3.3   Data Visualization

Visualization refers to any easy, understandable presentation of data or to any methodology that converts complicated data sets into clear presentable patterns (Shaw et al. 2001; Turban, Sharda, and Delen 2011). This technique has proven to be valuable in exploratory data analysis, especially when little is known about the raw data, and when goals of fraud detection are vague. Visualization can provide researchers with intuition and some guidance for them to interpret results from statistical analysis. Eick and Fyock (1996) show how researchers at Bell and AT&T Laboratories have exploited data visualization to detect fraud.

17.3.3.4   Other Techniques

Extensions of the techniques we discussed above as well as other techniques have been developed by researchers in statistics, information management, and decisions sciences to detect financial fraud. A non-exhaustive list of these techniques includes discriminant analysis and logistic discrimination methods (Hand (1981) and McLachlan (2004) are examples), adaptive neural networks (Ripley (2007), Hand (1997), Webb (2003) are examples), supervised learning algorithms (Clark and Niblett (1989), Quinlan (1990), and Cohen (1995) are examples), tree-based algorithms (Breiman et al. (1984) and Quinlan (2014) are examples), and meta-learning algorithms (that include combinations of one or more of the above techniques) as in Chan et al. (1999).

Some of these techniques can only be used to detect one particular type of fraud. For example, link analysis is used to detect large-scale money laundering schemes. This approach identifies persons of interest that are potentially linked to known criminals or money launders. Links to known criminals are identified by monitoring their bank accounts, financial records, market transactions, and even social media accounts. Link analysis first identifies methods and then distinguishes legitimate links from illegitimate ones. This technique exploits the fact that accounts that transact with known criminals (or money launderers) are inherently suspicious. Link analysis is used by Andrews and Peterson (1990) Senator et al. (1995), Goldberg and Senator (1998), and Chartier and Spillane (2000) to detect money laundering.

A technique that can only be used to detect securities fraud is used by the American National Association of Securities Dealers, Inc., which uses a rule pattern matcher and a time-sequence pattern matcher to detect financial fraud. Another example of a unique approach that can only detect insider trading fraud has been developed by SearchSpace (now Fortent-IBM) called MonITARS, and is deployed by the London Stock Exchange. This technique combines genetic algorithms, fuzzy logic, and neural network technology to detect insider dealing and market manipulation.

Audit trails can be used to detect only computer fraud. This technique relies on the fact that illegally accessing computers leaves audit trails that can be then tracked by researchers. An audit trail is a record of activities on a computer system that are logged in chronological order. Analysis of audit trails can be automated to be performed periodically to check the integration of the system. See Lee, Stolfo et al. (1998), Lippmann et al. (2000), and Shieh and Gligor (1991), among others, for examples.

17.3.4   Dynamic Misconduct Detection

Most of the analysis in academic work reviewed above is ex-post or 'retrospective' in nature. Once financial market misconduct has been discovered, such ex-post analysis is highly relevant for policymakers as well as litigators. However, regulators and market participants are also interested in ex-ante or 'prospective' analysis, where the aim is to proactively screen for financial market misconduct via dynamic surveillance.[26]

For such dynamic surveillance, regulators may pick any of the empirical methodologies discussed above, and use them repeatedly or continuously to monitor for financial markets misconduct. Continuous or repeated monitoring is required because even if the first tests reveal no evidence of misconduct, the regulator may wish to continue monitoring the market, or rerun the tests after new or additional data becomes available. The decision to continuously monitor markets can be at the discretion of the regulator or prompted by the complaints from market participants. Specifically, the regulator may decide to repeatedly monitor a particular market after some participants in that market complain of misconduct, perhaps through a whistleblower programme.

Given the potentially large cost of manually performing these empirical tests repeatedly, financial regulators and institutions may wish to automate the process. For the same reason, Harrington (2008) argues that automation should be a criteria for systematic screening of market data for detecting collusion or cartels.

When statistical tests are applied repeatedly, researchers should be wary of the 'multiple/sequential testing problem'. Chu, Stinchcombe, and White (1996) show that at a fixed significance level and with the conventional critical values, repeated applications of a statistical test will lead to false positives with a probability approaching one in the limit. In our context, this means that with repeated application, an empirical detection method based on classical hypothesis testing will eventually 'identify' some activity as suspicious, even when there was no financial market misconduct.

The following numerical example illustrates this problem. Assume one collects historical trading volume for a particular stock and aims to test if trading volume in

---

[26] This section is largely based on Deng (2017).

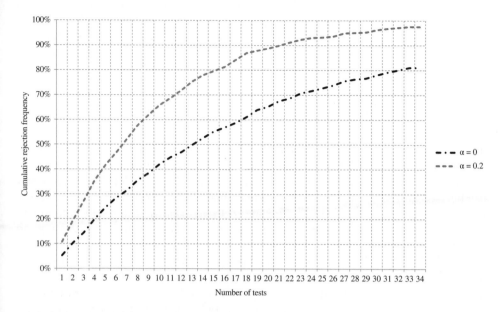

Figure 17.2 Cumulative rejection frequency.
Notes: This figure plots the cumulative rejection frequency (Type I error).

this stock is significantly different from the norm at certain dates and times (say to detect insider trading). We use an AR(1) process to simulate the trading volume in a stock. For simplicity and without loss of generality, we use an AR(1) process with a mean zero: $y_t = \alpha y_{t-1} + \epsilon_t$. Here, α is a constant and ϵ_t is follows a standard normal distribution with mean 0 and standard deviation 1.[27] We use two values of $\alpha \epsilon \{0, 0.2\}$ to simulate the data.

Further, assume this simulated data corresponds to demeaned monthly trading volume. We then choose to perform a standard one-shot F test (Chow test) every time we 'collect' six more data points, corresponding to trading volume data for six more months or every half a year. This simulation is repeated 1,000 times. Figure 17.2 shows the cumulative rejection frequencies across these simulations. The results show that after six tests or three years, we would find evidence of misconduct in nearly 30% of the cases when $\alpha = 0$, and in more than 45% of the cases when $\alpha = 0.2$. In addition, the persistence of the data matters. Data that is highly persistent yields substantially higher false positives using the one-shot test.

What can one do about this multiple testing problem? Fortunately, there is a solution. The key insight is that if the detection of false positive is a concern, then one should 'distribute' the type I error across time (or equivalently across the repeated

---

[27] One can think of y_t as the 'demeaned' version of the trading volume.
[28] While Chu, Stinchcombe, and White (1996) introduced the concept of distributing type I errors, there have been a number of extensions in recent years, including Zeileis et al. (2005) and Groen, Kapetanios, and Price (2013). More recent econometric research focuses on how the type I error should be distributed. Anatolyev and Kosenok (2012) proposed critical values so that the test size would be more uniformly distributed over the monitoring horizon. Most authors focus on purely statistical approaches. In the context of finance, Frisén (2008) provides an introduction to continuous financial surveillance.

applications of the test). This means that if one wants the overall critical size of the test to be 5%, then this 5% probability should be 'spread' out across each of the tests performed. As a result, intuitively, each individual test will need to have a critical value smaller than 5%.[28]

17.4   Conclusion

In this chapter, we have comprehensively reviewed empirical tools developed by academic researchers to investigate financial market misconduct. Six key lessons for future research emerge from our review. First, classical models of crime (e.g. Becker 1968) provide a structural framework to study financial market misconduct. This framework can be used to study misconduct both ex-ante (when the goal is to proactively discourage misconduct) and ex-post (when the goal is to quantify the extent of misconduct). However, these classical models of crime need to be updated to account for some puzzling empirical facts in the literature. For example, classical models for crime are static and do not explain why some markets experience periodic waves of financial market misconduct, despite no apparent changes in the incentives for and against misconduct. The model also does not offer a rationale for why frequency of financial market misconduct is often correlated with asset bubbles. Finally, current models suggest that incentives for engaging in financial misconduct should be inversely related to wealth or income of agents, and do not provide a good reason for why some of the agents engaged in financial market misconduct are also some of the most wealthy.[29]

Second, our review suggests that researchers have developed an overwhelming variety of tools and techniques to detect and quantify financial market misconduct. Most of these can be classified either as techniques that benchmark data or techniques that identify anomalous data patterns. Financial economists primarily compare (i.e. benchmark) the financial market data resulting from the alleged or suspected financial market misconduct with the data that is (or should be) generated when there is no misconduct. Researchers in other academic areas, especially those in management and information sciences, primarily look for anomalous data patterns to identify financial fraud. Some of the tools developed by researchers (such as neural networks to identify credit card fraud) are quite complex or require proprietary data to implement. Yet it is useful for non-experts, especially corporate executives and senior management, to be aware of these techniques so they can choose and implement the right tools to monitor misconduct.

Third, empirical techniques to detect and quantify financial market misconduct work best when researchers have access to both 'clean' (i.e. observations with no misconduct) as well as 'contaminated' (i.e. observations with misconduct) data. Some techniques may fail in the extreme case when observations with no misconduct (i.e. clean data) are missing from the sample. For example, consider the case of a financial market participant that has always engaged in a certain unique kind of misconduct. Benchmarking current data for such a participant to its historical values or even to other participants in this market will not help researchers identify misconduct. Of course, all hope is not lost. Regulators have significant authority to (randomly) sample

---

[29] For example, stock option backdating was engaged in by wealthy CEOs for relatively gains that were relatively small compared to their income or wealth.

data and demand more information (including additional data, internal documents, and electronic communications) in cases where they suspect misconduct. These can be used to identify hitherto unknown cases or methodologies of misconduct. Thus, one cannot overemphasize the role of a proactive regulator to prevent novel instances of financial market misconduct.

Fourth, the first-best outcome for a researcher interested in financial market misconduct is that his or her published, well-publicized academic research paper on financial market misconduct reduces the frequency of such misconduct. There is little incentive for market participants to engage in misconduct if it is widely known that regulators are constantly on the look-out for such behaviour. Ritter (2008) emphasizes the role the broader news media can play in highlighting the results of academic research in financial market misconduct, spurring the need for regulatory or policy changes. Similarly, Macey and O'Hara (2009) also discuss how, in some cases, regulations and public policy react to findings of the literature on financial market misconduct. If market participants' or regulators' attention to a particular kind of misconduct weakens, it is likely that some of it reappears. As an example, consider that many of the reforms aimed at addressing misconduct by mutual funds managers proposed by the SEC in 2003 were subsequently weakened when media or regulators' attention to the topic faded.[30]

Fifth, future researchers interested in financial market misconduct must take into account the Lucas' critique, which suggests that economic agents can and will rationally respond to specific empirical tools deployed to detect and quantify financial market misconduct. Thus, a downside of a well-publicized paper on financial market misconduct is that agents become aware of the exact empirical technique used to detect misconduct and such knowledge could make it easier to fool this system. Perhaps this is why in some instances the exact methodology to detect misconduct needs to be kept secret.[31]

Finally, research in financial market misconduct suffers from an embarrassing lack of data. In many instances researchers lack access to frequent data that can help them identify hidden actions or incentives. An example is the lack of detailed portfolio holdings for financial intermediaries at frequent intervals. Such data is at best available quarterly or yearly and only with a lag. Another example is the quantity and price information for many financial instruments such as bonds and credit default swaps that are traded in over-the-counter markets. The natural response of offenders is to increase data restrictions when faced with allegations of financial market misconduct.[32] The one clear lesson for regulators is to encourage data sharing to the maximum extent possible. The recent MiFiD II (Markets in Financial Instruments Directive), that requires financial intermediaries in Europe to post price information in almost real time for a large number of over-the-counter markets is a welcome step in this direction.

---

[30] The 2003 mutual fund scandal refers to the discovery of illegal late trading and market timing by some mutual and hedge fund managers prior to 2003. For more details see McCabe (2008).
[31] This is why the exact methodology used to detect bank and credit card fraud are closely guarded secrets, and lay readers are generally not aware of them.
[32] For example, Thomson Reuters restricted data access after Ljungqvist, Malloy, and Marston (2009) established a kind of misconduct using their data.

To conclude, our review suggests that regulators and policymakers often fail to police behaviour of agents engaged in misconduct. This is not a surprise, as by definition, misconduct involves illegal or unethical behaviour that violates implicit or explicit contracts, which agents actively work to hide from regulators and policymakers. In most cases, investigative journalists in the financial press are the first to present evidence of financial market misconduct, and then the systematic investigation of such misconduct is taken up by academics. Still, investigators often miss important instances of financial market misconduct. These missed opportunities suggests that academics and practitioners should, if anything, increase the time and effort to empirically analyse financial market misconduct.

References

Abrantes-Metz, R. M., Kraten, M., Metz, A. D. and Seow, G. S. (2012). Libor Manipulation? *Journal of Banking & Finance* 36: 136–150.

Acharya, V.V. (2009). A theory of systemic risk and design of prudential bank regulation. *Journal of financial stability* 5: 224–255.

Agarwal, V., Daniel, N.D. and Naik, N.Y. (2009). Role of managerial incentives and discretion in hedge fund performance. *The Journal of Finance* 64: 2221–2256.

Aghion, P. and Bolton, P. (1992). An incomplete contracts approach to financial contracting. *The Review of Economic Studies* 59: 473–494.

Agresti, A. (2003). *Categorical Data Analysis*. New York: Wiley.

Allen, L. and Saunders, A. (1992). Bank window dressing: Theory and evidence. *Journal of Banking & Finance* 16: 585–623.

Anatolyev, S. and Kosenok, G. (2012). Another numerical method of finding critical values for the Andrews stability test. *Econometric Theory* 28: 239–246.

Andrews, P.P. and Peterson, M.B. (1990). *Criminal Intelligence Analysis*. Loomis, CA: Palmer Enterprises.

Ayres, I. (1987). How cartels punish: A structural theory of self-enforcing collusion. *Columbia Law Review* 87: 295–325.

Banner, S. (1997). What causes new securities regulation – 300 years of evidence. *Wash. ULQ* 75: 849.

Becker, G.S. (1968). Crime and punishment: An economic approach. *Journal of Political Economy* 76: 169–217.

Beneish, M.D. (1999). The detection of earnings manipulation. *Financial Analysts Journal* 55: 24–36.

Bhojraj, S., Hribar, P., Picconi, M. and McInnis. J. (2009). Making sense of cents: An examination of firms that marginally miss or beat analyst forecasts. *The Journal of Finance* 64: 2361–2388.

Bollen, N.P. and Pool, V.K. (2009). Do hedge fund managers misreport returns? Evidence from the pooled distribution. *The Journal of Finance* 64: 2257–2288.

Bolton, R.J. and Hand, D.J. (2002). Statistical fraud detection: A review. *Statistical science* 17(3): 235–249.

Brause, R., Langsdorf, T. and Hepp, M. (1999). Neural data mining for credit card fraud detection. In *Tools with Artificial Intelligence, 1999. Proceedings. 11th IEEE International Conference on*, pp. 103–106. IEEE.

Breiman, L., Friedman, J., Stone, C.J. and Olshen, R.A. (1984). *Classification and Regression Trees*. Boca Raton, FL: CRC press.

Brunnermeier, M., Crockett, A., Goodhart, C.A., Persaud, A. and Shin H.S. (2009). *The Fundamental Principles of Financial Regulation*, vol. 11. ICMB, Internat. Center for Monetary and Banking Studies.

Burgstahler, D. and Dichev, I. (1997). Earnings management to avoid earnings decreases and losses. *Journal of accounting and economics* 24: 99–126.

Burns, N. and Kedia, S. (2006). The impact of performance-based compensation on misreporting. *Journal of financial economics* 79: 35–67.

Chan, P.K., Fan, W., Prodromidis, A.L. and Stolfo, S.J. (1999). Distributed data mining in credit card fraud detection. *IEEE Intelligent Systems and Their Applications* 14: 67–74.

Chartier, B. and Spillane, T. (2000). Money laundering detection with a neural-network. In *Business Applications Of Neural Networks: The State-of-the-Art of Real-World Applications* (eds. P.J.G. Lisboa, A. Vellido, B. Edisbury), 159–172. World Scientific.

Chawla, N.V., Bowyer, K.W., Hall, L.O. and Kegelmeyer, W.P. (2002). SMOTE: Synthetic Minority Over-sampling Technique. *Journal of Artificial Intelligence Research* 16: 321–357.

Chen, W.-S. and Du, Y.-K. (2009). Using neural networks and data mining techniques for the financial distress prediction model. *Expert systems with applications* 36: 4075–4086.

Chhikara, R.S. and McKeon, J. (1984). Linear discriminant analysis with misallocation in training samples. *Journal of the American Statistical Association* 79: 899–906.

Christie, W.G. and Schultz, P.H. (1994). Why do NASDAQ market makers avoid odd-eighth quotes? *The Journal of Finance* 49: 1813–1840.

Christie, W.G. and Schultz, P.H. (1995). Policy watch: Did Nasdaq market makers implicitly collude? *Journal of Economic Perspectives* 9: 199–208.

Chu, C.-S.J., Stinchcombe, M. and White, H. (1996). Monitoring structural change. *Econometrica: Journal of the Econometric Society* 64(5): 1045–1065.

Chye Koh, H. and Kee Low, C. (2004.) Going concern prediction using data mining techniques. *Managerial Auditing Journal* 19: 462–476.

Cici, G., Gibson, S. and Moussawi, R. (2010). Mutual fund performance when parent firms simultaneously manage hedge funds. *Journal of Financial Intermediation* 19: 169–187.

Clark, P. and Niblett, T. (1989). The CN2 induction algorithm. *Machine learning* 3: 261–283.

Coffee, J.C. (2005). A theory of corporate scandals: Why the USA and Europe differ? *Oxford Review of Economic Policy* 21: 198–211.

Cohen, W.W. (1995). Fast effective rule induction. In *Machine Learning Proceedings 1995*, 115–123. Elsevier.

Comerton-Forde, C. and Putniņš, T.J. (2015). Dark trading and price discovery. *Journal of Financial Economics* 118:70–92.

Corlytic (2017). The Corlytics Barometer – The Economic Crime Landscape. techreport, Corlytics.

Corwin, S.A., Larocque, S.A. and Stegemoller, M.A. (2017). Investment banking relationships and analyst affiliation bias: The impact of the global settlement on sanctioned and non-sanctioned banks. *Journal of Financial Economics* 124: 614–631.

Cumming, D. and Walz, U. (2010). Private equity returns and disclosure around the world. *Journal of International Business Studies* 41:727–754.

Degeorge, F., Patel, J. and Zeckhauser, R. (1999). Earnings management to exceed thresholds. *The Journal of Business* 72: 1–33.

Deloitte (2007). Ten things about financial statement fraud: A review of SEC enforcement releases 20002006. resreport, Deloitte Forensic Center.

Deng, A. (2017). Cartel detection and monitoring: A look forward. *Journal of Antitrust Enforcement* 5: 488–500.

Dewatripont, M. and Tirole, J. (1994). The prudential regulation of banks. ULB Institutional Repository, ULB – Universite Libre de Bruxelles.

Duda, R.O., Hart, P.E. and Stork, D.G. (2012). *Pattern Classification*. New York: Wiley.

Dyck, A. and Zingales, L. (2004). Private benefits of control: An international comparison. *The Journal of Finance* 59: 537–600.

Efendi, J., Srivastava, A. and Swanson, E.P. (2007). Why do corporate managers misstate financial statements? The role of option compensation and other factors. *Journal of Financial Economics* 85: 667–708.

Efron, B. and Tibshirani, R. (1991). Statistical data analysis in the computer age. *Science* 253: 390–395.

Eick, S.G. and Fyock, D.E. (1996). Visualizing corporate data. *AT&T Technical Journal* 75: 74–86.

Elton, E.J., Gruber, M.J. and Blake, C.R. (2003). Incentive fees and mutual funds. *The Journal of Finance* 58: 779–804.

Faccio, M., Masulis, R.W. and McConnell, J. (2006). Political connections and corporate bailouts. *The Journal of Finance* 61: 2597–2635.

Fama, E.F. (1970). Efficient capital markets: A review of theory and empirical work. *The Journal of Finance* 25: 383–417.

Fanning, K., Cogger, K.O. and Srivastava, R. (1995). Detection of management fraud: A neural network approach. *Intelligent Systems in Accounting, Finance and Management* 4: 113–126.

Fanning, K.M. and Cogger, K.O. (1998). Neural network detection of management fraud using published financial data. *International Journal of Intelligent Systems in Accounting, Finance & Management* 7: 21–41.

Frisén, M. (ed.)(2008). *Financial Surveillance*. Chichester: Wiley.

Gandhi, P., Golez, B.J., Jackwerth, C. and Plazzi, A.J. (2018). Financial market misconduct and public enforcement: The case of Libor manipulation. *Management Science, Forthcoming*.

Goldberg, H. and Senator, T. (1998). The FinCEN AI system: finding financial crimes in a large database of cash transactions. In: *Agent technology* (eds. R. Jennings and M. Wooldridge), 283–302. Berlin: Springer-Verlag.

Groen, J.J., Kapetanios, G. and Price, S. (2013). Multivariate methods for monitoring structural change. *Journal of Applied Econometrics* 28: 250–274.

Han, J., Pei, J. and Kamber, M. (2011). *Data Mining: Concepts and Techniques*. Waltham, MA: Elsevier.

Hand, D.J. (1981). *Discrimination and Classification*. Wiley Series in Probability and Mathematical Statistics. Chichester: Wiley.

Hand, D.J. (1997). *Construction and Assessment of Classification Rules*. Chichester: Wiley.

Harrington, J. (2008). Detecting cartels. In: *Handbook in Antitrust Economics* (ed. P. Buccirosi). Cambridge, MA: MIT Press.

Harris, M. and Raviv, A. (1988). Corporate control contests and capital structure. *Journal of Financial Economics* 20: 55–86.

Hassibi, K. et al. (2000). Detecting payment card fraud with neural networks. In *Business Applications Of Neural Networks: The State-of-the-Art of Real-World Applications* (eds. P.J.G. Lisboa, A. Vellido, B. Edisbury), 141–157. World Scientific.

Hay, G.A. and Kelley, D. (1974). An empirical survey of price fixing conspiracies. *The Journal of Law and Economics* 17: 13–38.

Heron, R.A. and Lie, E. (2007). Does backdating explain the stock price pattern around executive stock option grants? *Journal of Financial Economics* 83: 271–295.

Hill, T.P. (1995). Base-invariance implies Benford's law. *Proceedings of the American Mathematical Society* 123: 887–895.

Huang, J., Sialm, C. and Zhang, H. (2011). Risk shifting and mutual fund performance. *The Review of Financial Studies* 24: 2575–2616.

Hung, E. and Cheung, D.W. (1999). Parallel algorithm for mining outliers in large database. In *Proc. 9th International Database Conference (IDC'99), Hong Kong*. Citeseer.

Jensen, M.C. and Meckling, W.H. (1976). Theory of the firm: Managerial behavior, agency costs and ownership structure. *Journal of financial economics* 3: 305–360.

Jolls, C., Sunstein, C.R. and Thaler, R. (1998). A behavioral approach to law and economics. *Stanford Law Review* 50: 1471–1550.

Kedia, S. and Philippon, T. (2009). The economics of fraudulent accounting. *The Review of Financial Studies* 22.

Keys, B.J., Mukherjee, T., Seru, A. and Vig, V. (2010). Did securitization lead to lax screening? Evidence from subprime loans. *The Quarterly journal of economics* 125: 307–362.

Khwaja, A.I. and Mian, A. (2005). Do lenders favor politically connected firms? Rent provision in an emerging financial market. *The Quarterly Journal of Economics* 120: 1371–1411.

Kothari, S. (2001). Capital markets research in accounting. *Journal of Accounting and Economics* 31: 105–231.

Kuo, D., Skeie, D. and Vickery, J. (2012). A comparison of Libor to other measures of bank borrowing costs. *Federal Reserve Bank of New York, Working paper.*

Lachenbruch, P.A. (1974). Discriminant analysis when the initial samples are misclassified II: non-random misclassification models. *Technometrics* 16: 419–424.

Laffont, J.-J. and Tirole, J. (1993). *A Theory of Incentives in Procurement and Regulation.* Cambridge, MA: MIT Press.

Lee, W., Stolfo, S.J. et al. (1998). Data mining approaches for intrusion detection. In *USENIX Security Symposium*, 79–93. San Antonio, TX.

Lin, H.-w., and McNichols, M.F. (1998). Underwriting relationships, analysts' earnings forecasts and investment recommendations. *Journal of Accounting and Economics* 25: 101–127.

Lippmann, R.P., Fried, D.J., Graf, I., Haines, J.W., Kendall, K.R., McClung, D., Weber, D., Webster, S.E., Wyschogrod, D., Cunningham, R.K. et al. (2000). Evaluating intrusion detection systems: The 1998 DARPA off-line intrusion detection evaluation. In *DARPA Information Survivability Conference and Exposition, 2000. DISCEX'00. Proceedings*, vol. 2, 12–26. IEEE.

Liu, X. and Ritter, J.R. (2010). The economic consequences of IPO spinning. *The Review of Financial Studies* 23: 2024–2059.

Ljungqvist, A., Malloy, C. and Marston, F. (2009). Rewriting history. *The Journal of Finance* 64: 1935–1960.

Macey, J.R. and O'Hara, M. (2009). Regulation and scholarship: Constant companions or occasional bedfellows? *Yale Journal on Regulation* 26: 89–116.

Malenko, N. and Grundfest, J. (2014). Quadrophobia: Strategic rounding of EPS data. *Boston College, Working paper.*

Malmendier, U. and Tate, G. (2009). Superstar CEOs. *The Quarterly Journal of Economics* 124: 1593–1638.

Masters, B. and McCrum, D. (2012). Gulf between U.S. and U.K. Insider Trading. *Financial Times.*

McCabe, P. (2008). The economics of the mutual fund trading scandal. *Board of Governors of the Federal Reserve System,* Working paper.

McLachlan, G. (2004). *Discriminant Analysis and Statistical Pattern Recognition.* New York: Wiley.

Michaely, R. and Womack, K.L. (1999). Conflict of interest and the credibility of underwriter analyst recommendations. *The Review of Financial Studies* 12: 653–686.

Mollenkamp, C. (2008). Bankers cast doubt on key rate amid crisis. *The Wall Street Journal.*

Morey, M.R. and O'Neal, E.S. (2006). Window dressing in bond mutual funds. *Journal of Financial Research* 29: 325–347.

Nigrini, M.J. (1999). I've got your number. *Journal of accountancy* 187:79.

Nigrini, M.J. and Mittermaier, L.J. (1997). The use of Benford's law as an aid in analytical procedures. *Auditing* 16: 52.

Odom, M.D. and Sharda, R. (1990). A neural network model for bankruptcy prediction. In *Neural Networks, 1990., 1990 IJCNN International Joint Conference on,* 163–168. IEEE.

Oxley, M.G. (2003). Rebuilding Investor Confidence, Protecting U.S. Capital Markets: The Sarbanes–Oxley Act: The First Year. resreport, The Huron Consulting Group.

Posner, R.A. (1974). Theories of economic regulation. *Bell Journal of Economics* 5(2): 335–358.

Provost, F. and Fawcett, T. (2001). Robust classification for imprecise environments. *Machine learning* 42: 203–231.

Quinlan, J.R. (1990). Learning logical definitions from relations. *Machine learning* 5: 239–266.

Quinlan, J.R. (2014). *C4. 5: Programs for Machine Learning.* CA: Elsevier.

Reuter, J. (2006). Are IPO allocations for sale? Evidence from mutual funds. *The Journal of Finance* 61: 2289–2324.

Reuter, J. and Zitzewitz, E. (2006). Do ads influence editors? Advertising and bias in the financial media. *The Quarterly Journal of Economics* 121: 197–227.

Ripley, B.D. (2007). *Pattern Recognition and Neural Networks.* Cambridge University Press.

Ritter, J.R. (2008). Forensic finance. *Journal of Economic Perspectives* 22: 127–47.

Senator, T.E., Goldberg, H.G., Wooton, J., Cottini, M.A., Khan, A.U., Klinger, C.D., Llamas, W.M., Marrone, M.P. and Wong, R.W. (1995). Financial crimes enforcement network AI system (FAIS) identifying potential money laundering from reports of large cash transactions. *AI magazine* 16: 21.

Sharma, S. (1995). *Applied Multivariate Techniques.* New York: Wiley.

Shaw, M.J., Subramaniam, C., Tan, G.W. and Welge, M.E. (2001). Knowledge management and data mining for marketing. *Decision support systems* 31: 127–137.

Shieh, S.W. and Gligor, V.D. (1991). A pattern-oriented intrusion-detection model and its applications. In *Research in Security and Privacy, 1991. Proceedings, 1991 IEEE Computer Society Symposium on,* 327–342. IEEE.

Shleifer, A. and Vishny, R.W. (1994). Politicians and firms. *The Quarterly Journal of Economics* 109: 995–1025.

Snider, C.A., and Youle, T. (2010). Does the Libor reflect banks' borrowing costs? *University of California, Los Angeles, Working paper.*

Spathis, C.T. (2002). Detecting false financial statements using published data: Some evidence from Greece. *Managerial Auditing Journal* 17: 179–191.

Srivastava, A., Kundu, A., Sural, S. and Majumdar, A. (2008). Credit card fraud detection using hidden Markov model. *IEEE Transactions on dependable and secure computing* 5: 37–48.

Stigler, G.J. (1964). A theory of oligopoly. *Journal of Political Economy* 72: 44–61.

Stigler, G.J. (1971). The theory of economic regulation. *The Bell Journal of Economics and Management Science* 2: 3–21.

Tan, P.-N., Steinbach, M. and Kumar, V. (2005). *Introduction to Data Mining.* Pearson.

Turban, E., Sharda, R. and Delen. D. (2011). *Decision Support and Business Intelligence Systems.* India: Pearson Education.

Viaene, S., Derrig, R.A., Baesens, B. and Dedene, G. (2002). A comparison of state-of-the-art classification techniques for expert automobile insurance claim fraud detection. *Journal of Risk and Insurance* 69: 373–421.

Watts, R.L. and Zimmerman, J.L. (1978). Towards a positive theory of the determination of accounting standards. *Accounting Review* 53(1): 112–134.

Webb, A.R. (2003). *Statistical Pattern Recognition*. Chichester: Wiley.

White, H. (1989). Learning in artificial neural networks: A statistical perspective. *Neural Computation* 1: 425–464.

Wong, J.T. (2009). Libor left in limbo; A call for more reform. *NC Banking Inst.* 13: 365.

Yue, D., Wu, X., Wang, Y., Li, Y. and. Chu, C.-H. (2007). A review of data mining-based financial fraud detection research. In *Wireless Communications, Networking and Mobile Computing, 2007. WiCom 2007. International Conference on*, 5519–5522. Ieee.

Zeileis, A., Leisch, F., Kleiber, C. and Hornik, K. (2005). Monitoring structural change in dynamic econometric models. *Journal of Applied Econometrics* 20: 99–121.

Zhang, D. and L. Zhou (2004). Discovering golden nuggets: Data mining in financial application. *IEEE Transactions on Systems, Man, and Cybernetics* 34: 513–522.

Zhou, X. and Belkin, M. (2014). Semi-supervised learning. In *Academic Press Library in Signal Processing*, vol. 1, 1239–1269. Elsevier.

Zitzewitz, E. (2002). Regulation Fair Disclosure and The Private Information of Analysts. *Stanford Graduate School of Business, Working paper.*

Chapter 18

Benford's Law and Its Application to Detecting Financial Fraud and Manipulation

Christina Bannier
Justus Liebig University Giessen

Corinna Ewelt-Knauer
Justus Liebig University Giessen

Johannes Lips
Justus Liebig University Giessen

Peter Winker
Justus Liebig University Giessen

18.1   Introduction

Large data sets may contain relevant information about substantive relationships, but also provide indications of potential fraud, malpractice, and manipulation. In the digital age, the number of large data sets available for analysis is growing exponentially. Consequently, statistical methods to analyse such data sets in order to detect potential inconsistencies attracted growing interest.

We will focus, exemplarily, on a classical method used in this context, namely digital analysis based on Benford's law. When studying this approach more thoroughly, it becomes obvious that statistical methods cannot be expected to provide unequivocal evidence. This conclusion also applies to more refined methods, e.g. those based on machine learning, including deep learning. All these data-driven methods can only provide signals. These signals bear the risk of marking an incident as suspicious, even if it is not, or of missing a real case of fraud. This also cuts down the usefulness of these methods in legal proceedings.[1] Thus, statistical methods such as Benford's law are valuable tools for providing first indications of potential misconduct. However, without further evidence, they do not provide sufficient proof for a conviction. Therefore, it might be advisable to focus digital analysis on incidents where a priori a higher likelihood of fraud could be expected, so that the risk of false alarms will be reduced. Alternatively, such methods might be used as pre-screening procedures.

Even more important than taking the risk of misleading signals into account is the insight into detection methods fraudsters may obtain. Thus, if people are aware that some financial data will be inspected with regard to its fit to some distributional assumption such as Benford's law, one might even expect that manipulated data fit Benford's law better than real data, at least after some adjustment period. Therefore, it appears important to consider the predator-and-prey perspective when analysing the performance of data-based procedures for fraud detection. In fact, a reliable procedure should still work even though the potential fraudster is aware of its use. Otherwise, procedures must be elaborated in a way that they keep pace with the defrauders, a scenario which is more likely.

Inspired by the observation that the first pages of logarithmic tables wear out quicker than the last ones, the discovery of Benford's law dates back to the nineteenth century, when Newcomb (1881), in a short note, provided a mathematical model for the distribution of the first significant digit of numbers. In non-technical terms, it states

---

[1] See, for example, a decision by the Lower Saxony Finance Court rejecting the use of digital analysis as proof of manipulations (Niedersächsisches Finanzgericht 15. Senat, 17. November 2009, Az: 15 K 12031/08). Other German court decisions also refer to the normal or uniform distribution as potential benchmarks (FG Münster, 05.12.2002 – 8 V 5774/02 E,G,U, FG Münster, 14.08.2003 – 8 V 2651/03 E,U, FG Düsseldorf, 13.04.2004 – 11 V 632/04 A(U), FG Düsseldorf, 31.03.2008 – 14 V 4646/07 A(E,G,U,H(L))).

that smaller values of the first digit occur more often than larger values. The frequency decreases monotonically from about 30% for a 1 to less than 5% for a 9 as leading digit, while a uniform distribution would predict each digit to occur with the same frequency of about 11.1%. Not only did Benford (1938) provide a formal representation, but also empirical evidence for the law, based on 20,229 observed numbers from many different data-generating processes.[2] Hill (1995) provides a sound statistical base for Benford's law and, consequently, together with technological progress, contributed to an increasing number of applications. A comprehensive literature review of applications and extensions of Benford's law up to the early 2000s is provided by Hürlimann (2006).

According to a non-representative survey among practitioners Bierstaker, Brody, and Pacini (2006) using digital analysis software which addresses conformity with Benford's law was rated as quite effective for fraud detection in an accounting framework. In the same survey, it was listed number 33 out of 34 fraud prevention methods regarding its actual implementation. Bierstaker, Brody, and Pacini (2006) argue that this might be due to the resources required for implementing digital analysis software. Thus, there might be room for a broader implementation.

Considering applications in financial markets, for example, Durtschi, Hillison, and Pacini (2004) discuss when Benford's law might be an effective tool to detect fraud and when it might not be expected to perform well. In particular, they stress that real data conform to Benford's law if they are combinations of numbers from different sources, as is often the case with aggregate accounting information. By contrast, when only few observations are available, when the share of manipulated observations is small, or when the source of real data does not satisfy Benford's law, the tool loses efficiency. In our case study, we consider time series with only a small number of observations for each period. Thus, we analyse to what extent Benford's law is informative in this situation and suggest alternative methods.

This chapter contributes to the literature on digital analysis in two ways. First, it provides an overview of applications of Benford's law in the fields of accounting, controlling, taxation, finance, and related areas with a focus on opportunities and limitations. Second, the application to LIBOR (London Interbank Offered Rate) data will demonstrate whether the manipulation of LIBOR data might have been detected earlier under the use of Benford's law, or some generalization, and which alternative approaches could be used in this and similar settings.

The remainder of this chapter is organized as follows. Section 18.2 describes Benford's law and some basic limitations and straightforward generalizations to circumvent the limitations. The following Section 18.3 summarizes applications described in the literature in the domains of accounting, controlling, taxation, and finance. The application to LIBOR data is presented in Section 18.4, while Section 18.5 draws some policy conclusions on the use of digital analysis for fraud detection. Concluding remarks and an outlook for future research in the field are provided in Section 18.6.

---

[2] Diaconis and Freedman (1979) provide convincing evidence that Benford himself manipulated part of his data to obtain a better fit to the theoretically assumed distribution.

18.2   Benford's Law and Generalizations

18.2.1   The Basic Principle of Benford's Law

Newcomb (1881) had already discovered that the leading significant digits (meaning the first non-zero digit, regardless of the decimal separator) of naturally occurring numbers are not uniformly distributed, but follow a logarithmic distribution. The rediscovery of this property and the empirical evidence provided by Benford (1938) triggered research in this area and led to the attribution of this law to Benford. It is, thus, another example for Stigler's law of eponymy, which posits that many scientific discoveries are attributed and named after people other than their respective originators (Goodman 2016).

We start with the most elementary version of Benford's law, which considers only the first significant, i.e. non-zero digits. For example, the numbers 0.123, 123 and 123,000 all share the first significant digit of 1. Consequently, the set of possible outcomes for the first significant digit d_1 is given by the set $\{1, 2, \ldots, 9\}$. Benford's law assumes that the probability distribution of a randomly selected first digit D_1 is given by:

$$Prob(D_1 = d_1) = \log_{10}(d_1 + 1) - \log_{10}(d_1) = \log_{10}\left(\frac{d_1 + 1}{d_1}\right).$$

To provide an example for the calculation, according to this version of Benford's law for the first digit, the probability of observing a 1 as the first significant digit in a number is given by $Prob(D_1 = 1) = \log_{10}\left(\frac{1+1}{1}\right) = 0.3010$. Thus, it is straightforward to calculate the theoretically expected frequency distribution of the first significant digit according to Benford's law (see Table 18.1) and use it as a benchmark against which the observed empirical frequency of the digit can be tested.

Table 18.1   **Empirical distribution of first digits of house numbers in Great Britain from the OpenStreetMap (2018) database (third column) and the theoretical distribution according to Benford's law (second column). The observed absolute differences between the two distributions (right column) are rather small. Thus, the first digits for house numbers appear to be a prime example for naturally occurring numbers closely following Benford's law.**

Digit	Benford Distribution	Empirical Distribution	Absolute Difference
1	0.3010	0.3066	0.0056
2	0.1761	0.1828	0.0067
3	0.1249	0.1270	0.0021
4	0.0969	0.0953	0.0016
5	0.0792	0.0782	0.0010
6	0.0669	0.0654	0.0015
7	0.0580	0.0543	0.0037
8	0.0512	0.0480	0.0032
9	0.0458	0.0425	0.0033

18.2.2   Illustration of Benford's Law

To illustrate the application of Benford's law we apply it to a data set similar to one of those which were part of the original illustration in Benford (1938). Namely, we analyse the distribution of the first digits for house numbers in Great Britain which are part of the OpenStreetMap (2018) database. This results in a total of N=93,087 observations.[3] To compare the distribution of first digits with Benford's law, the first digit is extracted from each house number and the relative frequency is calculated.

Table 18.1 provides the expected frequencies for each possible first digit in the second column and the empirical frequencies found for the house numbers in the third column. The final column shows the absolute difference between the two frequencies. The similarity of both sets of frequencies is striking, which is also supported by the graphical representation in Figure 18.1. A possible explanation for the close conformity, implying high frequencies for low digits, is that in Great Britain the scheme of numbering houses in most cases starts with 1 for houses closest to the city centre. Thus, lower digits naturally have a higher prevalence than all of the larger digits, since the length of streets is finite and, whenever you have a 4, you had a 1 before, whenever you have a 22, you had 10, 11, . . . ,19 before, etc. However, only 11.6% of the numbers exceed 100 and only 20 or 0.02% of those are larger than 1000.

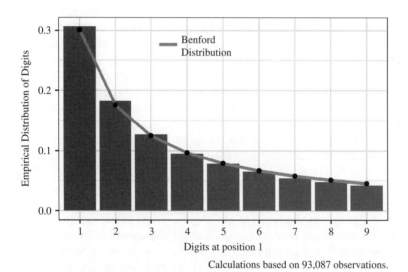

Calculations based on 93,087 observations.

Figure 18.1   The graphical display of the relative frequencies of first digits of house numbers in the UK (bars) and the theoretical expected distribution according to Benford's law (grey line) indicate the close conformity to Benford's law.

---

[3] It has to be noted that the OpenStreetMap (2018) data set does not include all house numbers in Great Britain, but only covers a subset.

18.2.3 Testing for Conformity with Benford's Law

The comparison of the empirical distribution of digits with the distribution implied by Benford's law is either carried out by means of graphical presentations of both distributions as shown in Figure 18.1 or based on statistical procedures. In the latter case, Pearson's chi-squared (x^2) test is an appropriate procedure. In the present setting, it tests the null hypothesis that the observed digits are generated in accordance with Benford's law. To this end, the empirical frequencies of all digits are compared with their theoretical counterparts, the probabilities from Benford's law. The test statistics is calculated by the below formula:

$$x^2 = \sum_{i=1}^{9} \frac{(ac_i - ec_i)^2}{ec_i}.$$

ac_i corresponds to the actual count of digit i, ec_i represents the expected count which is given by the probability of observing an i under Benford's law multiplied with the number of observations N, i.e. $ec_i = Prob(D_1 = i) \cdot N$. The x^2-test statistic takes on large values if these differences are large, while it should be small when the data are generated in accordance with Benford's law. Asymptotical critical values for the x^2-test statistics are obtained from the x^2-distribution with 9 degrees of freedom.[4] For the house number example, the x^2-test statistic amounts to 105.64. Provided that this value is larger than the critical value at the 5% level (and also above the 1% and 0.1% level), the null hypothesis of conformity of the distribution of the first digits with Benford's law has to be rejected despite the seemingly good fit shown in Figure 18.1.

In the context of searching fraud, malpractice, or misconduct, the fact that failing to reject the null hypothesis, i.e. apparent conformity of the data with Benford's law does not automatically imply that numbers occurred naturally and, thus, are not manipulated has to be considered. Alternatively, the number of observations might be too small to allow for a significant result, or the data might follow Benford's law despite manipulations, as the fraudsters might be aware of tests conducted.

On the other hand, large deviations resulting in a rejection of the null hypothesis do not prove manipulations either. For example, when testing at a significance level of 5%, such rejections occur at a rate of 5% even if the data follow Benford's law. Of course, a significant test result might also be owed to the fact that the true distribution does not comply with Benford's law for the specific data considered. Thus, finding significant deviations should only be a starting point for further investigations in order to find out if they can be attributed to fraudulent behaviour or if they arose otherwise.

---

[4] These critical values are 16.919, 19.023, and 21.666 for a level of significance of 0.1, 0.05, and 0.01, respectively. For the analysis of second or further significant digits, asymptotical critical values are obtained from the x^2-distribution with 10 degrees of freedom: 18.307, 20.483, and 23.209 for a level of significance of 0.1, 0.05 and 0.01, respectively.

Another important caveat in the application of the x^2-test statistic is the problem of excess power, as described by Nigrini (2012). This means that in cases where the number of observations becomes large, even small and practically irrelevant deviations from Benford's law will result in test statistics which exceed the critical values at the usual significance levels. This leads to the rejection of the null hypothesis and thus to the false conclusion that there is a relevant – and not just statistically significant – deviation from Benford's law. When applying the x^2-test statistic in an attempt to detect financial fraud, it is important to have a large sample available for analysis. This unwelcome aspect might be addressed by using stricter levels of significance, e.g. 1%, 0.1% or even below if the number of observations becomes very large.

An alternative indicator, which is used by Shi, Ausloos, and Zhu (2018), Judge and Schechter (2009), and Schündeln (2018) amongst others, is based on the Euclidian distance between the distributions and calculated as:

$$d^* = \frac{1}{M}\sqrt{\sum_{i=1}^{9}\left(\frac{ac_i}{N} - \frac{ec_i}{N}\right)^2},$$

where M is the maximum possible distance, which is obtained if all observed digits are equal to 9. The normalization with M guarantees that the values of d^* fall in the interval [0,1]. Values close to zero indicate conformity with Benford's law. While the measure has the advantage of not being sensitive to sample size and appears useful for comparing changes over time, it appears difficult to derive thresholds for deciding if a distribution follows Benford's law or not.

A further alternative has been proposed by Drake and Nigrini (2000). It might be used to determine the degree of conformity that an empirical distribution exhibits, namely the mean absolute deviation (MAD). This measure is the average of the absolute differences between the empirically observed relative frequencies and the ones determined in accordance with Benford's law. According to Drake and Nigrini (2000), it has the advantage of being less affected by the number of observations used in the analysis. Unfortunately, however, the MAD indicator does not follow a well-defined probability distribution. Therefore, Drake and Nigrini (2000) provide some simulated critical values and suggest the following conclusions. When considering only the first significant digit, they label values in the range up to 0.006 as 'close conformity', values above 0.006 and below 0.012 as 'acceptable conformity', values above 0.012 and below 0.015 as 'marginally acceptable conformity' and only values above 0.015 as 'nonconformity'.[5] For the house number example, the value of the MAD is obtained by adding up the absolute differences listed in the last column of Table 18.1 and dividing this sum by the number of digits considered (9). The resulting value is 0.0032 and thus, based on the categories by Drake and Nigrini (2000), we might assume 'close conformity' to Benford's law.

---

[5] The relevant intervals for second digits and the combination of first-two or first-three digits are provided in Table 18.3 in the Appendix.

18.2.4 Considering Further Digits with Benford's Law

Similar arguments that apply to the first digit also hold true for further significant digits. In particular, for the second significant digit d_2, the probability distribution over the set of possible values $\{0,1, \ldots, 9\}$ is calculated as follows:

$$Prob(D_2 = d_2) = \sum_{i=1}^{9} \log_{10}\left[1 + \frac{1}{10i + d_2}\right].$$

Accordingly, the probabilities decrease from 11.97% for a zero to 8.50% for a 9 as the second digit. However, the differences are much smaller compared to those of the first digit.

To illustrate this, we again use the house number data. The comparison between theoretical probabilities and empirical frequencies is shown in Figure 18.2. A first point to note is that there are fewer observations, only 70,446, for the second digit, which is due to the fact that some (small) house numbers only have one digit. The results for testing the conformity with Benford's law for the second digit are similar to the results obtained for the first digit, since with a χ^2-test statistic of 155.54, the null hypothesis of conformity between the empirically observed and theoretically expected frequencies has to be rejected. In contrast to this, the value of the MAD indicator of 0.00383 again indicates 'close conformity' according to the intervals provided in Table 18.3.

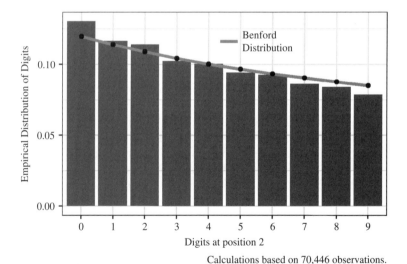

Calculations based on 70,446 observations.

Figure 18.2 The graphical display of the relative frequencies of second digits of house numbers in the UK (bars) and the theoretical expected distribution according to Benford's law (grey line) confirm the observation and still indicates the close conformity to Benford's law.

The following formula generalizes the probability distribution for all subsequent digits. For the n-th position in a number, when $n > 1$, the probability to observe a digit $d \in \{0,1, \ldots ,9\}$ is calculated as follows:

$$Prob(D_n = d) = \sum_{k=10^{n-2}}^{10^{n-1}-1} \log_{10}\left[1+\frac{1}{10k+d}\right].$$

It is important to note that, as might be expected, the theoretical distribution for subsequent digits gets closer to uniform when moving further to the right within the number. Already for the fourth significant digit, the probabilities for all digits range between 10.02% for a 0 and 9.98% for a 9, while they would all be 10% in case of a uniform distribution.

Since the first and second (and further) digits are not distributed independently, considering several significant digits in combination makes perfect sense in order to increase the discriminatory power of the analysis. Hill (1995) derives the formal generalization of the significant-digit law for the first k digits ($k > 1$). It states that for positive integers with k digits, all first digits $d_1 \in \{1,2, \ldots ,9\}$ in combination with subsequent digits $d_j \in \{0,1, \ldots ,9\}, j = 2, \ldots ,k$, should follow the joint probability distribution:

$$Prob(D_1 = d_1, \ldots , D_k = d_k) = \log_{10}\left[1+\left(\sum_{i=1}^{k} d_i \times 10^{k-i}\right)^{-1}\right].$$

To provide an example for the calculation according to this general version of Benford's law, the probability to observe a number with the first two significant digits being 1 and 2, e.g. 12, 125, or 1209, is given by $Prob(D_1 = 1, D_2 = 2) = \log_{10}\left(1+(12)^{-1}\right)$ $= 0.03476$.

Again, we use the example of house numbers in the UK to illustrate how this analysis is conducted. Figure 18.3 exhibits the empirical and the theoretically expected frequencies of a combination of the first two digits. It is apparent that the first two digits do not correspond to the generalized Benford's law. This evidence is underpinned by the calculated test statistics, which both result in a rejection of the null hypothesis of conformity with Benford's law. The x^2-test statistic takes on a value of 59,456, which has to be compared to the critical values of a x^2-distribution with 89 degrees of freedom (106.469, 112.022, and 122.942 for the 10%, 5% and 1%-level, respectively, and only 147.35 for the 0.01% level). The MAD indicator adds up to 0.004939326. This value clearly falls into the range of nonconformity according to the values provided in Table 18.3 in the appendix (above 0.0022).

Recently, Barabesi et al. (2018) propose a hierarchical sequence of tests starting with a joint test on the first k digits and, conditional on rejection, going down to smaller sets. They provide simulated critical values and demonstrate that the procedure helps reducing the rate of false alarms.

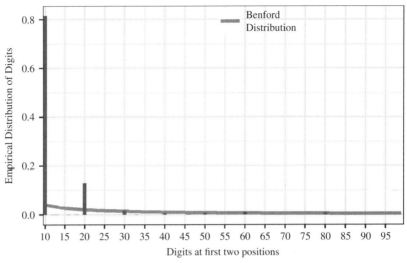

Calculations based on 729 observations.

Figure 18.3 **The graphical display of the relative frequencies of the first two digits of house numbers in the UK (bars) and the theoretical expected distribution according to Benford's law (grey line) indicate that the first two digits do not match the generalized Benford distribution. It is apparent that numbers with the leading digits 10 and 20 are much more frequently observed than any other digit combination.**

18.2.5 When Do Data Conform to Benford's Law?

Benford's law does not apply to all sets of numerical data. Thus, it is important to verify whether all necessary conditions are met. Nigrini and Mittermaier (1997) and Fewster (2009) describe the most essential of these conditions.

A first requirement refers to the range of values the numbers might take on. One of the most basic and most important findings is the fact that Benford's law provides a better fit if the distribution of the numbers covers several orders of magnitude (Raimi 1976; Smith 1997). The order of magnitude of a number can be described using the number of powers of 10 contained therein. The house numbers in our previous application ranging from 1 to 2,473 only cover four orders of magnitude since all numbers lie within the range from 1×10^0 to 1×10^4. According to Fewster (2009) a range of six might be sufficient to obtain a good approximation to Benford's law. He also provides an intuitive explanation and several examples for this requirement.

Second, the numbers should not be assigned but occur naturally. This implies that Benford's law might not work well considering personal income figures of a certain income tax bracket due to the arbitrary cut-off points. Consequently, the probabilities for certain digits might deviate considerably from Benford's law. Another example for assigned numbers in the same context are social security numbers, which follow a certain pattern as they are the result of human thought. By contrast, the total sales volume of firms should meet this requirement.

Third, as proved by Hill (1995), many naturally occurring numbers, which follow Benford's law, are mathematical combinations of numbers which are unbiasedly sampled from various distributions. This is also the explanation why Benford's law is often used to analyse accounting data at the firm level, since these accounting data are the result of the multiplication of randomly sampled numbers of, for example, quantities and prices and their summation.

In a prior contribution, Durtschi, Hillison, and Pacini (2004) provide an overview of applications of Benford's law in the context of financial accounting. They also give examples as to when the conditions for the application of Benford's law can be expected to hold. In particular, they stress the relevance of combinations of numbers, e.g. accounts receivable as product of quantity sold, times the prices for the products, and the advantage of large data sets, as even small deviations might become significant. However, as mentioned above, recently, this feature has been judged more ambivalently. Furthermore, a mean larger than the median, i.e. a positive skewness of the distribution, supports conformity to Benford's law (see also Wallace (2002)). Nigrini and Mittermaier (1997) suggest that auditors might assume that the data follow Benford's law when considering 'items, such as accounts receivable or payable, inventory counts, fixed asset acquisitions, daily sales, and disbursements'. Durtschi, Hillison, and Pacini (2004) state that Benford's law should not be applied when numbers are assigned, influenced by human thought, containing a large number of firm-specific numbers, or built-in minimum or maximum.[6] In addition, they point out that Benford's law and similar methods cannot be applied if fraud is conducted without any record, e.g. theft or kickbacks.

A more rigorous mathematical analysis of the conditions to be met for a set of numbers to follow Benford's law can be found in Boyle (1994), Dümbgen and Leuenberger (2008), Gauvrit and Delahaye (2011), Pinkham (1961), Wallace (2002), and Chenavier, Massé, and Schneider (2018).

18.2.6   Limitations of Using Benford's Law for Identification of Manipulations

The requirements stated above limit the range of possible applications of Benford's law for detecting fraud, malpractice, and manipulation in financial markets. If the distribution of non-manipulated data does not follow Benford's law, the test statistics introduced above will reject the null hypothesis too often and result in false alarms. Consequently, generalizations of the approach, which do not require conformity with Benford's law in the strict sense, might be more appropriate and are discussed below.

Furthermore, even if real data follow Benford's law closely enough, a substantial number of observations for potentially manipulated data is required for a powerful statistical test. This limits the applicability of the method as an early warning or real-time check, when only few observations become available in each time period,

---

[6] Lu and Boritz (2005) propose an adaptive version of Benford's law allowing to take artificial cut-off values into account.

e.g. aggregate earnings or profits at the firm level. Only after a sufficiently long period of malpractice, a retrospective analysis of the data might become feasible.

When considering fraud and manipulation of data, a further shortcoming of methods relying on Benford's law in the strict sense is their vulnerability under the predator-and-prey perspective, i.e. the observation that impostors will adjust their behaviour to the means used in surveillance. If potential manipulators become aware that such methods are commonly used for checking the integrity of data, they can decide either to stop manipulations or to adjust the way they produce manipulated data. Unfortunately, it does not present a challenge to produce data in compliance with Benford's law when using computer tools. There are even websites offering the generation of such data or providing a code for generating the data. For obvious reasons, we do not want to advertise these offers, but it is a rather safe bet to assume that potential manipulators will find and use them.[7] Therefore, relying on Benford's law as a stand-alone instrument for detecting fraud, malpractice, or manipulations is not recommendable.

18.2.7   Generalizations of Benford's Law for Identification of Manipulations

In order to deal with some of the limitations mentioned above, the literature proposes some generalizations and extensions. In the context of accounting, Winter, Schneider, and Yannikos (2012) propose using a modified Benford distribution which makes allowance for accounting limits. The resulting distribution should be closer to observed real numbers and, consequently, reduce the rate of false positives. A different and more general approach followed, amongst others, by Rodriguez (2004) and Hürlimann (2009) is to consider classes of distributions and to decide on the specific benchmark based on the fit to the available data. Again, having a closer approximation to the actual distribution should reduce the risk of false alarms.

Given that the digital analysis and the tests for homogeneity, i.e. equal distributions, are mainly non-parametric, a further straightforward extension consists in considering the empirical distribution of digits as a benchmark. If it can be assumed that the share of manipulated data is small, the distribution of digits over all available observations should represent a good approximation to the true distribution (Schräpler 2011). If the distribution for a subsample differs significantly, this generates a signal to look at the subsample more thoroughly.

Developing this idea further, it could be assumed that part of the available data is correct and could provide the benchmark distribution of digits, while the other part exhibits a different distribution of significant digits. A generalized procedure could try to identify both parts by an optimization procedure over different sample splits attempting to maximize the distance between the distributions of the two parts.

---

[7] In a laboratory experiment, Watrin, Struffert, and Ullmann (2008) provide evidence that the distribution of digits of manipulated numbers becomes more similar to Benford's law when the subjects are informed about its use. However, the differences were not found to be statistically significant.

However, such a procedure would be computationally complex and could not indicate a priori which of the two parts contains the manipulated data.

All three approaches, generalized parametric distributions, non-parametric approaches based on the empirical distribution of all available observations and non-parametric approaches derived from an optimization procedure share the advantage that the benchmark used for the analysis is not known a priori. Thus, potential manipulators do not know which benchmark to meet unless they have access to all data. Even if this were the case, the sketched optimization approach might still impose a hurdle for generating manipulated data, which might remain undetected. Finally, the idea of combining several indicators as proposed by Bredl. Winker, and Kötschau (2012) in the context of survey data, which focus on different aspects of data quality and not just on the distribution of digits, might help to improve discriminatory power.

18.3   Usage of Benford's Law for Detecting Fraud and Deviant Behaviour

Since the initial publication in 1881, the number of published research papers using or analysing Benford's law has increased considerably, in particular after 2000 with a peak during the financial crisis. Admittedly, following the financial crisis the number of publications decreased. Figure 18.4 provides a graphical representation of

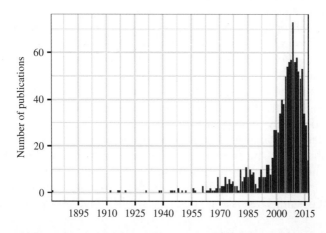

Figure 18.4   Development of the yearly number of academic publications using or analysing Benford's law. Initially, the first publication by Newcomb (1881) did not entail a lot of follow-up publications, and also the publication by Benford (1938) increased the interest in this topic only slightly. Only the availability of increasing computational resources and large digital data sets lead to an increasing usage of Benford's law in order to detect fraud and deviant behaviour resulting in a growing number of publications during the 1990s and the early 2000s. The figure is based on data provided by Berger, Hill and Rogers (2018).

this development and is based on a comprehensive listing by Hürlimann (2006) and Berger et al. (2018).[8]

Even though the applications of Benford's law are not restricted to the analysis of fraud and manipulations in financial markets, the number of publications in this particular area is quite substantial. Therefore, the literature review presented in this section has to be selective. It is organized along the topics (i) forensic accounting, auditing and internal control systems; (ii) finance; and (iii) surveys and research.

18.3.1   Forensic Accounting in the Context of Auditing, Internal Control Systems, and Taxation

Detecting fraud, malpractice, or manipulations is one of the main tasks of audits and internal control systems. Carslaw (1988) was the first who applied Benford's law on accounting data by hypothesizing that when important key indicators, such as net income, are slightly below specific 'psychological boundaries', managers typically round these numbers up to evoke the impression that they are larger (this rounding up phenomenon is also known as '$1.99 pricing phenomenon'). For instance, a net income of $187,000 or $9.54 million is rounded up to $200,000 or $10 million, respectively. This technically implies an increase of second digit 0s and a shortage of second digit 9s. Indeed, Carslaw (1988) found in a data set from New Zealand more second digit 0s and fewer second digit 9s than expected. This result is also in line with the observations of Thomas (1989), who found an excess of second digit 0s based on a rounding-up phenomenon in quarterly U.S. net income data, when companies report a positive net income. In contrast, when companies have negative net incomes, he observed fewer second digit 0s and more second digit 9s, meaning that firms avoid rounding losses. This effect also holds when analysing net income on a per share level (earnings per share – EPS). More precisely, multiples of 5 cents and 10 cents are more often used than expected when reporting EPS, while EPS ended less often than expected on the ending digit 9. Recently, Henselmann, Ditter, and Scherr (2015) add to this stream of literature by showing a high degree of deviation from Benford's law in suspect firm years (defined as firm-years just meeting or beating zero (last-year) earnings), compared to other firm-years that clearly miss or beat the thresholds. In the same vein, Amiram, Bozanic, and Rouen (2015) inter alia demonstrate that restated financial statements conform more closely to Benford's law compared to the respective misstated financial statements. In addition, they show that earnings persistence decreases, when divergence from Benford's law increases.

The detection of fraudulent behaviour conducted by individuals is mainly based on Hill (1988), who ran an experiment with 742 students asking them to randomly guess a six-digit number. The results show that the first digit 1 occurs more often than

---

[8] Hürlimann (2006) compiled an impressive list, which is continuously updated and provided at http://www.benfordonline.net/list/chronological by Berger, Hill, and Rogers (2018) and as of 09/25/2018 lists more than 1,000 publications. See also Mir and Ausloos (2018) for an in-depth bibliometric analysis of citations to Newcomb (1881) and Benford (1938).

expected, whereas the numbers 8 and 9 occur less often than expected as first digit based on Benford's law. Moreover, the second digits are distributed more uniformly than the first digits. This idea is picked up by Nigrini (1994) – as cited in Nigrini and Mittermaier (1997) – by hypothesizing that numbers made up by people will not conform to the expected digital frequency. In detail, he used cases of payroll fraud and found that fraudulent numbers deviated significantly from Benford's law. This effect is even more pronounced when individuals have more routine in faking numbers, because they get used to certain numbers. Nigrini and Mittermaier (1997) introduced Benford's law to a specific audit context. In detail, they show how digital and number tests can help to assess the authenticity of lists of numbers in the planning stages of audits. Durtschi, Hillison, and Pacini (2004) provide a practitioner's guide for auditors on when and how Benford's law can help to detect suspect accounts based on all available data. Nigrini and Miller (2009) introduce a 'second-order Benford test' to the auditing literature to find errors in transactional data. They show that digits of the differences between amounts approximate the frequencies of Benford's law for most data sets when the amounts are sorted from the smallest to the largest amounts. Moreover, Nigrini (2012) demonstrates how Benford's law can help to detect inconsistencies within the accounts receivables based on firm-wide invoice-level data. More recently, Benford's law has been used to detect target-driven earnings management especially by Ullmann and Watrin (2017).

Focusing on taxation, Christian, Gupta, and Lin (1993) investigate tax returns to detect whether tax payers reduced taxable income from above a tax table bracket to a taxable income below a tax table bracket (so called 'secondary evasion') to get a lower tax rate. They assume that that the ending digits of taxable incomes should be uniformly distributed over the 00 to 99 range and that the expected frequency of the third, fourth and fifth digits represent a near-uniform distribution. The results indicate a clear bias toward taxpayers having taxable incomes slightly below a specific tax table bracket. Regarding tax compliance, Nigrini (1996) shows that there was a bias towards lowering taxable income by using (1) low digits for interest received and high digits for interest paid. Watrin et al. (2008) show that Benford's law is a valuable tool to select firms for an on-site tax audit if the non-manipulated data conforms to the Benford distribution resulting in more efficient and effective on-site tax audits.

Barabesi et al. (2018) illustrate their hierarchical testing procedure to trade data reported by Italian traders. Since customs and value added tax are calculated based on these declared values, there is a considerable incentive to underreport. On the other hand, money laundering schemes might provide incentives to increase reported valuations. For two selected traders, the authors demonstrate that their hierarchical testing procedure allows for a better differentiation between false alarms and indeed suspicious cases.

18.3.2   Finance

In the finance context, Ley (1996) is one of the first to employ Benford's law. He finds that the series of daily returns on two of the most important U.S. stock indexes, the Dow Jones Industrial Average Index (DJIA) over the period 1900 to 1993 and the Standard and Poor's Index (S&P) over the period 1926 to 1993, follow Benford's law. His work followed earlier research studying the importance of certain numerical values of major stock indexes (Koedijk and Stork 1994; Ley and Varian 1994). While earlier papers mainly focused on the psychological impact of specific index levels (such as, e.g., multiples of 1,000) in order to predict future stock market movements, the application of Benford's law was subsequently employed to examine manipulative behaviour on financial markets. In this respect, Corazza, Ellero, and Zorzi (2010) discuss the S&P 500 stock market index and find that sequences of trading days not confirming with the Benford distribution are rather short. Moreover, they observe that days on which the stock index distribution does not follow Benford's law are related to extreme market events, such as the attack on the World Trade Center on September 11, 2001.

Relatedly, Rauch et al. (2011) use Benford's law to check the accuracy of governmental macroeconomic statistics relevant for compliance with the Stability and Growth Pact criteria of the European Union. They consider all relevant data from the 27 EU member states from 1999 to 2009. As macroeconomic data comes from different sources with different distributions, a Benford distribution is to be expected. Moreover, since the Benford distribution is the only distribution of first significant digits that is scale invariant, this property makes Benford's law particularly helpful in a macroeconomic context where data need to be converted from one currency to another. As might have been expected, Rauch et al. (2011) find the data reported by Greece to show the greatest deviation from Benford's law among all countries in the Euro area. Deleanu (2017) comes to a similar conclusion with respect to a data set of self-reported indicators of compliance and efficiency in the fight against money laundering among European Union member states. Her results, based on Benford's law, hint at potential manipulations of these indicators for countries that faced sufficient incentives and opportunities to misinform the community about their efforts to fight money laundering.

Nye and Moul (2007) apply Benford's law as a tool for assessing the quality of macroeconomic indicators on a broader scale. They focused on the GDP series of OECD countries and of certain African nations and find that only a subset of the data – particularly from the developing countries – shows non-conformity consistent with deliberate manipulation of the underlying series. In a follow-up study, Gonzalez-Garcia and Pastor (2009) enlarge the data set to 80 countries and report only little indication of a rejection of the first-digit law for most series. Even more importantly, they show that the observed deviations from Benford's law may be a result of structural breaks captured in the data series and caution against interpreting them as a signal of poor quality in macroeconomic data.

In contrast to this, current studies have found evidence in favour of strategic manipulation of macroeconomic data by governments. Michalski and Stoltz (2013), for instance, consider the balance of payments data from the IMF between 1989 and 2007. Since some countries have already been caught misreporting their information (e.g. Ukraine) to this data set, there is some valid reason to reconsider the full dataset. The authors find that there is evidence from Benford's law that countries which are more vulnerable to capital flow reversals (e.g. those with fixed exchange rates or countries with current account and fiscal deficits) show irregular, non-Benford behaviour of the first digits in their data series. Interestingly, China, which has often come under scrutiny for its official statistics on GDP development, has been shown to largely conform with Benford's law (Holz 2014).

Further applications of Benford's law have been inspired by observations of peculiar price movements in the financial crisis starting in 2007. Irregularities on reference rates such as the LIBOR have questioned the integrity of the interbank market and led to investigations using Benford's law (Mollenkamp, 2008; Mollenkamp and White-house, 2008; Abrantes-Metz, Villas-Boas, and Judge 2011). Our case study in Section 18.0 demonstrates how Benford's law can be employed in this context. Further analyses indicate that other reference rates, such as EURIBOR or TIBOR, may have been affected by manipulation as well (Rauch et al., 2013).

Hofmarcher and Hornik (2013) employ Benford-like distributions to CDS market data and find consistency for the US-CDS market but huge fluctuations in the distributions of first significant digits for the European market during the financial crisis. They attribute these differences to the reorganization procedures in bankruptcy that are much more lenient on borrowers in the US as compared to Europe. Ausloos, Castellano, and Cerqueti (2016) stress the importance of employing Benford's law for checking the credibility of CDS data whose pricing processes are often opaque and trading volumes highly variable. They examine the daily sovereign CDS spreads of 13 European countries between 2008 and 2015. Their results show that Benford's law tends to be violated more often in the more liquid CDS instruments and in the core European countries' (France, Germany, United Kingdom) CDS. The authors nevertheless point out that the development of CDS spreads is strongly affected by liquidity constraints, which might have a stronger impact than the underlying sovereign risk perception.

However, manipulations of interest rates appear to reflect only the tip of the iceberg as other benchmarks, e.g. deriving from commodity, currency, or other financial markets, seem to be affected as well (Wheatley 2012). In this respect, El Mouaaouy (2018) examines FX benchmarks via the use of Benford's law. He finds anomalies in several foreign exchange rates that were also exposed to the LIBOR rigging and blames coordinated interventions of market participants for influencing the benchmark rates to their advantage. In a similar analysis, Stenfors (2018) also utilizes Benford's law as a screening device in order to detect artificial patterns in FX data of USD/JPY and USD/NOK swap markets. The empirical results reveal patterns that suggest that some form of coordination between market participants has taken place.

El Mouaaouy and Riepe (2018) employ Benford's law to analyse capital allocation processes within firms. They consider publicly available segment-level data from the German banking industry from 2004 to 2011 and show that managerial interventions lead to stronger deviations from Benford's law with increasing complexity of the underlying business model. Similar results are obtained by Lin et al. (2018) with regard to earnings management in Taiwanese firms. They find stronger deviations from Benford's law for firms in which board members have the power to increase their own pay substantially.

18.3.3   Surveys and Research

Finally, two further fields of applications, which are at least indirectly related to financial markets, warrant a brief mentioning. The first are surveys, which often focus on topics related to financial markets, for instance investor expectations or household finance. Bredl, Storfinger, and Menold (2013) provide a recent review on the usage of Benford's law in this context. Second, there is a line of research testing whether academic research itself might be affected by possible manipulations or fraud.

With regard to surveys, in particular those on investor expectations, a first observation is that they do not lend themselves to a digital analysis as they include only a small number of questions, out of which a large part is rather qualitative ('stock prices will increase', 'stay constant', 'fall'). Hence, there are not enough metric variables with several digits in the dataset required for a good estimate of the empirical distribution of digits for a single interview or at least for all interviews conducted by one interviewer. Furthermore, the metric variables included in the data set should follow Benford's law in real data, which might be the case for many variables included in financial markets or household finance surveys. However, it is not sufficient that the real data conform to Benford's law. The actual numbers reported by respondents have to comply with Benford's law, too. At this level, it is well known that respondents tend to round numbers in a way that at least for non-leading digits a clustering at 0 and 5 can often be observed (see e.g. Schräpler (2011)). Obviously, this should not constitute a signal for possible fraud by interviewers. Therefore, care should be taken when deciding which digits from which variables to use for comparison with Benford's distribution in survey data.

Judge and Schechter (2009) and Schräpler (2011) use Benford's law for identifying suspect observations or interviewers. Both employ household surveys including a large number of metric variables related to agricultural production and monetary income components. They succeed in identifying suspicious cases. According to Schräpler (2011), a follow-up done for one interviewer actually resulted in discovering falsifications, which remained unnoticed as more traditional methods were used. In line with one of the generalizations of Benford's law discussed in Section 18.0, Schräpler (2011) suggests using the distribution of digits over all available observations as benchmark instead of Benford's distribution. Assuming that most observations are real, this might provide a better approximation to the underlying distribution, in particular when rounding is relevant. However, this method has to be refined in case of a large share of falsifiers, as e.g. found by Bredl, Winker, and Kötschau (2012). In a related application, Schündeln (2018) compares the conformity to Benford's law for repeated interviews on consumption expenditures in the Ghana Living Standards Survey. He finds smaller deviations for early responses and takes this finding for an indication of higher data quality resulting from early measurements.

In particular, if the analysis is based on only a limited number of metric variables as might be the typical setting in financial markets surveys, the standard approach will not withstand the predator-and-prey perspective. If falsifiers are aware of controls based on Benford's law, they have to exert just a minor additional effort to generate falsified data in line with Benford's law. Then, the test will lose its power for identifying suspicious cases. In order to overcome this limitation, Bredl et al. (2012) combine several indicators and used the multivariate distribution for discriminating groups of interviewers. In this way, the benchmark becomes higher dimensional and depends on the other interviewers, making it much more difficult for a cheater to replicate it (Winker 2016).

Finally, given that the peer-review process typically does not include a check of research data, there are incentives for researchers to manipulate their results in order to increase the possibility of publication of their research. Diekmann (2007) analyses empirical distributions of digits in statistical estimates, as they can often be found in empirical research. According to his analysis based on more than 1,000 regression coefficients, the first digit of these numbers closely follows Benford's law. The author uses students to fabricate regression coefficients, supporting a certain hypothesis. The results indicate that fabricated data most significantly differ not at the first digit, but rather at the subsequent ones. This is also in line with research by Mosimann, Wiseman, and Edelman (1995), and Mosimann et al. (2002).

Another strand of literature uses Benford's law to check the integrity of reported academic results and for example Tödter (2009) reports a substantial number of articles in his sample, which do not conform to Benford's law and are thus probably manipulated. He concludes that the empirical results presented in these articles might have been manipulated. In a direct response, Diekmann and Jann (2010) challenge the conclusions drawn by Tödter (2009) and doubt that Benford's law is an appropriate tool to distinguish between manipulated and untampered estimates. They especially highlight the relatively high probability of Type I error, i.e. 'false positives', when using Benford's law. This property was also analysed in more detail by Bauer and Groß (2011). They conclude that a comparison of research data with Benford's law can only provide indications for possible fraud, and these indications are only relevant if certain conditions are met.

18.4   A Case Study: Benford's Law and the LIBOR

This section provides a case study demonstrating possible ways to use Benford's law for identifying suspected fraud. During the climax of the financial crisis, in April and May 2008, first reports surfaced in the *Wall Street Journal* (WSJ), indicating possible problems with the reliability of the London Interbank Offered Rate (LIBOR) (Mollenkamp 2008; Mollenkamp and Whitehouse 2008).

Since the LIBOR is supposed to be a measure of the interest rate at which banks lend to each other, it can be used as an indicator of individual bank's risk, which is expected to rise when banks face higher risks. Thus, during the peak of the financial crisis individual banks had the incentive to report lower interest rates to mask their real borrowing costs and, consequently, to obscure the extent of their risk exposure towards the market. A further incentive for fraud, which a priori does not predetermine the direction of possible misreported interest rates, is the possibility that market participants with a large exposure to derivatives rated based on the LIBOR can profit by strategically moving the LIBOR into the desired direction.

Gyntelberg and Wooldridge (2008) raise the issue of reliability of interest rate fixings in connection with the drying up of liquidity in major interbank markets in the second half of 2007. By comparing spreads and correlations between interbank fixings, they are able to show that in the period between August 2007 and January 2008 the spreads widened considerably while LIBOR rose substantially less than similar interest rates fixes.

Monticini and Thornton (2013) use this as a starting point to check the effect of misreporting on the LIBOR rate and find significant breaks in the spread for the period from late 2007 to late 2008 and early 2009. Our case study focuses on the one month LIBOR for the US-$. For this series, we find a break as indication for suspected underreporting as shown in Figure 18.5, following the initial publication of the report in the WSJ on April 16, 2008 (date marked by the vertical line in Figure 18.5) that immediately increased the reported rate.

Abrantes-Metz, Villas-Boas, and Judge (2011)[9] use digital analysis based on Benford's law to analyse the submitted interest rates and try to discern possible patterns indicating the manipulation of the reported interest rates. Given the overall level of interest rates in the period under consideration, a manipulation of the first digit would be too obvious to remain undetected. Therefore, the authors focus their analysis on the second digit. They show that, in comparison with the years 1987 to 2005, in the run up and during the financial crisis from 2007 to 2008, the deviations between the empirical distribution of the second digits and the expected distribution according to Benford's law increased.

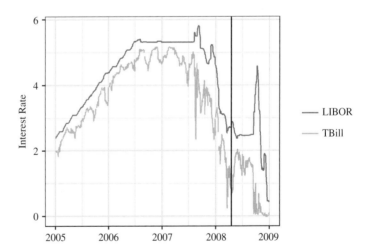

Figure 18.5 **Historical development of the one-month LIBOR and Treasury bill interest rate from 1/4/2005 to 12/31/2008 in percentage terms. The black vertical line indicates the initial release of the *Wall Street Journal* report on possible manipulations of the LIBOR submissions. It is found that the LIBOR interest rate follows the Treasury bill interest rate closely only until the beginning of the financial crisis. In September 2008, the spread becomes substantially larger than usual.**

---

[9] The working paper version Abrantes-Metz and Villas-Boas (2010) provides additional technical details on the analysis.

Obviously, as a test case to check whether Benford's law might be useful in detecting possible manipulations or fraud during this episode provides an interesting example. Ex post, it became apparent that the interest rates submitted by individual banks were often rigged in order to profit in the derivative markets or in order to understate their liquidity risk during the financial crisis (Ashton and Christophers 2015).

However, it has to be taken into account that interest rates cannot be expected to follow Benford's law closely as they do not fulfil most of the conditions discussed in Section 18.2. Thus, the following analysis does not mainly focus on the question if the LIBOR submissions follow Benford's law, but rather on the question whether Benford's law could act as a sensible benchmark against which the distribution of the digits can be checked. Therefore, the first step of our analysis shown in Figure 18.6 is just an illustration that the second significant digits of the interest rates under consideration are not distributed according to Benford's law. Nevertheless, the distribution of the second digits for the four weeks Treasury Bills (TBills) interest rates is much more similar to Benford's distribution than the LIBOR submissions during the period from 1/4/2005 to 12/31/2008. The analysis for the LIBOR is based on the submissions of interest rates for US Dollar lending with a maturity of one month from individual banks, which were published by Rogers in the *Guardian*. In order to provide a benchmark interest rate, the TBills secondary market interest rate[10] is used, which is supposedly less prone to human intervention in the determination of single digits.

In fact, the high proportion of the digit 3 for the LIBOR submissions is striking, while the TBills interest rate rather exhibits too high frequencies of larger values (5 to 9) compared to the distribution of the second digit according to Benford's law. The high frequency of digit 3 is caused by a long period from mid-2006 to mid-2007,

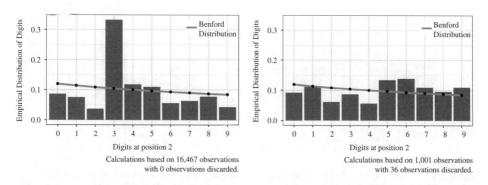

Figure 18.6   **Comparison of the distribution of second digits in the LIBOR submissions (left) and TBills interest rate (right) from 1/4/2005 to 12/31/2008 with the expected theoretical distribution based on Benford's law (grey line). The high share of digit 3 in the LIBOR submissions signals a clear departure from Benford's law, while the distribution of second digits in the TBills interest rates is much closer to the theoretical distribution according to Benford's law.**

---

[10] Data on the TBills interest rate provided by the Board of Governors of the Federal Reserve System (US) (2018) through their FRED economic data tool.

when the LIBOR was at about 5.3% and – as will be shown below – all submissions from individual banks were almost identical. This does not provide any proof for manipulation or fraud per se, but could have provided a first warning signal even before the first articles in the WSJ.

Figure 18.7 exhibits the distribution of the second significant digits for a more recent period starting with the newly created LIBOR submission regime and covering the period 2/3/2014 – 2/8/2017.[11] One of the major changes to increase transparency is that all individual submissions are made available after a three-month delay by the Intercontinental Exchange (ICE) London.[12] Still, the distribution does not conform to Benford's law, but deviations are much smaller than for the earlier period, and the overall shape becomes more similar to the one for the TBills interest rate.

The comparison of LIBOR submissions in each of the two subperiods as depicted in Figure 18.6, and Figure 18.7 shows that the transparency measures introduced after the LIBOR scandal appear to have led to a digit distribution more similar to Benford's distribution.

The formal tests based on the χ^2-statistics confirm the descriptive evidence that the empirical distributions would deviate significantly from the distribution if Benford's law applied. Table 18.2 reports the test statistics for both subperiods and the three pairs of distributions (TBills, LIBOR, and theoretical distribution according to Benford's law), which all exceed the critical value at the 1%-level of 23.209. However, the size of the test statistic differs substantially between LIBOR and TBills when it comes to the comparison with Benford's distribution. For the first subperiod, the value for LIBOR is larger than 10,000, providing a very strong signal for

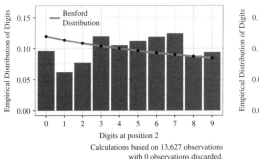
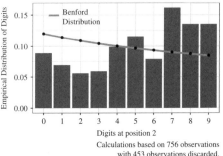

Figure 18.7 **Comparison of the distribution of second digits in the LIBOR submissions (left) and Treasury Bills interest rate (right) from 2/3/2014 to 2/8/2017 with the expected theoretical distribution based on Benford's law (grey line). The differences for the LIBOR rate become much smaller as compared to the earlier period shown in Figure 18.6.**

---

[11] During this period, the Treasury Bills interest rate became smaller than 0.1% for a substantial number of days including a few days when it actually reached zero. As only two decimal places are reported for the Treasury Bills rate, no second significant digit is available for these days. Therefore, the sample had to be restricted to those days with rates equal to or above 0.1% (303 out of 756 days).

[12] For more information on the newly created regime, please see https://www.theice.com/iba/libor and for detailed data please see https://www.theice.com/marketdata/reports/186.

Table 18.2 χ^2-test statistic for different periods and different underlying interest rate time series testing the goodness of fit between the distributions of second digits. Based on the χ^2-test statistic, the null hypothesis of equal distributions has to be rejected for all cases. Moreover, the MAD test statistic in all cases is above the threshold of 0.012 indication non-conformity between the pairs of distributions. The size of the χ^2-test statistic shrinks substantially for the second sample period, i.e. the distributions of second digits become more similar.

Distributions compared	χ^2-test statistic	MAD test statistic
2nd Digits LIBOR vs. Benford 2005–2008	10,185	0.05184
2nd Digits TBills vs. Benford 2005–2008	94	0.02733
2nd Digits TBills vs. LIBOR 2005–2008	463	0.06134
2nd Digits LIBOR vs. Benford 2014–2017	867	0.02135
2nd Digits TBills vs. Benford 2014–2017	57	0.03765
2nd Digits TBills vs. LIBOR 2014–2017	31	0.02707

deviation from Benford's law. This value shrinks to 867 for the second subperiod reflecting the descriptive evidence that the distribution became much closer to Benford's distribution. However, for both subperiods, the distance between the empirical distribution of second significant digits for the TBills and Benford's distribution is much smaller.

It is interesting to note that the χ^2-test cannot only be used to compare any empirical distribution with the one according to Benford's law, but also two empirical distributions like the TBills with the LIBOR. The large test statistics for this comparison, in particular for the first subperiod, provide further signals regarding a potential problem with the LIBOR data, as the null hypothesis that both distributions of second significant digits follow the same probability distribution for the period 2005 to 2008 has to be rejected at all conventional levels of significance. Therefore, either one has a good rationale why second significant digits should be distributed differently for two interest rates with otherwise similar properties or it has to be interpreted (with caution) as an indication of potential manipulations in at least one of the series. Apparently, the changes to the LIBOR submission regime had the desired impact and made the frequency distributions of the two interest rates much more similar, visible in the decrease of the χ^2-test statistic from 463 to 31.

The values of the MAD test statistic in Table 18.2 confirm the test results obtained by the χ^2-test, since for the second digit they are all well above the upper threshold provided in Table 18.3 in the Appendix. They thus indicate that the digits of both the LIBOR and the TBills do not conform to Benford's law. Nevertheless, they also indicate that the conformity of the LIBOR time series increased, since the value for the second period is considerably smaller. Additionally, the deviations between the LIBOR and TBills decreased from 0.06134 to 0.02707 which also indicates that the newly created regulatory regime might have improved the quality of the LIBOR as a proxy for short term interest rates.

In the first part of the analysis, it became apparent that the interest rates under consideration do not conform to Benford's law no matter whether they were based on real transactions such as the TBills or on submissions by individual banks. Nevertheless, since Benford's law offers an easily applicable benchmark it is possible to monitor the extent of these deviations from the benchmark over time, which might be used to detect suspicious changes.

In Figure 18.8, the change of these deviations is plotted against time. Each observation corresponds to one quarter of data. It becomes obvious that the deviations are largest over the period when the LIBOR rate was almost constant. In order to check whether this substantial increase of the deviations is triggered by particular banks, we repeat the analysis for the individual submissions of each bank separately. The results are provided in Figure 18.9. Apparently, for the last quarter of 2006 and the first two quarters of 2007 all banks exhibit the same level of deviation, as they reported the same interest rate of 5.32% for a substantial part of this period.

Comparing the quarterly development of the squared deviations between the empirical digit distribution and Benford's distribution in Figure 18.8 and Figure 18.10, it is important to note the overall decrease of deviations. The mean and median for these two periods decreased from 3,042 to 386 and 1,468 to 256, respectively. This can be regarded as an indication that the newly created regime to increase transparency – and perhaps also the information that academics used Benford's law to analyse historical submissions – led to a more similar distribution of digits and fewer deviations from Benford's law.

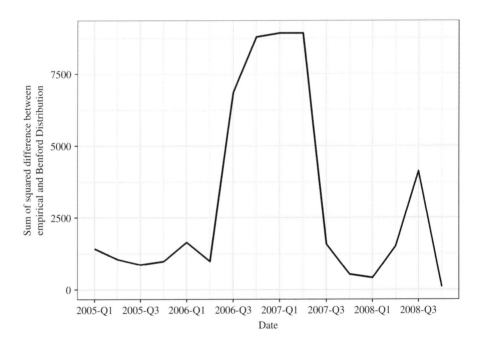

Figure 18.8 **Quarterly development of the sum of squared differences between the empirical and Benford's distribution of the second digit of the LIBOR interest rate submissions from January 2005 to December 2008. Interestingly, there is an unusually large deviation beginning in 2006 until the end of 2007.**

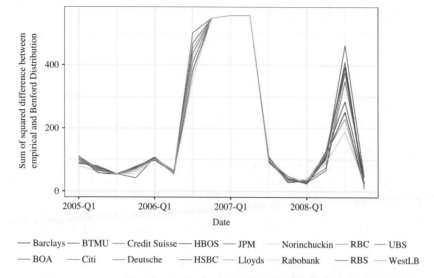

Figure 18.9   Quarterly development of the sum of squared differences between the empirical and Benford's distribution of the second digit of the LIBOR interest rate submissions per individual bank from January 2005 to December 2008. It becomes apparent that the large deviations from 2006 to the end of 2007 are not caused by one single bank, but are rather the result of a period when all banks submitted the exact same interest rate.

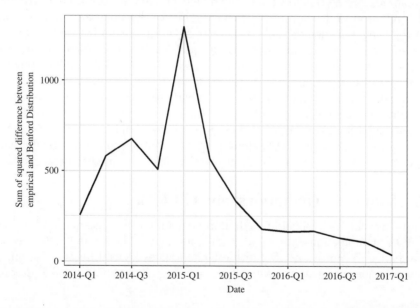

Figure 18.10   Quarterly development of the sum of squared differences between the empirical and Benford's distribution calculated for the second digits of the LIBOR interest rate submissions from February 2014 to February 2017. Although there are still substantial deviations it has to be noted that the absolute level of the sum of squared differences is much lower than during the period from 2005 to 2008.

18.5   Policy Implications

In order to make productive use of this type of digital analysis in identifying fraud and manipulations, they should be accompanied by further considerations. First, any misconduct – whether within companies or on financial markets – is typically triggered by an incentive to misrepresent the data at hand. It is therefore important to keep the incentive structure of the decision environment in mind when conducting an analysis based on Benford's law or similar statistical techniques. Particularly for decisions taken on upper management levels, a consideration of management compensation schemes will be important. In this respect, Morrison and Thanassoulis (2017) show that the fraud-related impact of compensation systems in firms is strongly dependent on the ethical standards of their employees so that strong incentives via bonuses are not necessarily harmful.[13] Second, and equally important, the increasing complexity of the decision environment will raise the ability of market participants to coordinate their behaviour in such a way that the manipulation of data can be concealed efficiently. Examining the conformity with a given dataset using Benford's law in combination with an assessment of the incentive and complexity structure of the corresponding decision should help to enhance the validity and informative power of the analysis' output.

Furthermore, the higher the interests at stake, the more likely it is that manipulators are aware of simple methods such as digital analysis based on Benford's law. From a predator-and-prey perspective, it would be naïve to rely on a routine application of such methods as manipulators could avoid detection at low cost. Instead, continuous effort is required to develop new statistical tools for detecting fraud and manipulation. While any new method, unknown to the agents in the field of application, might work well for some time, more sustainable effects can be achieved if the methods do not allow for an easy adjustment of manipulated data even if they were known. The generalizations of digital analysis based on Benford's law discussed in Section 18.2, which use empirical distributions as a benchmark, represent such an approach.

Finally, from a regulation point of view, it appears rather obvious that benchmarks with a financial impact such as the LIBOR (similar examples include inflation rates used in indexed contracts, GDP determining contributions to international organizations, credit ratings) should not be determined by agents immediately affected.

18.6   Summary, Limitations, and Outlook

Benford's law can be a valuable method to detect fraud, for instance with respect to the LIBOR manipulations. Therefore, regulators such as the United States Securities and Exchange Commission (SEC) or the United States Federal Reserve System (Fed) as well as other organizations with similar responsibilities should make use of tests

---

[13] Irrespective of compensation structures, there is a positive relation of certain individual personality traits, such as narcissism, with fraud (Rijsenbilt and Commandeur, 2013). However, effects of personality traits of individual decision makers will be much more difficult to assess as compared to a general incentive structure invoked by a compensation scheme. For a discussion of incentives and personal characteristics in the context of interviewer falsifications see, e.g. Winker et al. (2015) and Winker (2016).

relying on methods like Benford's law to detect fraudulent behaviour proactively. A stronger focus on statistical methods for fraud detection will also increase the number of lawsuits against companies and employees, which may have a deterrent effect on other potential offenders. Moreover, courts should encourage companies to use statistical methods for identifying first suspicions of a fraud case. However, there is always a risk of errors either due to the properties of a statistical test or due to the fact that not all data considered necessarily follow Benford's law (see also Cleary and Thibodeau (2005)). Therefore, not all significant deviations from the Benford distribution should be taken as conclusive evidence of manipulation. While fabrication of numbers often does result in a deviation (unless the fabricators are aware of checks based on Benford's law – in this case, one would not expect any deviation), even simple rounding can have the same effect. Consequently, non-conformity with Benford's law can be seen as a signal of potential misconduct that might warrant further investigation. As such, Benford's law has become a well-known pre-test in many different fields of manipulation detection. However, for sentencing companies or individuals, courts need a complete chain of evidence based on indisputable facts.

Focusing on fraud prevention in the future, digitalization of the accounting system and new technologies like blockchain technology might make data manipulations more difficult. In detail, blockchain technology can help to implement an automated accounting process especially across companies based on a joint register. In this joint register, all transactions are recorded and cryptographically sealed. Thus, the life cycle of each accounting incident is fully reflected in the blockchain and all relevant documents are stored in the blockchain making data manipulation practically impossible. However, even though the blockchain technology has a lot of potential, to date it is still in the experimental phase. Furthermore, it is recommendable to monitor the development of this technology with a focus on gateways for misconduct. In any case, until blockchain (or an alternative) technology is widely used, detecting fraud remains a crucial issue and, thus, statistical methods are of utmost importance.

Given the limitations of rather simple methods of digital analysis, such as Benford's law, further developments in this field are required. More advanced methods, including those mentioned as generalizations of Benford's law, require more data, e.g., several variables from financial statements. Then, both classical and more recent multivariate classification tools might be used, which exhibit the advantage of making it more difficult for manipulators to adjust their data in a way to remain undetected. Some of these tools require a supervised learning step, and it might be difficult to obtain appropriate data covering already identified manipulated data as well as correct data (Ravisankar et al. 2011). Consequently, the use of other – non-supervised – machine learning tools might be an interesting approach for future research.

References

Abrantes-Metz, R.M., and Villas-Boas, S.B. (2010). Tracking the LIBOR rate. Available at SSRN: https://ssrn.com/abstract=1646600.

Abrantes-Metz, R.M., Villas-Boas, S.B. and Judge, G. (2011). Tracking the LIBOR rate. *Applied Economics Letters* 18: 893–899.

Amiram, D., Bozanic, Z. and Rouen, E. (2015). Financial statement errors. Evidence from the distributional properties of financial statement numbers. *Rev Account Stud* 20: 1540–1593.

Ashton, P. and Christophers, B. (2015). On arbitration, arbitrage and arbitrariness in financial markets and their governance. Unpacking LIBOR and the LIBOR scandal. *Economy and Society* 44: 188–217.

Ausloos, M., Castellano, R. and Cerqueti, R. (2016). Regularities and discrepancies of credit default swaps. A data science approach through Benford's law. *Chaos, Solitons & Fractals* 90: 8–17.

Barabesi, L., Cerasa, A., Cerioli, A. and Perrotta, D. (2018). Goodness-of-fit testing for the Newcomb-Benford law with application to the detection of customs fraud. *Journal of Business & Economic Statistics* 36. 346–358.

Bauer, J. and Groß, J. (2011). Difficulties detecting fraud? The use of Benford's law on regression tables. *Journal of Economics and Statistics* 231: 734–748.

Benford, F. (1938). The law of anomalous numbers. Proceedings of the American Philosophical Society 78, 551–572.

Berger, A., Hill, T.P. and Rogers, E. (2018). Benford online bibliography. http://www.benfordonline.net. 09/25/2018.

Bierstaker, J.L., Brody, R.G. and Pacini, C. (2006). Accountants' perceptions regarding fraud detection and prevention methods. *Managerial Auditing Journal* 21: 520–535.

Board of Governors of the Federal Reserve System (US) (2018). 4-week Treasury bill. Secondary market rate [dtb4wk]. 09/25/2018.

Boyle, J. (1994). An application of Fourier series to the most significant digit problem. *The American Mathematical Monthly* 101: 879–886.

Bredl, S., Storfinger, N. and Menold, N. (2013). A literature review of methods to detect fabricated survey data. In: *Interviewers' deviations in surveys. Impact, reasons, detection and prevention* (eds. N. Menold, P. Winker and R. Porst), 3–24. Frankfurt am Main: Peter Lang.

Bredl, S., Winker, P. and Kötschau, K. (2012). A statistical approach to detect interviewer falsification of survey data. *Survey methodology* 38: 1–10.

Carslaw, C.A.P.N. (1988). Anomalies in income numbers. Evidence of goal oriented behavior. *The Accounting Review* 63: 321–327.

Chenavier, N., Massé, B. and Schneider, D. (2018). Products of random variables and the first digit phenomenon. *Stochastic Processes and their Applications* 128: 1615–1634.

Christian, C.W., Gupta, S. and Lin, S. (1993). Determinants of tax preparer usage. Evidence from panel data. *National Tax Journal* 46: 487–503.

Cleary, R. and Thibodeau, J.C. (2005). Applying digital analysis using Benford's law to detect fraud. The dangers of type i errors. *Auditing* 24: 77–81.

Corazza, M., Ellero, A. and Zorzi, A. (2010). Checking financial markets via Benford's law. The S&P 500 case. In: *Mathematical and Statistical Methods for Actuarial Sciences and Finance* (Eds. M. Corazza and C. Pizzi), 93–102. Milan: Springer Milan.

Deleanu, I.S. (2017). Do countries consistently engage in misinforming the international community about their efforts to combat money laundering? Evidence using Benford's law. *PLOS ONE* 12, e0169632.

Diaconis, P. and Freedman, D. (1979). On rounding percentages. *Journal of the American Statistical Association* 74: 359–364.

Diekmann, A. (2007). Not the first digit! Using Benford's law to detect fraudulent scientific data. *Journal of Applied Statistics* 34: 321–329.

Diekmann, A., and Jann, B. (2010). Benford's law and fraud detection. Facts and legends. *German Economic Review* 11: 397–401.

Drake, P.D. and Nigrini, M.J. (2000). Computer assisted analytical procedures using Benford's law. *Journal of Accounting Education* 18: 127–146.

Dümbgen, L. and Leuenberger, C. (2008). Explicit bounds for the approximation error in Benford's law. *Electronic Communications in Probability* 13: 99–112.

Durtschi, C., Hillison, W. and Pacini, C. (2004). The effective use of Benford's law to assist in detecting fraud in accounting data. *Journal of forensic accounting* 5: 17–34.

El Mouaaouy, F. (2018). Financial crime 'hot spots' – empirical evidence from the foreign exchange market. *The European Journal of Finance* 24: 565–583.

El Mouaaouy, F. and Riepe, J. (2018). Benford and the internal capital market. A useful indicator of managerial engagement. *German Economic Review* 19: 309–329.

Fewster, R.M. (2009). A simple explanation of Benford's law. *The American Statistician* 63: 26–32.

Gauvrit, N. and Delahaye, J.-P. (2011). Scatter and regularity imply Benford's law . . . and more. In: *Randomness Through Computation* (ed. H. Zenil), 53–69. London: World Scientific.

Gonzalez-Garcia, J. and Pastor, G.C. (2009). Benford's law and macroeconomic data quality. IMF Working Paper *WP/09/10*.

Goodman, W. (2016). The promises and pitfalls of Benford's law. *Significance* 13: 38–41.

Gyntelberg, J. and Wooldridge, P. (2008). Interbank rate fixings during the recent turmoil. *BIS Quarterly Review*, March 2008.

Henselmann, K., Ditter, D. and Scherr, E. (2015). Irregularities in accounting numbers and earnings management—a novel approach based on sec XBRL filings. *Journal of Emerging Technologies in Accounting* 12: 117–151.

Hill, T.P. (1988). Random-number guessing and the first digit phenomenon. *Psychological Reports* 62: 967–971.

Hill, T.P. (1995). A statistical derivation of the significant-digit law. *Statistical Science* 10: 354–363.

Hofmarcher, P. and Hornik, K. (2013). First significant digits and the credit derivative market during the financial crisis. *Contemporary Economics* 7: 21–29.

Holz, C.A. (2014). The quality of China's GDP statistics. *China Economic Review* 30: 309–338.

Hürlimann, W. (2006). Benford's law from 1881 to 2006. ArXiv Mathematics e-prints *arXiv:math/0607168*.

Hürlimann, W. (2009). Generalizing Benford's law using power laws. Application to integer sequences. *International Journal of Mathematics and Mathematical Sciences* 2009: 1–10.

Judge, G. and Schechter, L. (2009). Detecting problems in survey data using Benford's law. *Journal of Human Resources* 44: 1–24.

Koedijk, K.G. and Stork, P.A. (1994). Should we care? Psychological barriers in stock markets. *Economics Letters* 44: 427–432.

Ley, E. (1996). On the peculiar distribution of the US stock indexes' digits. *The American Statistician* 50: 311–313.

Ley, E. and Varian, H.R. (1994). Are there psychological barriers in the Dow-Jones index? *Applied Financial Economics* 4: 217–224.

Lin, F., Lin, L.-J., Yeh, C.-C. and Wang, T.-S. (2018). Does the board of directors as fat cats exert more earnings management? Evidence from Benford's law. *The Quarterly Review of Economics and Finance* 68: 158–170.

Lu, F. and Boritz, J.E. (2005). Detecting fraud in health insurance data. Learning to model incomplete Benford's law distributions. In: *Machine Learning: ECML 2005: 16th European Conference on Machine Learning, Porto, Portugal, October 3-7, 2005. Proceedings* (eds. J. Gama, R. Camacho, P.B. Brazdil, A.M. Jorge and L. Torgo), 633–640. Berlin, Heidelberg: Springer.

Michalski, T. and Stoltz, G. (2013). Do countries falsify economic data strategically? Some evidence that they might. *Review of Economics and Statistics* 95: 591–616.

Mir, T.A. and Ausloos, M. (2018). Benford's law. A 'sleeping beauty' sleeping in the dirty pages of logarithmic tables. *Journal of the Association for Information Science and Technology* 69: 349–358.

Mollenkamp, C. (2008). Bankers cast doubt on key rate amid crisis. *Wall Street Journal*, 04/16/2008: 16.

Mollenkamp, C. and Whitehouse, M. (2008). Study casts doubt on key rate. Wall street journal (WSJ) analysis suggests banks may have reported flawed interest data for LIBOR. *Wall Street Journal*, 05/29/2008.

Monticini, A. and Thornton, D.L. (2013). The effect of underreporting on LIBOR rates. *Journal of Macroeconomics* 37: 345–348.

Morrison, A.D. and Thanassoulis, J.E. (2017). Ethical standards and cultural assimilation in financial services. Available at SSRN: https://ssrn.com/abstract=2766996.

Mosimann, J.E., Dahlberg, J., Davidian, N. and Krueger, J. (2002). Terminal digits and the examination of questioned data. *Accountability in Research* 9, 75–92.

Mosimann, J.E., Wiseman, C.V. and Edelman, R.E. (1995). Data fabrication. Can people generate random digits? *Accountability in Research* 4: 31–55.

Newcomb, S. (1881). Note on the frequency of use of the different digits in natural numbers. *American Journal of Mathematics* 4: 39–40.

Nigrini, M. (1994). Using digital frequencies to detect fraud. The white paper (8), 3–6.

Nigrini, M.J. (1996). A taxpayer compliance application of Benford's law. *Journal of the American Taxation Association* 18: 72–91.

Nigrini, M.J. (2012). *Benford's law. Applications for Forensic Accounting, Auditing, and Fraud Detection*. Hoboken, NJ: Wiley.

Nigrini, M.J. and Miller, S.J. (2009). Data diagnostics using second-order tests of Benford's law. *Auditing* 28: 305–324.

Nigrini, M.J. and Mittermaier, L.J. (1997). The use of Benford's law as an aid in analytical procedures. *Auditing* 16: 52–67.

Nye, J. and Moul, C. (2007). The political economy of numbers. On the application of Benford's law to international macroeconomic statistics. *The B.E. Journal of Macroeconomics* 7: Article 17.

OpenStreetMap (2018). Planet dump retrieved from https://planet.Osm.Org.

Pinkham, R.S. (1961). On the distribution of first significant digits. *The Annals of Mathematical Statistics* 32: 1223–1230.

Raimi, R.A. (1976). The first digit problem. *The American Mathematical Monthly* 83: 521–538.

Rauch, B., Göttsche, M., Brähler, G. and Engel, S. (2011). Fact and fiction in EU-governmental economic data. *German Economic Review* 12: 243–255.

Rauch, B., Göttsche, M., El Mouaaouy, F. and Geidel, F. (2013). Empirical methods in competition analysis applying Benford's law to the western Australian petroleum market. Available at SSRN: https://ssrn.com/abstract=2364384.

Ravisankar, P., Ravi, V., Raghava Rao, G. and Bose, I. (2011). Detection of financial statement fraud and feature selection using data mining techniques. *Decision Support Systems* 50: 491–500.

Rijsenbilt, A. and Commandeur, H. (2013). Narcissus enters the courtroom. Chief executive officer (CEO) narcissism and fraud. *Journal of Business Ethics* 117: 413–429.

Rodriguez, R.J. (2004). First significant digit patterns from mixtures of uniform distributions. *The American Statistician* 58: 64–71.

Rogers, S. The LIBOR rate submissions by each bank, 2005 to 2008. *The Guardian*, 07/03/2012.

Schräpler, J.-P. (2011). Benford's law as an instrument for fraud detection in surveys using the data of the socio-economic panel (SOEP). *Journal of Economics and Statistics* 231: 685–718.

Schündeln, M. (2018). Multiple visits and data quality in household surveys. *Oxford Bulletin of Economics and Statistics* 80: 380–405.

Shi, J., Ausloos, M. and Zhu, T. (2018). Benford's law first significant digit and distribution distances for testing the reliability of financial reports in developing countries. *Physica A: Statistical Mechanics and its Applications* 492: 878–888.

Smith, S.W. (1997). *The Scientist and Engineer's Guide to Digital Signal Processing*. San Diego, CA: California Technical Publishing.

Stenfors, A. (2018). Bid–ask spread determination in the FX swap market. Competition, collusion or a convention? *Journal of International Financial Markets, Institutions and Money* 54: 78–97.

Thomas, J.K. (1989). Unusual patterns in reported earnings. *The Accounting Review* 64: 773–787.

Tödter, K.-H. (2009). Benford's law as an indicator of fraud in economics. *German Economic Review* 10: 339–351.

Ullmann, R. and Watrin, C. (2017). Detecting target-driven earnings management based on the distribution of digits. *Journal of Business Finance & Accounting* 44: 63–93.

Wallace, W.A. (2002). Assessing the quality of data used for benchmarking and decision-making. *The Journal of Government Financial Management* 51: 18–22.

Watrin, C., Struffert, R. and Ullmann, R. (2008). Benford's law. An instrument for selecting tax audit targets? *Review of Managerial Science* 2: 219–237.

Wheatley, M. (2012). *The Wheatley review of LIBOR*. Final report. London: HM Treasury.

Winker, P. (2016). Assuring the quality of survey data. Incentives, detection and documentation of deviant behavior. *Statistical Journal of the IAOS* 32: 295–303.

Winker, P., Kruse, K.-W., Menold, N. and Landrock, U. (2015). Interviewer effects in real and falsified interviews. Results from a large scale experiment. *Statistical Journal of the IAOS* 31. 423–434.

Winter, C., Schneider, M. and Yannikos, Y. (2012). Model-based digit analysis for fraud detection overcomes limitations of Benford analysis, 255–261. *2012 Seventh International Conference on Availability,* Reliability and *Security*.

18.A   Appendix

Table 18.3   Drake and Nigrini (2000) propose the mean absolute deviation (MAD) of digit frequencies as an alternative to the χ^2-statistic. Given that no theoretical results are available on the probability distribution of their statistics, categories corresponding to differing degrees of conformity to Benford's law are provided following their proposal.

Digits	Range	Conclusion
First Digits	0.000 to 0.006	Close conformity
	0.006 to 0.012	Acceptable conformity
	0.012 to 0.015	Marginally acceptable conformity
	Above 0.015	Nonconformity
Second Digits	0.000 to 0.008	Close conformity
	0.008 to 0.010	Acceptable conformity
	0.010 to 0.012	Marginally acceptable conformity
	Above 0.012	Nonconformity
First-Two Digits	0.0000 to 0.0012	Close conformity
	0.0012 to 0.0018	Acceptable conformity
	0.0018 to 0.0022	Marginally acceptable conformity
	Above 0.0022	Nonconformity
First-Three Digits	0.00000 to 0.00036	Close conformity
	0.00036 to 0.00044	Acceptable conformity
	0.00044 to 0.00050	Marginally acceptable conformity
	Above 0.00050	Nonconformity

Part V

Regulation and Enforcement

Chapter 19

The Enforcement of Financial Market Crimes in Canada and the United Kingdom

Anita Indira Anand*
University of Toronto

19.1   Introduction

Strong enforcement of the law governing financial markets improves investment, reduces information asymmetries among corporations and investors, and prevents adverse selection (Christensen et al. 2016; Coffee Jr. 2007). It has proven to be a deterrent, signalling to potential wrongdoers that criminal activity has serious consequences (Harvard Law Review 1979). It can also provide victims of crime with compensation for their losses (Luedtke 2014). Despite these benefits, developed market economies, including those under consideration here, struggle to develop

* My sincere thanks to Douglas Cumming and Kenneth Jull for comments and to Adil Abdulla, Jason Lamb, Tegan Valentine, Jamil Visram and Alvin Yau for excellent research assistance funded by the Law Foundation of Ontario. This article was written in 2018.

comprehensive systems which allow for the successful prosecution of financial crime. Indeed, the law of financial market crime is perhaps the most poorly enforced branch of criminal law.

This chapter undertakes a comparative analysis of the enforcement of financial market crimes in Canada and the United Kingdom. In both jurisdictions, financial market crimes have low enforcement rates for a multiplicity of reasons common to both jurisdictions. First, financial market crimes appear to be a relatively low priority for law enforcement officials who are required to devote increasing resources to violent crimes. Second, law enforcement infrastructure lacks financial resources which undermines the investigation and prosecution of financial market crime and fraud cases. Third, technology has allowed new types of fraud to develop, with insufficient human and financial resources to deal with them. Fourth, past treatment of financial market criminals as pillars of the community who have merely had a fall from grace has weakened public perceptions of the harm caused by these crimes (Archibald, Jull, and Roach 2015, INT-11; Soltes 2016, p. 29).

Despite the existence of agencies and regulators specially designated to address these issues, there seems to be no formal and effective strategy in either jurisdiction to tackle the problem of financial market enforcement. The problems with enforcement are not exclusively legal, and cannot be solved through legal reform alone (Anand 2008). Nevertheless, reform to the law is warranted in both jurisdictions. In particular, as this chapter argues, reform should dedicate greater resources to financial market criminal enforcement, introduce principles-based regulation, facilitate inter-agency coordination, and pursue other targeted regulatory reforms.

While there is no universally accepted definition of 'financial market crime,' the term typically refers to 'any non-violent crime that generally results in a financial loss' (IMF 2001). Building on this broad definition, this chapter will discuss these much-needed reform proposals after critically examining the relevant scholarship and comparative enforcement issues in Canada and the UK. Section 19.2 lays the groundwork by examining the key themes that emerge in existing academic writing. Section 19.3 focuses on the differing institutional and legal characteristics of each jurisdiction. Section 19.4 examines the viability of various reform proposals. Section 19.5 concludes.

19.2   Existing Scholarship

If one accepts that under-enforcement of financial market crimes is an issue, one must ask why this is the case. The literature provides many potential responses, including (i) the complexity of financial crimes, (ii) a lack of coordination among enforcement agencies, (iii) legislative reluctance to acknowledge the importance of corporate culture, (iv) the lack of public awareness of financial crime, and (v) the ability of corporations to evade prosecution.

First, some scholars argue that the complexity of financial market crimes, paired with the high burden of proof in criminal law, renders prosecution difficult and ultimately leads to lower enforcement. The first problem presented by complexity is detection. Kempa (2010) highlights the difficulty in this area, particularly for complex financial crimes like market manipulation and insider trading. He argues that these sophisticated offences are more difficult to detect, investigate, and prosecute than simpler financial crimes like fraud and money laundering, leading to lower rates of effective resolution for the more sophisticated crimes (Kempa 2010, p. 256).

In a cross-country analysis, La Porta et al. (2006) study various legal obligations, from criminal sanctions to disclosure requirements, to determine whether securities laws result in stronger capital markets and better investor protection. They find that outside of initial public offerings (IPOs), criminal sanctions were insignificant in promoting positive behaviour. They speculate that the inefficacy of deterrence may arise from the difficulty in proving criminal intent on the part of directors, distributors, and accountants who omit material information or make misrepresentations in disclosure (La Porta 2006, p. 21). Along these lines, Anand has argued that the difficulty of proving mens rea has important procedural implications, often pushing a case into an administrative tribunal where criminal sanctions cannot be applied because they are ultra vires the securities regulator's legislative authority (Anand 2007).

The problem of complexity as a barrier to enforcement of law relating to financial crime may be exacerbated by the question of corporate liability. Laws relating to corporate crime are often under-enforced, partly as a consequence of the costs associated with finding liability in a complex corporate structure. For example, Bittle and Snider (2011, p. 374) note that corporate criminal laws relating to workplace safety enacted in the early 2000s quickly fell into a state of 'virtual disuse'. They argue that the enforcement of corporate criminal liability for workplace safety was limited for both practical and ideological reasons, directed only at 'small companies where there was . . . little difficulty tracing the chain of responsibility throughout the organization', and therefore lower investigation costs (Bittle and Snider 2011, pp. 378–380). By contrast, multinational corporations – often characterized by multilayered decision-making and complex levels of accountability – complicate the process of assigning criminal responsibility (Bittle and Snider 2011, p. 380). Bittle and Snider (2011, p. 383) suggest that laws creating corporate liability for financial offences encounter similar issues.

Archibald, Jull, and Roach (2015) counter that Canada's Bill C-45 constitutes a fundamental change, if not a revolution, in corporate criminal liability. It effectively replaces the traditional legal concept of corporate liability based on the fault of the corporation's 'directing mind(s)', the board of directors and those with the power to set corporate policy, with liability tied to the fault of all of the corporation's 'senior officers'. (Archibald, Jull, and Roach 2015, INT:40:10) That definition includes all those employees, agents or contractors who play 'an important role in the establishment of an organization's policies' or who have responsibility 'for managing an important aspect of the organization's activities'. (Archibald, Jull, and Roach 2015 INT:40:10) It is no longer necessary for prosecutors to prove fault in the boardrooms or at the highest levels of corporations: the fault of even middle managers may suffice.

The first decision interpreting corporate criminal liability in Canada after the introduction of the new law was contained in *R c Pétrols Global Inc* [2012] JQ No 5437. The case was the first litigated case in Canada to test the parameters of the Criminal Code's corporate criminal liability provisions. Citing Archibald et al., Justice Tôth held that 'It will no longer be necessary for prosecutors to prove fault in the boardrooms or at the highest levels of a corporation: the fault even of middle managers may suffice'. On 17 April 2015, Justice Tôth imposed a $1 million fine on Global Fuels in *R c Pétrols Global Inc* 2015 QCCS 1618. This case's importance rests in its affirmation that corporations can be penalized for the actions of middle-level territory managers, even where there is no evidence that the head office of the company was aware of the misconduct.

The wide reach of organizational criminal liability is illustrated by the groundbreaking case of *R. v. Metron Construction Corp.* 2013 ONCA 541. Metron entered a plea of guilty to a count of criminal negligence causing death on the basis of the actions of an independent contractor who met the definition of a 'senior officer' of Metron by virtue of his management of an important aspect of the business at the site where workers were tragically killed. The Court of Appeal increased the fine imposed on Metron and, most importantly, observed that a corporation should not be permitted to distance itself from culpability due to the corporate individual's rank on the corporate ladder.

The case of *Metron* affirms the fundamental change brought by Bill C-45 and will have far-reaching effects in areas such as foreign corrupt practices where the hiring of agents is a major risk factor. In the context of workplace safety, criminal convictions against corporations underline the seriousness of workplace safety. In *R. v. Stave Lake Quarries Inc.* 2016 BCPC 377, a worker was killed at work when a rock hauler that she had been operating rolled over and crushed her to death. The defendant corporation was the worker's employer. The corporation entered a guilty plea to one count of criminal negligence causing the worker's death. By entering its guilty plea, the company acknowledged that, through one or more of its senior officers, it showed wanton or reckless disregard for the worker's life (Archibald Jull, and Roach 2015, INT:40:10).

A second factor that elucidates the enforcement problems inherent in the prosecution of financial crimes is the lack of coordination among different entities responsible for investigating and regulating financial crime. Canada has 50 entities (including public police, provincial regulators, and self-regulating organizations) involved in enforcement (Kempa 2010, p. 255). Effective coordination and information sharing among so many institutions are near impossible (Kempa 2010, p. 255). In the European Union and the UK, the story is similar. For example, Tupman (2010, p. 159) lists the EU Office de Lutte Antifraude (OLAF), the Court of Auditors, the Budgetary Committee of the European Parliament, Europol and Eurojust as all playing a role in financial market crime enforcement and argues that there are 'too many cooks in the kitchen'. The issue of reform, which will be addressed in Section 19.4 below, is very much a question of how to address financial markets with multiple regulatory institutions.

The third factor relates to the way in which external parties, particularly legislators, view corporate wrongdoing. Kempa, like Bittle and Snider, refers to malignant corporate cultures – notably prevalent in the Enron and WorldCom collapses – as the source for many financial market crimes. Yet legislation passed in response to these collapses fails to assign liability for stewardship of a corporation's culture (Bittle and Snider 2011, p. 379). Bittle and Snider (2011, p. 380) suggest that legislators have been inherently sympathetic to corporations, believing that they should not be restrained too stringently for fear of chilling profit-making activity. Kempa (2010, p. 256) argues that 'research suggests that unfair and unscrupulous trading practices create a broader culture of corruption and criminal behaviour in the market sphere, wherein individuals are likely to rationalize and neutralize their own criminal conduct.'

Fourth, the enforcement of financial market crimes may suffer due to a lack of awareness of these crimes on the part of the investing public. This is true despite the widespread impact of white collar crime on investors in the capital markets. The Canadian Securities Administrators (CSA) (2007) estimate that 1 in 20 Canadians have been victimized by investment fraud. In the United Kingdom, a 2017 survey estimates that the costs of fraud to the UK economy is £190 billion – an amount greater than the UK government's entire 2017 expenditure on healthcare (Sims 2017).

Despite significant costs to investors, research suggests that the public underestimates the prevalence of the problem, either because they are unaware or because they downplay the importance of financial crime (Bittle and Snider 2011). Button and Tunley (2015, p. 54) state that 'many victims of fraud do not know they are victims, or elect not to report the incident.' Meanwhile, prosecutors' focus has shifted from fraud investigation to asset recovery, which potentially means fewer investigations in proportion to resources spent (Gannon and Doig 2010, p. 57). In some cases, an increase in resources has meant a decrease in enforcement actions but the reasons for this decrease are unclear: they may be due to higher compliance rather than more effective and more active enforcement (Lohse, Pascalau, and Thomann 2014, p. 209).

The fifth and final factor that contributes to the ineffective enforcement of financial crimes is perhaps the most malign: corporations with large resources are in some cases able to avoid prosecutions by navigating and negotiating the enforcement process. Depending on the applicable laws, corporations can engage in informal arrangements and making tacit agreements with regulators or competitors (Bittle and Snider 2011, p. 383). Sometimes, attempts to avoid enforcement proceedings are explicit. Major players have the resources to devise sophisticated legal challenges and impossibly novel strategies of defiance, obstruction and delay – reducing enforcement effectiveness. Bittle and Snider (2011, p. 383) describe 'transnational corporations with entire departments dedicated to devising ever more sophisticated legal challenges and impossibly novel strategies of defiance, obstruction and delay', sometimes bringing the authorities 'death by 42 boxes of documents'. As Anand and Green (2018) demonstrate, these players often settle. One such strategy is litigation or prelitigation paperwork, including swamping the agency in paper, emails and memoranda that have nothing to do with the investigation (Anand and Green 2018). Kedia and Rajgopal (2011, p. 271) show that where firms think the SEC is more willing to invest resources into enforcement, firms are less likely to misreport income.

19.3   Comparative Analysis

After this review of some of the applicable literature, we move to consider the enforcement of financial market crimes in Canada and the United Kingdom from a comparative perspective. Much of the examination entails an analysis of the institutions that comprise each country's enforcement regimes.

19.3.1   Canada

Financial market crimes in Canada include illegal securities distributions, fraud, registrant misconduct, illegal insider trading, disclosure violations, and market manipulation (Canadian Securities Administrators 2016, p. 10). These crimes are not prosecuted by or under the CSA, which is merely an umbrella organization with no legal or constitutional authority. Instead, financial crimes in Canada are regulated under a combination of provincial securities laws (e.g. in Ontario, Sections 122 and 126.1 of the Securities Act), federal statutes (e.g. the offence of corruption/bribery in the Corruption of Foreign Public Officials Act), the Criminal Code (e.g. fraud under section 380 or insider trading under section 382), and civil liability offences (e.g. the tort of fraud). The burden of proof is high and the rules of criminal procedure apply if the trial takes place in a court room (Bittle and Snider 2011, p. 383). Fraud investigations often get bogged down in protracted and complex legal proceedings against well-funded corporations (Bittle and Snider 2011, p. 374).

But who enforces the law? The answer begins with the Constitution Act, which divides power over economic conduct between the federal and provincial governments. Under the Constitution Act 1867, the federal government has jurisdiction to make rules respecting 'the Regulation of Trade and Commerce' and 'the Criminal Law', while the provinces have jurisdiction to make rules respecting 'Property and Civil Rights in the Province.' A long line of cases proclaims the constitutional validity of provincial jurisdiction over securities regulation, meaning that each province and territory has its own securities regulator (*Renvoi relative à la réglementation pancanadienne des valeurs mobilières*, 2017 QCCA 756). This structure means that the rules relating to the enforcement of financial crime can (and do) differ as between provincial and territorial jurisdictions with the federal government playing a role given its authority in area of criminal law (Wise Persons' Committee 2003, p. 29). In *Reference Re Securities Act* 2011 SCC 66, the Supreme Court of Canada upheld this constitutional division of powers.

From a practical standpoint, the enforcement of financial market crimes in Canada thus draws on both provincial securities laws (the 'regulatory law') and the *Criminal Code* (the 'criminal law'). An enforcement action in Canada starts with a tip, passed on to criminal or regulatory authorities, that indicates some form of wrongdoing has occurred. This tip is then sent on to a self-regulatory organization (e.g. the Investment Industry Regulatory Organization of Canada), a provincial regulatory authority (e.g. the Ontario Securities Commission), or a law enforcement agency such as the IMET or local police officials (Canadian Securities Administrators 2007, p. 10). At this point, the relevant enforcement agency evaluates the potential wrongdoing, and determines whether the alleged misconduct should be subject to an administrative tribunal or court proceeding. This structure may change if a new cooperative market regulator, proposed by some provinces in tandem with the federal government, is implemented (Government of Canada et al. 2013; Department of Finance (Canada) 2014; Government of Canada 2014).

The Canadian system is often criticized for being inefficient especially when compared to nations such as the United States (Bhattacharya 2006; Coffee Jr 2007) or Australia (Barbiero 2008). Many argue that the absence of a centralized securities regulator results in inconsistent law across the country and leaves investors unsure of whether wrongdoing in one provincial jurisdiction would be classified as such in another (FAIR Canada 2014; Anand 2017). A clear example of Canadian enforcement inefficiency can be seen in fines and penalties collections. In 2016, Canadian securities enforcement officials heard a total of 109 cases, ordered \$62.1 million in fines and administrative penalties, and called for an additional \$349.7 million in disgorgement, restitution, and compensation fees (Canadian Securities Administrators 2017, pp. 12–16). This number is substantial, yet Canada's enforcement agencies have historically struggled to collect such fines. Analysts peg the current amount of unpaid securities fines in Canada at over \$1.1 billion (Robertson and Cardoso 2017). That number continues to increase, and the amount owed to securities regulators in Canada climbed 22.5% between 2015 and 2017 (Robertson and Cardoso 2017). The poor collection of financial market penalties is not unique to securities fines. In 2006, 36.5% of all fraud cases led to losses that were never recovered (Peltier-Rivest and Lanoue 2015).These disconcerting statistics, coupled with the anonymity regulators have granted fine paying corporations in the past (Nicol, Seglins, and Niles 2017), suggests that enforcement orders are not playing the deterrent role that they should in Canada's capital markets.

19.3.2 The United Kingdom

The UK's regulation of financial markets is not subject to the same somewhat disjointed constitutional structure as is present in Canada. The prosecution of financial market crimes in the UK is relegated to Members of Parliament, who have created a series of legal instruments to protect the public. The Financial Services Act 2012, c 21, Pt II, s 6 defines a 'financial crime' as 'any offence involving – fraud or dishonesty; misconduct in, or misuse of information relating to, a financial market; handling the proceeds of crime, or the financing of terrorism'. The Criminal Justice Act 1993 handles cases of insider trading, while the Bribery Act 2010 addresses situations involving corruption and bribery. Despite the fact that the UK voted in favour of independence from the EU under referendum, regulations set out by the EU are in effect throughout the UK at present. These regulations provide victims with avenues to seek civil compensation for losses suffered as a result of financial crime (*Regulation (EU) No 596/2014*).

As in Canada, the UK's enforcement regime is based on both criminal and regulatory law. Unlike Canada, the UK has centralized financial market regulation and is not subject to a complicated regional approach to securities regulation. In the UK, financial market crimes are enforced predominantly through three market regulation agencies: the Financial Conduct Authority (FCA), the Serious Fraud Office (SFO), and the Office of Financial Sanctions Implementation.

The FCA is a successor to the Financial Services Authority (FSA), which was formerly the sole regulatory body overseeing all market activities, a role now shared by the FCA and the Prudential Regulation Authority (PRA) run by the Bank of England. Both authorities were established on 1 April 2013 pursuant to the Financial Services Act 2012. The FCA acts as an independent conduct regulator, while also providing advice on financial crime. It oversees 58,000 financial services firms and financial markets in the UK and is the prudential regulator for over 18,000 of those firms whereas the PRA is the prudential regulator of around 1,500 banks, building societies, credit unions, insurers and major investment firms (Financial Conduct Authority 2018a). Within this framework, smaller, specialized offices exist to deal with more specific financial criminal offences such as bribery. For example, the Office for Professional Body Anti-Money Laundering Supervision (OPBAS) is a new regulator set up by the government to strengthen the UK's anti-money laundering (AML) supervisory regime and monitor existing professional body AML supervisors (Financial Conduct Authority 2018b).

Working closely with the FCA, the SFO deals with the 'top level of serious or complex fraud, bribery and corruption' (Serious Fraud Office 2018a). Moreover, the Office of Financial Sanctions Implementation is trusted with ensuring financial sanctions are property implemented and enforced (Swift 2013). These three bodies liaise with UK criminal law officials to investigate potential instances of financial market crime, evaluate wrongdoing, and impose punishment on offenders.

While the UK's approach to financial market regulation is more integrated than Canada's, the use of multiple agencies is a source of weakness (Fishman 1991). The occurrence of financial market crime in the UK is on the rise (fraudulent activities in the UK surpassed £1 billion in 2017) (Treanor 2017), yet the quantity and size of fines levied and collected by the various agencies has dropped (Patton and McHugh 2016). Critics have blamed the structure of the UK's financial market enforcement regime for this deficit, arguing that the sheer number of bodies involved in prosecuting a violation lends itself to inefficiency (Fishman 1991). Others have described the reduction in fines since 2015/2016 as a return to normal (Binham 2015; Ring 2017b). Analysts have called on the UK to adopt a streamlined, zealous approach to enforcement – with many calling for the country to extend its regime of corporate liability to match that of the more stringent American system (Ring 2017a).

Furthermore, as previously mentioned, Canada and the United Kingdom have dramatically different approaches to dividing up enforcement jurisdiction for financial market crimes. In Canada, while the federal government has the jurisdiction over the criminal law, each province or territory can regulate financial market crime within its borders, and this regulation can be supported by a variety of federal law enforcement agencies and specialty self-regulatory organizations (Kempa 2010, p. 255; Wise Persons' Committee 2003). Canada's multitude of agencies with overlapping mandates means that financial crimes that are not high-profile enough to attract national attention can slip through the cracks (Gray and McFarland 2013). Victims of financial crime are often shuffled from agency to agency, in an attempt to find someone with the time and expertise to investigate – a process further complicated by the fact that victims and regulators do not have a streamlined method to determine if the same crime is already being investigated in another province (Gray and McFarland 2013).

In the United Kingdom, Parliament possesses the authority to regulate financial markets, and financial market crime is prosecuted by three distinct market regulatory agencies. While market regulation is more centralized, both the UK and Canadian systems rely on multiple agencies – and require those agencies to work together for the system to properly function. Theoretically, this integrated approach to financial market crime enforcement should work. Yet in both countries, problems have arisen as regulators struggle to determine which agency (or agencies) should be responsible for tackling a specific financial crime, and handle issues of information sharing between national and local law enforcement teams (Wise Persons' Committee 2003). This lack of proper coordination has hampered officials in both Canada and the United Kingdom as they attempt to prosecute and prevent financial market crime.

Financial crime rates are on the rise and it is unclear whether the enforcement mechanisms in place in Canada and the UK effectively prevent and deter financial market crimes. Many of these recommendations are obvious (both countries need to allocate additional resources to financial crimes, both countries should clear up the jurisdictional clouds that hang over financial market crime prosecution), while others are decidedly less so (both countries should consider a movement towards principle-based regulation).

19.4   Reform

Having examined both the literature and the structure of the enforcement of financial market crimes in Canada and the UK, we move now to examine three reform proposals relating to: resource allocation; principles-based regulation; and, targeted regulatory reforms, including those aimed at stronger regulatory coordination. Some of the ways that coordinated enforcement mechanisms could bolster compliance include securing more convictions through concentrated expertise, and using resources more efficiently by combating information mismanagement.

19.4.1   Resource Allocation

While the unique regulatory frameworks of Canada and the UK have created their own distinct challenges, certain enforcement issues are common across jurisdictions. Notably, the enforcement of financial market crime in both countries has been hampered by the common issues of constrained resources and a general lack of clarity regarding which level of government or agency has jurisdiction over enforcement.

Studies suggest that allocating public resources to the enforcement of financial market crimes has a positive effect on an economy's activity in this sector (Jackson and Roe 2009, p. 237). Investing in enforcement not only allows for a system better to identify and prosecute wrongdoers but also attracts investors by signalling a commitment to market integrity. As a result, countries with strong financial market enforcement systems see a variety of economic benefits, including increases in stock market capitalization, trading volumes, the number of active domestic firms, and the number of IPOs launched within their borders (Jackson and Roe 2009; La Porta et al. 1998; La Porta et al. 1997). Allocating resources toward financial market enforcement has a positive impact on domestic markets. Specifically, Cumming, Johan, and Li (2011) find that trading activity is positively impacted by specificity in rules relating to insider trading and market manipulation, but is not significantly impacted by rules pertaining to broker–agency conflict. They conclude that having specific regulations surrounding insider trading and market manipulation are important for facilitating efficient trading activity and decreasing volatility in the market. In short, regulatory change increases stock market liquidity. (Cumming, Johan, and Li 2011; Cumming and Johan, 2017).

One of the key problems plaguing Canadian and UK financial market enforcement agencies is a general absence of adequate resources, fuelled by a combination of poor political support (Ring and Wild 2018), minimal financial investment, and a lack of adequate regulatory staffing. Increased funding would signal a stronger commitment to investor protection and would also improve each country's ability to conduct market surveillance, investigate firms for wrongdoing, bring about successful enforcement actions, and develop stronger regulatory rules. In their empirical work, Jackson and Roe find that countries allocate sharply differing levels of resources to financial oversight. Where financial activity plays a large role in the domestic economy, countries (such as Luxembourg and Hong Kong) allocate have the highest staffing and budgets (Jackson and Roe 2009, p. 216). But other countries have less 'regulatory intensity'. Canada reports nearly 39 regulators staffing their securities agency per million of population whereas Spain, with a comparable GDP, reports only slightly more than eight staffers per million of population (Jackson and Roe 2009). In short, the variation among countries in terms of resource allocation is significant.

Lacking adequate resources, enforcement agencies tend to be reactive – investigating and prosecuting financial crimes after the harm has been done to investors, creditors and the market (Dooley and Radke 2010). Though more resources would improve the ability of enforcement agencies to investigate and successfully prosecute offenders; more significantly, an increase in funding would allow agencies to invest in proactive measures by conducting better market oversight. Additional resources can be allocated to more in-depth and frequent reviews of market participants and their financial reports. As demonstrated by Kedia and Rajgopal, an increase in resources allocated to oversight activities is a valuable preventative measure, reducing the likelihood that firms misreport key financial results and stemming fraudulent activities before they cause harm to potential victims (Kedia and Rajgopal 2011, p. 271).

19.4.2   Principles-Based Regulation

As regulators in Canada and the UK attempt to prosecute financial crime, they are hamstrung by existing regulations, which are currently based around a collection of so-called 'bright-line rules'. These rules set out clearly defined standards, and leave little room for variation or judicial interpretation. While this approach may work for more conventional crimes, in constantly evolving and unpredictable areas of law like financial market crime, bright-line rules create legal loopholes, allowing wrongdoers to skirt the justice system (Ford 2010). Instead of the current system of bright-line rules, regulators in Canada and the UK should consider moving towards a less rigid, principles-based system of financial market governance.

As the term suggests, 'principles-based regulation' consists of guiding principles to be considered when making enforcement decisions. The goal of adopting principles-based regulation is to provide regulators, and courts, with a degree of flexibility, which combats the key failings associated with conventional rules-based systems (Ford 2010). Successful principles-based regulation systems in financial market crime exist in many countries and, according to Professor Ford, share three common characteristics. First, regulators in principles-based systems must have sufficient capacity to handle the volume of financial market crime. This includes capacity in terms of numbers, access to information, and expertise. Second, regulation in a principles-based system should focus on the impact of complexity on the financial markets, and on their regulation. Finally, in regulating financial market crime, regulators should move away from an expertise-based, technocratic model of regulation in favour of a broader participatory model (Ford 2010).

A rules-based system is often championed because it provides a clear standard of conduct that is easier to apply consistently and provides certainty for market participants. However, an endless list of rules can lead to gaps and inconsistencies in the regulation, and often encourages firms to engage in 'creative compliance', contravening the spirit of the rules (Black, Hopper, and Band 2007, p. 193). A principle operates differently; it expresses a high-level and substantive objective – for instance transparent communication with investors – but relies on firms to devise strategies in concert with the regulator to satisfy the requirement (Allen 2013, p. 187). In a principles-based system, the regulator's role in determining compliance becomes an assessment of whether the firm exercised reasonable judgment in fulfilling the objective of the principle (Allen 2013, p. 32). Principles can lead to more substantive compliance in line with the purpose of the rules, as opposed to a 'check-the-boxes' approach, because they require firms to think through how to best comply. As such, a principles-based system can be more effective in engaging senior management as opposed to reducing compliance to a task handled by a team of corporate lawyers (Black, Hopper, and Band 2007, p. 193).

Jurisdictions that employ a principles-based system detail three main benefits: responsiveness in that principles which focus on substantive outcomes are more able to adapt to a rapidly changing market environment than a system based on prescriptive rules; accessibility, since principles are far more accessible to senior management and smaller firms as opposed to a confusing list of detailed rules; and, fostering effective compliance, since principles are more effective in requiring firms to comply in a manner consistent with the spirit of the rules especially in cases where a large volume of detailed provisions often diverts attention towards adhering to the letter of the law (Financial Services Authority 2007, p. 6). A principles-based system is designed to increase the accountability of senior management and adapt to changing market circumstances. In theory, therefore principles then provide a wider range of prosecution opportunities for enforcement agencies when financial crimes are committed and prosecuted.

Beyond allowing for increased prosecution, adopting a more flexible approach to securities enforcement could have another beneficial impact on regulation in Canada and the UK – namely an increase in the speed of prosecution. In Canada, enforcement actions are often subject to long delays that 'consume valuable investigative and prosecutorial resources, making it more difficult to investigate and prosecute other cases of market misconduct' (Schwartz 2009, p. 342). Studies have shown that adopting a more flexible approach to financial market crime enforcement can address the legal procedural delays that often hinder effective and efficient law enforcement (Canadian Securities Administrators 2017). Adopting a principles-based model of regulation could alleviate some of the stress placed on both the Canada and UK system, allowing for a simplified prosecution process.

19.4.3   Targeted Regulatory Reforms

Perhaps the single largest challenge facing the prosecution of financial market crime in Canada and the UK is the complicated patchwork of laws that govern the subject. In Canada regulation of the capital markets largely falls within the jurisdiction of each province and territory. This results in enforcement challenges, as both regulations and their enforcement are to some extent inconsistent across jurisdictional lines (Lortie and Hockin 2011). Attempts have been made in the past to create a unified federal regulator. In *Reference Re Securities Act* 2011 SCC 66, the Supreme Court of Canada rejected the federal government's proposed statute on the basis that it fell outside the general trade and commerce power in the Constitution. However, the Court held that it is within the power of the federal and provincial governments to work together to create a 'cooperative market regulator'. The proposed Cooperative Capital Markets Regulatory System (CCMR) is the direct result of such cooperative efforts. The project, which is a joint initiative between federal government and 6 of Canada's 13 provinces and territories, was originally slated to take effect by 1 July 2018. Instead the proposed regulator has been hampered by various delays, and was the subject of a second Supreme Court of Canada case questioning the constitutionality of the CCMR (*Renvoi relative à la réglementation pancanadienne des valeurs mobilières*, 2017 QCCA 756).

In the UK, the regulatory and enforcement framework has also had a fragmented history but is not subject to the constitutional challenges that Canada has faced. This fragmentation necessarily impacts the quality of financial law enforcement. The transition from the unified FSA to the parallel FCA and PRA structure increases the risk of duplicative procedures and inattention to firms that are subject to dual regulation. The two agencies maintain a Memorandum of Understanding designed to minimize overlap in their relationship and facilitate information sharing. Each has committed to refrain from 'introducing, inadvertently, requirements which are inconsistent or conflict with those introduced by, or are under serious consideration by, another Authority' and to 'working closely together, and to communicating effectively and promptly in order to ensure that regulatory actions are coordinated' if a major participant in a payment system risks default (Financial Services (Banking Reform) Act 2013: Memorandum of Understanding 2018, paras 24, 26). While such high-level commitment suggests a concerted effort to avert an overly fragmented regulatory regime, the memorandum's remedy for persistent conflict among the authorities over strategies, requirements, or policy is to ensure that 'the issue [is] escalated to the senior management' (Financial Services (Banking Reform) Act 2013: Memorandum of Understanding 2018, para 27).

Relying on leadership to reconcile differences over enforcement strategies may lead to intractable disputes that distract from the purposes of the bifurcated system. For instance, an accused entity may be a major financial institution subject to dual regulation, the prosecution of which would serve the FCA's mandate to maintain the integrity of the capital markets but hinder the PRA's interest in ensuring the stability of such firms. The memorandum also allows each authority to depart from its arrangement under exceptional circumstances where urgent action is required, which may conceivably encompass enforcement actions against serious financial crimes (Financial Services (Banking Reform) Act 2013: Memorandum of Understanding 2018, para 38).

The proliferation of specialized enforcement offices within the FCA is further indicative of fragmentation. Despite the drawbacks of coordination across disparate entities, amalgamating agencies may also present difficulties. The Conservative majority government under Prime Minister Theresa May proposed folding the SFO and integrating it as part of the National Crime Agency (a law enforcement agency that targets 'serious and organized criminals') (National Crime Agency 2018). Commentators in the financial press have been critical about the lack of effective enforcement given the regulatory fragmentation in the UK and its associated lack of dedicated resources (Ring and Wild 2018; Tennant 2016).

Both Canada and the UK have moved toward allowing prosecutors to enter into 'deferred prosecution agreements' (DPAs) with offending corporations (Roach et al. 2017). The Government of Canada created a deferred prosecution programme following public consultations (Public Services and Procurement Canada 2018; Bill C-74). The deferred agreements are termed 'Remediation Agreements' which are defined as 'an agreement, between an organization accused of having committed an offence and a prosecutor, to stay any proceedings related to that offence if the organization complies with the terms of the agreement' (Criminal Code, s 715.3(1)). This is a complex new regime.

A DPA combines traditional financial market crime sanctions with mandated changes to an organization's structure (e.g. required education and training on ethics and best practices in addition to the creation of new or improved compliance programs). Proponents argue that the organizational changes made under a DPA not only allow corporations to better understand the consequences of financial crime, but create systems within corporations that make it more difficult for financial market crime to occur, and more obvious to detect (Serious Fraud Office 2018b). These DPAs represent a step in the right direction if efficiency is the main regulatory goal. But like most legal innovations, they are not without their flaws.

One drawback is that DPAs may lead to under-prosecution, undermining specific and especially general deterrence. Note that there are examples of severe penalties for non-cooperation (US Department of Justice 2014). Comparable systems such as American non-prosecution agreements allow offenders to avoid prosecution if they voluntarily offer information about their wrongdoing (Bildfell 2016; Xiao 2013). This voluntary system theoretically encourages disclosure, often results in serious conduct being penalized by fines and mandated monitors as well as participation in education and training programs (Gibson Dunn 2018). Fines themselves may not have a significant deterrent effect on financial crime and conduct but, especially in significant cases, holding companies accountable for criminal conduct sends a strong signal to the market (Gilchrist 2014; Schnell 2017).

In addition to robust DPA procedures, other mechanisms should be implemented/ strengthened through regulatory reform. Whistleblowing incentives encourage key witnesses to step forward (Minkes 2010, pp. 468, 471), and internal controls such as hotlines and ethics training improve prosecution rates and significantly curtail the prevalence of fraud (Peltier-Rivest and Lanoue 2015). While much of the under-enforcement of financial market crime in Canada and the United Kingdom can be attributed to regulatory issues, the absence of a culture of compliance has also played a significant role. In the UK, the Public Interest Disclosure Act 1998 (PIDA) provides protection for someone harmed or dismissed as a result of whistleblowing about a firm or individual. Yet commentary on the legislation has argued that it is insufficient to protect prospective whistleblowers since it does not offer anonymity for reporting parties or protection from retaliation (in the context of an employee whistleblower against their employer) (Thomson Reuters Foundation 2016). While the FCA may offer confidentiality for reporting parties, they may still be subject to PIDA and related European laws and restrictions Financial Conduct Authority 2016).

Similarly, in Canada, provincial securities regulators have encouraged whistle-blowing. In Ontario, the Office of the Whistleblower has offered rewards of up to $5 million CAD for information regarding misconduct. In contrast to the UK, the Ontario Securities Commission (OSC) allows for direct or anonymous whistleblow-ing through a lawyer acting as an intermediary. Furthermore, the OSC explicitly states that it may take action against employers who retaliate against whistleblow-ing from within their organization (Ontario Securities Commission 2018). Moving forward, both nations should seek to promote the reform of regulatory systems that deter financial market crime and encourage witnesses to step forward when it arises.

19.5 Conclusion

There is no single explanation for the under enforcement of financial market crime, yet this is a phenomenon that plagues both Canada and the United Kingdom. Reform appears to be necessary but would be undoubtedly complex given the institutional composition underpinning enforcement regimes in each country. As a first step, leg-islators in each country must seek to ensure coordination among existing domestic agencies. They must also consider reform initiatives – such as deferred prosecution agreements and whistleblowing – to enhance the efficacy of existing enforcement mechanisms.

References

Allen, J.P. (2013). *Securities Regulation of Ontario Venture Issuers: Rules or Principles?* (PhD Dissertation, Osgoode Hall Law School, 2013) [unpublished].

Anand, A. (2006). Carving the public interest jurisdiction in securities regulation: Contributions of Justice Iacobucci. Paper written for and delivered at Symposium in honour of Justice Frank Iacobucci, Faculty of Law, University of Toronto (Oct. 2006).

Anand, A. (2008). Securities law needs more enforcement, not more laws. *Lawyers Weekly* (24 March 2008), online: <https://www.law.utoronto.ca/blog/faculty/securities-law-needs-more-enforcement-not-more-laws>.

Anand, A. (2017). What about the investors? White Paper written for FAIR Canada (July 1, 2017).

Anand A. and Andrew Green, A. (2018). Securities settlements as examples of crisis-driven regulation. Int Rev L & Econ 55: 41–57.

Archibald, T.L., Jull, K.E., and Roach K.W. (2015). *Regulatory and Corporate Liability: From Due Diligence to Risk Management*. Toronto: Canada Law Book.

Barbiero, F. (2008). Federalizing Canada's securities regulatory regime: Insights from the Australian experience. *National Journal of Constitutional Law* 24: 89.

Bhattacharya, U. (2006). Enforcement and its impact on cost of equity and liquidity of the market, Vol. 6 in Canada Steps Up: Report of the Task Force to Modernize Securities Regulation in Canada 131.

Binham, C. (2015). Global regulators shift focus to risk and conduct. *Financial Times*, online: < https://www.ft.com/content/e965566c-f1b1-11e4-98c5-00144feab7de>.

Bittle, S. and Snider, L. (2011). 'Moral panics' deflected: the failed legislative response to Canada's safety crimes and markets fraud legislation. *Crime L & Social Change* 56(4): 373.

Black, J., Hopper, M. and Band, C. (2007). Making a success of principles-based regulation. *L & Fin Mkt's Rev* 1(3) 191.

Button, M. and Tunley, M. (2015). Explaining fraud deviancy attenuation in the United Kingdom. *Crime Law Soc Change* 63: 49.

Canada. Wise Persons' Committee to Review the Structure of Securities Regulation in Canada (2003). *It's Time*. (Vancouver: Department of Finance, 2003).

Canadian Securities Administrators (2007). *Canadian Securities Administrators Investor Study: Understanding the Social Impact of Investment Fraud*, Canadian Security Administrators, Executive Summary, online: <www.securities-administrators.ca>.

Canadian Securities Administrators (2016). 2016 Enforcement Report, online: < https://www.securities-administrators.ca/uploadedFiles/General/pdfs/CSA_AnnualReport2016_English_Final(1).pdf>.

Canadian Securities Administrators (2017) CSA Investor Index, online: < https://www.securities-administrators.ca/uploadedFiles/Investor_Tools/CSA07%20Investor%20Index%20Deck%20-%20Full%20Report%20-%2020171128.pdf>.

Christensen, H.B., Hail, L. and Leuz, C. (2016). Capital-market effects of securities regulation: prior conditions, implementation, and enforcement. *Rev Fin Stud* 29 (11) 2885.

Coffee, J.C. Jr, Law and the market: The impact of enforcement. *U Penn L Rev* 156: 229.

Comments Requested for CCMR Draft Regulations (May 14, 2018) *Advisor.ca*, online: <http://www.advisor.ca/news/industry-news/comments-requested-for-ccmr-draft-regulations-256721>.

Constitution Act, 1867 (UK), 30 & 31 Vict, c 3, reprinted in RSC 1985, Appendix II, No 5, ss 91(2), 91(27), 92(13).

Cumming, D., Johan, S. and & Dan Li, D. (2011). Exchange trading rules and stock market liquidity. *JFE 99(3)*. Available at SSRN: https://ssrn.com/abstract=1328553.

Cumming, D. and Johan, S. (2017). Capital-market effects of securities regulation: prior conditions, implementation, and enforcement revisited (26 December 2017). Available at SSRN: https://ssrn.com/abstract=3093580.

Department of Finance (Canada) (2014). Saskatchewan and New Brunswick agree to join the Cooperative Capital Markets Regulatory System, News Release (9 Jul 2014).

Dooley D.V. and Radke, M. (2010). Does severe punishment deter financial crimes? *Charleston L Rev* 4(3): 619.

Dunn, G. (2018). 2018 Mid-Year Update on Corporate Non-Prosecution Agreements (NPAs) and Deferred Prosecution Agreements (DPAs*)*, <https://www.gibsondunn.com/2018-mid-year-npa-dpa-update/>.

EC, *Regulation (EU) No 596/2014 of the European Parliament and of the Council of 16 April 2014 on market abuse (market abuse regulation) and repealing Directive 2003/6/EC of the European Parliament and of the Council and Commission Directives 2003/124/EC, 2003/125/EC and 2004/72/EC*, [2014] OJ, L173/1.

Ford, C. (2010). Principles-based securities regulation in the wake of the global financial crisis. *McGill L J* 55(2): 257.

Fair Canada (2014). A report on a Canadian strategy to combat investment fraud (11 August 2014), online: <http://faircanada.ca/wp-content/uploads/2014/08/FINAL-A-Canadian-Strategy-to-Combat-Investment-Fraud-August-2014-0810.pdf>.

Financial Conduct Authority (2018a). About the FCA (9 April 2018a), online: <https://www.fca.org.uk/about/the-fca>.

Financial Conduct Authority (2018b). Office for Professional Body Anti-Money Laundering Supervision (OPBAS) (30 April 2018b), online: <https://www.fca.org.uk/opbas>.

Financial Conduct Authority (2016). Whistleblowing: Our role (16 June 2016), online: <https://www.fca.org.uk/firms/whistleblowing/our-role>.

Financial Services Act 2012 (UK), c 21, Pt II, s 6 amending the *Financial Services and Markets Act 2000* (UK), c 8.

Fishman, J.J. (1991). Enforcement of securities laws violations in the United Kingdom. *Int'l Tax & Bus L* 9:131.

Gannon, R. and Doig, A. (2010). Ducking the answer? Fraud strategies and police resources. *Policing & Soc'y* 20(1): 39.

Gilchrist, G.M. (2014). The special problem of banks and crime. *U Colorado L Rev* 85:1.

Government of Canada (2009). Amended Agreement in Principle to Move Towards a Cooperative Capital Markets Regulatory System (9 Jul 2009) online: <http://www.fin.gc.ca/n14/docs/ccmr-rmc-eng.pdf>.

Government of Canada (2014). Prince Edward Island Agrees to Join the Cooperative Capital Markets Regulatory System (9 Oct 2014) online: <http://www.fin.gc.ca/n14/14-135-eng.asp>.

Government of Canada (2013). Province of Ontario, and Province of British Columbia, Agreement in Principle to Move Towards a Cooperative Capital Markets Regulatory System (19 Sep 2013), online: <http://www.fin.gc.ca/pub/ccmrs-scrmc/agreement-principle-entente-principe-eng.asp>.

Gray, J. and McFarland, J. (2013). Crime without punishment: Canada's investment fraud problem. *The Globe and Mail* (24 August 2013), online: <https://www.theglobeandmail.com/report-on-business/crime-and-no-punishment-canadas-investment-fraud-problem/article13938792/>.

Harvard Law Review (1979). Developments in the law – corporate crime: Regulating corporate behavior through criminal sanctions. *Harv L Rev* 92(6): 1227.

IMF Monetary and Exchange Affairs Department (2001). Financial system abuse, financial crime and money laundering – background paper. International Monetary Fund Paper, online: <https://www.imf.org/external/np/ml/2001/eng/021201.htm>.

Jackson, H.E. and Roe, M.J. (2009). Public and private enforcement of securities laws: Resource-based evidence. *J Fin Econ* 93: 207.

Kedia, S. and Rajgopal, S. (2011). Do the SEC's enforcement preferences affect corporate misconduct? *J Acc & Econ* 51(3): 259.

Kempa, M. (2010). Combating white-collar crime in Canada: Serving victim needs and market integrity. *J of Financial Crime* 17(2): 251.

La Porta, R.L., Lopez-de-Silanes, F., Shleifer, A. and Vishny, R.W. (1998). Law and finance. *J of Pol Econ* 106(6): 1113.

La Porta, R.L., Lopez-de-Silane, F., Shleifer, A. and Vishny, R.W. (1997). Legal determinants of external finance. *J Fin* 52(3): 1131.

La Porta, R., Lopez-de-Silanes, F. and Shleifer, A. (2006). What works in securities laws? *J Fin* 61(1) 1.

Lohse, T., Pascalau, R. and Thomann, C. (2014). Public enforcement of securities market rules: Resource-based evidence from the Securities and Exchange Commission. *J of Economic Behavior & Organization* 106: 197.

Lortie, P. and Hockin, T. (2011). Securities regulation in Canada: The case for effectiveness. IRPP 19.

Proposed *Canadian Securities Act*, as set out in Order in Council PC 2010-667 (26 May 2010) [proposed Act].

Public Interest Disclosure Act 1998, c 23.

Luedtke, D. (2014). Progression in the age of recession: restorative justice and white-collar crime in post-recession America. Brook J Corp Fin & Com L 9(1): 311.

Minkes, J. (2010). Silent or invisible? Governments and corporate financial crimes. *Crim & Pub Pol'y* 9(3): 467.

National Crime Agency (2018). About us, online: <http://www.nationalcrimeagency.gov.uk/about-us>.

Nicol, J., Seglins, D. and Niles, S. (2017). Manulife revealed as bank fined $1.15M for violating anti-money laundering reporting rules (27 February 2017) *CBC News*, online: <http://www.cbc.ca/news/business/fintrac-fine-name-secret-1.3999156>.

Ontario Securities Commission, Office of the Whistleblower (2018), online: <http://www.osc.gov.on.ca/en/whistleblower.htm>.

Patton, R. and McHugh, E. (2016). *Trends in Regulatory Enforcement in UK Financial Markets 2016/17 Mid-Year Report*. Nera Economic Consulting.

Peltier-Rivest, D. and Lanoue, N. (2015). Cutting fraud losses in Canadian organizations. J Fin Crim 22(3): 295.

Ring, S. (2017a). U.K. seeks tougher laws on corporate financial crime. (5 September 2017a) *Financial Post*, online: <http://business.financialpost.com/legal-post/u-k-seeks-tougher-laws-on-corporate-financial-crime>.

Ring, S. (2017b). FCA fines return to new normal with 10-fold increase in 2017 (10 December 2017b), *Bloomberg*, online: <https://www.bloomberg.com/news/articles/2017-12-11/fca-fines-return-to-new-normal-with-10-fold-increase-in-2017>.

Ring, S. and Wild, F. (2018). Britain's white-collar cops are getting too good at their job. *Bloomberg* (1 March 2018), online: <https://www.bloomberg.com/news/features/2018-03-01/britain-s-white-collar-cops-are-getting-too-good-at-their-job>.

Roach, K.W., Estabrooks, M.S., Shaffer, M. and Renaud, G. (2017). Will DPAs lead to better white collar compliance? *Crim L Q* 64: 225.

Robertson, G. and Cardoso, T. (2017). Canada's $1.1-billion problem: Regulators dish out big fines but only collect a fraction, *Globe and Mail* (22 December 2017), online: <https://www.theglobeandmail.com/news/investigations/billion-dollars-unpaid-fines-white-collar-crime/article37416140/>.

Schnell, B.D. (2017). No chance at immunity. *Western J Leg Stud* 7: 36.

Schwartz, R. (2009). A call for reform: Compelled questioning of witnesses in criminal securities fraud cases. *Crim L Q* 54: 341.

Serious Fraud Office (2018a). About Us, online: <https://www.sfo.gov.uk/about-us/>.

Serious Fraud Office (2018b). Guidance on deferred prosecution agreements, online: <https://www.sfo.gov.uk/publications/guidance-policy-and-protocols/deferred-prosecution-agreements/>.

Sims, B. (2017). Annual Fraud Indicator 2017 highlights UK footing £190 billion annual fraud bill. *Risk UK* (13 November 2017), online: <http://www.risk-uk.com/annual-fraud-indicator-2017-highlights-uk-footing-190-billion-annual-fraud-bill/>.

Swift, N. (2013). Enforcing white-collar crime in the UK (September 2013), *Financier Worldwide* (blog), online: <https://www.financierworldwide.com/enforcing-white-collar-crime-in-the-uk>.

Tennant, F. (2016). Whistleblowing in the UK *Financier Worldwide* (November 2016), online: <https://www.financierworldwide.com/whistleblowing-in-the-uk/>.

Thomson Reuters Foundation (2016). Protecting Whistleblowers in the UK: A New Blueprint (July 2016), online: <http://www.trust.org/contentAsset/raw-data/7161e13d-2755-4e76-9ee7-fff02f6584db/file>.

Treanor, J. (2017). UK fraud hits record £1.1bn as cybercrime soars (24 January 2017) *The Guardian*, online: <https://www.theguardian.com/uk-news/2017/jan/24/uk-fraud-record-cybercrime-kpmg>.

Tupman, W. (2010). Keeping under the radar: Watch out for 'Smurfs'. *J of Financial Crime* 17(1): 152.

UK Bribery Act 2010 (UK), c 23.

UK Financial Services Authority (2007). *Principles-based regulation: Focusing on the outcomes that matter* at 6, online: <http://www.fsa.gov.uk/pubs/other/principles.pdf>.

US Department of Justice (2014). Alstom pleads guilty and agrees to pay $772 million criminal penalty to resolve foreign bribery charges. *Justice News*, 22 December, < https://www .justice.gov/opa/pr/alstom-pleads-guilty-and-agrees-pay-772-million-criminal-penalty-resolve-foreign-bribery>.

Wise Persons Committee. Canada (2003). Minister of Finance, *Final Report of the Wise Persons Committee to Review the Structure of Securities Regulation in Canada* (Vancouver: Wise Persons Committee, 2003), online: <https://www.fin.gov.on.ca/en/publications/2003/5yr securitiesreview.pdf>.

Xiao, M.Y. (2013). Deferred/non-prosecution agreements: effective tools to combat corporate crime. *Cornell JL & Pub Pol'y* 23(1): 233.

Chapter 20

A Pyramid or a Labyrinth? Enforcement of Registrant Misconduct Requirements in Canada

Mary Condon
Osgoode Hall Law School*

20.1   Introduction

In the aftermath of the global financial crisis (GFC), a significant amount of attention has been paid in various jurisdictions to the question of whether conduct requirements imposed on financial intermediaries (especially those dealing with retail clients) remain adequate. While the UK's debates about this issue began before the crisis, they picked up significant traction afterwards.[1] Similar policy debates occurred

---

* Thanks to Jordan Routliff for his research assistance on this chapter.
[1] Andenas, M. and Chiu, I H-Y (201). *The Foundations and Future of Financial Regulation* Routledge at ch.8; Financial Conduct Authority *Financial Advice Market Review* (August 2015) https://www.fca.org.uk/firms/financial-advice-market-review-famr.

in the US and Australia and are still a live issue in Canada.[2] The focus of these debates is on matters such as whether a 'suitability' standard is rigorous enough to govern the advice that intermediaries give to investors about products or whether conflicts of interest in the activities of intermediaries are appropriately regulated. Such conflicts of interest could result from how advisors are paid to sell financial products by product manufacturers or the firms for which they work, or from the fact of limitations in the types of products they are registered to sell, which might drive their recommendations.

While these policy debates have many interesting dimensions, the question of whether the enforcement mechanisms to deal with *misconduct* by financial intermediaries are adequate or effective has received far less attention. This chapter attempts to provide a framework for addressing this question. It focuses on the variety of enforcement mechanisms to deal with financial intermediary misconduct in Canada and argues that significant problems of institutional design of the enforcement apparatus prevent visibility into the prevalence of the problem and may create an 'under-enforcement' concern. In particular, it argues that enforcement efforts in this area are fragmented, not just in the usual Canadian sense of being based on a securities regulatory jurisdiction that is provincially based, but in the more substantive sense of being fractured along a variety of dimensions, including among a number of different organizations who engage in enforcement, among a number of categories of registration, and among a variety of statutorily granted powers provided to the organizations who enforce conduct issues with respect to those categories. The situation is both confusing for investors and contributes to the inability to fully understand the extent and nature of registrant misconduct in Canada.

The argument will be developed as follows. In Section 20.2, I will define the parameters of the phenomenon I examine in the chapter. This definitional exercise is important to elucidate because the definitions of categories of financial registrants and their potential misconduct are themselves organized by regulatory silo and demonstrate the institutional and regulatory fragmentation to which I am alluding. In Section 20.3, I will review the academic literature on registrant misconduct and the broader debate about the so-called compliance/enforcement continuum in the white-collar crime context. In Section 20.4, I will identify the various statutory and self-regulatory routes and mechanisms by which enforcement of registrant misconduct can occur in Canada in order to support my argument about fragmentation. In Section 20.5, I will attempt to identify the types of misconduct that appear to be prevalent with respect to each enforcement route. Section 20.6 will draw out some of the implications of the fractured approach to registrant misconduct in Canada.

---

[2] See Financial Industry Regulatory Authority 'Report on Conflicts of Interest', October 2013, http://www.finra.org/sites/default/files/Industry/p359971.pdf; Royal Commission into Misconduct in the Banking, Superannuation and Financial Services Industry, https://financialservices.royalcommission.gov.au/Pages/default.aspx; Canadian Securities Administrators, 'Client Focused Reforms' Proposals for Amendment to NI 31-103, June 2018, https://www.osc.gov.on.ca/documents/en/Securities-Category3/rule_20180621_31-103_client-focused-reforms.pdf.

20.2   Definitional and Institutional Quagmires

From an investor's perspective, the question of who should be in the category of a financial intermediary who deals with or advises those investors, and who is therefore subject to general regulatory and enforcement requirements, should be relatively straightforward. In the UK, the Financial Conduct Authority (FCA), as its name implies, regulates the conduct of those selling products across the spectrum of consumer finance, including securities, mortgages, insurance, pensions, and credit products, as well as deposit-takers.[3] A similar situation exists in Australia.[4] This matter is not so simple in Canada. In this jurisdiction, the mechanisms and requirements of registration and the ongoing conduct regulation of registrants vary according to the instruments or investment products being sold or managed.

By way of background, it should first be noted that there are different legislative and institutional arrangements for banking, insurance, and securities markets in Canada. These arrangements are a product of Canada's constitutional history and, in particular, the division of legislative power in that Constitution between the federal government on the one hand and provincial and territorial governments on the other. Thus Canadian banks are regulated by the federal Bank Act, and the provisions of that legislation are implemented by the Office of the Superintendent of Financial Institutions (OSFI). Meanwhile, the operation of securities markets has historically been treated as a matter of provincial jurisdiction in Canada,[5] such that each province and territory enacts its own legislation and establishes its own regulatory agency. Some insurance companies are regulated federally by OSFI, whereas others are regulated by provincial agencies.

This landscape is further complicated by the fact that some provinces have merged the regulation of their securities markets with their insurance regulation so that in provinces like Quebec, New Brunswick, and Saskatchewan, a single provincial regulator has the authority to regulate a variety of financial products (not including banking products). In others like Ontario, a separate agency, the Ontario Securities Commission (OSC), regulates securities markets and products, as distinct from insurance and pension products, which is regulated by the Financial Services Commission of Ontario (FSCO), soon to become the Financial Services Regulatory Authority (FSRA). In the securities space, it is widely acknowledged that provincial and territorial jurisdiction creates coordination problems among regulators, since many financial services firms want to be able to operate across the country and investors want to invest nationally. Accordingly, an entity called the Canadian Securities Administrators (CSA) has been established, by voluntary agreement of the provincial and territorial regulators, to provide this coordinating role with respect to policy and rule-making.

---

[3] Note that Iain McNeil makes a similar argument about the problems of fragmentation with respect to conduct regulation in the UK, as while the FCA is the single regulatory agency, it uses four conduct of business sourcebooks to regulate different products and services; See McNeil, I. (2015). Rethinking Conduct Regulation. *Butterworths Journal of International Banking and Financial Law*, July/August 2015 413 at 418.
[4] Note that the Australian Securities and Investments Commission (ASIC) does not regulate pensions.
[5] The history of this constitutional treatment is well summarized in the Reference decision of the Supreme Court of Canada in 2011. See *Reference re Securities Act* [2011] 3 S.C.R. 837.

The CSA has an office and a small staff which provides project management support for rule and policy coordination. However, enforcement efforts remain overwhelmingly a matter of individual provincial and territorial jurisdiction.

In addition to this complicated governmental regulatory landscape, there are also two major self-regulatory organizations that operate in the securities space in Canada. Unlike their governmental counterparts, these are national organizations, who are legally recognized by provincial and territorial authorities. Their jurisdiction comes from the contractual obligation of their members to follow their requirements and the delegation to them by governmental authorities of ongoing oversight of certain categories of registrant. The Investment Industry Regulatory Organization of Canada (IIROC) is the self-regulatory organization for investment dealers in Canada. The Mutual Fund Dealers Association (MFDA) is the self-regulatory organization for mutual fund dealers. Finally, in the life and health insurance space, the Canadian Life and Health Insurance Association (CLHIA) is explicitly a body dedicated to ensuring that 'the views and interests of its diverse membership and of the public are equitably addressed' and to 'promote a legislative and regulatory environment favourable to the business of its members'.[6] It develops policies and guidelines concerning insurance products with investment features, such as segregated funds, which are explicitly endorsed by provincial insurance regulators.

Turning to the legal framework for regulating intermediaries in the securities markets who deal in securities or advise investors, provincial securities legislation (which regulates the trading of instruments called securities) creates different categories of registration. Those categories are (i) investment dealer, (ii) mutual fund dealer (MFD), (iii) exempt market dealer (EMD), (iv) portfolio manager (PM), (v) investment fund manager (IFM), and (vi) scholarship plan dealer (SPD). As noted, IIROC and the MFDA are primarily responsible for oversight of the first two of these categories, with provincial or territorial government regulators responsible for the remainder. As of 2016, there were 122,556 individual registrants in Canada, a number that is relatively consistent from 2011, when it was 123,121.[7]

Meanwhile the conduct of insurance agents, mortgage brokers, or retail banking agents are not regulated by securities regulators, but by either insurance regulators or banking regulators. Those who offer 'financial planning' services are not regulated by a government entity at all.[8] The empirical focus of this chapter is on those whose conduct is regulated by securities law, bearing in mind that this is only a partial

---

[6] CLHIA, https://www.clhia.ca/web/CLHIA_LP4W_LND_Webstation.nsf/page/6EBFE54D9D076C568525 780E0056B1BE!OpenDocument.

[7] CSA 2011 *Enforcement Report,* https://www.securities-administrators.ca/uploadedFiles/General/pdfs/ CSA_2011_English.pdf?n=2239 and CSA 2016 *Enforcement Report,* https://www.securities-administra tors.ca/uploadedFiles/General/pdfs/CSA_AnnualReport2016_English_Final(1).pdf; the number was not reported in 2010.

[8] Condon, M. (2014). A discipline in search of Itself? Contemporary challenges for securities law in Canada. *UNB Law Journal* 341–352; Ontario Expert Committee To consider Financial Advisory and Financial Planning Policy Alternatives, Final Report November 2016, https://www.fin.gov.on.ca/en/consultations/ fpfa/fpfa-final-report.pdf.

account of the full landscape of the regulatory and enforcement apparatus for those selling retail financial products.

A further definitional issue to canvass at the outset is the meaning being attributed to 'misconduct' in this chapter. It is, of course, possible that registrants may commit market-based offences such as fraud or insider trading, just like any other market participant or investor.[9] While there is some evidence that registrants may be sanctioned particularly harshly for these activities because of their professional roles within securities markets, those generally prohibited activities are not the focus of the present analysis. Rather the focus is on the specific misconduct that can occur in the interactions between dealers or advisers and their clients in the sale of investment products or the provision of advice about those products.[10] As noted above, these types of misconduct span problems of conflicts of interest, overcharging, poor or negligent advice, and so on.

20.3   The Compliance/Enforcement Continuum

A number of intersecting legal and financial literatures focus on the analysis of capital markets infractions. A foundational paper in the so-called 'law and finance' school purported to assess the relative importance of 'public' and 'private' enforcement as a strategy for growing a stock market.[11] The research contrasted the relative importance of plaintiff-friendly civil remedies (private) with the discretionary power of a regulatory supervisor to take enforcement action (public) across over 40 countries. The conclusion drawn by these researchers was that jurisdictions that exhibited strong and growing capital market involvement by investors were characterized by reliable plaintiff-friendly civil remedies (and rigorous ex ante disclosure requirements) rather than by broad discretionary powers granted to government regulators. In other words, private remedies were more correlated with growing stock markets than were public enforcement powers.[12] However, the focus of this research was on the enforcement of the disclosure obligations of issuers, not the conduct of financial intermediaries and the theory has not been tested in the latter context.[13] The implications of this theory as applied to intermediary misconduct would be that the preferred form of enforcement would be the ability of investors to sue the registrants with whom they invest for deficiencies in their conduct. The research design also did not distinguish consistently

---

[9] See for example, the cases of Cahill in Manitoba (CSA 2010 Enforcement report) and MacDonald in Alberta (CSA 2010 Enforcement report).

[10] This is a different definition from the one used by Skinner in her article on 'misconduct risk', which is focused on the possibility of manipulation among bankers (e.g. benchmark manipulation) causing systemic risk problems in the banking sector; see Skinner, Christina P. (2016). Misconduct Risk. *Fordham Law Review* 84 (4): 1559–1610 at 1596.

[11] La Porta, Lopez-de-Silanes, and Schliefer (2006). What works in securities laws? *Journal of Finance*, Vol LX1, No.1 (February 2006).

[12] This thesis is contested by a number of researchers, including, most notably, John Coffee. See Coffee, J. (2007). Law and the market: The impact of enforcement. *Univ of Penn LR* Vol 156: 229.

[13] Krug A. (2014). Downstream securities regulation *94 B.U.L. Rev* 1589.

among various avenues of public enforcement, ranging from criminal prosecution to the lower-visibility adjudicative decisions of a regulatory decision-maker.

There has been some empirical investigation of the extent of misconduct among financial advisers in the US. Egan et al. report that 7% of advisers in the US have misconduct records, with one-third of this group being repeat offenders.[14] It is notable that the data analysed in this study came exclusively from FINRA, the US self-regulatory organization that is equivalent to IIROC in Canada. A similar study that would focus only on IIROC cases in Canada would not capture the full picture of securities registrant activity or enforcement mechanisms.

Meanwhile, in the socio-legal literature, the relative merits of the so-called 'compliance' as opposed to 'deterrence-based' approaches as a way of achieving enforcement effectiveness have long been debated in the criminological and legal literatures dealing with white-collar or corporate crime. This debate maps on to underlying assumptions about the state's role in corporate regulation as well as competing theories about why law-abiding behaviour occurs.[15] Thus, according to Almond and Erp's taxonomy, critical corporate criminology 'does not share the more optimistic view of administrative sanctions and alternatives to prosecution held within regulation and governance research' but rather sees this as offering a 'purely cosmetic form of compliance' that retains the 'privileges surrounding the crimes of the powerful'.[16]

Those who advocate for a compliance-based approach to enforcement of regulatory requirements often start with Braithwaite's enforcement pyramid,[17] which proposes an escalation through a range of ever more serious sanctions for repeated offences. Such a pyramid is premised on the idea of a limited number of decision-makers intentionally wielding a variety of enforcement tools in a toolbox, rather than the kind of multifaceted and multi-institutional approach exhibited in the Canadian context.[18]

Ultimately, empirical testing of these alternative compliance or deterrence approaches in the context of financial market registrants has been limited in other jurisdictions, and non-existent in Canada. MacNeil notes that in the wake of the GFC, the UK regulator moved to achieve a goal of so-called 'credible deterrence', with a 'sharp rise' in penalties and compensation associated with misconduct.[19] Similarly,

---

[14] The research also finds that financial advisers who are found to have engaged in misconduct do not typically leave the industry but are re-employed by firms with retail client bases.

[15] Almond, Paul and van Erp, Judith (2018). Regulation and governance versus criminology: Disciplinary divides, intersections and opportunities. *Regulation and Governance*, https://onlinelibrary.wiley.com/doi/abs/10.1111/rego.12202.

[16] Ibid.

[17] Ayres, Ian and Braithwaite, John (1992). *Responsive Regulation: Transcending the Deregulation Debate*. NY: OUP; Parker, Christine (2012). Twenty years of responsive regulation: An appreciation and appraisal. *Regulation and Governance* 7 (1): 2–13.

[18] Masini, Peter (2012). Why was the enforcement pyramid so influential? And what price was paid? *Regulation and Governance* 7 (1).

[19] MacNeil at 413. Andenas et al. discuss 'post-sale consumer redress' which focuses only on extraordinary measures taken by regulators to deal with product misselling. See Andenas, M. and Chiu, I H-Y. (2012). *The Foundations and Future of Financial Regulation*. See also Moloney, N. (2012). The investor model underlying the EU's investor protection regime: Consumers or investors? *European Business Organization Law Review* 13: 169–193 at 191.

Skinner argues that jurisdictions mostly responded to banking misconduct with 'primarily an ex post enforcement approach'.[20] But there are several possible alternative meanings of an 'enforcement' approach in the financial intermediary context. As we will show below, an 'enforcement' approach in the Canadian context could mean a wide variety of avenues for sanction. This chapter argues that some 10 years after the GFC, it should be possible to have a more sophisticated debate about regulatory policy choices with respect to enforcement of registrant misconduct. A crucial first step in doing this is to understand the full panoply of authorities that have the power to sanction registrants, as well as the gamut of legal tools at their disposal.

20.4   Enforcement Options Available to Sanction Registrant Misconduct

If proactive financial intermediary conduct regulation is siloed according to the legal definition of the financial product being sold (e.g. a mutual fund regulated by securities regulators or a segregated fund regulated by insurance regulators), the same is true of the enforcement mechanisms that could be used to sanction misconduct. The focus of this chapter is on those required to be registered under securities law only, acknowledging once again that this is a partial lens in which to view the landscape of financial intermediary enforcement requirements.

The Criminal Code of Canada is a compilation of the most serious criminal offences and the most serious penalties for infringing those criminal prohibitions. There are a few offences therein that could apply to registrants in their dealings with clients. For example, s.380 makes it an offence to defraud the public... 'of a service'. S.397 involves the falsification of books and documents. S.380.1, dealing with aggravating sentencing factors, includes as such a factor the 'affecting of investor confidence'.

At a somewhat lower level of seriousness in the criminal realm, all provincial securities statutes create criminal offences which can be prosecuted in provincial courts. These offences, if proven, will attract lesser penalties than Criminal Code infractions, but will still involve the possibility of jail time and fines. While some provincial statutes identify specific substantive provisions of securities legislation whose breach can be prosecuted criminally, s.122 of the Ontario Securities Act (OSA) simply makes it an offence to breach Ontario securities law. This suggests that in Ontario any registrant who breached conduct requirements contained in the statute or rules implemented pursuant to the legislation,[21] such as, for example, the requirement to 'deal fairly, honestly and in good faith'[22] towards clients, could be prosecuted under OSA s.122.

---

[20]   Skinner, Ibid., at 1561.
[21]   Beginning in the mid-1990s, most provincial securities regulators obtained the power to pass rules that would be binding on market participants. These rules are subject to a requirement to allow public comment on the substance of the rules before they are final, and the possibility that the relevant government ministry might prevent their implementation (within a specific period of time).
[22]   OSC Rule 31–505.

Moving outside the criminal realm, all provincial and territorial securities legislation provides that the regulatory agency established under it, acting as an adjudicative
tribunal, can make an order in the public interest, following an adjudicative hearing
that begins with a notice of hearing and statement of allegations outlined by regulatory enforcement staff. Some of the orders that can be made are specifically directed
to registrants. For example, OSA s.127 provides that the Ontario Securities Commission can suspend or restrict the registration of a person or company or require a
market participant to 'submit to a review of his, her or its practices and procedures
and institute such changes as may be ordered by the Commission'. It may also make
an order that a person is prohibited from becoming or acting as an officer or director
of a registrant or an investment fund manager. These potential orders are in addition
to general sanctions that the Commission may impose relating to cease trade orders
or the levying of administrative penalties or disgorgement.

Yet these enforcement powers do not exhaust all the methods available in provincial securities law to enforce sanctions for intermediary misconduct in relation to
clients. Another option for dealing with registrant misconduct resides in the power of
the Executive Director of the regulatory agency, or in certain cases, the Director of
Compliance and Registration (CRR) (an operational branch of the regulatory agency)
to decide that a person or company is not suitable for registration and either refuse to
register them, place terms or conditions on registration, or revoke a registration.[23] By
virtue of s.8 of the OSA, a decision of the Director may be appealed to the tribunal,
which can confirm or vacate the original decision, or impose additional requirements.

More systemically, the same branch of the OSC, and by extension, other provincial securities agencies, issues compliance reviews related to the registrant categories
which they regulate directly, that is, EMDs, PMs, and IFMs. The reviews are published
in the form of a 'Staff Notice' which outlines broad themes from the individual examinations of regulated firms that are carried out by the CRR branch. These firm-based
reviews can result in the identification of areas of non-compliance with conduct
requirements that require 'corrective action'.[24]

IIROC and the MFDA also carry out an enforcement programme with respect to
the activities of those registrants who are required to be members of an SRO. At present, there are 29,284 approved persons overseen by IIROC and 80,834 individual
members of the MFDA.[25] The exercise of these powers stems from breaches of the
rules applicable to members of the organization.[26] Each of these organizations has
an enforcement division, and the capacity to hold hearings to determine breaches
of their rules and appropriate sanctions. By definition, these organizations will have
a primary focus on registrant misconduct as a category of inappropriate conduct, as

---

[23] OSA s.27; ASA s.76; QSA ss.151 and 152.
[24] For example, see OSC Notice 33-738 2012 *Annual Summary Report for Dealers, Advisers and Investment Fund Managers*.
[25] IIROC website: https://annualreport.iiroc.ca/2018/pdfs/IIROC_AR_2017-18_EN.pdf [date accessed:
February 17, 2019]; MFDA website: About http://mfda.ca/about/ [date accessed: February 3, 2019].
[26] For MFDA rules, see http://mfda.ca/policy-and-regulation/rules/mfda-rules/; For IIOC rules, see http://
www.iiroc.ca/industry/rulebook/Pages/default.aspx.

opposed to infractions such as insider trading or fraud, which can be committed by any market participant.

20.5   Empirical Information Available about Registrant Misconduct in Canada

Turning to the question of what we know about the frequency and type of registrant misconduct over the period 2010–2016, the data presented in this section comes from a variety of sources, including legal databases, enforcement reports published annually by the CSA, OSC Director decisions posted on the OSC website,[27] and SRO enforcement reports.

20.5.1   Criminal Enforcement

First, there appears to be very little criminal enforcement in Canada in connection with registrant misconduct. Despite the invocation of a strategy of 'credible deterrence' by the Chair of the CSA in the 2015 *Enforcement Report*,[28] Criminal Code prosecutions in the securities area were non-existent in the period 2010–2012. The 2013 and 2014 *Enforcement Reports* each describe one Criminal Code prosecution in British Columbia, neither of which involved a registrant. In 2015, there were four sentences handed down for Criminal Code offences; two in Quebec, one in Ontario, and one in BC. Only the Quebec matter involved a registered firm. The 2016 CSA *Enforcement Report* notes that there were three Criminal Code prosecutions in total concluded across the provinces, one each in BC, Ontario, and Quebec. Only one of these cases involved a registrant. The Quebec case involved an insurance representative who was not a securities registrant at the time of the prosecution,[29] while the Ontario prosecution involved a registered individual (a scholarship plan dealer) who participated in a scheme which used confidential information about new parents from a hospital database to generate sales leads for educational savings plans.[30]

Prosecutions under the quasi-criminal provisions of provincial securities legislation are somewhat more frequent during the time period under examination, with four or five cases being concluded each year across the four major provinces. Only one of these cases involved a registrant in any way; the 2016 *Morin* case from Quebec involving a former mutual fund dealer, who was also prosecuted under the Criminal Code.[31]

The small number of criminal prosecutions involving registrants provides some support for the claim that this form of misconduct is systematically addressed within

---

[27] The OSC's data on this avenue of pursuing registrant misconduct matters is singled out, as it is the largest province in the sample, with the largest number of registrants.

[28] CSA 2015 *Enforcement Report* at p. 5.

[29] Robert Morin (March 24, 2016).

[30] Nellie Acar/Esther Cruz.

[31] See Morin case, note 29 above. There was also a 2010 case from Manitoba involving a former mutual fund salesperson (Scott William Bradley Spence).

a non-criminal framework, that is, on the softer end of the compliance/deterrence continuum.

20.5.2   CSA Non-Criminal Enforcement

The annual CSA enforcement reports mostly recount enforcement actions taken by regulatory enforcement staff before a provincial tribunal, although as noted above, in some years, criminal prosecutions are recorded separately as well. These reports do not cover Directors' Decisions or appeals of those decisions to the appropriate provincial tribunal. The empirical information provided in these annual reports about enforcement cases is sorted into six substantive categories.[32] Enforcement reports from 2010 to 2016 were reviewed, in order to examine what types of matters were pursued by regulatory enforcement staff. The focus of inquiry was on the four large provinces only.[33]

By way of example, the definition of the category of 'misconduct by registrants' in the 2016 CSA Enforcement report is characterized as including unregistered activities, unauthorized or improper trading, conflict of interest or acting against client interest, unsuitable investments and/or recommendations, and failure to discharge 'know your client' (KYC) and suitability obligations. Earlier CSA enforcement cases regarding registrant misconduct concern issues such as overvaluing the net asset value (NAV) of a fund;[34] failure to deal fairly, honestly and in good faith;[35] failure to keep proper books and records;[36] and deficiencies in written business procedures.[37]

Overall, the data from these reports make clear that, for each year under examination, those cases involving illegal distributions by unregistered market participants and fraud significantly outstripped the number of registrants accused of, and sanctioned for, misconduct. Throughout this period, the number of concluded cases against respondents accused of registrant misconduct in the four largest jurisdictions remained typically in single figures, from a high of 11 in 2010[38] to 4 in 2016. The period from 2010 to 2014 for all provinces and territories shows that concluded registrant misconduct cases accounted for somewhere between 9% and 18% of all concluded cases. The number for 2015 was not reported at all, and for 2016, registrant misconduct cases declined so as to account for only 5 out of 109 cases. In 2014 in Ontario, 3 of the 8 concluded matters involving registrant misconduct centred on the activities of scholarship plan dealers.

One striking feature of the data on registrant misconduct presented in the CSA enforcement reports is that cases from Quebec account for a larger share of these totals of registrant misconduct cases than might be expected based on the relative

---

[32] These are illegal distributions, market manipulation, insider trading, disclosure violations, registrant misconduct, and a miscellaneous category.

[33] Alberta, BC, Ontario, Quebec.

[34] Retrocom case.

[35] NAM case.

[36] Hucal case.

[37] Heritage Education Funds.

[38] Though many of these cases involved multiple individual respondents.

numbers of registrants in the province. For example, in 2011 and 2012, 15 out of 21 and 17 out of 28 registrant misconduct cases were reported from Quebec. In general, it seems clear that, other than in Quebec, enforcement resources in the major provincial commissions are directed elsewhere than towards actions focused on registrant misconduct.

20.5.3   Director's Decision Data in Ontario

As noted above, one important feature of the governmental regulatory landscape with respect to registrant misconduct is that the Executive Director in a provincial or territorial agency, or in Ontario, the Director of the CRR branch, has discretion to make a variety of decisions with respect to registration, including refusing an initial registration, imposing terms and conditions on a registration, or revoking or suspending a registration.[39] The cases reported on the OSC website from the Ontario Director of CRR during this time period show that decisions were made under this head of discretionary power much more frequently than more formal enforcement actions. Thus, there were 78 opportunities to be heard in Ontario between 2010 and 2017, with 18 of those occurring in 2011 alone. During the sample period, the most common matters addressed related to deficiencies in applying KYC, know your product (KYP), and suitability requirements, with trading or advising without registration being the next most common deficiency. Other matters that recurred consistently included the use of false client documentation, misleading regulatory staff, and inadequate handling of conflicts of interest.

   As noted above, the Ontario Securities Act offers a right of appeal to a tribunal of the Commission from a Director's Decision.[40] There have been a handful of cases during the period 2010–2016 that are appeals from registrant misconduct decisions by the CRR Director,[41] but these are not captured at all in the CSA enforcement reports. In other words, appeal decisions of the tribunal involving registrant misconduct that was originally sanctioned by an Executive Director or a Director of CRR in a province are not tracked in the same way as other enforcement matters because they originate from a different head of regulatory authority focusing on the discretionary decision to grant, suspend, or remove registration. Equally, the sanctions available to the tribunal in this context do not include all those provided under OSA s.127 because the tribunal's authority is founded in a different provision of the Act.

   Finally, as noted above, the provincial or territorial regulator in the larger provinces issues notices reviewing the results of their compliance oversight of registrant firms. These notices indicate trends observed by the regulators in non-compliant behaviour. For example, in the 2015 notice from Ontario, the three most prominent forms of non-compliant behaviour were (i) inadequate collection, documentation

---

[39] In Ontario there is a procedural requirement for a right to be heard under OSA s.31 before any of these actions may be taken.
[40] OSA s.8(2).
[41] E.g. In the matter of Sanjiv Sawh and Vlad Trukula https://www.osc.gov.on.ca/documents/en/Proceedings-RAD/rad_20120801_sawh.pdf; In the Matter of Sterling Grace https://www.osc.gov.on.ca/documents/en/Proceedings-RAD/rad_20140904_sterling-grace.pdf.

and updating of KYC and suitability information, (ii) deficiencies in client account statements and missing information in trade confirmations, and (iii) other general deficiencies.[42]

20.5.4   SRO Enforcement

IIROC also publishes annual Enforcement reports. Throughout the same sample time period (2010–2016), the three most common complaints received by IIROC related to registrants making unsuitable investments on behalf of clients, unauthorized and discretionary trading, and misrepresentations. Of these three categories of complaint, unsuitability was the predominant one by a significant margin, especially after 2012. Cases from Ontario produce the single largest source of completed IIROC cases nationally.

Meanwhile, the MFDA only began to publish enforcement reports in 2012. It is clear from these reports that a continuum of issues related to 'blank signed forms' and 'signature falsification' are among the most common types of matters dealt with by MFDA enforcement authorities. The category of 'signature falsification' was only created in these reports in 2016, with earlier reports distinguishing between 'falsification' and 'blank signed forms'. Overall, however, the most prominent category of misconduct among MFDs relates to investment suitability. Here again the MFDA distinguishes among two types of suitability violation, one related to investment suitability and the other related to the suitability of leveraging. Other important categories include inadequate business standards, followed by 'unauthorized trading'.

20.6   Analysis

Turning first to the question of any trends that may be discerned about Canadian approaches to enforcement of registrant misconduct, it has been noted above that criminal enforcement of registrant misconduct is a rare event across the four largest provinces, suggesting that the strategy of 'credible deterrence' adopted in other jurisdictions does not include the application of criminal sanctions in Canada. More interestingly, within the realm of enforcement by way of non-criminal powers, the data examined in this paper suggests a divergence of approach among the two biggest provinces in Canada with respect to ways of accomplishing enforcement of registrant misconduct. While Quebec, as we have seen, addresses the issue through the same enforcement channel as instances of illegal distributions or fraud, i.e. by bringing cases to the adjudicative tribunal or the courts, Ontario tends to adopt an alternate regulatory track of having decisions rendered by the Director of CRR which are, on occasion, appealed to the tribunal under separate legal powers, with more limited possible sanctions. Further research is warranted to fully understand the factors that are at play to produce this divergence of enforcement philosophy. One interesting

---

[42] These include, for example, inadequate written compliance policies and procedures, inadequate or misleading marketing material, inadequate compliance reports to the board, and inaccurate calculation of excess working capital.

question that could be explored is whether the divergence is in part the result of the fact that the regulatory institutional design in Quebec is that of an integrated approach, whereby the same regulator (the AMF) regulates across a broader spectrum of financial products, beyond the securities realm.

More generally, this case study of the Canadian approach to enforcement of regulatory misconduct provokes reflection on the role of institutional design in crafting an effective enforcement strategy. The data presented here demonstrates clearly how fragmented and multi-institutional the Canadian design is, involving as it does a variety of routes spanning the criminal justice authorities, multiple branches and powers of governmental regulatory enforcement, as well as the involvement of self-regulatory organizations. Admittedly, the involvement of self-regulatory organizations is a peculiarly North American phenomenon, as European jurisdictions and Australia have largely abandoned this aspect of organizational design in the securities realm. The case study also calls into question the efficiency of the approach of creating separate enforcement channels according to the specific financial product being sold.

There are a number of other implications of the fragmented institutional design outlined above. They include the obvious implication that it may obscure the scope of the problem of registrant misconduct, because complaints and resolutions are dispersed over multiple regulatory organizations. This may contribute to a sense that the problems are not widespread, given the difficulty, demonstrated by the patchy data available, of uncovering trends across different platforms from a variety of sources. From an investor's perspective, the complicated institutional design may make it less likely that she or he would seek to question whether the service provided by the registrant reaches an acceptable threshold, especially given documented challenges of financial literacy among the consumer population.[43] The idea that an investor would need to know which category of registration was held by a financial advisor and therefore which regulator would regulate the conduct of that registrant in order to bring a problem to official attention is a situation that is often criticized by investor advocates in Canada.

A multi-institutional regulatory design for enforcement also impedes the ability of regulators to use evidence-based approaches to make informed decisions about the effectiveness of compliance-based or deterrence-based strategies. For example, the fact that there are two separate channels within the same governmental regulatory organization to sanction registrant misconduct (sanctions applied by the Director of CRR as well as sanctions applied by the regulatory tribunal following an enforcement hearing), with one channel being used more systematically than the other, might be a coherent approach to enforcement of intermediary conduct requirements by the OSC in Ontario. However, it clearly raises questions about the exercise of the discretionary power and the use of resources to push a matter through one channel or the other, as well as questions about how the exercise of discretion here aligns (or not) with approaches taken by other governmental and non-governmental organizations.

---

[43] Lusardi, Annamaria, and Mitchell, Olivia S. (2011). Financial literacy around the World: An overview. J *Pension Econ Financ* Oct 2011, 10(4): 497–508.

More generally, given fragmentation across different governmental and self-regulatory platforms of oversight, evidence from enforcement trends themselves cannot easily be used as a source of information to inform proactive policymaking about market failures in financial advisory services.[44] This issue about the challenges of amassing useful data to inform policymaking is one that many jurisdictions could face in different degrees. For example, while there are some gaps in the evidence presented above, the data gathered from the multiple sources explored appear to suggest that registrant misconduct in Canada over the last five or six years has converged on a few key deficiencies, most notably the lack of achievement of an appropriate standard of suitability in investment advice. The comparatively low visibility about this convergence has significantly delayed the development of a consistent approach to standard-setting and appropriate norms of investment advising and product selling across securities, insurance, and banking regulators.[45]

All these implications point to a more general commentary about the persistence of path dependency in the institutional design of an enforcement system. While the Canadian case may be considered an extreme case of such path dependency, other jurisdictions may also need to be concerned about whether their enforcement system for registrant misconduct is effective if it is dispersed across multiple institutions or heads of legal power. If such a design also produces idiosyncratic or partial as opposed to comprehensive approaches to data collection about misconduct, useful information about emerging problems or strategies of enforcement to address them will not easily be surfaced, to the detriment of financial consumers. Ten years after the GFC, financial regulators should pay closer attention to these questions.

---

[44] See, for example, Campbell et al. (2011). Consumer Financial Protection. *J of Econ Perspectives* 25(1): 91–114.

[45] Client-focused reforms proposed by the CSA may bring about some consistency in the securities realm in Canada, if they are ultimately passed into law.

Chapter 21

Judicial Local Protectionism and Home Court Bias in Corporate Litigation

Michael Firth
Lingnan University

Oliver M. Rui
China Europe International Business School

Wenfeng Wu
Shanghai Jiao Tong University

21.1   Introduction

China's economic transformation has involved a process of decentralization where there is a redistribution of power between the central government and local governments. This has led to regional yardstick competition, which entails regions facing similar external economic environments competing with one another on a (more or less) equal footing in a decentralized and non-specialized environment (Maskin, Qian, and Xu 2000). While this process gives local governments incentives to promote local economic growth and development, it can also lead to local protectionism. This can result in duplicative investments, surplus production, excessive industrial competition, and bias towards local businesses (Young 2000). China has been described as a case of de facto federalism, involving a decentralized economic system where each province can be considered an autonomous economic entity (Qian and Xu 1993). In political terms, decentralization increases bureaucratic, administrative, and judicial autonomy for the local officials. Judicial localism is more prevalent in China than in many other countries because the current organizational structure of the legal system makes judicial independence extremely difficult. One-party politics and high state involvement empower the local government's influence on courts. Local protectionism often runs counter to the rule of law. This localism can undermine legal supremacy and authority through incidents of corruption and self-dealing, the unwillingness to make and enforce judicial rulings, and a lack of bureaucratic coordination. Xiao Yang, a former Chairman of China's Supreme People's Court, considered local protectionism as the major reason for the difficulties in law enforcement, leading to what he called 'judiciary localism'.[1] Judiciary local protectionism biases the judgment in dispute resolution in favour of the party inside the jurisdiction of the court making the rulings. In a typical scenario of contract dispute between firm X in province 1 and firm Y in province 2, the court in province 1 likely rules in favour of firm X and the court in province 2 likely rules in favour of firm Y. Under judiciary local protectionism, contract and law enforcement are not impartial. The aim of our study is to find if there is any quantifiable evidence of judiciary local protectionism in China and what impact this has on firms and their stockholders.

In this chapter, we examine whether courts are biased toward a litigating firm (regardless of whether they are the plaintiff or defendant) that is domiciled in the same city or province as the court. Thus, we examine if there is a home bias or home court advantage. We take a market perspective and use stock prices to quantify the economic effects of litigation. In particular, we use abnormal stock returns and the appeals process to test our main hypothesis: whether firms have a home court advantage when cases are heard in the same province as where the firm is located. We investigate the appeals process and assess a defendant's likelihood to appeal and their success in obtaining better judgments. Based on an analysis of stock returns, we find that the stock market views litigation to be bad news for the defendants. However, litigation is regarded as less bad news for firms with home court advantage than for those without. We also show that the defendants without home court advantage are

---

[1] *People's Daily*, September 3, 1999.

more likely to appeal when they receive unfavourable verdicts in the first run trial. These appeals are based on perceived inequities from biased judgments. Overall, our findings are consistent with there being home court bias in China. Here, the local government tends to exert its influence on local courts to protect the interests of the firms that lie within its jurisdiction.

Our research contributes to the literature in the following ways. First, we add to the growing body of literature that studies the impact of political and economic institutions on the valuation of firms (Shleifer and Vishny 1994; Firth, Rui, and Wu 2011a; Cai et al., 2016). To date, however, there are few studies on the role of these institutions in influencing court behaviour in corporate litigation. Our chapter helps fill this void in the literature. In one-party states with government-controlled media, courts are subject to substantial pressure from government agencies. Thus, we examine the role of government influence in shaping the firm-court relationship. Second, our chapter examines a direct channel through which the local government protects local business through its influence on the courts. Third, we add to the international literature on court bias (Berkowitz and Clay 2006; Mai and Stoyanov 2014). Fourth, the chapter contributes to the literature on fiscal decentralization. Qian and Roland (1998) argue that a shift of fiscal power and responsibility to lower levels of government can enhance market incentives. In a similar line of inquiry, Lin and Liu (2000) argue that decentralization increases economic efficiency because governments at lower levels have informational advantages over the central government on issues such as resource allocation and market demand. However, decentralization could induce a higher incidence of corruption because government officials are in closer proximity to the businesspeople they deal with and regulate (Shleifer and Vishny 1993). In support of this view, Fan, Lin, and Treisman (2009) find that bribery is more frequent in those countries that have a large number of government or administrative tiers and a larger number of public employees. Our results indicate that the local government does sacrifice court independence to protect local firms and boost the local economy. This, in turn, may enhance the reputation of the local government bureaucrats. Thus, fiscal decentralization can play both a positive and a negative role in terms of economic efficiency. Finally, as international investors are increasing their investments in China's capital market,[2] our chapter helps investors better understand the workings of corporate litigation and its impact on shareholder wealth (He et al. 2014). Our study complements studies that examine whether home court bias exists at the national level. For example, Bhattacharya, Galpin, and Haslem (2007), Clermont and Eisenberg (2007), and Moore (2003) report evidence of home court bias that favours US defendants and plaintiffs over foreign litigants. In contrast, Clermont and Eisenberg (1996), in a study of civil cases in the US, find that foreigners win a higher percentage

---

[2] In 2003, the government introduced a QFII (Qualified Foreign Institutional Investor) scheme to allow foreign investors to invest directly in China's domestic stock market. Top international investment banks, such as Citigroup, Credit Suisse First Boston, Goldman Sachs, HSBC, and Nomura Securities promptly applied for, and received, their licenses to make direct portfolio investments in China. In Spring 2015, China further relaxed foreign investment by introducing a 'stock connect' programme with Hong Kong that allows foreigners to more easily buy shares in Chinese listed firms.

of cases than do domestic parties. Thus, the evidence on home court bias (US versus foreign litigants) in the US is mixed.

The rest of the chapter is organized as follows. Section 21.2 introduces the institutional background of China's economic reforms, the legal system, and judicial independence. Section 21.3 describes the research design and presents the empirical results. Section 21.4 concludes the chapter.

21.2   Institutional Background

21.2.1   Decentralization and Local Protectionism

China's economic reform has been characterized by regional decentralization (Qian and Xu 1993; Qian and Weingast 1996).[3] Until 1979, the Chinese economy was a centrally planned economy, with virtually all aspects of the economy being subject to centrally-imposed plans and material incentives and initiatives were completely suppressed. Under this system, regional governments collected all the surpluses from firms under their jurisdictions and transferred them to the central government. In turn, the central government then allocated budgets to the regional governments, but there was no obvious correlation between the surpluses handed over and the budgets allocated back. Under this system, there was no incentive for firms and industries to perform efficiently and nor was there any great incentive for the regional governments to protect local firms or industries. This situation changed dramatically after the economic reform initiated in 1979 and with it the introduction of the fiscal decentralization policy.

Regional decentralization can drive economic development in a process that is sometimes referred to as 'yardstick jurisdictional competition'. Maskin, Qian, and Xu (2000) define regional yardstick competition as competition among jurisdictions, where regions are compared and evaluated by a higher level of government in accordance with a set of standardized performance criteria, one of which is the region's economic performance relative to its peers. These results in incentives for regional governments to compete against each other by linking regional government officials' career paths with regional economic performance reflected in indicators such as the GDP growth rate (Maskin, Qian, and Xu 2000; Li and Zhou 2005).[4] The process is akin to tournament theory in labour economics (Lazear and Rosen 1981).

---

[3] For instance, Qian and Weingast (1996) assert that: 'The critical component of China's market-oriented reform, which began in 1979, is decentralization.' Montinola, Qian, and Weingast (1996) describe China's political system during the reform era as a 'market-preserving federalism', which has yielded net benefits to the country. Qian and Roland (1998, p.1156) argue that: 'one of the most distinct features of China's transition has been associated with devolution of authority from the central to local levels of government.'

[4] Maskin, Qian, and Xu (2000) document a positive relation between the political status of a Chinese province (measured by a province's per capita number of Central Committee members in the Party Congress) and the ranking of a province's economic growth rate one year before the Party Congress.

One consequence of yardstick jurisdictional competition is that it can lead to local protectionism. Using official statistics, Young (2000) finds an increasing similarity in the structure of economic activities among China's regions, which implied a rise of local protectionism. Here, each province sought to have its own steel works, car manufacturing plant, and so on, regardless of the merits of each case. Using industry data from 1985 to 1997, Bai et al. (2004) show the degree of industrial agglomeration at first decreased and then increased during the sample period and they conclude that both the market forces for specialization and the forces for local protectionism against specialization were at play.

The decentralization reforms reinforced China's de facto economic federalism as more regulatory responsibilities, ownership of firms, and economic and financial powers were entrusted to the provincial governments. Under the guise of assistance to the local economy, local governments used their increased administrative powers to implement a multiform protection of firms under their authority (Zhao and Zhang 1999; Wong, 2003). Furthermore, Blanchard and Shleifer (2001) argue that local government may be more easily captured or influenced by special interest groups under its authority.

An important component of economic reform in China is the corporatization of SOEs, which were initially solely owned by the central government and local governments. The corporatization process legitimized the concept of profit and has allowed SOEs to sell shares to the public. These shares are listed on the Shanghai Stock Exchange or the Shenzhen Stock Exchange, which were established in 1990 and 1991, respectively. Although new shares issued by the firm are sold to individual and institutional investors, the state and its various entities kept most of their existing shares, which were sufficient to retain control of the SOEs (Errunza and Mazumdar 2001). In conjunction with the SOE corporatization process, the central government has transferred their control rights in many SOEs to local governments to encourage them to develop their local economies. Of the 2,524 Chinese A-share firms at the end of 2012, 1048 (41.25%) were SOEs, of which 368 (14.6%) were central SOEs which were ultimately controlled by the central government, and 680 (26.9%) were local SOEs ultimately controlled by local governments. The decentralization policy granted local government officials great autonomy over their economies, including the responsibility to set prices, to make investments with surplus or borrowed funds, and the autonomy to restructure their firms and issue business licenses to newly established firms. Local enterprises often have close ties with the local government, which has led to bribery and blackmailing practices and lobbying for more economic protection. Local government also has the incentives, the tools, and, some would say, the obligation to lend a helping hand to firms under its jurisdiction in order to develop the local economy.

21.2.2 Judicial Independence

One way for the regional and city government to protect local firms is through its strong influence on the local courts. Under judicial local protectionism, contract and law enforcement are not impartial and may, instead, be biased in favour of a local enterprise, organization, or person. Formally, judicial independence is a recognized principle in the Chinese Constitution and laws. Article 126 of the Constitution states that the people's courts shall exercise judicial power independently and in accordance with the stipulations of the law, and free from any interference by administrative agencies, social organizations, or individuals. However, in practice, judicial power may not be exercised independently (Peerenboom, 2010). Even the supreme people's courts' activities are not free from political and other influences. This is because of the way the current judicial system is set up. China is a communist-party-dominated socialist country and there is no separation of powers.[5] The People's Congress is the basic organization of the nation's political power. According to the Constitution, the National People's Congress (NPC) is the highest body of state power and is required to be under the leadership of the communist party. Though defined as the nation's top judiciary body, the supreme people's court is required to report to the NPC. Below the NPC, there are local people's congresses at the province and county level to which the lower people's courts report to and to which the courts are beholden to for funding.

There are also other characteristics of the legal system that affect the independence of the judiciary. According to Article 11 of the Judge Law in China, the presidents of the various levels of local courts are appointed and dismissed by the local People's Congress.[6] Therefore, judges need to maintain the favour of the Party and government officials to keep their positions. The court personnel are not much different from an ordinary cadre in the bureaucratic system under the Communist Party rule. Supreme and high court judges are selected from lower level judges with at least five years' experience, and from legal academics and senior lawyers. At the basic court level, presidents in the past were often appointed based on their political background rather than their legal skills. Nowadays, presidents are supposed to meet the qualification requirements for judges and to be selected from the best judges in the court.

Each level of court is essentially responsible to the local political power at the same level, a responsibility that is reinforced by local control over court finances. The expenses of the People's courts are included in the local government's budget, which is examined and approved by the People's congresses at each level. Zhang (2002) states that one of the judicial syndromes in China is the lack of funding from the central government and the reliance on the local government to meet court expenses. The judge's salary and the funds for court operations come mostly from the local

---

[5] The Chinese Communist Party takes the leading position in China's politics, economy, and society. As the ruling party, it leads and coordinates the work of the People's congresses and their standing committees, executives, the People's court, and the People's procuratorates.

[6] The vice-president, chief judge, and vice-chief judge of tribunals and their judges are appointed and removed by the standing committee of the People's congress at the equivalent level. The Organization Law of People's Courts provides the People's congress with the power to remove the president of the People's court at its equivalent level.

government budget and are subject to the threat of reduction whenever the court decisions adversely affect the local interest.[7]

The lack of professional ethics and judicial corruption can affect judicial independence (Yang 2013).[8] In China, personal relationships or 'back-door' connections play significant roles in all aspects of society. This can often be observed in the adjudication of court proceedings. For example, many lawyers spend a lot of their time trying to gain easy access to the presiding judge instead of concentrating their efforts on traditional legal analysis.

Another system defect is the internal managerial system of the people's courts. Within the people's courts, the president of each court is both the chief judge and the chief executive. The president has the power to influence the promotion and demotion of any judge in the court. In most cases, the local people's court president is a political appointee of the local government. Although cases are tried by a collegial panel, the panel's decision is subject to review by the trial committee consisting of the president, vice presidents, and division directors.[9] Thus, the ability of the judge or collegial panel to reach an independent decision on a case is considerably constrained.

The effectiveness of any legal system depends on the skills and integrity of its lawyers and judges. At the beginning of China's reforms in the 1990s, the legal training of judges was very weak. According to Zhang (2002), only 19.1% of the presidents and vice-presidents of the people's courts received a bachelor's degree or higher qualification. Many who did have a law degree did so through continuing education rather than through a period of intense full-time study. The government recognized this state of affairs and has instituted major judicial reforms, which include those relating to the education and training of lawyers and judges (Yang 2013; State Council 2012). He and Su (2013) report that the numbers of judges, lawyers, and law schools have increased substantially in recent years. However, they also opine that 'corruption and favouritism are rampant and judicial independence remains largely on paper' (p. 123). Despite the much better training of lawyers, their independence and freedom from bias is still a matter of concern (Yang 2013). This lack of judicial independence can lead to home bias in the court room.

The heavy government impact on the local court leads to legal localism which manifests itself in terms of delaying the prosecution, and increased fees and onerous procedures for non-local plaintiffs. The main research question addressed in this chapter is whether local firms have an advantage in local courts in corporate litigations. We define local firms based on where the headquarters are located. If home

---

[7] The Xinhua news agency reports that local protectionism made it difficult for the courts to make and enforce unbiased rulings, because local governments control the receipts and expenditures of courts. According to Li Daoming, the president of the Henan Provincial Higher People's Court, inadequate funding led to failures in enforcing the law. For example, in 2002, staff members in 101 courts in Henan were owed 47.57 million RMB in unpaid salaries. This led to low morale and likely slowed down the courts' work.

[8] For example, according to the Supreme People's Court 2002 Work Report, 995 judges and judicial personnel violated laws and rules in 2001.

[9] When hearing a case in accordance with the Civil Procedure Law, the people's court shall form either a collegial panel consisting of an odd number of both judges and judicial assessors (jurors) or judges alone.

bias exists, we would expect that the abnormal stock return will be more positive (or less negative) for the local defendant than it is for the non-local defendant, and there is a higher probability for a local defendant to win the case. This hypothesis also implies that if a non-local defendant loses its case, there is a higher probability for them to file an appeal. Here, the non-local defendant believes there is local bias against them, which they hope will be recognized in an appeal.

21.2.3   The Heterogeneity of the Legal Environment across Regions

There is great heterogeneity in institutional quality across the various regions in China (Qian and Xu 1993; Jin, Qian, and Weingast 2005), which makes it a natural labora-tory for a cross-sectional investigation of whether and how the institutional environ-ment affects the independence of the courts. This heterogeneity is partly the result of the decentralization reforms undertaken since 1978 (Jin, Qian, and Weingast 2005; Qian and Weingast 1996; Qian and Xu 1993; Firth, Rui, and Wu 2011a). The signifi-cant variation in legal environment across regions could have a significant impact on local government incentives to protect local firms through its influence on the local court.

We use an index constructed by Fan, Wang, and Zhu (2003, 2007) to control for the quality of the legal environment in each province. The legal environment index includes five aspects that are closely related to the extent of investor protection. It measures the development of market intermediaries, protection of property rights, protection of copyrights and consumers, and an index of professional lawyers that measures the number of qualified lawyers as a percentage of the population in the province. Allen, Qian, and Qian (2005) argue that the supply of qualified legal profes-sionals is crucial for an effective law enforcement system, which is closely correlated with the investor protection of the province. Therefore, these indexes are effective instruments for investor protection in a province in China. A court located in a well-developed legal environment should face less interference from the government. Therefore, we expect that home court bias should be mitigated in a well-developed legal environment.

21.3   Empirical Evidence

Measuring directly the extent of local protectionism is very difficult. While some pro-tectionist policies are specific and quantifiable, others are subtle and indirect. For example, to protect the local automobile industry, some regions blatantly list locally made cars as the only choice for taxi service firms within that jurisdiction, while other regions give a long list of technical specifications such as the size of the engine and the rate of emissions that effectively narrows down the choice set in favour of locally made cars. Bai et al. (2004) use the benefits from protecting local firms and industries as indirect measures for the extent of local protectionism. Local governments obtain more financial benefits from industries with higher profit and tax margins, and they derive more control benefits from state-owned enterprises (Shleifer and Vishny 1994). We use a different approach to quantify local protectionism. Specifically, we use changes in stock prices to measure investors' perceptions of the benefits and costs of litigation to the plaintiff and to the defendant. We then examine whether the stock market reaction is conditioned on the location where the case is heard. We also examine the propensity to appeal a court's verdict and the results of the appeal to see if there are differences between home courts and non-home courts. These tests allow us to make inferences about home court bias and judiciary local protectionism.

21.3.1   Sample

We hand collect data on litigations that involve listed firms either as plaintiffs or as defendants. This process requires a comprehensive search of company announcements and financial statements for the years 1999 through 2012. Listed firms disclose the litigations through specific corporate announcements and in their periodic financial statements. In total, we identify 5,436 litigation cases over the sample period. In order to conduct the event study, we restrict our analysis to announcements where we are able to identify when and where the litigations take place and when there is no other major firm-specific event taking place around the same time as the litigation announcement. A total of 2,419 cases enter our final sample. There are 1,467 cases involving defendants and 952 cases involving plaintiffs.

To examine home bias we need information on the location where the trial takes place, the headquarters location of the defendant, and the headquarters location of the plaintiff. We identify 31 locations that have litigation cases involving listed firms. The locations reflect the major administrative regions of China[10] and are made up of provinces and four major municipalities or cities. For ease of exposition we use the term 'provinces' to represent these different administrative regions even though four of them are cities. The provinces administer courts that are situated in that province. According to the Civil Procedure Law, a lawsuit based on a contract dispute shall be under the jurisdiction of the people's court of the place where the defendant has his domicile or where the contract is performed. A lawsuit involving real estate should be under the jurisdiction of the people's court in the place where the estate is located. A lawsuit involving an infringement act shall be under the jurisdiction of the people's court in the place where the infringing act took place or where the defendant has his or her domicile. A lawsuit based on claims for damages caused by a railway, road, water transport, or air accident shall be under the jurisdiction of the people's court in the place where the accident occurred or where the vehicle or ship first arrived after the accident or where the aircraft first landed after the accident, or where the defendant has his domicile. Thus, in very general terms, territorial jurisdiction is often determined by the defendant's domicile. This jurisdiction doctrine is commonly characterized as the plaintiff accommodating the defendant. As we will see, however, this is a very general rule and many cases are not heard on the defendant's home turf. Some court location decisions seem to defy the provisions in the Civil Procedure

---

[10] The Chinese political system is broadly composed of five layers of state administration: the centre, provinces, municipalities, counties, and townships. The administrative regions consist of 23 provinces, 5 autonomous regions, 4 centrally administered municipalities, and 2 special administrative regions, Hong Kong and Macao. Under them are 2,862 county-level administrative units.

Law; however, we are not privy to all the details and factors leading up to the court location decision.

21.3.2   Basic Statistics

In Table 21.1 we present descriptive statistics for the lawsuit filings by year, the type of opposing parties, the type of legal issue, the type of litigation, the level of court, and location. Panel A of Table 21.1 shows that the number of litigation cases in our sample at first increased and then decreased during the sample period, with the peak in 2005. There are 638 observations in 2004 and 2005, making up 26 percent of total observations during period 1999 to 2012. During 2004 and 2005, banks were under pressure from the government to improve their balance sheets and they resorted to litigation to recover overdue principal and interest; this might help explain the increase in cases in these years. For those cases involving defendants and plaintiffs who are located in different provinces, there are 464 cases that are filed at the defendant's home court, and 284 cases that are filed at the opponent's home court. For 489 cases, both defendant and plaintiff are headquartered in the same province. The remaining 230 cases are filed at neither the defendant's nor the plaintiff's province. Thus, the doctrine of 'plaintiff accommodating the defendant' is a somewhat weak explanation or gross generalization of court location. For those cases involving plaintiffs, there are 247 cases that are filed at the plaintiff's home court, and there are 244 cases filed in the opponent's province. For 329 cases, both defendants and plaintiffs are headquartered in the same provinces. The remaining 132 cases are filed at neither the defendant's nor the plaintiff's home province.

Panel B of Table 21.1 shows the number of observations for filing against defendants (plaintiffs) categorized by the type of opponents and by the court location. We classify the type of opponent into six categories: bank, government agency, a non-listed firm, another listed firm, foreign firm, and private individual. For those cases involving defendants, the largest number of filings is for bank lawsuits (where banks sue their customers, clients, and suppliers), followed by disputes with a non-listed firm. For bank lawsuits, the numbers of cases that are filed at the defendant's home court, the plaintiff's home court, both defendant's and plaintiff's home court, and neither the defendant's nor the plaintiff's home court, are 299, 39, 188, and 105, respectively. For cases involving plaintiffs, the largest number of filing announcements occurs for inter-firm disputes with non-listed businesses. Among the 777 disputes with non-listed firms, the number of cases filed at the plaintiff's home court, the defendant's home court, both the defendant's and the plaintiff's home courts (that is, the defendant and plaintiff are from the same province), and neither the defendant's nor the plaintiff's home courts, are 195, 191, 283, and 108, respectively.

Panel C of Table 21.1 shows the defendant and plaintiff filings by the type of cases and court location. The filing announcements cover different legal issues. We read each case to identify what is the real issue in the dispute. We identify five types of cases: breach of contract, breach of loan covenants, breach of a loan guarantee agreement, asset transactions, and others. The most common types of disputes involve issues of breach of contract, breach of loan covenant, and breach of loan guarantee agreement.

Table 21.1 Descriptive statistics of the sample.

Panel A: Sample by year

This panel reports descriptive statistics for filings according to whether the firm is a defendant or a plaintiff, by year and by the location of the court. Based on the location of the court where the case is heard, we classify the type of the court's location into four categories: the firm's home province, the opponent's home province, both the firm's and the opponent's home province, and neither the firm's nor the opponent's home province.

	Defendant					Plaintiff				
	Home court	Opponent's court	Both parties' court	Neither of the two parties' courts	Total	Home court	Opponent's home court	Both parties' court	Neither of the two parties' courts	Total
1999	35	6	34	5	80	2	3	9	0	14
2000	41	17	23	11	92	7	5	21	0	33
2001	37	10	25	4	76	18	3	16	6	43
2002	38	20	24	8	90	21	17	29	3	70
2003	40	15	37	11	103	16	10	28	16	70
2004	101	22	47	16	186	30	13	19	16	78
2005	78	32	91	52	253	28	24	49	20	121
2006	14	18	48	21	101	19	25	34	6	84
2007	18	20	30	23	91	17	18	26	4	65
2008	21	24	35	28	108	18	16	20	15	69
2009	12	25	40	20	97	18	32	28	18	96
2010	12	22	26	14	74	24	33	17	13	87
2011	11	25	15	10	61	14	16	20	6	56
2012	6	28	14	7	55	15	29	13	9	66
Total	464	284	489	230	1467	247	244	329	132	952

(continued)

Table 21.1 (Continued)

Panel B: Sample by the type of opponent

This panel reports descriptive statistics for filings according to whether the firm is a defendant or a plaintiff, by type of opponent and by the location of the court. We classify the type of opponent into six categories: bank, government agency, a non-listed firm, another listed firm, foreign firm and individual.

	Defendant					Plaintiff				
	Home court	Opponent's home court	Both parties' court	Neither of the two parties' courts	Total	Home court	Opponent's home court	Both parties' court	Neither of the two parties' courts	Total
Bank	299	39	188	105	631	9	5	7	5	26
Government	3	9	16	4	32	4	10	13	4	31
Non-listed firm	110	164	248	99	621	195	191	283	108	777
Listed firm	8	17	23	8	56	9	11	20	6	46
Foreign firm	7	12	1	3	23	8	10	0	5	23
Individual	37	43	13	11	104	22	17	6	4	49
Total	464	284	489	230	1467	247	244	329	132	952

Panel C: Sample by the type of cases

This panel reports descriptive statistics for filings according to whether the firm is a defendant or a plaintiff, by type of cases and by the location of the court. We classify the type of cases into five categories: breach of contract, breach of loan covenants, breach of loan guarantee agreement, asset transaction, and others. The breach of contract means the litigation is related to product and service contracts with the named parties.

	Defendant					Plaintiff				
	Home court	Opponent's home court	Both parties' court	Neither of the two parties' courts	Total	Home court	Opponent's home court	Both parties' court	Neither of the two parties' courts	Total
Contract	101	101	146	60	408	113	101	148	61	423
Loan covenants	138	48	153	70	409	34	41	62	24	161

	Defendant					Plaintiff				
	Home court	Opponent's home court	Both parties' court	Neither of the two parties' courts	Total	Home court	Opponent's home court	Both parties' court	Neither of the two parties' courts	Total
Loan guarantee	174	35	108	52	369	9	14	18	6	47
asset transaction	14	25	26	8	73	23	17	21	9	70
others	37	75	56	40	208	68	71	80	32	251
Total	464	284	489	230	1467	247	244	329	132	952

Panel D: Sample by the type of litigation

This panel reports descriptive statistics for filings according to whether the firm is a defendant or a plaintiff, by type of litigation and by the location of the court. We classify the type of litigation into three categories: civil lawsuit, administrative lawsuit, and arbitration.

	Defendant					Plaintiff				
	Home court	Opponent's home court	Both parties' court	Neither of the two parties' courts	Total	Home court	Opponent's home court	Both parties' court	Neither of the two parties' courts	Total
Civil Lawsuit	449	262	459	213	1383	230	220	302	113	865
Administrative Lawsuit	4	6	9	2	21	4	7	2	1	14
Arbitration	11	16	21	15	63	13	17	25	18	73
Total	464	284	489	230	1467	247	244	329	132	952

Panel E: Sample by the level of court

This panel reports descriptive statistics for filings according to whether the firm is a defendant or a plaintiff, by level of court and by the location of the court. We classify the level of court into four categories: basic people's court, intermediate people's court, higher people's court, and others.

	Defendant					Plaintiff				
	Home court	Opponent's home court	Both parties' court	Neither of the two parties' courts	Total	Home court	Opponent's home court	Both parties' court	Neither of the two parties' courts	Total
Basic	84	69	108	55	316	57	64	62	30	213
Immediate	279	107	252	72	710	122	71	149	39	381

(continued)

Table 21.1 (Continued)

	Defendant					Plaintiff				
	Home court	Opponent's home court	Both parties' court	Neither of the two parties' courts	Total	Home court	Opponent's home court	Both parties' court	Neither of the two parties' courts	Total
Higher	60	24	55	23	162	23	22	32	9	86
Others	41	84	74	80	279	45	87	86	54	272
Total	464	284	489	230	1467	247	244	329	132	952

Panel F: Sample by which province the firm is located in

This panel reports descriptive statistics for filings according to whether the firm is a defendant or a plaintiff, by the province where the firm is located. MLegal score is an index to capture the legal environment of each province in China. The index is measured from the following: (1) the development of intermediary organizations, such as lawyers, and accountants; (2) the protection of manufacturers; (3) the protection of intellectual property; and (4) the protection of customers. The higher the score, the better the legal environment of the province is. CExpense is the per capita average annual local fiscal expenditure on the public security, procuratorial work and the court of justice (unit: 100 RMB) of each province during our sample period.

			Defendant		Plaintiff	
Province	MLegal Score	Per capita CExpense	Number of cases	Ratio of cases (%)*	Number of cases	Ratio of cases (%)*
Shanghai	12.23	5.14	220	10.43	124	5.88
Zhejiang	10.26	2.54	77	4.65	95	5.74
Beijing	9.71	5.79	97	6.04	64	3.99
Guangdong	9.25	2.84	248	8.99	146	5.29
Jiangsu	8.92	2.09	56	3.57	46	2.94
Tianjin	7.72	3.56	30	7.85	12	3.14
Liaoning	5.69	2.22	59	8.23	22	3.07

Fujian	5.64	1.72	41	5.86	61	8.71
Shandong	5.35	1.29	106	8.54	30	2.42
Sichuan	4.60	1.26	109	12.18	69	7.71
Heilongjiang	4.58	1.70	28	7.16	22	5.63
Hubei	4.47	1.41	44	5.01	24	2.73
Jilin	4.36	1.88	29	6.49	19	4.25
Chongqing	4.31	1.58	81	21.60	23	6.13
Anhui	4.27	0.96	9	1.32	8	1.17
Shanxi	4.10	1.61	8	2.17	6	1.63
Hebei	4.03	1.28	17	3.70	10	2.18
Xinjiang	3.97	2.51	15	3.77	14	3.52
Neimenggu	3.95	2.25	1	0.41	5	2.06
Henan	3.94	1.00	15	2.83	10	1.89
Hainan	3.77	2.15	30	10.20	23	7.82
Jiangxi	3.71	1.19	2	0.61	3	0.92
Shaanxi	3.70	1.41	23	5.78	14	3.52
Hunan	3.55	1.18	60	9.45	24	3.78
Guangxi	3.53	1.33	22	6.88	34	10.63
Yunnan	3.49	1.60	2	0.65	9	2.90
Ningxia	3.22	2.15	12	7.95	5	3.31
Guizhou	2.87	1.35	4	1.77	14	6.19
Gansu	2.87	1.24	7	2.73	11	4.30
Qinghai	2.39	2.53	2	1.55	4	3.10
Xizang	2.05	6.22	13	11.30	1	0.87

*This is the percentage of cases to the total firm-year observations in a province/city.

Panel D of Table 21.1 tabulates defendant and plaintiff filings by the type of litigation and court location. We classify the type of litigation into three categories: civil lawsuit, administrative lawsuit, and arbitration. The largest number of filings is for civil lawsuits, which account for 94% (91%) of observations for defendants (plaintiffs). Panel E of Table 21.1 reports defendant and plaintiff filings by court level and court location. There are four levels of court: basic people's court, intermediate people's court, higher people's court, and the supreme people's court, representing county, prefecture, province, and national levels, respectively. Most of the lawsuits are filed at the intermediate people's court level, followed by the basic people's court level. Table 21.1, Panel F, shows that the observations are unevenly distributed across the different provinces. As a proportion of the number of listed firms in a province, the defendants are more likely to be located in Chongqing, Sichuan, Shanghai, and Xizang, while plaintiffs are more likely to be located at Guangxi, Fujian, Hainan, and Sichuan. For example, there are 81 cases in Chongqing and there are 375 firm-year observations of listed firms in Chongqing (approximately 27 firms per year times 14 years). This means that about 21.6% of total firm-year observations (375) are involved in litigation as a defendant. Panel F also shows two statistics relating to the legal environment of each province. The MLegal score is taken from Fan, Wang, and Zhu (2003, 2007) and it represents the sophistication and development of the legal system in each province. A high score represents a more highly developed legal environment. We use MLegal in our regression tests. Per capita CExpense represents the money spent by each province on the legal system divided by the population of the province. A higher judicial budget may indicate higher quality courts (Berkowitz and Clay 2006). We use CExpense as an alternative to MLegal in our regression analyses.

21.3.3   The Wealth Effect for Defendants and Plaintiffs around the Filing Announcements at Different Courts

Prior US research finds that defendants suffer significant wealth losses when a lawsuit is filed, while plaintiff firms experience no significant changes in wealth. For example, Bhagat, Bizjak, and Coles (1998) analyse a large sample of lawsuits in which at least one side, plaintiff or defendant, is a corporation. They find that the average wealth loss for a defendant is 0.97% of the market value of the equity, or $15.96 million. These losses are in the forms of fines, penalties, restitution, prohibitions on commercial practices, and damaged reputation. However, it has proved difficult to obtain precise estimates of these different costs (Bhagat and Romano 2002; Helland 2006; Karpoff, Lott, and Wehrly 2005; Prince and Rubin 2002).

We use the event study methodology to measure how news of the litigation affects the stock market values of the defendant and plaintiff firms. The event date is the first reported announcement of any lawsuit filing by listed firms. To isolate the effect of the litigation, we delete those firms with multiple news events during the event window. The abnormal return for security i on event date t is given by:

$$AR_{i,t} = R_{i,t} - E\left(R_{i,t} \mid I_t\right) \tag{1}$$

where $AR_{i,t}$, $R_{i,t}$, and $E(R_{i,t}|I_t)$ are the abnormal, actual, and expected returns for time period t, respectively. I_t is the information set on which the expected return depends. We use both the market adjusted returns model (where the actual market return is used as the expected return on the individual stock) and the market model (where we use a firm's systematic risk and the market return to generate its expected stock return) in our study and they give similar results and conclusions. For brevity's sake, we just report the results using the market adjusted returns model.[11] We cumulate $AR_{i,t}$ to obtain cumulative abnormal returns (CARs).

Table 21.2 shows the market adjusted stock returns for defendants, plaintiffs, and for a portfolio of matched opponents (where both the plaintiff and the defendant are listed firms) during the 21-day event period. For plaintiffs and defendants on their own, the cumulative abnormal return when the filing is announced represents the change in expectation about both the wealth transfer and the costs of litigation. The mean (median) CAR (−10, +10) for defendant firms is −2.73% (−2.01%). The t-statistic is significant, which implies a rejection of the null hypothesis of zero abnormal returns. The Wilcoxon signed-rank test and the Fisher sign test show that the negative median returns and the percentage of negative returns are statistically significant. The negative returns for defendant firms are consistent with evidence from the US The mean and median changes in firm value for the defendant shareholders are −RMB 63.87 million and −RMB 25.08 million.[12] The market considers litigation to be bad news for the defendant.

The average abnormal stock returns for the plaintiff firms around the lawsuit filings are negative and statistically significant. The negative returns for plaintiffs contrast with the positive returns reported in the US (Bizjak and Coles 1995). The mean (median) stock returns of −0.82% (−1.10%) is significantly different from zero. The Wilcoxon signed-rank test and the Fisher sign test are statistically significant. The mean and median changes in firm value for the plaintiff shareholders are −RMB52.35 million and −RMB22.30 million, respectively. One explanation for the negative abnormal returns for a plaintiff is that any positive effect from the judgment is offset on average by the expected litigation costs. A second interpretation of the results is that the litigation announcement tells investors for the first time that the firm has been injured and may not be able to fully recoup all of its losses. Thus, the expected damages received might be less than the losses suffered. Our results indicate that plaintiffs can inflict economic damage on defendants through litigation, but the plaintiffs do not gain from the defendants' losses. Figure 21.1 plots the CARs for the defendants and plaintiffs over a 20-day event period centred on the announcement of the litigation. There is a general downward drift in the CARs of the defendants over the event window and a less pronounced downward drift for plaintiffs.

---

[11] We use both equal- and value-weighted market returns. They give similar conclusions and we therefore just report the results using equally weighted market returns. We also use the Scholes-Williams (1977) and Dimson (1979) methods to alleviate concerns about the impact of non-synchronous trading. The results from these alternative estimation methods give similar results to those reported here.

[12] The exchange rate during our sample period ranges from US $1 = RMB8.3 to US $1 = RMB6.5.

Table 21.2   Abnormal stock returns and wealth effect.
This table reports abnormal stock returns around lawsuit filings for defendant, plaintiff, and a paired sample of firms. If both the defendant and plaintiff of the same case are listed firms, they are classified as a paired defendant and plaintiff. The average CAR of the matched sum-sample is the weighted sum of the CARs of the defendants and plaintiffs (where the weights are based on the relative market values of the two listed firms). The CARs are for day −10 to day +10 around the announcement of the filing of the lawsuit. The dollar change in shareholder wealth is calculated by multiplying the CAR by the market value prior to the announcement.

Panel A: Cumulative abnormal stock returns around lawsuit filings for defendant, plaintiff, and a paired sample of firms

	Defendant	Plaintiff	Matched Defendant & plaintiff
Average CAR(−10, +10)	−2.73%	−0.82%	−4.15%
T-statistic (p-value)	−8.02 (0.00)	−2.50 (0.01)	−2.13 (0.03)
Median CAR (−10, +10)	−2.01%	−1.10%	−2.66%
Wilcoxon Signed-Rank p-value	0.000	0.001	0.044
Number of positive CARs	578	387	35
Fisher sign test p-value	0.000	0.000	0.087
Mean change in shareholder wealth (RMB million)	−63.87	−52.35	−61.53
Median change in shareholder wealth (RMB million)	−25.08	−22.30	−51.28
Sample size	1408	909	83

Panel B: Cumulative abnormal returns around the lawsuit filing date for defendants classified by the court's location.

	Mean of CAR	Median of CAR	t-statistics	Fisher sign test p-value	Wilcoxon Signed-Rank p-value	Number of positive CAR	Sample size
Home court	−1.67%	−1.04%	−2.66***	0.072	0.030	204	447
Opponent's court	−2.52%	−2.20%	−3.60***	0.000	0.000	93	250
Both parties' court	−3.61%	−2.68%	−6.00***	0.000	0.000	188	498
Neither parties' court	−3.17%	−2.32%	−3.84***	0.075	0.001	93	213
F-value			1.92				
Kruskal-Wallis value			7.48*				

Table 21.2 (Continued)

Panel C: Cumulative abnormal returns around the lawsuit filing date for plaintiffs classified by the court's location.

	Mean of CAR	Median of CAR	t-statistics	Fisher sign test p-value	Wilcoxon Signed-Rank p-value	Number of positive CAR	Sample size
Home court	−0.58%	−0.88%	−0.82	0.105	0.194	97	219
Opponent's court	−1.18%	−1.13%	−1.72*	0.025	0.076	98	231
Both parties' court	−0.73%	−1.45%	−1.39	0.002	0.034	141	341
Neither parties' court	−0.84%	−0.78%	−1.07	0.167	0.148	51	118
F-value			0.15				
Kruskal-Wallis value			0.09				

***, ** indicates statistical significance at the 0.01 and 0.05 levels, respectively.

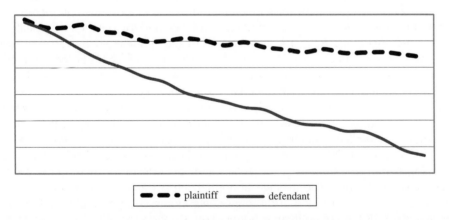

Figure 21.1 The Market-adjusted cumulated abnormal returns around the filing date (%)

A question arises why a plaintiff might institute a lawsuit when the returns from doing so, on average, are negative. We have several conjectures on this. Litigation is a relatively rare occurrence for a firm and the plaintiff's managers feel very confident about their case. These managers are probably not aware of the typical reaction of investors to plaintiff litigation and, in any event, they feel confident about the merits of their own case. This confidence may be borne of hubris on the part of the plaintiffs' managers. Another conjecture is that the litigation may in fact result in less negative returns compared to what would happen if there was no action (once the firm's injury and 'no action' is revealed).

We also measure the combined wealth effect for the defendants and plaintiffs when both firms are listed. To do this, we follow Bhagat, Brickley, and Coles (1994) and calculate a weighted return, where the weight for each firm is equal to its proportion of the combined market value of the two firms' common stock at the end of the fiscal year just prior to the year in which the event occurred. On average, the combined market value of the firms' common stock drops by a statistically significant 4.15%. The average combined reduction in the firms' stock values is RMB61.53 million. The median combined return is −2.66%, and the median decline in firm value is RMB51.28 million. The Wilcoxon signed-rank test and the Fisher sign test are significant at conventional levels.

Our parametric and non-parametric tests show substantial joint wealth losses for firms upon the filing of a lawsuit in China. The results imply that lawsuits represent a significant breakdown in the bargaining process between the litigating parties and result in significant combined losses.

21.3.4   The Impact of Court Location on the Wealth Effect

The major focus of this study is on whether a firm has an advantage if the case is heard in a court that is situated in the same province as the firm. We report the impact of court location on the wealth effect around the filing announcement in Panel B of Table 21.2. The average CAR for a defendant in a case heard in its opponent's court (where the court is located in the plaintiff's province and the defendant is located in another province) is −2.52%. The average CAR for a defendant when the case is heard at its own home court is −1.67%, while the CAR for a defendant at the same court as its opponent (where both have home court advantage) is −3.61%. Thus, litigation is regarded as less bad news for defendants with home court advantage. The average CAR for a defendant whose case is heard at neither its own nor its opponent's home court is −3.17%. All these CARs are statistically significant. However, the standard F-test does not reject the null hypothesis that the CAR is the same between the defendants with and without home court advantages (however, the Kruskal-Wallis statistic gives some marginal support at the 10% significance level for there being a difference). For the plaintiff, the average abnormal returns are a statistically significant −1.18% if the cases are filed at the opponents' home courts (Panel C, Table 21.2). The average CAR for a plaintiff at its home court is not statistically significant. To help illustrate the numbers in Table 21.2, Figure 21.2 and 21.3 plot the CARs overtime and across court jurisdictions. Visually, at least, firms have higher stock returns when cases are heard in their local courts.

21.3.5   Regression Analysis of the Wealth Effects from a Filing Announcement

There is great heterogeneity in the lawsuits and firm and lawsuit characteristics may mask the impact of home court bias. In order to isolate the impact of home court bias we develop a regression model with controls for a firm's characteristics, share

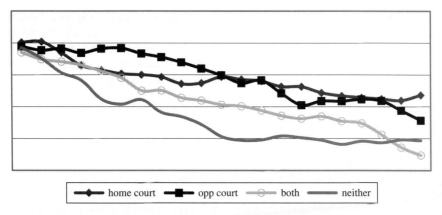

Figure 21.2   The defendant's market-adjusted cumulated abnormal returns around the filing date grouped by court location (%).

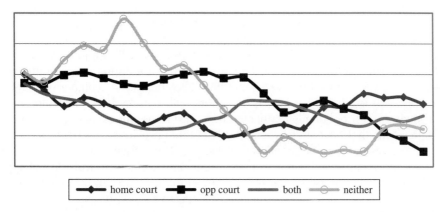

Figure 21.3   The plaintiff's market-adjusted cumulated abnormal returns around the filing date grouped by court location (%).

ownership, political connections, legal environment, type of opponent, type of case, type of litigation, and the seniority level of the court. Firms that are controlled by the state (where the state or an agency of the state is the largest shareholder) and firms that have political connections to the state may receive biased judgments (Firth, Rui, and Wu 2011b). Political connections are identified if the CEO or chairperson are family members of government officials or have previously held a senior position in central or local government (Fan, Wong, and Zhang 2007). We also control for firm size, which is a proxy for direct legal costs, and the relative size of the litigation. Amount is defined as the ratio of the dollar (RMB) amount requested in the filing by the plaintiff normalized by the book value of equity at the beginning of the year.

We also control for a firm's closeness to financial distress. Using US data, Cutler and Summers (1988) and Bhagat, Brickley, and Coles (1994) show that a firm's near- ness to bankruptcy helps explain the stock market's reaction to litigation involving the firm. We measure nearness to financial distress using the bankruptcy prediction model of Wu and Lu (2001). They construct a logistic model to estimate the probability of bankruptcy for a China listed firm. We use the parameter estimates from Wu and Lu (2001) and the accounting data from our sample firms, to estimate the probability of bankruptcy.[13],[14] We calculate the probability of bankruptcy for the fiscal year immediately before the year in which the announcement of litigation is made.

Table 21.3 presents the parameter estimates for the regression models. In each case, the dependent variable is the filing event-window CAR for the defendant or plaintiff firm, which extends from 10 days before the filing to 10 days after. Explanatory variables include dummy variables to control for state ownership, political connections, the type of the lawsuit, the type of opponent, the type of litigation, the level of the court, and the financial distress variable. We use heteroskedasticity-robust standard errors corrected for clustering of observations at the firm level and provincial level (Petersen 2009). Year and industry controls are added although the coefficients are not reported in the tables. Multicollinearity does not seem to be a problem in the model, as the maximum variance inflation factor of the coefficients is 1.5.

We first briefly discuss the basic results (Model 1 in Panels A and B) without considering court location. Many of the dummy variables are not significant in any of the regressions except for those that capture the type of case. The coefficients on ROA and Log(Amount) are significant. The findings are consistent with the previous US studies that the firms' performance and litigation amount are important determinants of defendants' stock returns around lawsuit filings. Defendants have higher stock returns if the opponent is a foreigner. This is consistent with a home bias against foreigners. We also control for politically connected firms and firms whose major stockholder is the state. Firms that have a chairperson or CEO that previously worked for the government is considered to be politically connected. The evidence in Table 21.3, Panel A, shows that state-owned defendants and politically connected firms do not appear to be favoured. In contrast, earlier research by Firth, Rui, and Wu (2011b) found that politically connected defendant firms had less negative stock returns. We re-examine this issue in more detail later when we report the results of the interaction effects.

We include court location in Model 2 of Panel A. The coefficient on the home court variable (Home court) is positive and significant. This indicates that the defendant firms with home court advantage experience less wealth decline around the

---

[13] The model is similar to the one developed by Ohlson (1980) using US data. Bhagat, Bizjak, and Coles (1998) and Bizjack and Coles (1995) use a similar approach.

[14] The bankruptcy probability is defined as the probability of bankruptcy, whose calculation is based on the model of Wu and Lu (2001). Wu and Lu (2001) construct a logistic model similar to Ohlson (1980) to estimate the probability of bankruptcy for a China listed firm. Using the Wu and Lu (2001) parameter estimates and accounting data for the sample firms, our estimate of bankruptcy probability, $\phi_{j,t}$ is calculated as follows:

$$\phi_{j,t} = \left[1 + \exp\left(-y_{j,t}\right)\right]^{-1}$$

where $y_{jt} = -0.867 + 2.5313\ CHIN_{jt} - 40.2785\ NITA_{jt} + 0.4597\ CLCA_{jt} + 3.2293\ LLTA_{jt} - 3.9544\ WCTA_{jt} - 1.7814\ SLTA_{jt}$, and NI_{jt} = Net Income, $CHIN_{jt} = (NI_{jt} - NI_{jt-1})/(|NI_{jt}| + |NI_{jt-1}|)*2$, $NITA_{jt} = NI_{jt}$ / total assets, $CLCA_{jt}$ = current liabilities/ current assets, $LLTA_{jt}$ = long-term liabilities/ total assets, $WCTA_{jt}$ = working capital/ total assets, $SLTA_{jt}$ = sales/total assets.

Table 21.3 Multivariate analysis of wealth effects for defendants and plaintiffs around the filing announcement.

This table reports the estimated coefficients of the model of CAR(−10,+10) for the defendants and plaintiffs regressed on variables measuring firm ownership (state-controlled or not), politically-connected managers, the type of opposing parties, the type of case, the type of litigation, the level of court, firm size, ROA (profit/asset), Log (bankruptcy probability), and log (Litigation Amount). The Litigation Amount is defined as the ratio of money amount requested in the filing by the plaintiff normalized by the book value of equity at the beginning of the year. In Model 2 we add the court location dummies. Home court dummy equals one if the court is located in the listed company's province, otherwise zero. Opponent court dummy equals one if the court is located in the opponent's province and not in the listed company's province; otherwise zero. We use DMLegal or DCExpense to capture the legal environment where the court is located. MLegal score is an index to capture the legal environment of each province in China. CExpense is the per capita average annual local fiscal expenditure on the public security, procuratorial work and the court of justice (unit: 100 RMB) of each province during our sample period. We divide the sample into two groups based on the legal environment index MLegal scores (CExpense) and create a dummy DMLegal (DCExpense) which equals one if the MLegal (CExpense) score is above the median value, otherwise it is coded zero. In Model 3 we add the interaction terms between the DMLegal with home court and opponent court dummies. In Model 4 we add the interaction terms between the CExpense with home court and opponent court dummies. In Model 5 we add the interaction terms between political connections and home or opponent court dummies.

Panel A: Listed companies as defendant

	Model 1	Model 2	Model 3	Model 4	Model 5
Intercept	0.164	0.155	0.138	0.130	0.152
	(0.102)	(0.122)	(0.168)	(0.194)	(0.129)
Size	−0.012*	−0.011*	−0.011*	−0.011*	−0.011*
	(0.063)	(0.066)	(0.072)	(0.084)	(0.059)
ROA	0.010***	0.011***	0.011***	0.011***	0.011***
	(0.005)	(0.003)	(0.003)	(0.003)	(0.003)
Log (Bankruptcy probability)	−0.002	−0.002	−0.002	−0.002	−0.002
	(0.384)	(0.347)	(0.356)	(0.216)	(0.253)
State-owned	0.002	0.002	0.000	−0.001	0.001
	(0.797)	(0.840)	(0.994)	(0.903)	(0.929)
With politically-connected managers	−0.001	−0.002	−0.003	−0.003	0.017
	(0.901)	(0.825)	(0.737)	(0.711)	(0.153)
DMLegal	0.007	0.008	0.026**		
	(0.379)	(0.339)	(0.020)		
DCExpense				0.031***	
				(0.007)	
Opponent					
Bank	0.012	0.007	0.009	0.004	0.005
	(0.613)	(0.766)	(0.704)	(0.853)	(0.823)
Government	0.000	0.002	−0.001	−0.003	−0.002
	(0.989)	(0.962)	(0.972)	(0.933)	(0.959)
Non-listed firm	0.008	0.008	0.009	0.007	0.008
	(0.713)	(0.733)	(0.687)	(0.776)	(0.734)

(continued)

Table 21.3 (Continued)

	Model 1	Model 2	Model 3	Model 4	Model 5
Foreign firm	0.077**	0.072*	0.075**	0.076**	0.073*
	(0.041)	(0.057)	(0.048)	(0.044)	(0.053)
Individual	0.044	0.038	0.044	0.039	0.038
	(0.127)	(0.186)	(0.129)	(0.175)	(0.187)
Type of case					
Breach of contract	−0.022	−0.023	−0.021	−0.022	−0.023
	(0.153)	(0.131)	(0.158)	(0.153)	(0.125)
Breach of loan covenants	−0.027*	−0.027*	−0.024	−0.024	−0.025
	(0.097)	(0.095)	(0.134)	(0.137)	(0.120)
Breach of loan guarantee agreement	−0.009	−0.010	−0.010	−0.010	−0.010
	(0.606)	(0.543)	(0.551)	(0.554)	(0.551)
Tangible and intangible assets transactions	−0.039*	−0.038	−0.037	−0.035	−0.036
	(0.099)	(0.105)	(0.114)	(0.130)	(0.127)
Type of litigation					
Administrative lawsuit	−0.038	−0.045	−0.042	−0.040	−0.051
	(0.384)	(0.304)	(0.334)	(0.365)	(0.249)
Arbitration lawsuit	−0.010	−0.011	−0.012	−0.011	−0.009
	(0.651)	(0.617)	(0.579)	(0.630)	(0.697)
Court					
Basic people's court	0.013	0.012	0.010	0.013	0.014
	(0.385)	(0.423)	(0.485)	(0.392)	(0.355)
Intermediate people's court	0.012	0.010	0.008	0.010	0.012
	(0.354)	(0.448)	(0.559)	(0.427)	(0.370)
Higher people's court	0.018	0.015	0.013	0.015	0.016
	(0.272)	(0.353)	(0.433)	(0.367)	(0.318)
Log (Amount)	−0.007***	−0.006***	−0.006***	−0.006***	−0.006***
	(0.003)	(0.006)	(0.008)	(0.005)	(0.008)
Home court		0.018**	0.040***	0.043***	0.028***
		(0.045)	(0.001)	(0.000)	(0.008)
Opponent court		0.002	0.014	0.006	0.011
		(0.877)	(0.379)	(0.701)	(0.411)
Home court * DMLegal			−0.046***		
			(0.007)		
Opponent court * DMlegal			−0.024		
			(0.292)		
Home court * DCExpense				−0.057***	
				(0.001)	
Opponent court * DCExpense				−0.006	
				(0.783)	
Home court * With political connections					0.037**
					(0.048)
Opponent court * With political connections					−0.040
					(0.122)
Adjusted R²	0.038	0.040	0.044	0.048	0.042

Industry and Year controls are included. The *p*-value of *t*-statistics is given in the parentheses below the coefficient estimate. ***, **, * indicates statistical significance at the 0.01, 0.05, and 0.10 levels, respectively.

Table 21.3   (Continued)

Panel B: Listed companies as plaintiff

	Model 1	Model 2	Model 3	Model 4	Model 5
Intercept	−0.055	−0.059	−0.053	−0.038	−0.067
	(0.547)	(0.520)	(0.561)	(0.681)	(0.463)
Size	0.004	0.005	0.005	0.004	0.005
	(0.290)	(0.277)	(0.250)	(0.341)	(0.204)
ROA	0.016*	0.017*	0.017*	0.017*	0.016*
	(0.067)	(0.062)	(0.053)	(0.054)	(0.070)
Log (Bankruptcy probability)	−0.003**	−0.003**	−0.003**	−0.002**	−0.003**
	(0.032)	(0.033)	(0.034)	(0.039)	(0.024)
State-owned	0.003	0.003	0.004	0.003	0.003
	(0.698)	(0.699)	(0.682)	(0.689)	(0.757)
With politically-connected	0.008	0.007	0.008	0.007	0.004
managers	(0.349)	(0.356)	(0.350)	(0.400)	(0.706)
DMLegal	0.009	0.009	−0.007		
	(0.263)	(0.279)	(0.501)		
DCExpense				0.006	
				(0.570)	
Opponent					
Bank	0.004	0.004	−0.001	0.005	0.005
	(0.890)	(0.888)	(0.960)	(0.848)	(0.840)
Government	0.007	0.007	0.003	0.006	0.008
	(0.836)	(0.828)	(0.937)	(0.861)	(0.798)
Non-listed firm	0.010	0.010	0.007	0.010	0.010
	(0.554)	(0.566)	(0.677)	(0.548)	(0.563)
Foreign firm	−0.031	−0.032	−0.035	−0.032	−0.032
	(0.256)	(0.244)	(0.208)	(0.247)	(0.248)
Individual	−0.010	−0.009	−0.014	−0.009	−0.008
	(0.686)	(0.705)	(0.573)	(0.703)	(0.725)
Type of case					
Breach of contract	−0.014	−0.015	−0.016	−0.016	−0.014
	(0.147)	(0.140)	(0.114)	(0.116)	(0.161)
Breach of loan covenants	0.000	−0.001	−0.001	−0.002	−0.001
	(0.973)	(0.952)	(0.928)	(0.875)	(0.958)
Breach of loan guarantee	−0.003	−0.004	−0.003	−0.004	−0.003
agreement	(0.851)	(0.811)	(0.862)	(0.813)	(0.861)
Tangible and intangible assets	−0.015	−0.016	−0.015	−0.014	−0.016
transactions	(0.352)	(0.328)	(0.353)	(0.384)	(0.324)
Type of litigation					
Administrative lawsuit	−0.002	−0.004	−0.004	0.000	−0.006
	(0.962)	(0.932)	(0.942)	(0.993)	(0.912)
Arbitration lawsuit	−0.013	−0.013	−0.015	−0.015	−0.014
	(0.389)	(0.397)	(0.348)	(0.346)	(0.380)
Court					
Basic people's court	−0.014	−0.014	−0.011	−0.012	−0.014
	(0.251)	(0.273)	(0.356)	(0.314)	(0.269)
Intermediate people's court	0.008	0.009	0.009	0.009	0.007
	(0.439)	(0.393)	(0.409)	(0.425)	(0.495)

(continued)

Table 21.3   (Continued)

	Model 1	Model 2	Model 3	Model 4	Model 5
Higher people's court	−0.032**	−0.031**	−0.033**	−0.031***	−0.033**
	(0.028)	(0.032)	(0.024)	(0.032)	(0.023)
Log (Amount)	0.002	0.002	0.002	0.002	0.002
	(0.299)	(0.312)	(0.314)	(0.268)	(0.288)
Home court		−0.003	−0.015	−0.005	−0.006
		(0.707)	(0.211)	(0.640)	(0.607)
Opponent court		0.005	−0.016	−0.014	−0.002
		(0.587)	(0.212)	(0.299)	(0.888)
Home court * DMLegal			0.025		
			(0.187)		
Opponent court * DMlegal			0.046**		
			(0.015)		
Home court * DCExpense				0.003	
				(0.861)	
Opponent court * DCExpense				0.039**	
				(0.042)	
Home court * With political connections					0.002
					(0.923)
Opponent court * With political connections					0.017
					(0.409)
Adjusted R^2	0.051	0.049	0.055	0.054	0.047

Industry and Year controls are included. The p-value of t-statistics is given in the parentheses below the coefficient estimate. **, * indicates statistical significance at the 0.05 and 0.10 levels, respectively.

lawsuit filing. The evidence is consistent with that in Table 21.2, Panel B, and home court advantage reduces the negative impact of the litigation announcement.

There is great heterogeneity in the legal environment across the different regions in China and this could have a significant impact on local government incentives to protect local firms through its influence on the local court. We therefore include a measure of the sophistication of the legal environment in each province into our model. To do this, we make use of an index, which we compile from the survey research of Fan, Wang, and Zhu (2003, 2007). This index, which we call MLegal, is constructed from the following sub-indexes: (i) the development of intermediary organizations, such as lawyers, and accountants; (ii) the protection of manufacturers; (iii) the protection of intellectual property; and (iv) the protection of customers. The higher the MLEGAL score, the better the legal environment of the province. The Fan, Wong & Zhu (2003, 2007) indexes have been extensively used in prior China-based research (for example, Firth, Rui, and Wu 2011a).

We partition provinces with above-median MLegal index scores from those with below-median index scores. DMLegal is coded one if the legal environment score is above the median and is coded zero otherwise. In model 3 (Table 21.3, Panel A), we include DMLegal and its interactions with Home court and Opponent court. We find that the interaction term Home court*DMLegal has a significant and negative coefficient. This implies that a court located in a better legal environment is less likely to protect local firms. One interpretation of this result is that local government located in a better legal environment is less able or less likely to exert its influence on the local court. As a robustness check, we use CExpense as an alternative measure of legal environment. CExpense is denoted as the per capita average annual local fiscal expenditure on the public security, procuratorial work, and the court of justice for each province. We partition provinces into those with above-median CExpense (DCExpense = 1) and those with below-median CE expense (DCExpense = 0) and include this variable and its interactions with Home court and Opponent court in Model 4. We find that the coefficient on the interaction term, Home court*DCExpense, is negative and significant. Thus, our two proxies for high legal development, MLegal and CExpense, help reduce home court bias that favours defendants. We create an interaction term between home court and political connections and find a positive and significant coefficient. While Firth, Rui, and Wu (2011b) find a positive coefficient on political connections, this study shows the effect is limited to cases heard in the defendant's home court. As political connections can include local connections, the benefits from these connections for firms arise mostly when the litigation occurs in the firm's home province.

We carry out a similar analysis using the plaintiffs' CARs on the explanatory variables. The results are reported in Panel B of Table 21.3. Most of the control variables are not significant. However, profitable firms (ROA) have higher returns, which may indicate their strength in being able to absorb the legal costs involved in litigation. Consistently, firms near to bankruptcy have negative returns, which imply they might not have the resources to follow through on the lawsuits. We find that the coefficients on home court and opponent court are not significant. This indicates that investors do not perceive that local plaintiffs have any advantage in the corporate litigation. State-owned plaintiffs and politically connected plaintiffs have no advantages in litigation (as reflected in stock returns). These findings mirror those in Firth, Rui, and Wu (2011b). The legal environment variable, DMLegal, is not significant. However, the interaction of DMLegal with cases heard in an opponent's court has a positive coefficient. This suggests that investors perceive that the opponent court located in a better legal environment is less likely to be biased against the non-local plaintiffs. We obtain a similar result when we use CExpense as an alternative proxy for the legal environment (DMLegal). The results echo what we found in Panel A that home court bias is mitigated in a well-developed legal environment.

21.3.6   Heckman Two-Step Analysis of Sample Selection Bias

Lawsuits are not random because plaintiffs only file a case if they believe the benefits from suing outweigh their costs (and outweigh the benefits from settlement). Similarly, defendants have to make a decision whether to settle with the plaintiff or go to trial. To address the sample selection bias, we apply Heckman's (1979) selection bias model and present the results in Table 21.4. The first stage uses all firms, sued or not, to estimate the probability of a lawsuit occurring. We have 19,865 non-sued firm-year observations during our data period. We model the probability of a lawsuit as:

$$P_{Li} = N[X_i] = N[\alpha_0 + \alpha_1 * SIZE_i + \alpha_2 * ROA_i + \alpha_3 * Bankruptcy_i + \alpha_4 * State - owned_i$$
$$+ \alpha_5 * Politically\, Connected_i + \alpha_6 * Board\, Independence_i + \alpha_7 * DMLegal_i] \qquad (2)$$

where P_{Li} is the probability of litigation for firm i, N(x) is a standard normal cumulative density function (CDF) evaluated at x, X is a matrix of independent variables, including firm size (SIZE), performance (ROA), probability of bankruptcy (Bankruptcy), legal environment index (DMLegal or DCExpense), and the proportion of independent directors on the board (board independence). The probability of a firm going to litigation rather than making a settlement depends in part on the relative number of the independent directors. Independent directors give a more dispassionate and balanced view of the litigation matter and may have more experience of lawsuits and settlements. However, the proportion of independent directors is unlikely to affect the court's decision. We also control for whether the firm's major shareholder is some agency of the state (State-owned) and whether the firm has politically connected managers (Politically Connected). We do not include the location of the court as a variable in the first stage model as the non-sued firm-year observations do not have such data. The first stage model generates the inverse Mills ratio, which is a measure of the self-selection bias. The inverse Mills ratio is an input into the second stage model. The results are shown in Table 21.4. ROA has negative coefficients in the Litigation dummy regression, which suggests that more profitable firms are less likely to be defendants. Consistent evidence is given by the coefficients on the Log (Bankruptcy probability) variable. Board independence is significant in the first-stage regression (of whether to litigate or not), indicating that firms with boards that are more independent are less likely to be sued. Independent boards may be more inclined to settle outside of court. Firms are less likely to be defendants if they are state owned (significant at the 0.01 level) and if they are politically connected (significant at the 0.05 level).

Even after controlling for self-selection bias using the inverse Mills ratio, the coefficient on Home court in Panel A is still significantly positive. This shows that the abnormal stock market loss at the announcement of litigation is less for the home court-located firms. In general, shareholders react less negatively when a firm with home court advantage is sued than when a firm without home court advantage is sued. The coefficient on the interaction between home court and legal environment is negative and significant. The home court advantage is more prominent if the defendant is politically-connected.

We regress the plaintiffs' CARs on the explanatory variables in Panel B. The coefficient on home court is not significant. The interaction between opponent court and the quality of the legal environment is positive. Thus, plaintiffs' cases heard in the opponents' courts are less biased if the quality of the court is high (however, the p-values of the t-statistics are 0.108 for opponent court*DMLegal and 0.107 for opponent court*DCExpense). Overall, the results in Table 21.4, which control for self-selection bias, are consistent with those in Table 21.3.

Table 21.4   Heckman two-step analysis of CAR for sample selection bias.
In the first step, we estimate the probability of a lawsuit occurring. A litigation dummy (coded one if litigation occurs and zero otherwise) is modelled as a function of firm characteristics (size, ROA, log (bankruptcy probability), state-ownership, political connections, and board independence). The first stage generates an inverse Mills ratio which is added to the second step equation (of CAR) as a control for self-selection bias. The second step reports the estimated coefficients of the model of CAR(−10,+10) for the defendants and plaintiffs regressed on variables measuring the type of opposing parties, the type of case, firm ownership (state-controlled or not), politically-connected managers, the type of litigation, the level of court, firm size, ROA (profit/asset), Log (bankruptcy probability), Lamda (the inverse Mills ratio generated in step 1), and log (Litigation Amount). The Litigation Amount is defined as the ratio of money amount requested in the filing by the plaintiff normalized by the book value of equity at the beginning of the year. Home court dummy equals one if the court is located in the listed company's province, otherwise zero. Opponent court dummy equals one if the court is located in the opponent's province and not in the listed company's province; otherwise zero. We use DMLegal or DCExpense to capture the legal environment where the court is located. In Model 1 we add the interaction terms between the DMLegal with home court and opponent court dummies. In Model 2 we add the interaction terms between the CExpense with home court and opponent court dummies. In Model 3 we add interaction terms between political connections of the firms with home or opponent courts.

Panel A: Listed companies as defendant

	Model 1		Model 2		Model 3	
	Litigation Dummy	CAR	Litigation Dummy	CAR	Litigation Dummy	CAR
Intercept	0.943	0.129	1.044	0.141	0.943	0.135
	(0.144)	(0.216)	(0.107)	(0.176)	(0.144)	(0.192)
Size	0.002	−0.010**	−0.003	−0.011**	0.002	−0.011**
	(0.942)	(0.025)	(0.919)	(0.017)	(0.942)	(0.020)
ROA	−0.402***	−0.001	−0.416***	−0.001	−0.402***	−0.002
	(0.000)	(0.806)	(0.000)	(0.822)	(0.000)	(0.779)
Log (Bankruptcy probability)	0.075***	0.006**	0.076***	0.005*	0.075***	0.005*
	(0.000)	(0.043)	(0.000)	(0.050)	(0.000)	(0.050)
State-owned	−0.009***	0.000	−0.009***	0.000	−0.009***	0.000
	(0.000)	(0.178)	(0.000)	(0.218)	(0.000)	(0.137)
With politically-connected managers	−0.139**	0.005	−0.142**	0.007	−0.139**	0.041***
	(0.048)	(0.570)	(0.045)	(0.487)	(0.048)	(0.001)
Board independence	−0.705***		−0.812***		−0.705***	
	(0.003)		(0.001)		(0.003)	
DMLegal	0.077	0.024**			0.077	0.013
	(0.246)	(0.042)			(0.246)	(0.165)
DCExpense			0.175**	0.021*		
			(0.010)	(0.089)		
Lamda (Inverse Mills ratio)		0.089**		0.085**		0.088**
		(0.039)		(0.041)		(0.041)

(continued)

Table 21.4   (Continued)

	Model 1		Model 2		Model 3	
	Litigation Dummy	CAR	Litigation Dummy	CAR	Litigation Dummy	CAR
Opponent						
Bank		0.000		0.000		−0.004
		(0.985)		(0.982)		(0.856)
Government		−0.017		−0.016		−0.028
		(0.589)		(0.604)		(0.375)
Non-listed firm		−0.005		−0.006		−0.009
		(0.790)		(0.782)		(0.678)
Foreign firm		0.031		0.031		0.027
		(0.342)		(0.353)		(0.404)
Individual		0.017		0.016		0.011
		(0.507)		(0.526)		(0.661)
Type of case						
Breach of contract		−0.013		−0.012		−0.014
		(0.335)		(0.366)		(0.316)
Breach of loan covenants		−0.034**		−0.034**		−0.033**
		(0.023)		(0.025)		(0.030)
Breach of loan guarantee agreement		−0.014		−0.014		−0.014
		(0.380)		(0.380)		(0.368)
Tangible and intangible assets transactions		−0.037		−0.038*		−0.035
		(0.093)*		(0.092)		(0.117)
Type of litigation						
Administrative law-suit		−0.005		−0.003		−0.016
		(0.902)		(0.940)		(0.702)
Arbitration lawsuit		−0.012		−0.010		−0.007
		(0.576)		(0.637)		(0.751)
Court						
Basic people's court		0.010		0.012		0.013
		(0.463)		(0.402)		(0.358)
Intermediate people's court		0.008		0.011		0.011
		(0.494)		(0.376)		(0.360)
Higher people's court		0.013		0.016		0.016
		(0.378)		(0.297)		(0.285)
Log (Amount)		−0.006***		−0.006***		−0.006***
		(0.005)		(0.004)		(0.008)
Home court		0.023**		0.016**		0.039***
		(0.049)		(0.049)		(0.000)
Opponent court		0.043		0.035		0.041*
		(0.115)		(0.102)		(0.092)
Home court * DMLegal		−0.011**				
		(0.047)				
Opponent court * DMLegal		−0.037*				
		(0.082)				

Table 21.4　(Continued)

	Model 1		Model 2		Model 3	
	Litigation Dummy	CAR	Litigation Dummy	CAR	Litigation Dummy	CAR
Home court * DCExpense			−0.013** (0.050)			
Opponent court * DCExpense			−0.019 (0.367)			
Home court * With political connections						0.077*** (0.000)
Opponent court * With political connections						−0.056 (0.187)

Industry and Year controls are included. The *p*-value of *t*-statistics is given in the parentheses below the coefficient estimate. ***, **, * indicates statistical significance at the 0.01, 0.05 and 0.10 levels, respectively.

Panel B: Listed companies as plaintiff

	Model 1		Model 2		Model 3	
	Litigation Dummy	CAR	Litigation Dummy	CAR	Litigation Dummy	CAR
Intercept	−0.841 (0.222)	0.100 (0.814)	−0.506 (0.463)	0.001 (0.998)	−0.841 (0.222)	0.087 (0.832)
Size	0.037 (0.270)	0.001 (0.892)	0.019 (0.563)	0.003 (0.513)	0.037 (0.270)	0.001 (0.892)
ROA	0.006 (0.926)	0.017 (0.186)	−0.017 (0.808)	0.018* (0.083)	0.006 (0.926)	0.016 (0.192)
Log (Bankruptcy probability)	−0.035*** (0.002)	0.002 (0.727)	−0.032*** (0.004)	0.001 (0.816)	−0.035*** (0.002)	0.002 (0.746)
State-owned	0.007*** (0.000)	0.000 (0.744)	0.007*** (0.000)	0.000 (0.752)	0.007*** (0.000)	0.000 (0.735)
With politically-connected managers	0.074 (0.309)	−0.007 (0.720)	0.072 (0.320)	−0.005 (0.709)	0.074 (0.309)	−0.007 (0.724)
Board independence	−0.253 (0.295)		−0.505** (0.044)		−0.253 (0.295)	
DMLegal	0.059 (0.394)	−0.009 (0.606)			0.059 (0.394)	0.005 (0.739)
DCExpense			0.290*** (0.000)	−0.010 (0.744)		
Lamda (Inverse Mills ratio)		−0.180 (0.541)		−0.123 (0.450)		−0.172 (0.541)
Opponent						
Bank		0.007 (0.809)		0.009 (0.719)		0.010 (0.734)
Government		0.005 (0.886)		0.006 (0.843)		0.007 (0.832)

(continued)

Table 21.4   (Continued)

	Model 1		Model 2		Model 3	
	Litigation Dummy	CAR	Litigation Dummy	CAR	Litigation Dummy	CAR
Non-listed firm		0.014		0.016		0.016
		(0.468)		(0.325)		(0.397)
Foreign firm		−0.020		−0.018		−0.017
		(0.530)		(0.498)		(0.571)
Individual		−0.008		−0.005		−0.005
		(0.774)		(0.821)		(0.856)
Type of case						
Breach of contract		−0.014		−0.014		0.014
		(0.186)		(0.134)		(0.188)
Breach of loan		−0.002		−0.002		−0.002
covenants		(0.866)		(0.833)		(0.905)
Breach of loan guaran-		0.007		0.006		0.006
tee agreement		(0.735)		(0.733)		(0.748)
Tangible and intangi-		−0.012		−0.012		−0.013
ble assets		(0.527)		(0.480)		(0.498)
transactions						
Type of litigation						
Administrative lawsuit		−0.024		−0.026		−0.026
		(0.637)		(0.562)		(0.600)
Arbitration lawsuit		−0.012		−0.011		−0.010
		(0.510)		(0.456)		(0.537)
Court						
Basic people's court		−0.004		−0.005		−0.007
		(0.760)		(0.693)		(0.596)
Intermediate people's		0.018		0.019		0.017
court		(0.135)		(0.066)*		(0.129)
Higher people's court		−0.025		−0.023		−0.024
		(0.132)		(0.093)*		(0.129)
Log (Amount)		0.003		0.003		0.003
		(0.197)		(0.094)*		(0.184)
Home court		−0.009		−0.002		0.003
		(0.508)		(0.846)		(0.773)
Opponent court		−0.011		−0.010		0.003
		(0.482)		(0.453)		(0.788)
Home court * DMLegal		0.023				
		(0.264)				
Opponent court * DMLegal		0.034				
		(0.108)				
Home court * DCExpense				0.008		
				(0.633)		
Opponent court * DCExpense				0.029		
				(0.107)		

Table 21.4   (Continued)

	Model 1		Model 2		Model 3	
	Litigation Dummy	CAR	Litigation Dummy	CAR	Litigation Dummy	CAR
Home court * With political connections						−0.005 (0.799)
Opponent court * With political connections						0.008 (0.695)

Industry and Year controls are included. The *p*-value of *t*-statistics is given in the parentheses below the coefficient estimate. ***, **, * indicates statistical significance at the 0.01, 0.05 and 0.10 levels, respectively.

21.3.7   The Impact of Court Location on the Likelihood to Appeal

If there exists a home court bias, defendants who have their cases heard at the opponent's court are more likely to receive unfavourable verdicts. An alternative approach to test the home court bias is to investigate whether there is a higher likelihood for a defendant without home court advantage at the first round trial to file an appeal when the initial verdict is not favourable.[15] Judicial proceedings occur in two instances, trial and appeal, in China. The appeal must be filed at a court which is higher than the initial trial court. A decision made by an appellate court is final, and no further appeal is allowed. Of the 1,191 defendants for which we have data, 214 chose to appeal (note that unlike the abnormal stock return analyses, the sample is not constrained by the need to have non-contaminated stock prices at day 0). Panel A of Table 21.5 shows that the probability for a firm to file an appeal when the case is heard at its home court in the initial trial is 19.63%, while the probability of appeal for a defendant firm where the plaintiff and defendant share the same home court is 14.63%. The probability for a firm to appeal when the first case is heard at its opponent's home court is 29.14%. The probability for a defendant firm appealing when the case is held at neither party's home court is only 12.42%. The *F*-test and KW-test show that the difference in likelihood to file an appeal for firms at home courts and firms at their opponents' courts is statistically significant. The results suggest that the original court is more likely to issue a biased verdict to defendants if the case is heard at their opponents' courts. The result is consistent with home court bias.

We also use a logit model to measure the likelihood of an appeal. Here, the dependent variable is coded one if the defendant appeals the court's ruling. The model allows us to control for other factors that might affect the decision to appeal. The results from the logit regression model are reported in Table 21.5, Panel B. Firm size is negatively related to the propensity to appeal. Cases involving breach of contract and breach of loan covenants are less likely to be appealed. Lawsuits relating to arbitration cases are also less likely to be appealed. The significant positive coefficient

---

[15] There are relatively few appeals by plaintiffs and so we concentrate our analysis on defendants.

Table 21.5   The analysis of the impact of home bias on the likelihood to appeal.
Panel A: Univariate analysis of the likelihood to appeal partitioned by the location of the court. The variable 'appeal' is set equal to one if the firm appeals when it loses in the first-round ruling. If the firm does not appeal when they lose in the first-round filing, the variable is set to zero. The table reports the percentage of firms that choose to appeal when they lose.

	n	Mean
Home court	428	19.63%
Opponent's court	151	29.14%
Both parties' court	451	14.63%
Neither parties' court	161	12.42%
F-value		6.87***
Kruskal-Wallis value		20.32***

Panel B: Logit analysis of the likelihood to appeal
We employ a logit regression on the variable 'appeal'. The independent variables measuring the type of opposing parties, the type of case, the type of litigation, the level of court, firm size, ROA (profit/asset), Log (bankruptcy probability), state-ownership, politically connected management, and log (Litigation Amount). Home court dummy equals one if the court is located in the listed company's province, otherwise it is coded zero. Opponent court dummy equals one if the court is located in the opponent's province and not in the listed company's province; otherwise it is coded zero. We use DMLegal or DCExpense to capture the legal environment where the court is located. In Model 2 we add the interaction terms between the DMLegal with home court and opponent court dummies. In Model 3(4) we add the interaction terms between the CExpense (political connections) with home court or opponent court dummies.

	Model 1	Model 2	Model 3	Model 4
Intercept	5.211**	5.416**	4.249*	4.913*
	(0.040)	(0.033)	(0.094)	(0.051)
Size	−0.329***	−0.352***	−0.320***	−0.319***
	(0.006)	(0.003)	(0.008)	(0.007)
ROA	0.104	0.106	0.088	0.104
	(0.385)	(0.377)	(0.462)	(0.384)
Log (Bankruptcy probability)	0.010	0.012	0.012	0.011
	(0.281)	(0.176)	(0.167)	(0.228)
State-owned	0.223	0.229	0.290	0.279
	(0.232)	(0.221)	(0.123)	(0.135)
With politically connected managers	−0.407*	−0.392*	−0.465**	−1.099
	(0.070)	(0.084)	(0.045)	(0.144)
DMLegal	−0.708***	0.156		
	(0.001)	(0.789)		
DCExpense			0.974	−0.393*
			(0.100)	(0.067)
Opponent				
Bank	−0.886	−0.863	−0.865	−0.815
	(0.105)	(0.113)	(0.114)	(0.132)
Government	0.332	0.386	0.208	0.294
	(0.649)	(0.595)	(0.778)	(0.686)

Table 21.5   (Continued)

	Model 1	Model 2	Model 3	Model 4
Non-listed firm	0.297	0.363	0.299	0.333
	(0.583)	(0.499)	(0.579)	(0.534)
Foreign firm	15.128	15.242	14.685	14.847
	(0.984)	(0.983)	(0.985)	(0.985)
Individual	0.415	0.473	0.392	0.275
	(0.652)	(0.612)	(0.672)	(0.762)
Type of case				
Breach of contract	−1.418***	−1.423***	−1.554***	−1.413***
	(0.001)	(0.001)	(0.001)	(0.001)
Breach of loan covenants	−1.271***	−1.289***	−1.367***	−1.263***
	(0.001)	(0.001)	(0.001)	(0.001)
Breach of loan guarantee agreement	−0.386	−0.405	−0.466	−0.385
	(0.310)	(0.286)	(0.217)	(0.311)
Tangible and intangible assets	−0.524	−0.612	−0.656	−0.447
transactions	(0.352)	(0.284)	(0.256)	(0.430)
Type of litigation				
Administrative lawsuit	−14.48	−14.62	−14.35	−14.16
	(0.989)	(0.989)	(0.989)	(0.989)
Arbitration lawsuit	−2.759**	−2.766**	−2.878**	−2.728**
	(0.026)	(0.021)	(0.018)	(0.021)
Court				
Basic people's court	−0.379	−0.414	−0.410	−0.396
	(0.313)	(0.271)	(0.272)	(0.286)
Intermediate people's court	0.373	0.376	0.340	0.298
	(0.263)	(0.259)	(0.303)	(0.363)
Higher people's court	1.484***	1.445***	1.470***	1.517***
	(0.001)	(0.001)	(0.001)	(0.001)
Log (Amount)	−0.241***	−0.235***	−0.245***	−0.247***
	(0.001)	(0.001)	(0.001)	(0.001)
Home court	0.117	0.503	0.856*	−0.091
	(0.697)	(0.179)	(0.062)	(0.782)
Opponent court	0.723**	0.744*	1.119**	0.548*
	(0.045)	(0.095)	(0.037)	(0.067)
**Home court * ** DMLegal		−1.168*		
		(0.060)		
**Opponent court * ** DMlegal		−0.085		
		(0.908)		
**Home court * ** DCExpense			−1.716***	
			(0.005)	
**Opponent court * ** DCExpense			−0.619	
			(0.388)	
**Home court * ** With political connections				0.671
				(0.395)
**Opponent court * ** With political connections				1.031
				(0.260)
Adjusted R²	0.168	0.172	0.169	0.162

Industry and Year controls are included. The *p*-value of *t*-statistics is given in the parentheses below the coefficient estimate. ***, **, * indicates statistical significance at the 0.01, 0.05 and 0.10 levels, respectively.

on opponent court indicates that a firm whose case is heard at its opponent's court is more likely to file an appeal when the initial verdict is unfavourable. Appeals are also more likely from a higher people's court judgment. Our logit model does not include factors that reflect the initial judgment as it is impossible to quantify variables such as the merit of the case and the fairness of the judgment. We also include the interaction between home court and legal environment (DMLegal and DCExpense) to capture the impact of the legal environment on home court bias in Models 2 and 3. The coefficients on the interactions are negative and significant. This indicates that a strong legal environment can mitigate the home court bias. The interactions of political connections and home and opponent courts are not significant.

We analyse the impact of court location on the appeal results in Table 21.6. If there is a home court bias, the appealing firms are more likely to obtain a favourable verdict at the appellate court. This is predicated on the belief that home bias is less likely to be present at a higher court, especially as the appellant is likely to highlight the bias from the lower court during the appeal hearing. We define the variable 'favour' as equal to one if the appealing listed firm gets a better second-round ruling result than the first-round ruling result, i.e. the loser in the initial trial becomes the winner, or the appealing firm gains more (or pays less) in the second-round ruling. If the second-round ruling result has not changed or becomes worse, favour is set equal to zero. The sample sizes are smaller than in Table 21.5 because many appeal cases have not yet been completed. Overall, about 31.5% of appealing firms receive some benefit from the appeal process (this is the weighted average of the means in Panel A, Table 21.6). The univariate result shown in Panel A, Table 21.6, indicates that 40.0% of appealing firms, whose original trials take place at their opponents' courts, obtain a better second-round result, while only 30.88% of appealing firms whose original trials take place at their own home court achieve a better result. These raw results indicate that firms with home court advantage in the first trial receive more favourable judgments (biased judgments) than those without home court advantage. Thus, the biased judgments are overturned (or made less onerous) on appeal. However, the F-test and KW-test show that the difference in the appeal results for firms at different courts is not statistically significant.

The results from the logit regression model reported in Table 21.6, Panel B shows that a firm is more likely to obtain a better result after filing an appeal if the original trial takes place at its opponent's court (Models 2 and 3). The results also show that successful appeals are less likely in the intermediate people's court. State-owned firms tend to have better appeal results. We also include the interaction between home court and legal environment to capture the impact of legal environment on home court bias in Models 2 and 3. The coefficients are negative and significant, indicating home bias is reduced when the legal environment is good.

21.3.8 Sensitivity Tests

The results reported in this paper use the full sample data (1999–2012). In 2007, China introduced a new property rights law that spelt out new rules on mortgages, liens, pledges, and other aspects of property law. To see if this change in law has an impact on our results, we redo our analyses using the subsample periods 1999–2006

Table 21.6   The analysis of the impact of home bias on the appeal results.
Panel A: Univariate analysis of appeal results partitioned by the location of the court
In order to test whether state-owned firms have an advantage in the appeal ruling, we set the variable 'favour' equal to one if the appealing listed firms get a better second-round ruling result than the first-round ruling result. If the second-round ruling result has not changed or becomes worse, favour is set equal to zero. The table gives the percent of appealing firms obtaining better appeal ruling results.

	n	Mean
Home court	68	30.88%
Opponent's court	45	40.00%
Both parties' court	65	29.23%
Neither parties' court	25	24.00%
F-value		0.76
Kruskal-Wallis value		2.31

Panel B: Logit analysis for appeal results
We employ a logit regression on the variable 'favour'. The independent variables measuring the type of opposing parties, the type of case, the type of litigation, the level of court, firm size, ROA (profit/asset), Log (bankruptcy probability), state-ownership, politically connected management, and log (Litigation Amount). Home court dummy equals one if the court is located in the listed company's province, otherwise it is coded zero. Opponent court dummy equals one if the court is located in the opponent's province and not in the listed company's province; otherwise it is coded zero. We use DMLegal or DCExpense to capture the legal environment where the court is located. In Model 2 we add the interaction terms between the DMLegal with home court and opponent court dummies. In Model 3(4) we add the interaction terms between the CExpense (political connections) with home court or opponent court dummies.

	Model 1	Model 2	Model 3	Model 4
Intercept	−1.921	−4.490	−4.130	−1.972
	(0.752)	(0.479)	(0.505)	(0.739)
Size	0.087	0.143	0.081	0.053
	(0.760)	(0.624)	(0.775)	(0.848)
ROA	−0.148	−0.045	−0.136	−0.165
	(0.608)	(0.875)	(0.625)	(0.560)
Log (Bankruptcy probability)	−0.072	−0.076	−0.079	−0.076
	(0.447)	(0.455)	(0.423)	(0.432)
State-owned	1.363***	1.400***	1.207**	1.335***
	(0.004)	(0.005)	(0.010)	(0.004)
With politically connected managers	−0.220	−0.126	−0.451	−11.41
	(0.675)	(0.816)	(0.375)	(0.955)
DMLegal	−1.772***	1.280		
	(0.001)	(0.372)		
DCExpense			1.385	−1.294**
			(0.336)	(0.011)

(continued)

Table 21.6   (Continued)

	Model 1	Model 2	Model 3	Model 4
Opponent				
Bank	0.348	1.050	1.024	1.050
	(0.812)	(0.518)	(0.506)	(0.489)
Government	1.908	2.640	2.251	2.135
	(0.223)	(0.117)	(0.185)	(0.186)
Non-listed firm	−0.438	0.079	−0.062	0.207
	(0.717)	(0.953)	(0.962)	(0.871)
Foreign firm	−0.870	−0.749	−0.345	−0.632
	(0.689)	(0.728)	(0.878)	(0.758)
Individual	−0.769	−0.495	0.084	−0.194
	(0.654)	(0.787)	(0.962)	(0.907)
Type of case				
Breach of contract	0.929	1.201	1.088	1.122
	(0.269)	(0.180)	(0.220)	(0.192)
Breach of loan covenants	−1.155	−1.481	−0.961	−0.750
	(0.208)	(0.129)	(0.325)	(0.421)
Breach of loan guarantee agreement	−0.428	−0.594	−0.251	−0.010
	(0.663)	(0.565)	(0.811)	(0.992)
Tangible and intangible assets	1.843*	1.651	1.738	2.044**
transactions	(0.066)	(0.128)	(0.106)	(0.044)
Type of litigation				
Administrative lawsuit	−1.941	−2.630	−2.374	−2.373
	(0.263)	(0.151)	(0.208)	(0.184)
Arbitration lawsuit	−3.135	−3.981*	−2.869	−3.531*
	(0.255)	(0.093)	(0.248)	(0.099)
Court				
Basic people's court	−1.849*	−1.829*	−1.996**	−2.036**
	(0.057)	(0.068)	(0.032)	(0.030)
Intermediate people's court	−1.957**	−2.036**	−1.853**	−2.117**
	(0.021)	(0.018)	(0.022)	(0.012)
Higher people's court	−1.358	−1.601	−1.363	−1.552
	(0.174)	(0.122)	(0.155)	(0.111)
Log (Amount)	−0.066	−0.008	−0.055	−0.017
	(0.645)	(0.958)	(0.698)	(0.903)
Home court	0.567	2.137**	1.749	−0.041
	(0.476)	(0.041)	(0.126)	(0.958)
Opponent court	1.347	2.118*	2.447*	0.692
	(0.150)	(0.075)	(0.056)	(0.437)
Home court * DMLegal		−3.954**		
		(0.014)		
Opponent court * DMlegal		−1.907		
		(0.270)		
Home court * DCExpense			−3.245**	
			(0.039)	
Opponent court * DCExpense			−2.389	
			(0.158)	

Table 21.6   (Continued)

	Model 1	Model 2	Model 3	Model 4
Home court *				10.733
With political connections				(0.958)
Opponent court *				12.054
With political connections				(0.953)
Adjusted R²	0.292	0.320	0.282	0.273

Industry and Year controls are included. The *p*-value of *t*-statistics is given in the parentheses below the coefficient estimate. ***, **, * indicates statistical significance at the 0.01, 0.05 and 0.10 levels, respectively.

and 2007–2012. The results are similar across the two subperiods and so the introduction of the new law has no significant impact on our conclusions regarding home bias. We also run subsample tests across other judicial reform periods and find that our main findings on home bias remain.

Subsample tests are also used to help control for the split-share reform programme instituted in 2005 to 2007. The reform is aimed at improving corporate governance by making state shareholders act more like private shareholders (Firth, Lin, and Zou 2010). It is possible that the corporate governance reform could have an influence on our results. However, we find that our results are similar across the pre- and post-reform periods.

In supplementary tests we omit bank-related lawsuits, use the ownership percentage of the state shareholders (rather than using a 0/1 dummy variable), and distinguish between central government ownership (0/1 and percentage) and local government ownership (0/1 and percentage). We also differentiate between local-level and national-level political connections and rerun our tests. The results and conclusions from using the alternative specifications of the variables are very similar to the results reported in Tables 21.3 to 21.6. Adding controls for corporate governance (chairperson-CEO duality, board size, and institutional ownership) has no material effect on our results.

21.4   Conclusion

Some scholars attribute China's unorthodox economic growth to its de facto economic federalism. However, one of its drawbacks is that the yardstick jurisdictional competition that often arises from economic federalism leads to local protectionism. Local governments use their administrative powers to implement a multiform protection of firms under their authority. Given that judicial independence is weak in China, local governments can exert their strong influence on local courts. However, quantifying whether there is local protectionism is a major challenge.

Bias in judicial localism can be manifested in local firms having an advantage when litigations are heard in local courts. In this paper, we provide systematic evidence that the rulings of courts are indeed biased in favour of local firms. We find that shareholders react less negatively when a local firm (where a court case is heard in the same province as where the firm is located) is sued rather than when a non-local firm is sued. We also show that a non-local firm is more likely to appeal a case when it receives an unfavourable verdict in the first-run trial. This implies that the non-local firms are disadvantaged in the local courts. Our results are consistent with the view that economic federalism that induces increased competition can lead to local protectionism that distorts incentives and hurts economic efficiency. The findings are also consistent with the theory that the 'haves' (in our case, litigants in the same locale as the court) come out ahead of the 'have nots' (Galanter 1974; He and Su 2013). We believe that home court bias is a very real and important legal and economic concern in China.

Possible solutions to the home bias exhibited in courts include a rethink about how courts are financed and giving increased publicity to favouritism towards local litigants. Currently, courts are financed by cities and provinces and this leaves them open to local influence. Some change in the way courts are financed could lead to less local bias. Greater publicity given to the prevalence of and the effects of home bias might lead to better conduct in the courts. While economic federalism has its benefits, prolonged local bias could lead to lower investment by foreign firms, less inter-regional trade, and a reduction in economic efficiency. All told, China needs to be concerned by any form of judicial bias. In this study, we document evidence of the existence of home bias, induced by decentralized federalism, whereby the courts favour local litigants.

References

Allen, F., Qian, J. and Qian, M. (2005). Law, finance, and economic growth in China. *Journal of Financial Economics* 77: 57–116.

Bai, C., Du, Y., Tao, Z. and Tong, S. (2004). Local protectionism and regional specialization: Evidence from China's industries. *Journal of International Economics* 63: 397–417.

Berkowitz, D. and Clay, K. (2006). The effect of judicial independence on courts: Evidence from the American states. *Journal of Legal Studies* 35: 399–440.

Bhagat, S., Brickley, J. and Coles, J. (1994). The wealth effects of interfirm lawsuits: Evidence from corporate lawsuits. *Journal of Financial Economics* 35: 221–247.

Bhagat, S., Bizjak, J. and Coles, J. (1998). The shareholder wealth implications of corporate lawsuits. *Financial Management* 27: 5–27.

Bhagat, S. and Romano, R. (2002). Event studies and the law – Part I: Technique and corporate litigation. *American Law and Economics Review* 4: 141–167.

Bhattacharya, U., Galpin, N. and Haslem, B. (2007). The home court advantage in international corporate litigation. *Journal of Law and Economics* 50: 625–659.

Bizjak, J. and Coles, J. (1995). The effect of private antitrust litigation on the stock market valuation of the firm. *American Economic Review* 85: 436–461.

Blanchard, O. and Shleifer, A. (2001). Federalism with and without political centralization: China versus Russia. *IMF Staff Papers* 48: 171–179.

Cai, C., Chau, F., Wang, J. and Ye, J. (2016). Corporate governance and creditor lawsuit: Evidence from bank loan litigation. *Journal of International Financial Markets, Institutions and Money*, forthcoming.

Clermont, K.M. and Eisenberg, T. (1996). Xenophilia in American courts. *Harvard Law Review* 109: 1120–1143.

Clermont, K.M. and Eisenberg, T. (2007). Xenophilia or xenophobia in U.S. courts? Before and after 9/11. *Journal of Empirical Legal Studies* 4: 441–464.

Cutler, D. and Summers, L. (1988). The costs of conflict resolution and financial distress: Evidence from the Texaco-Pennzoil litigation. *Rand Journal of Economics* 19: 157–172.

Dimson, E. (1979). Risk measurement when shares are subject to infrequent trading. *Journal of Financial Economics* 7: 197–226.

Errunza, V. and Mazumdar, S. (2001). Privatization: a theoretical framework. *Journal of International Financial Markets, Institutions and Money* 11: 339–362.

Fan, C., Lin, C. and Treisman, D. (2009). Political decentralization and corruption: Evidence from around the world. *Journal of Public Economics* 93: 14–34.

Fan, G., Wang, X. and Zhu H. (2003). *National Economic Research Institute Index of Marketization of China's Provinces 2002 Report*. Beijing: Economic Science Press.

Fan, G., Wang, X. and Zhu, H. (2007). *National Economic Research Institute Index of Marketization of China's Provinces 2006 Report*. Beijing: Economic Science Press.

Fan, J., Wong, T.J. and Zhang, T.Y. (2007). Politically connected CEOs, corporate governance and post-IPO performance of China's partially privatized firms. *Journal of Financial Economics* 84: 330–357.

Firth, M., Lin, C. and Zou, H. (2010). Friend or foe? The role of state and mutual fund ownership in the split share structure reform in China. *Journal of Financial and Quantitative Analysis* 45: 685–706.

Firth, M., Rui, O.M. and Wu, W.F. (2011a). Cooking the books: Recipes and costs of falsified financial statements in China. *Journal of Corporate Finance* 17: 371–390.

Firth, M., Rui, O.M. and Wu, W.F. (2011b). The effects of political connections and state ownership on corporate litigation in China. *Journal of Law and Economics* 54: 573–607.

Galanter, M. (1974). Why the 'Haves' come out ahead: Speculations on the limits of legal change. *Law & Society Review* 9: 95–160.

He, H., Chen, S., Yao, S. and Ou, J. (2014). Financial liberalization and international market interdependence: Evidence from China's stock market in the post-WTO accession period. *Journal of International Financial Markets, Institutions and Money* 33: 434–444.

He, X. and Su, Y. (2013). Do the 'Haves' come out ahead in Shanghai courts? *Journal of Empirical Legal Studies* 10: 120–145.

Heckman, J. (1979). Sample selection bias as a specification error. *Econometrica* 47: 153–161.

Helland, E. (2006). Reputational penalties and the merits of class action securities litigation. *Journal of Law and Economics* 49: 365–395.

Jin, H., Qian, Y. and Weingast, B.R. (2005). Regional decentralization and fiscal incentives: federalism Chinese style. *Journal of Public Economics* 89 (9–10): 1719–1742.

Karpoff, J., Lott, J. and Wehrly, E. (2005). The reputational penalties for environmental violations: Empirical evidence. *Journal of Law and Economics* 48: 658–675.

Lazear E. and Rosen, S. (1981). Rank-order tournaments as optimum labor contracts. *Journal of Political Economy* 89: 841–864.

Li, H. and Zhou L. (2005). Political turnover and economic performance: The incentive role of personnel control in China. *Journal of Public Economics* 89(9–10): 1743–1762.

Lin, J.Y. and Liu, Z. (2000). Fiscal decentralization and economic growth in China. *Economic Development and Cultural Change* 49(1): 1–21.

Mai, J. and Stoyanov, A. (2014). Home country bias in the legal system: Empirical evidence from the intellectual property rights protection in Canada. Working paper, York University.

Maskin, E., Qian, Y. and Xu, C. (2000). Incentives, information, and organizational form. *Review of Economic Studies* 67 (2): 359–378.

Montinola, G., Qian, Y. and Weingast, B.R. (1996). Federalism, Chinese style: The political basis for economic success. *World Politics* 48: 50–81.

Moore, K. (2003). Xenophobia in American courts. *Northwestern University Law Review* 97: 1497–1550.

Ohlson, J. (1980). Financial ratios and the probabilistic prediction of bankruptcy. *Journal of Accounting Research* 18: 109–131.

Peerenboom, R. (2010). *Judicial Independence in China*. New York: Cambridge University Press.

Petersen, M.A. (2009). Estimating standard errors in finance panel data sets: Comparing approaches. *Review of Financial Studies* 22: 435–480.

Prince, D. and Rubin, P.H. (2002). The effects of product liability litigation on the value of firms. *American Law and Economics Review* 4: 44–87.

Qian, Y. and Roland, G. (1998). Federalism and the Soft Budget Constraint, *American Economic Review* 85(5): 1143–1162.

Qian, Y. and Xu, C. (1993). Why China's economic reforms differ: The M-Form hierarchy and entry/expansion of the non-state sector. *Economics of Transition* 1 (2) June: 135–170.

Qian, Y. and Weingast, B.R. (1996). China's transition to markets: Market-preserving federalism, Chinese style. *Journal of Policy Reform* 1: 149–185.

Scholes, M., Williams, J. (1977). Estimating betas from nonsynchronous data. *Journal of Financial Economics* 5: 309–327.

Shleifer, A. and Vishny, R. (1993). Corruption. *Quarterly Journal of Economics* 108: 599–617.

Shleifer, A. and Vishny, R. (1994). Politicians and firms. *Quarterly Journal of Economics* 109: 995–1025.

State Council (2012). *Judicial Reform in China*. Beijing: Information Office of the State Council.

Wong, C. (2003). Economic growth under decentralization: Old wine in new bottles? Another look at fiscal incentives in China, Working Paper.

Yang, J. (2013). Legal services reform in China: Limitations, policy perspectives, and strategies for the future. *The Journal of Political Risk* 1: 1–13.

Young, A. (2000). The razor's edge: Distortions and incremental reform in the People's Republic of China. *Quarterly Journal of Economics* 115 (4): 1091–1135.

Wu, S.N. and Lu, X.Y. (2001). The prediction model of financial distress of China listed firms. *Economic Research* June: 46–55. (In Chinese).

Zhao, X.B. and Zhang, L. (1999). Decentralization reforms and regionalism in China. A review. *International Regional Science Review* 22: 251–281.

Zhang, M. (2002). International civil litigation in China: A practical analysis of the Chinese judicial system. *Boston College International and Comparative Law Review* 25: 59–96.

Index